Multilevel Modeling
of Educational Data

A volume in
Quantitative Methods in Education and the Behavior Sciences:
Issues, Research, and Teaching
Ronald C. Serlin, *Series Editor*

EDITORIAL BOARD

Multilevel Modeling of Educational Data

Edited by

Ann A. O'Connell
Ohio State University

and

D. Betsy McCoach
University of Connecticut

INFORMATION AGE PUBLISHING, INC.
Charlotte, NC • www.infoagepub.com

Library of Congress Cataloging-in-Publication Data

Multilevel modeling of educational data / edited by Ann A. O'Connell and D. Betsy McCoach.
    p. cm. – (Quantitative methods in education and the behavioral sciences: issues, research, and teaching)
  Includes bibliographical references.
  ISBN 978-1-59311-684-2 (pbk.) – ISBN 978-1-59311-685-9 (hardcover)
1. Educational statistics. 2. Quantitative methods. 3.
Education–Statistical methods. I. O'Connell, Ann A. II. McCoach, D. Betsy.

  LB2846.M767 2008
  370.2'1–dc22

                                                    2008000849

Printed in the United States of America

To our families
Nathan, Delaney, and Meseret Morphew
and Del and Jessica Siegle.

CONTENTS

Series Introduction ix
　Ronald C. Serlin

Acknowledgements.. xi

PART I

DESIGN CONTEXTS FOR MULTILEVEL MODELS

1 Introduction: Pedagogy and Context for Multilevel Models 3
　Ann A. O'Connell and D. Betsy McCoach

2 The Use of National Datasets for Teaching and Research............... 11
　Laura M. Stapleton and Scott L. Thomas

3 Using Multilevel Modeling to Investigate School Effects................ 59
　Xin Ma, Lingling Ma, and Kelly D. Bradley

4 Modeling Growth Using Multilevel and Alternative
　Approaches 111
　Janet K. Holt

5 Cross-Classified Random Effects Models 161
　S. Natasha Beretvas

6 Multilevel Logistic Models for Dichotomous and Ordinal Data.... 199
Ann A. O'Connell, Jessica Goldstein, H. Jane Rogers, and C. Y. Joanne Peng

PART II
PLANNING AND EVALUATING MULTILEVEL MODELS

7 Evaluation of Model Fit and Adequacy.. 245
D. Betsy McCoach and Anne C. Black

8 Power, Sample Size, and Design 273
Jessaca Spybrook

PART III
EXTENDING THE MULTILEVEL FRAMEWORK

9 Multilevel Methods for Meta-Analysis.............................. 315
Sema A. Kalaian and Rafa M. Kasim

10 Multilevel Measurement Modeling 345
Akihito Kamata, Daniel J. Bauer, and Yasuo Miyazaki

PART IV
MASTERING THE TECHNIQUE

11 Reporting Results from Multilevel Analyses 391
*John M. Ferron, Kristin Y. Hogarty, Robert F. Dedrick,
Melinda R. Hess, John D. Niles, and Jeffrey D. Kromrey*

12 Software Options for Multilevel Models 427
J. Kyle Roberts and Patrick McLeod

13 Estimation Procedures for Hierarchical Linear Models 469
Hariharan Swaminathan and H. Jane Rogers

About the Contributors **521**

SERIES INTRODUCTION

Quantitative Methods in Education and the Behavioral Sciences: Issues, Research and Teaching is a unique book series sponsored by the American Educational Research Association's Special Interest Group Educational Statisticians. Motivated by the groups central purpose—to increase interaction among educational researchers interested in the theory, applications, and teaching of statistics in the social sciences—the new series is devoted to didactically oriented presentations that introduce, extend, and clarify state-of-the-art quantitative methods for students and researchers in the social and behavioral sciences. As such, the current series aims to present selected topics in a technically sophisticated yet didactically oriented format. This allows for the individual volumes to be used to enhance the teaching of quantitative methods in course sequences typically taught in graduate behavioral science programs. Although other series and journals exist that routinely publish new quantitative methodologies, this book series is dedicated to both the teaching and applied research perspectives of specific modern quantitative research methods through each volumes' relevant and accessible topical treatments. In line with this educational commitment, royalties from the sale of series' volumes will be used in large part to support student participation in annual special interest group conference activities.

Ronald C. Serlin, *Series Editor*
University of Wisconsin – Madison

ACKNOWLEDGEMENTS

We wish to thank Ron Serlin, Series Editor for *Quantitative Methods in Education and the Behavioral Sciences: Issues, Research and Teaching*, as well as the entire editorial board—Gabriella Belli, Greg Hancock, Charles Stegman, Sharon Weinberg, Joe Wisenbaker, and Bruno Zumbo—for their confidence in our co-editorship and their support of our efforts during the development of this volume. In particular, we extend our gratitude to Ron Serlin, Greg Hancock, and Ralph Mueller for their humor, ready availability, and expert guidance on many aspects of the editorial process. Thank you!

We wish to thank the many students from EPSY 440, our multilevel modeling class at the University of Connecticut, who read and re-read numerous versions of the chapters contained herein. Your comments and suggestions greatly enhanced the quality of the final volume. Special thanks go to Jill Adelson, Stephanie Allen, Anne Black, Jessica Goldstein, Xing Liu, Christina Peretti, Karen Rambo, and Kate Zhao for their editorial assistance throughout the preparation of the book. Finally, we would like to thank all of the chapter reviewers, who provided numerous comments and suggestions that improved the quality and readability of the chapters. A full list of the chapter reviewers is contained at the end of the volume.

PART I

DESIGN CONTEXTS FOR MULTILEVEL MODELS

CHAPTER 1

INTRODUCTION

Pedagogy and Context
for Multilevel Models

Ann A. O'Connell and D. Betsy McCoach

INTRODUCTION

Hierarchies abound. Once you start to view the world through a multilevel lens, the importance of context or place and its impact on individuals becomes apparent in nearly every human setting. The use of multilevel analyses to examine differences across groups or contexts—such as classrooms, schools, neighborhoods, hospitals, or prisons—on individual outcomes has burgeoned over the course of the past few decades. Yet the widespread adoption of multilevel models to represent these hierarchical systems and address questions of critical social and educational significance continues to present fascinating and complex challenges to the applied research community, particularly to those of us who teach in this field.

Our goal in this book is to provide a comprehensive and instructional resource text on multilevel analysis for graduate students and professors of quantitative methods courses, as well as for quantitative researchers who plan to use multilevel techniques in their work. We have linked our book

Multilevel Modeling of Educational Data, pages 3–10
Copyright © 2008 by Information Age Publishing
All rights of reproduction in any form reserved.

to a website (http://www.infoagepub.com/serlinfiles_multilevel) containing data that can be used to replicate the examples presented in most of our chapters, creating an opportunity for readers to learn by doing. Consequently, our book provides an accessible and practical treatment of methods appropriate for use in a first and/or second course in multilevel analysis.

Historically, the treatment of hierarchical data has its roots in sampling designs where information is collected from clusters or groups of individuals who experience some common phenomena or event. This "common phenomena" could arise from simply living in the same neighborhood or attending the same class, school, or community health clinic. Alternatively, group membership could be manipulated. This might occur, for example, when students are assigned to work in small collaborative groups to examine the effects of collaboration and increasingly difficult puzzle tasks on individual solution strategies. Of central importance in these scenarios is that information obtained from individuals who are clustered within a population—either in naturally occurring or intentionally formed groups—tends to be more similar within the groups in comparison to information obtained from individuals in other groups. The degree to which individuals within a group or cluster are similar is measured through the intraclass correlation coefficient (ICC). The ICC is found through decomposition of total variance in an outcome into its within-group and between-group components, and represents the proportion of variance that is between-groups (Raudenbush & Bryk, 2002). As a measure of similarity or homogeneity, the ICC reflects the correlation between pairs of individuals randomly selected from within the same randomly selected group or cluster (Snijders & Bosker, 1999). Data that are wholly independent and contain no within-cluster similarity yield an ICC of zero. Thus, the presence of positive ICC indicates dependency within the dataset.

Just as observations taken from individuals within a group or cluster tend to be similar to each other, so do observations taken repeatedly across individuals. Thus, repeated measures designs or longitudinal studies are suspect to the same intra-unit dependency problems as data collected from clustered-sample designs. Multilevel models applied to longitudinal data accommodate this clustering or intra-individual correlation; hierarchically, each person in the longitudinal design simply functions as his or her own "cluster."

The effects of a lack of independence on statistical analyses and subsequent conclusions have been known for some time (see Kenny & Judd, 1986, for a review), and sampling statisticians have long accommodated the presence of intraclass correlation in analyses using cluster or multi-stage data collection designs (Donner, Birkett, & Buck, 1981; Fowler, 1993; Kish, 1965, 1995; Murray & Hannon, 1990; Sudman, 1985). Ignoring the clustered structure inherent within the data offers no distinction between the between- and within-group variance. Thus, when the clustering is ignored, the variances of estimates derived from that sample tend to be much smaller than what would realistically be expected if the clustered structure of the data had been incorporated into the calculation. The variance inflation factor (VIF), also referred to as the design effect, provides information regarding the degree to which the variance of an estimate tends to increase (for clustered samples) over what might be obtained if a simple random sample of the same size were conducted in the same population (Donner, et al., 1981; Kish, 1965, 1995; Murray, 1998; Snijders & Bosker, 1999). The amount of variance inflation is directly related to the intraclass correlation—as the ICC increases, the VIF also increases. The amount of variance inflation is also related to the average cluster size. As the size of the average cluster increases, the VIF increases. Therefore, treating cluster-sampled data as if it were obtained using simple random sampling will result in variance estimates (and standard errors) that are too low.

This situation, well-known from the sampling literature, has great implications for how hierarchical data should best be analyzed. In short, when considering variance from data obtained through grouped or clustered designs, the hierarchical sources of variability cannot be ignored without seriously contributing to errors of inference, compromising the validity of results and research conclusions. Statisticians use variance estimates in nearly all statistical tests and analyses, so ignoring the structure of a research setting or the sample design adversely affects these variance estimates and increases the likelihood of Type I errors for any comparisons, contrasts, or effects we wish to assess. Multilevel modeling accommodates the structure of many familiar research settings—such as data collected from children within multiple schools or classrooms, or data collected from patients within multiple health clinics—and helps to protect the validity of statistical conclusions drawn from our analyses.

Often, however, the existence of clustering is not simply a nuisance to be overcome. In fact, differences in *relationships* among individual-level variables may exist between the clusters or contexts themselves, representing an additional source of variability over and above that present at the individual level. Multilevel analyses are uniquely designed to capture and model this variability across multiple levels, allowing for a better understanding of the influence that contexts—such as classrooms, schools or neighborhoods— may have on individual outcomes.

Perhaps there is no more obvious setting for consideration of multilevel systems than schools. Given the current era of accountability, educators and policymakers are especially interested in the effects of classroom, school, or district level variables on students' academic achievement. Multilevel modeling techniques lend themselves to the exploration of these and other educational issues, but as with all observational or non-experimental studies where random assignment is constrained, causal conclusions need to be tempered. Causality requires far more than a sophisticated statistical model, and the use of multilevel modeling does not imply that causality can be readily assumed or inferred. Multilevel modeling does provide a valuable tool for analyzing and understanding data that arise from non-independent or clustered samples; however, the use of this technique in and of itself does not lead to identification of direct causal links. When the data are collected from cluster-randomized designs, i.e., where entire clusters are the randomized elements, multilevel modeling can be used to make inferences about the efficacy of a treatment. However, when the data result from non-randomized designs, any causal claims attributed to the variables of interest may be far more speculative. The focus for this book is on methodology and applications of multilevel modeling for hierarchical data structures; these structures can occur within experimental or non-experimental settings. Our book is not designed to emphasize assessment of causal claims; readers with further interests in issues of causality within hierarchical designs are referred to Hong and Raudenbush (2005), Bloom (2005), and Kawachi and Berkman (2003) for some informative reading in this area.

STRUCTURE OF THE BOOK

This book is pedagogical in nature, and is intended to provide a cogent introduction to the area of multilevel modeling for applied researchers as well as advanced graduate students. It is our hope that readers and professors of educational statistics courses will use this book as a guide and a tutorial on multilevel modeling techniques in educational research. Overall, the chapter topics range from basic to advanced, yet each chapter is designed to be able to stand alone as an instructional unit on its respective topic, with an emphasis on application and interpretation.

The first section in the book, *Design Contexts for Multilevel Models*, provides foundational information on some of the most common applications of multilevel modeling. Following the initial chapter, Chapter 2 serves as an introduction to sampling methods in relation to multilevel analysis designs and provides an overview of several existing national survey databases housed within the National Center for Education Statistics. Stapleton and Thomas describe how multilevel modeling could be used to explore these datasets and provide recommendations and suggested avenues for research utilizing these extensive public-access databases. Chapter 3 provides an introduction to multilevel modeling in the context of school effects research, with broader applications to organizational models in general. Ma, Ma, and Bradley frame their discussion of school effects within the input-process-output (IPO) model, first proposed by Good and Brophy (1986) to measure behavioral as well as perceptional processes that function within the school and classroom. Chapter 4 provides an overview and comparison of three popular methods of analyzing longitudinal data: multilevel modeling, latent growth curve modeling (using SEM), and growth mixture modeling. Through applications involving different growth modeling scenarios, Holt compares and contrasts the assumptions, strengths, and weaknesses of these alternative longitudinal methods.

Sometimes data are simultaneously nested within two or more crossed hierarchies. For example, students are nested within teachers at a single grade level, but cross-classified by teacher across two or more grade levels. In Chapter 5, Beretvas contrasts cross-classified structures with purely hierarchical structures, and introduces cross-classified random effects models through detailed examples, descriptions of data/model set-ups, and model interpretations.

The final chapter in this section deals with dependent variables that are categorical or ordinal in nature. In Chapter 6, O'Connell, Goldstein, Rogers and Peng extend generalized linear models to the multilevel framework and provide readers with details on estimating hierarchical logistic and ordinal models. This chapter provides in-depth examples of logistic and ordinal models, extensions to other educational contexts, and a brief review of some software considerations for hierarchical generalized linear models.

The two chapters in the second section, *Planning and Evaluating Multilevel Models*, detail issues that every researcher must consider when designing and implementing multilevel models in educational research. Chapter 7 reviews methods for the evaluation of model fit and model adequacy within the multilevel framework. McCoach and Black cover issues such as deviance and model selection criteria, the impact of full versus restricted maximum likelihood estimation on assessment of model fit, nestedness, and variance reduction statistics, and they review the controversies surrounding model fit concerns in multilevel analyses. Chapter 8 provides an introduction to statistical power analysis within the multilevel framework. Spybrook focuses on randomized experiments and illustrates the use of the *Optimal Design* software to determine the power or necessary sample sizes for several different kinds of multilevel designs.

Extending the Multilevel Framework moves from traditional studies utilizing multilevel models to those involving meta-analytic studies and measurement applications. In Chapter 9, Kalaian and Kasim introduce meta-analysis using random or mixed-effects from a multilevel perspective, and contrast these approaches with typical fixed-effects meta-analyses. The authors then detail the steps necessary to conduct univariate and multivariate meta-analysis using the HLM software program to synthesize the results of multiple research studies. In another extension of traditional multilevel analyses, Kamata, Bauer, and Miyazaki discuss how items from a psychological or educational test or inventory can be viewed as being nested within subscales. In Chapter 10, these authors compare traditional measurement models to measurement models based within a more flexible multilevel framework, where within- as well as between-cluster variations of the data are accommodated. They also demonstrate how covariates and interaction effects can conveniently be incorporated into the measurement model.

The final section of the book is called *Mastering the Technique*, and deals with three critical topics in multilevel research: presenting results from complex analyses, rapidly changing software options, and choice of parameter estimation methods. Chapter 11 provides guidelines for interpreting results and writing about multilevel models. Ferron, Hogarty, Dedrick, Hess, Niles, and Kromrey have developed a comprehensive checklist for researchers to use when preparing manuscripts for publication. Without being overly prescriptive, the authors offer helpful suggestions for what results to present and how to use text, tables and figures to best present these results. Chapter 12 contains a comparison of some of the most commonly used multilevel software programs. Along with a brief historical review of software development in this area, Roberts and McLeod discuss the strengths and weaknesses of many available multilevel packages. The authors include data examples, output and interpretations, syntax, and directions for further information on each statistical package reviewed. Finally, Chapter 13, by Swaminathan and Rogers, is the most mathematically rigorous chapter in this volume. Beginning with a small and simple dataset appropriate for hand-calculation of some of the procedures presented, the authors review and explain various estimation methods used in the field of multilevel modeling. Although the content is extensive, this chapter serves as a framework and starting point for the motivated reader who seeks a comprehensive initial understanding of estimation procedures for hierarchical models.

A Note on Notation

In general, the notation in this volume follows the conventions contained in Raudenbush & Bryk, 2002. For simplicity, in this chapter, we consider an unconditional means model (also referred to as a one-way analysis of variance model with random effects), in which there are no level-1 or level-2 predictors. (Subsequent chapters present the notation for multilevel models containing level-one and level-two variables). The outcome variable, Y, for person i in cluster j, Y_{ij}, is a function of the cluster level intercept, which randomly varies across clusters, and a residual term, r_{ij}, which captures the deviation of person $_{ij}$ from his or her cluster's intercept. Then, the collection of cluster level intercepts, β_{0j}, are modeled at level two through the grand mean intercept in the population, γ_{00}, where u_{0j} is the deviation of cluster

j's intercept from the grand intercept. At level one, the within-cluster variability is represented as $\mathrm{Var}(r_{ij}) = \sigma^2$, with variability assumed to be homogeneous across clusters; and at level two, the between-cluster variability is represented as $\mathrm{Var}(u_{0j}) = \tau_{00}$.

This unconditional model can be expressed as two separate equations, as shown below.

$$Y_{ij} = \beta_{0j} + r_{ij} \tag{1.1}$$

$$\beta_{0j} = \gamma_{00} + u_{0j} \tag{1.2}$$

Alternatively, the two separate equations can be combined into one equation:

$$Y_{ij} = \gamma_{00} + u_{0j} + r_{ij} \tag{1.3}$$

Although the combined equation more accurately portrays the computational process being used when estimating multilevel models, the multiple equation layout is often simpler for novice multilevel modelers to grasp. Therefore, throughout most of this volume the multiple equation layout is presented, but the combined format is used in many examples to demonstrate the equivalence of these two approaches to presenting a system of multilevel equations. Departures from the conventions used by Raudenbush and Bryk (2002) are noted and explained within each chapter as necessary.

REFERENCES

Bloom, H.S. (Ed.). (2005). *Learning more from social experiments: Evolving analytic approaches*. New York: Russell Sage Foundation.

Donner, A., Birkett, N., & Buck. C. (1981). Randomization by cluster: Sample size requirements and analysis. *American Journal of Epidemiology, 114,* 283–286.

Fowler, F.J. (2001). *Survey research methods* (3rd ed.). Newbury Park: Sage Publications.

Good, T. L., & Brophy, J. E. (1986). School effects. In M. Wittrock (Ed.), *Third handbook of research on teaching* (pp. 570–602). New York: Macmillan.

Hong, G. & Raudenbush, S.W. (2005). Effects of kindergarten retention policy on children's cognitive growth in reading and mathematics. *Educational Evaluation and Policy Analysis, 27,* 205–224.

Kawachi, I. & Berkman, L.F. (Eds.). (2003). *Neighborhoods and health.* New York: Oxford University Press.

Kenny, D.A., & Judd, C.M. (1986). Consequences of violating the independence assumption in analysis of variance. *Psychological Bulletin, 99,* 422–431.

Kish, L. (1965, 1995). *Survey sampling.* New York: John Wiley & Sons.

Leyland, A.H., & Goldstein, H. (2001). *Multilevel modeling of health statistics.* New York: John Wiley & Sons.

Murray, D. M. (1998). *Design and analysis of group-randomized trials.* New York: Oxford.

Murray, D.M., & Hannan, P.J. (1990). Planning for the appropriate analysis in school-based drug-use prevention studies. *Journal of Consulting and Clinical Psychology, 58,* 458–468.

Raudenbush, S.W., & Bryk, A.S. (2002). *Hierarchical linear models* (2nd ed.). Newbury Park, CA: Sage.

Snijders, T. & Bosker, R. (1999). *Multilevel analysis.* Thousand Oaks, CA: Sage.

Sudman, S. (1985). Efficient screening methods for the sampling of geographically clustered special populations. *Journal of Marketing Research, 22,* 20–29.

CHAPTER 2

THE USE OF NATIONAL DATASETS FOR TEACHING AND RESEARCH

Sources and Issues

Laura M. Stapleton and Scott L. Thomas

INTRODUCTION

Students who recently have been exposed to instruction in multilevel modeling techniques often hunt for data on which to wield their newfound knowledge and skills. We hope this chapter can be used as a starting point in a search for appropriate data for example analyses, and with this goal in mind, we hope to accomplish several things. First, we introduce the reader to some basic issues in sampling theory, including the concepts of cluster sampling, stratification, and disproportionate sampling. Each of these concepts are used to a great extent in the sampling designs for survey programs run by the National Center for Education Statistics ([NCES], 2006), and data from these survey programs will be featured in this chapter. Second, we provide detailed descriptions of three popular publicly-available datasets that have been collected under complex sampling designs and that

Multilevel Modeling of Educational Data, pages 11–57
Copyright © 2008 by Information Age Publishing
11

might be useful for application in a course that covers issues in multilevel modeling. For these datasets, we provide basic information, including the sampling plan, the content covered, and how the data and documentation can be obtained. We also highlight several other datasets that may be of interest to readers in an appendix. Next, we discuss important issues to consider when working with some of these datasets, including the incorporation of sampling weights, the handling of missing data, and a variety of other technical issues. In the chapter's final section, we provide a few recommendations for readers undertaking research using national survey datasets. While these recommendations for practice cannot be all-encompassing and suitable for every situation, we hope that the basic steps we provide will simplify the process for newer users.

This chapter serves as a resource for instructors and students of multilevel modeling to generate ideas, suggests avenues of access to data, and provides references to applied examples for demonstration of multilevel modeling techniques. Readers should note that working with these datasets is not an easy task, and there is no way that we can provide all the detailed knowledge necessary to address the complexities in the data in this short chapter. We strongly recommend that readers review the references and websites provided here for additional information.

While the wide availability of national datasets provides important opportunities for modeling multilevel phenomena, these data also have significant limitations in terms of testing theory. The primary goal of the collection of such data is, more often than not, to enable a representative description of a specific population. The variables in these datasets, therefore, are developed with this end in mind and often force the researcher interested in the testing of theories to rely on gross proxies to define constructs central to the ultimate substantive issues of interest. This reality can be every bit as important as the many technical concerns we raise throughout the remainder of this chapter. Accordingly, we strongly encourage the researcher to devote considerable attention to the development of his or her constructs and models in ways that best facilitate adequate theoretical tests.

In this chapter, we assume a basic knowledge of the concept of sampling and of how the sample selection process used in national data collection may differ from that of simple random sampling. Additionally, we assume that the reader has some degree of familiarity with concepts such as parameter estimation, sampling error, and confidence intervals.

BASIC ISSUES IN SAMPLING THEORY

There are two basic data collection problems encountered when collecting large-scale sample survey data. First, with many large-scale surveys, no simple sampling frame (i.e., a single list from which we can choose our sample members randomly) for our target population exists. Second, even if a sampling frame existed, we most likely would want to ensure that our sample has a sufficient number of respondents with certain characteristics (e.g., certain racial/ethnic groups, from different types of schools or colleges). Many researchers are interested in research focusing on these smaller segments of a population; thus, a simple random sample (SRS), in which one forms the sample by selecting a pre-specified number of respondents randomly (and in which all potential respondents have an equal probability of being selected for the sample), might not yield adequate numbers of observations in the subpopulations of interest.

Both of these data collection problems—lack of a sampling frame and need for adequately sized subpopulations of interest—are addressed by stratified multi-stage cluster sampling strategies. Such strategies usually involve sampling in several stages to overcome the problem of not having a single list for the entire population as well as oversampling individuals with certain characteristics who need to be included in sufficient numbers for purposes of analysis. The process of oversampling results in certain elements or participants being sampled at a higher probability of selection than is the case for others in the sample. Sampling in stages as well as oversampling are design issues that need to be accommodated during the analysis phase.

Most NCES survey samples involve several stages of selection (such as the random selection of schools from a list and then, in a second stage, the random selection of students from those schools), and this selection may be stratified on many different variables at each level of sampling. For example, selection of schools might be stratified by sector to include specifically both public and private schools, or selection of students might be stratified by both gender and grade to include specifically third-grade girls, third-grade boys, fourth-grade girls, and fourth-grade boys.

The implications of complex sampling designs play out in analyses during estimation of standard errors for parameter estimates, such as a mean or a regression coefficient. For example, consider the use of a cluster sample to collect data. In many situations, the characteristics of population members within a cluster (e.g., students in a school) are more similar than are the characteristics of population members across clusters. So, sampling several students within the same school does not describe the population as precisely as sampling a range of students from different types of schools. For a given variable of interest, a measure of the amount of dependency among members of a cluster is called the intraclass correlation (ICC), with values ranging from approximately 0 to a maximum of 1. Values near zero indicate that the individuals within clusters are no more similar to each other on the variable of interest than individuals across clusters. ICC values close to 1.0 indicate that the individuals within clusters are nearly identical to each other on the variable of interest. Because of possible dependency within clusters, the use of a cluster sampling design tends to yield standard errors that are larger than would have been obtained with an SRS of the same size (Lee, Forthofer, & Lorimor, 1989). For any complex sampling designs (be they multistage, stratified, etc.), a measure of the difference in standard errors that would result between the complex sample data and simple random sample data is called the design effect (Kalton, 1983). Design effects (DEFF) greater than 1.0 indicate that the complex sampling design is not as efficient (yields greater standard errors) as a simple random sample of the same size. Specifically, the design effect is the ratio of an estimate's sampling variance (its squared standard error) under the actual complex sample design to the estimate's variance that would have resulted under simple random sampling assumptions (see Thomas & Heck, 2001; Rust, 1985; Wolter, 1985; Woodruff, 1971):

$$\text{DEFF} = \frac{SE^2_{\text{COMPLEX SAMPLE}}}{SE^2_{\text{SRS}}}. \tag{2.1}$$

In the following sections, we provide an overview of the details associated with these particular types of sampling strategies (multi-stage, stratified, and disproportionate selection) and consider the implications of common sample characteristics for multilevel analyses.

Cluster and Multistage Sampling

Cluster sampling is one of the most common strategies for sample selection and often is used when groups are sampled more easily than individual units are. Some example situations in which cluster sampling might be beneficial include sampling children who are clustered or nested within classrooms or schools, sampling teachers who are nested within schools, and sampling faculty who are nested within universities. With nested data, the sampling process usually is undertaken in multiple stages. Generally, each level defines a discrete stage of the sampling process, and each stage has its own set of probabilities defining population members' likelihood for inclusion. In the first stage of selection, the primary sampling units (PSUs), generally the higher-level groups or clusters, are selected. For example, this might involve obtaining a random sample of classrooms, schools, or universities. In the second or subsequent stages, participants are selected from within those sampled clusters; for example, children or teachers from the selected schools would be included in the final sample. Technically, the term "cluster sample" denotes the situation in which all of the elements in a selected PSU are included in the sample (Kalton, 1983; Kish, 1965). Thus, in a cluster sample of teachers, if schools were selected as PSUs, then all the teachers in a selected school would be included in the sample. When only some of the elements from a selected PSU are included, the sampling design is termed "multistage sampling" (Kalton, 1983).

Clustered data often leads to violation of the common assumption in many statistical models that modeled residuals are independent across observations. Consequently, observed variance within clusters is usually less than variance observed between clusters, leading to underestimates of overall variance. This homogeneity of variance within clusters introduces inefficiencies in estimation and requires adjustments that we address in this chapter. As is well known to sampling theorists and multilevel modelers, when a sample has been collected via multistage or cluster sampling, the estimates of single-level parameters (such as regression coefficients, means, or correlations) typically will be less precise (i.e., be associated with more sampling variance or larger standard errors) than had a sample of the same size been collected through simple random sampling (Lee, et al., 1989; Skinner, Holt, & Smith, 1989). Moreover, if clustered data are analyzed assuming independence of observations, that is, ignoring the clustering, the standard errors for estimates (and thus the confidence intervals around the estimates) will be underestimated, or too narrow, and the degree of this bias will depend on the homogeneity of the response variable(s) across clusters (Lee et al., 1989). This homogeneity can be measured via the ICC. For example, if one were working with a cluster sample of fourth-grade students nested in schools and surveyed in September, the variable "age" likely would yield an ICC value close to zero. There is little reason to expect that children's ages would be more similar within schools than across schools. However, the variable of "achievement" might show an ICC value close to .2 or .3, suggesting that about 20 or 30 percent of the variability in "achievement" could be explained by knowing what school a child attended. This non-zero ICC results in biased standard error estimates for statistics, such as overall mean achievement or regression coefficients, if the traditional formulas for standard errors of these statistics are applied. Standard errors, just like means or regression coefficients, are estimates. Specifically, they estimate the amount of variability in the statistic being estimated that one would expect over repeated sampling. The standard error is subject to possible bias with important consequences. In hypothesis testing, an underestimated standard error will result in rejection of the null hypothesis more often than would be appropriate (the actual Type I error rate would be higher than the nominal rate chosen, such as .05). Calculating the ICC value or knowing the size of the design effect can provide important information about how biased the traditional estimate of the standard error might be. Simply, the larger the ICC and for DEFF values farther from 1.0, the greater the difference between standard errors adjusted for the sample design and traditional estimates ignoring the design features.

Stratification

In the literature, less attention has been paid to the issue of stratification in complex sample data. Many sampling designs used in the collection of national data sets include a process by which the elements in the population are stratified into mutually exclusive categories and then explicitly or implicitly sampled from these strata in order to ensure representation of each category in the sample. For example, a sample of schools might be stratified by school type (private and public) and/or by U.S. Census region (Northeast, South, Midwest, and West) and then schools are sampled explicitly or implicitly from each of the stratification categories. Explicit sampling involves selecting a specified number or percentage of elements within each stratum (Kalton, 1983). Implicit sampling is accomplished by sorting all of the elements in the sampling frame by stratum and then choosing every ith element on the list, where i is a predetermined interval defined as the ratio of the number of elements in the sampling frame over the number of elements to be sampled (Kalton, 1983). This systematic movement by a specified interval through an entire sorted list typically will result in each of the strata being represented proportionately to the distribution in the population. When database documentation manuals refer to sorting the elements in the sampling frame by a specific set of variables and then using systematic sampling, the documentation is referring to an implicit stratification process.

Stratification can be used at any or all levels of a multistage sampling design. For example, suppose that to obtain a sample of fourth-grade students in U.S. elementary schools, first counties are sampled, then schools in those selected counties are chosen, and then the children in those selected schools are sampled. At the first stage of selection, the counties might be stratified by U.S. Census region and the resulting sample of counties will include some counties from each region of the country. At the second stage of selection, the schools in the selected counties might be stratified by public/private status and sorted by school size, resulting in the use of explicit stratification on school type and implicit stratification on size. At the final stage of selection, the students might be stratified by gender and/or free lunch qualification status.

How does stratification typically affect parameter estimates? In general, any time stratification is used as part of the sampling design and the response variable is homogenous within strata, the estimates from the sample will be more precise than had a sample of the same size been obtained through simple random sampling (Kalton, 1983; Kish, 1965; Lee et al., 1989). This increase in precision is related to the guarantee that different types of people (or units) will be included in the sample—it will be nearly impossible to obtain a "bad," non-representative, sample with an extreme parameter estimate. Related to this increase in precision of estimates, analyses ignoring the fact that stratification was used tend to result in overestimates of the standard errors associated with parameter estimates and a subsequent Type I error rate lower than the nominal rate. In essence, the result is the converse of that found with multistage or cluster sampling. The use of stratification alone would result in a design effect less than 1.0 (Kalton, 1983). However, most sampling designs include both stratification and multistage sampling and the increase in precision of estimates resulting from stratification is smaller than the decrease in precision found with multistage sampling (Kalton, 1983). Consequently, the issue of stratification has received less attention than the issue of cluster sampling in recent modeling literature.

Disproportionate Sampling

If not properly accounted for in the analysis, disproportionate selection of elements into the sample can affect the resulting estimates from an analysis adversely. This brief section introduces the concepts surrounding disproportionate selection and sampling weights; methods to accommodate these sampling weights into an analysis will be discussed in the third section of this chapter. At various stages of the sampling design, the elements (such as schools and students) typically are selected at different sampling rates. There are many reasons for the use of disproportionate sampling rates, and three types of disproportionate sampling are discussed here: probability proportionate to size (PPS) sampling, over-sampling by stratum, and post-stratification adjustments. First, consider the example of a simple two-stage sampling design. Suppose we want to obtain a sample of 20,000 seniors from public high schools in the U.S. In fall, 2000, there were about 2,700,000 12th-grade students in the U.S. in about 27,000 public schools (Snyder, Tan, & Hoffman, 2003). One way to obtain a sample of 20,000 students would be just to sample 20,000 students randomly out of the total pool of 2,700,000 students. If we wanted to do this, we would be using a selection probability of $\pi = 20,000/2,700,000 = .0074$ (or 74 out of every 10,000 students). We could, for example, take a list of 2,700,000 students, select every 135th name on the list, and we would obtain a sample of 20,000 names; each of the names had a .0074 chance of being selected into the sample. The sampling interval of 135 was obtained by dividing the total population (2,700,000) by the number of desired sample elements

(20,000). Note that this sampling interval is also the reciprocal of the selection probability: $1/.0074 = 135$. The reciprocal of the selection probability also is referred to as the "sampling weight." Each person in our hypothetical sample represents 135 people from the original population.

There is a complication in our example, however, in that we do not have a list of all students at every school, so it is not logistically feasible for us to conduct a simple random sample to obtain .74% of the 2,700,000 students. An approach that has been developed to work around this problem of not having a complete list or frame of all students in the target population is to sample in two stages: first sample a group of schools, asking those selected schools for a list of their students, and then take a selection of those listed students. The difficulty with this approach, however, is that we now need to determine two selection probabilities, one for the schools (π_j) and one for the students within the selected schools $(\pi_{i|j})$. In order to obtain a sample of 20,000 students, the product of these two probabilities must equal the overall selection probability of .0074. We arbitrarily can select a value for one of these probabilities, and the other value will, therefore, be determined. For example, suppose we decide to sample 5% (or .05) of the students within each selected school. That would mean that we would need to select 14.8% of the schools because $.148 \times .05 = .0074$. So, if we sample 14.8% of the schools $(\pi_j = .148)$ and sample 5% of the students at each selected school $(\pi_{i|j} = .05)$, we would obtain a sample with an expected size of 20,000 and each element in the population would have an overall selection rate of .0074 $(\pi_{ij} = \pi_j \times \pi_{i|j} = .148 \times .05 = .0074)$. But note that the number of students typically varies across schools and that with this proposed process we might sample a relatively large number of students in very large schools (for example, with a sampling rate of 5% and 1,000 12th-grade students in a school, we would have a sample of 50 students at that school) and only 1 student at another school (because there might be only 20 12th-grade students at the school). It is usually more administratively efficient to conduct surveys in a standardized manner across schools. With this sampling plan of using a fixed sampling rate within all schools, we could not guarantee a specific size of the sample at each school. Within-school sample size has important implications for reliability and power when analyzing clustered data with multilevel models. In short, small within-unit sample sizes will undermine the overall reliability of estimates and compromise the researcher's ability to detect variability in person-level effects between the groups (Snidjers, 2005). We address this challenge in subsequent sections of this chapter and refer the reader to a more complete treatment of power and sample size issues in Chapter 8 of this volume (Spybrook, 2008).

In many of the typical national designs, the sample developers plan to administer the surveys or assessments to about the same number of students at each site for standardization purposes. Looking across the sample designs for the publicly-available data from the National Center for Education Statistics (NCES), it is apparent that this number is often around 20 to 25 participants per site. Therefore, an alternate plan might be to sample schools at a fixed selection rate and then to sample a specified number of students at each school, for example, 20 students. With this two-stage sampling design and taking a specified number of participants at each site, the students in small schools have a very high probability of selection into the sample if their school is chosen. For the example school of size 20 given above, the selection rate would be (π_{ilj} = 20/20 = 1.00. Conversely, students who are in very large schools have a relatively small chance of being selected for the sample if their school is chosen. Students in the large school of size 1000 would have a selection rate of π_{ilj} = 20/1000 = .02. If the schools are sampled with equal probabilities (say, π_j = .148), then students from these two different schools would have very different overall rates of selection: $\pi_{ij} = \pi_j \times \pi_{ilj}$ = .148 × 1.00 = .148 for students in the small school and $\pi_{ij} = \pi_j \times \pi_{ilj}$ = .148 × .02 = .00296 for students in the large school. Consequently, students in small schools would be over-represented in the sample (selected at 50 times the rate of the students in the larger schools!). A way to avoid having unequal numbers of selected students per school or unequal selection probabilities for individual students across schools is to select schools with a method that samples large schools at higher rates and smaller schools at lower rates, rather than sample schools with equal probability. This method, called probability proportionate to size (PPS) sampling, commonly is used in national data collection. With PPS sampling, the overall selection probabilities for students (π_{ij}) will tend to be equivalent, but their conditional probabilities (π_{ilj}) within their respective schools will differ. For example, suppose with our previous example that we want to select about 20 students at each school no matter the size of the school. A school with 20 12th graders would need to have a .0074 chance of selection into the sample (that is, π_j = .0074), to result in an overall probability of inclusion for a student in that school of .0074 ($\pi_{ij} = \pi_j \times \pi_{ilj}$ = .0074 × 1.0 = .0074). Alternately, a school with 1,000 12th graders would need to have a chance of selection of .37 in the sample (that is, π_j = .37), to result in an overall selection probability for the students in those schools of .0074 ($\pi_{ij} = \pi_j \times \pi_{ilj}$ = .37 × .02 = .0074).

In addition to accounting for differing sizes of initial sampling units, disproportionate sampling also may be used to obtain sufficient numbers of elements to undertake subgroup reporting. For example, special interest might lie in reporting estimates for Asian American students or teachers (as is the case in the Early Childhood Longitudinal Study of kindergarten students and the Schools and Staffing Survey involving teachers; Tourkin et al., 2004; U.S. Department of Education, 2006). When the desire is to report estimates by subgroup, sample designers might employ a higher rate of sampling in certain strata than the rate used in other strata. Thus, with NCES datasets, it is not unusual to find sampling weights that differ for teachers or students within the same school or for teachers or students across school types (for example, public and private).

Finally, similar to the approach of over-sampling, post-stratification weighting adjustments might be employed by the survey designers to adjust for non-response. Non-response to the survey might result in differing proportions of participants in the respondent sample as compared to the desired sample. Although equal selection probabilities might have been used for all elements in the initial sampling plan, some groups typically respond at lower rates. For example, women tend to respond to surveys at higher rates than men (Dillman, 2000), and in a survey of faculty, although men and women might have been sampled at an equal rate, women might have responded at a higher rate. After survey data are collected, sampling weights for responses from men would be set higher to reflect their true proportion in the population (if it is known or can be approximated), and women's responses would be associated with smaller sampling weights.

It is important to note that the appropriate use of post-stratification weighting for non-response can be somewhat controversial (Lohr, 1999). The survey weighting literature reveals at least four classes of solutions to post-stratification weighting: (a) cell weighting (Kalton & Flores-Cervantes, 2003), (b) raking (Deming & Stephan, 1940; Little & Wu, 1991), (c) regression estimation (Lohr, 1999), and (d) more complex schemes such as hierarchical regression weighting (Gelman, 2005). Each of these methods incorporates auxiliary information to make adjustments for non-response. For example, the simplest of these, cell weighting, brings key response cells into line with known population estimates and operates on the assumption that data are missing at random. More complex forms of post-stratification weighting relax the assumption of randomly missing data and rely on the use of more complex information than cell weighting. Assumptions and choices of auxiliary information form the grounds for controversy when devising and using post-stratification weights. The reader is encouraged to consult the literature for more information about these issues.

Statistically, the use of sampling weights to address non-response reduces bias resulting from non-response but does so at the expense of precision (Kalton, 1983; Skinner et al., 1989). If the non-response is unrelated to the response variable, then no bias will exist in the parameter estimate, thus rendering the use of weights for non-response unnecessary. By including weights (either developed through post-stratification adjustment or due to initial disproportionate selection probabilities), estimated standard errors will be larger than if they had been estimated from an equal probability of selection sample. Therefore, the weighted analysis becomes less powerful. A primary (and familiar) challenge for the analyst is to find the appropriate trade-off between biased standard error and biased coefficient estimates.

We will return to these issues of disproportionate selection rates in the third section of this chapter when we discuss the use of sampling weights in analyses. Given these brief descriptions of reasons for disproportionate sampling or unequal sampling weights, we hope data users will be more comfortable when they encounter discussions of weights in technical manuals or journal articles or the weights themselves on the data set.

PUBLICLY AVAILABLE DATASETS FOR USE IN MULTILEVEL MODELING

In this section, we provide descriptions of three education-related datasets from NCES that are available to the public and that can be used for research as well as in multilevel courses for demonstration purposes. We present one cross-sectional database (Schools and Staffing Survey [SASS]) and two longitudinal databases (Early Childhood Longitudinal Study—Kindergarten Cohort [ECLS-K] and National Educational Longitudinal Study of 1988 [NELS:88]). For each dataset, we provide information on the important aspects of the sampling design used for data collection, a review of the content of the collected data, where to obtain the data, example articles that use multilevel methods with the dataset, and special concerns with the dataset structure or required analysis approach of which we are aware. In an appendix, we provide a brief list of additional datasets that may be of interest to multilevel modelers. We cannot stress enough that the few paragraphs that we provide here are not a replacement for a careful reading of the user's guides that are associated with each of these data sets. Our goal here is simply to put those user's guides in a more accessible and helpful context. Documentation on the NCES (2006) website should be consulted for further information on the surveys discussed below.

In most of these datasets, there are three general types of data available: sample design data, questionnaire responses or assessment results for participants, and derived variables created by the study administrators. The sample design information includes data about the sample elements or higher-level units that are available prior to data collection, such as Census region, public or private status of schools, and urban/rural location of the schools. The great bulk of the variables on any dataset are specific responses to questionnaires that were administered to the participants; copies of these questionnaires are usually available in technical manuals written for the specific dataset. For participants who are too young to complete written questionnaires (such as the youngest children who participate in the ECLS-K), results from interviewer-administered standardized assessments typically are provided. Finally, on any dataset, the study developers usually include derived variables, which can be extremely useful for research and analysis purposes. An example might be socio-economic status (SES); on NCES datasets, this variable typically is created from participant and/or parent/guardian responses to questions about their income, their education level, and their occupation. Researchers should be careful to note whether a derived variable they plan to use in their research was created based on another variable they might be including in the analysis (for example, the use of both income and SES in the same analysis might not be advisable due to multicollinearity issues).

Before we present our discussion of specific databases, we note that two different databases are usually available for any given dataset: publicly-available and restricted-use datasets. There is concern that if all available data for participants were provided to the public, it might be possible to identify particular individuals. For example, within the SASS dataset, there might be an Asian American female teacher from North Dakota who responded to the set of questionnaires. If data were available about the state and level of the school, coupled with the school enrollment size, the discipline in which she teaches, and her age, we very well might be able to pinpoint the exact individual who must have answered the questionnaire, compromising the confidentiality of her responses. Therefore, on its publicly-available datasets, NCES masks some of the data by either removing it from the database or by categorizing continuous variables. In this example, perhaps the variable, "discipline in which the respondent teaches," would not be available on the public-use dataset. Additionally, the variable "age" might be recorded as an ordinal variable with categories of "less than 25," "25 to 30," "31 to 40," "41 to 50," and "51 and over." As a precaution, researchers should not assume that all data collected with the questionnaires will be available to the end-user on the public-use data files. If a particular piece of data is crucial to an analysis, a researcher has the option to apply for a restricted-use license. To obtain such a license, the researcher must document the security procedures that will be in place to keep the data confidential. More information is available at the NCES website: http://nces.ed.gov/statprog/rudman/

The datasets described below are available free to the public on compact discs. These CDs usually contain documentation .pdf files, .pdf files that contain copies of the questionnaires or interview scripts used in data collection, the raw data (usually in ASCII format), and an electronic codebook application (referred to as the ECB). After using the CD to install the ECB on his or her computer, the researcher or analyst then can use the ECB to identify and "tag" variables of interest. Once all variables needed for analysis are tagged, the user can request the creation of SAS or SPSS syntax for extraction of the data (note that STATA syntax generation is also available for the ECLS-K dataset described below). This syntax then is written by the ECB, and the user can run the syntax file to extract the needed data from the CD and save it into a permanent SAS or SPSS data file (in many cases the user may need to edit this syntax slightly). The extracted data file created with the ECB-generated code will contain the user-tagged variables, typically accompanied by selected sampling design variables that the database designers at NCES deem important for all analysts to have (e.g., sample design information or sampling weights, etc.).

Example Dataset 1: Schools and Staffing Survey

Sampling Design

The Schools and Staffing Survey (SASS) is a cross-sectional survey that involves the collection of data at two levels: at each selected school, responses are obtained from a sample of teachers (level one) and responses are provided by the principal and by an administrative contact (level two) (Tourkin, et al., 2004). This survey is conducted periodically, and the most recent data available to the public are from the 1999–2000 school year (released April, 2005). Two separate sampling processes were undertaken to obtain the sample: one for public schools and one for private schools (and thus there is explicit stratification on school type). For the public school sample, the goals of sampling included the desire to report both national and state estimates of school and teacher characteristics at both the elementary and secondary level and to over-sample schools with a higher percentage of Native American enrollments so that national estimates for these schools might be produced. Some schools (such as public charter schools) were selected with certainty (they automatically were included in the sample). For the remainder of the schools in the public school sampling frame, several levels of stratification were used; schools were divided into Native American schools (19.5% or more of the enrolled students were Native American), schools in Nevada, West Virginia, or Delaware (which required a different sampling strategy given the school system structure), and all other schools (all Alaskan schools were placed in this third group regardless of Native American enrollment). At the second level of stratification, in general, the schools were stratified by state or state and district. At the third level of stratification, within states, the schools were grouped into categories of elementary, secondary, or combined (spanning at least grades 6 and 9) schools. Within each of these strata, the public schools were sorted by region, highest grade, percent minority, and enrollment. Systematic PPS sampling then was used to select schools. Disproportionate rates of sampling of schools were used across the explicit strata, and as an example, the sampling rates for states ranged from .051 in Illinois to .429 in the District of Columbia. Using this sampling process, a total of 11,139 public schools were selected.

To develop the private school sample, a list of schools was developed as the sampling occurred; 120 PSUs (counties) were chosen across the U.S.

in pairs within 60 strata defined by region. Within these PSUs, all private schools were attempted to be identified using a variety of methods (because no inclusive list already existed for all private schools in the U.S.). The goals of the sample allocation included the ability to provide estimates for each of 20 school affiliations and provide national comparisons of private versus public schools. Schools were stratified explicitly by affiliation and school grade level (elementary, secondary, and combined). Within PSUs, schools were sorted by affiliation, highest grade in school, location type and enrollment. Systematic PPS sampling then was used to select schools. In all, 3,560 private schools were selected for the sample.

For each sampled public and private school, a list of current teachers was obtained and stratified into one of five categories: teachers who are Asian or Pacific Islander (API), teachers who are American Indian or Alaskan Native (AIAN), teachers who are assigned to teach limited English proficient (LEP) classes, teachers with fewer than 4 years of experience, and teachers who have 4 or more years of experience. Teachers falling into more than one category were placed in the first as listed above. The sampling rates of teachers within a school depended on the selection rates for the school, resulting in approximately equal overall rates of selection for all teachers in the sampling frame. A maximum of 20 teachers were intended to be selected from a school, with oversampling of API, AIAN and LEP teachers. Within private schools, new teachers were sampled at higher rates than experienced teachers. Across all categories of schools, a total of 72,058 teachers were selected for the sample. Approximately 80% of teachers responded to the survey; the final dataset contains data for 42,086 public school teachers from 8,712 schools, and 7,098 private school teachers from 2,504 schools.

Content

The publicly-available dataset contains hundreds of variables on school, principal, and teacher characteristics (also district data, but due to confidentiality concerns, these data are not easily merged with school data and thus are not discussed here). The dataset contains teacher respondent information, such as satisfaction with class size, job security, and salary (measured on Likert-type scales), classes assigned and grade levels, income and benefits, licensure and academic preparation, perceived professional development support and availability, demographic information, the teacher's career path, and instructional practices, including hours spent on specific subjects in class and computer use. Principal respondent information includes the principal's career path and demographic information, goals for the school and an assessment of how close to the goals the school is perceived to be, responses to questions pertaining to levels of influence of various in-school and out-of-school forces on school policies and practices, problems with student behavior and teacher performance, activities undertaken as principal in the last month, and whether the school had or had not met standards and, if not, the required action. School-level data, which were provided by a contact at the school (who may or may not have been the principal), contain information on grade levels at the school, enrollments by race/ethnicity and gender, absentee information, admission requirements, program availability (such as Advanced Placement and technical preparatory programs), student scheduling policies (use of tracking, block schedules, team teaching, etc.), school calendar, student outcomes after graduation, parental involvement activities and levels of participation, security and violence prevention policies, staffing numbers, and vacancies.

Summary of Data Structure

The available data lend themselves to many two-level modeling examples, using principal and school data as level-two variables and teacher data at level-one. The number of teachers per school is somewhat low, however, ranging from 1 to 19 with an average of about 4.4. The distribution of schools by number of sampled teachers is shown in Table 2.1.

In general, this dataset would be useful for two-level contextual analyses, given the simple structure of teachers within schools. However the number of teachers within a school may have implications for some multilevel analyses. Most immediately, the number of within-cluster observations (teachers in this case) has an impact on the reliability with which the population

TABLE 2.1   Number and Percent of Schools by Size of Teacher Sample from the SASS Dataset

Teachers per school	#	%
1	1,006	9.0
2	1,710	15.3
3	2,116	18.9
4	1,974	17.6
5	1,404	12.5
6	1,011	9.0
7	691	6.2
8	463	4.1
9	298	2.7
10	214	1.9
11	125	1.1
12 or more	204	2.0
Total number of schools	11,216	100.0

means for each cluster, and relations within each cluster, are estimated. Smaller within-cluster samples yield relatively less reliable estimates of these population parameters than do larger within-cluster samples. Because sample sizes within each level-two unit (schools in this case) are likely to differ, reliability will vary across level-two units, also. Some multilevel modeling programs (e.g., HLM) provide a summary measure of these reliabilities that takes the form of the average reliability across all level-two units. While the ICC provides a sense of the degree to which variability exists between level-two units, the reliability of these within-school estimates determines the degree to which observed differences between-groups are representative of real population differences rather than sampling error. It should be clear that the ICC and associated reliabilities are related directly to the ability to detect between-unit differences at level two (i.e., power) (Heck & Thomas, 2000). A discussion of power issues in multilevel data is provided in the last section of this chapter, and a more comprehensive treatment of these issues can be found in Chapter 8 of this volume (Spybrook, 2008).

A user should note that when data are extracted using the ECB-generated SAS or SPSS syntax with the SASS data, several datasets are provided, one for each type of survey respondent (public school, public principal, public teacher, private school, private principal, and private teacher). The public and private datasets need to be appended (vertically concatenated into one file); these files already contain the same variable names, and thus concatenating the files is generally a simple process. Depending on the multilevel software to be used (see Chapter 12 of this volume (Roberts & McLeod, 2008)), the principal and/or school information can be merged with the teacher data by SCHCNTL, a school identification code. Individuals within schools are identified by a personal identification number, CNTLNUM.

On each of the SASS datasets, there is a unique sampling weight, and thus separate weights exist for the school, principal, and teacher levels. These weights represent the reciprocal of the overall selection rates of the element in the sample. School and principal rates are not necessarily the same, due to principal non-response.

Example Articles

The following articles provide examples of research using the SASS data with a multilevel analysis:

- Ballou, D., & Podgursky, M. (1997). What makes a good principal? How teachers assess the performance of principals. *Economics of Education Review, 14,* 243–252.
- Liu, X. S., & Meyer, J. P. (2005). Teachers' perceptions of their jobs: A multilevel analysis of the Teacher Follow-up Survey for 1994–95. *Teachers College Record, 107,* 985–1003.

- National Center for Education Statistics. (1997). *Teacher professionalization and teacher commitment: A multilevel analysis* (NCES 97-069). Washington, D.C.: U.S. Department of Education.

Where to Obtain More Information

More information about the SASS dataset is available at: http://nces.ed.gov/surveys/sass/

At the website, a user can obtain copies of the questionnaires, along with more information about the data collection process, summary data tables, and a listing of all the reports that the NCES has produced using this dataset. In the documentation, a User's Guide provides the estimated design effects for key variables across the sample design (see Appendix G of the SASS User's guide). A review of these design effects may help to identify variables that will likely show larger intraclass correlations. Note that NCES considers its data CDs as "publications," so a user can click on "publications" and choose "data products" and a list of data CDs that can be requested for free from the U.S. Department of Education will appear.

Example Dataset II: Early Childhood Longitudinal Study—Kindergarten Cohort

Sample Design

In 1998, the U.S. Department of Education began a longitudinal assessment of cognitive and non-cognitive abilities of children, along with a collection of information about their home environments. This study began with a sample of kindergarten children and has assessed these children repeatedly at different times over the first 6 years of their school careers (kindergarten through approximately fifth grade), with plans to assess them again in year 9 of their school careers (approximately eighth grade). Briefly, the ECLS-K sampling design includes three stages of sampling: PSUs of single counties or groups of counties, schools within those counties, and students within the selected schools. First-stage strata were defined by a combination of Census Metropolitan Statistical Area, Census region, proportion of the population of a specific race/ethnicity, size of the PSU and average per capita income of the PSU. One hundred PSUs were selected within these strata and within each of the PSUs, schools were stratified by public/private status and then were sampled with further implicit stratification on size of the school and proportion of Asian/Pacific Islander (API) students. Finally, within 1,280 sampled schools, students were selected using two strata: API students and non-API students. API students were selected at a rate 3 times greater than non-API students (when population numbers allowed), for a target size of 24 students per school.

Several follow-up data collection waves have occurred for the kindergarten cohort. After the kindergarten students were assessed initially in the fall of 1998, the students were again assessed in the spring of 1999. In the subsequent year, a 30% subsample was selected in the fall of the first grade to facilitate the assessment of "summer loss" in achievement. In the spring of 2000, a "freshened" sample of the original cohort of students, now mostly in first grade, was assessed. The freshened sample included "new cases added to a longitudinal sample plus the retained cases from the longitudinal sample used to produce cross-sectional estimates of the population at the time of a subsequent wave of longitudinal data collection" (NCES, 2007). A freshened sample was required to capture students who were now in first grade but had not been enrolled in kindergarten the prior year (and thus did not have a chance to be selected in the original cohort). Two years later, in the spring of 2002, the freshened sample again was assessed. NCES refers to this data collection period as "third-grade collection," but not all students were in the third grade; 89% of the respondents were actually in third grade, 8% were in second grade, and the remaining students were in other grades or not enrolled. Data from the wave of data collection in spring 2004 were released in 2006 and is referred to as the fifth-grade follow-up, although just 87% are actually in fifth grade. In spring of 2007, data were collected on these students but has not yet been released; NCES refers to this data collection period as the eighth-grade follow-up, although not all students actually were in eighth grade.

Content

During each of the data collection stages, data are collected from the child, the child's parent or guardian, the teacher of the child, and the principal or school administrator. In the data collection that took place in kindergarten and first grade, children were assessed as they took part in cognitive and non-cognitive tasks. In the third and fifth grade, in addition to the assessments, students also were asked to complete questionnaires about their perceptions of their abilities and their interest and attitudes toward school subjects and learning. Using item-response theory, summary scores were created from the assessment information for the cognitive and non-cognitive tasks and are available on the data set.

Parents were interviewed to obtain data, including information about the home, past day care arrangements, family structure, child behaviors and activities, as well as information to assess the parent's level of depression and family functioning. Teachers provided information using a self-administered questionnaire on their own teaching practices and background as well as an evaluation of the child's cognitive and non-cognitive development. School staff were asked to provide information about student attendance, transfer, and individual educational plans, if applicable.

Summary of Data Structure

Out of the 17,565 records on the kindergarten to fifth-grade longitudinal dataset, nearly 16,000 are reported as starting in Round 1 of the longitudinal study (the remaining records are part of the freshened samples for spring of kindergarten and spring of first grade). Of these fall 1998 kindergarten students, the initial cohort, data for 75% are available up to the third-grade data collection period. Moreover, about 62% of the initial cohort was available to be assessed in the subsequent spring, the spring of first grade, the spring of third grade, and the spring of fifth grade, making for a fairly large set of complete longitudinal data. Note that some students were not available to be assessed and dropped from the study at various time points. For most of the children who participated in all data collection periods, their parent and teacher data are available as well at the time points they were assessed.

Of interest to multilevel modelers is the number of students for whom data are available within each school. Because of student movement across schools and the existence of students on the dataset who were not part of the initial kindergarten sample, it can be somewhat difficult to examine the number of students per school for longitudinal analysis, but Table 2.2 provides the school distribution by number of children for whom data are available from the school for the children who were in the initial cohort of fall kindergarten students.

In the fall of kindergarten, data were available for 15,848 students across 926 schools, resulting in an average of about 17 students per school, and this number ranged from 1 to 26 students per school. The majority of schools had data available for between 11 and 20 or more students. Over time, as students transferred to new schools, the number of schools with data available for only 1 student rose dramatically across the data collection waves. By design, students were followed, even if they changed schools. The number of schools with higher numbers of students per school decreased slowly over time so that by the fifth-grade data collection point, there were few schools ($n = 13$) with greater than 20 students in the sample. In the ECLS-K, when a student changed schools, he or she typically entered a school that was not already in the study and, therefore, created a new school in the sample with only 1 student. The reliabilities of schools represented by a single respondent are, of course, quite low, and algorithms in most multilevel modeling programs place very little weight on the contributions of these schools to level-one estimates. The decision to include or exclude level-two units with small sample sizes should depend on the goals of the analysis. Snijders (2005) writes:

> A primary qualitative issue is that, for testing the effect of a level one variable, the level one sample size...is of main importance; for testing the effect of a

TABLE 2.2 Number and Percent of Schools by Size of Student Sample and Wave of Data Collection for the Initial Cohort from the ECLS-K Dataset

Number of students for whom data are available per school	Fall kindergarten		Spring kindergarten		Spring first grade		Spring third grade		Spring fifth grade	
	#	%	#	%	#	%	#	%	#	%
1	12	1.3	192	17.2	822	42.6	1,550	56.0	1,187	53.7
2–5	32	3.5	47	4.2	238	12.3	405	14.6	318	14.4
6–10	54	5.8	53	4.7	82	4.3	244	8.8	316	14.3
11–15	177	19.1	187	16.7	254	13.2	338	12.2	270	12.2
16–20	399	43.1	436	39.0	426	22.1	205	7.4	108	4.9
21–26	252	27.2	203	18.2	107	5.6	27	1.0	13	0.6
Total number of schools	926	100.0	1,118	100.0	1,929	100.0	2,769	100.0	2,212	100.0

level two variable it is the level two sample size, etc.... A second qualitative issue is that for testing fixed regression coefficients, small cluster sizes are not a problem.... What is limited by this low average cluster size, is the power for testing random slope variances at the school level, i.e., between-school variances of effects of classroom- or pupil-level variables; and the reliability of estimating those characteristics of individual schools, calculated from [student] variables, that differ strongly between schools. (p. 2)

Sample freshening boosts the cross-sectional within-school samples but does not address within-school attrition in the original panel. Thus, analysts interested in modeling school-level effects on children's growth over time may need to focus only upon those children who remain in the same school for the duration of the study. Note that this type of analysis limits the population of inference to non-movers, and results from such an analysis should not be generalized to all students. Another possible approach to modeling the data when students move to different schools is to use a cross-classified analysis, allowing students to be nested under more than one school. This approach to modeling is discussed in detail in Chapter 5 of this volume (Beretvas, 2008), but be cautioned that adjusting for cross-classification does not fully address the sparseness issue created with 1 student per school.

Researchers might be interested in examining a finer distinction in levels of data in ECLS-K. On average, there are about 3 teachers per school, with the actual range from 1 to 15 teachers, depending on the data collection wave. While within-school attrition can make longitudinal analyses difficult, the freshened cross-sectional data provide opportunities for models nesting students within teachers and teachers within schools. Although this provides analytic opportunities to develop three-level models, there are also design threats of clustering and stratification that need to be acknowledged whether or not these are incorporated into the analytical model. Again, it is important to be aware of the data structures resulting from the various waves of these longitudinal surveys.

Users also must be cognizant of their population of interest, whether it be kindergarten students, first graders, etc. For any analysis, the panel of data to be used from the dataset will depend on the population of inference. Analyses using the kindergarten data and any longitudinal analyses that start with students in kindergarten will be representative of all kindergarten students in the U.S. in 1998; teacher data from such analyses are nationally representative of teachers of kindergarten students and the school-level data represent all schools with kindergartens. Data for first graders (from the spring 2000 follow-up) are representative of all first-grade students in the U.S. (because of the use of a freshened sample), but the teacher and school-level data are not representative of all U.S. first-grade teachers and schools. The spring 2002 and 2004 follow-up data are *neither* representative of all students in the third or fifth grade, nor all teachers of third or fifth graders, nor all schools with third or fifth grades. These data are intended to be used for longitudinal purposes and not for cross-sectional analyses. Results from any cross-sectional analyses undertaken with these data on third or fifth graders only can be generalized to students who were formerly kindergarten students in 1998.

Another possible complication in the use of the ECLS-K data is that not all students are assessed at the same time point. It is not feasible to have assessment personnel visit all 16,000 students at the same time. In fact, the assessments are spread out across a few months. For example, in the spring 1999 data collection, students were assessed anytime between March and July. Most students (92%) were assessed in April and May, but others were outside that time window. With the cognitive growth that is occurring in children at these ages, the difference between March and July assessments might be quite large. There is a section of the fifth-grade Combined User's Manual (NCES, 2006) that discusses measuring gains (section 3.1.6) when students are assessed at differing time points across data collection waves, and the NCES cautions users to consider child age and assessment date when comparing gains within relatively short periods of time (such as within-in-grade or across a 1-year time point).

Unlike the SASS dataset that contains just one sampling probability weight variable for each observation, the kindergarten to fifth-grade longitudinal ECLS-K dataset contains 28 sampling probability weights for each child record in the dataset. Because there are several sources of information about each child (child, parent, teacher, school) and because there are several data collection times, the appropriate weight to use will depend on whether the analysis model includes certain kinds of variables. In section 4.7.5 of the User's Manual, cross-sectional weights are described, and Chapter 9 of the User's Manual contains a discussion on longitudinal analysis strategies including weighting options (NCES, 2006).

On some of the ECLS-K CDs, there may be several databases available (such as child-based data, teacher-based data, etc.), and on some of the longitudinal CDs (such as the longitudinal fifth-grade CD) the data already are combined. The linking process across the school, teacher, and student databases in ECLS-K will depend on whether the researcher's question is cross-sectional or longitudinal in nature. For example, examining kindergarten-classroom and school effects on spring kindergarten outcomes requires the base-year data CD, and this CD contains separate data catalogs for schools, teachers, and children. In the School file, each school is identified with an identification code labeled S_ID. In the Teacher file, each teacher is identified with a unique number labeled T_ID, and each teacher record includes a school link, S_ID. In the Child file, each kindergartener has a unique CHILDID code and also has identification codes of T1_ID, T2_ID, S1_ID, and S2_ID. The first of these codes, T1_ID, represents the teacher identification number from the fall data collection, and the second, T2_ID, represents the teacher identification number from the spring data collection. It is possible that a student switched teachers during the school year. Similarly, the S1_ID and S2_ID codes represent the fall and spring school identification codes. To merge data across the catalogs or to prepare a file that multilevel software such as HLM can use, some renaming of variables may be necessary since variable names must be identical across all data files.

As another example, the fifth-grade longitudinal ECLS-K data only has the child data catalog available. Teacher and school information already is merged with the child record, and on this child record are identification codes for teachers for each of the six possible data collection points (for example, T4_ID, T5_ID), as well as identification codes for schools for each of the six possible data collection points (S2_ID, S5_ID, etc.). To use this data set, an analyst may need to split the data into level-two and level-one data files, depending on the software used. Also, it is possible that an analyst may want to extract some teacher-specific information, for example, from the spring kindergarten Teacher catalog, to merge with the longitudinal file.

Example Articles

The following articles provide examples of research using the ECLS data with a multilevel analysis:

- Datar, A., & Sturm, R. (2004). Physical education in elementary school and body mass index: Evidence from the Early Childhood Longitudinal Study. *American Journal of Public Health, 94,* 1501–1506.
- Finn, J. D., & Pannozzo, G. M. (2004). Classroom organization and student behavior in kindergarten. *Journal of Educational Research, 98,* 79–92.
- McCoach, D.B., O'Connell, A.A. Reis, S.M., & Levitt, H.A. (2006). Growing readers: A hierarchical linear model of children's reading growth during the first 2 years of school. *Journal of Educational Psychology, 98,* 14–28.
- Xue, Y., & Meisels, S. J. (2004). Early literacy instruction and learning in kindergarten: Evidence from the Early Childhood Longitudinal Study—Kindergarten Class of 1998–1999. *American Educational Research Journal, 41,* 191–229.

Where to Obtain More Information

More information about the dataset is available at: http://nces.ed.gov/ecls/kindergarten.asp At the website, a user can obtain copies of the questionnaires, along with more detailed information about the data collection process, summary data tables, and a listing of all the reports that the NCES has produced using this dataset. The user's guide provides the estimated design effects for key variables across the sample design (see Tables 9-3 through 9-6 of the User's Manual (NCES, 2006)).

Example Dataset III: National Education Longitudinal Study 1988

Sample Design

As of this writing, the National Education Longitudinal Study (NELS) 1988 eighth-grade cohort has been followed longitudinally for five collection periods, with the most recent collection occurring in the year 2000. The NELS:88 data collection is intended to provide policy-relevant information about the experiences of high school students in the U.S. through the 1990s. The NELS dataset contains data for a cohort of students who were enrolled in the eighth grade in 1988. The sampling design was a stratified two-stage sample with selection of schools as PSUs and then sampling of students within the selected schools. School strata were defined by school type (public or private), geographic region, and location type. For public schools, the strata also were divided into percent minority categories. Once the stratified list of schools was created, a PPS sample of schools was drawn with implicit stratification by enrollment. To provide efficient national estimates for students from private schools, private schools were selected at a higher sampling rate than public schools. Some schools were specifically excluded from the sample, such as special education schools and schools for U.S. military dependents overseas. Within the sampled schools, eighth-grade students were selected from three strata: Asian, Hispanic, and all other students (Asian and Hispanic students were over-sampled). The final sample contained responses from nearly 25,000 students in 1,052 schools (815 public and 237 private). In 1990, 2 years later, NCES conducted a follow-up study in which they located the students (most students had changed schools) and included the initial cohort as well as a freshened sample to ensure that the sample was representative of all 10th-grade students in the U.S. After another 2 years, during the 1991–92 school year, the initial cohort was surveyed, and a freshened sample was used to obtain a representative sample of 12th graders in the U.S. In 1994, to control costs, a sub-sample of just 15,964 participants was selected and surveyed, and a fourth follow-up took place in 2000, again using sub-sampling.

Content

At the first wave of data collection (eighth grade), information was collected from students, parents, teachers, and principals. Students completed a cognitive test covering reading, mathematics, science, and social studies, as well as a questionnaire that asked about school experiences, attitudes about themselves (such as self confidence), behaviors (such as homework practices and use of alcohol and cigarettes), and home characteristics (for example, whether an adult was at home when the student arrived home from school). Parents were asked to provide information about student activities, the parent's relationship with the school, and characteristics of the family. For each student, two teachers were selected (in the topics of math, science, English or social studies, depending on the sampling design), and they were asked to provide information on their teaching emphasis in class, time spent on specific activities, as well as various ratings of the student. Principals provided information about the school and administrative records for the student, such as attendance and grade records.

In the first follow-up, when most students were high school sophomores, the same general types of elements were collected; however, no information was obtained from parents. In the second follow-up (1992), when most students were seniors in high school, a final cognitive assessment was made, and parents, teachers, and principals again were contacted. At this follow-up, a large amount of information for students who dropped out of school also was collected. In 1994, when most students had graduated from high school, the participants were asked questions regarding employment and postsecondary education, and finally, in 2000, when most respondents were 26 years of age, the fourth follow-up centered on educational and social issues, community integration, marriage, and family formation, and the data collection also included collection of postsecondary transcripts.

Summary of Data Structure

The NELS data can be useful for both contextual and longitudinal analyses, and the information on the number of students per school depends on whether a cross-sectional or longitudinal analysis is desired. Either way, there appear to be sufficient data for multilevel analyses given the students per school (at least until they leave school). Table 2.3 contains the distribution of number of schools by the number of students in the sample at that school for the base year and first follow-up.

In the base year, there were almost 25,000 students in 1,052 schools, for an average of over 23 students per school. In the first follow-up of these students from the original cohort, 17,465 were sub-sampled, located, and in school and were spread across 1,628 schools, with an average of almost 11 students per school (note that the change from 8th to 10th grade usually includes a change from middle-school to high-school; thus, each sub-sampled student was required to be located at the new high-school).

Several NELS:88 CDs are available for public use, and the data needs will determine the CD that the researcher should obtain for use. If a researcher is interested in a cross-sectional analysis for 8th, 10th, or 12th graders, then the CD titled *N2P* would be appropriate (the *N* stands for NELS, the

TABLE 2.3 Number and Percent of Schools by Size of Student Sample and Wave of Data Collection for the Initial Cohort from the NELS Dataset

Students per school	Eigth grade (base year)		First follow-up	
	#	%	#	%
1	5	0.5	486	29.9
2–5	16	1.5	196	12.0
6–10	35	3.3	159	9.8
11–15	32	3.0	187	11.5
16–20	162	15.4	345	21.2
21–25	544	51.7	195	12.0
26–30	151	14.4	33	2.0
>30	107	10.2	27	1.7
Total number of schools	1,052	100.0	1,628	100.0

2 stands for 1992 data collection, and the *P* represents the public dataset). If a researcher is interested in following any of these cohorts to the year 1994, then the CD titled *N4P* should be used. Finally, if interest is in the full longitudinal file, which follows students to the year 2000, then the CD titled *N0P* would be appropriate.

Again, just as with the ECLS-K data, users must be cognizant of their population of interest, whether it be eighth graders, schools, etc. For any analysis, the panel of data to be used from the dataset will depend on the population of inference. Files from the base year (1988) can be used for analysis to be nationally representative of eighth-grade students as well as schools that enroll eighth-grade students, and while the 1990 and 1992 follow-up datasets hold data that are nationally representative for 10th- and 12th-grade students respectively, the data for the sample of schools is not nationally representative of all 10th- and 12th-grade schools.

For multilevel analyses that are longitudinal (and thus use data across time for individuals), analysts will need to undertake some data manipulation to prepare files for analysis because all the data across time are on one record. Once the user downloads the data, he or she will then need to split the data into separate occasion-specific records and keep the person unique identifier, STU_ID, on each record. To run a contextual school analysis, there are school IDs on the file for both the base year (eighth grade) and the first year follow-up (10th grade). SCH_ID is the base-year school identification number, and F1SCH_ID is the first-year follow-up school identification number.

Example Articles

The following articles provide examples of research using the NELS data with a multilevel analysis:

- Lee, V., & Smith, J.B. (1997). High school size: Which works best, and for whom? *Educational Evaluation and Policy Analysis, 19,* 205–227.
- Morgan, S.L. and Sorensen, A.B. (1999). Parental networks, social closure, and mathematics learning: A test of Colemen's social capital explanation of school effects. *American Sociological Review, 64,* 661–681.
- Pong, S. (1998). The school compositional effect of single-parenthood on 10th-grade achievement. *Sociology of Education, 71,* 24–43. [Won the 1999 Willard Waller Award from the American Sociological Association.]
- Wiley, S. (2001). Contextual effects on student achievement: School leadership and professional community. *Journal of Educational Change, 2,* 1–33.

Where to Obtain More Information

More information about the dataset is available at: http://nces.ed.gov/surveys/nels88/ Copies of the questionnaires used in all data collection waves for students, parents, teachers, school administrators, and students who have dropped out of school are available at this website. In addition, researchers can obtain an annotated bibliography of research that has been undertaken on this dataset (both single-level and multilevel).

Additional Information: Datasets and Training

In the appendix, we have provided a list of additional datasets that may be of interest to readers. For those readers who are interested in more targeted training in learning how to work with NCES data sets, NCES provides training opportunities. Each summer, the NCES offers workshops to learn how to work with a specific database. These opportunities typically are announced at the following website: http://nces.ed.gov/whatsnew/conferences/ in the "Workshop/Training & Technical Assistance" section. Another source of training is the American Educational Research Association's Institute on Statistical Analysis for Education Policy. This program consists of 3 days of training, in conjunction with the association's annual meeting, covering the use of a specific statistical technique with a specific database from NCES or the National Science Foundation. Current information about this institute is available at the following website: http://www.aera.net/grantsprogram/ res_training/stat_institute/SIFly.html Finally, technical assistance always can be sought by contacting the staff at NCES who work in the specific survey program area.

ISSUES WHEN WORKING WITH THESE DATASETS

In this section, we focus on several important analytic issues for researchers working with datasets such as the national studies we have described above. These issues include the use of sampling weights, the accommodation of missing data, the careful consideration of the level of analysis including power, and attention to the sampling design.

Sampling Weights

Probably one of the most challenging aspects of working with these NCES datasets is determining the appropriate way to accommodate sampling weights into the analysis. First, we review a simple single-level research situation, and then we extend the use of weights to multilevel designs. Suppose that data were collected using a simple stratified sampling design. Specifically, 100 children were sampled from a school of 1,000 children. In the population, there were 800 non-Hispanic children and 200 Hispanic children. For the sample, however, explicit stratification by ethnicity was used, and 50 non-Hispanic children and 50 Hispanic children were sampled. The probability of selection for a non-Hispanic child was 50/800 = .0625 and the probability of selection for a Hispanic child was 50/200 = .25. After data were collected, suppose interest lies in using the data to estimate the mean level of student achievement. We hope that it is clear from our discussion to this point in the chapter that the disproportionate selection in the sampling design demands attention.

To obtain unbiased parameter estimates, the observations in the sample dataset most likely should be weighted to bring the intentionally biased sample proportions back in correspondence with the known population proportions. Failure to apply sample weights will result in an artificial influence of groups that were oversampled. For example, Hispanic children were oversampled at a rate of 4:1 (the sampling rates were .25 for Hispanic children compared with .0625 for non-Hispanic children), failure to weight the sample back to the correct proportion will result in any estimates being biased toward the characteristics of the Hispanic children in the sample— that is, Hispanic children will be accorded disproportionate weight in any estimates made directly from the unweighted sample. If Hispanic children perform higher on the achievement test of interest, then the overall esti-mated mean will be biased upward by the effective quadruple-counting in the sample, and thus the estimate will not be reflective of the true overall population mean on that test. The weights used to "balance" such quadru-ple-counting resulting from the sample design simply reflect the inverse of any sample element's overall probability of their inclusion in the sam-ple. Thus, after applying the sampling weights in this simple single-level example, a response from a Hispanic student will be accorded a weight of 1/.25 (or 4), and a response from a non-Hispanic student will be accorded a weight of 1/.0625 (or 16). These weights will be used in determining the parameter estimate.

A consequence of disproportionate sampling is that observations select-ed with higher probabilities (i.e., oversampled) will have smaller raw weight values. For any dataset, summing the raw weights across all observations yields the population N:

$$\sum_{i=1}^{n} w_i = N. \tag{2.2}$$

While statistical packages vary in the way they use weights to calculate certain statistics, most calculate the weighted mean as follows:

$$\bar{x} = \sum_{i=1}^{n} w_i x_i \Big/ \sum_{i=1}^{n} w_i, \tag{2.3}$$

which is the sum of the products of each observation's raw weight and value for x, divided by the sum of the raw weights, N. Notice that the sum of the raw weights ($\sum w_i$), or the size of the target population, now becomes what is referred to as the "effective sample size" in this calculation.

A consequence of using the raw weights supplied with most complex survey data is that, when calculating SE estimates, some statistical packages (SPSS included) are fooled into believing that the sample size is much larg-er than it really is. While use of the raw weights yields an unbiased point esti-mate for the mean in all software packages, in some software packages, like SPSS, analyses using the raw weights result in an effective sample size that is the same as the population N. The use of this inflated effective sample size seriously can compromise some calculations, such as standard errors and sampling variances as well as variances and covariances. The effect of using this inflated effective sample size becomes an especially critical point when one wishes to test hypotheses using weighted data—most every difference or coefficient becomes statistically significant when using statistical pack-ages that are blind to the actual sample size. Recall that the standard error is a function of variance over sample size; with an effective sample size of N in the denominator, the standard error will be incredibly small!

This difficulty can be avoided in any statistical package, however, with a simple scaling of the raw weights. In order to preserve the effective sample size as the actual sample size while still adjusting for oversampling, we can create what is termed as *relative* weights by dividing the raw weights by their mean,

$$w_{relative_i} = w_i / \overline{w}, \tag{2.4}$$

where $\overline{w} = \sum w_i / n$. Note that the sum of these relative weights is equivalent to the sample size $(\sum w_{relative_i} = n)$.

This issue of weight scaling extends directly to multilevel analyses; however, weighting in the multilevel context brings additional challenges. Some software packages automatically rescale the raw sample weight while others do not. The user is encouraged to review the most recent technical manual that is available for the software to be sure the weight is being handled in an expected manner. For most types of analyses, multilevel modeling software offers researchers the opportunity to provide sampling weights at each of the levels of their model. The ability to weight at different levels of the model requires a consideration of the ways in which disproportionate sampling occurs at different levels and in how combining weights at these different levels can affect parameter estimates. To this point in the chapter, we have considered weighting issues in the context of a single level of analysis. As we hope to make clear in this section, multilevel analyses require a more complex way of thinking about the purpose and behavior of sample weights. On which level(s) should one apply weights? Which weights are appropriate—weights that reflect the sampling rate of the school, weights that reflect the conditional sampling rate of the student, or weights that combine those sampling rates? These are crucial issues to consider when using data from complex samples in multilevel analyses.

Considerable debate exists about the correct choice of weights to use for a multilevel analysis. The central features of that debate include the appropriate scaling of the weight and the best estimation method for the parameter and variance components with models incorporating sampling weights. Simulation studies have been conducted, and no method is clearly the most appropriate under all circumstances; success of the methods depend on conditions such as whether the response variable is correlated with the sampling weights (referred to as informative sampling weights), whether the model includes continuous or dichotomous outcomes, and the sample sizes at level one and level two (Asparouhov, 2005; Pfeffermann, Skinner, Holmes, Goldstein, & Rasbash, 1998; Rabe-Hesketh & Skrondal, in press).

To clarify some of the decisions that a researcher must address, let us examine an example. Suppose that we draw a stratified sample from a school district. In the population, there are five public schools with 300 students enrolled in each of them and 25 private schools, each with just 20 students enrolled, for a total population of 2,000 students (1,500 public and 500 private). We select two schools, using explicit stratified sampling and select one public school at a probability of $\pi_1 = 1/5 = .2$ and one private school at a probability of $\pi_2 = 1/25 = .04$. The respective raw sampling weights at the school level for these two schools are $w_1 = 1/.2 = 5$ and $w_2 = 1/.04 = 25$. The public school represents five schools, and the private school represents 25 schools. Once the schools are selected, 10 students are selected from each. Students in the public school are selected with a probability of $\pi_{i|1} = 10/300 = .033$, and students at the private school are selected at a probability of $\pi_{i|2} = 10/20 = .5$. The conditional raw sampling weight for students in the public school is $w_{i|1} = 1/.033 = 30$; thus, each public-school student in the sample represents 30 students in the population from that specific school. In the private school the conditional raw sampling weight is $w_{i|2} = 1/.5 = 2$; thus, each private-school student in the sample represents just 2 students from that specific school in the population. Overall sampling weights can be calculated by taking the product of the school-level and conditional student-level weights. These overall weights indicate the number of students in the overall population represented by each student selected for the sample, after adjusting for strata (public or private school). Thus, the selected students from the public schools each represent $w_{i1} = w_1 \times w_{i|1} = 5 \times 30 = 150$ students from the original school district population, and the selected students from the private schools each represent $w_{i2} = w_2 \times w_{i|2} = 25 \times 2 = 50$ students from the original school district population. Given this scenario, the typical weight provided on an NCES database would be 150 for public school students and 50 for private school students (NCES usually provides overall weights on databases and not within-school conditional sampling weights).

Assuming we had access to the overall sampling weight and each of the conditional weights, on which level of a multilevel analysis does one specify the weight? Most multilevel software now will allow users some options: to provide a weight at level one only, a weight at level two only, or weights at both levels of the analysis. Using the HLM software as an example, if we provide our overall raw sampling weights at level one ($w_{i1} = 150$ for public school students and $w_{i2} = 50$ for private school students) and no weight information at level two, the software accurately will assume that the level-one weights provided are overall sampling weights. In the HLM software, these weights then will be scaled as relative weights by dividing each overall weight by the average of the weights:

$$w_{relative_{ij}} = w_{ij} / \bar{w} . \tag{2.5}$$

In this example, the average weight is 100, and thus, the new, scaled relative weight for students from public schools becomes 1.5, and the new, scaled relative weight for private school students becomes .5. Note that these new weights will sum to the actual sample size, thus allowing for more appropriate standard error estimation than if unscaled raw weights were used. However, appropriate scaling is still under investigation in a multi-level context (Asparouhov, 2005; Rabe-Hesketh & Skrondal, in press). In obtaining level-one parameter estimates, data from public-school students in our example will weigh more heavily in the estimation than data from private-school students since their relative weight is larger. However, at level two, because we provided no weight information (it was incorporated into the overall relative weight), school-level relations would be determined considering the information from each of the schools as equally informative.

Alternatively, in this example we could choose to provide weights at both level one and level two. With this approach, the HLM software will make the assumption that the weights at level one are conditional weights (i.e., within level two). Unfortunately, this assumption would be incorrect for most analyses using publicly-available data from NCES; recall that NCES typically only provides overall sampling weights. However, the violation of this assumption is relatively benign. For example, if we provide the overall sampling weights to HLM ($w_{ij} = 150$ for public school students and $w_{ij} = 50$ for private school students), HLM automatically will rescale the weights within each level-two unit such that the sum of the weights within a level-two unit equals the sample size within that level-two unit. The HLM software does this by dividing each raw weight by the average of the weights within each level-two unit, similar to the previously-described scaling procedure. For public-school students in our example, their raw weights would be divided by 150, resulting in a relative weight of 1 ($150/150 = 1$), and for private-school students, this scaling would result in each raw weight being divided by 50, resulting in a relative weight of 1 ($50/50 = 1$). Note that if we had access to the conditional sampling weights (of 30 and 2 respectively) to provide to HLM, the relative weights still would have been equal to 1. The distinction between marginal and conditional weights is meaningless for this rescaling because the overall sampling probability weight differs from the conditional probability weight only by a constant for all elements within a level-two unit,

With weighting at both level one and level two in the analysis, the level-one relations will be estimated based on equal weighting of the data on students from public and private schools; however, the level-one estimation is moderated by the weights applied at level two. When raw weights are provided at level two (in this example, 5 and 25 for public and private schools, respectively), HLM will rescale these weights by dividing each school-level weight by the sum of the school weights (i.e., yielding relative weights). In our simple case, each raw school weight would be divided by 15 to result in new, scaled relative weights of .33 for public schools and 1.67 for private schools. These new school-level relative weights will sum to the actual sample size at level two. To obtain estimates of school-level relations that can be generalized to the population of schools in this district, the data for the private school will be weighted more heavily than the public school. Thus, the level-two estimates will play a role in level-one estimation.

Finally, a third option for weighting is to provide sampling weights at level two only. In HLM, the weights would be rescaled automatically at level two as described above (i.e., relative weights) and responses from individuals within the level-two units are assumed to contribute to the estimation equally. This method may appear to result in the same approach as providing both level-one and level-two weights as described above; however, this similarity is a result of a simplified example. If unequal weighting is applied *within*-schools (some students selected at higher rates than others), then the two approaches would yield different estimates, assuming the responses differed across strata of students.

Estimation methods and accommodations for addressing weights in multilevel software appear to be changing with each new version of software, so users are encouraged to consult the manuals for the appropriate version of their software before deciding on which weighting approach to use. For example, the weighting options and assumptions in the MLwiN software are similar to those provided with HLM; however, MLwiN appears a little more flexible. MLwiN allows the user to model with raw weights (instead of rescaling automatically to use relative weights, although the rescaling is available) and will estimate level-two weights from overall inclusion weights at level one.

The examples presented above reveal that the estimates a user obtains for level-one and level-two regression coefficients can differ depending on the weighting approach chosen. In light of these differences, perhaps the safest approach is to analyze the model with and without weights and for the various level-weighting combinations that can be attempted (Aitkin & Sheih, 2002). If the interpretations of model estimates do not differ across these various analyses, then the researcher can be confident in reporting either set of estimates, at least to the extent that the model is assumed to be specified correctly. If the interpretations do differ, then the researcher should clarify the weighting approach chosen and might opt to present and discuss the differential results in the manuscript or research report (Aitkin & Sheih, 2002).

Regression estimates that are dependent on the weighting scheme selected provide evidence that the stratification variables (which led to the disproportionate selection probabilities) are related to the response variable, and thus the sampling weights are informative. Including salient stratification variables in the analysis may help to remove the apparent discrepancy between weighted and unweighted results. For example, a researcher might choose to include a public/private indicator variable in the level-two equations. The idea here is that one can control for variation on the stratification elements by including these in the model itself. In most complex sample surveys, the incorporation of all such sample design variables is unrealistic. Nonetheless, the thoughtful inclusion of design elements most central to the analysis (such as public/private school stratum indicators or demographic stratum indicators at the student-level) can prove helpful in understanding potential biases and in obtaining a relevant, interpretable model.

Depending on the type of database (cross-sectional or longitudinal) and the types of respondents (student, parent, teacher, etc.), the sampling probability weights can be easy or quite complex to select. NCES attempts to provide weights to handle the representation of any particular observation that may be in an analysis. An assortment of different types of weights for different kinds of analyses is included in NCES databases and is explained in all NCES user's guides. For example, a user might be analyzing data from the ECLS-K database to examine children's cognitive growth from the spring of kindergarten to the spring of first grade and only intend to include child-provided information, such as assessment data in the analysis. Thus, the researcher needs to use weights specifically designed to represent the sampling probability for child data that were collected in spring of kindergarten and first grade. The suitable weight in this case is contained in the variable called C24CW0, and children with non-zero values for this weight will yield a nationally representative sample suitable for studying children's growth from kindergarten to first grade. However, suppose that the analyst also wanted to include data that the parent and teacher had provided. For some of these students, the teacher and/or parent may not have provided information; thus, using the C24CW0 weight may not yield the most representative accounting of the relations for hypotheses involving national estimates. In this case, a more suitable weight would contain values of 0 for children who have no responses from teachers and parents. In the User's Manuals, NCES typically explains the set of weights available to the researcher and also provides example analyses that would be appropriate for each type of weight. In some cases, however, an analysis may not fit with any of the pre-specified weights, and a choice must be made among those available. This process of choosing a weighting strategy based on the availability of data (i.e., from teachers, from parents, etc.) must be used with caution since it assumes that the researcher does not want to model incomplete observations or wants to exclude people who may have left the study in later years. Future research should examine the use of modeling with different types of weights on NCES datasets in conjunction with the missing data methods available in software for multilevel analysis.

Theoretically, as alluded to earlier, it is possible to avoid using the sampling weights entirely by including the components of the sampling design into the analysis. For example, suppose you were working with a dataset that had been collected by stratified sampling on gender and that males and females were sampled at disproportionate rates. Further, suppose that you desired to calculate the (overall) mean income from this sample. An analysis not using sampling weights (disregarding the disproportionate rates of selection) would lead to a biased estimate of the mean if income differed across gender in the population. That is, the mean would be more reflective of the group that was oversampled. However, if appropriately derived sampling weights were used in the calculation of the sample mean, then this estimate of the population mean would be unbiased. Using weights in a statistical analysis is referred to as a "design-based" analysis (Kalton, 1983). An alternative to using the sampling weights is to include the stratum information in the statistical model. Such an approach would be considered a "model-based" analysis (including the sampling design into the analytic model). For example, one could regress income on gender without using sampling weights and thus obtain two appropriate estimates; assuming gender was effect-coded (i.e., using codes of 1 and –1 for each gender), this regression would yield an intercept "baseline" income estimate as well as an estimate of the incremental income associated with being male (or female). Note that we no longer would have one estimate of overall average income but two estimates (the intercept and an incremental gender coefficient), therefore answering a somewhat different research question than originally posed. Instead of asking, "What is the average income?" we would be asking two questions: "What is the average income, and does it differ between men and women?" Given a population difference in income between genders, perhaps this statistical model leads to more appropriate inference about average income. However, the descriptions of the sampling designs provided in the first section of this chapter suggest that it would be extremely difficult to include all of the many elements of typical NCES sampling designs into the statistical model without losing some clarity in interpretation of the model. In summary, the correct application of carefully constructed weights will obviate the need for the incorporation of additional variables controlling for elements of the sampling design—elements that may have little or no part in the substantive analysis of the question at hand.

Non-Response and Non-Response Coding

Missing data can occur at both the respondent/occasion level and at the item level. On its datasets, NCES provides flags on records to indicate whether a certain respondent provided data for a particular wave of the data collection. The NCES user's guides provide the user with information on weights and on how to use these weights to choose the appropriate records when there is non-response during data collection.

Missing data can arise in various ways: a respondent may miss an entire wave of data collection; a respondent might have missed, ignored, or refused to answer a particular item (item non-response); or a respondent may have been re-routed through a section of the survey based on known non-applicability of a particular item or items—known as a "legitimate skip." On most NCES datasets, these missing item-level data are given codes that are negative numbers. It is extremely important that data users understand this coding and properly recode the data or identify the values as missing values to the analysis software being used. Without such action, erroneous estimates would be obtained. As an example, there is a variable in the ECLS-K database from the parent survey that holds the response to "In a typical week, how often does {CHILD} use the computer? Would you say...", and the parent is offered the response options of *never, once or twice a week, three to six times a week,* or *everyday.* This question was asked in spring 1999, spring 2000, spring 2002, and spring 2004; P2COMPWK is the variable holding the response from the spring 1999 parent-interview. In the dataset, there were 16,099 records with the frequency distribution shown in Table 2.4.

Note that the only way to know the context for a question and whether or not the non-response categories represent legitimate skips or otherwise is to review the questionnaire and item wording carefully. For this question, a sizable portion of the respondents (7,120) are in the "Not applicable" category because they actually have no computer in the home, as determined by their answer to an earlier item during the interview. Since the question was in reference to how often the child used the home computer, it was not asked of respondents who indicated they did not have a home computer,

TABLE 2.4 Frequency of Parent Response Level to P2COMPWK on the ECLS-K Database, Spring 1999

P2COMPWK Value	Response Label	Frequency
1	Never	283
2	Once or twice a week	4,008
3	3–6 times a week	3,281
4	Every day	1,390
−1	Not applicable	7,120
−7	Refused	0
−8	Don't know	11
−9	Not ascertained	6

and thus, these 7,120 responses are legitimate skips. According to the data, no parents refused to answer the question on home computer usage, 11 parents were not sure how many days a week their child used the computer, and an answer was not obtained for 6 parents, possibly because the interview was ended prematurely. The analyst must decide how to treat each of these responses for each of the variables used in any analysis with great care. For this example, the researcher might opt to recode the response of "not applicable" to be 1 (*never* use the computer in the home) and consider the "don't know" and "not ascertained" responses to be truly missing values. The recoding will depend on the intended analysis to be undertaken, but analysis results must be interpreted according to how any recoding was conducted.

A full discussion on how to accommodate missing data in multilevel analyses is beyond the scope of this chapter. For those who need a basic introduction to the topic of missing data, we highly recommend the coverage provided by Graham and Hofer (2000). Regarding choices for treatment of missing data during multilevel modeling, researchers should investigate the options available in the software program being used (and these procedures may change as software versions are updated). Alternatively, researchers can consider approaches to managing missing data that are handled outside of existing multilevel software packages or procedures, such as the development and use of multiply imputed datasets. For example, the PAN program (named for its original use in modeling panel data), designed for use with S-PLUS, is freely available for multivariate imputation with panel or clustered data (Schafer & Yucel, 2002), as is NORM, a free windows-based stand-alone application for multiple imputation (Schafer & Graham, 2002). Information on these programs can be accessed through: http://www.stat.psu.edu/%7Ejls/misoftwa.html

Bias, Power, and Sample Size in Multilevel Analyses

Among the most frequently asked questions by researchers and students working with multilevel data is, "How many groups and how many within-group observations do I need?" Questions about appropriate level-one and level-two sample sizes tend to be focused on two issues: the sample size required to ensure that estimates of fixed effects and variances are unbiased, and the sample size required to ensure detection of an hypothesized effect if, in fact, one exists. Chapter 8 in this volume (Spybrook, 2008) provides extensive coverage of sample size and power considerations for school- and classroom-based intervention research. Here, we discuss some of these issues as they relate to the use of large-scale national survey databases. We'll assume a hierarchical system of regression equations, with a continuous dependent variable regressed on a single level-one predictor within each of J groups.

Bias

The bulk of the research examining the issue of sample size and bias for multilevel analyses suggests that the number of observations or groups, J, sampled at the higher level of the design tends to have the greatest impact on precision of estimation. Mok's (1995) simulations suggest that for smaller overall sample sizes (e.g., $N < 800$, which might occur with 20 students sampled from each of $J = 40$ schools or 40 students sampled from each of $J = 20$ schools), level-one fixed estimates (the regression coefficients) are less biased when the number of groups is increased at the expense of the number of observations within each group, as opposed to the other way around. For larger overall samples (about $N > 800$), bias in the fixed-effects tends towards zero. Similarly, estimates of the variance components at level two are less biased with a larger number of groups, holding overall sample size constant (Mok, 1995).

When thinking about precision, researchers might be tempted to believe that better estimation may result by increasing the size of the groups (and thereby reducing the number of groups). But as Snijders (2005) points out, for the same overall sample size, it is generally more desirable to have a larger number of groups with fewer within-group observations than to increase the number of observations obtained from within a smaller number of groups. Maas and Hox (2005) examined the accuracy of parameter estimates from multilevel models under a range of conditions and arrived at a similar conclusion. Their work is noteworthy because it ties much of the literature in this area together and then provides a simulation that yields a useful set of guidelines for the multilevel analyst. The essence of their findings is that while regression coefficients and variance components are unbiased under a range of realistic conditions (i.e., number of groups, within-groups sizes, and realistic ICCs), estimates of standard errors of level-two variances tend to be biased downward when there are 30 or fewer level-two units. Overall, their findings are consistent with a number of other simulations, suggesting that group-level sample size is generally more important than individual-level sample size when estimating fixed-effects at the individual level. What makes the Maas and Hox (2005) piece most useful is the range of conditions and estimates they examine and their treatment of previous related work. Importantly, they suggest that while the regression coefficients and level-one variance components are generally unbiased, the bias in group-level variance components is simply too great when using 10 or fewer groups—regardless of within-group sample sizes and degree of ICC. Typically, a researcher using any of the large-scale national datasets discussed here need not worry about possible bias in fixed level-one estimates resulting from a low number of level-two units, since one of the greatest advantages to using these datasets is the availability of a large number of clusters utilized during the sampling phase of these national surveys.

Power

The ability to detect an effect if it exists is understood as power: the probability of rejecting the null hypothesis (i.e., no effect or difference) when it is not true. Many of the determinants of the power of a multilevel analysis (such as sample size and effect size) are out of the researcher's control when working with existing large-scale national datasets. Staff at the NCES already have determined the appropriate sample sizes for their intended uses of the data and, for the most part, already have defined how the intended constructs will be measured. Regardless, we consider it appropriate that readers understand the components that define the power of any multilevel analysis prior to undertaking the research. In a single-level context, most researchers know that the significance level, effect size, and sample size are determinants of the power of a statistical test. However, there are at least two other considerations that inform estimates of power in a multilevel context: sample size at each level and the ICC (Kaplan, 1995; Kreft, 1996; Muthén & Satorra, 1995). While the impact of sample size at each level might be more immediately intuitive, the role of the ICC deserves more explanation. As we have reviewed earlier, the design effect in cluster samples can be calculated from Equation 2.1, which is equivalent to:

$$\text{DEFF} = 1 + (n-1) \times \text{ICC}, \qquad (2.6)$$

where n represents the average cluster size. From this formula, it is apparent that as the ICC increases, the design effect (or loss of efficiency) increases, holding group size constant (see Muthen & Satorra, 1995, for a more complete discussion). When the groups themselves are internally homogeneous such that the outcomes from the members of the same group tend to be more similar than outcomes of members from different groups, little information is gained with each additional group member. Thus, power to detect level-one effects decreases with increasing ICC, holding the sample size constant at all levels. Further, the power to detect level-two effects is much more sensitive to the number of groups in the sample as opposed to the number of observations within groups.

As designs become more complex, the need for larger samples at both levels increases. Bassiri (1988) suggested that the power necessary to detect cross-level interactions might require at least 30 groups with 30 observations within each group ($N = 900$). Kreft and de Leeuw (1998) advised that when the number of groups is large (perhaps as large as 150 or so), as few as five observations per unit or group could yield power at the 0.90 level to detect significant fixed effects at level one. Fortunately, many excellent resources are available in order to help the researcher plan responsible analyses and understand the connections between power, sample size at multiple levels of a design, and ICC. In his chapter on sample sizes and power, Hox (2002) walks though examples of power estimation for certain analyses, using a method outlined by Raudenbush and Liu (2000) as well as a program called PinT (Snijders & Bosker, 1993). The software and manual for PinT are freely available at http://stat.gamma.rug.nl/Pint21_UsersManual.pdf Finally, in this volume, Chapter 8 (Spybrook, 2008) contains a demonstration of the *Optimal Design Software* (http://sitemaker.umich.edu/group-based), which is primarily useful for planning studies rather than working with public-use databases.

Through all of the above, we encourage the analyst to understand that the number of groups and the number of observations within groups depends largely on the needs of the research and the complexity of the model being tested. For purposes of analysis of NCES datasets such as those described in this chapter, it is important to recognize that while no firm rules of thumb exist regarding adequate sample sizes at various levels, there are useful resources to help guide decisions in this area. We encourage the reader to review the references cited above for additional information.

Accommodating Other Aspects of the Sample Design

When researchers choose to use multilevel modeling to answer a specific research question, they usually have to make choices about the levels to include in the analysis and the predictor variables to include at each level. Based on the research question, the analyst may or may not incorporate all of the important features of the sample design (such as school strata indicators and student demographic strata indicators) into the analysis (see earlier discussion on model-based versus design-based analysis). When the analysis model does not include all sampling design information, researchers should be careful to temper their interpretation of the results according to the complexities of the sample data. For example, the NELS dataset was collected using a two-stage sampling design: schools were selected, and then students within those schools were sampled. Given the two stages, a two-level analysis appropriately would account for clustering effects. On the other hand, the ECLS-K sample is a product of a three-stage sampling design: counties were selected, then schools, then students. A two-level analysis of students within schools would disregard the dependence of schools within counties; therefore, it is possible that standard errors of parameter estimates might be downwardly biased. Additionally, although the use of sampling weights can account for disproportionate selection across strata in a sampling design, it does not address the effect of stratification on standard error estimation. For the NELS data, schools were selected from within categories of public/private status, region, and location type (urban/suburban/rural); thus, one can assume that if the response variable is homogenous within these categorizations, efficiencies would be gained by this stratified sampling design (Kalton, 1983). However, an analysis not including these stratum indicators likely would overestimate standard errors. We hope from this discussion that the challenges of modeling all parts of the sampling design are apparent and that the reader recognizes that not every analysis can accommodate all of the potentially available information. This difficulty, however, does not relieve the researcher from the responsibility of reporting the possible problems associated with these sampling issues.

SUMMARY WITH RECOMMENDATIONS FOR PRACTICE

Our intent in this chapter was to provide readers with the basic knowledge necessary to begin working confidently with large-scale complex survey data, freely available through national, public-use databases. Our examples were designed to help readers locate data suitable to develop and answer research questions requiring multilevel modeling, either for a contextual analysis or a longitudinal analysis. We would like to conclude this chapter with some suggestions for practice.

First, for any given database, researchers carefully must consider the substantive nature of the variables on the data file before jumping into data management and analysis tasks. These tasks often consume a fair amount of time and energy and will tend to yield only disappointment if variable definition and identification is not given careful and thoughtful attention. We have noted the temptation that well-designed multilevel datasets present to some analysts. Once the power of the multilevel model is understood, exuberance sometimes blinds researchers from the hard realities defined by variables available on a given dataset. No matter how well the sample design may lend itself to multilevel exploitation, the lack of proper variables for the substantive research question at hand quickly will grind this exuberance to a halt.

Second, review the user's guide that comes with the database. A quick read will provide a general overview of the sampling design and help the user identify whether there are any design variables, other than the clustering, that will need to be accommodated in the analysis. In addition, the user's guide will provide information regarding whether the sample size is sufficient given the levels included in the intended analysis. A detailed reading of the guide is not necessary at this initial stage (it will be later), but reviewing this information early will save valuable time, compared to finding out later, after extensive work with the ECB and database programming, that the data set will not support the intended analysis.

Third, before starting to use the ECB to identify specific variables for analysis, read through the questionnaires used during data collection. The variables on these datasets number in the hundreds or thousands, and the variables in the ECB can be alluring. As you look through the list of variables in the ECB to determine which to tag for extraction to an SPSS or other software package, suddenly every one of them will look interesting even though they may be ancillary to the research question. In addition, the ECB sometimes contains only partial wording for an interview or questionnaire item, and the items on the ECB may not be in the same order as they appear in the questionnaires or interviews. Before extracting items to address a substantive research question, it is important to understand exactly how the items were worded, what the response alternatives were, and the order in which each item was asked of the respondent in order to appreciate fully the measurement issues or the possibility of order effects.

Fourth, once you have an understanding of the general sampling design, data collection procedure, and actual question responses with which you would like to work, install the ECB and find the variables to tag. While installation and operation of the ECB appears straightforward, we do not want to understate the challenges that beset many users when working with the ECB. It takes time to become oriented to the program's functions and the steps necessary to identify, examine, and download the proper variables and/or program code. We encourage the reader not to underestimate the time that such orientation may require. With that caveat in mind, most of the electronic codebooks from NCES allow for a simple click on a variable name to obtain basic aggregate descriptive information, such as the mean, range, and/or frequency distribution. Reviewing this descriptive information for each variable is useful in identifying potential problems with missing data that might be overwhelming and preclude further analysis using that variable. Also, at this time, users should identify the variables needed to accommodate the sampling design appropriately, including probability weights. Detailed sections in the user's guides cover selection of sample weights and variance estimation; in brief, it is better to extract more sample-design or weighting-related variables than you may use eventually for any specific analysis.

Fifth, when you extract your data and before you begin to model, examine the frequency distributions or other descriptive statistical information for the extracted dataset. In order to identify any possible problems in creating the dataset, determine whether the distributions and basic descriptive statistics for the variables in your dataset match what was reported in the ECB, and verify the adequacy of your sample size. Next, be sure to note the value labels. It can be dangerous to assume that you know what each value of a variable represents on a public-use database. For example, in the ECLS-K dataset, the variable T5GLVL represents the grade level that the student was in at the fifth data collection wave. The values of this variable are –9, 1, 2, 3, 4, 5, 6, and 7. Unfamiliar users may assume that the value of "4" represents fourth grade. In fact, it (non-intuitively) represents third grade. Without carefully examining your data and the documentation provided with it, such mistakes will be easy to make.

Finally, carefully evaluate the sufficiency of the data in terms of the issues we have laid out in this chapter. What is the level of ICC for the dependent variable of interest? Is sufficient data available to ensure desired power to detect effects (which requires consideration of the ICC and the number of observations at each level)? What are the missing data codes for the variables of interest, and how will these be recoded appropriately? Remain aware of the lack of firm resolution about weighting in the multilevel context and about the availability and appropriateness of weights themselves. Moreover, remember that the estimation procedures being used by the various software programs can and do differ, and that there is likely to remain some controversy about which procedure is most appropriate under specific circumstances. Careful thought to questions and issues such as these will better enable profitable use of large-scale datasets, such as those we have outlined in this chapter.

REFERENCES

Aitkin, M., & Shieh, Y.-Y. (2002, April). *Longitudinal modeling of incomplete response data from clustered and stratified survey designs.* Paper presented at the annual meeting of the American Educational Research Association, New Orleans, Louisiana.

Asparouhov, T. (2005). Sampling weights in latent variable modeling. *Structural Equation Modeling, 12,* 411–434.

Bassiri, D. (1988). *Large and small sample properties of maximum likelihood estimates for the hierarchical model.* Unpublished Doctoral Dissertation, Michigan State University, East Lansing.

Beretvas, S. N. (2008). Cross-classified random effects models. In A. A. O'Connell and D. B. McCoach (Eds.), *Multilevel modeling of educational data* (pp. 161–197). Charlotte, NC: Information Age Publishing.

Deming, W.E., & Stephan, F.F. (1940). On a least squares adjustment of a sample frequency table when the expected marginal total are known. *Annals of Mathematical Statistics, 11,* 427–444.

Dillman, D. A. (2000). *Mail and internet surveys: The tailored design method.* New York: John Wiley & Sons, Inc.

Gelman, A. (2005). Struggles with survey-weighting and regression modeling. Unpublished manuscript, Department of Statistics and Department of Political Science, Columbia University, New York. Retrieved October 1, 2006, from http://www.stat.columbia.edu/~gelman/research/unpublished/model-weights3.pdf

Graham, J. W., & Hofer, S. M. (2000). Multiple imputation in multivariate research. In T. D. Little, K. U. Schnabel, & J. Baumert (Eds.), *Modeling longitudinal and multilevel data* (pp. 201–218). Mahwah, NJ: Lawrence Erlbaum Associates.

Heck, R.H., & Thomas, S.L. (2000). *An introduction to multilevel modeling techniques.* Mahwah, NJ: Lawrence Erlbaum Associates.

Hox, J. J. (2002). *Multilevel analysis: Techniques and applications.* Mahwah, NJ: Lawrence Erlbaum Associates.

Kalton, G. (1983). *Introduction to survey sampling.* Newbury Park: Sage Publications.

Kalton, G., & Flores-Cervantes, I. (2003). Weighting methods. *Journal of Official Statistics, 19*(2), 81–97.

Kaplan, D. (1995). Statistical power in SEM. In R. Hoyle (Ed.), *Structural equation modeling: Concepts, issues, and applications* (pp. 100–117). Newbury Park, CA: Sage Publications.

Kish, L. (1965). *Survey sampling.* New York: John Wiley & Sons, Inc.

Kreft, I. (1996). *Are multilevel techniques necessary? An overview, including simulation studies.* Retrieved August 30, 2005, from http://www.calstatela.edu/faculty/ikreft/quarterly/quarterly.html

Kreft I., & deLeeuw, J. (1998). *Introducing multilevel modeling.* Newbury Park, CA: Sage Publications.

Lee, E. S., Forthofer, R. N., & Lorimor, R. J. (1989). *Analyzing complex survey data.* Newbury Park, CA: Sage Publications.

Little, R.J.A., & Wu, M. (1991). Models for contingency tables with known margins when target and sampled populations differ. *Journal of the American Statistical Association, 86*, 87–95.

Lohr, S. (1999). *Sampling: Design and Analysis.* Pacific Grove, CA.: Duxbury.

Maas, C. J. M., & Hox, J. J. (2005). Sufficient sample sizes for multilevel modeling. *Methodology, 1*, 86–92.

Mok, M. (1995). Sample size requirements for 2-level designs in educational research. *Multilevel Modelling Newsletter, 7*(2). Retrieved January 16, 2007, from *http://www.cmm.bristol.ac.uk/learning-training/multilevel-m-support/new7-2.pdf*

Muthén, B. O., & Satorra, A. (1995). Complex sample data in structural equation modeling. In P. V. Marsden (Ed.), *Sociological methodology* (pp. 267–316). Washington, D.C.: American Sociological Association.

National Center for Education Statistics (2006). *Early childhood longitudinal study, kindergarten class of 1998–99 (ECLS-K): Combined user's manual for the ECLS-K fifth-grade data files and electronic codebooks.* (NCES 2006-032). Washington, CD: Author.

National Center for Education Statistics (2007). *NCES Statistical Standards.* Retrieved January 16, 2007, from http://nces.ed.gov/statprog/2002/glossary.asp

National Center for Education Statistics (2006). *Survey and Program Areas.* Retrieved October 13, 2006, from http://nces.ed.gov/surveys/

Pfeffermann, D., Skinner, C. J., Holmes, D. J., Goldstein, H., & Rasbash, J. (1998). Weighting for unequal selection probabilities in multilevel models. *Journal of the Royal Statistical Society, Series B, 60*, 23–40.

Rabe-Hesketh, S., & Skrondal, A. (in press). Multilevel modeling of complex survey data. *Journal of the Royal Statistical Society, Series B.*

Raudenbush, S. W., & Liu, X. (2000). Statistical power and optimal design for multisite randomized trials. *Psychological Methods, 5,* 199–213.

Roberts, J. K., & McLeod, P. (2008). Software options for multilevel models. In A. A. O'Connell and D. B. McCoach (Eds.), *Multilevel modeling of educational data* (pp. 427–467). Charlotte, NC: Information Age Publishing.

Rust, K. (1985). Variance estimation for complex estimators in sample surveys. *Journal of Official Statistics, 4,* 381–397.

Schafer, J. L., & Yucel, R. M. (2002). Computational strategies for multivariate linear mixed-effects models with missing values. *Journal of Computational and Graphical Statistics, 11,* 437–457.

Skinner, C. J., Holt, D., & Smith, T. M. F. (1989). *Analysis of complex surveys.* Chichester, England: John Wiley & Sons.

Snijders, T.A.B. (2005). Power and sample size in multilevel linear models. In B.S. Everitt & D.C. Howell (Eds.), *Encyclopedia of Statistics in Behavioral Science. Volume 3,* (pp. 1570–1573). Chices-ter (etc.): Wiley, 2005.

Snijders, T.A.B. & Bosker, R.J.(1993). Standard errors and sample sizes for two-level research. *Journal of Educational Statistics, 18,* 237–259.

Snyder, T.D., Tan, A.G., & Hoffman, C.M. (2004). *Digest of Education Statistics 2003* (NCES 2005–025). Washington, DC: U.S. Department of Education, National Center for Education Statistics.

Spybrook, J. (2008). Power, sample size, and design. In A. A. O'Connell and D. B. McCoach (Eds.), *Multilevel modeling of educational data* (pp. 273–311). Charlotte, NC: Information Age Publishing.

Thomas, S. L., & Heck, R.H. (2001). Analysis of large-scale secondary data in higher education: Potential perils associated with complex sample designs. *Research in Higher Education, 42,* 517–540.

Tourkin, S. C., Pugh, K. W., Fondelier, S. E., Parmer, R. J., Cole, C., Jackson, B., Warner, T., Weant, G., & Walter, E. (2004). *1999–2000 Schools and Staffing Survey (SASS) Data File User's Manual* (NCES 2004-303). Washington, DC: U.S. Department of Education, National Center for Education Statistics.

U.S. Department of Education. (2006). *Early Childhood Longitudinal Study, Kindergarten Class of 1998–99 (ECLS-K): Combined User's Manual for the ECLS-K Fifth Grade Data Files and Electronic Codebooks* (NCES 2006-032). Washington, DC: Institute for Education Sciences.

Wolter, K.M. (1985). *An introduction to variance estimation.* New York: Springer.

Woodruff, R.S. (1971). A simple method for approximating the variance of a complicated estimate. *Journal of the American Statistical Association, 66,* 411–414.

APPENDIX

Other Publicly Available Datasets
(some will require application for a restricted license)

The following is a short list of other datasets that readers may find useful for undertaking multilevel modeling. All but one of these studies are conducted by NCES, and more information for these data sets can be found at http://nces.ed.gov/surveys/

The *Baccalaureate and Beyond Longitudinal Study* (B&B) is a survey of about 11,000 students who completed their bachelor's degree in 1992–93 and were surveyed in 1994, 1997, and 2003. Information collected in 1994 included immediate post-graduate plans and transcript information from the undergraduate years. In 1997, information about graduate school attendance and workforce outcomes were collected.

Beginning Postsecondary Student Longitudinal Study (BPS) follows students from their first attendance in college (in 1997), to 1 year later, to a final follow up in 2001. About 9,000 students attending 800 institutions are included in the study, and interest lies in examining college persistence, financial aid, college transfer behavior, and work status.

High School and Beyond (HS&B) followed two cohorts, one of which were high school sophomores in 1980. They were followed up in 1982, 1984, 1986, and for a final time in 1992. Topics include the educational attainment, employment outcomes, and family formation of these young adults during the 12 years after their sophomore year in high school.

The IEA *Civic Education Study* (CivEd) is a 28-country data set that contains information about the level of civic knowledge and skills as well as attitudes toward social issues of 14-year-old students. The sampling included whole-class cluster sampling within selected schools. Across all countries, over 90,000 students participated in the study. For the U.S., there are 2,811 students from 124 schools.

The *National Study of Postsecondary Faculty* (NSOPF) is a cross-sectional survey of faculty at colleges and universities in the U.S. The study has been repeated several times, with the most recent being in 2003–2004. The sample contains 35,000 teaching and research faculty from 1,080 postsecondary institutions. Questions pertaining to job satisfaction, workload, scholarly productivity, and career plans are covered. Data are available at the institution level as well as the faculty level.

The *National Longitudinal Study of Adolescent Health* (Add Health), housed at the University of North Carolina Population Research Center, is a longitudinal data set that examines the correlates of health-related behaviors of adolescents in grades 7 through 12. Data at the individual, family, school, and community levels have been collected for three waves, in 1994, 1996, and 2001–2002.

CHAPTER 3

USING MULTILEVEL MODELING TO INVESTIGATE SCHOOL EFFECTS

Xin Ma, Lingling Ma, and Kelly D. Bradley

In this chapter, we demonstrate the most fundamental multilevel procedures in estimating school effects. Schools are perhaps one of the most highly organized institutions in society. Therefore, statistical analyses of school effects parallel those of organizational effects. While we concentrate on school effects in this chapter, these modeling procedures easily can be translated to organizational-effects research.

School effects indicate the relationship between school characteristics and schooling outcomes. School characteristics often can be classified into two types of variables: context and climate. Context variables describe the "hardware" of the school, with characteristics descriptive of the physical background (e.g., school location and resources), the student body (e.g., school socioeconomic and racial-ethnic compositions), and the teacher body (e.g., levels of teacher education and teaching experience). Climate variables, often referred to as evaluative variables, describe the "software" of the school, with characteristics descriptive of the learning environment (e.g., administrative policies, instructional organization, school operation,

Multilevel Modeling of Educational Data, pages 59–110
Copyright © 2008 by Information Age Publishing

59

and attitudes, values, and expectations of students, parents, and teachers). From a conceptual perspective, the key to a successful evaluation of school effects is the distinction between school context and school climate (Raudenbush & Willms, 1995; Teddlie & Reynolds, 2000).

School effects research usually focuses on school climate because it is under the direct control of parents, teachers, and administrators. For example, administrators can use school policies to create, amend, or reform school climate to provide teachers and students with a positive environment in which to engage in teaching and learning. In contrast, school context is out of the direct control of parents, teachers, and administrators. Although school contextual effects are informative to educational policy, most researchers use them as a control for refining the influence of school climatic variables. In other words, the effects of school climate may be adjusted for school context, reducing the dependence of educational policy implications on school context. This is the logical and analytical position presented in this chapter. We demonstrate an application of multilevel modeling to school effects research as we analyze the American sample from the Programme for International Student Assessment (PISA) 2000 using the HLM (Hierarchical Liner Modeling) software package (Raudenbush, Bryk, Cheong, & Congdon, 2004).

INTRODUCTION

Brief Review of Research Literature

Early school-effects research (Coleman et al., 1966; Jencks et al., 1972) suggested that manipulable variables, such as per-student expenditures and the nature of the curriculum, had very small effects on student achievement when compared with the effects of family background. This finding led to the pessimistic conclusion that schools do not make a difference and provoked three decades of research on school effects. Recent advances in statistical modelling, data analysis, and the measurement of schooling outcomes (Ma, 1999; Ma & Ma, 2005; Raudenbush & Willms, 1991, 1995) and the inclusion of a wide range of variables related to classroom practice and school climate (Brand, Felner, Shim, Seitsinger, & Dumas, 2003; Bryk, Lee, & Smith, 1990; Ma, 2002; Phillips, 1997; Raudenbush, Rowan, & Kang, 1991) have led to a general agreement that schools do provide some "added value" to educational outcomes (Everson & Millsap, 2004; Lee, Zuze, & Ross, 2005; Opdenakker & Van Damme, 2006).

Specifically, students learn more and better in schools where (a) principals effectively "buffer the technical core" (minimize the extraneous and disruptive effects that keep teachers from teaching and students from learning) (Bell, Jones, & Johnson, 2002; Blase & Roberts, 1994; Kelley, Thornton, & Daugherty, 2005; Riehl, 2000), (b) staff have high expectations for student performance (Gottfredson, Marciniak, Birdseye, & Gottfredson, 1995; Reyes, Scribner, & Scribner, 1999; Rosenholtz, 1989; Trouilloud, Sarrazin, Bressoux, & Bois, 2006), (c) teachers minimize classroom disruptions and maximize time spent teaching (Baker, 2005; Joubert, de Waal, & Rossouw, 2004; Ma & Willms, 2004; Tulley & Chiu, 1995), (d) there is a high level of parental involvement (Hong & Ho, 2005; Jeynes, 2003, 2005; Ma, 1999), (e) reforms give teachers greater professional autonomy (Bryk & Schneider, 2002; Darling-Hammond, 1996; Little, 1995; Pearson & Moomaw, 2005), (f) teachers actively commit themselves to their work (Lee & Loeb, 2000; Ma & Willms, 1999; Park, 2005; Tsui & Cheng, 1999), (g) liberal policies of curriculum access are practiced (Gamoran & Hannigan, 2000; Lamb, 1996; Lewin, Mavers, & Somekh, 2003; Tomlinson, 2005), (h) a narrow curriculum composed mostly of academic courses is offered (Finn, Gerber, & Wang, 2002; Lee & Smith, 2001; Lee, Croninger, & Smith, 1997; Lee, Smerdon, Alfeld-Liro, & Brown, 2000), and (i) early access to advanced curriculum is encouraged (Burris, Heubert, & Levin, 2004; Carraher, Schliemann, Brizuela, & Earnest, 2006; Ma, 2005; Shapka, Domene, & Keating, 2006).

Importance of Research on School Effects

In general, school-effects research explores differences in students' educational outcomes, both among students within schools and across schools. Specifically, school-effects research often focuses on four principal questions (Willms, 1992): (a) To what extent do schools vary in their schooling outcomes? (b) To what extent do schooling outcomes vary for students of differing status (e.g., socioeconomic status, race-ethnicity, or ability level)? (c) What school policies and practices improve the levels of schooling outcomes? (d) What school policies and practices reduce inequalities in schooling outcomes between high status and low status groups? The first two questions pertain to quality and equity issues of education. The last two questions concern the impact of school-level variables on educational quality and equity. In answering these questions, researchers identify both effective and ineffective schools in terms of quality and equity in schooling outcomes and determine school characteristics that make these schools effective or ineffective. Obviously, such information bears important implications for educational policy.

Research on school effects plays a critical role in many on-going educational reforms. The enactment of the No Child Left Behind ([NCLB], 2002) federal legislation requires states to develop content-based standards, to annually assess students' academic performance on tests linked to those standards, and to hold schools accountable for substandard student outcomes. Multilevel analysis can play an important role in evaluating the NCLB outcomes because it can help disentangle school effects from the effects of intake characteristics of students who attend a school. Under the NCLB, all schools are required to make annual progress beyond a common standard in key school subjects, such as reading and mathematics. Inadequate progress of a school often is associated with characteristics of school context and school climate. Although school contextual effects are typically beyond the direct control of the school, school climatic effects may indicate direct ways of reforming school policies and practices to improve students' academic performance. In the ever-growing system of educational accountability, it is imperative that studies of school effects examine the way that schools can use climatic characteristics to influence students' academic performance (Ma & Klinger, 2000; Ma & Willms, 2004; Willms, 1992).

Theoretical Model of School Effects

One category of organizational studies typically examines working groups and teams to explore the nature of explanatory mechanisms that mediate between-team inputs and outcomes. Attention to process as the link between inputs and outputs brought about the input-process-output (IPO) model (see Ilgen, Hollenbeck, Johnson, & Jundt, 2004). Purkey and Smith (1983) first adopted the IPO model for school-effects research. Good and Brophy (1986) used this model to emphasize the need of measuring both behavioral and perceptional processes that function within the "black box" of schools and classrooms. Since then, the IPO model has been used in many studies of school effects to guide the selection of variables and specification of statistical models (Caldas, 1999; Edmonds, Branch, & Mukherjee, 1994; Hargreaves, 2001; Ma & Crocker, in press; Scheerens, 2001; Sidani & Sechrest, 1999; Teddlie, Reynolds, & Sammons, 2000; Willms, 1992; Willms & Raudenbush, 1989).

In the IPO model, students are seen as bringing into their schools different individual and family characteristics as well as different cognitive and affective conditions; schools are viewed as channeling or processing, through school context and school climate, students with differing background into different categories of schooling outcomes, such as performance, coursework selection, attitude, and aspiration (i.e., students under different school context and school climate demonstrate different educational attainment). Researchers who use this model carefully control the characteristics of student background, examine the distribution of outcomes across students and schools, and identify salient school contextual and climatic characteristics that process students into different categories of outcomes.

The IPO model has been commonly adopted (Sammons, 1999), but it is not the only theoretical framework to use for examining school effects. Other theories, such as contingency, catastrophe, systems, and public choice, also have been borrowed as theoretical models in school effects research (Creemers & Scheerens, 1994; Scheerens, 1992; Scheerens & Bosker, 1997). We favor the IPO model because its emphasis on school context and school climate bears direct policy implications for policymakers, administrators, teachers, and parents.

Although the nature of this theoretical model is logically sound, we provide a historical perspective on the problems that some researchers have identified in the application of this model in research on school effects. As early as 1989, Willms and Raudenbush pointed out the lack of adequate statistical control over school characteristics, asserting that many previous analyses of school effects were done without any understanding of the educational processes at the school level. Additionally, much of the previous research on school effects overlooked the interaction effects between student-level variables as well as between school-level variables (Byrne & Gallagher, 2004). In this chapter, it is our intention to consider these criticisms as a reminder of the importance of these issues both analytically and practically.

Importance of Multilevel Analysis to Research on School Effects

Although many studies in the social and behavioral sciences have data with a multilevel or hierarchical structure, not all researchers realize the importance of multilevel analysis. School education systems provide an obvious example of a hierarchical structure, with students nested within classes, classes nested within schools, schools nested within districts, and so on. With these grouping effects, students are no longer independent in subsequent analyses. In other words, due to grouping, students' responses are correlated, resulting in the loss of independence among observations, a serious violation of a key assumption underlying a large majority of parametric statistical procedures (Goldstein, 1995; Hox, 2002; Kreft & de Leeuw, 1998; Raudenbush & Bryk, 2002; Snijders & Bosker, 1999). Therefore, many traditional statistical techniques are unsuitable for research on school effects. Failure to recognize the hierarchical nature of educational data leads to unreliable estimation of the effectiveness of schools and their practices, which could lead to misinformed educational policies (Goldstein, 1995; Rasbash et al., 2000; Raudenbush & Bryk, 2002).

Multilevel modeling is an extension of a standard and well-proven method of statistical analysis known as multiple regression. With simultaneous multiple regressions at different levels, multilevel analysis specifically accounts for correlated responses at levels where dependencies of observations (or clustering effects) occur; hence, it overcomes the difficulty in analyzing hierarchical data, as the assumption of independence of observations is relaxed. Ma (2001) summarized the advantages of multilevel modeling, stating that it is a significant step further in the solution of persistent problems in the analysis of hierarchical data, accounting for (a) the dilemma of unit of analysis, (b) the problem of dependencies of individual responses within groups, (c) confounding variables at both within- and between-group levels, (d) detection of cross-level interactions, and (e) the manipulation of random coefficients. Multilevel analysis has been growing in popularity in research on school effects because of its ability to account for the hierarchical structure of educational data (Opdenakker & Van Dammer, 2000).

OVERVIEW OF MULTILEVEL MODELS FOR RESEARCH ON SCHOOL EFFECTS

The objective of research on school effects is often to uncover how the contextual and climatic structure of a school influences schooling outcomes of students over and above the influence of students' own individual and family background. Several multilevel models can be specified and tested to answer questions, such as whether and why schools are different from each other in students' schooling outcomes (see earlier discussion for general research questions concerning school effects). In this chapter, we use mathematics achievement as the outcome measure and examine the effects of school context and school climate (as well as their interaction effects) on students' mathematics achievement through five multilevel models. We begin by introducing these multilevel models statistically. In the next section, we apply these models to the estimation of school effects.

The Null Model of School Effects

Kreft and de Leeuw (1998) define a null model as containing only an outcome variable and no independent variables except an intercept. Statistically, it is equivalent to a one-way random-effects analysis of variance (ANOVA) (see Raudenbush & Bryk, 2002). The level-one model is

$$Y_{ij} = \beta_{0j} + r_{ij}, \tag{3.1}$$

where Y_{ij} is the mathematics achievement for student i in school j, β_{0j} is the average mathematics achievement for school j, and r_{ij} is the error term representing a unique effect associated with student i in school j. Statistically, r_{ij} measures the level-one random effect assumed to have a normal distribution with a mean of zero and a constant level-one variance σ^2. The level-two model is

$$\beta_{0j} = \gamma_{00} + u_{0j}, \tag{3.2}$$

where γ_{00} is the intercept, which represents the grand mean, or overall average, of mathematics achievement and u_{0j} is the error term representing a unique effect associated with school j. Statistically, u_{0j} measures the level-two random effect assumed to have a normal distribution with a mean of zero and a level-two variance τ_{00}. The level-one and level-two models can be combined into a single equation by a simple substitution of β_{0j}:

$$Y_{ij} = \gamma_{00} + r_{ij} + u_{0j}. \tag{3.3}$$

This null model essentially serves two research purposes. One is to estimate the grand mean of mathematics achievement with adjustment for clustering of students within schools and for different sample sizes across schools, and the other is to estimate variance components at the student and school levels. Because of the data hierarchy, the null model decomposes the total variance in mathematics achievement into variance attributable to students (within-school variance) and variance attributable to schools (between-school variance). The latter is a good indicator of the existence of school effects. Statistically significant between-school variance (or variance at the school level) indicates that school average mathematics achievement varies significantly across schools. Therefore, some schools have significantly better (and some schools have significantly worse) average mathematics achievement. The proportion of variance in the outcome that is between schools is the intraclass correlation. In other words, it is the proportion of variance at the school level in relation to the total variance (i.e., between-school variance, τ_{00}, divided by the total variance, $\sigma^2 + \tau_{00}$). The proportion of variance at the school level is always positive, ranging from 0 to 1 in magnitude, with higher proportions indicating larger between-school variance. Finally, the null model is used as the baseline model to compare with the results of more elaborate models.

The Student Model of School Effects

The premise of including student-level variables in models of school effects is the adequate control for characteristics of students attending each school. The student model is developed based on the null model to capture as many critical student characteristics (individual differences) as possible that may be confounded with school effects. In doing so, school effects are estimated over and above individual differences. The student model, with an empty school model at the second level that contains no school-level variables, can be expressed as

$$Y_{ij} = \beta_{0j} + \sum_{q=1}^{Q} \beta_{qj} X_{qij} + r_{ij} \tag{3.4}$$

$$\beta_{0j} = \gamma_{00} + u_{0j}$$

$$\beta_{1j} = \gamma_{10}$$

$$\beta_{2j} = \gamma_{20}$$

$$......$$

$$\beta_{Qj} = \gamma_{Q0}.$$

The summation sign in the level-one (student-level) model indicates that a number of student-level variables can be used in the model. X_{qij} is the qth student-level variable $(q = 1, 2, \ldots Q)$, and the slope or coefficient, β_{qj}, associated with X_{qij} measures the relationship between the student-level variable and mathematics achievement (the effects of the student-level variable on mathematics achievement). "The key feature of this model is that only the intercept parameter in the level-1 model, β_{0j}, is assumed to vary at level 2" (Raudenbush & Bryk, 2002, pp. 102–103). Under this model, student-level variables are assumed to have the same influences across schools. This means that each student-level variable has a fixed slope or fixed effect across all schools. In other words, individual differences associated with each student-level variable are the same across all schools.

Researchers who use the student model as a means of control usually do not interpret this model; rather, they use it as a basis to build various models at the school level to examine school effects. Occasionally, researchers treat the effects of individual-level variables (e.g., SES, IQ, gender) on mathematics achievement as random effects rather than fixed effects, implicitly assuming that the effects of individual differences vary across schools. When such a student model is specified, researchers obtain estimates of the average magnitude of the effect of individual differences among schools (fixed effect) and the extent to which the effect of these individual differences varies across schools (random effect). One such student model can be expressed as

$$Y_{ij} = \beta_{0j} + \sum_{q=1}^{Q} \beta_{qj} X_{qij} + r_{ij} \qquad (3.5)$$

$$\beta_{0j} = \gamma_{00} + u_{0j}$$

$$\beta_{1j} = \gamma_{10} + u_{1j}$$

$$\beta_{2j} = \gamma_{20}$$

$$\beta_{3j} = \gamma_{30}$$

$$\cdots\cdots$$

$$\beta_{Qj} = \gamma_{Q0},$$

where γ_{10} is the fixed effect of X_{1ij} and u_{1j} is the random effect of X_{1ij}. Certainly, there can be more than one random effect in the student model. Nevertheless, we caution against specifying random effects unless estimating the variability in the effect of individual differences across schools is the primary research question. Thum and Bryk (1997) stated that "either all coefficients should be fixed or the random slopes should be objects of study" (p. 105). Even though research questions may dictate the specification of random effects, we caution, based on our experiences, that a multilevel model with too many random effects may fail to converge (i.e., produce estimates) because of the complexity of the model.

The Contextual Model of School Effects

Traditionally, a contextual model is defined as a regression model containing two types of variables: individual-level variables and aggregated contextual variables, such as school means or medians (Kreft & de Leeuw, 1998). This definition statistically operationalizes school contextual effects as we discussed earlier. The contextual effects associated with socioeconomic status (SES) are often of interest to researchers. With students nested within schools, students' mathematics achievement is affected not only by students' individual SES but also by the mean SES of the school that they attend. Therefore, SES is used twice, once as an individual (student-level) variable and once as an aggregated (school-level) variable. A contextual model that examines the impact of school socioeconomic composition over and above individual socioeconomic differences typically contains SES at the student level and school mean SES at the school level:

$$Y_{ij} = \beta_{0j} + \beta_{1j} SES_{ij} + r_{ij} \tag{3.6}$$

$$\beta_{0j} = \gamma_{00} + \gamma_{01} SchoolMeanSES_j + u_{0j}$$

$$\beta_{1j} = \gamma_{10}.$$

We note that SES is treated as fixed in the above contextual model, resulting in $\beta_{1j} = \gamma_{10}$ at the school level. Researchers who are interested in estimating school socioeconomic composition effects on educational outcomes often fix SES slopes, as in the present case. SES can be treated as random if researchers believe that socioeconomic gaps are different from school to school. In that case, $\beta_{1j} = \gamma_{10} + u_{1j}$, where γ_{10} estimates the average effect of SES and u_{1j} estimates the unique portion of the SES slopes for the jth school, describing how the effects of SES vary across schools. Researchers who are interested in examining within-school socioeconomic gaps in educational outcomes often leave the SES slopes random.

The effect of SES on mathematics achievement also can be adjusted for other student characteristics or student-level variables, X_{qij} ($q = 2, 3, \ldots Q$), resulting in a more complex contextual model.

$$Y_{ij} = \beta_{0j} + \beta_{1j} SES_{ij} + \sum_{q=2}^{Q} \beta_{qj} X_{qij} + r_{ij} \tag{3.7}$$

$$\beta_{0j} = \gamma_{00} + \gamma_{01} SchoolMeanSES_j + u_{0j}$$

$$\beta_{1j} = \gamma_{10}$$

$$\beta_{2j} = \gamma_{20}$$

$$\beta_{3j} = \gamma_{30}$$

$$\ldots\ldots$$

$$\beta_{Qj} = \gamma_{Q0}$$

Again, SES can be treated as either fixed or random at the discretion of the researchers. Functioning mainly to adjust the effects of SES, other student-level predictors usually are fixed in the contextual model.

The contextual model, as suggested by the name, aims to examine school contextual effects. As discussed earlier, to some researchers, these contextual effects bear important implications for educational policy. For example, students from low SES families may be disadvantaged twice in schooling outcomes, once by their own SES and once by school mean SES, as they often attend low SES schools (see Dundas & Ma, 2006).

By traditional definition, only a regression analysis with aggregated contextual variables is considered a contextual model. If information about schools is directly available, school context can be measured more precisely than by aggregation of student information to the school level. Obviously, aggregation creates cross-level dependencies of variables. For example, SES at the student level is related to school mean SES at the school level, which is obtained by averaging the SES of sampled students within each school. In fact, when school context can be better defined and measured, the effects of school context can be better estimated and adjusted. We propose a general contextual model that extends the traditional SES-related context to school context as a whole (which also fits into our broader theoretical definition of school context discussed earlier). Therefore, besides school mean SES or other direct measures of school socioeconomic composition, such as the percent of students eligible for the reduced or free lunch program, other school contextual variables can be added to portray a whole picture of school context (e.g. the physical background, the student body, and the teacher body).

$$Y_{ij} = \beta_{0j} + \beta_{1j} SES_{ij} + \sum_{q=2}^{Q} \beta_{qj} X_{qij} + r_{ij} \qquad (3.8)$$

$$\beta_{0j} = \gamma_{00} + \sum_{s=1}^{S} \gamma_{0s} Context_{sj} + u_{0j}$$

$$\beta_{1j} = \gamma_{10}$$

$$\beta_{2j} = \gamma_{20}$$

$$\beta_{3j} = \gamma_{30}$$

......

$$\beta_{Qj} = \gamma_{Q0}$$

School contextual variables are used to explain the variation in, for example, school mean mathematics achievement or school means adjusted for student-level predictors. Given that school context (e.g., school location) is often difficult to change, researchers often use these contextual effects as an important control to refine estimates of the effects of school climate, which are changeable through actions of students, parents, teachers, and administrators. Stated differently, the effects of school climate are adjusted for school context, which leads us to the evaluative model of school effects.

The Evaluative Model of School Effects

Based on this general contextual model, variables descriptive of school climate are added to explain the variation in school mean mathematics achievement after controlling for school contextual effects, producing the evaluative model. The purpose of this model is to evaluate the impacts of school climatic variables on schooling outcomes, such as academic achievement.

$$Y_{ij} = \beta_{0j} + \sum_{q=1}^{Q} \beta_{qj} X_{qij} + r_{ij} \tag{3.9}$$

$$\beta_{0j} = \gamma_{00} + \sum_{s=1}^{S} \gamma_{0s} Context_{sj} + \sum_{r=S+1}^{R} \gamma_{0r} Climate_{rj} + u_{0j}$$

$$\beta_{1j} = \gamma_{10}$$

$$\beta_{2j} = \gamma_{20}$$

......

$$\beta_{Qj} = \gamma_{Q0}$$

As one can see in the evaluative model, the effects of school climate are adjusted for school context. This adjustment is important to ensure that educational policy implications are applicable to all schools, regardless of school contextual characteristics.

The Interactive Model of School Effects

As Byrne and Gallagher (2004) correctly pointed out, few researchers have paid attention to interaction effects among school characteristics. Such an emphasis is an important recognition of the complexity of school effects on students' schooling outcomes. For example, the same disciplinary climate may produce a larger improvement on schooling outcomes of students attending high SES than low SES schools. A good starting point is to examine interactions between school context and school climate, recognizing that the effects of school climate may depend on school context.

$$Y_{ij} = \beta_{0j} + \sum_{q=1}^{Q} \beta_{qj} X_{qij} + r_{ij} \tag{3.10}$$

$$\beta_{0j} = \gamma_{00} + \sum_{s=1}^{S} \gamma_{0s} Context_{sj} + \sum_{r=S+1}^{R} \gamma_{0r} Climate_{rj} + \sum_{t=R+1}^{T} \gamma_{0t} Context_{tj} * Climate_{tj} + u_{0j}$$

$$\beta_{1j} = \gamma_{10}$$

$$\beta_{2j} = \gamma_{20}$$

......

$$\beta_{Qj} = \gamma_{Q0}$$

With the presence of interaction effects between school context and school climate, main effects of school context and school climate are not of primary importance unless corresponding interaction effects are not statistically significant. The interactive model emphasizes the effectiveness of educational policy conditional on school context. Such a model identifies where attention is necessary when applying educational policy implications. Such models may provide more detailed information leading to reasoned and pointed actions to improve the effectiveness of schools and their practices.

APPLICATION OF MULTILEVEL MODELING TO RESEARCH ON SCHOOL EFFECTS: THE CASE OF PISA

As an application, we present a series of multilevel analyses in which we use mathematics achievement as the outcome measure and examine how school context, school climate, and their interactions affect students' mathematics achievement through the multilevel models that we discussed earlier. We first describe the data and the variables at the student and school levels and then interpret the results of our multilevel data analyses.

Data Source

Data for the present analysis came from the American sample of the Programme for International Student Assessment (PISA) 2000 (see www. pisa.oecd.org). The PISA national samples were obtained through a stratified random sampling approach with schools as primary sampling units. Once schools were selected at random, students (at the age of 15) were drawn randomly from each sampled school (Adams & Wu, 2002). Such a sampling procedure establishes a data hierarchy with students nested within schools, and multilevel analysis becomes necessary for such hierarchical data. A multilevel approach also takes into account differences in sample size across schools. This is important because when sample size is different from school to school, the precision of level-one effects varies across groups, thus affecting the estimation of school effects.

The American PISA sample contains 2,135 students from 110 schools. Sampling weights for students and schools were used in the present analysis to make the sample reflective of the population (see Chapter 2 of this volume (Stapleton & Thomas, 2008) for information on sampling and sampling weights). In PISA, to capture students' capacity to manage real-life challenges, assessments of reading, mathematical, and scientific literacy were administered to students, and the PISA staff used student and school questionnaires to obtain student and school background information.

PISA contains a number of scales that describe school context (including resources) and school climate (including practices) and that can be used to examine school effects on mathematics achievement.

Outcome Measure

Student mathematics achievement scores were the outcome measure. This is the "O" component in the IPO model. PISA defines mathematics literacy as students' ability to solve mathematical problems that they encounter in real-life situations. To reduce the length of the test but still cover a comprehensive set of mathematical knowledge, PISA applied what is often referred to as matrix sampling, in which several short but different tests are administered to students. Because students complete different tests, mathematics achievement cannot be obtained through traditional test scores but are obtained in, what we call, plausible values (Adams & Wu, 2002). Simply put, plausible values measure a student's ability parameter. There are usually two ways to estimate this parameter: one is to use a point estimate for this parameter, which is a traditional test score for each student; the other is to estimate a probability distribution for this parameter empirically derived from the observed values on students' tests and their background variables. Plausible values then are drawn at random from this probability distribution for each student. Therefore, plausible values are not test scores and need to be combined properly for statistical analysis (see Chapter 9 of Raudenbush, Bryk, Cheong, & Congdon, 2004, for formulas and discussion). In PISA, each student had five plausible values to estimate mathematics achievement (Adams & Wu, 2002). Fortunately, the HLM program is capable of handling plausible values as the outcome measure (Raudenbush et al., 2004).

Student-Level Variables

In the present analysis, gender, SES, family structure (number of parents), family size, home educational resources, family cultural possession, and family cultural activity were selected as student characteristics. Gender came from student self-report, coded as a dichotomous variable that compared females (a value of one) with males (a value of zero). The PISA staff used parental occupations to generate an international socioeconomic index of occupational status that was used as a continuous variable. Family structure was coded as a dichotomous variable comparing single-parent families (a value of one) with two-parent families (a value of zero). Family size represented the number of siblings living together with each sampled student.

The PISA staff derived the three index variables that we used to measure home environment. Home educational resources measured the availability of dictionaries, books, and calculators, as well as a place and a desk to study. Family cultural possession measured the availability of books of poetry and classic literature as well as works of art at home. Family cultural activity measured the participation of students' families in cultural activities, including visiting a museum or art gallery; attending an opera, ballet, or classical symphony concert; and watching live theatre. We note that these student-level variables represent the "I" component in the IPO model; namely, these individual and family characteristics are what students bring into their schools. School effects need to be assessed after controlling for these student-level variables. Therefore, in the present analysis, the average mathematics achievement for a school was adjusted for the student-level variables included in the model.

Descriptive statistics for all student-level (and school-level) variables are provided in Appendix A, with additional measurement information in a later section.

Context, Climate, and Interaction Variables at the School Level

At the school level, we included variables descriptive of school context and school climate. School enrollment size, school location, school socioeconomic composition, shortage of teachers, school material resources, and school instructional resources served as school context variables; disciplinary climate, academic pressure, teacher support, student-teacher relationship, and school autonomy were used as school climate variables. The meanings of these school-level variables are self-explanatory, and items used to measure them are presented in Appendix B. School context variables came from the school questionnaire usually completed by principals, and school climate variables were aggregated measures from the student-level data obtained from the student questionnaire. The PISA staff created the index variables or composite variables using questionnaire items.

It is possible for school context and school climate to influence schooling outcomes of students interactively. Because these interaction effects are between variables at the same level (the school level in our case), they are referred to as same-level interactions. The construction and interpretation of these interactions is similar to how we examine interaction effects in a single-level multiple regression analysis. In a multilevel analysis, same-level interactions can be contrasted with cross-level interactions that occur when we use school-level variables to model the slopes or coefficients estimated at the student level (see Figure 3.1 for an illustration of randomly varying slopes).

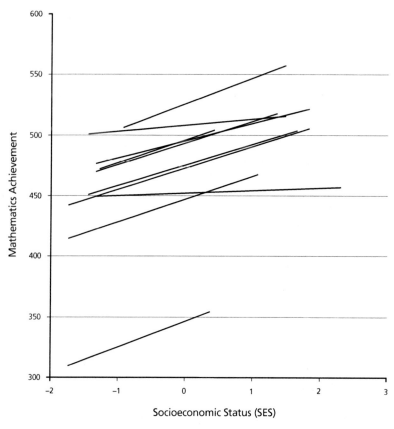

Figure 3.1 Random Socioeconomic Status (SES) Slopes for 10 Schools.

Consider the following multilevel model for mathematics achievement, Y_{ij}, with students nested within schools (for simplicity, we will assume here that the intercepts are fixed across schools):

$$Y_{ij} = \beta_{0j} + \beta_{1j} X_{ij} + r_{ij} \qquad (3.11)$$

$$\beta_{0j} = \gamma_{00}$$

$$\beta_{1j} = \gamma_{10} + \gamma_{11} W_j + u_{1j}.$$

Following our discussion earlier about various multilevel models, we note that β_{1j} is the slope associated with the student-level variable, X_{ij}, which measures the effects of this variable on mathematics achievement. In the above multilevel model, these effects vary from school to school, with u_{1j} being the random effect of X_{ij}, measuring the extent to which these effects vary across schools. In addition, γ_{10} is the fixed effect of X_{ij} and γ_{11} is the coefficient for the school-level variable, W_j. We use W_j as a school-level predictor to assess whether this variable is contributing to variation in the effects associated with X_{ij} across schools. If so, this would represent a cross-level interaction between X_{ij} and W_j, and γ_{11} is a measure of this interaction effect. We naturally see this definition if we combine the student- and school-level models, as presented in Equation 3.11, by substituting β_{0j} with γ_{00} and β_{1j} with $\gamma_{10} + \gamma_{11}W_j + u_{1j}$ into the student model:

$$Y_{ij} = \gamma_{00} + \gamma_{10}X_{ij} + \gamma_{11}X_{ij} * W_j + u_{1j}X_{ij} + r_{ij}. \qquad (3.12)$$

It is now clear that γ_{11} is the coefficient for the interaction effect between X_{ij} and W_j. We refer to this as a cross-level interaction because X_{ij} is a student-level variable and W_j is a school-level variable. From this combined model, it should also be clear that γ_{10} represents the fixed effect of X_{ij}, and u_{1j} represents the random effect of X_{ij}.

If we introduce additional variables at the school level, W_{1j} and W_{2j} for example, we can create a same-level interaction between W_{1j} and W_{2j}. In the following multilevel model (here, assuming fixed slopes), γ_{03} represents the same-level interaction between W_{1j} and W_{2j} because W_{1j} and W_{2j} both are school-level variables:

$$Y_{ij} = \beta_{0j} + \beta_{1j}X_{ij} + r_{ij} \qquad (3.13)$$
$$\beta_{0j} = \gamma_{00} + \gamma_{01}W_{1j} + \gamma_{02}W_{2j} + \gamma_{03}W_{1j} * W_{2j} + u_{0j}$$
$$\beta_{1j} = \gamma_{10}.$$

In this chapter, we model same-level interaction effects between school context and school climate. Although interaction effects rarely are explored in research on school effects, we believe that the examination of interaction effects can imply policy-sensitive educational strategies. In fact, as we argued earlier, interaction effects between variables descriptive of school context and school climate capture the complexity of school effects. In our analyses, we examine interaction effects between school enrollment size, school location, and school socioeconomic composition and school climate variables. These school-level variables (including their interaction effects) constitute the "P" component in the IPO model. That is, school context and school climate, as well as their interactions, are "process" variables, which may cause students to perform differently in mathematics achievement. Research on school effects aims to uncover how these school contextual and climatic variables and their interactions impact the schooling outcomes of students.

Data Manipulation and Analysis

The descriptive statistics on student-level and school-level variables used in our data analysis are reported in their original PISA measurement scales in Appendix A. For this analysis, we standardized all continuous student-level variables to have a mean of zero and a standard deviation of one. Specifically, each student-level variable was standardized across schools (standardization based on the national sample), implying that the national mean of that variable was the reference against which each student was assigned a measure. When there is a need to standardize student-level variables, unless dramatically different school systems are present (e.g., public, private, and religious schools), standardization across schools is appropriate (see Kreft & de Leeuw, 1998; Raudenbush & Bryk, 2002). In the present analysis, the decision to standardize continuous variables was based on the fact that these continuous variables do not share the same measurement scale. Standardization unified different scales by setting one unit as one standard deviation. We also standardized school socioeconomic composition (i.e., school mean SES) at the school level.

In addition, we centered all dichotomous variables at the student level and remaining variables at the school level around their (grand) means. Similar to the case of standardization, each dichotomous student-level variable was centered across schools (centering based on the national sample). The difference between grand mean centering ($X_{ij} - \overline{X}_{..}$ where $\overline{X}_{..}$ is the grand mean or sample mean) and standardizing

$$\frac{X_{ij} - \overline{X}_{..}}{SD_{..}}$$

where $SD_{..}$ is the grand standard deviation or sample standard deviation) is that a centered variable has a mean of zero but keeps its original standard deviation, whereas a standardized variable has a mean of zero and a standard deviation of one. We have more discussion on centering variables later in this chapter.

Finally, we have adopted the notion of absolute and relative effects in our multilevel data analyses. Whenever there are multiple variables to be examined at the student level, we first test each student-level variable one at a time (i.e., examining its absolute effects). Statistically significant student-level variables then are introduced together at the student level to examine their relative effects (i.e., in the presence of other student-level variables). Working with this augmented model, we remove variables that are no longer statistically significant one by one, starting with the variable with the largest p value and continuing until all remaining variables in the model are statistically significant. School-level variables can be treated in the same manner. Such a statistical practice aims to reduce the complexity of a multilevel model by focusing on those variables that have both absolute and relative effects on the outcome measure.

Statistical Results from the Null Model

Table 3.1 presents statistical results from the null model estimated based on the following HLM syntax command:

$$\text{Level 1 Model:} \tag{3.14}$$

$$MathAchievement = \beta_{0j} + r_{ij}$$

Level 2 Model:

$$\beta_{0j} = \gamma_{00} + u_{0j}.$$

American students demonstrated mean mathematics achievement of about 484 points. Given that PISA mathematics achievement has an international scale with 500 points as the mean and 100 points as the standard deviation, American students scored marginally below the international average. The statistically significant between-school variance indicates that average mathematics achievement varied across American schools ($\tau_{00} = \text{var}(u_{0j}) = 2714.12$, $\chi^2(109) = 960.63$, $p = 0.00$). Intraclass correlation shows that 34% of the total variance in mathematics achievement is attributable to schools, while 66% (i.e., $100\% - 34\%$) is attributable to students.

TABLE 3.1 Statistical Results of the Null Model of School Effects on Mathematics Achievement

	Fixed effects			
	Coefficient	SE	t-ratio	p
Intercept (mathematics achievement) γ_{00}	483.89	6.10	79.28	0.00
	Random effects			
	Variance	df	Chi-square	p
Between-school variability (Intercept)	2714.12 τ_{00}	109	960.63	0.00
Within-school variability	5206.31 σ^2			
Reliability (Intercept)			0.68	
Intraclass Correlation			0.34	

2714

2714+52 0.6

Although the majority of the variation in mathematics achievement lies between students, a large portion of the variation lies between schools. This is a good indication that school effects do exist.

The intercepts of the null model, β_{0j}, indicate average mathematics achievement for the J schools ($j = 1, 2, \ldots J$), and as identified above, these intercepts vary at the school level. The reliability for β_{0j} measures the extent to which we can discriminate among schools in their average mathematics achievement. Statistically, the overall reliability for $\hat{\beta}_0$ is defined as

$$\frac{1}{J} \sum_{j=1}^{J} \tau_{00} / (\tau_{00} + v_{00j}), \qquad (3.15)$$

where τ_{00} is the variance in average mathematics achievement across schools and v_{00j} is the sampling variance associated with average mathematics achievement for the jth school (Raudenbush & Bryk, 2002). In general, this sampling variance differs among the J schools because of the differences in sample size. The reliability is an overall summary measure across the J schools. It represents the degree to which the schools (level-two units) can be discriminated between using the ordinary least squares estimates of β_{0j} (Raudenbush & Bryk). We note that low reliability does not invalidate the results of a multilevel analysis. Rogosa, Brandt, and Zimowski (1982) stated that "low reliability does not necessarily mean lack of precision" (p. 744). It is possible to have both precise estimates of school average mathematics achievement and a low reliability coefficient if schools are not reasonably distinguishable (see Rogosa & Willett, 1983, 1984; Willett, 1988).

In our null model, the reliability is a good indicator of how well each school's sample mean estimates the unknown parameter, β_{0j}. A low reliability for the intercept would suggest that it is difficult to discriminate among schools on the basis of their average mathematics achievement. Because the reliability coefficient ranges from zero to one, the magnitude of 0.68 is reasonable. Given that the goal is to model school effects, we would like the reliability coefficient to be fairly high.

Statistical Results from the Student Model

To develop the student model, we then added the (standardized) student-level variables to the null model. As discussed earlier, each student-level variable can be treated as either a fixed effect, assuming that the effects of the variable are the same across schools, or a random effect, assuming that the effects of the variable are different across schools. We treated all student-level variables as fixed effects. Such a treatment is appropriate if random effects are not a part of the research questions (Raudenbush & Bryk, 2002; Thum & Bryk, 1997). For example, because this analysis aims to identify school-level variables that are responsible for variation in mathematics achievement among schools, without any attempt to investigate within-school gender differences in mathematics achievement across schools, gender as a student-level variable is fixed. Fixing this effect corresponds with the assumption that within-school gender gaps are the same across schools. Treating gender as a random effect implies that within-school gender gaps vary across schools. Thum and Bryk (1997) argue, however, that including this random variation would distort school effects on mathematics achievement because of the correlation between school average mathematics achievement and within-school gender gaps in mathematics achievement.

Table 3.2 shows statistical results from the student model based on the following HLM syntax command:

Level 1 Model: (3.16)

$$MathAchievement_{ij} = \beta_{0j} + \beta_{1j}(EducationalResources)_{ij} +$$

$$\beta_{2j}(FamilyPossession)_{ij} + r_{ij}$$

Level 2 Model:

$$\beta_{0j} = \gamma_{00} + u_{0j}$$

$$\beta_{1j} = \gamma_{10}$$

$$\beta_{2j} = \gamma_{20}.$$

Both slopes were held fixed in this model (see the next section for a case in which a slope is allowed to be random). When student-level variables are treated as fixed effects, it is not necessary to interpret the student model at this stage because it is an intermediate step in the model building process, especially if school effects are the focus of data analysis. However, we do so here for pedagogical purposes. The student model lays the foundation for researchers to build models at the school level. Once a multilevel model is fit at both student and school levels, the effects of student-level variables can be interpreted more meaningfully. Nevertheless, we found two statistically significant student-level variables: home educational resources and family culture possession. The addition of these two significant student-level variables reduced the variance at both student and school levels. The proportion of variance explained by the student model, in which only the intercept is allowed to vary randomly, can be calculated at both student and school levels by comparing the variance

TABLE 3.2 Statistical Results of the Student Model of School Effects on Mathematics Achievement

	Fixed effects			
	Coefficient	SE	t-ratio	p
Intercept (mathematics achievement) γ_{00}	484.23	5.48	88.33	0.00
Student-level variables				
Home educational resources γ_{10}	13.55	3.10	4.37	0.00
Family possession related to classical culture γ_{20}	16.48	2.80	5.88	0.00
	Random effects			
	Variance	df	Chi-square	p
Between-school variability (Intercept)	2060.70	109	819.60	0.00
Within-school variability	4777.26			
	Proportion of Variance Explained			
At the school level (between schools)	0.24			
At the student level (within schools)	0.08			

components from the null and student models. The following formulas were used in this case, and this process can be extended to comparisons of more complex models as well:

The proportion of within-school variance explained by the student model is

$$\frac{\sigma^2_{(null)} - \sigma^2_{(student)}}{\sigma^2_{(null)}}. \qquad 0.08 \qquad (3.17)$$

The proportion of between-school variance in the intercepts explained by the student model is

$$\frac{\tau_{00(null)} - \tau_{00(student)}}{\tau_{00(null)}}. \qquad 0.24 \qquad (3.18)$$

For these data, in comparison to the null model, the student model explained 8% of the variance at the student level and 24% of the variance at the school level. The intercepts for the student model, β_{0j}, represent adjusted means for each school. School average mathematics achievement becomes more homogeneous after it is adjusted within each school for home educational resources and family culture possession. This explains the substantial reduction in the variance at the school level even though no school-level variables are present.

Statistical Results from the Contextual Model

The top half of Table 3.3 presents statistical results from a model that fits the traditional definition of a contextual model with individual SES at the student level and school mean SES (aggregated from the student level) at the school level (SES slopes are held fixed in this model). The HLM syntax command is

Level 1 Model: $\qquad$ (3.19)

$$MathAchievement_{ij} = \beta_{0j} + \beta_{1j}(SES)_{ij} + r_{ij}$$

Level 2 Model:

$$\beta_{0j} = \gamma_{00} + \gamma_{01}(SchoolSES)_j + u_{0j}$$

$$\beta_{1j} = \gamma_{10}.$$

Student (or individual) SES did not show statistically significant effects on mathematics achievement, but school mean SES was statistically significant in favor of schools with high average SES. Specifically, the contextual effects, coming from the school level, indicated that a one standard deviation increase in school mean SES was associated with an increase of about 36 points in mathematics achievement. Relative to the null model, this contextual model with SES as a fixed effect explains 57% of the between-school variance in the intercepts and 1% of the variance in math achievement within schools.

As mentioned earlier, random, rather than fixed, slopes may be the focus of study. For example, some researchers may decide to treat individual SES as a random effect in order to examine if within-school socioeconomic gaps in mathematics achievement vary significantly across schools. To demonstrate, we allowed the slopes for SES to vary randomly across schools by adding a residual term to Equation 3.19: $\beta_{1j} = \gamma_{10} + u_{1j}$ (see results presented in the lower half of Table 3.3). We found that the within-school socioeconomic gap was about 13 points and was, indeed, statistically significantly different across schools ($\tau_{11} = \text{var}(u_{1j}) = 129.97$). Therefore, in some schools, students from socially disadvantaged families would be expected to perform much more poorly in mathematics than those from socially advantaged families, which implies socioeconomic inequity in mathematics achievement. However, in other schools, such a so-

TABLE 3.3 Statistical Results of the Typical Contextual Model of School Effects on Mathematics Achievement

	Contextual Model with Coefficient (Slope) of Socioeconomic Status (SES) Fixed			
	Fixed effects			
	Coefficient	SE	t-ratio	p
Intercept (mathematics achievement) γ_{00}	487.31	4.62	105.40	0.00
Student-level variables				
SES γ_{10}	5.70	5.36	1.06	0.29
School-level variables on Intercept				
School mean SES γ_{01}	36.48	5.31	6.87	0.00
	Random effects			
	Variance	df	Chi-square	p
Between-school variability (Intercept)	1177.14	108	583.52	0.00
Within-school variability	5135.12			
	Proportion of variance explained			
At the school level (between schools)		0.57		
At the student level (within schools)		0.01		

	Contextual Model with Coefficient (Slope) of SES Random			
	Fixed effects			
	Coefficient	SE	t-ratio	p
Intercept (mathematics achievement) γ_{00}	487.34	4.62	105.41	0.00
Student-level variables				
SES γ_{10}	13.17	2.74	4.80	0.00
School-level variables on Intercept				
School mean SES γ_{01}	33.12	4.95	6.69	0.00
	Random effects			
	Variance	df	Chi-square	p
Between-school variability (Intercept)	1213.31	108	536.20	0.00
Between-school variability (SES slope)	129.97	109	154.81	0.00
Within-school variability	4827.16			
	Reliability			
Intercept (random at the school level)		0.49		
SES slope (random at the school level)		0.17		

cioeconomic gap may not be large at all, implying socioeconomic equity in mathematics achievement.

Just as a random intercept has an estimable reliability, a multilevel model also generates a reliability estimate for a random slope. In the current case, when $\beta_{1j} = \gamma_{10} + u_{1j}$, the reliability estimate for $\hat{\beta}_1$ is calculated as

$$\frac{1}{J} \sum_{j=1}^{J} \tau_{11} / (\tau_{11} + v_{11j}), \qquad (3.20)$$

where τ_{11} is the variance in the slopes of SES across schools and v_{11j} is the sampling variance associated with the slope for SES for the jth school (Raudenbush & Bryk, 2002). The sampling variance may differ among the J schools because of the different sample sizes. In our current example, the reliability for the SES slopes was 0.17 (lower half of Table 3.3); thus, it may be difficult to distinguish schools on the basis of their (within-school) socioeconomic gaps in mathematics achievement. Raudenbush et al. (2004) suggest that researchers consider fixing a slope if it shows a low reliability, around 0.10 or less, because the slopes may not usefully discriminate among schools.

Another noticeable difference between the two models presented in Table 3.3 is that the effect of student SES is not statistically significant when treated as a fixed effect but is statistically significant when treated as a random effect. This indicates that the decision to specify random effects in a multilevel model needs to be thought out carefully because this choice may influence the results and subsequent interpretation dramatically. In the current case, when within-school variation in the effect of individual SES was taken into account, student SES showed a positive and statistically significant effect (a one standard deviation increase in individual SES was related to an increase of about 13 points in mathematics achievement); however, it was associated with only a 5-point increase in the fixed model. Consequently, the fixed-SES model indicates a stronger effect of school mean SES relative to its effect in the random-SES model (36.48 points versus 33.12 points, respectively).

Let us go back for a moment to the student model presented earlier in Table 3.2. Re-specifying home educational resources as a random effect, for example, allows for an opportunity to examine whether (and to what extent) within-school mathematics achievement gaps created by home educational resources vary across schools. However, one tradeoff with this approach is that with random effects for level-one predictors in the model, the estimates of explained proportions of variance relative to the null model are no longer unique, as they were in the case where the intercept was the only random component. Instead, in a random slopes model, the variance estimates exist for each slope; in addition, the variability in these slope effects depends on where the predictors are centered (see Kreft & de Leeuw, 1998). Thus, for our random SES example we did not calculate the proportions of variance explained by the contextual model. In the series of models we are developing here, we chose to view the student-level model as a means of controlling for student-level effects in order to examine school effects; thus, the standardized student-level predictors are treated as fixed effects for demonstration purposes. We provide an additional example later in which this assumption is relaxed.

Table 3.4 presents statistical results from a more complex contextual model, in which we return to our model with individual SES treated as a fixed effect and investigate any adjustment to the effect of individual SES based on inclusion of additional student-level variables. With the addition of the two predictors measuring home educational resources and family possessions related to classical culture, individual SES remained non-statistically significant and, thus, was removed from the model. The resulting model indicated that home educational resources and family culture possession had positive effects on mathematics achievement. The HLM syntax command is

Level 1 Model: (3.21)

$$MathAchievement_{ij} = \beta_{0j} + \beta_{1j}(EducationalResources)_{ij} +$$

$$\beta_{2j}(FamilyPossession)_{ij} + r_{ij}$$

Level 2 Model:

$$\beta_{0j} = \gamma_{00} + \gamma_{01}(SchoolSES)_j + u_{0j}$$

$$\beta_{1j} = \gamma_{10}$$

$$\beta_{2j} = \gamma_{20}.$$

Specifically, a one standard deviation increase in home educational resources was related to an increase in mathematics achievement of about 13 points with control for family culture possession; and a one standard deviation increase in family culture possession was associated with an increase in mathematics achievement of about 16 points, holding home educational resources constant. For the sake of space, in our subsequent discussion, we will simplify the interpretation of effects at both student and school levels by omitting phrases that are generally understood, such as holding other variables in the model constant.

The contextual effects of school mean SES remained statistically significant in the new model. As in the previous contextual model, schools with high mean SES outperformed schools with low mean SES. A one standard

TABLE 3.4 Statistical Results of the Contextual Model of School Effects on Mathematics Achievement with Adjustment at the Student Level

	Fixed effects			
	Coefficient	SE	t-ratio	p
Intercept (mathematics achievement) γ_{00}	486.72	4.33	112.45	0.00
Student-level variables				
Home educational resources γ_{10}	13.18	3.11	4.23	0.00
Family possession related to classical culture γ_{20}	15.78	2.76	5.72	0.00
School-level variables on the Intercept				
School mean socioeconomic status γ_{01}	32.79	4.43	7.40	0.00
	Random effects			
	Variance	df	Chi-square	p
Between-school variability (Intercept)	1003.24	108	538.74	0.00
Within-school variability	4767.42			
	Proportion of variance explained			
At the school level (between schools)	0.63			
At the student level (within schools)	0.08			

deviation increase in school mean SES was related to an increase in mathematics achievement of about 33 points. Adding school mean SES dramatically reduced the variance at the school level. Relative to the null model (Table 3.1), this contextual model explained 63% of the variance at the school level. Without further specification at the student level, the proportion of variance explained at the student level remained at 8% (see statistical results from the student model).

At the school level, we proceeded to add other school contextual variables in addition to school mean SES, creating what we termed as the "general contextual model." With the exception of the aggregate measure of school mean SES, all level-two predictors were centered at the grand mean. Non-significant effects were removed from the level-two model. In addition to school socioeconomic composition (i.e., school mean SES), school location had a statistically significant impact on mathematics achievement in favor of rural schools (see Table 3.5). The HLM syntax command is

Level 1 Model: (3.22)

$$MathAchievement_{ij} = \beta_{0j} + \beta_{1j}(EducationalResources)_{ij} +$$

$$\beta_{2j}(FamilyPossession)_{ij} + r_{ij}$$

Level 2 Model:

$$\beta_{0j} = \gamma_{00} + \gamma_{01}(SchoolSES)_j + \gamma_{02}(SchoolLocation)_j + u_{0j}$$

$$\beta_{1j} = \gamma_{10}$$

$$\beta_{2j} = \gamma_{20}.$$

A one standard deviation increase in school socioeconomic composition was related to an increase in mathematics achievement of about 37 points. Rural schools outperformed city schools in mathematics achievement with

TABLE 3.5 Statistical Results of the Contextual Model of School Effects on Mathematics Achievement with Adjustment at Both Student and School Levels

	Fixed effects			
	Coefficient	SE	t-ratio	p
Intercept (mathematics achievement) γ_{00}	480.83	3.92	122.63	0.00
Student-level variables				
Home educational resources γ_{10}	13.01	3.09	4.21	0.00
Family possession related to classical culture γ_{20}	15.89	2.72	5.84	0.00
School-level variables on intercept				
School mean socioeconomic status γ_{01}	36.48	3.97	9.19	0.00
School location (urban versus rural) γ_{02}	−50.47	9.07	−5.57	0.00
	Random effects			
	Variance	df	Chi-square	p
Between-school variability (Intercept)	676.89	107	421.09	0.00
Within-school variability	4752.66			
	Proportion of variance explained			
At the school level (between schools)		0.75		
At the student level (within schools)		0.09		

a difference of about 50 points. Overall, school context demonstrated substantial effects on students' mathematics achievement. This general contextual model explained 9% of the variance at the student level and 75% of the variance at the school level, relative to the null model.

Before we proceed to discuss the evaluative model, we note that, in the same way that we modeled the adjusted average mathematics achievement (intercept) among schools with school-level variables, we can also model a random slope at the school level if the slope varies significantly across schools. To demonstrate this procedure, we go back to the earlier contextual model with the random SES slopes (lower half of Table 3.3). In that example, we found that the SES slopes varied significantly across schools, and thus we can use school-level variables to explain this variation. The HLM syntax command is provided below with results shown in Table 3.6:

Level 1 Model: (3.23)

$$MathAchievement_{ij} = \beta_{0j} + \beta_{1j}(SES)_{ij} + r_{ij}$$

Level 2 Model:

$$\beta_{0j} = \gamma_{00} + \gamma_{01}(SchoolSES)_j + u_{0j}$$

$$\beta_{1j} = \gamma_{10} + \gamma_{11}(TeacherShortage)_j + \gamma_{12}(SchoolInstructionalResources)_j + u_{1j}.$$

We found that teacher shortage and school instructional resources both had statistically significant effects on the SES slopes. Teacher shortage had a positive coefficient (i.e., a larger value in teacher shortage was associated with a larger SES slope), indicating that in schools with greater teacher shortage, the socioeconomic gap in mathematics achievement among students becomes larger (i.e., worse socioeconomic equity). A one scale point increase in the teacher shortage index was related to an increase of about 6 points in the within-school SES gap in mathematics achievement (recall that all school-level variables were grand mean centered rather than standardized, with the exception of school mean SES). Meanwhile, school instructional resources had a negative coefficient (i.e., a smaller value in school instructional resources was associated with a larger SES slope), indicating that in schools with poorer instructional resources, the socioeconomic gap in mathematics achievement among students was larger (i.e., worse socioeconomic equity). We found that a one scale point increase in the school instructional resources index was associated with an increase of about 8 points in the within-school SES gap in mathematics achievement.

TABLE 3.6 Statistical Results of a Random Slope Model of School Effects on Mathematics Achievement

	Fixed effects			
	Coefficient	SE	t-ratio	p
Intercept (mathematics achievement) γ_{00}	487.15	4.59	106.22	0.00
Student-level variables				
Socioeconomic status (SES) γ_{10}	13.54	2.07	6.54	0.00
School-level variables on Intercept				
School mean SES γ_{01}	33.28	4.67	7.13	0.00
School-level variables on SES slope				
Teacher shortage γ_{11}	6.02	2.19	2.74	0.01
School instructional resources γ_{12}	−7.98	2.38	-3.35	0.00
	Random effects			
	Variance	df	Chi-square	p
Between-school variability (Intercept)	1198.32	108	534.09	0.00
Between-school variability (SES slope)	37.35	107	157.15	0.00
Within-school variability	4849.53			
Between-school variability (SES slope)	37.35	107	157.15	0.00

Statistical Results from the Evaluative Model

We now return to our previous contextual model with educational resources and family possessions at the student level, treated as fixed rather than random. The evaluative model is built upon this contextual model by introducing school climatic variables, providing us with an opportunity to assess the effects of school climate. Among five variables descriptive of school climate (disciplinary climate, academic pressure, teacher support, student-teacher relationship, and school autonomy), student-teacher relationship and school autonomy showed statistically significant absolute effects (i.e., in the absence of other school-level variables). However, in the presence of the two significant contextual variables contained in the previous model (school location and school socioeconomic composition), the climate effects became non-statistically significant. We kept them in the model only to illustrate how the effects of school climate may be evaluated and reported (see Table 3.7). The HLM syntax command for the evaluative model is

Level 1 Model: $\hspace{4cm}$ (3.24)

$$MathAchievement_{ij} = \beta_{0j} + \beta_{1j}(EducationalResources)_{ij} +$$

$$\beta_{2j}(FamilyPossession)_{ij} + r_{ij}$$

Level 2 Model:

$$\beta_{0j} = \gamma_{00} + \gamma_{01}(SchoolSES)_j + \gamma_{02}(SchoolLocation)_j +$$

$$\gamma_{03}(StudentTeacherRelationship)_j + \gamma_{04}(SchoolAutonomy)_j + u_{0j}$$

$$\beta_{1j} = \gamma_{10}$$

$$\beta_{2j} = \gamma_{20}.$$

TABLE 3.7 Statistical Results of the Evaluative Model of School Effects on Mathematics Achievement

	Fixed effects			
	Coefficient	SE	t-ratio	p
Intercept (mathematics achievement) γ_{00}	480.85	3.90	123.30	0.00
Student-level variables				
Home educational resources γ_{10}	12.94	3.10	4.17	0.00
Family possession related to classical culture γ_{20}	15.86	2.74	5.78	0.00
School-level variables on Intercept				
School mean socioeconomic status γ_{01}	34.97	3.95	8.84	0.00
School location (urban versus rural) γ_{02}	−46.17	9.87	−4.68	0.00
Student–teacher relationship γ_{03}	3.09	3.36	0.92	0.36
School autonomy γ_{04}	4.07	3.70	1.10	0.27
	Random effects			
	Variance	df	Chi-square	p
Between-school variability (Intercept)	685.95	105	403.89	0.00
Within-school variability	4751.04			
	Proportion of variance explained			
At the school level (between schools)		0.75		
At the student level (within schools)		0.09		

School climatic effects can be interpreted in the same way as school contextual effects—a one scale point increase in a school climatic variable is associated with an estimated increase (or decrease) in mathematics achievement of a certain number of points, represented by the slope (coefficient) for the school climatic variable. Because none of the school climatic variables were statistically significant, the proportions of variance explained at the student and school levels remained unchanged from the general contextual model in Table 3.5.

We want to emphasize that the pattern of results found in the present analysis regarding the effects of school climate is not uncommon in research on school effects. That is, school climate variables often show null or weak effects on students' educational outcomes, particularly in the presence of school context variables. This situation does not mean that school climate does not have any impact on students' educational outcomes. Variance at the school level is measured as over and above variance at the student level (this is why school effects are described as over and above the effects of student-level variables). It is typical that variance in students' educational outcomes is small among schools, relative to that among students within schools (see Table 3.1). In fact, both between- and within-school variance are reduced after student-level variables and school contextual variables are entered into the model (see Table 3.5). Many measures of school climate are not sensitive enough to detect the subtle variation in educational outcomes among schools associated with climatic differences. School climate variables that are statistically significant in the presence of student-level variables and school context variables represent salient school climatic effects that bear important educational policy implications.

Statistical Results from the Interactive Model

To demonstrate same-level interactions, we tested three groups of interaction effects between school context and school climate. The first group pertains to the interactions between school enrollment size and school climatic variables; we used our original selection of five climatic variables tested through the previous evaluative model. Specifically, we tested five interaction effects at the school level (among $J = 110$ schools): $SchoolEnrollmentSize_j \times DisciplinaryClimate_j$, $SchoolEnrollmentSize_j \times AcademicPressure_j$, $SchoolEnrollmentSize_j \times TeacherSupport_j$, $SchoolEnrollmentSize_j \times StudentTeacherRelationship_j$, and $SchoolEnrollmentSize_j \times SchoolAutonomy_j$. Similarly, the second group pertains to the interactions between school location and the five school climatic variables (also yielding five interaction effects), and the third group pertains to the interactions between school socioeconomic composition (i.e., school mean SES) and the five school climatic variables (yielding five interaction effects).

This approach to constructing interaction effects focuses on identifying potential interaction effects between statistically significant contextual and climatic variables. We created interaction terms between all five of the climate variables and the two statistically significant context variables from the evaluative model. A theoretical approach can also be used to construct interaction effects within both context and climate, as well as between them. We felt that the context variable of school enrollment might interact with school climate, and thus created five additional interaction terms involving the same collection of five climate variables.

We examined these 15 interaction effects separately with their corresponding main effects. Individually, we found three statistically significant interaction effects between school location and (a) teacher support, (b) student-teacher relationship, and (c) school autonomy (see Figures 3.2 to 3.4 for graphical illustrations of these interaction effects).

We then jointly tested the three interaction effects reported earlier, and found that only two of them remained statistically significant: interactions between school location and (a) teacher support and (b) school autonomy.

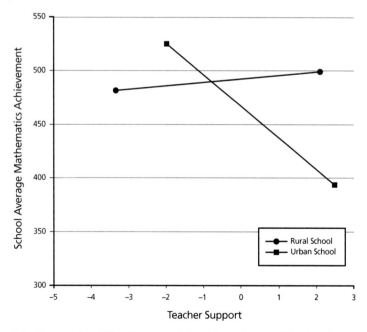

Figure 3.2 Interaction Effect Between School Location and Teacher Support.

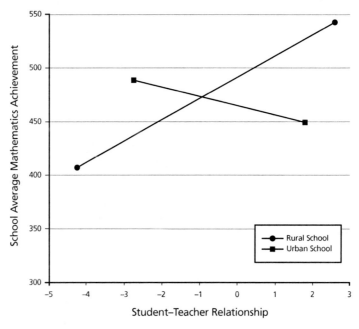

Figure 3.3 Interaction Effect Between School Location and Student–Teacher Relationship.

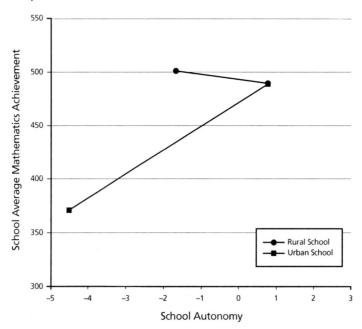

Figure 3.4 Interaction Effect Between School Location and School Autonomy.

Results of a model including these two interaction effects, together with their corresponding main effects, are presented in Table 3.8. The HLM syntax command is

Level 1 Model: $\hspace{8cm}$ (3.25)

$$MathAchievement_{ij} = \beta_{0j} + \beta_{1j}(EducationalResources)_{ij} +$$
$$\beta_{2j}(FamilyPossession)_{ij} + r_{ij}$$

Level 2 Model:

$$\beta_{0j} = \gamma_{00} + \gamma_{01}(SchoolLocation)_j + \gamma_{02}(TeacherSupport)_j +$$
$$\gamma_{03}(SchoolAutonomy)_j + \gamma_{04}(SchoolLocation_j * TeacherSupport_j) +$$
$$\gamma_{05}(SchoolLocation_j * SchoolAutonomy_j) + u_{0j}$$
$$\beta_{1j} = \gamma_{10}$$
$$\beta_{2j} = \gamma_{20}.$$

We found that the effects of teacher support on mathematics achievement depended on school location. Specifically, because city schools were coded as 1 (rural schools were coded as 0), the negative interaction indicated that the effects of teacher support were significantly larger in rural schools than city schools. With a 1 scale point increase in teacher support, rural schools were predicted to outperform city schools in mathematics achievement by 29 additional points. We also found that the effects of school autonomy depended on school location. Specifically, because city schools were coded as 1, the positive interaction indicated that the effects of school autonomy were significantly larger in city schools than rural schools. A 1 scale point increase in school autonomy resulted in a gain of 24.57 points for city schools over and above the gain for rural schools. These findings imply that city schools tend to be more sensitive to school autonomy whereas rural schools tend to be more sensitive to teacher support.

Some Critical Issues in Multilevel Analysis of School Effects

One of the important issues in multilevel analysis of school effects involves determining sample size (i.e., student sample and school sample). The power chapter in this volume (Spybrook, 2008) contains a detailed description on sample size and statistical power under the multilevel analytical framework. We emphasize briefly here that the primary concern of research on school effects is investigating the impact schools have on the

TABLE 3.8 Statistical Results of the Interactive Model of School Effects on Mathematics Achievement

	Fixed effects			
	Coefficient	SE	t-ratio	p
Intercept (mathematics achievement) γ_{00}	487.94	5.04	96.78	0.00
Student-level variables				
Home educational resources γ_{10}	13.59	3.09	4.39	0.00
Family possession related to classical culture γ_{20}	16.62	2.79	5.97	0.00
School-level variables on Intercept				
School location (urban versus rural) γ_{01}	−17.92	10.27	−1.74	0.08
Teacher support γ_{02}	−5.62	5.05	−1.11	0.27
School autonomy γ_{03}	2.50	5.69	0.44	0.66
School location × teacher support γ_{04}	−28.97	10.90	−2.66	0.01
School location × school autonomy γ_{05}	24.57	10.02	2.45	0.01
	Random effects			
	Variance	df	Chi-square	p
Between-school variability (Intercept)	1588.36	104	681.77	0.00
Within-school variability	4776.47			
	Proportion of variance explained			
At the school level (between schools)	0.41			

development of students in many areas, such as cognition and affect. Given that the precision of estimates at the school level will depend on the number of schools, we would want to have as many schools as possible in any multilevel analysis of school effects. We now turn our focus to other analytical concerns.

Centering Variables

Scaling or centering is a critical issue in multilevel analysis of school effects. In general, centering variables is a good analytical practice when building a multilevel model. Centering makes the interpretation of multilevel results more meaningful and "removes high correlations between random intercepts and slopes, and high correlations between first- and second-level variables and cross-level interactions" (Kreft & de Leeuw, 1998, p. 114). Centering can take the form of grand-mean centering ($X_{ij} - \bar{X}$ where $\bar{X}$ is the grand mean) or group-mean centering ($X_{ij} - \bar{X}_j$ where $\bar{X}_j$ is the group mean or level-two mean) (Raudenbush & Bryk, 2002). Grand-mean centering essentially produces a model mathematically equivalent to the raw score model without any centering. This means that the coefficients (including intercepts) can be transformed back and forth between the two models. Because the two models are equivalent, estimates obtained from the grand-mean centered model correspond to the raw score model, and the research questions each model addresses are quite similar. In this sense, the process of grand-mean centering is not likely to alter the research questions relative to raw score form.

In our multilevel analyses, we grand-mean centered variables at both student and school levels (standardizing is a form of centering). We note that grand-mean centering of school-level variables is important to reduce collinearity between predictive variables and interactive variables containing these predictors at the school level because centering makes these two groups of variables orthogonal. Similarly, grand-mean centering of student-level predictor variables is also important if interaction effects among these predictors are considered at the student level. However, we caution that, as a linear transformation of variables, grand-mean centering does not alter the overlap or shared variance of individual predictors with one another.

Collinearity among predictive variables at each level needs to be examined regardless of the analytical decision on centering. A correlation analysis is often sufficient to identify pairs of predictive variables that are highly correlated. This issue of collinearity is especially critical in research on school effects because many variables tend to correlate highly at both student and school levels. In our case, although we did not report correlations among the student-level variables, we did examine the correlation matrix at the student level. The highest correlation was 0.43 between family culture possession and family culture activity, which raises no alarms for our data analysis. In the case of very high correlations (more than 0.90) among student-level variables, one solution is to combine highly correlated variables into a composite variable by means of either theoretically or factor-analytically grouping variables. This same procedure can be carried out with highly correlated school-level variables.

In general, grand-mean centering is recommended for most multilevel analyses of school effects, with the advantage that, under grand-mean centering, the subsequent models are always mathematically equivalent to the raw score model. On the other hand, group-mean centering produces a model that is not mathematically equivalent to the raw score model so that the coefficients (including intercepts) can no longer be transformed back and forth between the two models; in other words, we arrive at a totally different model after group-mean centering. Because the two models are nonequivalent, estimates obtained from the group-mean centered model do not correspond with those from the raw score model.

The major impact of centering is at the school level. Kreft and de Leeuw (1998) demonstrated that although standard errors of fixed effects may not change much, the parameter estimates may change dramatically (even to the degree of alteration in the signs of the estimates). Nevertheless, they discuss a method of correction that re-introduces group means as a school-level variable when developing models at the school level (this group mean variable always accompanies other school-level variables when modeling school effects).

Although grand-mean centering often is preferred for school effectiveness research, group-mean centering does have some unique statistical advantages. Raudenbush and Bryk (2002) stated that group-mean centering makes the interpretation of an intercept meaningful because the intercept now takes the form of the predicted mean on the outcome variable for each school. Dichotomous student-level variables also can be interpreted meaningfully with group-mean centering. For example, when we group-mean center the eligibility of students within a school for the federal free lunch program (yes coded as 1 and no coded as 0), the centered variable becomes the proportion of eligible students in that school, and its slope (coefficient) now represents the average effect of the free lunch program for that school.

Some unique school effects are impossible to identify with the more popular grand-mean centering. One critical issue associated with school effects often is referred to as the "fish pond" or "frog pond" effect that deals with the development of a student's full potential. Is it better to be a small fish in a big pond or a big fish in a small pond? The underlying idea is contextual, acknowledging that the wellbeing (e.g., academic performance) of a student is conditional on the average wellbeing of students in the school that this student attends. Hox (1995) considered group-mean centering as the analytical procedure to address the "fish pond" effect:

> Centering around the group means makes very explicit that the individual scores should be interpreted relative to their group's mean. Another advantage of centering around the group means is that the group-centered individual deviation scores have a zero correlation with the disaggregated group means, which has statistical advantages. (p. 4)

The "fish pond" effect clearly emphasizes a school's environment surrounding a student, particularly relevant to the contextual characteristics of the school.

Another issue closely related to group-mean centering is the so-called "sector effect" that describes a unique impact of the private school sector on the relationship between academic achievement and SES. Raudenbush and Bryk (1986) reported that lower SES students perform better in Catholic schools whereas higher SES students perform better in public schools (see also Bryk, Lee, & Holland, 1993). Kreft and de Leeuw (1998) replicated these patterns with another database and emphasized that group-mean centering is essential to identifying the "sector effect." When schools are dramatically different, the relative position of a student in his or her own school on those characteristics (i.e., group-mean centering) can be used to capture school effects far better than the relative position of a student in the entire sample (grand-mean centering).This is why group-mean centering is often the method of choice when comparing public and Catholic (or other private or religious) schools—the systems are fundamentally different in most aspects of school life (e.g., educational philosophy, educational expectation, educational policy, student intake, and curriculum and instruction). Paccagnella (2006) presents a good discussion on the role of group-mean centering in the assessment of group effects (see also Hofmann & Gavin, 1998; Kreft, de Leeuw, & Aiken, 1995).

In summary, researchers should be guided by the nature of their research questions when faced with centering decisions. Here, we used standardization, a form of grand-mean centering, since our primary interest was in the identification and interpretation of school effects on mathematics achievement after adjusting for student-level effects across the entire sample.

Selecting the Number of Levels

Structurally, educational data can be quite complex, in that many levels may be present in the data, such as student, group, class, school, district, state, and country. When multiple levels are present in educational data, the decision to include or not to include some levels may impact the multilevel results. We note that there are sometimes serious consequences to ignoring levels in a multilevel structure. Opdenakker and Van Damme (2000) found that ignoring an important top or intermediate level in research on school effects can lead to different research conclusions, with significant impacts on fixed coefficients, variance components, and their corresponding standard errors (see also Moerbeek, 2004). A safe measure is to include all levels corresponding to random sampling strata. Therefore, classroom should not be ignored as a level if random selection is carried out among classes within schools. Although researchers are encouraged, in general, to avoid ignoring levels, they need to bear in mind that statistical programs have different capacities in handling the number of levels (see Chapter 12 of this volume (Roberts & McLeod, 2008) for more details on software capacities), as well as to understand the impact that ignoring a given level may have on the utility, credibility, and validity of the research findings.

Assessing Multilevel Models from the IPO Perspective

There are a number of statistical procedures available to assess the aptness of multilevel models. For example, Snijders and Bosker (1999) proposed a six-question approach to evaluate the assumptions of multilevel analysis (p. 121). Here, we emphasize the importance of assessing the aptness of multilevel analysis from the theoretical or practical perspective. In particular, we reiterate the concern of Willms and Raudenbush (1989) that adequate statistical control over school characteristics is essential for research on school effects. Once more, we also echo the criticism of Byrne and Gallagher (2004), who assert that interaction effects between school characteristics cannot be ignored in multilevel analysis of school effects.

We propose the following questions for researchers to consider as a way to assess the aptness of a multilevel model for research on school effects: (a) Do outcome measures vary among students and across schools (focusing on the "O" component of the IPO framework, via the null model)? (b) If outcome measures vary among students, can student-level variables account for this variation (focusing on the "I" component of the IPO framework, via the student model)? (c) If outcome measures vary across schools, can school-level variables account for this variation (focusing on the "P" component of the IPO framework, via the contextual and evaluative models)? (d) Do within-school parameters (i.e., slopes of student-level variables or within-school individual differences) vary across schools (focusing on the "I" and "O" components, via the student model)? (e) If these parameters vary across schools, can school-level variables account for these variations (focusing on the "P" component, via the contextual and evaluative models)? (f) Are there interaction effects among school-level variables (focusing on the "P" component, via the interactive model)? In this chapter, we have provided examples of models and corresponding interpretations for each of these six questions. In general, adequate attention to these questions can help researchers ensure the aptness of their resulting multilevel model. We emphasize, however, that a good multilevel model demonstrates not only statistical (or analytical) fitness but also practical (or theoretical) fitness. Chapter 7 in this volume (McCoach & Black, 2008) contains information helpful in clarifying issues of overall model fit.

FINAL REMARKS

School effects research represents a macro-level empirical investigation that focuses on the effectiveness of educational policy and practice in promoting positive educational outcomes for students. Schools are differentially effective in capitalizing on educational policy and practice because they have different school context and climate. Therefore, conditionality is important in school effects research, and implications for educational policy and practice drawn from multilevel analysis must recognize this complexity.

The Theoretical Recap

We believe that the IPO model is a sound approach to account for the educational conditionality of schools. In the IPO model, student intake and school characteristics are both responsible for educational outcomes. When this model is applied within the multilevel analytical framework, educational quality (how well students within a school perform) and educational equity (how equitably students with differing background within a school perform) become functions of student intake and school characteristics (see the four principal questions for school effects research presented at the beginning of this chapter). The IPO model easily can be extended, when there are appropriate data, to include community as a higher level (e.g., neighborhoods, school districts, or regions) so that student intake, school characteristics, and community conditions all can be examined in relation to educational outcomes.

When applying the IPO model to school effects research, adequate measures of school context and climate are always important to ensure the validity of educational policy and practice implications. This requires the identification and inclusion of critical school contextual and climatic variables that either facilitate or hamper the implementation of educational policy and practice. Although the PISA data do not contain measures on all components that may be of interest, we reiterate our emphasis on the hardware of the school with the physical background (e.g., school resources), the student body (e.g., student intakes), and the teacher body (e.g., teacher conditions) as major components of school context; and we reiterate also our emphasis on the software of the school with school operation (e.g., principal leadership, school autonomy), school environment (e.g., disciplinary climate, parental involvement), and classroom practice (e.g., enacted curriculum, instructional practice) as major components of school climate. Teddlie and Reynolds (2000) have identified many additional key school-level factors that school-effects researchers should consider in order to capture contextual and climatic characteristics of a school fully (see also Willms, 1992).

Considering interaction effects between school context and climate is another important way to appreciate the conditionality of educational policy and practice. As we have demonstrated, school climatic effects do depend on school context. When policy intervention variables are present in educational data, it is especially critical to take into account interaction effects between policy intervention and school context and climate simply because the effectiveness of policy intervention may depend on school context and climate. The bottom line is that educational policy and practice implications drawn from multilevel analysis must be sensitive to the different contextual and climatic conditions that schools endure in educating students, as well as the interactive conditions between contextual and climatic factors. These conditions are important for all types of evaluation of school effects, and for all kinds of efforts that attempt to identify effective or ineffective schools for various purposes.

The Analytical Recap

Although there is a natural fit between the IPO model and the multi-level analytical framework, careful attention always is needed with regard to model specification, estimation, and interpretation. We have developed five multilevel models (i.e., null, student, contextual, evaluative, and interactive). With increasing complexity, these models serve as building blocks for statistical analysis as well as guides for exploring different issues in school-effects research. We advocate an orderly process of model development because this progressive model-building approach is both theoretically and statistically sound. We have described briefly a related issue on model building critically important to multilevel analysis; that is, school effects can be distorted if relevant levels of data hierarchy are ignored. Researchers must assess the adequacy of incorporating—or ignoring—any of the levels in their multilevel analyses carefully. We concur with the established practice that the intercept in the student-level model be the only random component at the school level unless educational equity issues (e.g., gender differences or socioeconomic differences) form part of the research questions (see Raudenbush & Bryk, 2002; Thum & Bryk, 1997). One advantage of this modeling approach is the ability to calculate proportions of variance explained at both student and school levels relative to the null model—a critical way to evaluate how well our multilevel model fits our hierarchical data.

Throughout our examples, we have discussed how centering of the predictors generates multiple statistical benefits of which school-effects researchers should take advantage. These benefits include reducing the collinearity when same-level interaction effects are present, eliminating the cross-level collinearity when cross-level interaction effects are present, and improving interpretation of analytical results. We have discussed how grand- and group-mean centering can produce different (sometimes unexpected) school effects. Although there is no rule of thumb as to when to use which form of centering, grand-mean centering or the standardization approach that we used here is simple to apply, produces meaningful estimates, and addresses research questions critical to school-effects research. Alternatively, group-mean centering often can be justified when schools come from totally different societal sectors or when dramatically innovative educational interventions are applied to schools in an experimental design (with control schools). In any research design, however, decisions on centering must be made prior to data analysis—experimenting with centering in a data-mining fashion can undermine the researcher's efforts to estimate school effects appropriately.

Finally, using a series of multilevel models applied to the PISA database, we have shown that building up from the null model, to the student model, to the contextual model, to the evaluative model, and finally to the interactive model, provides a convenient framework from which to assess school effects. Our approach was based on the IPO theoretical framework applied to school effectiveness research but easily could be adopted for other organizational studies and settings as well.

REFERENCES

Adams, R., & Wu, M. (Eds.) (2002). *Programme for International Student Assessment (PISA): PISA 2000 technical report.* Paris: Organization for Economic Cooperation and Development.

Baker, P. H. (2005). Managing student behavior: How ready are teachers to meet the challenge? *American Secondary Education, 33*(3), 51–64.

Bell, G., Jones, E., & Johnson, J. (2002). School reform: Equal expectations on an uneven playing field. *Journal of School Leadership, 12,* 317–336.

Blase, J., & Roberts, J. (1994). The micropolitics of teacher work involvement: Effective principals' impact on teachers. *Alberta Journal of Educational Research, 40,* 67–94.

Brand, S., Felner, R., Shim, M., Seitsinger, A., & Dumas, T. (2003). Middle school improvement and reform: Development and validation of a school-level assessment of climate, cultural pluralism, and school safety. *Journal of Educational Psychology, 95,* 570–588.

Bryk, A. S., Lee, V. E., & Holland, P. B. (1993). *Catholic schools and the common good.* Cambridge, MA: Harvard University Press.

Bryk, A. S., Lee, V. E., & Smith, J. B. (1990). High school organization and its effects on teachers and students: An interpretative summary of the research. In W. H. Clune & J. F. Witte (Eds.), *Choice and control in American education. Volume 1: The theory of choice and control in education* (pp. 135–226). London: Falmer.

Bryk, A.S., & Schneider, B.L. (2002). *Trust in schools: A core resource for improvement.* New York: Russell Sage Foundation.

Burris, C., Heubert, J., & Levin, H. (2004). Math acceleration for all. *Educational Leadership, 61*(5), 68–71.

Byrne, G., & Gallagher, T. (2004) Systemic factors in school improvement. *Research Papers in Education, 19,* 161–183.

Caldas, S. (1999). Multilevel examination of student, school, and district-level effects on academic achievement. *Journal of Educational Research, 93,* 91–100.

Carraher, D., Schliemann, A., Brizuela, B., & Earnest, D. (2006). Arithmetic and algebra in early mathematics education. *Journal for Research in Mathematics Education, 37,* 87–115.

Coleman, J. S., Campbell, E. Q., Hobson, C. J., McPartland, J., Mood, A. M., Wienfield, F. D., & York, R. L. (1966). *Equality of educational opportunity.* Washington, DC: US Government Printing Office.

Creemers, B.P.M., & Scheerens, J. (1994). Developments in the educational effectiveness research program. *International Journal of Educational Research, 21,* 125–140.

Darling-Hammond, L. (1996). The quiet revolution: Rethinking teacher development. *Educational Leadership, 53*(6), 4–10.

Dundas, T., & Ma, X. (2006, April). *Double jeopardy in mathematics achievement for socially disadvantaged students.* Paper presented at the annual meeting of the American Educational Research Association. San Francisco, CA.

Edmonds, G. S., Branch, R. C., & Mukherjee, P. (1994). A conceptual framework for comparing instructional design models. *Educational Technology Research and Development, 42*(4), 55–72.

Everson, H., & Millsap, R. (2004). Beyond individual differences: Exploring school effects on SAT scores. *Educational Psychologist, 39,* 157–172.

Finn, J., Gerber, S., & Wang, M. (2002). Course offerings, course requirements, and course taking in mathematics. *Journal of Curriculum & Supervision, 17,* 336–366.

Gamoran, A., & Hannigan, E. C. (2000). Algebra for everyone? Benefits of college-preparatory mathematics for students with diverse abilities in early secondary school. *Educational Evaluation and Policy Analysis, 22,* 241–254.

Goldstein, H. (1995). *Multilevel statistical models* (2nd ed.). London: Edward Arnold.

Goldstein, H. (1997). Methods in school effectiveness research. *School Effectiveness and School Improvement, 8,* 369–395.

Good, T. L., & Brophy, J. E. (1986). School effects. In M. Wittrock (Ed.), *Third handbook of research on teaching* (pp. 570–602). New York: Macmillan.

Gottfredson, D. C., Marciniak, E. M., Birdseye, A. T., & Gottfredson, G. D. (1995). Increasing teacher expectations for student achievement. *Journal of Educational Research, 88,* 155–163.

Hargreaves, D. H. (2001). A capital theory of school effectiveness and improvement. *British Educational Research Journal, 27,* 487–503.

Hofmann, D. A. & Gavin, M. B. (1998). Centering decisions in hierarchical linear models: Implications for research in organizations. *Journal of Management, 24,* 623–641.

Hong, S., & Ho, H. (2005). Direct and indirect longitudinal effects of parental involvement on student achievement: Second-order latent growth modeling across ethnic groups. *Journal of Educational Psychology, 97,* 32–42.

Hox, J. J. (1995). *Applied multilevel analysis.* Amsterdam, Netherlands: TT-Publikaties.

Hox, J. J. (2002). *Multilevel analysis: Techniques and applications.* Mahwah, NJ: Lawrence Erlbaum.

Ilgen, D. R., Hollenbeck, J. R., Johnson, M., & Jundt, D. (2004). Teams in organizations: From input-process-output models to IMOI models. *Annual Review of Psychology, 56,* 517–543.

Jencks, C. S., Smith, M., Acland, H., Bane, M. J., Cohen, D., Ginitis, H., Heyns, B., & Michelson, S. (1972). *Inequality: A reassessment of the effect of family and schooling in America.* New York: Basic Books.

Jeynes, W. (2003). A meta-analysis: The effects of parental involvement on minority children's academic achievement. *Education and Urban Society, 35,* 202–218.

Jeynes, W. (2005). A meta-analysis of the relation of parental involvement to urban elementary school student academic achievement. *Urban Education, 40,* 237–269.

Joubert, R., de Waal, E., & Rossouw, J. P. (2004). Discipline: Impact on access to equal educational opportunities. *Perspectives in Education, 22*(3), 77–88.

Kelley, R. C., Thornton, B., & Daugherty, R. (2005). Relationships between measures of leadership and school climate. *Education, 126,* 17–24.

Kreft, I., & de Leeuw, J. (1998). *Introducing multilevel modeling.* Thousand Oaks, CA: Sage.

Kreft, I., de Leeuw, J., & Aiken, L. (1995). The effect of different forms of centering in hierarchical linear models. *Multivariate Behavioral Research, 30,* 1–22.

Lamb, S. (1996). Gender differences in mathematics participation in Australian schools: Some relationships with social class and school policy. *British Educational Research Journal, 22,* 223–240.

Lee, V. E., Croninger, R. G., & Smith, J. B. (1997). Course-taking, equity, and mathematics learning: Testing the constrained curriculum hypothesis in US secondary schools. *Educational Evaluation and Policy Analysis, 19,* 99–121.

Lee, V. E. & Loeb, S. (2000). School size in Chicago elementary schools: Effects on teachers' attitudes and students' achievement. *American Educational Research Journal, 37,* 3–31.

Lee, V. E., Smerdon, B. A., Alfeld-Liro, C., & Brown, S. L. (2000). Inside large and small high schools: Curriculum and social relations. *Educational Evaluation and Policy Analysis, 22,* 147–71.

Lee, V. E., & Smith, J. B. (2001). *Restructuring high schools for equity and excellence: What works.* New York: Teachers College Press.

Lee, V. E., Zuze, T., & Ross, K. (2005). School effectiveness in 14 sub-Saharan African countries: Links with 6th graders' reading achievement. *Studies in Educational Evaluation, 31,* 207–246.

Lewin, C., Mavers, D., & Somekh, B. (2003). Broadening access to the curriculum through using technology to link home and school: A critical analysis of reforms intended to improve students' educational attainment. *Curriculum Journal, 14,* 23–53.

Little, D. (1995). Learning as dialogue: The dependence of learner autonomy on teacher autonomy. *System, 23,* 175–181.

Ma, L., & Ma, X. (2005). Estimating correlates of growth between mathematics and science achievement via a multivariate multilevel design with latent variables. *Studies in Educational Evaluation, 31,* 79–98.

Ma, X. (1999). Dropping out of advanced mathematics: The effects of parental involvement. *Teachers College Record, 101,* 60–81.

Ma, X. (2001). Stability of school academic performance across subject areas. *Journal of Educational Measurement, 38,* 1–18.

Ma, X. (2002). Early acceleration of mathematics students and its effect on growth in self-esteem: A longitudinal study. *International Review of Education, 48,* 443–468.

Ma, X. (2005). A longitudinal assessment of early acceleration of students in mathematics on growth in mathematics achievement. *Developmental Review, 25,* 104–131.

Ma, X., & Crocker, R. (in press). Provincial differences in reading achievement. *Alberta Journal of Educational Research.*

Ma, X., & Klinger, D. A. (2000). Hierarchical linear modelling of student and school effects on academic achievement. *Canadian Journal of Education, 25,* 41–55.

Ma, X., & Willms, J. D. (1999). Dropping out of advanced mathematics: How much do students and schools contribute to the problem? *Educational Evaluation and Policy Analysis, 21,* 365–383.

Ma, X., & Willms, J. D. (2004). School disciplinary climate: Characteristics and effects on eighth grade achievement. *Alberta Journal of Educational Research, 50,* 169–189.

McCoach, D.B., & Black, A. (2008). Evaluation of model fit and adequacy. In A. A. O'Connell and D. B. McCoach (Eds.), *Multilevel modeling of educational data* (pp. 245–271). Charlotte, NC: Information Age Publishing.

Millman, J. (Ed.) (1997). *Grading teachers, grading schools: Is student achievement a valid evaluation measure?* Thousand Oaks, CA: Corwin.

Moerbeek, M. (2004). The consequence of ignoring a level of nesting in multilevel analysis. *Multivariate Behavioral Research, 39,* 129–149.

Opdenakker, M. C., & Van Damme, J. (2000). The importance of identifying levels in multilevel analysis: An illustration of ignoring top or intermediate levels in school effectiveness research. *School Effectiveness and School Improvement, 11,* 103–130.

Paccagnella, O. (2006). Centering or not centering in multilevel models? The role of group mean and the assessment of group effects. *Evaluation Review, 30,* 66–85.

Park, I. (2005). Teacher commitment and its effects on student achievement in American high schools. *Educational Research & Evaluation, 11,* 461–485.

Pearson, L., & Moomaw, W. (2005). The relationship between teacher autonomy and stress, work satisfaction, empowerment, and professionalism. *Educational Research Quarterly, 29,* 38–54.

Phillips, M. (1997). What makes schools effective? A comparison of the relationships of communitarian climate and academic climate to mathematics achievement and attendance during middle school. *American Educational Research Journal, 34,* 633–662.

Purkey, S. C., & Smith, M. S. (1983). Effective schools: A review. *Elementary School Journal, 83,* 426–452.

Rasbash, J., Browne, W., Goldstein, H., Yang, M., Plewis, I., Healy, M., Woodhouse, G., Deaper, D., Langford, I., & Lewis, T. (2000). *A user's guide to MLwiN.* University of London.

Raudenbush, S. W., & Bryk, A. S. (1986). A hierarchical model for studying school effects. *Sociology of Education, 59,* 1–17.

Raudenbush, S. W., & Bryk, A. S. (2002). *Hierarchical linear models* (2nd ed.). Newbury Park, CA: Sage.

Raudenbush, S. W., Bryk, A. S., Cheong, Y. F., & Congdon, R. (2004). *HLM6: Hierarchical linear and nonlinear modeling.* Chicago, IL: Scientific Software International.

Raudenbush, S. W., Bryk, A. S., Cheong, Y. F., & Congdon, R. (2004). *HLM6: Hierarchical linear and nonlinear modeling.* Chicago, IL: Scientific Software International.

Raudenbush, S. W., Rowan B., & Kang S. J. (1991). A multilevel multivariate model for studying school climate with estimation via the EM algorithm and application to U.S. high-school data. *Journal of Educational Statistics, 16,* 295–330.

Raudenbush, S. W., & Willms, J. D. (Eds.) (1991). *Schools, classrooms, and pupils: International studies of schooling from a multilevel perspective.* San Diego, CA: Academic.

Raudenbush, S. W., & Willms, J. D. (1995). The estimation of school effects. *Journal of Educational and Behavioural Statistics, 20,* 307–335.

Reyes, P., Scribner, J. D., & Scribner, A. P. (1999). *Lessons from high-performing Hispanic schools: Creating learning communities.* New York: Teachers College Press.

Riehl, J. C. (2000) The principal's role in creating inclusive schools for diverse students: A review of normative, empirical, and critical literature on the practice of educational administration. *Review of Educational Research, 70,* 55–81.

Roberts, J. K., & McLeod, P. (2008). Software options for mutilevel models. In A. A. O'Connell and D. B. McCoach (Eds.), *Multilevel modeling of educational data* (pp. 427–467). Charlotte, NC: Information Age Publishing.

Rogosa, D. R., Brandt, D., & Zimowski, M. (1982). A growth curve approach to the measurement of change. *Psychological Bulletin, 90,* 726–748.

Rogosa, D. R., & Willett, J. B. (1983). Demonstrating the reliability of the difference score in the measurement of change. *Journal of Educational Measurement, 20,* 335–343.

Rogosa, D. R., & Willett, J. B. (1984). Understanding correlates of change by modeling individual differences in growth. *Psychometrika, 50,* 203–228.

Rosenholtz, S. (1989). *Teachers' workplace.* White Plains, New York: Longman.

Sammons, P. (1999). *School effectiveness: Coming of age in the twenty-fist century.* Lisse, Netherlands: Swets & Zeitlinger.

Scheerens, J. (1992). *Effective schooling: Research, theory and practice.* New York: Cassell.

Scheerens, J. (2001). Monitoring school effectiveness in developing countries. *School Effectiveness and School Improvement, 12,* 359–384.

Scheerens, J., & Bosker, R. (1997). *The foundations of educational effectiveness.* Oxford, United Kingdom: Pergamon.

Shapka, J., Domene, J., & Keating, D. (2006). Trajectories of career aspirations through adolescence and young adulthood: Early math achievement as a critical filter. *Educational Research & Evaluation, 12,* 347–358.

Sidani, S., & Sechrest, L. (1999). Putting program theory into operation. *American Journal of Evaluation, 20,* 227–238.

Snijders, T. A. B., & Bosker, R. J. (1999). *Multilevel analysis.* Thousand Oaks, CA: Sage.

Spybrook, J. (2008). Power, sample size, and design. In A. A. O'Connell and D. B. McCoach (Eds.), *Multilevel modeling of educational data* (pp. 273–311). Charlotte, NC: Information Age Publishing.

Stapleton, L.M, & Thomas, S.L. (2008). The use of national datasets for teaching and research: Sources and Issues. In A. A. O'Connell and D. B. McCoach (Eds.), *Multilevel modeling of educational data* (pp. 11–57). Charlotte, NC: Information Age Publishing.

Teddlie, C., & Reynolds, D. (Eds.). (2000). *The international handbook of school effectiveness research.* London: Falmer.

Teddlie, C., Reynolds, D., & Sammons, P. (2000). The methodology and scientific properties of school effectiveness research. In C. Teddlie & D. Reynolds (Eds.), *The international handbook of school effectiveness research* (pp. 55–133). London: Falmer.

Thum, Y. M., & Bryk, A. S. (1997). Value-added productivity indicators: The Dallas system. In J. Millman (Ed.), *Grading teachers, grading schools: Is student achievement a valid evaluation measure?* (pp. 100–109). Thousand Oaks, CA: Corwin.

Tomlinson, C. (2005). Quality curriculum and instruction for highly able students. *Theory into Practice, 44,* 160–166.

Trouilloud, D., Sarrazin, P., Bressoux, P., & Bois, J. (2006). Relation between teachers' early expectations and students' later perceived competence in physical education classes: Autonomy-supportive climate as a moderator. *Journal of Educational Psychology, 98,* 75–86.

Tsui, K., & Cheng, Y. (1999). School organizational health and teacher commitment: A contingency study with multi-level analysis. *Educational Research & Evaluation, 5,* 249–268.

Tulley, M., & Chiu, L. (1995). Student teachers and classroom discipline. *Journal of Educational Research, 88,* 164–171.

Willett, J. B. (1988). Questions and answers in the measurement of change. In E. Rothkopf (Ed.), *Review of research in education 1988–89* (pp. 345–422). Washington, DC: American Educational Research Association.

Willms, J. D. (1992). *Monitoring school performance: A guide for educators.* Washington, DC: Falmer.

Willms, J. D., & Raudenbush, S. (1989). A longitudinal hierarchical linear model for estimating school effects and their stability. *Journal of Educational Measurement, 26,* 209–232.

APPENDIX A

Descriptive Statistics of Student-Level and School-Level Variables

	N	Mean	SD
Student-level variables			
Gender (male = 0, female = 1)	2135	0.52	0.50
Socioeconomic status (SES) (international rating)	1788	45.57	17.08
Family structure (both parents = 0, single parents = 1)	1995	0.23	0.42
Family size (number of siblings)	2013	2.45	1.61
Home educational resources (scale index)	2014	−0.30	1.19
Family cultural possession (scale index)	2009	−0.16	1.04
Family cultural activity (scale index)	1999	0.20	0.96
School-level variables			
Context			
School enrollment size (number of students)	114	1180.82	869.95
School location (urban = 1, rural = 0)	119	0.66	0.48
Shortage of teachers (scale index)	121	−0.12	0.97
School material resources (scale index)	121	−0.17	0.81
School instructional resources (scale index)	121	−0.37	0.87
Climate			
Disciplinary climate (scale index)	147	2.19	0.24
Academic pressure (scale index)	147	2.99	0.22
Teacher support (scale index)	147	3.07	0.32
Student-teacher relationship (scale index)	147	2.84	0.23
School autonomy (scale index)	121	1.03	0.92

Note. Another school-level variable, school mean SES, is created as a standardized aggregation of individual SES within each school. Both student-level and school-level index variables reported here are in their original PISA measurement scales that are standardized based on international mean and standard deviation (except for SES). For the purpose of data analysis in this chapter, student-level index variables and school mean SES are standardized based on the US national mean and standard deviation; all other variables at both student and school levels are centered around their grand means.

APPENDIX B

Description of School-Level Variables

School Context

School enrollment size represents the total enrollment of students in a school. It is used as a continuous variable.

School location contains six categories: (a) village, hamlet, or rural area (fewer than 3,000 people); (b) small town (3,000 to 15,000 people); (c) town (15,000 to 1,000,000 people); (d) city (1,000,000 people); (e) close to the center of a city with over 1,000,000 people; and (f) elsewhere in a city with over 1,000,000 people. It is used as a dichotomous variable comparing city schools (a value of one, with city defined as the last three categories) with countryside schools (a value of zero, with countryside defined as the first three categories).

School mean SES is an average measure of SES of students within each school. It is used as a continuous variable.

Shortage of teachers is an index variable created by the PISA staff which measures the extent to which learning by 15-year-old students is hindered by: (a) shortage or inadequacy of teachers in general and (b) shortage of teachers in reading, mathematics, or science. It is used as a continuous variable, with a lower value indicating a more serious problem of teacher shortage.

School material resources is an index variable created by the PISA staff which measures the extent to which learning by 15-year-olds is hindered by: (a) poor condition of buildings, (b) poor heating and cooling and/or lighting systems, and (c) lack of instructional space (e.g., classrooms). It is used as a continuous variable, with a lower value indicating a lower quality of school physical infrastructure.

School instructional resources is an index variable created by the PISA staff to measure the extent to which learning by 15-year-olds is hindered by: (a) lack of instructional materials, (b) not enough computers for instruction, (c) lack of instructional materials in the library, (d) lack of multi-media resources for instruction, (e) inadequate science laboratory equipment, and (f) inadequate facilities for the fine arts. It is used as a continuous variable, with a lower value indicating a lower quality of school educational resources.

School Climate

Disciplinary climate is an index variable created by the PISA staff to measure the frequency with which: (a) the teacher has to wait a long time for students to quiet down, (b) students cannot work well, (c) students do not listen to what the teacher says, (d) students do not start working for a long time after the lesson begins, (e) there is noise and disorder, and (f) at the start of class more than five minutes are spent doing nothing. It is used as a continuous variable, with a lower value indicating a poorer disciplinary climate.

Academic pressure is an index variable created by the PISA staff to measure the frequency with which: (a) the teacher wants students to work hard, (b) the teacher tells students that they can do better, (c) the teacher does not like it when students deliver careless work, and (d) students have to learn a lot. It is used as a continuous variable, with a lower value indicating a lower academic pressure from teachers.

Teacher support is an index variable created by the PISA staff to measure the frequency with which: (a) the teacher helps students with their work, (b) the teacher continues teaching until the students understand, (c) the teacher does a lot to help students, and (d) the teacher helps students with their learning. It is used as a continuous variable, with a lower value indicating a lower level of teacher support.

Student–teacher relationship is an index variable created by the PISA staff to measure the extent to which students agree with the following statements: (a) students get along well with most teachers, (b) most teachers are interested in students' well being, (c) most teachers really listen to what students have to say, (d) if students need extra help they will receive it from their teachers, and (e) most teachers treat students fairly. It is used as a continuous variable, with a lower value indicating a worse student-teacher relationship.

School autonomy is an index variable created by the PISA staff to measure whether schools are responsible for: (a) appointing teachers, (b) dismissing teachers, (c) establishing teachers' starting salaries, (d) determining teachers' salary increase, (e) formulating school budgets, (f) allocating budgets within the school, (g) establishing student disciplinary policies, (h) establishing student assessment policies, (i) approving students for admittance to school, (j) choosing which textbooks to use;, (k) determining course content, and (l) deciding which courses are offered. It is used as a continuous variable, with a lower value indicating a lower degree of school autonomy.

CHAPTER 4

MODELING GROWTH USING MULTILEVEL AND ALTERNATIVE APPROACHES

Janet K. Holt

In recent years, the array of linear growth modeling techniques has expanded greatly, from traditional methods of univariate or multivariate repeated measures analysis to more flexible random coefficients models that include multilevel growth models, latent growth curve models, and growth mixture modeling. This chapter provides general descriptions of and contrasts methods across three classes of growth models: multilevel growth modeling, including linear, quadratic, piecewise, and shift models; latent growth curve models, including models for linear, quadratic, and estimated growth curves; and growth mixture models, including estimation and prediction of latent growth classes as well as prediction of distal outcomes. While not an exhaustive list of growth modeling methods, this is a comparison of some of the more popular, cutting-edge methods in the literature. In this chapter, I demonstrate how analysts can use these classes of growth models in longitudinal or developmental studies to model change across time, describe how to use each of these models to address substantive questions about change, and summarize the strengths/weaknesses, assumptions, and data

Multilevel Modeling of Educational Data, pages 111–159
Copyright © 2008 by Information Age Publishing
111

requirements for each of these classes of models. I begin with a general discussion of each approach and provide examples from the research literature. For selected models, an applied demonstration of the technique is also included.

MULTILEVEL MODELING

Reconceptualizing Longitudinal Models As Multilevel Models

Traditional approaches for analyzing longitudinal data utilize repeated measures ANOVA or MANOVA techniques; however, these methods place severe constraints on the form of the data. The two most problematic constraints in repeated measures analyses are that all subjects must have an equal number of data points and that the data collection schedule needs to be *time-structured*, such that the planned schedule of data collection must be at the same times for all individuals. By default, these traditional longitudinal analyses use listwise deletion to discard participants without full data for all time points. This often results in a much-reduced data set that does not accurately represent the originally sampled population and that is likely to be biased.

In contrast, in multilevel modeling (MLM), the data are a series of observations nested within the individual; therefore, the structure of the data can be person-specific and much more flexible. This approach allows for data that are collected at unequally-spaced waves of data collection and that are *time-unstructured* (i.e., different data collection schedules for different individuals) and *unbalanced* (i.e., different number of observations for each individual). This flexibility also can translate to person-specific growth trajectories. Analysts can estimate the variation in growth patterns and investigate relationships with covariates to model both the intra- and inter-person variability. This reconceptualization of growth modeling results in a flexible modeling approach that more aptly captures the inherent complexity in growth processes.

Multilevel Linear Growth Models

Analysts can use the basic multilevel linear growth model to assess both initial status and linear change over time. Equations 4.1 and 4.2 describe this model with random coefficients:

$$y_{ti} = \pi_{0i} + \pi_i (time - time_1)_{ti} + e_{ti} \tag{4.1}$$

$$\pi_{0i} = \beta_{00} + r_{0i}$$

$$\pi_{1i} = \beta_{10} + r_{1i}$$

(4.2)

for $i = 1,\ldots, n$ subjects across $t = 1,\ldots, T$ waves. The growth parameters, π_{0i} and π_{1i}, represent the intercept and linear rate of change, respectively, for person i, and e_{ti} is the within-person residual not accounted for by the specified growth parameters. If time 1 is the initial time point assessed in the data, then the intercept represents the initial value on the dependent variable. The level-one equation (see Equation 4.1) is the individual growth model and specifically describes the outcome at time 1, the intercept and the rate of change for person i, and random fluctuations around the linear growth trajectory. The level-two equations (see Equation 4.2) describe the between-person variability in the growth parameters: the intercepts, π_{0i}, and the linear slopes, π_{1i}. The level-two residuals, r_{0i} and r_{1i}, represent the random, between-person differences in the growth parameters, π_{0i} and π_{1i}, respectively; and the fixed effects in this model, β_{00} and β_{10}, represent the average intercept and the average rate of growth, respectively. The level-two equations allow us to model the variability in the growth parameters across persons. Together, Equations 4.1 and 4.2 represent the unconditional linear growth model with random slopes and intercepts.

Data Requirements and Assumptions

Data Requirements

MLM allows the analysis of incomplete data as long as data are missing at random (MAR; i.e., the missingness pattern can be related to observed values of other variables in the data set; Little & Rubin, 2002). As previously mentioned, multilevel growth models do not require the data to be time-structured or balanced. However, these models do require one more wave of data than the number of growth parameters in the level-one growth model (see Equation 4.1). Therefore, a linear model with two growth parameters in the level-one equation, π_{0i} and π_{1i}, would require at least three waves of data. This is the minimum requirement, but one can estimate the parameters with greater precision with additional waves of data.

Assumptions

MLM makes assumptions regarding both the random components of the level-one and level-two models as well as specification assumptions about the relationship of the variables to the random components. For a detailed explanation of assumptions, see Raudenbush and Bryk (2002, pp. 255–256). One important assumption is that both level-one and level-two residuals are independently and normally distributed. Nonnormality introduced at level one will bias the standard errors at both levels one and two. Examination of the residuals with normal probability plots is an accepted procedure for checking whether the data meet this assumption. Analysts need to construct separate normal probability plots for each level of residuals (e.g., e_{it}, r_{0i}, r_{1i}). To normalize the data and resolve many nonnormality problems, analysts can use common data transformation procedures. (See Judd & McClelland, 1989, for an excellent discussion of data transformations.)

Form of the Data

General data analysis software typically lays out data on repeated observations in a multivariate, or *wide*, format, where each observation is represented by a different variable in a separate column within the database. For example, Figure 4.1 presents an SPSS screen shot of data on reading achievement for a sample of children across five waves of data collection: 1, 2, 3, 4, and 8. In this dataset, described in more detail in a later section,

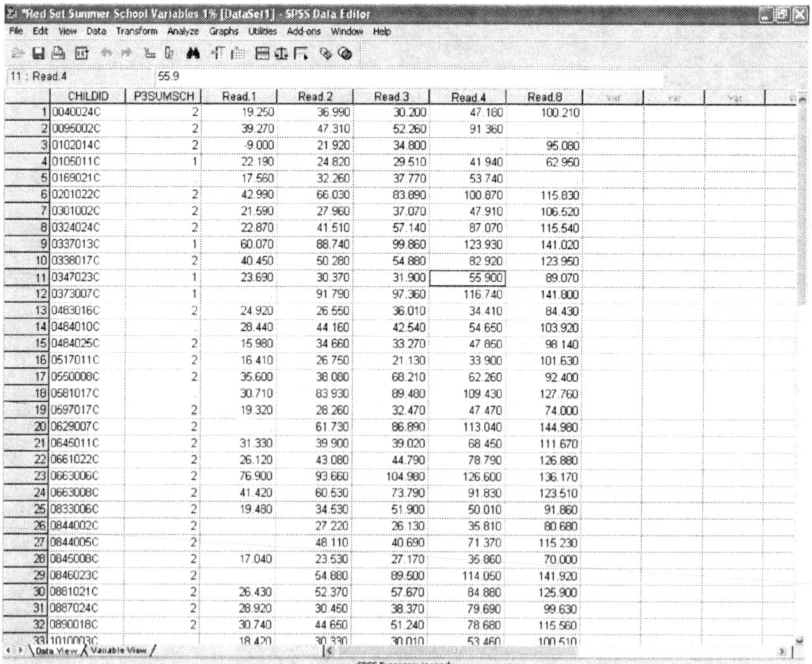

	CHILDID	P3SUMSCH	Read.1	Read.2	Read.3	Read.4	Read.8
1	0040024C	2	19.250	36.990	30.200	47.180	100.210
2	0095002C	2	39.270	47.310	52.260	91.360	.
3	0102014C	2	-9.000	21.920	34.800	.	95.080
4	0105011C	1	22.190	24.820	29.510	41.940	62.950
5	0169021C	.	17.560	32.260	37.770	53.740	
6	0201022C	2	42.990	66.030	83.890	100.870	115.830
7	0301002C	2	21.590	27.960	37.070	47.910	106.520
8	0324024C	2	22.870	41.510	57.140	87.070	115.540
9	0337013C	1	60.070	88.740	99.860	123.930	141.020
10	0338017C	2	40.450	50.280	54.880	82.920	123.950
11	0347023C	1	23.690	30.370	31.900	55.900	89.070
12	0373007C	1	.	91.790	97.360	116.740	141.800
13	0483016C	2	24.920	26.550	36.010	34.410	84.430
14	0484010C	.	28.440	44.160	42.540	54.650	103.920
15	0484025C	2	15.980	34.660	33.270	47.850	98.140
16	0517011C	2	16.410	26.750	21.130	33.900	101.630
17	0550008C	2	35.600	38.080	68.210	62.260	92.400
18	0581017C	.	30.710	83.930	89.480	109.430	127.760
19	0597017C	2	19.320	28.260	32.470	47.470	74.000
20	0629007C	2	.	61.730	86.890	113.040	144.980
21	0645011C	2	31.330	39.900	39.020	68.450	111.670
22	0661022C	2	26.120	43.080	44.790	78.790	126.880
23	0663006C	2	76.900	93.660	104.980	126.600	136.170
24	0663008C	2	41.420	60.530	73.790	91.830	123.510
25	0833006C	2	19.480	34.530	51.900	50.010	91.860
26	0844002C	2		27.220	26.130	35.810	80.680
27	0844005C	2		48.110	40.690	71.370	115.230
28	0845008C	2	17.040	23.530	27.170	35.860	70.000
29	0846023C	2		54.880	89.500	114.050	141.920
30	0881021C	2	26.430	52.370	57.670	84.880	125.900
31	0887024C	2	28.920	30.450	38.370	79.690	99.630
32	0890018C	2	30.740	44.650	51.240	78.680	115.560
33	1010003C		18.420	30.330	30.010	53.460	100.510

Figure 4.1 Multivariate, or *wide*, data layout.

data were collected at five "terms," that is, fall and spring of kindergarten, fall and spring of first grade, and spring of third grade. Note that the analyst formatted each measure of reading achievement as a separate column in this data layout and that there is only one row per person or child ID. However, when conducting growth analyses, it is helpful to represent each time point as a separate case. Additionally, if the data are not time-structured and different persons have different data structures, it is cumbersome to structure the data in a multivariate format. For these reasons, analysts organizing repeated measures data for MLM often use a person-period, or *long*, data set. A person-period data set has multiple rows per person, one for each time point at which the person has a measurement. The analyst enters a variable coding the passing of time (e.g., wave, time, age, term, grade) as a separate variable in the data set. In this data layout, the number of rows equals the number of observations, whereas in a multivariate format, the number of rows equals the number of persons. Figure 4.2 compiles the time-varying measures of reading achievement into a single column called "read," and in this format, the variable "term" indicates the wave in which data collection occurred. Also note that there now are five rows of data per child, one for each time period of data collection.

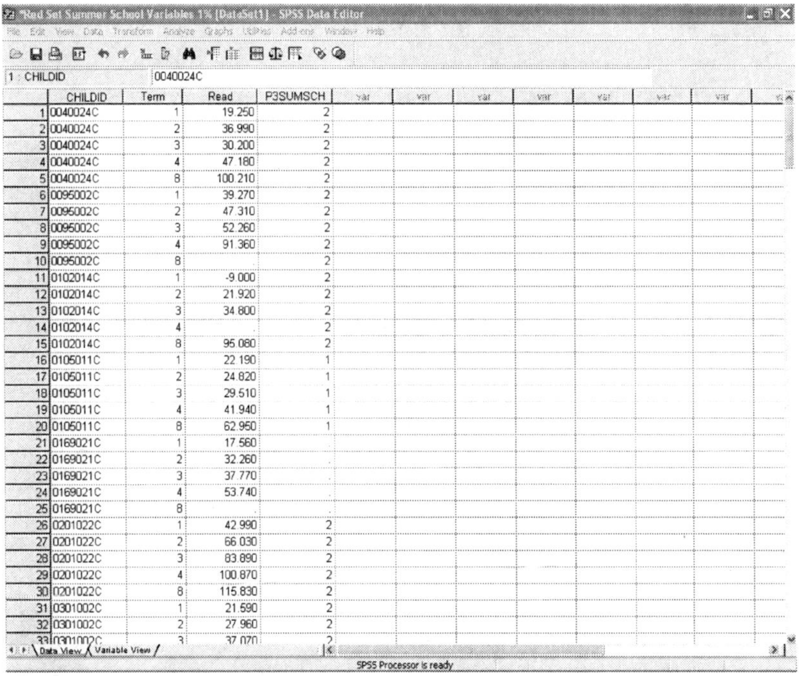

	CHILDID	Term	Read	P3SUMSCH
1	0040024C	1	19.250	2
2	0040024C	2	36.990	2
3	0040024C	3	30.200	2
4	0040024C	4	47.180	2
5	0040024C	8	100.210	2
6	0095002C	1	39.270	2
7	0095002C	2	47.310	2
8	0095002C	3	52.260	2
9	0095002C	4	91.360	2
10	0095002C	8	.	2
11	0102014C	1	-9.000	2
12	0102014C	2	21.920	2
13	0102014C	3	34.800	2
14	0102014C	4	.	2
15	0102014C	8	95.080	2
16	0105011C	1	22.190	1
17	0105011C	2	24.820	1
18	0105011C	3	29.510	1
19	0105011C	4	41.940	1
20	0105011C	8	62.950	1
21	0169021C	1	17.560	.
22	0169021C	2	32.260	.
23	0169021C	3	37.770	.
24	0169021C	4	53.740	.
25	0169021C	8	.	.
26	0201022C	1	42.990	2
27	0201022C	2	66.030	2
28	0201022C	3	83.890	2
29	0201022C	4	100.870	2
30	0201022C	8	115.830	2
31	0301002C	1	21.590	2
32	0301002C	2	27.960	2
33	0301002C	3	37.070	2

Figure 4.2 Person-period, or *long*, data layout.

Treatment of Time

To measure the passing of time, analysts typically enter a variable for time into the level-one equation, as in Equation 4.1. However, depending on the research scenario, the analyst may use an alternate variable for time that more closely corresponds to the research design and occasions of measurement. For instance, the analyst may use age, denoted in years, months, or even days, for developmental research studies; on the other hand, in school-based studies, analysts frequently use grade level to describe the passage of time.

No matter the variable chosen to denote the passage of time, the analyst should give careful consideration to centering this variable in multilevel modeling because the interpretation of the intercept, β_{00}, and all other lower-order growth parameters depends on the centering point. For instance, if the time series ranges from 24 months of age to 36 months of age and has data available at 3-month intervals, then depending on the centering of age, β_{00} could represent the average outcome at the onset of the data collection period (i.e., 24 months), at the midpoint (i.e., 30 months), or at the end of the data collection period (i.e., 36 months). Biesanz, Deeb-Sossa, Papakakis, Bollen, and Curran (2004) suggest that the coding of time in multilevel modeling should facilitate interpretability and should focus on the main period of interest in the study.

To illustrate the effects of centering, consider the situation in which a researcher is studying the effects of test coaching by monitoring test scores just prior to the coaching sessions, and at the quarterly periods during and immediately following the 12-week coaching session. Centering at 0 weeks (i.e., initial status), 6 weeks (i.e., midpoint), and 12 weeks (i.e., final status) will result in different interpretations of β_{00}. If the researcher coded the first week as 0, β_{00} would represent the expected value of coaching at initial status, just prior to the onset of coaching. This may not be the most desired interpretation for β_{00} because it is before the treatment actually occurs. In contrast, centering at 6 weeks would require recoding the origin to ($week - 6$) and would result in an intercept that is the average outcome midway through coaching, an interesting time point if the growth process is of interest. Centering at final status would require recoding the origin to ($week - 12$) and would allow an interpretation of the intercept after coaching is complete, which may be most appropriate if the final outcome is of greatest interest.

Centering the time variable does not affect β_{10} in a linear growth model because β_{10} is a constant linear rate of growth across time—in this example, from 0 to 12 weeks. Likewise, centering time does not affect the within-person variance or the residual variance in rate of change; it can, however, drastically affect both the variance of the intercept and the covariation between the intercept and rate of change. Therefore, if coaching reduces the variability in test scores, then the random variance in the intercept and the correlation between the intercept and growth rate would decrease as the centering point moves from initial status to midpoint to final status. Thus, decisions regarding centering should take into consideration the impact of the centering point on the interpretation of the intercept, the residual variance of the intercept, and the correlation between the intercept and rate of change.

Variance-Covariance Structures

The unconditional growth model in Equations 4.1 and 4.2 has an implied variance of e_{ti} equal to σ^2, the within-person residual variance, and a variance/covariance structure of the unique person effects, r_{0i} and r_{1i}, equal to:

$$\mathbf{T} = \begin{bmatrix} \tau_{00} & \tau_{01} \\ \tau_{10} & \tau_{11} \end{bmatrix} \qquad (4.3)$$

(Raudenbush & Bryk, 2002). **T**, referred to as the tau matrix, is the level-two covariance structure for the model that Equations 4.1 and 4.2 describe. Assuming time is centered at initial status, the variance terms, τ_{00} and τ_{11}, describe the variance in initial status and rate of growth across individuals, respectively, whereas the covariance term, τ_{01} or τ_{10}, describes the covariation between initial status and rate of growth across individuals, which also can be expressed as a correlation. With data from three or more time points (multiwave data), the correlation between initial status and rate of growth provides an estimate of the correlation between true initial status and growth rate (Raudenbush & Bryk, 2002), although floor or ceiling effects at particular time points can influence the estimate. As noted previously, this correlation can vary with a change in centering point. Depending on the software package used, various options are available for modeling alternative covariance structures within a multilevel framework. These are more fully described under software options.

Modeling Change with Covariates

The structure of the multilevel model allows the incorporation of covariates at levels one and two. Consequently, analysts can use time-varying covariates at level one to account for variation in observations within individuals, and time-invariant covariates at level two to account for variation in growth parameters across individuals. Combined, both types of covariates allow for the formulation of rich models of change.

Time-Varying Covariates

Analysts can incorporate covariates into level one of the model to account for within-person changes that occur across observations. The level-two equations will model each of the level-one parameters. For example, Equation 4.4 (with *time* centered at $time_1$) adds a time-varying covariate, a_{ti}, to level one, and Equation 4.5 models the associated parameter, π_{2i}, in a new level-two equation. Depending on whether r_{2i} has significant variation across individuals, the analyst is able to fix the equation (i.e., remove this residual from the level-two equation) or treat it as random (i.e., keep the residual in the level-two equation). Analysts can use a significance test of the variation of the r_{2i} residuals to inform this decision. However, for models with more than two or three random effects, estimation difficulties may occur as **T** becomes increasingly complex. The number of elements in the tau matrix is $r*(r+1)/2$, where r is the number of random effects at level two, because we normally estimate the variances for each random effect as well as the covariances between all pairs of random effects. For this reason, parsimony is an important consideration when determining which level-one predictors to include as random and which effects to fix at level two.

$$y_{ti} = \pi_{0i} + \pi_{1i}(time - time_1) + \pi_{2i}a_{ti} + e_{ti} \qquad (4.4)$$

$$\pi_{0i} = \beta_{00} + r_{0i}$$
$$\pi_{1i} = \beta_{10} + r_{1i} \qquad (4.5)$$
$$\pi_{2i} = \beta_{20} + r_{2i}$$

Time-Invariant Covariates

One of the strengths of multilevel modeling is the ability to model cross-level effects, or interactions between variables measured at different levels of analysis. Within a growth modeling framework, this allows for modeling the relationships between effects that are repeated measures (i.e., measured within-persons) and individual-level effects (i.e., measured at the person level). Covariates assessed at the person level are termed time-invariant covariates, and analysts easily can incorporate them into the level-two equations of the multilevel growth model. Examples of time-invariant covariates include gender, or race/ethnicity. As an alternative to Equation 4.5, Equation 4.6 is a series of level-two equations that analysts could formulate to model the growth parameters in Equation 4.4. The addition of X_i, a time-invariant covariate, to the level-two equations allows the introduction of a person-level variable to study the effects of that variable on the intercept via

β_{01}; the effects of X_i on the linear growth rate via β_{11}, and the effects of X_i on the time-varying covariate via β_{21}. These latter two parameters represent the cross-level interactions of a person-level variable, X_i, with the within-person effects of Equation 4.4. Note that Equation 4.6 includes the same predictor in all level-two equations; however, the analyst may choose to include different time-invariant predictors within any of the level-two models.

$$\pi_{0i} = \beta_{00} + \beta_{01}X_i + r_{0i}$$
$$\pi_{1i} = \beta_{10} + \beta_{11}X_i + r_{1i} \tag{4.6}$$
$$\pi_{2i} = \beta_{20} + \beta_{21}X_i + r_{2i}$$

Modeling Change in Growth Rates

Although a simple linear model of change is appropriate for many growth scenarios, there are instances in which the linear model is not the best fit, and the analyst should examine other alternatives. Consider the situation in which subjects grow in a linear trajectory but then growth slows and the rate of change lessens (i.e., decelerates) or, alternatively, the growth increases (i.e., accelerates) over time. As this description illustrates, more complex growth curves may involve changes in the growth rate. Alternately, the change in growth rate may be abrupt, and thus represent separate phases of growth. Deviations from a constant linear rate of growth may be due to physical, cognitive, or other internal developmental processes or can be due to transitions that occur in the society or institutions to which the subjects belong. Whatever the cause, analysts often can examine resultant changes in growth rates by using growth models that extend beyond the simple linear form. The following sections on polynomial multilevel growth models and multiphase multilevel growth models will consider these alternatives to simple linear growth.

Polynomial Multilevel Growth Models
The addition of terms that include higher-order time variables (e.g., time-squared, time-cubed) can be used to account for changes in growth rates. A quadratic growth curve includes the square of the time variable, and the corresponding coefficient represents the degree of acceleration or deceleration in growth that occurs over time; that is, whether or not the curve is tapering off (decelerating) or rapidly increasing (accelerating) as the time variable increases. Typically, analysts test the quadratic model with a likelihood ratio test to determine if it provides a better fit than the linear model. This is done by constructing an hypothesis test comparing the restricted model (e.g., linear model) to the more complex alternative model

(e.g., quadratic model). The likelihood ratio test compares deviances and *df* for these two nested models using the χ^2 difference test. A statistically significant χ^2 test indicates that the more complex model is warranted. (See McCoach & Black, 2008, Chapter 7 this volume for more details about the chi-square difference test). Equation 4.7 describes the unconditional quadratic growth model:

$$y_{ti} = \pi_{0i} + \pi_{1i}(time - time_1) + \pi_{2i}(time - time_1)^2 + e_{ti}$$
$$\pi_{0i} = \beta_{00} + r_{0i}$$
$$\pi_{1i} = \beta_{10} + r_{1i}$$
$$\pi_{2i} = \beta_{20} + r_{2i}$$

(4.7)

In this model, the interpretation of the linear coefficient changes somewhat from the linear growth model. Recalling that time is centered at the first time-point of data collection, the intercept, π_{0i}, remains the initial status for person *i*. However, π_{1i} now represents the rate of change *at initial status* (i.e., when $time - time_1 = 0$) for person *i*. We refer to this effect as the *instantaneous* rate of change at initial status. This change in interpretation arises because the quadratic model no longer has a single linear rate of change; instead, there is a different rate of change at every time point. Rates of change in a quadratic model are estimated by the slopes of lines tangent to the growth curve at each point on the curve. These "simple-slopes" change across the entire time-span of the growth curve. In a polynomial model, the simple-slopes are equivalent to the first derivative, with respect to time, of the level-one equation evaluated at each specific value of time; for the quadratic model, the equation for these simple-slopes is: $\pi_{1i} + 2\pi_{2i}(time - time_1)$. Because time is centered at $time_1$ in this example, analysts can interpret π_{1i} as the instantaneous rate of growth *at initial status*. If the analyst recentered the data to the midpoint, then π_{1i} would represent the instantaneous rate of change *at the midpoint*. The interpretation of π_{1i} depends on the placement of the origin for time (Biesanz, et al., 2004).

The new level-one parameter, π_{2i}, represents the acceleration/deceleration apparent in the growth curve for person *i* across time. When π_{2i} is positive, acceleration is occurring, and the growth curve is convex to the time axis (i.e., the instantaneous linear growth rates are increasing). In contrast, if π_{2i} is negative, then deceleration is occurring, and the growth curve is concave to the time axis (i.e., the instantaneous linear growth rates are slowing). This new parameterization of growth requires at least four time points because there are three growth parameters in the level-one equation of the quadratic growth model: π_{0i}, π_{1i}, and π_{2i}.

The level-two equation for π_{2i} is a model for the acceleration/deceleration parameter for person i, and describes its variation as a function of the grand mean for acceleration/deceleration, β_{20}, and the unique effects of the person (see Equation 4.7). Overall, the person-level parameters, β_{00}, β_{10}, and β_{20}, represent the population average intercept at initial status, the average instantaneous rate of growth at initial status, and the average acceleration/deceleration across time, respectively. The residuals, r_{0i}, r_{1i}, and r_{2i}, are the unique effects of person i on their initial status, instantaneous growth at initial status, and acceleration/deceleration rates, respectively.

The unconditional quadratic growth model has random slopes and intercepts, an implied variance of e_{ti} equal to σ^2, and a variance/covariance structure of r_{0i}, r_{1i}, and r_{2i} equal to:

$$\mathbf{T} = \begin{bmatrix} \tau_{00} & \tau_{01} & \tau_{02} \\ \tau_{10} & \tau_{11} & \tau_{12} \\ \tau_{20} & \tau_{21} & \tau_{22} \end{bmatrix} \tag{4.8}$$

(Raudenbush & Bryk, 2002). Analysts could expand this model further to include individual effects on the mean growth parameters (i.e., a conditional growth model) by incorporating level-two time-invariant covariates, similar in structure to Equation 4.6. As with the linear model, the level-two covariates of the different growth parameters do not need to be the same. Additionally, organizational effects on the person-level parameters can be assessed through a three-level model (e.g., time nested within individuals, nested within organizations) by incorporating level-three time-invariant covariates.

Analysts also can formulate more complex polynomial growth models. For example, a cubic model includes a parameter for time-cubed. The parameter for the cubed term represents the change in the acceleration or deceleration that is occurring over time. If examined graphically, a cubic model has one inflection point, indicating that the quadratic acceleration/deceleration pattern is changing. In multilevel polynomial growth models, analysts interpret the highest-order term (e.g., cubic parameter) across the full range of the time variable, whereas they interpret the lower-order terms (e.g., intercept, linear, and quadratic parameters) at the centering point. Researchers need to weigh the advantages of modeling a more complex model with the added data requirements. For instance, a minimum of five waves would be needed to test a cubic model. However, if this is not a trend that they would expect or be interested in, researchers may opt to forego the more complex model and analyze a less complex polynomial model that could be estimated with greater precision.

Examples From The Literature

Using data from the Longitudinal Study of American Youth (LSAY), Ma (2005) studied both student and school effects on the rate of mathematics achievement growth from 7th through 11th grade using a three-level linear growth model. Level one modeled the intra-individual variation across time, level two modeled the inter-individual variation within schools, and level three modeled the inter-school variation. The outcome variable was mathematics achievement, and the student-level predictors included gender, race, age, and other demographic variables. The school-level predictors included measures of both school context and school climate. Ma compared growth rates and effects of the student-level demographic variables, and effects of school-level context and climate variables, on mathematics achievement growth between students who experienced early acceleration in their mathematics instruction and those who did not, as well as among those in regular, honors, and gifted classes.

In a growth study of the onset of tense marking (a measure of grammatical development in young children), Hadley and Holt (2006) constructed quadratic growth models to estimate the growth rates in tense marking from 24 to 36 months of age in a sample of slow-developing language learners, assessed at 3-month intervals. The positive coefficients for both the linear and the quadratic components indicated that growth was increasing and accelerating across time. Hadley and Holt expected that children's changes over time in their mean length of utterance (MLU) also would affect their developmental trajectories in tense marking. Including the time-varying covariate, MLU, which also was assessed in 3-month intervals from 24 to 36 months, controlled for the variation in children's growth in tense marking that was not due solely to the child's developmental growth over time but also to the individual child's change in MLU. The researchers also modeled the interaction between MLU and time in order to determine if the tense marking growth rate covaried with changes in MLU.

Hadley and Holt (2006) also examined the influence of several time-invariant covariates on the growth parameters to determine if environmental factors (e.g., maternal education) or maturational factors (e.g., family history of speech, language, or learning disabilities) covaried with the average level of tense marking and its linear growth rate in slow-developing language learners. They assessed the time-invariant covariates at the initial evaluation and modeled their influence on the growth parameters as well as on the time-varying covariates.

Application—Linear and Quadratic Growth Models

To assess growth in reading achievement from kindergarten through third grade, I used a subsample of data from the kindergarten cohort of the Early Childhood Longitudinal Survey (ECLS-K; $n = 16,400$). The students completed cognitive reading assessments in the fall and spring of kindergarten, fall and spring of first grade, and the spring of third grade. These data were not gathered at equal intervals: students did not complete the assessments in the fall and spring of second grade or the fall of third grade. Furthermore, a subsample of only 30% of the base-year cohort completed the assessment in the fall of first grade (National Center for Education Statistics, 2004). Therefore, not all subjects had an equal number of data collection points. To simplify the presentation of this illustrative example, I did not use sampling weights in the current analyses. Full maximum likelihood was used for parameter estimation.

I formulated multilevel polynomial growth models to 1) determine the growth trajectory for reading achievement from kindergarten through third grade, 2) determine whether a time-varying covariate, changing schools between terms, affects the reading achievement, and 3) determine whether the growth parameters and the effect of changing schools vary depending on the time-invariant predictor, gender. Figure 4.3 graphs a random sample of 1% of the cases by gender. It is apparent that reading achievement

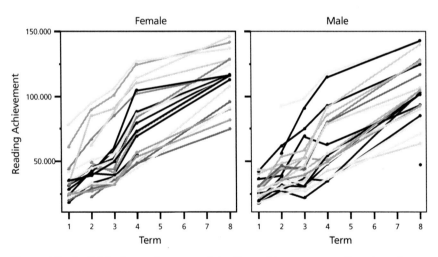

Figure 4.3 Individual growth curves of reading achievement as a function of gender for a selected sample from kindergarten through third grade.

growth is decelerating (slowing down) from kindergarten to third grade and that a linear growth model would not account for this deceleration. In these graphs, time ranges from 1 to 8, representing each term from fall and spring of kindergarten to fall and spring of third grade.

Although the graph of individual growth curves can illustrate general trends, a multilevel statistical analysis directly addresses the questions of interest. To assess reading achievement growth, I first formulated a two-level linear growth model (Model 1). Next, I formulated a quadratic growth model (Model 2) and tested the difference in the deviances to determine if the more complex quadratic model yielded a significantly better fit to the data. I then added the time-varying covariate (1 = school change, 0 = no school change) to the quadratic growth model (Model 3) to determine if there was a significant relationship between changing schools and reading achievement, controlling for growth, as well as if the growth remained statistically significant after controlling for the effect of changing schools. Finally, I entered the level-two covariate, gender (1 = male, 0 = female) as a predictor of the growth parameters and of the impact of the time-varying covariate (changing schools) on reading achievement (Model 4).

Results for the four models are presented in Table 4.1. Equation 4.9 represents the most complex model, Model 4; those parameters not included in Models 1—3 would be set to zero in this general model. Time was measured by *term*, and centered at fall of first grade. Note that Equation 4.9 contains a separate level-two equation for each time-varying effect at level one.

$$Reading\ Ach_{ti} = \pi_{0i} + \pi_{1i}(term - term_{F1st})_{ti} + \tag{4.9}$$

$$\pi_{2i}\left(term - term_{F1st}\right)_{ti}^{2} + \pi_{3i}(school\ change)_{ti} + e_{ti}$$

$$\pi_{0i} = \beta_{00} + \beta_{01}(gender)_i + r_{0i}$$

$$\pi_{1i} = \beta_{10} + \beta_{11}(gender)_i + r_{1i}$$

$$\pi_{2i} = \beta_{20} + \beta_{21}(gender)_i + r_{2i}$$

$$\pi_{3i} = \beta_{30} + \beta_{31}(gender)_i + r_{3i}$$

There was significant variation in the linear growth trajectories, as indicated by τ_{11} in Model 1 (See Table 4.1) The mean linear growth rate in reading achievement from kindergarten through third grade, as estimated by β_{10}, was positive and statistically significant. This growth rate implies that a child whose reading growth is one standard deviation above average can be expected to improve at a rate of $11.77 + \sqrt{5.09} = 11.77 + 2.26 = 14.03$ points per term (unconditional linear growth rate + 1 SD in growth rate).

In Model 2, I added the quadratic term, π_{2i}, as noted in Equation 4.9. The quadratic growth model provided a significantly better fit than the lin-

TABLE 4.1 Multilevel Growth Curve Modeling of Reading Achievement

Fixed Effects	Model 1	Model 2	Model 3	Model 4
Avgerage Achievement				
Intercept, β_{00}	49.68***	51.59***	51.63***	53.17***
Gender, β_{01}				-3.01***
Linear Effect				
Intercept, β_{10}	11.77***	13.05***	13.09***	13.45***
Gender, β_{11}				-0.71***
Quadratic Effect				
Intercept, β_{20}		-0.40***	-0.39***	-0.44***
Gender, β_{21}				0.10***
School Change				
Intercept, β_{30}			-3.15***	-3.68***
Gender, β_{31}				1.05†

Random Effects	Variance Components and Deviance Statistics			
Level one error	100.61	64.60	63.66	63.66
Intercept, τ_{00}	212.61***	321.20***	321.48***	319.19***
Linear growth, τ_{11}	5.09***	13.01***	13.15***	13.02***
Quadratic growth, τ_{22}		0.69***	0.68***	0.67***
School change, τ_{33}			30.45*	29.77*
Deviance	539,631.1	529,291.1	528,927.1	528,788.3
Number of parameters	6	10	15	19

***$p < .001$, **$p < .01$, *$p < .05$, †$p < .07$

ear model according to the likelihood ratio test comparing the two models, $\chi^2(4) = 10,340$, $p < .001$; therefore, I retained the quadratic parameter in subsequent growth models. There was significant random variation in the quadratic parameter, as indicated by τ_{22} (See Table 4.1). The linear parameter in Model 2, β_{10}, is positive, indicating a positive mean instantaneous growth rate at fall of first grade. However, the quadratic parameter, β_{20}, is negative, indicating that this growth rate is not constant but instead tends to diminish over time. Specifically, predictions for reading achievement tend to change by a factor of $(-.40)*(term - term_{F1st})^2$, evidence of a decelerating growth pattern.

In Model 3, I added the time-varying covariate, school change, as a predictor of reading achievement. The coefficient, β_{30}, was statistically significant and negative, indicating that, given the instantaneous linear growth and deceleration effects, a child who changed schools would be expected to score approximately 3 points lower in reading achievement after the switch. This effect significantly varied across students, as indicated by τ_{33}.

Finally, in Model 4 I added the time-invariant covariate, gender, to determine if gender was related to average reading achievement at the fall of first grade (for a child who did not change schools during terms); to the instantaneous rate of growth in reading achievement at the fall of first grade; to the deceleration effect; or to the effect of school change on reading achievement (i.e., β_{01}, β_{11}, β_{21}, and β_{31}, respectively; see Equation 4.9). The results indicate that, relative to females, males (*gender* = 1) who did not change schools (*schoolchange* = 0) had significantly lower reading scores at the beginning of first grade ($p < .001$), significantly lower instantaneous rates of change at the fall of first grade ($p < .001$), and significantly less deceleration in growth from kindergarten through third grade ($p < .001$). Finally, these results also showed that the negative effect of changing schools did not vary significantly between boys and girls, although there is the suggestion that females may experience the negative effect of changing schools slightly more strongly than males ($p < .07$).

In summary, the results demonstrate that the instantaneous rate of change in reading achievement is positive at the fall of first grade (i.e., indicating an increasing trend at this time-point), but across the span of kindergarten to third grade there is a deceleration in reading growth over time. Those children who changed schools had lower reading achievement scores on average, although the growth in reading was still statistically significant after accounting for school change. Finally, there were different growth trajectories for females and males and a tendency for the effect of school change to be moderated by gender, although this effect failed to reach statistical significance.

In this example, multilevel modeling allowed the estimation of achievement growth across a time period in which data were not collected at equal intervals and where data were incomplete for some individuals in the sample. Furthermore, the multilevel model allowed for variation in growth trajectories when estimating average growth, producing a growth model that better reflected the individual differences in growth patterns.

Multiphase Multilevel Growth Models

When the growth follows a continuous pattern without abrupt transitions, analysts tend to prefer the previously described multilevel linear and quadratic growth models or latent growth curve models (described in a later section). In some situations, however, growth may occur in phases and people may exhibit fairly distinct growth patterns between phases. The figures below (4.4a through 4.4c) contain examples of these patterns of

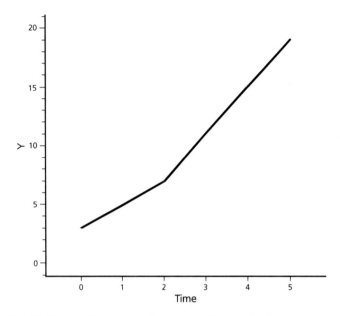

Figure 4.4a Multiphase linear growth patterns: Change in slope.

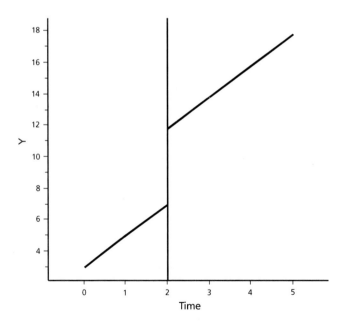

Figure 4.4b Multiphase linear growth patterns: Change in elevation.

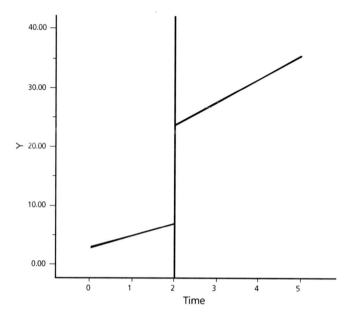

Figure 4.4c Multiphase linear growth patterns: Change in slope and elevation.

abrupt change. Either internal factors (e.g., transitioning to a new physical or developmental phase) or external factors (e.g., relocating, moving to next grade level) may cause the change in growth trajectories. Regardless of the cause, an abrupt change in the growth trajectory at the time that the transition occurs characterizes a multiphase model. This type of growth pattern can be explored using a method that explicitly models differential growth across phases.

Piecewise Linear Models

Piecewise linear growth models can capture linear growth that occurs in phases such that the slopes of the linear growth pattern distinctly change when transitioning from one phase to another. In this type of growth model, the change in linear slope occurs at the same measurement point for everyone in the model. As illustrated in Figure 4.4a, the linear growth rate changes dramatically at *time* = 2; therefore, the analyst can conceive the growth rate as having two separate phases. In this case, the first phase occurs from times 0 to 2, and the second phase occurs from times 2 to 5. In the two-piece linear model, the analyst uses two separate variables to describe growth across the two distinct phases. This is in contrast to the single linear phase of growth implied by Equation 4.1. As a substantive example, consider achievement growth, which may change abruptly when students move from high school to college. A piecewise model to capture this change would include two rates of growth: the first reflecting a rate of achievement growth in high school, and the second reflecting a rate of achievement growth in college. Singer and Willett (2003) suggest another appropriate use of this method, modeling distinct phases in an experimental study (e.g., baseline, experimental, and follow-up phases). The piecewise approach works best, however, when there are a limited number of phases, and when data are available at multiple time points within each phase.

Fitting a piecewise growth model requires developing a set of codes representing the hypothesized pattern of change for each phase of linear growth. Raudenbush and Bryk (2002) suggest two methods of coding piecewise growth. The first uses a two-rate method, in which the analyst codes each linear phase separately. The second method uses an increment/decrement approach, in which the analyst codes a linear rate of growth for the entire duration, and then creates a second set of codes to account for any increment or decrement from that linear growth during one of the phases.

To illustrate the first method of coding, consider the Hadley and Holt (2006) data described earlier in the example for quadratic growth. Their study measured the onset of tense marking for children from 24 to 36 months old, collected at 3-month intervals. The data seem to support a rapid increase in tense marking occurring at about 30 months of age. Assume that age is centered at initial status, i.e., 24 months. If phase-1 growth occurs between 24 and 30 months, and phase-2 growth occurs between 30 and 36 months, then a reasonable coding scheme for the variable marking growth over time during phase 1 is $a_{1i} = 0, 1, 2, 2, 2$, and for growth over time during phase 2 is $a_{2i} = 0, 0, 0, 1, 2$, for time $t = 24, 27, 30, 33$, and 36 months, respectively. The resulting model is shown in Equation 4.10. Alternatively, if the data are centered at the midpoint, i.e., 30 months, the corresponding codes for these two phases of growth are $-2, -1, 0, 0, 0$ for phase 1 and $0, 0, 0, 1, 2$ for phase 2. With either coding scheme, the coefficient for phase-1 growth represents the linear growth from 24 to 30 months, and the coefficient for phase-2 growth represents the linear growth from 30 to 36 months.

$$y_{ti} = \pi_{0i} + \pi_{1i}a_{1ti} + \pi_{2i}a_{2ti} + e_{ti} \qquad (4.10)$$

When using the increment/decrement method for these time scores, centered at initial status, the corresponding codes are 0, 1, 2, 3, 4 for the overall linear growth and 0, 0, 0, 1, 2 for the increment/decrement from the linear growth. Here, the coefficient for phase 1 of the increment/decrement coding denotes the linear growth from 24 to 36 months, and the coefficient for phase 2 denotes the increment or decrement to that linear growth which occurs in the period from 30 months to 36 months.

Application—Piecewise Linear Growth

As an illustration, I used a selected group of 511 students from the LSAY data set. The students were in seventh grade at the onset of data collection in 1987, and researchers collected data yearly through 11th grade; hence, five waves of data were available for analysis. The question of interest was, "How did the math achievement growth rates differ between early secondary school, as defined by grades 7 through 9 (phase 1), from that in later secondary school, as defined by grades 9 through 11 (phase 2)?" A further goal of the study was to investigate whether the predictors of math achievement growth were different across the two phases. The predictors studied were math track placement and family SES.

For these analyses, I used the two-rate method, and I centered the data at initial status, seventh grade. In addition to the intercept, I estimated two growth parameters to model the change in math achievement during phase 1 and phase 2, respectively. I modeled the growth in the two phases with the time scores, 0, 1, 2, 2, 2 for phase 1, and 0, 0, 0, 1, 2 for phase 2. As with earlier examples, I fit a series of models to the data. Equation 4.11 is the most complex model used for these analyses, where I coded *Linear 1* as the variable for linear growth in phase 1, and *Linear 2* as the variable for linear growth in phase 2. These are added as time-varying covariates in level one. In this model, β_{10} and β_{20} denote the mean phase-1 and phase-2 linear growth estimates, respectively, controlling for math track placement and SES of the family. Results (using restricted maximum likelihood estimation) are presented in Table 4.2.

$$Math\ Ach_{ti} = \pi_{0i} + \pi_{1i}\left(Linear\ 1_{ti}\right) + \pi_{2i}\left(Linear\ 2_{ti}\right) + e_{ti} \qquad (4.11)$$

$$\pi_{0i} = \beta_{00} + \beta_{01}\left(Math\ Track_i\right) + \beta_{02}\left(SES_i\right) + r_{0i}$$

$$\pi_{1i} = \beta_{10} + \beta_{11}\left(Math\ Track_i\right) + \beta_{12}\left(SES_i\right)$$

$$\pi_{2i} = \beta_{20} + \beta_{21}\left(Math\ Track_i\right) + \beta_{22}\left(SES_i\right) + r_{2i}$$

Piecewise Linear Model of Math Achievement

Model 1 is the unconditional model with all slopes random. However, the slope for the linear growth in phase 1 did not vary significantly across individuals, $\iota_{11} = 1.98$, $\chi^2(452) = 453$, $p > .05$ therefore, I fixed that slope in Models 2 and 3 (see Table 4.2). Model 2 represents the unconditional model with fixed slope for phase 1. Model 3 is the fully conditional model that tests the relationships of math track placement with initial status and phase-1 and phase-2 growth, as denoted by β_{01}, β_{11}, and β_{21}, respectively, controlling for SES; and similarly for β_{02}, β_{12}, and β_{22}, which represent the relationships of SES to initial status and phase-1 and phase-2 growth, respectively, controlling for math track placement.

TABLE 4.2 Piecewise Linear Model of Math Achievement

Fixed Effects	Model 1	Model 2	Model 3
Avg. Achievement			
Intercept, B_{00}	51.15^{***}	51.13^{***}	51.15^{***}
Math Track , B_{01}			3.22^{***}
SES, B_{02}			1.73^{**}
Phase 1 slope			
Intercept, B_{10}	2.79^{***}	2.84^{***}	2.77^{***}
Math Track, B_{11}			0.31^{*}
SES, B_{12}			0.24
Phase 2 slope			
Intercept, B_{20}	0.58^{*}	$0.54^{\dagger}$	0.44
Math Track, B_{21}			0.81
SES, B_{22}			0.16

Random Effects	Variance Components and Deviance Statistics		
Level one error	40.68	42.24	41.90
Intercept, τ_{00}	65.62^{***}	88.77^{***}	41.87^{***}
Linear phase 1, τ_{11}	1.98	—	—
Linear phase 2, τ_{22}	14.59^{***}	16.52^{***}	13.81^{***}
Deviance	16,245.2	16,286.3	15,936.0
Number of parameters	7	4	4

Note: The linear phase 1 component was fixed in both Models 2 and 3.
Estimation was done through restricted maximum likelihood.
$^{***}p < .001$, $^{**}p < .01$, $^{*}p < .05$, $^{\dagger}p < .07$

In Model 2, results indicated that there was a slight change in growth pattern between phases 1 and 2. The linear growth rate was statistically significantly different from zero in phase 1 ($p < .001$), but did not reach statistical significance in phase 2 ($p < .07$, see Table 4.2). This effect diminished in the conditional model, Model 3, in which growth in phase 1 was statistically significant ($p < .001$) but phase-2 growth was not. For those students in a low math track and with SES at a measured value of zero, moving up one grade in phase 1 corresponded to an increase of 2.77 points in math achievement, whereas in phase 2 there was only a 0.44-point increase in math achievement for each step in grade. The phase-1 growth rate was more than six times as steep as the phase-2 growth rate, indicating a leveling off of math achievement growth in later high school. Both math track placement and SES were significant predictors of math achievement in seventh grade (i.e., for the intercept); math track was a significant predictor of linear growth in phase 1. These results indicate the continuing importance of math track placement and the diminishing role of SES for later math growth. Additionally, relative to Model 2, the covariates of math track placement and family SES accounted for 53% of the variance in mean math achievement [i.e., $(88.77 - 41.87)/88.77 = .53$] and 16% of the variance in phase-2 math achievement growth [i.e., $(16.52 - 13.81)/16.52 = .16$].

Shift Models

The piecewise model adequately captures the pattern of growth if there is a distinct change in slope, but not if there is an abrupt change in the average outcome after an event occurs. In some situations, there may be a shift in average level of the outcome in the second phase (see Figure 4.4b) while the overall rate of change remains unchanged, or there may be both a shift in elevation as well as a change in slope (see Figure 4.4c). To model the shift in elevation, it is necessary to know when the change takes place between the growth phases, and to measure this change. Analysts typically do this with a time-varying binary indicator in which 0 specifies that no shift has occurred and 1 signifies that the shift has occurred. The resulting model, with the time-varying predictor of shift-change at level-one of the model, is referred to as the intercept-shift model. One advantage of using multilevel techniques to model this shift in the intercept is that the shift does not have to occur at the same time for all individuals.

As an example of a shift in elevation that might occur for all individuals at the same time, consider children undergoing a summer tutoring program for reading achievement. All students would be receiving the intervention during the summer, and consequently, one might expect average reading achievement, and possibly reading achievement growth rate, to increase as a result of the intervention at the beginning of the next grade. In contrast, students with reading difficulty might enroll in a private after-school tutoring program to improve their reading comprehension. In this second case, students would enroll at different times; hence, one might expect exposure to tutoring, the intervention, to cause a shift in average reading achievement at different times for different individuals. As long as the data include the time of enrollment into the tutoring program, the analyst can use a random coefficients shift model to assess the change in reading achievement as a consequence of the tutoring intervention. And, as alluded to earlier, the change across phases could elicit not only a change in elevation but also a change in slope (see Figure 4.4c). In this case, the linear growth rate changes across phases, and there is a concomitant abrupt change in elevation. Analysts can model the simultaneous change in elevation and change in slope by combining a piecewise slope model with an intercept shift model.

As another example of a shift model where the level-one covariate is not time itself but instead is another time-varying variable, consider the prediction of driving ability from hours spent in supervised driving, which can operate as a time-varying covariate. The relationship between hours spent in supervised driving and driving ability for new drivers might exhibit a moderate positive relationship until the new drivers spend a critical amount of time in supervised driving. After they reach this critical level, one might expect the relationship between hours spent in supervised driving and driving ability to increase (i.e., slope change), as students have learned basic driving skills and driving becomes more intuitive for them. An increase in average driving ability (i.e., elevation change) also is likely to occur at this point; therefore, we would see a pattern very similar to Figure 4.4c, in which the x-axis would denote hours spent in supervised driving, the y-axis would denote driving ability, and the dashed line would represent the number of hours that it takes for new drivers to acquire the basic driving skills. For further discussion of these types of discontinuity models, see Singer and Willett (2003).

Advantages and Disadvantages: Multilevel Modeling

Researchers easily can understand the multilevel growth modeling approach as an extension of linear regression analysis. In this respect, it is a method that is accessible to researchers with a good foundation in regression analysis. The modeling process is less complex than alternatives, such as growth mixture modeling. Multilevel growth modeling is well suited to studying cross-level interactions, and researchers can adapt their models to include higher levels, as in the Ma (2005) study. Furthermore, like other random coefficients methods, multilevel growth modeling has a distinct advantage over typical repeated measures analyses; it does not require time-structured or balanced data.

Multilevel growth modeling works best when the outcome is an observed variable that is directly assessed. However, given that multilevel growth modeling is limited to analyzing change in one outcome measure at a time, a latent growth modeling approach would be more appropriate if the outcome is a construct with multiple indicators. Further limitations of the multilevel modeling approach are that some statistical packages for multilevel modeling offer limited options for covariance structures (see software options for more detail), there are limited measures of model fit, and multilevel modeling requires complete data (or the use of imputation techniques) at higher-levels of the analysis.

Software Options for Multilevel Modeling

Several software packages for multilevel analyses are continually being updated. Current versions of some of the popular programs for multilevel analysis are SAS PROC MIXED and PROC GLIMMIX (SAS version 9.1), MLwiN (version 2.01), and HLM (version 6.04). Hierarchical linear modeling has gained popularity since 1992, when Bryk and Raudenbush released the first version of their HLM software. In the current HLM software (Raudenbush, Bryk, & Congdon, 2007), the user can conduct two- or three-level growth models using HLM (the standard hierarchical linear modeling analysis), or they can opt for HMLM (hierarchical multivariate linear models) analysis, which assumes complete data but has more options for covariance structure modeling. Options also are available for nonlinear models when modeling categorical outcomes.

In SAS and SPSS, the data from both levels need to be in one file. Although HLM does not require a separate file for level-two data, it is beneficial when the level-one file is large. SPSS, SAS, and HLM require the level-one file to be in a person-period format (see Singer and Willett, 2003). If the analyst has a separate level-two data file for HLM, the level-two file should have one row per person that contains all the time-invariant covariates at the person level. Both files should contain a person-level ID, which the program uses to align the information between the two data files, and the data must be sorted by the ID. If the analyst is conducting a three-level analysis, then level one is a person-period data set, level two is the individual-level data, and level three contains organizational-level data, which is structured with one row per organization. With three-level models, the data need two IDs, a person-level ID in levels one and two and an organization-level ID in all levels, so the program can align the three data sets. The analyst should conduct a nested sort of the level-two and level-three IDs.

The options available for modeling alternate covariance structures vary depending on the software package. SPSS Mixed Procedure in SPSS version 14 allows up to 17 forms for covariance structure (Peugh & Enders, 2005), and SAS PROC MIXED in SAS version 9.1.3 allows more than 20 covariance structures (SAS Institute, 2005). See Singer and Willett (2003) for a comparison of some of the more commonly used covariance structures in longitudinal research. Within the HLM6 program, users can model heterogeneous variances either by using the HMLM algorithm, which allows the modeling of various covariance structures but requires time-structured data, or by modeling the heterogeneity of variance as a function of another variable in the study (Raudenbush et al., 2007).

LATENT GROWTH CURVE MODELS

Another option for analysts is the use of latent growth curve (LGC) models to estimate linear or curvilinear growth over time. Meredith and Tisak (1984, 1990) formalized this methodology, and McArdle and colleagues (see McArdle, 1986; McArdle & Epstein, 1987), Muthén (see Muthén 1991, 1993), and Muthén and Curran (1997), among others, expanded upon it. Whereas multilevel modeling builds on the regression tradition, LGC is an extension and specification of structural equation modeling (SEM). Although one also can view LGC modeling as random coefficients modeling, there are similarities and differences with MLM that result in different strengths and limitations when comparing the two approaches. However, as Bauer (2003) has described, many of the differences between MLM and SEM-based approaches are based on tradition rather than the inherent limitations of either method. Furthermore, it is clear that with some reparameterization, analysts can generate equivalent estimates of most MLM models from a SEM framework. However, the process can be much more cumbersome with latent growth curves, particularly with unbalanced and time-unstructured data (Bauer, 2003; Curran, 2003).

The multilevel growth model can be reformulated as a latent variable model such that the growth parameters in the multilevel linear model, π_{0i} and π_{1i}, are now regarded as latent variable growth factors in the latent growth curve model. Equation 4.12 gives the equations for a latent growth curve model with one time-invariant covariate, X_i:

$$Y_{ti} = \lambda_{0t}(intercept)_i + \lambda_{1t}(slope)_i + e_{ti} \qquad (4.12)$$

$$intercept_i = \beta_{00} + \beta_{01}X_i + u_{0i}$$

$$slope_i = \beta_{10} + \beta_{11}X_i + u_{1i}$$

The latent growth curve framework treats the growth parameters from the multilevel linear model, π_{0i} and π_{1i}, (see Equations 4.1 and 4.6) as latent variable growth factors, $intercept_i$ and $slope_i$, respectively, which vary across individual i. The λ_{0t} and λ_{1t} vectors contain the factor loadings for the intercept and slope, respectively, across t times. The analyst sets the intercept factor loadings to 1, and typically fixes the slope factor loadings (i.e., time scores) to represent a linear slope: $0, 1, 2, \ldots, t-1$. These slope loading values represent the desired coding for time. For example, when assessing growth from 24 to 36 months in 3-month intervals, outcomes are measured across five time points: 24, 27, 30, 33, and 36 months. By fixing the loadings for the slope at 0, 1, 2, 3, 4, the analyst makes the assumption that for every 3-month interval, there is an equal change in Y. Hence, this models a linear growth trajectory.

Analysts can adapt this approach to accommodate a polynomial model with a quadratic growth factor by including the quadratic growth factor and its factor loadings on time in the equation for Y_{ti}. Like the process of creating the quadratic terms for time in the polynomial model for growth, we must add an additional term (λ_{2t}) by squaring the corresponding codes for λ_{1t}. Consequently, an additional equation can be used to model variance in the quadratic growth factor. Overall, the LGC approach allows for flexible modeling of growth curves. In addition, analysts may choose to use a latent-basis method for estimation growth; by estimating the factor loadings empirically, analysts can model a greater variety of growth trajectories (Bollen & Curran, 2006; Duncan, Duncan, & Stryker, 2006).

Data Requirements and Assumptions

Data Requirements

Estimation of LGC with maximum likelihood (ML) methods provides proper inferences when data are MAR. Typical LGC models, as formulated in Equation 4.12, do not allow for individually-varying times of observation; that is, λ_{0t} and λ_{1t} vary across time but not individuals. However, recent developments using individual data vector-based SEM approaches allow for proper estimation of growth parameters with time-unstructured data, such that the estimates produced are identical to those produced with MLM (Mehta & West, 2000; Neale, Boker, Xie, & Maes, 2002).

Assumptions

Under ML estimation procedures, the likelihood function typically is structured assuming a multivariate normal distribution (Neale et al., 2002). However, several researchers have developed procedures for working with nonnormal data in SEM analyses (Bollen & Curran, 2006; Satorra & Bentler, 1994). LGC analyses require additional assumptions regarding the form of and interrelationships among the errors. For a detailed explanation of these LGC assumptions, see Bollen & Curran (2006, p. 20).

Form of the Data

Analysts applying LGC models typically lay out data in a multivariate, or wide format, in which each case is a separate row in the data set, with separate columns for each measurement at time t (see Figure 4.1). In this layout, time is not an explicit variable in the data set; observations across time are captured as distinct variables displayed in separate columns of the data set.

Treatment of Time

Centering

As described above, analysts typically set the values for $\lambda_{1t} = 0, 1, 2, \ldots t-1$ in a latent growth curve model, and thus interpret the intercept factor as the mean response value at the first measurement occasion, $\lambda_{1t} = 0$, i.e., *time* 1. However, the analyst can alter these values to center the data at a different time point. For instance, to center at *time* 2, the analyst would set the time scores to $\lambda_{1t} = -1, 0, 1, \ldots t - 2$, and thus would interpret the intercept factor at *time* 2.

Unstructured Data

In some instances, the data are not time-structured, and individuals have different data collection schedules. Time-unstructured data may also arise in a sequential cohort design, where entire cohorts of individuals are each followed over an overlapping limited number of data collection schedules; thus, not all cohorts would have data at every time point. As a result, the analyst must invoke methods of estimating the LGC with missing data (see Bollen & Curran, 2006, pp. 79–81). Alternately, the analyst can use vector-based SEM methods to allow the measure of time to vary across individuals (Mehta & West, 2000; Neale et al., 2002)

Latent Basis Model

To allow flexibility in the estimation of the shape of the growth curve, a latent basis model estimates the factor loadings on time from the data (Meredith & Tisak, 1990). Using this approach does not restrict the growth curve to a linear, quadratic, or other specified form. In the case in which the five time points from 24 to 36 months are being assessed, the analyst can either fix specific slope factor loadings, as in the linear model previously shown, or estimate them from the data. For instance, if an intercept and a growth factor are specified, the analyst would need to fix two of the time factor loadings for identification purposes. One strategy is to fix the first factor loading at 0, which becomes the centering point, and the next factor loading at 1. The analyst can estimate the other time scores from the data and interpret them relative to the growth from $t = 0$ to $t = 1$. For example, if the analyst wanted to estimate the growth pattern across five time points, 24 months through 36 months at 3-month intervals centered at initial status, s/he could specify 0, 1, λ_3, λ_4, λ_5 as the factor loadings, or basis coefficients, for the slope factor. This would allow the last three factor loadings to be estimated from the data. The interpretation of the mean slope factor, however, would be the mean change in the outcome between 24 and 27 months. Alternately, the analyst could specify the fixed factor loadings at the first and last time points, 0, λ_2, λ_3, λ_4, 1. With this model, the interpretation of the mean slope would be the average change in the outcome from 24 to 36 months. Another approach might be to center at the midpoint, or 30 months, and specify the following time scores: λ_1, λ_2,

0, λ_4, 1. The resulting mean slope would represent the mean change in outcome from 30 to 36 months. The likelihood function remains the same across the different forms of the latent basis model; however, the values of estimated factor loadings will depend on the choice of the fixed factor loadings. This approach works as long as two points (the centering point and an additional time point) are fixed when two growth factors (i.e., intercept and slope factor) are being specified and there are a sufficient number of observations at each time point. In general, this approach allows the analyst tremendous flexibility in estimating the shape of the growth trajectory that best fits the data.

Piecewise Linear Growth

In the LGC framework, analysts also can construct a piecewise model, like the one described earlier in the section on multiphase multilevel growth models, by modeling each phase as a separate growth factor or slope. The coding system would be the same as for the multilevel model. The analyst specifies the factor loadings for each growth factor to reflect linear growth during each phase. For instance, if one expects an abrupt two-phase change in growth between $t = 3$ and $t = 4$, then the fixed factor loadings for the first growth factor would be 0, 1, 2, 2, 2; and the second phase growth factor loadings would be 0, 0, 0, 1, 2. This would result in two growth factors, one for phase-1 growth from $t = 1$ to 3 and one for phase-2 growth from $t = 3$ to 5.

Variance-Covariance Structures

In LGC, the specified model determines the model-implied covariance matrix, $\Sigma(\theta)$, including the estimated and fixed factor loadings for λ_t. The discrepancy between the model-implied and the sample covariance matrix estimated from the data, **S**, can be used to gauge the fit of the model. Based on the assumptions of LGC, analysts put restrictions on the variance/covariance matrix, but LGC analysis can be extended to situations in which the repeated measures are correlated in some manner, such as in an autoregressive pattern. Curran and Bollen (2001) combined the autoregressive and LGC approaches in their autoregressive latent trajectory (ALT) model. Modeling alternate covariance structures generally is not problematic in SEM and related data analysis approaches, such as LGC, and therefore allows much flexibility when error correlations are time-dependent, as often is the case with repeated measures data.

Modeling Change with Covariates

Analogous to a conditional multilevel growth model, the latent growth curve model can contain both time-varying and time-invariant covariates. In the example in Equation 4.12, the time-invariant covariate, X_i, is used to explain variability in the intercepts and slopes across individuals. The expression in Equation 4.12 for Y_{ti} is analogous to a SEM measurement model with the growth factors measured by multiple indicators over time (eg., Y_t), whereas the next two lines in Equation 4.12 are equivalent to the structural component of a SEM model, relating the growth curve factors to other variables or factors in the model. Alternatively, a graphical expression of this model is provided in the path diagram shown in Figure 4.5, in which Y_t denotes the outcome at multiple time points, Z_t denotes the time-varying covariate, and X denotes the time-invariant covariate. The path diagram fixes both the intercept (Int.) and slope (Slp.) growth factors for each of the time points. If the analyst constrains the error variances to be equal across time and fixes the error covariances at 0, the resulting LGC is identical to the multilevel growth model, and will produce the same results as a comparable multilevel analysis (Hox, 2002).

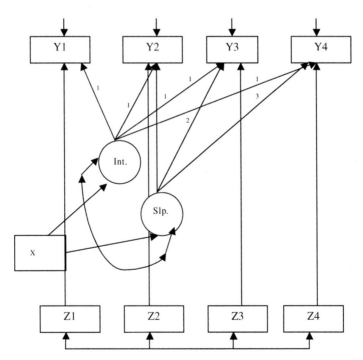

Figure 4.5   Path diagram of latent growth curve model with a time-invariant and time-varying predictor.

Advantages and Disadvantages: Latent Growth Curves

As Bollen and Curran (2006) point out, latent growth curves and multilevel models each have their strengths. It is easier to model time-unstructured data with MLM. Although a vector-based approach is available in LGC, the modeling of time-unstructured data is not as seamless in LGC as in MLM. Contrary to expectations regarding large sample size requirements for SEM, latent growth curve modeling does not require large samples; sample size requirements are essentially the same as MLM. This follows from the notion that growth estimated with identically-specified latent growth curves and multilevel models yield essentially identical parameter estimates when using full information maximum likelihood (FIML).

The LGC approach does offer substantial advantages to growth modelers. First, latent growth curves can be used to model growth within the larger SEM framework; thus, models can include multiple-indicator latent factors, mediating variables between exogenous variables and growth factors or among the growth factors, time-invariant moderator variables, and prediction of future outcomes (Curran & Hussong, 2002). This flexibility allows for much more complex modeling possibilities. For instance, one could posit a time-invariant predictor of growth that is a latent factor assessed with multiple indicators. Alternately, the growth factors may predict later growth processes and distal outcomes, and one can test these complex relationships within one model. In addition, the LGC approach does not assume normality and homoscedasticity across all waves of data and generally relies on the robustness of the ML estimator to nonnormality (Bollen & Curran, 2006). Currently, the LGC approach is more capable than MLM of modeling alternate covariance structures. In sum, it currently is easier to incorporate a growth model within a larger modeling framework that can accomodate complex error structures with a LGC approach rather than with a MLM approach. Yet, as Bollen and Curran (2006), Bauer (2003), and others have noted, the distinctness of the two traditions is likely to fade over time as methodologists develop newer methods to merge the strengths of the two approaches.

Examples from the Literature

Some of the many examples of using LGC models to address questions of change include the following: George's (2000) study of the change in science attitudes among middle to high schoolers; Colder, Chassin, Stice, and Curran's (1997) study of adolescents' heavy drinking behavior; and Li, Duncan, and Acock's (2000) study of the prevention of problem behaviors among middle-school students. These studies illustrate various substantive applications of LGC and also emphasize different aspects of the growth modeling methodology (i.e., use of time-varying and time-invariant covariates, mediational growth models, and interactions among growth factors). In particular, they demonstrate the flexibility of the LGC approach as part of the larger SEM framework.

George (2000) used LGC to formulate models of growth that included both time-invariant predictors of science attitude (i.e., background variables) and time-varying variables (i.e., peer science push, parent academic push, teacher science push, achievement motivation, science self-concept, science anxiety, and science activity) as predictors of initial status and rate of change in science attitudes. This analysis typifies the use of both time-invariant and time-varying covariates in studying latent growth curves.

Colder et al. (1997) used LGC analysis to test a model of alcohol expectancies as mediators of the relationship between parents' alcohol use and adolescent heavy alcohol usage. In the LGC framework, they represented adolescent alcohol usage by latent growth factors of initial status and linear growth in heavy drinking behavior. This application provides an example of how analysts use LGC modeling to test the mediational effects on both of the growth factors.

Finally, Li et al. (2000) used LGC analysis to study the prevention of problem behavior among middle school students. Participants provided self-report data about parenting practices, family interactions, youth problem behavior, and peer behavior at four time points. The researchers assumed missing data to be MAR and imputed the values. They predicted adolescent antisocial behaviors from parental rule-setting, parental monitoring, and their interaction. Then, using LGC, they tested two interaction models. In the first model, they predicted the change in behavior from the two static predictors and their interaction. In the second model, they used the change in rule setting and the change in parental monitoring, as well as their interaction, to predict changes in antisocial behavior. Their analysis demonstrates the use of LGC to study interaction effects of both time-invariant and time-varying covariates on a growth process.

Application—Latent Growth Curve Models

I constructed latent growth curve models of the ECLS-K reading achievement data for a subsample of children (n = 4,371) assessed at fall of kindergarten (term = 1), spring of kindergarten (term = 2), fall of first grade (term = 3), and spring of first grade (term = 4). Figure 4.6 presents individual growth patterns for a sample of cases across the four time points.

I constructed and compared two latent growth curve models. First, I constructed the linear model with λ_t = 0, 1, 2, 3 for the four time points.

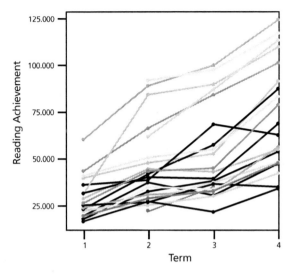

Figure 4.6 Individual growth curves of reading achievement from kindergarten through first grade.

TABLE 4.3   Latent Growth Curves Modeling of Reading Achievement Data

	Linear	Latent basis
χ^2	3,685***	742***
CFI	.79	.96
TLI	.75	.92
AIC	135,183	132,245
RMSEA	.41	.24
λ_1	0	0
λ_2	1	1
λ_3	2	1.56***
λ_4	3	3.40***
Mean intercept	25.6	25.5
Mean slope	11.2	12.1

***$p < .001$

The second model was a latent basis model with estimated factor loadings for the last two time points: $\lambda_t = 0$, 1, λ_3, λ_4. As seen in Table 4.3, which presents the results of these analyses, the mean slope factor for the linear model equals 11.2, which represents the mean change in reading achievement across terms, whereas the mean slope factor for the latent basis model equals 12.1, which represents the mean change in reading achievement from fall of kindergarten to spring of kindergarten. As expected, the fit of the latent basis model is a significant improvement over the fit of the linear model because the latent basis model has fewer constraints placed on it. To test whether the change in λ_t between the fixed linear model and the estimated scores in the latent basis model are significantly different, I conducted a t-test of the difference in λ_3 between the two models. The results indicate that the latent basis model produced a significantly different λ_3 from the linear model, $t = (1.56 - 2)/.013 = -33.8$, $p < .001$, implying that the two models provide different estimates of λ_3. The estimated factor loadings for λ_t indicate that, compared to the linear model, there was deceleration in growth from spring of kindergarten to fall of first grade (i.e., 1.56 vs. 2), as well as a rapid acceleration between fall and spring of first grade (i.e., 3.4 vs. 3).

Software Options for Latent Growth Curve Models

Various software options are available for modeling latent growth curves. They vary from stand-alone structural equation modeling programs to procedures integrated into comprehensive statistics software packages. Some of the more well known structural equation modeling programs integrated into major statistical packages include: Amos (Analysis of Moment Structures; SPSS Inc., 2007), which is now fully integrated into SPSS, and the CALIS (Covariance Analysis and Linear Structural Equations; SAS Institute Inc., 2004) procedure in SAS/STAT. These two programs have the advantage of seamless compatibility with a major statistical package. Although most of the programs now include a graphical interface, Amos was among the first programs to do so and has a fairly well-developed graphical user interface. Other stand-alone packages include: EQS 6.1 (Equations; Bentler, 2003); LISREL 8.8 (Linear Structural Relations; Jöreskog, Sörbom, Du Toit, S., & Du Toit, M., 2001) distributed by Scientific Software, International; M*plus* 4.21 (Muthén & Muthén, 2006); and Mx Graph 1.66b (Matrix; Neale, Boker, Xie, & Maes, 2002). EQS has the capability to conduct exploratory statistical analyses and includes a thorough set of estimation procedures to handle nonnormal data. LISREL was one of the first entrants into the SEM software market. It originally required matrix input but now has incorporated user-friendly wizards and a graphical interface. The LISREL suite includes a group of related programs for preparing the data for SEM analyses and conducting exploratory analyses. The M*plus* program has been at the forefront of the incorporation of algorithms for categorical outcomes, multilevel data structures, and growth mixture modeling (see next section).

The Mx Graph program is available as a free download over the internet and is widely used in medical and genetics research.

GROWTH MIXTURE MODELING

Growth mixture modeling (GMM) is a second generation of growth modeling, in which categorical and continuous latent variables are combined within one analysis to model unobserved heterogeneity in growth or development. Although the popularity of GMM in education is due primarily to Muthén and colleague's developments in this area, including the M*plus* program (Muthén, 2001a, 2001b, 2004a; Muthén & Muthén, 2006; Muthén & Shedden, 1999), other authors also have made significant contributions to the development of GMM (Nagin, 1999; Verbeke & LeSaffre, 1996). The key conceptual distinction between GMM and LGC is that although growth parameters are allowed to vary, LGC assumes individuals come from one population. As a result, analysts can estimate a mean growth curve using all individuals. In contrast, GMM assumes different subpopulations with qualitatively different growth trajectories in order to account for heterogeneity in development across subpopulations; thus, different latent growth classes capture these population-specific growth trajectories.

Methodologists developed growth mixture modeling from the more general class of finite mixture models. Two distinct purposes exist for finite mixture models: 1) to estimate distinct classes of individuals and, consequently, estimate parameters separately for these different classes; and 2) to approximate complex distributions with a limited number of simpler distributions (Bauer & Curran, 2003). The use of GMM in education and social science research almost always is for the first purpose. However, as Bauer and Curran (2003) demonstrated, the distinct distributions of different latent growth trajectories estimated though GMM simply may be components of a more complex and unitary distribution and not derived from multiple separate normally distributed populations.

For predicting the growth classes, growth mixture modeling incorporates methods from both LGC and categorical data analysis. These growth classes are latent variables formed based on the patterns of growth trajectories represented in the data. GMM assumes that there are c unobserved classes of growth that occur; each class is described by a different set of growth parameters.

Before analysis, it is necessary to specify the number of latent growth classes, as the solution will depend on the number of growth classes. Software packages, such as M*plus* (Muthén & Muthén, 2006), produce a number of indices that are helpful in deciding the number of classes to specify.

The Bayesian Information Criterion (BIC; Schwartz, 1978) can help discern the relative fit among competing models. BIC is defined as:

$$BIC = -2LL + p * \ln(n) \tag{4.13}$$

where $-2LL$ is the model deviance or -2 times the log likelihood, p is the number of free parameters, and n is the sample size. BIC is scaled such that smaller values indicate increasingly better fit. Alternately, analysts can use an entropy measure to assess the quality of the classification of individuals among competing models with different numbers of classes. Entropy is defined as:

$$E_K = 1 - \left(\frac{\sum_i \sum_k \left(-\hat{p}_{ik} * \ln(\hat{p}_{ik}) \right)}{n * \ln(K)} \right) \tag{4.14}$$

where $K =$ the number of latent classes, p is the class probability for person i in class k, and n is the sample size (Muthén, 2005; Ramaswamy, Desarbo, Reibstein, & Robinson, 1993). Entropy values range between 0 and 1, with a larger value indicating a better classification. In terms of model selection, there is simulation evidence which suggests that BIC performs well for over-identified models in finite mixture analyses, as does another fit index, the Consistent Akaike Information Criterion (CAIC; Jedidi, Jagpal, & Desarbo, 1997a). However, these same researchers also found that entropy, goodness of fit indices (GFI), and root mean square residuals (RMR) do not. One strategy for choosing the number of classes is to begin with a limited number (e.g., 2) and increase until the model indices indicate a certain number of classes (Muthén, 2001c). However, Bauer and Curran (2003) caution that concluding a particular number of latent classes is optimal for a GMM solution based on BIC or entropy does not *prove* that the parent population is comprised of a mixture of distributions.

To estimate parameters, GMM uses maximum likelihood estimation procedures via the EM algorithm (Muthén, 2001a). For a given solution, GMM estimates growth class membership. Muthén (2004a) emphasizes the importance of using a fully specified model with covariates when estimating class membership. He suggests that class membership in a conditional model with covariates could be quite different from the estimated class membership from an unconditional model if, as hypothesized, the covariates are related to growth patterns. For technical details of GMM, interested readers are referred to Muthén and Shedden (1999).

Data Requirements and Assumptions

Data Requirements

Data requirements parallel those for LGC, as both are developed within the SEM tradition and use ML estimation methods. Hence, LGC allows missing data as long as they are MAR. If missing data patterns are non-ignorable, then analysts need to use alternate procedures to classify the pattern of missingness (Muthén, Jo, & Brown, 2003). Analysts can use data that are not time-structured as long as they use the time scores as data rather than parameters in the model (Muthén, 2004b).

Assumptions

Unlike multilevel modeling and latent growth curve analysis, growth mixture modeling does not assume overall normality at each time point, however, it does assume that observations within each latent class are normally distributed. When observations are combined across classes, it can result in quite nonnormal outcomes. In fact, as Bauer and Curran (2003) have described, GMM expects nonnormality in the aggregate distribution in order for the solution to be non-trivial. Therefore, an assumption in estimating multiple latent growth trajectory classes using GMM is that the distinct growth classes arise because there is a set of subpopulations of growth classes rather than a unitary population distribution. This assumption is necessary because GMM analyses cannot confirm that separate subpopulations truly exist (Bauer & Curran).

Form of the Data

For GMM, analysts must arrange data in a multivariate, or wide, format, in which each case is a separate row in the data set with separate columns for each measurement at time t (see Figure 4.1). In this layout, time is not an explicit variable in the data set; observations across time are captured as distinct variables displayed in separate columns within the data set.

Treatment of Time

As in LGC, analysts typically use time as a parameter in the model, and specify the time scores or factor loadings for the slope factor to indicate a linear slope. In this way, they do not specify time as a variable but rather as fixed parameters specifying the loadings of the repeated measures variable on the slope factor. Analysts also specify the centering of the time scores.

Variance-Covariance Structures

Analysts test the variance-covariance structure implied by the model against the covariance structure estimated from the sample data. In GMM, however, because there are different latent classes, different mean and covariance structures may exist across classes. The key to accurate estimation in GMM lies in specifying an accurate within-class covariance structure (Muthén, 2004a). In addition, the restrictions placed on the covariance structure within classes can stabilize the estimation process (Blåfield, 1980; Dolan & van der Maas, 1998; Jedidi, Jagpal, & Desarbo, 1997b, as cited in Bauer & Curran, 2004). Hence, it is advantageous to specify carefully the restrictions of the covariance structure within classes.

Modeling Change with Covariates

As with the other approaches reviewed here, analysts can use covariates to predict latent class membership. Effective antecedent covariates should influence the growth trajectory. For accurate prediction of the number of classes, it is important to have a properly specified model. Contrary to typical procedures in multilevel modeling in which the analysts first specifies an unconditional model, in GMM the analyst specifies the conditional model with the antecedent covariates prior to testing for the optimal number of classes.

Distal Outcomes

The longitudinal growth models discussed so far are appropriate when the goal is to explain a pattern of growth. Yet, analysts also can use growth modeling to predict later outcomes that may result because of the growth. For example, Holt, Ennis, and Vaughn (2006) found that middle-school through high-school math achievement growth is an important predictor of choosing a college major in science, engineering, or math for both males and females. Holt et al., used math achievement growth, not just average math achievement, as a predictor of a later categorical outcome, college major. In many situations, changes in growth may occur prior to significant changes in the average outcome because growth must first occur in order to realize changes in status. In this respect, growth, whether measured by growth curve parameters or by growth class, can be an important predictor variable of later outcomes. In GMM, analysts can accommodate these patterns by predicting distal outcomes or sequential growth processes (Muthén, 2004a). That is, the latent class can be used as a predictor of these outcomes or growth processes. In fact, Muthén and colleagues (Muthén, 2001a, 2001b; Muthén, Khoo, Francis & Boscardin, 2003) have described various educational applications of GMM in which latent class membership better predicts later outcomes than traditional methods of growth curve analysis do.

Advantages and Disadvantages: Growth Mixture Modeling

There are several advantages to GMM. First, GMM allows the prediction of fairly complex growth processes within a larger SEM framework. Because GMM does not assume growth trajectories of subgroups to be from the same population, analysts can identify class-specific growth trajectories. Additionally, it is not necessary to identify *a priori* the groups that define the classes; instead these groups emerge from the data. In addition, analysts can model sequential outcomes or growth processes from the latent trajectory class.

Growth mixture modeling has its limitations, however. It involves complex estimation procedures, and convergence problems due to data singularities are not uncommon in estimation. Also, there is a problem with GMM as with other analytic procedures that produce clusters or classes: they are prone to local solutions that provide inferior estimates of parameters (Hipp & Bauer, 2006; Muthén & Shedden, 1999). This tendency is particularly problematic for complex models with random effects within classes. Hipp and Bauer suggested that the default number of start values in common software programs for GMM (i.e., 10) is not sufficient; they suggest that analysts should specify a larger range of start values (i.e., 50–100) to obtain accurate parameter estimation with complex models. A further limitation when estimating the number of classes in GMM is the difficulty in distinguishing a unitary population distribution with nonnormal features from a non-unitary population with separate sub-population distributions (Bauer & Curran, 2003).

Examples From The Literature

Orcutt, Erickson, and Wolfe (2004) used GMM to determine whether or not different growth trajectories of post-traumatic stress disorder (PTSD) occurred within a sample of Gulf War veterans, and if gender and other covariates could predict group membership. They collected data on a sample of 2,949 veterans at time 1, and attrition reduced the sample to 1,327 by time 3. Theory led the researchers to postulate that there would be two different growth trajectories. Their analyses using GMM also suggested the existence of 2 classes; using BIC, they determined that the optimal number of classes from their data was two. The first group was the less symptomatic group: these veterans had fewer symptoms at time 1 and a slower growth rate in the number of symptoms from time 1 to time 3. Additionally, the initial status of symptoms was not correlated with growth in symptoms for this group. In contrast, the second group of veterans had a greater number of symptoms at time 1, and a steeper slope for growth in number of symptoms from time 1 to time 3. For this group, the initial status and growth of symptoms had a significant positive correlation. The model classified approximately 57% of the veterans into group 1 and 43% into group 2.

Next, the authors tested the significance of possible antecedent variables as predictors of the latent class membership. They found that gender, race, education, and combat exposure were significant predictors of latent class membership. Specifically, men, Whites, those with higher education, and those with less combat exposure were more likely to be in the less symptomatic group (Orcutt et al., 2004).

An educational example of growth mixture modeling focused on the development of reading skills in early elementary school children (Muthén et al., 2003). Initially, the researchers used GMM to classify the growth trajectories of kindergartners in phonemic awareness (PA), a hypothesized predictor of later reading skills. Four growth trajectory classes emerged. Class 1, which contained 21% of the children, exhibited a low level of PA upon exit from kindergarten, and no kindergarten growth. Class 2, which contained 7% of the children, also had low levels of PA upon exit of kindergarten, but rapid acceleration in PA was the key characteristic. Class 3, which contained 49% of the children, had average PA skills upon exit from kindergarten, and class 4, which contained 23% of the children, had above-average PA skills upon exit from kindergarten. The researchers used multinomial regression to regress class membership on an early covariate (letters, sounds, and naming skills in early kindergarten) as a proxy variable for literacy support and early instruction. This covariate was predictive of class membership; for example, children with literacy support one standard deviation below average were more likely to fall into class 1 in their PA development in kindergarten.

Next, the researchers used class membership to predict a distal outcome: word recognition (WR) skills in first grade. There was significant variation in WR based on growth trajectory class. Children in classes 3 and 4 continued to perform well in WR in first grade, while children in class 2 performed better than children in class 1, indicating the importance of rapid acceleration in PA skills in kindergarten. Together, the results from both stages of analysis suggested that early reading development begins in the home. Those children with poor literacy support in early kindergarten were more likely to have both low levels and poor growth in PA in kindergarten, which was more likely to result in poor WR skills in first grade. This method may be useful for identification of at-risk children very early in their formal educational experience. Interestingly, the researchers also analyzed the same data with conventional growth curve modeling and did not find the PA slope to be predictive of later WR skills in first grade. Only by allowing for separate growth trajectories for different latent growth classes did this pattern emerge.

In the PTSD example, it is interesting to note that the number of classes that the model identified was consistent with theory. Further, this example highlights the use of predictor variables of growth trajectory class to advance theory about a developmental process that occurred because of life events. The PA development example demonstrated how analysts can use GMM to model developmental growth and a later outcome, and the advantage that this provides over conventional growth modeling.

Application—Growth Mixture Modeling

The goal of these analyses was to predict reading achievement in third grade, a time at which many children begin to read fluently. Specifically, the analyses addressed the growth patterns in reading achievement that emerge between kindergarten and first grade, and whether growth classes based on these different patterns predict later reading achievement in third grade. I used selected cases from the ECLS-K ($n = 3,973$) to form latent growth classes based on early reading development. Then, I used these latent growth classes to predict the distal outcome, third-grade reading achievement, using growth mixture modeling. Figure 4.7 illustrates the growth model proposed to test these questions. I included gender in the model to control for gender differences in growth rate. The distal outcome, third-grade reading achievement, was an ordinal variable specifying the quartile of their spring third-grade reading achievement scores. Results are provided in Table 4.4.

I compared the BIC, adjusted BIC, and entropy measures across one-, two-, and three-class models. The first two measures decreased with an increasing number of classes (see Figure 4.8), and entropy increased with increasing numbers of classes, $E_2 = .769$, $E_3 = .859$. A four-class model was not estimable; therefore, I chose the three-class model because it had the lowest BIC and adjusted BIC and the highest entropy.

As Table 4.4 indicates, three growth classes emerged to describe reading growth in kindergarten through first grade. There was an uneven probability of membership in the three growth classes, with P(membership) = .077

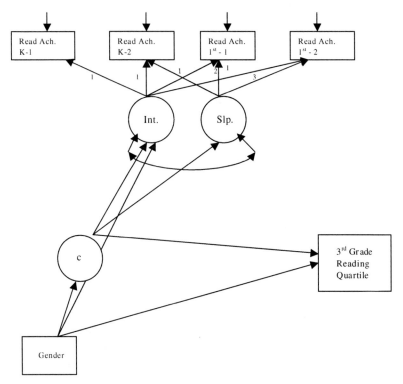

Figure 4.7 Path diagram of growth mixture model to predict third-grade reading achievement.

TABLE 4.4 Growth Mixture Analysis of Reading Achievement

	Class 1	Class 2	Class 3
Probability of membership	.077	.619	.305
Mean intercept	50.393***	26.343***	16.809***
Mean slope	18.988***	11.419***	7.275***
Third-Grade Reading Category Probabilities			
Category 1	.000	.000	.811***
Category 2	.007	.311***	.185***
Category 3	.174***	.383***	.003
Category 4	.820***	.306***	.000

Note: category 1 < Q1, category 2 between Q1 and Q2, category 3 between Q2 and Q3, and category 4 > Q3.
*** $p < .001$.

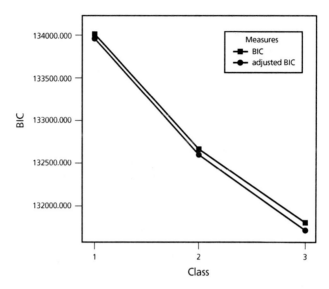

Figure 4.8 BIC values for growth mixture models with different numbers of classes.

for class 1, .619 for class 2, and .305 for class 3. Intercepts and slopes differed across the three classes. The highest average achievement and the steepest average growth rate during the period of early reading development distinguished class 1; the lowest average achievement and flattest growth rate characterized class 3; class 2 mean achievement and slope fell in the middle of those for classes 1 and 3. According to the probability of classification into the third-grade reading quartiles, the members of class 1 were likely to be in the third or fourth reading quartile; members of class 2 were likely to be in the second through fourth reading quartiles; and members of class 3 were likely to be in the first and second reading quartiles. Together, these results portray a picture of three classes of readers in kindergarten and first grade: the slow learners (class 3), who start at a below-average level of reading achievement and grow slowly and, as a result, are at the lowest quartiles of reading in third grade; the average learners (class 2), who begin at about an average level of reading achievement in kindergarten, have more or less average growth, and end up between an average to above-average reading quartile in third grade; and the fast learners (class 1), who start at an above-average level in reading achievement, have rapid reading achievement growth, and end up in the highest reading quartiles in third grade.

This model could be expanded to include additional covariates to account for variation in the growth classes. As Muthén (2005) suggests, models with different antecedents of class membership and growth factors will yield different classes and different probabilities of membership in the classes; therefore, from the onset, analysts should include in the model any covariates that would be useful for prediction.

Software Options

M*plus* software (Muthén & Muthén , 2006) is a SEM software program that is at the forefront in analysis of categorical outcomes, multilevel SEM, and growth modeling options, including GMM. Bengt Muthén is professor emeritus at UCLA, and Linda Muthén is the director of product development and runs an impressive open-access listserv for M*plus* support. The developers provide web training and conduct workshops on the use of the software. The M*plus* program is in its fourth version, the first version having been released in 1998.

Another software option for GMM is Latent Gold 4.0 (Vermunt & Magidson, 2005), developed by Jay Magidson at Statistical Innovations. He specifically designed Latent Gold 4.0 for latent class and finite mixture modeling, and targeted it toward marketing research. It has three separate modules for cluster, factor, and regression models. The software developers have online courses and workshops and provide extended support for an annual fee. For further comparison of the software programs with regard to specifying proper start values, see Hipp and Bauer (2006).

COMPARISONS OF ANALYSIS METHODS

This chapter covered three approaches to growth modeling: multilevel models, latent growth curves, and growth mixture modeling. Table 4.5 summarizes the key differences among these approaches in terms of data requirements, assumptions, strengths, and limitations.

Multilevel modeling is a flexible enough approach that allows for modeling both continuous and discontinuous growth models using a variety of strategies for defining patterns of growth. Conceptually, the assumption that observations are nested within individuals in multilevel models distinguishes multilevel models from LGC and GMM. MLM more readily allows data to be time-unstructured without complicated modifications. Theoretically, any slope can randomly vary in a multilevel model; however, allowing a number of slopes to vary randomly can result in convergence problems. The major distinguishing feature between multilevel modeling and SEM-based approaches is that MLM is based on a regression approach in which there is one observed outcome that is modeled with covariates. In this respect, it is more limiting than SEM-based approaches, which can allow for latent outcomes measured by a series of indicators, and which can be placed

TABLE 4.5 Strengths and Limitations of Three Growth Modeling Methods

Criteria	Multilevel models	Latent growth curve models	Growth mixture models
Data structure	• Allows unequal spacing between data waves • Allows unbalanced data • Allows time-unstructured data • Long data set format	• Allows unequal spacing between data waves • Allows unbalanced and time-unstructured data with some modification • Wide data set format	• Allows unequal spacing between data waves • Allows unbalanced and time-unstructured data with some modification • Wide data set format
Missing data assumptions	• MAR assumption for missing data at level one • Higher levels must have complete data	• MAR assumption for missing data	• MAR assumption for missing data
Normality assumption	• Assumption of multivariate normality	• Assumption of multivariate normality	• Assumption of normality within each latent class, however observed distributions may be nonnormal
Time-varying covariates	• Allows time-varying covariates	• Allows time-varying covariates	• Allows time-varying covariates which may differ across latent classes
Time-invariant covariates	• Allows time-invariant covariates	• Allows time-invariant covariates	• Allows time-invariant covariates which may differ across latent classes
Strengths	• Flexibly handles different data structures of time points and variance structure of time-varying covariates. • Noncovergence problems occur with a large number of random effects	• Allows for modeling of many covariance structures • Can model within a larger SEM model including antecedent covariates and moderating and mediating relationships • Test and indices of overall model fit are provided	• Allows modeling of unknown subpopulations with different growth trajectories • Can model within a larger SEM model • Ideal for modeling sequential growth processes

TABLE 4.5   Strengths and Limitations of Three Growth Modeling Methods (continued)

Criteria	Multilevel models	Latent growth curve models	Growth mixture models
Limitations	• Covariance structures limited in some software programs • Complete data required at person and organization levels. • No overall test and indices of model fit	• Modeling time unstructured data more cumbersome than multilevel models. • Need to understand SEM framework. • As compared to GMM, only models one population growth trajectory.	• Statistical sophistication may be needed to run models • May be difficult to reach estimable solutions with complex models. • May need to provide a wide range of start values. • Can result in misleading findings when data is from a nonnormal unitary population.

within a larger structural model involving mediating variables and parallel and sequential processes with multiple groups and complex variance structures. However, a related disadvantage for the LGC and GMM approaches is that analysts would benefit from a sophisticated understanding of SEM methodology in order to wisely apply these growth models.

Whereas both LGC and MLM assume a unitary population distribution, GMM assumes a mixture of different distributions. In GMM, the mixture of latent classes can produce a nonnormal observed distribution, although GMM assumes normality within each latent class. All three of the methods covered here allow for time-invariant as well as time-varying covariates; however, analysts more seamlessly can model time-unstructured data with time-varying covariates in MLM.

Growth mixture modeling often requires an added layer of complexity to arrive at a proper solution. First, there is difficulty in getting results to converge when there is singularity in the data. A second, less obvious problem is that solutions may not always be what they seem due to problems with obtaining an optimal solution. In LGC, the solutions typically are not dependent on the starting values for the maximum likelihood estimation; however, in GMM, they are. As Hipp and Bauer (2006) demonstrated, if a large number of varied starting values is not provided, the solution is likely to converge on a local solution that is not globally optimal, resulting in an inaccurate model. Although not an insurmountable problem, it would be necessary to override the default starting values to circumvent this problem, and less experienced users may have more difficulty navigating this issue. Despite these problems, the GMM approach adds a new dimension to the growth modeling possibilities by creating latent growth classes that analysts can use to describe different patterns of growth as well as predict distal outcomes and sequential growth processes.

The random coefficients models used in the methods described here are powerful and flexible tools for modeling growth. As this chapter demonstrates, the appropriate choice of modeling method needs to be based on a match of the assumptions of the methodology to the data structure and the type of growth pattern being investigated. With traditional approaches to the analysis of repeated measures, data that are time-unstructured or unbalanced severely limits the analyst's choices. Fortunately, advances in the use of random coefficients models not only allow for the investigation of time-unstructured data and complex growth patterns, but also capitalize on this structural variation in the data to estimate growth models that more accurately capture the real complexity inherent in much growth research in psychology, education, and other fields.

REFERENCES

Bauer, D. J. (2003). Estimating multilevel linear models as structural equation models. *Journal of Educational and Behavioral Statistics, 28*, 135–167.

Bauer, D. J., & Curran, P. J. (2003). Distributional assumptions of growth mixture models: Implications for overextraction of latent trajectory classes. *Psychological Methods, 8*, 338–363.

Bauer, D. J., & Curran, P. J. (2004). The integration of continuous and discrete latent variable models: Potential problems and promising opportunities. *Psychological Methods, 9*, 3–29.

Bentler, P.M. (2003). EQS 6.1 for Windows [Computer software]. Encino, CA: Multivariate software.

Biesanz, J. C., Deeb-Sossa, N., Papakakis, A., A., Bollen, K. A., & Curran, P.J. (2004). The role of coding time in estimating and interpreting growth curve models. *Psychological Methods, 9*, 30–52.

Blåfield, E. (1980). *Jyvaskyla studies in computer science, economics & statistics 2: Clustering of observations from finite mixtures with structural information.* Jyvaskyla, Finland: Jyvaskyla University.

Bollen, K. A., & Curran, P. J. (2006). *Latent curve models: A structural equation approach.* Hoboken, NJ: John Wiley & Sons.

Colder, C. R., Chassin, L., Stice, E. M., & Curran, P. J. (1997). Alcohol expectancies as potential mediators of parent alcoholism effects on the development of adolescent heavy drinking. *Journal of Research on Adolescence, 7*, 349–374.

Curran, P. J. (2003). Have multilevel models been structural equation models all along? *Multivariate Behavioral Research, 38,* 529–569.

Curran, P. J., & Bollen, K. A. (2001). The best of both worlds: Combining autoregressive and latent curve models. In. L. M. Collins & A. G. Sayer (Eds.), *New methods for the analysis of change* (pp. 107–135). Washington, DC: American Psychological Association.

Curran, P. J., & Hussong, A. M. (2002). Structural equation modeling of repeated measures data: Latent curve analysis. In Moskowitz & S. L. Hershberger (Eds.), *Modeling intraindividual variability with repeated measures data: Methods and applications* (pp. 171 - 201). Mahwah, NJ: Lawrence Erlbaum Associates.

Dolan, C. V., & van der Maas, H. L. J. (1998). Fitting multivariate normal finite mixtures subject to structural equation modeling. *Psychometrika, 63,* 227–253.

Duncan, T. E., Duncan, S. C., & Strycker, L. A. (2006). *An introduction to latent variable growth curve modeling: Concepts, issues, and applications* (2nd ed.) Mahwah, NJ: Lawrence Erlbaum Associates.

George, R. (2000). Measuring change in students' attitudes toward science over time: An application of latent variable growth modeling. *Journal of Science Education, and Technology, 9,* 213 - 225.

Hadley, P. A., & Holt, J. K. (2006). Individual Differences in the Onset of Tense Marking: A Growth Curve Analysis. *Journal of Speech, Language, and Hearing Research, 49,* 1 - 17.

Hipp, J., & Bauer, D. J. (2006). Local solutions in the estimation of growth mixture models. *Psychological Methods, 11,* 36–53.

Holt, J.K., Ennis, C., & Vaughn, M. (2006, April). *Keeping women in the science, technology, engineering, and mathematics pipeline: A growth modeling analysis.* Paper presented at the annual meeting of the American Educational Research Association.

Hox, J. (2002). *Multilevel analysis: Techniques and applications.* Mahwah, NJ: Lawrence Erlbaum Associates.

Jedidi, K., Jagpal, H. S., & Desarbo, W. S. (1997a). Finite-mixture structural equation models for response-based segmentation and unobserved heterogeneity. *Marketing Science, 16,* 39–59.

Jedidi, K., Jagpal, H. S., & DeSarbo, W. S. (1997b). STEMM: A general finite mixture structural equation model. *Journal of Classification, 14,* 23–50.

Jöreskog, K. G., Sörbom, D., Du Toit, S., & Du Toit, M. (2001) *LISREL 8: New statistical features.* Chicago, IL: Scientific Software.

Judd, C. M. and McClelland, G.H. (1989). *Data analysis: A model-comparison approach.* San Diego, CA: Harcourt Brace Jovanovich.

Li, F., Duncan, T. E., & Acock, A. (2000). Modeling interaction effects in latent growth curve models. *Structural Equation Modeling, 7,* 497–533.

Little, R. J. A., & Rubin, D. B. (2002). *Statistical analysis with missing data* (2nd ed.). Hoboken, NJ: Wiley.

Ma, X. (2005). A longitudinal assessment of early acceleration of students in mathematics on growth in mathematics achievement. *Development Review, 25,* 104–132.

McArdle, J. J. (1986). Latent growth within behavior genetic models. *Behavioral Genetics, 16,* 163–200.

McArdle, J. J., & Epstein, D. (1987). Latent growth curves within developmental structural equation models. *Child Development, 58*, 110–133.

McCoach, D.B., & Black, A. (2008). Evaluation of model fit and adequacy. In A. A. O'Connell and D. B. McCoach (Eds.), *Multilevel modeling of educational data* (pp. 245–271). Charlotte, NC: Information Age Publishing.

Mehta, P. D., & West, S. G. (2000). Putting the individual back into individual growth curves. *Psychological Methods, 9*, 301–303.

Meredith, W., & Tisak, J. (1984). *On "Tuckerizing" curves*. Presented at the annual meeting of the Psychometric Society, Santa Barbara, CA.

Meredith, W., & Tisak, J. (1990). Latent curve analysis. *Psychometrika, 55*, 107–122.

Miller, J. (1995). *Longitudinal study of American youth: Overview of study design and data resources*. DeKalb, IL: Northern Illinois University.

Muthén, B. O. (1991). Analysis of longitudinal data using latent variable models with varying parameters. In L. C. Collins & J. L. Horn (Eds.), *Best methods for the analysis of change* (pp. 1–17). Washington, DC: APA.

Muthén, B. O. (1993). Latent variable modeling of growth with missing data and multilevel data. In C. M. Cuadras & C. R. Rao (Eds.), *Multivariate analysis: Future directions 2* (pp. 199–210). Amsterdam: North Holland.

Muthén, B. O. (2001a). Latent variable mixture modeling. In G. A. Marcoulides & R. E. Schumacker (Eds.), *New developments and techniques in structural equation modeling* (pp. 1–33). Mahwah, NJ: Lawrence Erlbaum Associates.

Muthén, B. O. (2001b). Second-generation structural equation modeling with a combination of categorical and continuous latent variables. In L. M. Collins & A. Sayer (Eds.), *New methods for the analysis of change* (pp. 291–322). Washington, DC: APA.

Muthén, B. O. (2001c, January 9). Latent variable mixture modeling: LCA: Choosing initial conditional probabilities and number of classes [Msg 2]. Messages posted to http://www.statmodel.com/discussion/messages/13/98.html

Muthén, B. O. (2004a). Latent variable analysis: Growth mixture modeling and related techniques for longitudinal data. In D. Kaplan (Ed.), *The Sage handbook of quantitative methodology for the Social Sciences* (pp. 345–368). Thousand Oaks, CA: Sage.

Muthén, L. K. (2004b, April 6). Latent variable mixture modeling: Data distribution assumptions with version 2.0 [6:02 pm]. Message posted to http://www.statmodel.com/discussion/messages/13/116.html?1081282034.

Muthén, B. O. (2005, March). *Modeling with categorical latent variables using Mplus*. *Mplus* short course presented at Johns Hopkins University, Baltimore, MD.

Muthén, B. O., & Curran, P. J. (1997). General longitudinal modeling of individual differences in experimental designs: A latent variable framework for analysis and power estimation. *Psychological Methods, 2*, 371–402.

Muthén, B. O., Jo, B., & Brown, C. H. (2003). Comment on the Baranard, Rangakis, Hill & Rubin article, Principal stratification approach to broken randomized experiments: A case study of school choice vouchers in New York City. *Journal of the American Statistical Association, 98*, 311–314.

Muthén, B. O., & Khoo, S. T., Francis, D. J., Boscardin, C. K. (2003). Analysis of reading skills development from kindergarten through first grade: An application of growth mixture modeling to sequential processes. In S. P. Reise & N.

Duan (Eds.), *Multilevel modeling: Methodological advances, issues, and applications* (pp. 71–89). Mahwah, NJ: Lawrence Erlbaum Associates.

Muthén, L.K., & Muthén, B.O. (2006). M*plus*: Statistical analysis with latent variables (Version 4.21) [Computer software]. Los Angeles, CA: Muthén & Muthén.

Muthén, B. O., & Shedden, K. (1999). Finite mixture modeling with mixture outcomes using the EM algorithm. *Biometrics, 55,* 463–469.

Nagin, D. (1999). Analyzing developmental trajectories: A semi-parametric, group-based approach. *Psychological Methods, 5,* 23–43.

National Center for Education Statistics. (2004). *User's manual for the ECLS-K third grade public-use data file and electronic code book* (NCES Publication No. 2004-001). Washington DC: Author.

Neale, M. C., Boker, S. M., Xie, G., & Maes, H. H. (2002). *MX: Statistical modeling* (6th ed.). Richmond, VA: Virginia Commonwealth University, Department of Psychiatry.

Orcutt, H. K., Erickson, D. J., & Wolfe, J. (2004). The course of PTSD symptoms among Gulf War veterans: A growth mixture modeling approach. *Journal of Traumatic Stress, 17,* 195–202.

Peugh, J. L., & Enders, C. K. (2005). Using the *SPSS* mixed procedure to fit cross-sectional and longitudinal multilevel models. *Educational and Psychological Measurement, 65,* 717–741.

Raudenbush, S. W., & Bryk, A. S. (2002). *Hierarchical linear models: Applications and data analysis methods* (2nd ed.). Newbury Park, CA: Sage.

Raudenbush, S., Bryk, A. & Congdon, R. (2007). HLM for windows (Version 6.04) [Computer software]. Lincolnwood, IL: Scientific Software International.

Ramaswamy, V., Desarbo, W. S., Reibstein, D. J., & Robinson, W. T. (1993). An empirical pooling approach for estimating marketing mix elasticities with PIMS data. *Marketing Science, 12,* 103–124.

SAS Institute Inc. (2005). SAS OnlineDoc 9.1.3. Retrieved September 10, 2006, from the SAS Web site: http://support.sas.com/onlinedoc/913/docMainpage.jsp

SAS Institute Inc. (2004). *SAS/STAT* 9.1. [Computer software]. Cary, NC: Author.

Satorra, A., & Bentler, P. M. (1994). Corrections to test statistics and standard errors in covariance structure analysis. In A. von Eye & C. Clogg (Eds.), *Latent variable analysis in developmental research* (pp. 285–305). Newbury Park, CA: Sage.

Schwartz, G. (1978). Estimating the dimension of a model. *The Annals of Statistics, 6,* 461–464.

Singer, J. D., & Willett, J. B. (2003). *Applied longitudinal data analysis: Modeling change and event occurrence.* New York, NY: Oxford.

SPSS Inc. (2007) *Amos 7.0.* [Computer software]. Chicago, IL: Author.

Verbeke, G., & Lesaffre, E. (1996). A linear mixed-effects model with heterogeneity in the random-effects population. *Journal of the American Statistical Association, 91,* 217–221.

Vermunt, J. K., & Magidson, J. (2005). *Latent Gold Choice 4.0 user's manual.* Belmont, MA: Statistical Innovations.

Willett, J. B., & Sayer, A. G. (1994). Using covariance structure analysis to detect correlates and predictors of individual change over time. *Psychological Bulletin, 116,* 363–381.

CHAPTER 5

CROSS-CLASSIFIED RANDOM EFFECTS MODELS

S. Natasha Beretvas

CROSS-CLASSIFIED RANDOM EFFECTS MODELS

Multilevel modeling techniques now commonly are used to model the clustering inherent in social science research settings (such as students within classrooms grouped in schools and patients tended by nurses grouped in hospitals). In addition, the range of possible models has expanded quickly. One of the more complicated extensions involves the modeling of what are termed cross-classified random effects. The multilevel models that have been presented so far in this text are examples of purely nested data structures. Data do not always qualify as fitting a pure hierarchy. A classic example of a cross-classified data structure that is commonly encountered in educational research is students' cross-classification by neighborhood and school (Garner & Raudenbush, 1991). Schools are not purely clustered by neighborhood, nor are neighborhoods purely clustered within schools. In other words, students who attend a certain set, or cluster, of schools do not typically all come from a single neighborhood. Similarly, students from a cluster of neighborhoods do not all attend the same school. Rather, students are cross-classified by neighborhood and school. This cross-classifi-

Multilevel Modeling of Educational Data, pages 161–197
Copyright © 2008 by Information Age Publishing
All rights of reproduction in any form reserved.

cation can be modeled appropriately using cross-classified random effects modeling (CCREM).

Even though it is mentioned in most multilevel modeling textbooks (for example, Hox, 2002; Raudenbush & Bryk, 2002; Snijders & Bosker, 1999) and despite increasing use of CCREM in fields such as medicine (Rasbash & Browne, 2001) and in sociometric research (Hox, 2002; Pickery, Loosveldt, & Carton, 2001; Snijders & Bosker, 1999), this form of modeling is still only rarely used in educational research (for exceptions, see Fielding, 2002; Garner & Raudenbush, 1991; Goldstein & Sammon, 1997). The technical sophistication of the model seems to discourage its common use. Cross-classified (C-C) data structures, however, provide a commonly encountered reality that needs to be modeled appropriately.

This chapter distinguishes examples of purely nested versus C-C data structures. Formulation of the model and assumptions made are presented, starting with the simplest two-level model (with two C-C factors at level two) with extensions to three-level examples. The distinction between pure, hierarchical data structures and C-C data structures is presented using tables (Goldstein, 2003) and network graphs (Rasbash & Browne, 2001). There are already several very useful textbook chapters on CCREM, and the reader is encouraged to reference each of them (Goldstein; Hox, 2002; Rasbash & Browne, 2001; Raudenbush & Bryk, 2002; Snijders & Bosker, 1999). The current chapter contributes to these pedagogical expositions by offering two worked examples that detail how to use software to estimate the relevant CCREM parameters as well as how to interpret the relevant output.

The examples provided include a two-level CCREM in which students (level one) are cross-classified by junior high and high schools (level-two C-C factors). In the three-level example, measurement occasions (level one) are nested within examinees (level two), who are cross-classified by rater and classroom (the two level-three C-C factors). Explanatory variables at the measurement occasion, individual student, junior high school, and/ or high school level can be explored as sources of the possible variability. Estimation of the relevant parameters is demonstrated and interpretation of results provided using simulated data sets. Use of HLM software (version 6.0; Raudenbush, Bryk, & Congdon, 2004) for estimation of CCREM parameters is demonstrated with the two-level models. Use of SAS (SAS Institute Inc., 1999) is demonstrated for the two- and three-level models.

Data Structures

Pure Hierarchy, Two-level Data

Researchers commonly assume that their data structures involve *pure* clustering of units within groups. Some research questions are studied appropriately using a two-level model. For example, a researcher might be interested in investigating the impact of school effects on students' performance on a high school exam. Use of the two-level model involves the assumption that each student has been enrolled in a single high school. Using Raudenbush and Bryk's (2002) formulation of the two-level unconditional model, at level one, the outcome, Y_{ij}, representing the score of student i from school j, would be modeled such that

$$Y_{ij} = \beta_{0j} + r_{ij} \tag{5.1}$$

and at level two

$$\beta_{0j} = \gamma_{00} + u_{0j}, \tag{5.2}$$

or together as

$$Y_{ij} = \gamma_{00} + u_{0j} + r_{ij}. \tag{5.3}$$

Table 5.1 provides an example of a small, purely hierarchical dataset consisting of 12 students (A through L) attending four schools.

Figure 5.1 provides a network graph that provides an alternative (to Table 5.1) depiction of this pure nesting for the same dataset.

As can be seen in Table 5.1 and Figure 5.1, the data's structure is a pure clustering such that students are clustered within *only one* high school.

TABLE 5.1 Table of Pure Hierarchy of Students (Level One) Clustered within Schools (Level Two)

School 1	School 2	School 3	School 4
A, B, C			
	D, E, F		
		G, H, I	
			J, K, L

Note: Students attending a certain school are identified by alphabetic letter.

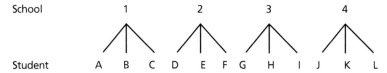

Figure 5.1 Network graph of pure hierarchy of students (level one) clustered within schools (level two).

Pure Hierarchy, Three-Level Data

A researcher might be interested in extending the model to consider the possible dependency associated with schools clustered in the same neighborhood (as well as that of students within the same school). Clearly, a three-level model could be considered in which level one represents students, level two represents the high schools in which they are enrolled, and level three models the neighborhoods from which schools enroll their students. Inclusion of this additional level necessitates the addition of an extra index, k, to represent neighborhood. The three-level unconditional model would be at level one

$$Y_{ijk} = \pi_{0jk} + e_{ijk}, \tag{5.4}$$

at level two

$$\pi_{0jk} = \beta_{00k} + r_{0jk}, \tag{5.5}$$

and at level three

$$\beta_{00k} = \gamma_{000} + u_{00k}, \tag{5.6}$$

or as a combined equation

$$Y_{ijk} = \gamma_{000} + u_{00k} + r_{0jk} + e_{ijk}. \tag{5.7}$$

Table 5.2 provides an example of a dataset that would meet the assumption of the pure nesting of students within schools and of schools within neighborhoods.

Figure 5.2 depicts the pure clustering of students within schools and the pure clustering of schools within neighborhoods in the dataset detailed in Table 5.2.

TABLE 5.2   Pure Hierarchy of Students (Level One) Grouped Within Schools (Level Two) Clustered Within Neighborhoods (Level Three)

Neighborhood i		Neighborhood ii	
School 1	School 2	School 3	School 4
A, B, C			
	D, E, F		
		G, H, I	
			J, K, L

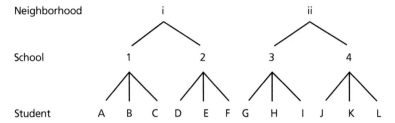

Figure 5.2   Network graph of pure hierarchy of students (level one) grouped within schools (level two) clustered within neighborhoods (level three).

Cross-Classified Hierarchy

In both Table 5.2 and Figure 5.2, the pure clustering within levels is again evident. However, the structure of real educational datasets frequently does not mimic this pure clustering. For the two-level example given here, it is unlikely that schools draw their students only from a single neighborhood. In other words, students from neighborhood *i* might attend a school that students from neighborhood *ii* also attend. Similarly, it is unlikely that neighborhoods send their students to only a single school. Table 5.3 lists an alternative data structure for the same 12 students (to that depicted in Table 5.2 and Figure 5.2).

TABLE 5.3   Cross-Classified Data Structured with Students Grouped Within Cross-Classifications of School and Neighborhood

	School			
Neighborhood	1	2	3	4
i	A, B	E		
ii	C	D	G, I	
iii		F	H	J
iv				K, L

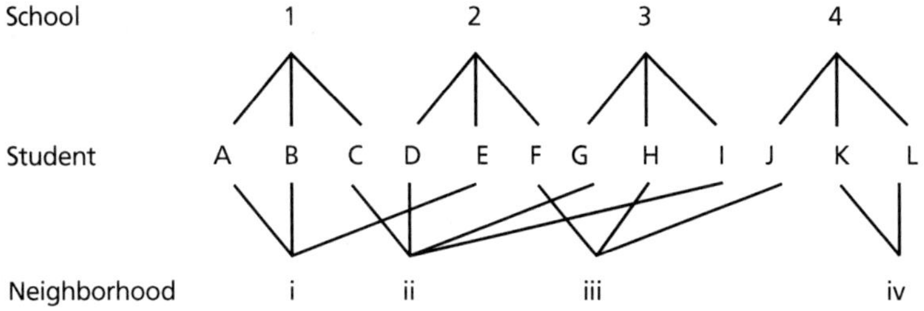

Figure 5.3   Network graph of cross-classified data structured with students grouped within cross-classifications of school and neighborhood.

Figure 5.3 more clearly depicts the lack of pure clustering of schools within neighborhoods.

As displayed in Table 5.3 and Figure 5.3, schools are not purely clustered within neighborhoods, nor are neighborhoods purely nested within schools. This means that there might be a cross-classification in the dataset; specifically, students are *cross-classified* by schools and neighborhoods. In this example, the cross-classification occurs at level two.

Consequences of Ignoring Cross-Classified Data Structures

Before discussing how to model C-C data structures, methods used by researchers to handle these more complex data structures are described. The first and most commonly encountered alternative would involve the researcher's ignoring of one of the cross-classification factors. For example, the researcher might only model the high school attended and ignore the possible effects of neighborhoods, thereby mis-specifying the model and possibly leading to spurious conclusions.

As a second alternative, for each neighborhood with the cross-classification of students by neighborhood and school, the school(s) with the smallest sample of students would be deleted leaving a set of schools purely clustered within each neighborhood. Table 5.4 contains the remaining data (from that in Table 5.3) that could be analyzed after the data were modified to obtain the pure nesting of students grouped within schools housed within neighborhoods. This second alternative can lead to an unnecessarily reduced dataset with a concomitant lack of statistical power and a reduction in the generalization of the resulting inferences.

Use of the CCREM avoids these analytic and inferential issues and provides the appropriate model to use with C-C data structures. The next section provides the formulation of a two-level CCREM, demonstrates the estimation of an actual model, and provides the interpretation of the estimated parameters.

TABLE 5.4 Deletion of Data to Convert Cross-Classified Data Structure in Table 3 to Purely Nested Dataset

Neighborhood	School			
	1	2	3	4
i	A, B			
ii			G, I	
iii		F		
iv				K, L

Models for Cross-Classified Data

The first example will extend that given above (see Figure 5.3 and Table 5.3) for C-C data structures for which the level-one units are cross-classified by two factors. An example of students cross-classified by school and neighborhood can be found in Raudenbush and Bryk (2002). Another education example of C-C data is of that wherein students (level one) are cross-classified by junior and high schools attended (level-two C-C factors). It is convenient to conceptualize both of these data structures as examples of a two-level model with C-C factors at level two.

The example involving junior and high schools as the cross-classified level-two factors will be used here to demonstrate formulation and interpretation of a two-level CCREM. In order to gauge the partitioning of variance into its various components, as is done with purely hierarchical data, the first model typically investigated in the CCREM is the fully unconditional model. At level one, the model is

$$Y_{i(j_1 j_2)} = \pi_{0(j_1 j_2)} + e_{i(j_1 j_2)}, \tag{5.8}$$

where $Y_{i(j_1 j_2)}$ represents the outcome (say, a math achievement test score) for student i in junior high school j_1 and high school j_2. The intercept, $\pi_{0(j_1 j_2)}$, represents the predicted math achievement score for students from the specific combination of junior high school j_1 and high school j_2. The residual $e_{i(j_1 j_2)}$, represents the deviation of a student's score from the student's junior high and high schools' predicted intercept value (assumed normally distributed with mean zero and variance, σ^2).

In the current chapter, formulation of the CCREM employs a mixture of the notations of Raudenbush and Bryk (2002), Hox (2002), and Rasbash and Browne (2001). Raudenbush and Bryk's levels' formulation will be used, and indices appearing together within parentheses (such as j_1 and j_2, here) will represent C-C factors, per Hox (2002). Then, using Rasbash and Browne's (2001) notation, the same letter (j) is used to identify C-C factors at the same level (here, level two). The factors themselves are only distinguished by the subscripted number associated with the index (thus, j_1 versus j_2). Last, another notational difference is necessary to facilitate interpretation of CCREM parameters. Coefficients for one of the C-C factors (for junior high school, here) are identified with a different Greek character (γ) than are used for the other C-C factor (β is used for high school). Yet another Greek character, θ, is used for parameters common across the two C-C factors.

At level two, the level-one intercept is modeled as a random effect in the unconditional model

$$\pi_{0(j_1 j_2)} = \theta_{000} + b_{0j_1 0} + c_{00j_2} + d_{0(j_1 j_2)}. \tag{5.9}$$

Note that in the two-level CCREM, three subscripts are needed. The first subscript represents the level-one unit (here, student) and two more subscripts are needed to identify each of the cross-classified factors (here, junior high and high school). The overall intercept, θ_{000}, represents the grand mean math achievement score. The junior high school residual, $b_{0j_1 0}$, represents the junior high school effect for school j_1 (averaged across high schools) and is assumed normally distributed with a mean of zero and variance of τ_{b00} (Raudenbush & Bryk, 2002; Snijders & Bosker, 1999). Similarly, the high school residual, c_{00j_2}, represents the high school effect for high school j_2 (averaged across junior high schools) and is assumed $\sim N(0, \tau_{c00})$. The random interaction effect, $d_{0(j_1 j_2)}$, represents the residual beyond that predicted by the grand mean, θ_{000}, and the two random main effects, $b_{0j_1 0}$ and c_{00j_2}, and is assumed $\sim N(0, \tau_{d00})$. Typically, the sample size per cell is insufficient to provide a good estimate of τ_{d00} as distinct from the student-level (within C-C cells) variance, σ^2 (Raudenbush & Bryk, 2002). This random effect, $d_{0(j_1 j_2)}$, and thus estimation of τ_{d00}, frequently is omitted from the CCREM (for example, in the CCREM chapters of the Hox, 2002; Rasbash & Browne, 2001; and Raudenbush & Bryk, 2002 textbooks) and will be omitted for the remainder of this chapter (where omission of its estimation implies setting its value to zero).

The level-one and level-two equations (Equations 5.6 and 5.7) can be combined to provide the overall model of interest

$$Y_{i(j_1 j_2)} = \theta_{000} + e_{i(j_1 j_2)} + b_{0j_1 0} + c_{00j_2}, \tag{5.10}$$

which clearly demonstrates the partitioning of the variability in students' math achievement scores into the component between junior high schools, $b_{0j_1 0}$, the component between high schools, c_{00j_2}, and the remaining variability between students within cells, $e_{i(j_1 j_2)}$.

Similar to analyses of purely hierarchical data, the variance components can be used to describe the proportions of variability at each level (Raudenbush & Bryk, 2002). The correlation between test scores for students in the same junior high school, j_1, who have attended different high schools, j_2 and j_2' (where $j_2 \neq j_2'$), can be estimated using

$$\rho_{Y_{ij_1 j_2}, Y_{i'j_1 j_2'}} = \frac{\tau_{b00}}{\tau_{b00} + \tau_{c00} + \sigma^2}. \tag{5.11}$$

The corresponding correlation for students who attended the same high school, j_2, although who are attending different junior high schools, j_1 and j_1', would be

$$\rho_{Y_{j_1 j_2}, Y_{i'j_1 j_2}} = \frac{\tau_{c00}}{\tau_{b00} + \tau_{c00} + \sigma^2}.$$ (5.12)

Lastly the proportion of the total variability that is within cells can be found by estimating

$$\rho_{Y_{j_1 j_2}, Y_{i'j_1 j_2}} = \frac{\sigma^2}{\tau_{b00} + \tau_{c00} + \sigma^2},$$ (5.13)

which provides the correlation between scores for students attending the same high and junior high schools.

If substantial within cross-classification (level-one) variability is found, then a student-level descriptor can be added to the model (in Equation 5.8) to explain some of that variability. For example, a researcher might be interested in investigating the relationship between students' grand-mean centered math self-concept[1], X, and their performance on a math achievement test. Equation 5.8 would become

$$Y_{i(j_1 j_2)} = \pi_{0(j_1 j_2)} + \pi_{1(j_1 j_2)} X_{i(j_1 j_2)} + e_{i(j_1 j_2)}.$$ (5.14)

And at level two, the coefficient, $\pi_{1(j_1 j_2)}$, describing the relationship between X and the outcome, could be modeled to vary randomly across junior high and high schools

$$\begin{cases} \pi_{0(j_1 j_2)} = \theta_{000} + b_{0 j_1 0} + c_{00 j_2} \\ \pi_{1(j_1 j_2)} = \theta_{100} + b_{1 j_1 0} + c_{10 j_2} \end{cases},$$ (5.15)

leading to the inclusion of two random effects, $b_{1 j_1 0}$, and $c_{10 j_2}$. Alternatively, the researcher might wish to model the covariate, X, as a fixed effect, in which case Equation 5.15 would become

$$\begin{cases} \pi_{0(j_1 j_2)} = \theta_{000} + b_{0 j_1 0} + c_{00 j_2} \\ \pi_{1(j_1 j_2)} = \theta_{100} \end{cases}.$$ (5.16)

In Equation 5.16, the residuals represent deviations around the intercept, θ_{000}. And because X is grand-mean centered, θ_{000} in equations 5.15 and 5.16 now represent the predicted math achievement score for a student with the average self-concept score. Therefore, here θ_{000} is an adjusted mean math achievement score.

If substantial variability remains in the intercept between high schools (τ_{c00}) and junior high schools (τ_{b00}), then descriptors of those C-C factors can be added to the model. For example, it might be hypothesized that a measure of a junior high school's resources for math classrooms, Z, could explain some of the variability in achievement test scores after controlling for self-concept. Thus, the level two-model (Equation 5.15) becomes

$$
\begin{cases}
\pi_{0(j_1 j_2)} = \theta_{000} + \gamma_{010} Z_{j_1} + b_{0 j_1 0} + c_{00 j_2} \\
\pi_{1(j_1 j_2)} = \theta_{100} + b_{1 j_1 0} + c_{10 j_2}
\end{cases}
\tag{5.17}
$$

As would be expected, inclusion of the junior high school predictor changes interpretation of the intercept, θ_{000}. If Z is grand-mean centered, θ_{000} now represents the adjusted (for student math self-concept) math achievement score for a student from a junior high school with the average amount of math resources. The relationship between the C-C factor (junior high school predictor, Z) and the intercept could be modeled in several ways. The slope could be modeled as fixed across levels of the other C-C factors (i.e., across high schools). Or, the relationship between a junior high school's math resources and a student's adjusted math achievement score (i.e., the coefficient, γ_{010}) could be modeled to vary randomly across high schools (Snijders & Bosker, 1999). In this case, Equation 5.17 becomes

$$
\begin{cases}
\pi_{0(j_1 j_2)} = \theta_{000} + (\gamma_{010} + c_{01 j_2}) Z_{j_1} + b_{0 j_1 0} + c_{00 j_2} \\
\pi_{1(j_1 j_2)} = \theta_{100} + b_{1 j_1 0} + c_{10 j_2}
\end{cases}
\tag{5.18}
$$

where $c_{01 j_2}$ represents the variability across high schools in the coefficient for Z. Last, a high school descriptor such as average high school class size, W, could be added to Equation 5.18 to explain some of the variability in students' math achievement between high schools in the relationship between achievement (controlling for self-concept) and junior high school math resources:

$$
\begin{cases}
\pi_{0(j_1 j_2)} = \theta_{000} + (\gamma_{010} + \gamma_{011} W_{j_2} + c_{01 j_2}) Z_{j_1} + b_{0 j_1 0} + c_{00 j_2} \\
\pi_{1(j_1 j_2)} = \theta_{100} + b_{1 j_1 0} + c_{10 j_2}
\end{cases}
\tag{5.19}
$$

Remember that grand mean-centered student math self-concept, X, was added as a level-one predictor (see Equation 5.14), thereby changing interpretation of the intercept to represent the predicted math achievement for a student with average math self-concept. This intercept was modeled to vary across both junior high and high schools (Equation 5.16). The quantity of junior high school math resources, Z, was added to explain some of the variability in this intercept across junior high schools (Equation 5.17). The relationship between the junior high school predictor, Z, and the intercept was then modeled to vary across high schools (see Equation 5.18). Some of the variability among high schools in the relationship between Z and the intercept is modeled as being explained by high school class size, W

(in Equation 5.19). The addition of the high school predictor, W, to explain variability between junior highs' Z slope is formally equivalent to adding an interaction between W and Z to the model (Raudenbush & Bryk, 2002). In other words, the first line of Equation 5.19 can be used to assess whether W moderates the relationship between Z and the intercept. Finally, the intercept in Equation 5.19 now represents the predicted math achievement score for a student with average math self-concept controlling for junior high math resources and high school class size.

The relationship between students' adjusted math achievement and a high school's average class size, W, (grand-mean centered) could also be investigated. The high school descriptor could be added to the level-two equation (Equation 5.17) for the intercept

$$
\begin{cases}
\pi_{0(j_1 j_2)} = \theta_{000} + \gamma_{010} Z_{j_1} + \beta_{001} W_{j_2} + b_{0 j_1 0} + c_{00 j_2} \\
\pi_{1(j_1 j_2)} = \theta_{100} + b_{1 j_1 0} + c_{10 j_2}
\end{cases}
, \tag{5.20}
$$

such that W's coefficient, β_{001}, is modeled as fixed across junior high schools. Alternatively, the relationship between a high school's average class size and achievement could be modeled to vary randomly across junior high schools

$$
\begin{cases}
\pi_{0(j_1 j_2)} = \theta_{000} + \gamma_{010} Z_{j_1} + (\beta_{001} + b_{0 j_1 1}) W_{j_2} + b_{0 j_1 0} + c_{00 j_2} \\
\pi_{1(j_1 j_2)} = \theta_{100} + b_{1 j_1 0} + c_{10 j_2}
\end{cases}
. \tag{5.21}
$$

Or, as in Equation 5.19, an interaction could be introduced into Equation 5.21 to explain variability among junior high schools in the relationship between high school class size and math achievement. This would change the set of coefficients in front of W_{j_2} in Equation 5.21 from $(\beta_{001} + b_{0 j_1 1})$ to $(\beta_{001} + \gamma_{011} Z_{j_1} + b_{0 j_1 1})$ and further complicate estimation and interpretation of the model parameters. In Equation 5.21, the math achievement score predicted for a student with average math self-concept is modeled to vary across junior and senior high schools. Variability in this intercept across these two C-C factors is modeled as being explained partly by junior high math resources, high school class size, and the interaction of the two predictors.

The original unconditional model (Equation 5.10) has been expanded to include C-C factors' descriptors designed to explain variability in the intercept (see Equation 5.21). It also includes a level-one predictor, X, modeled in Equation 5.21 such that its relationship with Y varies randomly across junior high and high schools. As was demonstrated with the intercept, relevant descriptors also could be added to explain variability across junior and senior high schools in the relationship between student math self-concept (X) and math achievement (Y). The reader is cautioned, however, that while it might be tempting to take advantage of the sophisticated flexibility of CCREMs, addition of multiple covariates and associated random effects make the models increasingly difficult to estimate and interpret (Raudenbush & Bryk, 2002). As with any kind of modeling, parsimony is strongly encouraged (Snijders and Bosker, 1999).

The next section demonstrates the use of HLM software (version 6) (Raudenbush, Bryk, & Congdon, 2004) to estimate the parameters of a two-level CCREM. The content of the datasets were simulated to match the example just provided. It should be noted that HLM software currently only can be used to estimate two-level CCREMs with two C-C factors at the higher level. SAS and MLwin (Goldstein et al., 1998) can be used to estimate CCREMs with additional levels and C-C factors. However, HLM software is a common choice of multilevel modelers, and thus, its use is demonstrated here.

Two-Level CCREM Example

An educational researcher might be interested in the relationship between students' performance on math achievement and descriptors of the student and of the junior high and high school that the student attended. This simulated dataset contains information for 829 students consisting of student, junior high and high school IDs, and scores on the following variables: the outcome variable (math achievement scores), a student-level predictor (math self-concept), a junior high school measure (school math resources), and a high school measure (average class size). The C-C nature of the dataset in which students are cross-classified by junior high and high school attended can be seen in Table 5.5. As evidenced in Table 5.5, there are no students attending some of the combinations of high and junior high school. For example, no students attend high school 1 and junior high schools 11 through 17. The number of students per cell ranged from 8 to 22 with an average per-cell (including the empty cells) sample size of 14.8.

As when using HLM software for purely hierarchical datasets, the user must construct a dataset for each level. SPSS was used to construct the datasets for the examples here. With a two-level CCREM analysis, the user must construct three datasets, one for the level-one information (*2Lvl_L1.SAV*) and one for each C-C factor (*2Lvl_JH_L2.SAV* and *2Lvl_HS_L2.SAV*). When units are cross-classified at a higher level, the level-one dataset should identify each case with identifiers for each of the relevant C-C factors. For the current dataset, this means that each student's information should be associated with the student's junior high and high school identifiers. For example, 17 students were identified as having attended Junior High School 1

TABLE 5.5 Cross-Classification of Students by Junior High and High School Attended

HS	Junior High School																	Total
	1	2	3	4	5	6	7	8	9	10	11	12	13	14	15	16	17	
1	17	17	13	13	12													72
2	13				16	15		15										59
3	17	15	14			20	15	13										94
4	21				11	20			20									72
5					15		8		8	18								49
6		14						11	18	16								59
7					15		16	11		19								61
8		11	14	16		13				17								71
9											11	18	14	22				65
10											14		18	12	14	13		71
11											21	14	10	18	16	14	12	105
12											18	15		18				51
Total	68	57	41	29	69	68	39	50	46	70	64	47	42	70	30	27	12	829

Note: HS = High school. Empty cells indicate no students in the dataset were from the associated combination of junior high and high school.

and High School 1 (see Table 5.5). The junior high school dataset contains only the junior high school identifier and junior high school information. Similarly, the high school dataset contains the high school identifier and associated high school information. Each dataset should be sorted by the higher levels' identifiers (i.e., by junior high and high school identifiers).

After constructing the datasets, the user must construct a multivariate data matrix (MDM) file for the HLM analysis. In the HLM package, after clicking on *FILE*, requesting *Make new MDM File*, and identifying *Stat Package Input*, the user will see the screen displayed in Figure 5.4. The default for this screen is *HLM2*; however, the user needs to click on *HCM2* to indicate that the MDM being constructed is for a C-C dataset.

Next, similar to modeling for purely hierarchical data, a screen appears (see Figure 5.5) from which the user must identify relevant files.

After naming the MDM file and selecting the relevant level-one file, the user clicks on *Choose Variables* to identify the relevant id variables and variables to be included in the later modeling. However, the *Choose variables* screen that appears for C-C datasets is a little different (see Figure 5.6).

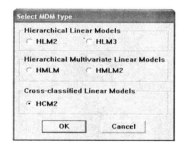

Figure 5.4 Window for selection of cross-classified data structure when building MDM file.

Figure 5.5 Window for identification of relevant files when constructing MDM file.

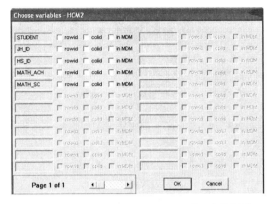

Figure 5.6 Choose variables screen when constructing MDM for cross-classified dataset.

The HLM manual (Raudenbush et al., 2004) recommends using the C-C factor with fewer units as the "row" factor and the other factor as the "column" factor. (See Tables 5.3 through 5.5 to understand what is meant by "row" and "column.") In the current dataset, there are 17 junior high schools and 12 high schools. Thus, high school was selected as the row variable and junior high as the column variable when constructing the MDM. Therefore, when *Choosing variables* for the level-one file, the user should choose *JH_ID* as the *colid* (column identifier) and *HS_ID* as the *rowid.* In addition, the user should be careful to select the high school dataset as the *Row-level File Name* and the junior high dataset as the *Column-level File Name* (see Figure 5.5). The remaining point-and-click commands are the same as for purely hierarchical datasets.

Estimating a Model in HLM Software

The first model to be estimated is the fully unconditional model (see Equations 5.6 and 5.7, summarized in Equation 5.10). First, the outcome is identified by clicking on *Math_Ach* and selecting the only available option, thereby indicating that *Math_Ach* is the desired dependent variable. The default is to model the unconditional model in which the intercept is treated as randomly varying across the two C-C factors (see Figure 5.7).

The model then can be saved and run. Part of the relevant output follows. The reader should note that in HLM output whichever C-C factor is the "row" variable (here, high school) is associated with the b random effects and the other factor (here, junior high) is associated with the c random effects. Full maximum likelihood (FML) is the estimation procedure used. Important values in the HLM output are bold and underlined.

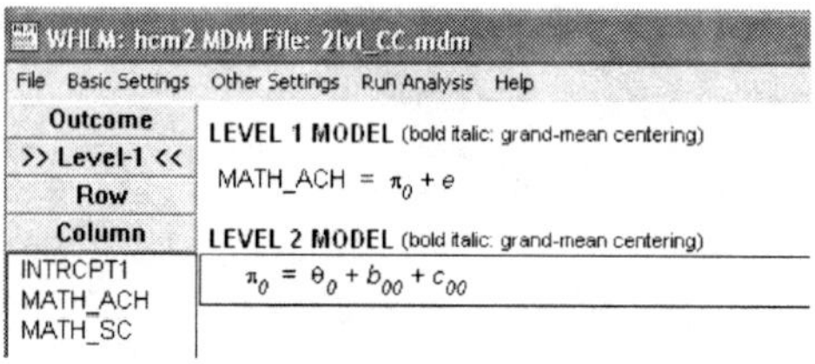

WHLM: hcm2 MDM File: 2lvl_CC.mdm	
File Basic Settings Other Settings Run Analysis Help	
Outcome	**LEVEL 1 MODEL** (bold italic: grand-mean centering)
>> Level-1 <<	MATH_ACH $= \pi_0 + e$
Row	
Column	**LEVEL 2 MODEL** (bold italic: grand-mean centering)
INTRCPT1 MATH_ACH MATH_SC	$\pi_0 = \theta_0 + b_{00} + c_{00}$

Figure 5.7 Unconditional two-level CCREM in HLM.

```
Final estimation of fixed effects:
----------------------------------------------------------------
                                  Standard  Approx.
Fixed Effect          Coefficient Error     T-ratio  d.f.  P-value
----------------------------------------------------------------
For INTRCPT1, P0
INTERCEPT, theta0      50.289203   1.205361  41.721   828   0.000
----------------------------------------------------------------
```

```
Final estimation of row and level-1 variance components:
----------------------------------------------------------------
Random Effect    Standard    Variance    df   Chi-square   P-value
                 Deviation   Component
----------------------------------------------------------------
INTRCPT1, b00    3.03681      9.22223    11   114.39596    0.000
level-1, e       8.99703     80.94655
----------------------------------------------------------------
```

```
Final estimation of column level variance components:
----------------------------------------------------------------
Random Effect    Standard    Variance    df   Chi-square   P-value
                 Deviation   Component
----------------------------------------------------------------
INTRCPT1, c00    3.06941      9.42131    16   132.11424    0.000
----------------------------------------------------------------
```

```
Statistics for current covariance components model
--------------------------------------------------
Deviance = 6048.168896
Number of estimated parameters = 4
```

The results of interest also are summarized in the CCREM unconditional model column of data in Table 5.6. The fixed effects variance estimates and tests of statistical significance appear as the first results in the output followed by the random effects results. The random-effects values can be used (see Equations 5.11, 5.12, and 5.13) to obtain the partitioning of the vari-

TABLE 5.6 Some of the Parameters for the Models Estimated with the Two-Level Cross-Classified Dataset

		CCREM						HLM model	
		Uncond.	Model 1	Model 2	Model 3			Uncond.	Model 1
Fixed effects						**Fixed effects**			
Intercept	θ_{000}	50.3**	50.3**	50.4**	49.9**	Intercept	γ_{00}	50.1**	50.0**
Math_SCc	θ_{100}		0.2**	0.2**	0.2**	Math_SCc	γ_{10}		0.2**
Math_ResC	β_{010}			0.6*	0.6*				
HS_CSize	γ_{010}				0.02				
Random effects						**Random effects**			
Student	$e_{i(j_1j_2)}$	80.9	78.4	78.4	78.4	Student	r_{ij}	89.0	86.6
Junior high	c_{00_2}	9.4**	9.7**	6.1**	6.1**	High school	u_{0j}	10.3**	10.9**
High school	b_{00_1}	9.2**	9.6**	9.5**	9.5**				
Model deviance		6,048	6,023	6,017	6,017			6,097	6,076

Note: CCREM results appear first, followed by HLM model results. Fixed effects are point estimates of the specified coefficients. Random effects provide variance estimates of the specified residuals. Only the statistical significance of the fixed effects is noted in this table. Math_MSc = Math self-concept (centered). Math_ResC = Math resources (centered). HS_CSize = High school class size. Uncond. = unconditional; Model 1 includes *Math_MSc* as a fixed level-one predictor; Model 2 includes *Math_MSc* as a fixed level-one predictor and *Math_ResC* as a fixed (C-C factor) predictor; Model 3 is the same as Model 2 except including *HS_CSize* as a fixed (C-C factor) predictor.
** $p < .001$; * $p < .05$

ability. The total variance (the denominator in the three Equations) was calculated by summing together $(\sigma^2 + \tau_{b00} + \tau_{c00})$, yielding: $80.9 + 9.2 + 9.4 = 99.5$. Using Equation 5.13, the variability within cells (i.e., within cross-classifications of junior high and high schools once junior high and high school effects have been partialled out) was estimated to be 81.3% (80.9/99.5). There was a substantial amount of variability found between high schools (9.3% from 9.2/99.5) as well as between junior high schools (9.4% from 9.4/99.5), supporting the importance of modeling the cross-classification. The fixed effect estimate of the coefficient for the intercept was 50.3, providing the predicted average math achievement score (found to differ significantly from zero, $p < .001$).

To demonstrate the results of mis-specifying the multilevel model by ignoring the clustering of students within junior high schools, a purely hierarchical model was estimated using a two-level HLM. Students (level one) were modeled as clustered within high schools (level two), and the junior high enrollment was ignored. An unconditional model was estimated with the fixed and random effect coefficient estimates. The results appear in the right-hand portion of Table 5.6. The calculation of the intraclass correlation coefficient (Raudenbush & Bryk, 2002) revealed that when junior high school cross-classification was not modeled, the proportion of variability between high schools remained around the same (10.4%, from 10.3/[89.0 + 10.3]). However, the proportion of variability between students was higher (89.6%, from 89.0/[89.0 + 10.3]) than the CCREM's estimate of 81.3% by almost the same percent of variability that was found between junior high schools in the appropriately modeled two-level CCREM ($c_{00j_2} = 9.4$ in Table 5.6). The ignored variability between junior high schools gets re-distributed such that the majority appears as variability between students (within cross-classifications). This clearly could impact the statistical significance testing and interpretation of results when the C-C structure is modeled (using CCREM) versus when it is ignored (and the HLM model is assumed).

Returning to the CCREM analysis, the researcher might add the student-level covariate (grand-mean centered math self-concept score) to the unconditional model (Equations 5.14 and 5.15) to explain some of the variability found at each level. To do this in HLM software, simply click on the relevant predictor (*Math_SC*) and specify it as grand-mean centered. The result is the screen shown in Figure 5.8.

The default in HLM6 is for predictors added to a model to be fixed effects (seen in Figure 5.8, in which the font of the slope's random effects [b_{10j_1} and c_{10j_2}] is only very faintly visible, and resulting in the model in Equation 5.16 rather than Equation 5.15). Clicking on each of these effects (b_{10j_1} and c_{10j_2}) will convert the slope to be modeled as varying randomly across junior high and high schools (see Figure 5.9), which is necessary if theoretically warranted.

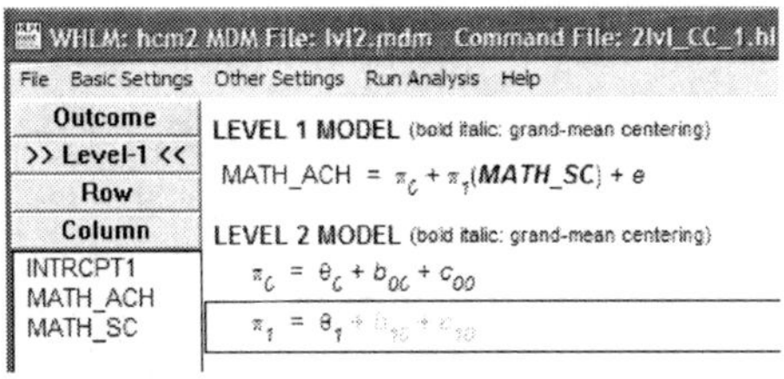

Figure 5.8 Conditional CCREM (with a fixed level-one predictor) in HLM software.

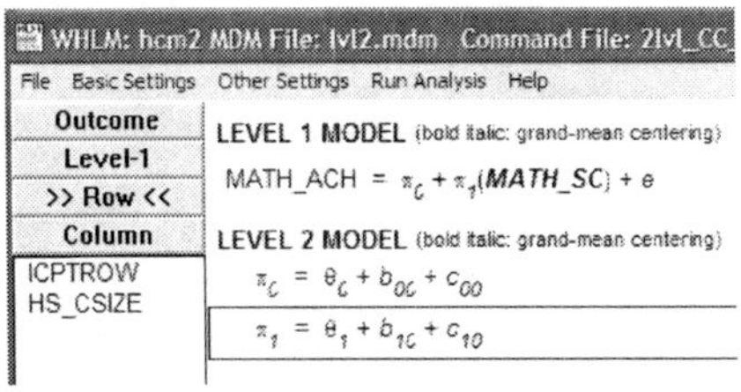

Figure 5.9 Conditional CCREM (with a randomly varying level-one predictor) in HLM software.

Due to the increased number of random effects being estimated, additional iterations were required to reach convergence. (The unconditional model's estimation took a mere 6 iterations as compared with 392 for the model depicted in Figure 5.9.) The output appears below.

```
Final estimation of fixed effects:
-------------------------------------------------------------------
                                  Standard  Approx.
Fixed Effect         Coefficient  Error     T-ratio  d.f.  P-value
-------------------------------------------------------------------
For INTRCPT1, P0
   INTERCEPT,theta0   50.324654   1.227643   40.993   827   0.000
For MATH_SC, P1
   INTERCEPT,theta1    0.227581   0.049063    4.639   827   0.000
-------------------------------------------------------------------


Final estimation of row and level-1 variance components:
-------------------------------------------------------------------
Random Effect       Standard    Variance    df  Chi-square  P-value
                    Deviation   Component
-------------------------------------------------------------------
INTRCPT1, b00        3.09350     9.56974     11   605.86476   0.000
MATH_SC slope, b10   0.07157     0.00512     11    18.18698   0.077
level-1, e           8.83385    78.03696
-------------------------------------------------------------------
```

```
Final estimation of column level variance components:
------------------------------------------------------------------
Random Effect        Standard     Variance    df   Chi-square   P-value
                     Deviation    Component
------------------------------------------------------------------
INTRCPT1, c00        3.15288      9.94064     16   127.62838    0.000
MATH_SC slope, c10   0.01263      0.00016     16    15.49900    >.500
------------------------------------------------------------------


Statistics for current covariance components model
--------------------------------------------------------
Deviance = 6020.224079
Number of estimated parameters = 9
```

The relationship between *Math_SC* and the outcome was significantly positive ($\hat{\theta}_{100}$ = 0.2, p < .001) and reduced the unexplained level-one variance, $\hat{\sigma}^2$, from 80.9 to 78.0 (by 3.6%). The value of this regression coefficient, $\hat{\theta}_{100}$, indicates that the higher students' reported math self-concept, the better their math achievement score would be predicted to be. In addition, given student A has a math self-concept score that is 1 point higher than student B's, then student A's math achievement test score would be predicted to be 0.2 points higher. The change in the deviance from the unconditional model (deviance = 6,048) to the model including the level-one predictor, which added five parameters to those estimated in the unconditional model (deviance = 6,020), was statistically significant [$\Delta\chi^2(5) = 28$, $p < .001$], indicating that the model including the level-one predictor resulted in a significant *improvement* in model-fit. The small values found in the output for the slope's variability across junior high and high schools (.00016 and .00512, respectively) and their lack of statistical significance ($p > 0.05$) indicate that the effect might be better modeled as fixed rather than random.

The model that included *Math_SC* as a fixed effect (see Equations 5.14 and 5.16 and Figure 5.8) was estimated next, and results are shown in Table 5.6 under model 1. No difference was found in the estimates of the resulting fixed effects (see Model 1 of CCREMs in Table 5.6). Only slight differences were found in the variance estimates between Model 1 ($\hat{\sigma}^2$ = 78.4, $\hat{\tau}_{b00}$ = 9.6, $\hat{\tau}_{c00}$ = 9.7) and the unconditional model ($\hat{\sigma}^2$ = 80.9, $\hat{\tau}_{b00}$ = 9.4, $\hat{\tau}_{c00}$ = 9.2). The deviance estimate for the model with *Math_SC* fixed across junior high and high schools was 6,023. The difference in the deviances between the model in which *Math_SC* was modeled as random versus fixed across junior high and high schools was not statistically significant ($\Delta\chi^2(4) = 3$, $p > .05$), supporting the fit of this more parsimonious (fixed slope) model.

A substantial amount of variability between junior high and high schools remained unexplained in the intercept (predicted math achievement

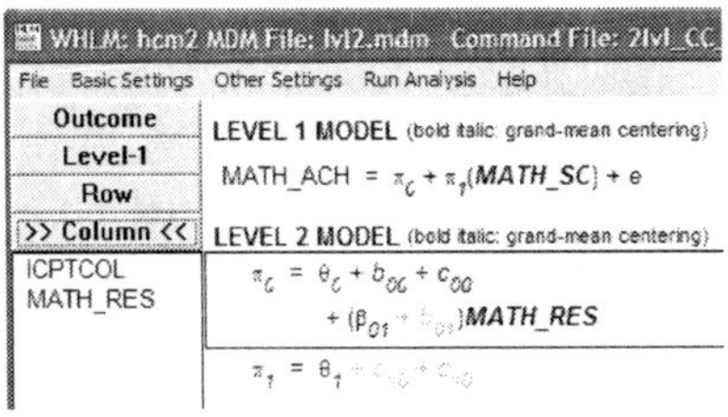

Figure 5.10 Conditional CCREM (with fixed level-one and cross-classified factor predictors) in HLM software.

scores adjusted for math self-concept scores). To address this, the measure of a junior high school's math resources (*Math_Res*) was added as a grand-mean centered variable[1] to the level-two equation for the intercept. Initially, the coefficient for the relationship between *Math_Res* and the outcome was modeled as fixed across high schools (see Equation 5.17). This is accomplished in HLM software by ensuring that the list of "column" (i.e., junior high) variables is listed on the left of the screen. Then, *Math_Res* was selected as a grand-mean centered predictor. Again, the default is that the predictor is fixed (as demonstrated in Figure 5.10).

The results for this model appear under Model 2 in Table 5.6. The fixed effect estimates from the output appear below.

```
Final estimation of fixed effects:
---------------------------------------------------------------------
                                     Standard   Approx.
Fixed Effect        Coefficient      Error      T-ratio   d.f.   P-value
---------------------------------------------------------------------
For INTRCPT1, P0
  INTERCEPT,theta0   50.428433       1.129441   44.649    826    0.000
MATH_RES, B01         0.625973       0.240469    2.603    826    0.010
For MATH_SC, P1
  INTERCEPT,theta1    0.227409       0.044453    5.116    826    0.000
---------------------------------------------------------------------
```

As the results in Table 5.6 indicate, the addition of *Math_Res* did not substantially change the fixed effect estimate of the relationship between *Math_SC* and *Math_Ach* ($\hat{\theta}_{100}$). The estimate of the intercept, ($\hat{\theta}_{000} = 50.4$, $p < .05$), now represents the predicted score for a student, controlling for *Math_SC* scores *and* for *Math_Res*. *Math_Res* was found to have a significantly positive relationship ($\hat{\gamma}_{010} = 0.6$, $p < .05$) with *Math_Ach* (controlling for *Math_SC*), indicating that the more math resources a junior high school offered, the better a student tended to perform on the math achievement test. More specifically, students with the same *Math_SC* scores at junior high schools that differ by 1 point on the *Math_Res* measure would be predicted to differ on their math achievement test scores by 0.6 points. The junior high school variance component (see Table 5.6) was reduced from 9.4 (in the unconditional model) to 6.1 (in Model 2), indicating that *Math_Res* explained about 35% of the variability in math achievement scores (controlling for *Math_SC*).

To assess how much the relationship between junior high math resources and the intercept varied across high schools, Equation 5.18 was estimated (instead of Equation 5.17). To change the model in this way using HLM6, the faint b_{01j_1} should be clicked on until it becomes dark as appears in Figure 5.11.

The resulting estimates are not shown in Table 5.6. However, with the addition of the random effects, estimation of the model required over 300 iterations to converge on a solution. No change was noted in the fixed effect estimates. The deviance statistic of this model was 6,017.2 compared with 6,017.3 (for the fixed *Math_Res* model in Equation 5.17, i.e., Model 2). Fit of the model was not significantly improved by the addition of the two extra parameters (the variance of b_{01j_1} and its covariance with b_{00j_2}).

The variability between high schools has not yet been explored. High school class size (*HS_CSize*) was added to the level-two equation as a grand-mean centered, fixed effect predictor[1] of the intercept (see Equation 5.20). To accomplish this in HLM, the user must ensure that variables describing this C-C factor identified as the "row" variable appear on the left-hand side of the HLM window (click on *Row* so it becomes "<<*Row*>>"). Next, select the *HS_CSize* variable and add it as a fixed (across junior high schools), grand-mean centered predictor of the intercept, resulting in the HLM window shown in Figure 5.12. The estimates resulting from this final model appear under Model 3 in Table 5.6.

In this dataset, high school class size was not related to the intercept ($\gamma_{010} = 0.02$, $p > 0.05$). This also is reflected in the lack of change in the between-high school variance of the residuals, $\hat{\tau}_{c00}$, which was 9.5 before and after inclusion of *HS_CSize* in the model. Note that the deviance is unchanged between models 2 and 3.

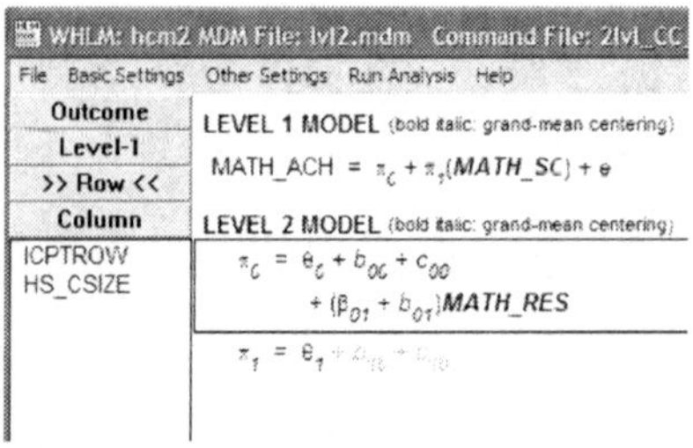

Figure 5.11 Conditional CCREM (with a fixed level-one and a random cross-classified factor predictor) in HLM software.

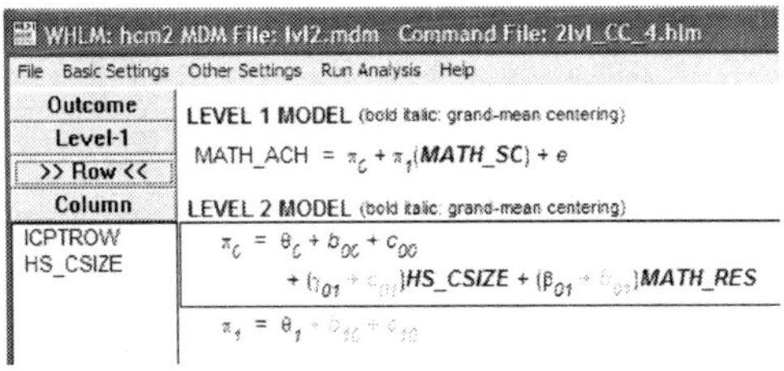

Figure 5.12   Conditional CCREM (with a fixed level-one and fixed cross-classified factor predictors) in HLM software.

Overall, these results suggest the selection of Model 2. In Model 2, there was a positive relationship between math self-concept and math achievement, and the relationship can be assumed fixed across junior high and high schools. In addition, the amount of math resources in a junior high also had a positive relationship with students' math achievement scores (even after controlling for students' math self-concept). A substantial proportion (9.5%) of variability remained unexplained between high schools ($\hat{\tau}_{b00} = 9.5$, $p < 0.05$) and between junior high schools (6.1%; $\hat{\tau}_{c00} = 6.1$, $p < 0.05$), as well as between students within cross-classifications by junior high and high school (78.4%). Additional sources of variability in mathematics achievement, particularly among individual students, should be investigated.

CCREM Dataset Construction for Analysis Using SAS PROC MIXED

The graphical user interface (GUI) along with the levels' formulation in HLM software favors its use with new multilevel modelers. However, use of SAS PROC MIXED is easier in some ways than HLM software for estimating multilevel models and in particular CCREMs. (A new user of SAS is strongly encouraged to work through Singer's 1998 article describing estimation of purely hierarchical multilevel models before embarking on the use of SAS for estimation of CCREMs).

When using SAS to estimate multilevel models, only a single dataset is needed. This single dataset should have identifying variables distinguishing each unit and cross-classified factor. Thus, in the current two-level example, identifiers for students, high schools, and junior highs are needed. Aligned with each combination of identifiers are each case's values on the relevant level-one and level-two predictors. In addition, variables requiring centering must be transformed prior to inclusion in PROC MIXED. Here, *Math_SCc* and *Math_RESc* refer to grand-mean centered versions of these variables.

Once the dataset is input, the commands below are needed to estimate the two-level unconditional CCREM in Equation 5.10.[3]

```
PROC MIXED DATA=DATA_2LVL_CC METHOD = ML COVTEST INFO IC UPDATE;
    CLASS JH_id HS_id;
    MODEL MATH_ACH = /solution ddfm=kr;
    RANDOM int/ sub=JH_id;
    RANDOM int/ sub=HS_id;
    run;
```

Be sure to identify the dataset with the "DATA=" command. Use the "CLASS" command to indicate the identifier variables that distinguish the different C-C factors (here, junior high and high school). As can be seen in the SAS code, there is no need to identify the data's structure as cross-classified. The cross-classification is recognized by SAS from the dataset's structure, and a CCREM will be estimated if the cross-classified factors are identified with the "CLASS" command.

For estimation of the unconditional CCREM, the user only needs to use the "MODEL MATH_ACH = /solution" statement to specify the outcome variable (here, *Math_Ach*) and to request final parameter estimates. Each of the "RANDOM int/" commands is used to present the level-two (C-C factors') equations, one for junior high schools and one for high schools. These two equations specify the intercept as varying randomly across the relevant factor.

Using SAS to estimate the unconditional model, the following fixed effect results correspond to those from HLM software:

```
Solution for Fixed Effects
```

Effect	Estimate	Standard Error	DF	t Value	Pr > |t|
Intercept	*50.2891*	1.2062	21.5	41.69	<.0001

The random effects estimates also correspond:

```
Covariance Parameter Estimates
```

Cov Parm	Subject	Estimate	Standard Error	Z Value	Pr Z
Intercept	jh_id	*9.4168*	4.0207	2.34	0.0096
Intercept	hs_id	*9.2170*	4.3668	2.11	0.0174
Residual		*80.9475*	4.0412	20.03	<.0001

Estimation of the model in which student *Math_SCc* is added as a grand-mean centered, fixed predictor of the intercept (see Equations 5.12 and 5.14) can be accomplished through modification of the "MODEL" statement as follows: "MODEL MATH_ACH = MATH_SCC/solution ddfm=kr;". The variance estimates and the fixed effect estimates (shown below) correspond with those from HLM (see Model 1 in Table 5.6).

```
Solution for Fixed Effects
```

		Standard			
Effect	Estimate	Error	DF	t Value	Pr > |t|
Intercept	*50.3060*	1.2231	21.6	41.13	<.0001
Math_SCc	*0.2253*	0.04447	807	5.07	<.0001

The SAS commands that can be used to estimate the model in which *Math_SCc* is assumed to vary randomly across both junior high and high schools (see Equation 5.15) are the same as for the fixed *Math_SCc* model except that the two RANDOM statements must be modified to identify that both the intercept and the slope (for *Math_SCc*) are being modeled as randomly varying. The two RANDOM statements become: "RANDOM INT MATH_SCC/ SUB=JH_ID;" and "RANDOM INT MATH_SCC/ SUB=HS_ID;". The results of the HLM analysis had indicated that the resulting slope residuals for junior highs, $\hat{\tau}_{b00}$, and for high schools, $\hat{\tau}_{c00}$, were very small. SAS reported that the G matrix (containing the variance components) was non-positive definite and, thus, failed to provide estimates of the two variances. This happens in scenarios such as the current one in which variance components' values are very close to zero. The SAS output for the variance components appears below, although the estimates' values are questionable (and thus, not highlighted) due to the problem with the G matrix.

```
Covariance Parameter Estimates
```

		Standard	Z	
Cov Parm Subject	Estimate	Error	Value	Pr Z
Intercept jh_id	9.6696	4.1037	2.36	0.0092
Math_SCc jh_id	0	.	.	.
Intercept hs_id	9.5699	4.4986	2.13	0.0167
Math_SCc hs_id	0	.	.	.
Residual	78.3822	3.9133	20.03	<.0001

To estimate a model in which a C-C factor predictor (for example, grand-mean centered, junior high *Math_RESc*) explains some of the variability in the intercept (as in Equation 5.17), the variable should be added to the "MODEL" statement which becomes: "MODEL MATH_ACH = MATH_SCC MATH_RESc/SOLUTION DDFM=KR;".

Including a Cross-Level Interaction

In the current model, variability was not substantial across junior high schools or high schools in the slope for *Math_SCc*. If variability had been substantial, then a researcher might use a C-C factor descriptor, *Z*, to explain some of that variability in the slope. In that case, Equation 5.17 would become

$$\begin{cases} \pi_{0(j_1 j_2)} = \theta_{000} + \gamma_{010} Z_{j_1} + b_{0 j_1 0} + c_{00 j_2} \\ \pi_{1(j_1 j_2)} = \theta_{100} + \gamma_{110} Z_{j_1} + b_{1 j_1 0} + c_{10 j_2} \end{cases}. \qquad (5.22)$$

When using SAS, the user should be aware[3] that the moderating variable translates into an interaction ($Z*X$) between the level-two variable, Z, and the level-one variable, X (*Math_SCc*). The cross-level interaction is easier to envision when the levels' equations (here, Equations 5.14 and 5.22) are combined into a single equation

$$Y_{i(j_1 j_2)} = \theta_{000} + \gamma_{010} Z_{j_1} + b_{0 j_1 0} + c_{00 j_2} + \qquad (5.23)$$

$$(\theta_{100} + \gamma_{110} Z_{j_1} + b_{1 j_1 0} + c_{10 j_2}) X_{i(j_1 j_2)} + e_{i(j_1 j_2)}.$$

The SAS commands needed to estimate the model that includes the cross-level interaction (see Equation 5.23) follow. (The reader should note the term "MATH_SCC*MATH_RESC" represents the cross-level interaction $Z*X$).

```
PROC MIXED DATA=DATA_2LVL_CC METHOD = ML COVTEST INFO IC UPDATE;
CLASS JH_id HS_id;
MODEL MATH_ACH = math_scC MATH_RESC math_scC*math_resc/solution
ddfm=kr;
RANDOM int math_scC/ sub=JH_id;
RANDOM int math_scC/ sub=HS_id;
run;
```

There are many other examples of two-level CCREMs that can be estimated and additional educational research data structures that necessitate their use. To complement this introduction to CCREM, an example of a three-level C-C data structure in which the cross-classification occurs at the highest level is presented along with a demonstration of the use of SAS to estimate the CCREM's parameters.

Three-Level CCREMs

A simple extension of the two-level C-C data structure described above could lead to the need to estimate a three-level CCREM. For example, a longitudinal analysis of students' achievement across secondary schools should consider the impact of junior high and high schools on that growth. In such a model, measurement occasions (level one) are considered nested within students (level two), who are cross-classified by junior high and high schools attended (C-C, level three factors).

Another example of a three-level CCREM could include modeling change over time in students' scores on a writing test. Each test might be

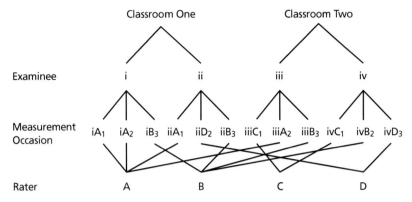

Figure 5.13 Network graph of cross-classified data structured with measurement occasion (level one) nested within examinee (level two) and cross-classified by rater and classroom (level three C-C factors).

graded by several raters who are not assigned to specific classrooms, and thus, students are cross-classified by classroom and rater. Figure 5.13 depicts this example (for a tiny sample solely used for clarification purposes) where the cross-classification occurs at the third level. Specifically, measurement occasions (level one) are nested within examinees (level two), who are cross-classified by raters and classroom (level three, C-C factors).

The next section provides the formulation of the three-level CCREM depicted in Figure 5.13. It also will demonstrate use of SAS PROC MIXED for estimating fixed and random effects parameters of a three-level CCREM in which the cross-classification (by two factors) occurs at level three. The contents of the dataset were simulated to match the three-level CCREM example just described.

Three-Level CCREM Example

The dataset being used to demonstrate estimation of the model in Figure 5.13 consists of 500 examinees with scores at four time points spaced 1 month apart. (Note the model depicted in Figure 5.13 only contains three times points). The *Time* variable is scored such that a zero represents the initial time point and it increases by a value of 1 (month) for each consecutive time point. The outcome variable, *Write*, is the student's score on a measure of writing ability. Identification variables distinguishing students, raters, and classrooms are included in the dataset. The dataset also includes the following variables: student's *Gender* (coded such that *Gender* = 0 for boys and *Gender* = 1 for girls), a measure of the rater's experience as a rater

(*Exper*), and a measure of the SES of students in the classroom (*SES*). For the *SES* variable, a higher value indicates a higher *SES* for the classroom.

To simplify the example, and because only four time points of data are available, the change over time in *Write* scores is assumed linear. The baseline unconditional model for a linear growth model would be, at level one,

$$Y_{ij(k_1k_2)} = \pi_{0j(k_1k_2)} + \pi_{1j(k_1k_2)}Time_{ij(k_1k_2)} + e_{ij(k_1k_2)}. \tag{5.24}$$

Four subscripts are needed for this three-level CCREM, such that $Y_{ij(k_1k_2)}$ is the writing score at time point i, for student j, in classroom k_2, and assessed by rater k_1. At the student level (two), in the unconditional model, the intercept and slope would be modeled as varying across students as follows:

$$\begin{cases} \pi_{0j(k_1k_2)} = \beta_{00(k_1k_2)} + u_{0j(k_1k_2)} \\ \pi_{1j(k_1k_2)} = \beta_{10(k_1k_2)} + u_{1j(k_1k_2)} \end{cases}. \tag{5.25}$$

Lastly, at level three (the cross-classification level), the intercept and slope would be modeled to vary randomly across raters (b_{00k_10} and b_{10k_10}, respectively) and classrooms (c_{000k_2} and c_{100k_2}, respectively):

$$\begin{cases} \beta_{00(k_1k_2)} = \theta_{0000} + b_{00k_10} + c_{000k_2} \\ \beta_{10(k_1k_2)} = \theta_{1000} + b_{10k_10} + c_{100k_2} \end{cases}. \tag{5.26}$$

As with linear models for change, the intercept represents the predicted outcome (here, writing score) when *Time* = 0. Thus, the intercept in the current model would represent the predicted *Write* score at the first measurement occasion. The slope represents the linear change in writing scores over time (given a change in *Time* of one unit).

A researcher might hypothesize that there are gender differences in the initial writing score (intercept) and in the linear change over time (slope). If that were the case, this level-two (examinee) descriptor could be added (uncentered) to Equation 5.25:

$$\begin{cases} \pi_{0j(k_1k_2)} = \beta_{00(k_1k_2)} + \beta_{01(k_1k_2)}Gender_{j(k_1k_2)} + u_{0j(k_1k_2)} \\ \pi_{1j(k_1k_2)} = \beta_{10(k_1k_2)} + \beta_{11(k_1k_2)}Gender_{j(k_1k_2)} + u_{1j(k_1k_2)} \end{cases}, \tag{5.27}$$

thereby introducing additional parameters that need to be considered at the third level. The researcher might hypothesize that the effect of *Gender* across raters and across classrooms is fixed, and thus, the following level-three model would need to be estimated:

$$\begin{cases} \beta_{00(k_1k_2)} = \theta_{0000} + b_{00k_10} + c_{000k_2} \\ \beta_{01(k_1k_2)} = \theta_{0100} \\ \beta_{10(k_1k_2)} = \theta_{1000} + b_{10k_10} + c_{100k_2} \\ \beta_{11(k_1k_2)} = \theta_{1100} \end{cases} \qquad (5.28)$$

Last, the researcher might be interested in exploring the relationship between a rater's (grand-mean centered) degree of experience and the examinee's initial score while controlling for possible classroom (grand-mean centered) *SES* differences in the starting point and in students' rate of change over time in their writing scores. If this were the case, Equation 5.28 would become

$$\begin{cases} \beta_{00(k_1k_2)} = \theta_{0000} + \gamma_{0010} Exper_{k_1} + \lambda_{0001} SES_{k_2} + b_{00k_10} + c_{000k_2} \\ \beta_{01(k_1k_2)} = \theta_{0100} \\ \beta_{10(k_1k_2)} = \theta_{1000} + \lambda_{1001} SES_{k_2} + b_{10k_10} + c_{100k_2} \\ \beta_{11(k_1k_2)} = \theta_{1100} \end{cases} \qquad (5.29)$$

Estimating a Three-level CCREM Using SAS PROC MIXED

The HCM2 function of HLM software's version 6 only can be used to estimate two-level CCREMs. SAS PROC MIXED (or MLwin) can be used to estimate parameters of CCREM that include additional levels. Use of SAS PROC MIXED to estimate a three-level CCREM is relatively simple and involves only the addition of the relevant additional "classes" (levels).

The SAS commands needed to estimate the baseline individual growth model (see Equations 5.21, 5.22, and 5.23) are

```
PROC MIXED DATA=DATA_3LVL_CC METHOD = ML COVTEST INFO IC UPDATE;
    CLASS STUDENT RATER CLASS;
    MODEL WRITE = /solution ddfm=kr;
    RANDOM int TIME / sub=STUDENT;
    RANDOM int TIME / sub=RATER;
    RANDOM int TIME / sub=CLASS;
    run;
```

The reader should notice that, again, the CLASS statement should be used to identify the ID distinguishing each of the levels. In the current model, level two is the student level, and at "level three" we have the two cross-classified factors (rater and classroom). Computation time increases as the models become more complex. It took over 14 minutes to estimate this simplest baseline unconditional model. The random effects estimates are recorded in the bottom rows of the unconditional model's estimates appearing in Table 5.7. The SAS output for the variance estimates appears below.

```
Covariance Parameter Estimates
```

Cov Parm	Subject	Estimate	Standard Error	Z Value	Pr Z
Intercept	student	24.4145	1.8802	12.99	<.0001
time	student	24.3558	1.6616	14.66	<.0001
Intercept	rater	27.5732	10.1623	2.71	0.0033
time	rater	3.9558	1.8083	2.19	0.0143
Intercept	class	20.5342	7.8731	2.61	0.0046
time	class	13.6660	5.1747	2.64	0.0041
Residual		6.2836	0.2808	22.38	<.0001

The results suggest that substantial variability existed in the initial *Write* score across students ($\hat{\tau}_{u00} = 24.4$, $p < .0001$), raters ($\hat{\tau}_{b000} = 27.6$, $p < .01$), and classrooms ($\hat{\tau}_{c000} = 20.5$, $p < .01$). There also was substantial variability in students' linear growth over time in *Write* scores across students ($\hat{\tau}_{u11} = 24.4$, $p < .0001$), raters ($\hat{\tau}_{b100} = 4.0$, $p < .05$), and classrooms ($\hat{\tau}_{c100} = 13.7$, $p < .01$). The fixed effects estimates appear below.

```
Solution for Fixed Effects
```

Effect	Estimate	Standard Error	DF	t Value	Pr > |t|
Intercept	19.2487	1.7161	29.9	11.22	<.0001
time	6.4299	1.0605	23.6	6.06	<.0001

Interpretation of the fixed effects estimates indicate that the average initial (*Time* = 0) *Write* score, predicted to be 19.2, differed significantly from zero ($p < .0001$). Table 5.7 includes the fixed and random effects estimates from the baseline unconditional, three-level CCREM.

Estimation of the model in which *Gender* is added to address possible gender differences in the intercept and growth over time (see Equation 5.28) can be accomplished using the following syntax

```
PROC MIXED DATA=DATA_3LVL_CC_3 METHOD = ML COVTEST INFO IC UPDATE;
    CLASS STUDENT RATER CLASS;
    MODEL WRITE = TIME GENDER GENDER*TIME/solution ddfm=kr;
    RANDOM int TIME/ sub=STUDENT;
    RANDOM int TIME/ sub=RATER;
    RANDOM int TIME/ sub=CLASS;
    run;
```

For this model (Model A in Table 5.7), *Gender* has been added as a predictor of the intercept (by including *Gender* in the MODEL WRITE = statement).

TABLE 5.7   Parameter Estimates for the Three-Level CCREMs

			Model estimated		
		Uncond.	Model A	Model B	Model C
Fixed effects					
First time point					
Intercept	θ_{0000}	19.2**	17.8**	18.6**	18.5**
Student *Gender*	θ_{0100}		2.9**	2.9**	2.9**
Rater *Exper*	γ_{0010}			1.3*	1.3*
Class *SES*	γ_{0001}			−0.5	
Time slope					
Intercept	θ_{1000}	6.4**	6.0**	6.1**	6.0**
Student *Gender*	θ_{1100}		0.8	0.8	0.8
Class *SES*	γ_{1001}			−2.5	
Random effects					
Intercept					
Student	τ_{u00}	24.4	22.3	22.3	22.3
Rater	τ_{b000}	27.6	28.1	13.0	12.8
Class	τ_{c000}	20.5	19.4	19.6	19.8
Time slope					
Student	τ_{u11}	24.4	24.1	24.1	24.1
Rater	τ_{b100}	4.0	3.9	3.9	3.9
Class	τ_{c100}	13.7	13.5	12.0	13.5

Note: Uncond. = unconditional. Model A is described by Equations 5.21, 5.27, and 5.28; Model B is described by Equations 5.21, 5.27, and 5.29; Model C is the same as Model B but does not include SES as predictor of the slope or the intercept.
**$p < .001$; *$p < .05$

Addition of the interaction term *Gender*Time* to the MODEL WRITE = statement line models *Gender* as a predictor of the growth in *Write* over time. The relationship between *Gender* and *Write* is modeled as fixed across raters and classrooms. Estimates of the model follow and are presented in Table 5.7.

Covariance Parameter Estimates

		Standard	Z	
Cov Parm Subject	Estimate	Error	Value	Pr Z
Intercept student	*22.2791*	1.7424	12.79	<.0001
time student	*24.1282*	1.6462	14.66	<.0001
Intercept rater	*28.0976*	10.3005	2.73	0.0032
time rater	*3.8833*	1.7788	2.18	0.0145
Intercept class	*19.4152*	7.4559	2.60	0.0046

time class	*13.5033*	5.1167	2.64	0.0042
Residual	*6.2933*	0.2816	22.35	<.0001

Solution for Fixed Effects

Effect	Estimate	Standard Error	DF	t Value	Pr > |t|
Intercept	*17.7770*	1.7209	31	10.33	<.0001
time	*6.0246*	1.0789	25.8	5.58	<.0001
gender	*2.8603*	0.4731	478	6.05	<.0001
time*gender	*0.8042*	0.4604	482	1.75	0.0813

These results indicate that *Gender* was not a statistically significant predictor of students' linear growth in *Write* scores ($\hat{\theta}_{1100} = 0.8$, $p > .05$). However, there appears to be a significant difference between boys and girls in their initial *Write* scores ($\hat{\theta}_{0100} = 2.9$, $p < .0001$). Given *Gender* is coded with *Gender* = 0 for boys and *Gender* = 1 for girls, the positive effect indicates that girls are predicted to have initial *Write* scores that are almost 3 points higher than boys. Adding *Gender* as a predictor reduced the student-level variance ($\hat{\tau}_{u00}$) from 24.4 to 22.3. Last, given the small gender effect in the slope, it is not surprising that the value of the slope ($\hat{\theta}_{1000} = 6.0$) was not changed much with the inclusion of *Gender* as a predictor of the slope from the unconditional model's estimate of θ_{1000}.

For the sake of completeness, if a researcher wished to estimate a model in which the *Gender* effect (on both slope and intercept) varied randomly across raters and classrooms, then the last two statements would be modified to be "RANDOM int GENDER GENDER*TIME TIME/ sub=RATER;" and "RANDOM int GENDER GENDER*TIME TIME/ sub=CLASS;".

Given the slight gender difference detected in students' growth in *Write* over time, *Gender* was retained in the model as a fixed predictor of the intercept and the slope (see Equation 5.27). In addition, a rater's grand-mean-centered level of experience (*Exper*) and classroom grand-mean-centered *SES* were added as predictors of the intercept. Last, grand-mean-centered *SES* also was added as a predictor of students' growth in *Write* over time (see Equation 5.29 for the level-three model). The following SAS syntax was used to estimate this model:

```
PROC MIXED DATA=DATA_3LVL_CC_3
METHOD = ML COVTEST INFO IC UPDATE;
    CLASS STUDENT RATER CLASS;
    MODEL WRITE = TIME GENDER GENDER*TIME EXPER SES SES*TIME
        /solution ddfm=kr;
    RANDOM int time/ sub=STUDENT;
    RANDOM int time / sub=RATER;
    RANDOM int time / sub=CLASS;
    run;
```

The fixed- and random-effects estimates appear below in the SAS output format. They also are reported under Model B in Table 5.7.

Covariance Parameter Estimates

Cov Parm Subject	Estimate	Standard Error	Z Value	Pr Z
Intercept student	22.2906	1.7436	12.78	<.0001
time student	24.1332	1.6468	14.65	<.0001
Intercept rater	12.9557	5.4188	2.39	0.0084
time rater	3.8681	1.7739	2.18	0.0146
Intercept class	19.6079	7.6391	2.57	0.0051
time class	12.0328	4.6248	2.60	0.0046
Residual	.2933	0.2816	22.35	<.0001

Solution for Fixed Effects

Effect	Estimate	Standard Error	DF	t Value	Pr > |t|
Intercept	18.5557	1.4540	30	12.76	<.0001
time	6.0998	1.0388	26.3	5.87	<.0001
gender	2.8844	0.4730	478	6.10	<.0001
time*gender	0.8019	0.4604	482	1.74	0.0822
exper	1.2965	0.3293	14.8	3.94	0.0014
SES	-0.4730	2.4242	16.9	-0.20	0.8476
time*SES	-2.4712	1.8576	17.1	-1.33	0.2009

The results indicate that *SES* was not a statistically significant predictor of the intercept ($\hat{\gamma}_{0001} = -0.5$, $p > .05$) nor of the slope ($\hat{\gamma}_{1001} = -2.5$, $p > .05$). A final model in which *SES* was removed from the level-three equations for the intercept and slope then was estimated:

$$\begin{cases} \beta_{00(k_1 k_2)} = \theta_{0000} + \gamma_{0010} Exper_{k_1} + b_{00k_1 0} + c_{000k_2} \\ \beta_{01(k_1 k_2)} = \theta_{0100} \\ \beta_{10(k_1 k_2)} = \theta_{1000} + b_{10k_1 0} + c_{100k_2} \\ \beta_{11(k_1 k_2)} = \theta_{1100} \end{cases} \quad (5.30)$$

The parameter estimate results appear below and in Model C's column in Table 5.7.

Covariance Parameter Estimates

Cov Parm Subject	Estimate	Standard Error	Z Value	Pr Z
Intercept student	22.2927	1.7438	12.78	<.0001
time student	24.1281	1.6462	14.66	<.0001

Intercept rater	*12.8270*	5.3082	2.42	0.0078
time rater	*3.8876*	1.7798	2.18	0.0145
Intercept class	*19.8014*	7.6417	2.59	0.0048
time class	*13.5065*	5.1177	2.64	0.0042

Solution for Fixed Effects

Effect	Estimate	Standard Error	DF	t Value	Pr > |t|
Intercept	*18.5464*	1.4544	29.9	12.75	<.0001
time	*6.0294*	1.0791	25.8	5.59	<.0001
gender	*2.8849*	0.4730	478	6.10	<.0001
time*gender	*0.8031*	0.4604	482	1.74	0.0817
exper	*1.3045*	0.3259	15.1	4.00	0.0011

SES was not a statistically significant predictor of the slope nor of the intercept; therefore, it is not surprising that the results do not change much between Models B and C. A significant *Gender* difference in initial *Write* that favors girls over boys was identified ($\hat{\theta}_{0100} = 2.9$, $p < .0001$). No significant *Gender* difference was found in monthly growth in Write scores ($\hat{\theta}_{1100} = 0.8$, $p > .05$). The experience of the rater was related significantly to initial *Write* scores ($\gamma_{0010} = 1.3$, $p < .01$).

If Model C were chosen as the final model, the researcher likely would investigate additional rater and classroom descriptors to help explain the variability across raters and classrooms in students' first *Write* score and in their monthly change in *Write* scores, and in their monthly change in write scores. Over and above model B, only some of the variability across raters was explained (using the measure of a rater's experience) in this final model. The remaining random effects estimates did not change significantly from the initial unconditional model after the addition of the relevant predictors.

SUMMARY

This chapter has described general scenarios in which C-C data structures might be encountered and the corresponding basic formulation of the two- and three-level CCREM. Use of HLM software for estimation of parameters in a two-level CCREM was described. Use of SAS PROC MIXED also was detailed for estimation of two- and three-level models in which the cross-classification occurred at the highest level. The reader is encouraged to explore these same analyses using MLwin software, another commonly used multilevel modeling program.

The CCREMs discussed here are of the simplest form. They only involved two cross-classified factors at a single level and only one level of C-C factors.

The reader is encouraged to read additional texts that describe modeling of these more complex models that commonly are encountered in educational research. Another simplification encountered in this chapter is the modeling only of interval-scaled outcomes. The CCREM also is useful for modeling dichotomous and ordinal outcomes for variables, such as graduation or recidivism, or as another extension of the multilevel measurement model for use with multiple-choice item scores (Beretvas, Meyers, & Rodriguez, 2005).

The CCREM also might be extended for scenarios in which units are cross-classified by *more than one unit of a C-C factor*. For example, given the educational accountability movement and the interest in value-added assessment, longitudinal analyses of students' achievement scores frequently are analyzed. The modeling of students within junior high and high schools (as demonstrated in the two-level model, above) would work *only* if students had attended only one junior high and one high school. This is unrealistic as many students attend (are cross-classified by) more than one junior high and/or high school. The value added by each school should be modeled appropriately. Models in which units are cross-classified by more then one unit of a C-C factor are termed "multiple membership" models. Readers are referred to Goldstein (2003) and to Rasbash and Browne (2001) to see more demonstrations of the utility and estimation of multiple membership models.

The sophistication and flexibility of CCREMs are useful in modeling some of the data structures commonly encountered in educational research. However, there are always tradeoffs. Estimation of these models is computationally very complex and, thus, is time-consuming. While the ability to estimate these models is facilitated greatly by easy implementation with various multilevel software packages, the user still must be dedicated to ensuring full understanding of the models' parameters and assumptions. In addition, due to the complexity of these models, much larger overall and per-cell sample sizes are needed for precise and accurate estimation of the parameters (Meyers & Beretvas, in press). Despite these caveats and considerations, CCREMs allow researchers to model data that is not purely hierarchical since cross-classified structures occur quite frequently within educational data. Therefore, CCREMs provide an important analytic addition to the multilevel modeling arsenal of modeling tools. See this volume's website for access to all simulated data used for the examples presented here.

NOTES

1. Scores on some predictors in the applied examples are centered (either using grand-mean centering or uncentered) to facilitate interpretation of the relevant model's parameters. The reader is encouraged to review the intro-

ductory chapters in this book that provide detailed expositions of the use of centering.
2. See chapter 12 and/or Littell et al., 2006 for additional information on the use of SAS for mixed models.
3. The reader is encouraged to review the sections of introductory chapters in this book and other sources (such as Snijders & Bosker, 1999) that discuss cross-level interactions.

REFERENCES

Beretvas, S. N., Meyers, J. L., & Rodriguez, R. A. (2005). The cross-classified multilevel measurement model: An explanation and demonstration. *Journal of Applied Measurement, 6*, 322–341.

Fielding, A. (2002). Teaching groups as foci for evaluating performance in cost-effectiveness of GCE Advanced Level provision: Some practical methodological innovations. *School Effectiveness and School Improvement, 13*, 225–246.

Garner, C. L., & Raudenbush, S. W. (1991). Neighborhood effects on educational attainment: A multilevel analysis. *Sociology of Education, 64*, 251–262.

Goldstein, H. (2003). *Multilevel statistical models* (3rd ed.). London: Edward Arnold/New York: Halsted.

Goldstein, H., Rasbash, J., Plewis, I., Draper, D., Browne, W., Yang, M., et al. (1998). *A user's guide to MLwiN.* London: University of London, Multilevel Models Project.

Goldstein, H., & Sammons, P. (1997). The influence of secondary and junior schools on sixteen year examination performance: A cross-classified multilevel analysis. *School Effectiveness and School Improvement, 8*, 219–230.

Hox, J. J. (2002). *Multilevel analysis: Techniques and applications.* Mahwah, NJ: Lawrence Erlbaum Associates.

Meyers, J. L., & Beretvas, S. N. (in press). The impact of the inappropriate modeling of cross-classified data structures. *Multivariate Behavioral Research.*

Pickery, J., Loosveldt, G., & Carton, A. (2001). The effects of interviewer and respondent characteristics on response behavior in panel surveys. *Sociological Methods & Research, 29*, 509–523.

Rasbash, J., & Browne, W. J. (2001). Modeling non-hierarchical structures. In A. H. Leyland & H. Goldstein (Eds.), *Multilevel modeling of health statistics* (pp. 93–105). Chichester: John Wiley & Sons.

Rasbash, J., Browne, W. J., Goldstein, H., Yang, M., Plewis, I., Healy, M., et al. (2000). *A user's guide to MLwiN.* London: University of London, Multilevel Models Project.

Raudenbush, S. and Bryk, A.S. (2002). *Hierarchical linear models: Applications and data analysis methods* (2nd edition). Thousand Oaks, CA: Sage Publications, Inc.

Raudenbush, S. W., Bryk, A.S., and Congdon, R. (2004). *HLM6: Hierarchical linear and nonlinear modeling* [Computer software]. Chicago: Scientific Software International.

SAS Institute Inc. (1999). *The SAS system for Windows Release 8.02* [Computer software]. Cary, NC: SAS Institute Inc.

Singer, J. (1998). Using SAS PROC MIXED to fit multilevel models, hierarchical models, and individual growth models. *Journal of Educational and Behavioral Statistics, 23*, 323–355.

Snijders, T. and Bosker, R. (1999). *Multilevel Analysis*. Thousand Oaks, CA: Sage Publications, Inc.

CHAPTER 6

MULTILEVEL LOGISTIC MODELS FOR DICHOTOMOUS AND ORDINAL DATA

Ann A. O'Connell, Jessica Goldstein, H. Jane Rogers, and C. Y. Joanne Peng

INTRODUCTION

So far, the models covered in this book have assumed a normal or approximately normal distribution for the outcome of interest, and thus for the errors across the multiple levels of the model. However, many response variables of interest in education and the social sciences do not fit the normal distribution framework; most often, these non-normal outcomes involve dependent variables with discrete or limited response categories. Common statistical approaches for analyzing these kinds of data are drawn from a class of linear models where the outcomes follow a distribution from the exponential family. These models are referred to as *generalized linear models* and can be applied to binary outcomes, count data, and ordinal or categorical data. In fact, models for normally distributed outcomes—often referred to as *general linear models*—are simply a special case of the generalized linear model where the normal distribution is used to describe the distribution of model errors. In the generalized case, binary outcomes typically are

Multilevel Modeling of Educational Data, pages 199–242

analyzed using the logistic distribution; count data by Poisson distribution; and ordinal/categorical data by the cumulative logistic or multinomial logistic models. This chapter presents models for two types of categorical responses: logistic models for (a) binary response variables and (b) ordinal response variables.

Consistent with the literature for single-level response models, multilevel analyses for categorical, count, or other types of non-normal data often are referred to as *hierarchical generalized linear models* (HGLM), although they also have been called *generalized linear mixed models* (Fielding, 2003; McCulloch & Searle, 2001). The application of generalized linear models in a multilevel framework parallels their applications in single-level research designs. For example, studies on factors related to dropping out of school, attaining proficiency for specific academic tasks, or enrolling in advanced placement courses in high school involve dichotomous outcomes that are analyzed best through logistic regression procedures.[1] When data is collected across individuals in the same classrooms, schools, or regions, we expect these dichotomous outcomes to contain a within-context dependency, yielding a situation that requires statistical adjustment for the cluster effect through multilevel research designs and analyses. In some research situations, group- or context-level variables such as teacher preparation, school-funding, or school-climate may be used to help explain differences across contexts in the relationships between individual-level variables and the outcome of interest. In short, the logistic regression coefficients are presumed to vary across contexts, and HGLM provides the methodology with which to model this variation. The use of a multilevel approach to analyze dichotomous and other forms of non-normal data is a direct extension of the application of these kinds of models for single-level data.

Our presentation of HGLM analyses uses HLM version 6.04 (Raudenbush, Bryk, Cheong & Congdon, 2004). Our multilevel perspective was adapted from Dobson's (2002) single-level approach for describing generalized linear models. Accordingly, throughout our examples we emphasize four elements of multilevel model building:

1. expressing the outcome of interest in terms of a collection of explanatory or predictor variables,
2. parameter estimation and interpretation,
3. assessing quality of fit of the multilevel model to the data, and
4. statistical inference and hypothesis testing.

We begin with some background on the data set used for our examples and then provide a brief review of single-level generalized linear models for categorical data. Next, we provide the conceptual background for multilevel logistic models for dichotomous outcomes and the multilevel proportional odds model for ordinal outcomes. After setting the stage conceptually, we present specific data examples in-depth for each of these two multilevel models, highlighting critical aspects of each approach. Extensions to these models in other educational contexts are discussed in the final section, along with a brief review of some software considerations.

BACKGROUND: THE EARLY CHILDHOOD LONGITUDINAL STUDY—KINDERGARTEN COHORT

The data for the examples contained in this chapter were drawn from the Early Childhood Longitudinal Study-Kindergarten Cohort (ECLS-K),[2] which tracks the arithmetic and reading progress of a nationally representative sample of kindergarten children through the completion of eighth grade (eighth-grade data are expected to be released in 2008). In the ECLS-K, random samples of children were drawn from selected schools. The examples in this chapter analyze proficiency data for a subsample of these children as they neared the end of first grade.

The ECLS-K is a program of the U.S. National Center for Education Statistics (NCES) that, in part, assesses student proficiency in early literacy, mathematics, and general knowledge as a series of "stepping-stones," which reflect an ordinal set of skills that form the foundation for further learning (West, Denton, & Germino-Hausken, 2000). In the kindergarten and first-grade releases of the ECLS-K, proficiency for early numeracy is defined using a series of five hierarchical skills outlined in Table 6.1. Proficiency for these skills is assumed to follow the Guttman model so that mastering one skill requires the mastery of the previous skills (NCES, 2002).[3] The proficiency assessment contains clusters of items representing each hierarchical skill, and proficiency criteria were met if a child successfully answered three out of the four items within each cluster. The highest proficiency level attained by each child was recorded in the database, with level 0 indicating

TABLE 6.1   Proficiency Categories for the ECLS-K Measures for Early Numeracy

Proficiency category	Brief description
0	Did not pass level 1
1	Can identify numbers and shapes
2	Can understand relative size and recognize patterns
3	Can understand ordinality and sequencing
4	Can solve simple addition and subtraction problems
5	Can solve simple multiplication and division problems

that the first level had not been reached successfully.[4] This ordinal proficiency variable is referred to here as PROFMATH and has six levels. We also used this variable to create a dichotomous version of proficiency, PROF45, with levels 4 and 5 representing "proficient in computation" versus all lower levels as "not proficient." Accordingly, our multilevel logistic examples use PROF45 as the outcome, and our multilevel proportional odds examples use the entire range of the ordinal scale, PROFMATH.

GENERALIZED LINEAR MODELS

Although this chapter assumes that the reader has a basic understanding of logistic regression methods for single-level data, such as covered in Cizek and Fitzgerald (1999), Fox (1997), Menard (1995), and Pampel (2000), a brief introduction to logistic models is included here. More comprehensive treatments of logistic regression may be found in Agresti (1990, 1996), Hosmer and Lemeshow (2000), and McCullagh and Nelder (1989). In addition, O'Connell (2000, 2006) and Peng and Nichols (2003) provide instructive applications of logistic and logit-type models to ordinal and multinomial single-level data, respectively. In this chapter, our discussion centers around multilevel extensions of single-level logistic models for binary and ordinal response variables with applications to education data. For additional background on these models, readers may want to review Wong and Mason (1985), who provide technical and historical information for multilevel logistic models; Hedeker and Gibbons (1994) and Hedeker and Mermelstein (1998) do the same for multilevel ordinal models.

The terminology and estimation strategies for fitting HGLMs are fairly straightforward extensions of those used for HLMs, coupled with modifications for the nature of the response variable. We will begin, however, with a single-level characterization of a generalized linear model (GLM). GLMs are characterized by three related model components:

- A *random component*, for which the dependent variable Y follows one of the distributions from the exponential family, such as the normal, binomial, or inverse Gaussian;
- A *linear component*, which describes how a function, η, of the dependent variable Y depends on a collection of explanatory variables; and
- A *link function*, which describes the transformation of the expected value of the dependent variable Y to η (Fox, 1997).

The distribution of the random component will define the kind of generalized linear model that is used to represent the data (Liao, 1994).

When the random component is specified by the normal distribution, the standard linear regression model for the response variable Y is obtained through the *identity* link function:

$$E(Y_i) = \eta_i = \beta_0 + \beta_1 X_{i1} + \beta_2 X_{i2} + \dots \beta_q X_{iq}. \tag{6.1}$$

The *identity* link does not transform the dependent variable; the expected values for Y are summarized over the collection of explanatory variables, and there is a linear relationship between the expected values and the regression coefficients. Further, the errors from this model, $Y_i - E(Y_i)$, are assumed to be $N(0, \sigma^2)$ as well as homoscedastic.

For categorical dependent variables, such as dichotomous or ordinal outcomes, these familiar assumptions of the standard linear regression model no longer hold. However, if a suitable transformation of the dependent variable is applied, many of the useful model building strategies and interpretive properties of standard linear regression are still applicable. For generalized linear models, these transformations are from the exponential family (Fox, 1997; Liao, 1994; McCullough & Nelder, 1989; Nelder & Wedderburn, 1972). Preferences for specific distributions and kinds of link functions exist, but one of the most commonly selected link functions is the logit link; other options are described in McCullough and Nelder (1989). The logit link offers a connection between odds and probability, which are natural and familiar quantities for describing the distribution of a categorical variable. By definition, the logit is the natural log of the odds. These terms are explained below.

We focus the remainder of our discussion in this section on dichotomous variables and then describe extensions to ordinal outcomes in a later section. The usual approach to analyzing dichotomous outcomes is to begin by identifying and coding the two possible outcomes as either success ($Y = 1$) or failure ($Y = 0$). Thus, the mean value of Y becomes a *conditional* probability, $P(Y = 1 \mid \underline{x})$; that is, the expected value represents the estimated proportion of successes given a particular set of values, $\underline{x}$, for the explanatory variables (or a local average if a predictor is continuous rather than discrete). However, since there are only two possible outcomes for the dependent variable, the errors from a model that seeks to predict probability of success are not normally distributed. In fact, the errors are heteroscedastic; the variance itself depends on the predicted values.

The probability distribution often associated with a dichotomous outcome is the *Bernoulli* distribution, which is a special case of the *binomial* distribution. The binomial distribution arises from counts of the number of successes in m attempts or trials. The Bernoulli distribution refers to a situation in which there is only one trial per person, and thus this single observation can be classified as either "success" or "failure." This is typically the case for most dichotomous data; that is, we don't count the number of times a student reaches proficiency for a specific arithmetic skill. Rather, we observe and record whether or not a student has attained proficiency at the time of data collection. In a Bernoulli distribution, the mean or expected value of Y is the proportion of observations possessing the characteristic of interest, such as $Y = 1$; the proportion or mean is written as $\pi(\underline{x})$ for the proportion of successes given a specific set of values for the collection of explanatory variables, $\underline{x}$. For a Bernoulli random variable, the variance is a function of the mean, $\pi(\underline{x})*(1 - \pi(\underline{x}))$; this is the probability of success times the probability of failure.

Predicting the probability of success seems like a reasonable goal for the analysis of a dichotomous variable, but the relationship between probability of success and the collection of explanatory variables is inherently non-linear, requiring data transformations or other adjustments to aid in the process of deriving a good prediction model. If standard linear regression were applied to the dichotomous outcome data (i.e., the linear probability model), we would find that predictions could fall below 0 or exceed 1; these would be implausible values for predictions of probability. Generally, a non-linear relationship between predicted probability and the predictors is expected, where probability predictions begin to taper off somewhat and approach zero or one more gradually than the predictions provided by a straight-line model (Agresti, 1990; Hosmer & Lemeshow, 2000). The resulting pattern of this gradual trend is referred to as an S-shaped curve. Figure 6.1 illustrates this pattern for a hypothetical explanatory variable and probability of "success" for a dichotomous variable Y.

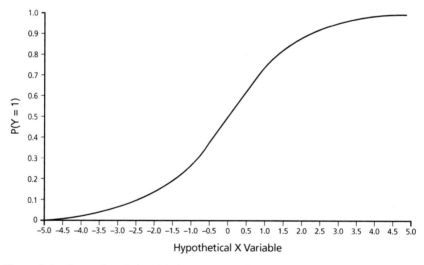

Figure 6.1 Example relationship between continuous predictor and probability of "success."

These three issues—(1) probability predictions needing to be constrained between 0 and 1, (2) heteroscedastic errors, and (3) an S-shaped relationship of interest—can be addressed by applying models that allow a curvilinear relationship between $\pi(\underline{x})$ and $\underline{x}$. The logistic distribution is one of the most useful distributions for modeling this non-linear relationship between probability and a collection of predictors, primarily because it tends to be very easy to use and results in a fairly straightforward interpretation of predictor effects.

Logistic analyses for binary outcomes attempt to model the odds of an event's occurrence and to estimate the effects of explanatory variables on these odds. The odds for an event is a quotient that conveniently compares the probability that an event occurs (referred to as "success") to the probability that it does not occur (referred to as "failure," or the complement of success). When the probability of success is greater than the probability of failure, the odds are greater than 1.0; if the two outcomes are equally likely, the odds are 1.0; and if the probability of success is less than the probability of failure, the odds are less than 1.0.

For the ECLS-K data described above, we are interested in studying the attainment of mathematics proficiency category 4 (addition and subtraction) or 5 (multiplication and division) among children at the end of first grade. The outcome can be described as binary: a child attains proficiency in category 4 or 5 (success) or the child does not (failure). The odds of proficiency are computed from the sample data by dividing the probability of reaching categories 4 or 5 (scored as $Y = 1$) by the probability of not reaching categories 4 or 5 (scored as $Y = 0$):

$$\text{Odds} = \frac{P(\text{``success''})}{P(\text{``failure''})} = \frac{P(Y=1)}{P(Y=0)} = \frac{P(Y=1)}{1-P(Y=1)}. \tag{6.2}$$

To examine the impact on the odds of an independent variable, such as gender or the number of family risk characteristics, we construct the odds-ratio (OR), which compares the odds for different values of the explanatory variable. For example, if we want to compare the odds of reaching proficiency between males (coded $x = 1$) and females (coded $x = 0$), we would compute the following ratio:

$$OR = \frac{Odds(\text{success} \mid male)}{Odds(\text{success} \mid female)} = \frac{\dfrac{P(Y=1 \mid x=1)}{1-P(Y=1 \mid x=1)}}{\dfrac{P(Y=1 \mid x=0)}{1-P(Y=1 \mid x=0)}}. \tag{6.3}$$

Odds ratios are bounded below by 0 but have no upper bound; thus, they can range from 0 to infinity. An OR of 1.0 indicates that an explanatory variable has no effect on the odds of success; that is, the odds of success for males are the same as the odds of success for females. Small values of the OR (< 1.0) indicate that the odds of success for the persons with the value of x used in the denominator (0 = females) are greater than the odds of success for the persons with a higher value of x used in the numerator (1 = males). The opposite is true for values of the OR that exceed 1.0; in that case, the odds for males of being proficient are greater than the odds for females. The nature and type of coding used for the explanatory variables becomes important in interpretation; we use simple dummy or referent coding in the examples in this chapter. Other approaches to coding categorical independent variables can change the interpretation of that variable's effect in the model; discussions of alternative approaches to categorizing qualitative data in logistic regression models can be found in Hosmer and Lemeshow (2000).

The OR is a measure of association between the binary outcome and an explanatory variable that provides an indication of how odds for the outcome ($Y = 1$) change as the explanatory variable increases or decreases. Although we seek a model for the probability of success, we use logistic regression to model the odds or, more specifically, to model the natural (base e) log of the odds, referred to as the *logits* of a distribution. These logits then can be used to determine variable effects and predicted probabilities given the collection of explanatory variables.

The logit transformation has many desirable properties. First, it eliminates the skewness inherent in estimates of the OR (Agresti, 1996), which can range from zero to infinity with a value of one indicating the *null* case of *no change in the odds*. The logit ranges from negative infinity to positive infinity, which eliminates the boundary problems associated with both the OR and probability. The logit model is linear in the parameters, which means that the effects of explanatory variables on the log of the odds are additive. The null case of no change in the odds is characterized by a parameter estimate of zero in the logit metric, since $\ln(1) = 0$, so that statistical tests around a null hypothesis of zero are conceptually familiar. Thus, the model is easy to work with and allows for application of model-building strategies that mirror those of ordinary linear regression.

This process can be extended to include more than one explanatory variable. If we let $\pi(Y = 1 \mid X_1, X_2, \ldots X_q) = \pi(\underline{x})$ represent the probability of "success," or the outcome of interest (e.g., a child being in proficiency category 4 or 5), for a given set of q explanatory variables, then the logistic model can be written as

$$\ln(Y') = \text{logit}\left[\pi(\underline{x})\right] = \ln\left(\frac{\pi(\underline{x})}{1 - \pi(\underline{x})}\right) = \beta_0 + \beta_1 X_1 + \beta_2 X_2 + \ldots \beta_q X_q. \quad (6.4)$$

In this expression, Y' is simply a convenient way to emphasize the odds as a transformed outcome variable: rather than predicting Y directly, we are predicting the (log of the) odds of $Y = 1$. The link function describes the process of "linking" the original Y to the transformed outcome: $\eta = \ln(Y') = \ln[\pi(\underline{x})/(1 - \pi(\underline{x}))]$, which is referred to as the *logit link*. Solving for $\pi(\underline{x})$ gives us the familiar expression for the logistic regression model for the probability of success:

$$\pi(\underline{x}) = \frac{\exp(\beta_0 + \beta_1 X_1 + \beta_2 X_2 + \ldots \beta_q X_q)}{1 + \exp(\beta_0 + \beta_1 X_1 + \beta_2 X_2 + \ldots \beta_q X_q)} \tag{6.5}$$

$$= \frac{1}{1 + \exp[-(\beta_0 + \beta_1 X_1 + \beta_2 X_2 + \ldots \beta_q X_q)]}.$$

For the ith person in a sample, the predicted logit can be written as

$$Logit_i(\pi(\underline{x})) = \eta_i = b_0 + b_1 X_{i1} + b_2 X_{i2} + \ldots b_q X_{iq}. \tag{6.6}$$

The logit, η_i, represents the log of the odds of "success" for the ith person, conditional on the set of predictors, and it provides a convenient metric in which to work: logits are continuous, and the logit model is linear in the parameters. A shorthand expression for estimating probability based on the predicted logit for the ith person is

$$\pi(\underline{x}) = \frac{\exp(\eta_i)}{1 + \exp(\eta_i)}. \tag{6.7}$$

Note that Equation 6.6 contains no specific error term. In the binomial distribution, the variance is a function of the conditional mean, $\pi(\underline{x})$, and thus the errors are described already by the choice of the binomial distribution rather than estimated separately (Hosmer & Lemeshow, 2000).

Parameter estimation in logistic regression is based on principles and methods of maximum likelihood and thus involves special iterative methods. This approach yields parameter estimates that "maximize the probability of obtaining the observed set of data" (Hosmer & Lemeshow, 2000, p. 8). A value of −2 times the log-likelihood (−2LL) for a particular fitted model can be used to assess quality of fit through a general likelihood ratio test for comparison of competing models. The "deviance" of a model often is referred to as −2LL and, in a sense, represents how poorly a model fits the data. If deviance is reduced by a competing nested model, the competing model is preferred. A discussion of different approaches to assessing model fit for single-level logistic regression models is outside the scope of this chapter (see Menard, 2000, for work in this area), but we shall return to some of these ideas as we examine the models and applications of HGLMs.

THE MULTILEVEL LOGISTIC MODEL
FOR DICHOTOMOUS OUTCOMES

So far, we have reviewed logit models for the analysis of single-level dichotomous data. In many research situations, however, observations are clustered within groups; educational data provide the most obvious context. Typically, children are nested within classrooms or schools, and schools are nested within districts or larger metropolitan units. It is likely that group-level variables might have an effect on an individual's response outcome, thus requiring a multilevel perspective of the data. Continuing our earlier example, if we let Y_{ij} represent the proficiency response (0 or 1) for the ith child in the jth school, where 1 indicates the child having reached proficiency level 4 or 5, then the expected value of Y is likely to vary based on child characteristics as well as by school characteristics. The sampling distribution for this collection of dichotomous data is Bernoulli, with $E(Y_{ij} \mid \pi_{ij}) = \pi_{ij}$ and $\text{Var}(Y_{ij} \mid \pi_{ij}) = \pi_{ij}(1 - \pi_{ij})$, where π_{ij} is the probability of reaching proficiency for the ith child in the jth school. The proportion of children reaching proficiency for a given school, P_j, will vary across schools depending on the proficiency outcomes for the randomly selected children sampled from within that school. The commonly used model for the link function is the logit link, and the resulting multilevel model resembles the single-level model, although now the regression coefficients from level one are allowed to vary across the different schools in the sample.

$$\text{Level 1:} \quad \eta_{ij} = \beta_{0j} + \beta_{1j}X_{1ij} + \beta_{2j}X_{2ij} + \ldots \beta_{qj}X_{qij}. \tag{6.8}$$

$$\text{Level 2:} \quad \beta_{qj} = \gamma_{q0} + \sum_{s=1}^{S_q} \gamma_{qs}W_{sj} + u_{qj}.$$

This is the most general expression for the multilevel logistic model. A model in combined form can be written but is too bulky to include here; however, we provide these expressions for each of our specific examples below. The distribution of regression coefficients at the school level is assumed to be normal, with the collection of residuals at level two described through covariance matrix T:

$$\underline{u}_{qj} \sim N(\underline{0}, T). \tag{6.9}$$

THE MULTILEVEL PROPORTIONAL ODDS MODEL
FOR ORDINAL OUTCOMES

Explanatory models for ordinal outcome data collected during a single time frame are not new to educational, social, or behavioral research, but they often are under-utilized. Some recent examples of applications of multilevel ordinal analyses can be found in the literature. Bell and Dexter (2000) used multilevel proportional odds models to establish comparability of educational examinations in the UK. Plewis (2002) described the fitting of multilevel ordinal data comparing two approaches—continuation odds and proportional odds—for a reanalysis of data from an experiment on young children's search strategies. Analysis strategies for multilevel ordinal data are extensions of those for single-level ordinal data, mirroring the process of adapting logistic regression procedures for multilevel dichotomous data. Reviews of different methods for analyzing ordinal data can be found in Agresti (1989, 1990, 1996), Bender and Benner (2000), Clogg and Shihadeh (1994), Long (1997), McCullagh (1980), and O'Connell (2000, 2006). Several well-known multilevel texts include sections pertaining to the analysis of ordinal data, such as Goldstein (2002), Leyland and Goldstein (2001), Raudenbush and Bryk (2002), and Snijders and Bosker (1999). For the most part, multilevel methods for analyzing continuous and dichotomous outcomes are far more developed than multilevel methods for ordinal data. However, as estimation methods for multilevel ordinal analyses improve, substantive aims and the needs of more complex data structures may be met more aptly (Fielding, 2003).

The examples in this chapter focus on the application and interpretation of the multilevel proportional odds (PO) model, a particular type of analysis for ordinal data that sometimes is referred to as the cumulative odds model. The PO approach is based on the most commonly used representation of ordinal categories for analyzing single-level ordinal data. It characterizes a sequence of cumulative outcomes explained in more detail below and uses a *cumulative logit link*, which is an extension of the logit link typically applied to dichotomous data (Agresti, 1996; Armstrong & Sloan, 1989; Long, 1997; McCullagh, 1980).

The assumption of proportionality is useful in the analysis of ordinal data primarily because of its resulting parsimony, and it corresponds naturally to models in which the interest may be in ascertaining the likelihood of a response being at or below a given outcome category. The resulting model assumes proportional odds across successive cumulative categories. For example, Table 6.1 shows the six possible proficiency outcomes for early numeracy within the ECLS-K on an ordinal scale: 0, 1, 2, 3, 4, and 5. Cumulatively, the data can be partitioned into five "splits" as follows: $Y \leq 0$, $Y \leq 1, Y \leq 2, Y \leq 3, Y \leq 4$ (where Y represents each of the sequential response category possibilities). Since all observations are contained in what could be called the final split, $Y \leq 5$, this last cumulative representation is not necessary. Now, if we imagine a series of binary logistic regressions across all of these cumulative splits—each split being used to estimate the probability of a child's proficiency level being at or below that specific response category—the assumption of proportionality implies that the effect of any explanatory variable remains constant regardless of the response value identifying each split. For example, this means that the effect of gender is assumed to be the same whether we are referring to the probability of a response being less than or equal to category 0 or to a response being less than or equal to category 3.

Proportionality is restrictive in the sense that equal log-odds ratios for the explanatory variables across all of the successive cumulative comparisons are assumed, which means that the log-odds of proficiency do not depend on response category. In many research situations involving single-level data, this assumption is a reasonable one. Hosmer and Lemeshow (2000) state that "inferences from fitted proportional odds models lend themselves to a general discussion of direction of response and do not have to focus on specific outcome categories" (p. 298). By extension, the same may be said for multilevel ordinal models, but it is incumbent on researchers to verify the reasonableness of any model they choose to apply to their data. Most software for the analysis of multilevel data will fit the PO model, although other link options, such as the complementary log-log link for continuation ratio models, as well as methods for allowing partial-proportional odds, are available. Models in which some explanatory variables exhibit non-proportional odds are referred to as "partial" proportional odds models; non-proportional odds models are those in which all of the explanatory variables exhibit non-proportionality. Hedeker and Mermelstein (1998) form extensions of hierarchical models for ordinal outcome data that allow for non-proportional odds for subsets of the explanatory variables. Their examples are based on a skin-cancer prevention intervention using the transtheoretical model (Prochaska & Velicer, 1997), a well-known stage-based behavior change theory.

In a proportional odds analysis, the (log of the) odds of a response at or below each of the ordinal response categories form the quantities of interest. For example, with a six-category ordinal outcome such as the numeracy proficiency levels for the ECLS-K study, which has $K = 6$ response outcomes ranging from 0 to 5, the 5 $(K-1)$ formulas shown in Table 6.2 can be used to compute the *cumulative probabilities* and, consequently, the *cumulative odds*. The cumulative probability is the probability that the response for the ith student in the jth school, which we can write as R_{ij}, is at or below a given proficiency level. As in logistic regression, the odds are a quotient comparing the probability of an event occurring to the probability

TABLE 6.2 Cumulative Odds Model for K = 6 (k = 0, 1,...5), Where R_{ij} Represents the Proficiency Outcome (Response) for the ith Student in the jth School

Category	Cumulative probability	Cumulative odds $[Y'_{kij}]$	Probability comparison
$k = 0$ (Proficiency 0)	$P\left(R_{ij} \leq 0\right)$	$\dfrac{P\left(R_{ij} = 0\right)}{P\left(R_{ij} > 0\right)}$	Proficiency 0 versus all levels above
$k = 1$ (Proficiency 1)	$P\left(R_{ij} \leq 1\right)$	$\dfrac{P\left(R_{ij} \leq 1\right)}{P\left(R_{ij} > 1\right)}$	Proficiency 0 and 1 combined versus all levels above
$k = 2$ (Proficiency 2)	$P\left(R_{ij} \leq 2\right)$	$\dfrac{P\left(R_{ij} \leq 2\right)}{P\left(R_{ij} > 2\right)}$	Proficiency 0,1,2 combined versus 3, 4, 5 combined
$k = 3$ (Proficiency 3)	$P\left(R_{ij} \leq 3\right)$	$\dfrac{P\left(R_{ij} \leq 3\right)}{P\left(R_{ij} > 3\right)}$	Proficiency 0,1,2,3 combined versus 4,5 combined
$k = 4$ (Proficiency 4)	$P\left(R_{ij} \leq 4\right)$	$\dfrac{P\left(R_{ij} \leq 4\right)}{P\left(R_{ij} > 4\right)}$	Proficiency 0,1,2,3,4 versus Proficiency 5

of an event not occurring. Accordingly, the cumulative odds $[Y'_{kij}]$ represent the odds that the response for the ith child in the jth school would be, at most, in category k (rather than beyond category k). From Table 6.2 we see that the cumulative odds, in order, correspond to the probability of being in proficiency level 0 relative to all categories above it; the probability of being in proficiency level 0 or 1 relative to all above it; and so on until arriving at the probability of being in categories 0, 1,...4 relative to being in category 5. The Kth, or final, cumulative probability always would be 1.0 (probability of being at or below the last possible level); therefore, its probability and associated odds are not included in the table. It is common to refer to the values marking each of these binary comparisons as "cutpoints" or cumulative splits. For example, the cutpoint for the first comparison is 0 (proficiency level 0 versus above 0); the cutpoint for the second comparison is 1 (proficiency 0 and 1 versus above 1), etc.

To better understand how the multilevel PO model works, imagine if the separate comparisons indicated in the last column of Table 6.2 were investigated using corresponding multilevel dichotomous-outcome logistic regressions for each of the associated cumulative splits. The *simultaneous* fitting of each of these separate $K - 1$ (in this example, $K - 1 = 5$) logistic models represents the overall PO approach. The validity of this approach rests upon a critical assumption. As mentioned previously, this "assumption of proportionality" states that the effects of the explanatory variables cannot be statistically different across these separate comparisons. This assumption also is called the cumulative odds assumption or the equal slopes assumption and may be very restrictive for certain research situations. For single-level data, the assumption of equal slopes easily can be tested within statistical packages that provide a score test for the proportional odds assumption (for discussions of this test see, for example, Brant, 1990; Hosmer & Lemeshow, 2000; Long, 1997; SAS, 1997). However, direct tests of this assumption within a multilevel context currently are not available. An ad hoc approach can be applied that investigates the consistency of slope estimates across the cumulative splits described in Table 6.2. This approach, taken by Bell and Dexter (2000), is one we follow here. We shall discuss this approach and the implications related to the plausibility of the equal slopes assumption later in this chapter.

For the ith student in the jth school, the multilevel proportional odds model is based on the cumulative logit link and fit according to the following equations (Raudenbush & Bryk, 2002):

$$\text{Level 1:} \quad \eta_{kij} = \ln(Y'_{kij}) = \ln\left(\frac{P(R_{ij} \leq k)}{P(R_{ij} > k)}\right) = \beta_{0j} + \sum_{q=1}^{Q} \beta_{qj} X_{qij} + \sum_{k=2}^{K-1} D_{kij}\delta_k \quad (6.10)$$

$$\text{Level 2:} \quad \beta_{qj} = \gamma_{q0} + \sum_{s=1}^{S_q} \gamma_{qs} W_{sj} + u_{qj}.$$

In these expressions, the level-one equations represent the child-level models and the level-two equations represent the school-level models. For the ith child in the jth school, Y'_{kij} represents the cumulative odds for each category k, with $k = 1, \ldots, K-1$ levels of the ordinal response and based on $q = 1, \ldots, Q$ child-level explanatory variables. The expression on the left side of the level-one equation is the natural log of the cumulative odds for each category k, and is referred to as the logit for the cumulative distribution. The expression in the middle represents the two specific probability comparisons being made in the determination of the (log of the) odds, where R_{ij} represents the proficiency outcome (i.e., response) for the ith child in the jth school. The first set of terms on the far right side of the level-one equation can be interpreted similarly to the regression coefficients in the multilevel logistic regression model, with β_{0j} representing the intercept for the jth school and the β_{qj} representing the collection of school-specific slopes for the jth school in terms of the expected change in the logit for each 1-unit change in the respective within-school explanatory variable, X_{qij}.

Across each of the $K-1$ underlying cumulative representations of the outcome data, these logit effects are assumed to be constant within each school; this is the proportional or cumulative odds assumption. For each school, the slope parameters, β_{qj}, are restricted to be constant for the qth explanatory variable across the separate possible cumulative splits derived according to the second column of Table 6.2. The level-two equations model the between-schools variability in these overall slope effects for each of the explanatory variables and the intercept at level one. Errors at level two are assumed to be multivariate normal and distributed as in Equation 6.9 for the multilevel logistic model, that is, $u_{qj} \sim N(\underline{0}, T)$.

The collection of estimates at the farthest right of the level-one equation are referred to as thresholds or "delta" coefficients, and they operate as deviations from the baseline intercept for each of the $K-1$ separate cumulative comparisons beyond the first, with β_{0j} as the baseline intercept (i.e., for the first comparison). D_{kij} is an indicator variable for the kth outcome category beyond the first. In other words, each cumulative comparison has its own intercept while the effects of the explanatory variables are assumed to be constant across each comparison.

The general level-two equation presented in Equation 6.10 describes how the within-school effects (level-one estimates) may vary based on selected school- or group-level characteristics. For example, γ_{q0} represents the intercepts for each of the $Q+1$ level-two models (one each for the qth predictor from level one plus the intercept). This is the best estimate for each of the regression coefficients from level one, "averaging" across all schools and when any school-level variables are set to 0. For each specific level-two equation, the γ_{qs} represent effects of each predictor for the qth equation at level two. As in the multilevel logistic model, parameter estimates at level two are in the log-odds metric. The exponentiation of these logit-slopes provides the estimate of the effect of the associated group-level predictor on the cumulative odds.

In the PO model, the likelihood (or odds) of a child's response falling into category k or below is assessed based on the collection of level-one and level-two explanatory variables. The multilevel PO analysis predicts a transformation of the odds, i.e., the cumulative logit, which is the log of the cumulative odds. A predicted cumulative logit of zero corresponds to a cumulative odds of 1.0, which implies that there is no difference between the probability of a child being in a certain category (or below) and being above that category (e.g., .5/.5 = 1.0, ln(1.0) = 0). A *positive* cumulative logit implies that the likelihood of being in *lower* categories is greater (e.g., .7/.3 = 2.33, log(2.33) = .85), and a *negative* cumulative logit implies that the likelihood of being in *higher* categories is greater (e.g., .3/.7 = .43, log(.43) = −.85). Estimated cumulative logits can be exponentiated and transformed to predicted cumulative probabilities using Equation 6.7. Our examples will make this process clear.

ESTIMATION AND MODEL COMPARISONS FOR HGLM

As mentioned earlier, single-level non-linear models require iterative maximum likelihood procedures for estimation of the regression parameters. When these regression parameters are allowed to vary across contexts, as in HGLM analyses, we need to estimate not just the fixed effects portions of the model but also the random effects—i.e., the variability between groups such as schools. Different computer software packages use different approaches that may vary in terms of computational intensity; however, for HGLM, the complexity of the estimation required yields a reliance on approximation methods for the maximum likelihood (Raudenbush & Bryk, 2002). The most common approaches use quasi-likelihood strategies. Fielding (2003) describes some options and current research on estimation strategies for HGLMs, and Raudenbush and Bryk (2002) detail estimation procedures for quasi-likelihood and numerical integration approaches to estimation. In this chapter, our emphasis is on intuitive understanding of analyses involving HGLM's, regardless of statistical package; however, our examples use HLMv6.04, and the methods available there are discussed briefly here.

In HLMv6.04, hierarchical models for binary data are estimated through either restricted or full penalized quasi-likelihood strategies (PQL or Full PQL, respectively) or using a more computationally intensive Laplace transformation. Ordinal models can be estimated using either form of PQL, but Laplace estimation is not available. The default for non-linear models in HLMv6.04 is PQL, which results in empirical Bayes, generalized least squares and approximate ML estimates for the random level-one coefficients, level-two fixed effects and level-two variance components, respectively. Neither the restricted nor the full PQL approximation yields a reliable deviance statistic that can be used to compare competing models (Snijders & Bosker, 1999). However, the advantages of using PQL are its simplicity and its ability to converge. Fixed effect estimates and variance components have been reported to be negatively biased if the level-two variances are very large and if the targeted probability is very small or very large (Raudenbush et al., 2004; Snijders & Bosker, 1999). Estimation through the Laplace transformation overcomes this bias and does produce a reliable deviance statistic for binary response models but may have convergence problems for some data sets.

In the examples presented here, we used the default PQL in order to provide some consistency in estimation for the binary and ordinal models, and we note in our tables the deviance under Laplace estimation for each of the binary models. Parameter estimates for those models were similar between PQL and Laplace methods. Under the Laplace method, goodness-of-fit can be assessed through comparison of deviances between nested binary models, similar to deviance comparisons for standard HLMs (see McCoach & Black, 2008 for details on goodness-of-fit).

DATA STRUCTURES FOR OUR EXAMPLES

Our examples focus on the prediction of proficiency in early numeracy. As described in the introduction, we used a collection of student-level and school-level predictors drawn from the public-use first-grade and follow-up third-grade sample of the ECLS-K.[4] All of the data analyzed here are available through the NCES, and the subsample data created for our examples can be found on our website (http://multilevel.education.uconn.edu). Our examples were derived solely for the purpose of explicating the technical and methodological use of multilevel logistic and ordinal regression models. Although they are informative, these examples are not meant to provide a complete picture of early arithmetic skill for first-grade children.

We based our analyses on first-grade children who were native English speakers (non-English Language Learners) and who were not repeating first grade or retained in kindergarten. We selected only those schools that had at least 5 children included in the national ECLS-K study and that had no missing data on the school-level variables of interest. Our resulting data set had $N = 7377$ children from $J = 569$ schools. Missing data for some of the student-level variables reduced our level-one data set further to $N = 6539$ for the multilevel analyses (when creating the MDM file for HLMv6.04, we selected the option for deleting missing data when making the MDM file in order to maintain the same sample for all analyses). The average number of children per school in this sample was $M = 11.5$ ($SD = 4.2$).

The dependent variables analyzed here are PROFMATH (the six-level ordinal response variable described in Table 6.1 and coded from 0 (lowest possible proficiency level) to 5 (highest possible proficiency category)) and PROF45 (a dichotomization of PROFMATH, where students in the highest proficiency categories of 4 and 5 were considered "success"). Overall, 77.3% of the children in our sample had attained proficiency in levels 4 or 5 by the end of the first grade.

Explanatory variables at the student level included gender (MALE; 1 = male, 0 = female) and a count of the number of family risk factors a child had experienced prior to entering kindergarten (NUMRISK; 0 to 4 as described below). For our sample, the distribution of gender was approximately even (49% male). Earlier studies suggested that children entering kindergarten from families with particular characteristics (living in a single parent household, living in a family that receives welfare payments or food stamps, having a mother with less than a high school education, or having parents whose primary language is not English) tended to be at risk for poor performance (Zill & West, 2001). The NUMRISK variable is a sum of the number of these four risk characteristics present for each child in the analytic sample and ranges from 0 to 4. The mean number of risks for our sample was .39, with a standard deviation of .72. Table 6.3 contains descriptive information on our analytic sample regarding the dependent and predictor variables at the child level.

We used two school-level variables to demonstrate the development and interpretation of HGLMs. First, we used factor analysis to create a neighborhood climate variable, NBHOODCLIM, which represents a composite of principal's perceptions of the severity of six specific problems in the vicinity of their school, including extent of litter, drug activity and gang activity in the area, crime, violence, and existence of vacant lots or vacant homes. The resulting scale scores for NBHOODCLIM ranged from 0 to 12, with $M = 1.73$ ($SD = 2.49$). School sector recorded as either public or private (PUB-PRIV2; private = 1, public = 0) also was selected as a school-level predictor. In our sample, 18% of the schools were private schools, and no distinction was made among different types of private schools. Table 6.4 contains de-

TABLE 6.3 Student-Level Descriptive Statistics for the Analytic Sample, N = 6539

Proficiency level (PROFMATH)	0	1	2	3	4	5	Total
Student level	$N = 9$	$N = 53$	$N = 192$	$N = 1231$	$N = 3188$	$N = 1866$	$N = 6539$
Cumulative proportion[a]	.11%	.95%	3.88%	22.71%	71.47%	100%	—
MALE							
% Male	33.33%	52.83%	48.44%	49.39%	46.55%	54.39%	49.4%
NUMRISKS							
M	1.11	1.15	.90	.55	.40	.19	.39
(SD)	(1.17)	(1.06)	(.97)	(.82)	(.72)	(.50)	(.72)

[a] $P(R \leq \text{cat. j})$, where R = proficiency level (response variable), and j = 0, 1, 2,...5 possible values for proficiency.

TABLE 6.4 School-Level Descriptive Statistics for the Analytic Sample, J = 569

Variable	Mean	SD	Minimum	Maximum
Neighborhood problems (NBHOODCLIM)	1.73	2.49	0.00	12.00
Private (PUBPRIV2)[a]	18%	—	—	—

[a] Public = 0; Private = 1.

scriptive information on our analytic sample regarding the predictor variables at the school level.

We created two data files to correspond to the levels of analysis of the data. The level-one data file contains the child-level outcomes, MALE and NUMRISKS, with the dependent variable of numeracy proficiency score recorded as a dichotomous (PROF45) and ordinal (PROFMATH) response variable for each child at the end of first grade. The level-two data file contains the school-level characteristics used for our demonstration, NBHOODCLIM and PUBPRIV2. We present data applications for two-level models, although three-level logistic and ordinal models are also available in HLMv6.04 as well as other software packages.

MODELING THE PROFICIENCY OUTCOMES (DICHOTOMOUS AND ORDINAL)

In our dichotomous-outcome examples, success refers to a child having achieved proficiency by performing at levels 4 or 5 on the early numeracy measure. For the ordinal analyses, we use the entire range of proficiency scores rather than the dichotomized version. We ran a series of multilevel models on these data. The first five are examples of multilevel logistic models for dichotomous data and used PROF45 as the outcome. The next two used multilevel ordinal regression based on the proportional odds model and use PROFMATH as the outcome. The collection of models applied and interpreted here are as follows:

1. Logistic empty model (no predictors at either level);
2. Logistic random coefficients model with MALE and NUMRISKS as level-one predictors of proficiency;
3. Logistic reduced model, allowing only the intercepts to vary randomly across schools (the slopes for MALE and NUMRISKS were both fixed);
4. Logistic reduced model, with only NUMRISKS as a fixed level-one predictor (MALE was removed from the model);
5. Logistic contextual model with NBHOODCLIM and PUBPRIV2 as school-level predictors of the intercepts;
6. Ordinal empty model; and
7. Ordinal contextual model with NUMRISKS as a fixed level-one predictor and NBHOODCLIM and PUBPRIV2 as school-level predictors of the intercepts.

DATA EXAMPLES FOR DICHOTOMOUS OUTCOMES

Empty Model and Unit-Specific versus Population Average Results

The dichotomous outcomes model we present uses PROF45 as the response variable, based on a child reaching proficiency on the arithmetic assessment in either category 4 or category 5: being able to solve simple addition and subtraction problems or simple multiplication and division problems (see Table 6.1). In multilevel logistic regression, the model constructed for the outcome is linear based on log-odds (the logits, or the natural log of the odds) and includes a random effect for the school. The empty model, i.e., the model with no predictors at either the child or school level, provides an overall estimate of the likelihood of proficiency for this sample, as well as information about the variability in the probability of proficiency between schools. The following equations define each level of the empty model:

$$\text{Level 1:} \quad \eta_{ij} = \beta_{0j} \tag{6.11}$$

$$\text{Level 2:} \quad \beta_{0j} = \gamma_{00} + u_{0j}.$$

In combined form, this becomes: $\eta_{ij} = \gamma_{00} + u_{0j}$. With no explanatory variables in the model, the β_{0j} represent the log-odds of success for children in the jth school. These school-average, or unit-average (Raudenbush & Bryk, 2002), log-odds vary across schools, with $\text{var}(u_{0j}) = \tau_{00}$, where γ_{00} represents the average log-odds of attaining proficiency across all schools.

For hierarchical generalized linear models, a distinction can be made between unit-specific (here, school-specific) results and population-average results. For the school-specific results, the empty model estimates the probability of attaining proficiency for a school with a value of zero for u_{0j}, that is, for a "typical" school. To find this estimated probability, Equation 6.7 can be applied, as shown below. The unit-specific model, or what Hosmer and Lemeshow (2000) refer to as a "cluster-specific model," is similar to the structure of a standard HLM in that "the goal is to provide inferences incorporating individual subject covariate values" (p. 312). Since this is our goal in these analyses, we use the unit-specific results throughout this chapter. An alternative approach is to report population-average effects. Population-average models generally will be more useful when the desired inferences focus on group-level variables rather than the varying effects of individual-level covariates, or when population-level causal inferences are desired. Differences between the two models may be great. The population average model does not "condition on (or "hold constant") the random effect, u_{0j}"

(Raudenbush et al., 2004, p. 110); rather, the estimates are averaged over all possible values for the level-two error terms. On the other hand, the unit-specific model provides an expected value conditioning on the level-two error terms. The HLM software provides unit-specific and population-average results for most of the HGLM analyses; for ordinal and multinomial hierarchical models, only unit-specific results are currently available in HLMv6.04 (Raudenbush et al., 2004).

Results of the (unit-specific) empty model in terms of estimated logits and corresponding odds ratios are provided in Table 6.5. The predicted logit for a typical school in this sample is $\gamma_{00} = 1.27$ (s.e. $= .044$). Significance testing for fixed and random effects corresponds to the standard HLM; thus, this average logit is statistically different from zero, $t(568) = 28.49$, $p < .001$. In addition, there was found to be considerable variability around the intercepts for this collection of schools, $\tau_{00} = .55$, $\chi^2 (568) = 1180.52$, $p < .001$. Estimated odds of attaining proficiency for students within a typical school is $\exp(1.27) = 3.56$, and thus the estimated probability of attaining proficiency for these students is

$$\frac{\exp(1.27)}{1+\exp(1.27)} = \frac{3.56}{4.56} = .78.$$

This estimate is close to the overall proportion of children (ignoring school variability) who achieved proficiency in categories 4 or 5 for this sample (i.e., $(3188 + 1866)/6539 = .77$; see data in Table 6.3). Under the model's assumption that the errors at level two follow a normal distribution, we can estimate that about 95% of schools in this sample have logits between -1.27 $+/- 1.96*(.55)^{1/2}$, or $(-.19, 2.72)$. Again applying Equation 6.7, this corresponds to estimated probabilities between .45 and .94. Thus, some schools have a considerable percentage of students who did not reach proficiency in early numeracy by the end of first grade.

TABLE 6.5   Multilevel Logistic Empty Model[a]

Fixed effects	Coefficient (SE)	Odds ratio	t (df)	p
Model for numeracy proficiency (β_0)				
Intercept (γ_{00})	1.27 (.04)	3.55	28.49 (568)	.000
Random effects (var. components)	**Variance**	**df**	**Chi-square**	
Var. in numeracy proficiency (τ_{00})	.55	568	1180.52 (.000)	

[a] Deviance, under Laplace estimation: 18804.739, parameters = 2

Intraclass Correlation Coefficients

An appealing characteristic of nearly all multilevel models involves the determination and interpretation of the intraclass correlation coefficient. Snijders and Bosker (1999) discuss two approaches to estimating an ICC for dichotomous outcomes. The first involves fitting a multilevel linear probability model by specifying an empty model and applying standard HLM to the dichotomous (0, 1) outcomes. Using this approach for our data, the

$$\text{ICC} = \frac{\tau_{00}}{\tau_{00} + \sigma^2}$$

and is approximately .11. The second method utilizes an empty logistic model and assumes that the outcome, Y, is a dichotomization of an unknown latent continuous variable, $\tilde{Y}$, with a level-one residual that follows the logistic distribution (Snijders & Bosker, 1999). The mean and variance of the logistic distribution are 0 and 3.29 (i.e., $\pi^2/3$), respectively (Evans, Hastings, & Peacock, 2000). Accordingly, the ICC based on this approach is

$$\frac{\tau_{00}}{\tau_{00} + 3.29} = .14.$$

For this example, these two results are quite similar, and under both estimations the variability attributed to schools is larger than zero, indicating that a multilevel analysis is appropriate due to a strong clustering effect. Reaching proficiency is more similar within schools than an independence model (i.e., one ignoring the clustering effect) would assume. Readers are referred to Browne, Subramanian, Jones, & Goldstein (2005) for extensions of these methods when overdispersion may exist in the response variable.

Logistic Random Intercept and Random Coefficient Models

As in the standard HLM, level-one coefficients in HGLM can be specified as fixed, randomly varying, or non-randomly varying. Thus the strategies used to model the logit for proficiency are familiar and straightforward. We selected two child-level predictors, gender (MALE) and the number of family risk characteristics (NUMRISKS), to determine how these factors might relate to proficiency, PROF45. Table 6.6 contains the estimated coefficients and corresponding odds ratios for the resulting random intercepts model based on results from a series of random coefficient models fit to these data. For those models, we first specified MALE and NUMRISKS as child-level predictors of success with respect to proficiency. No between-schools

TABLE 6.6 Logistic Random Coefficients Model with NUMRISKS, No Slope Variation[a]

Fixed Effects	Coefficient (SE)	Odds ratio	t (df)	p
Model for the intercepts (β_0)				
Intercept (γ_{00})	1.45 (.05)	4.26	31.14 (568)	.000
Model for NUMRISKS slope (β_1)				
Intercept (γ_{10})	–.42 (.04)	.66	–9.96 (6537)	.000

Random effects (var. components)	Variance	df	Chi-square
Intercept (τ_{00})	.41	568	1022.19 (.000)

[a] Deviance, under Laplace estimation: 18,713.20 parameters = 3

variability in the slopes was found for either explanatory variable ($p > .50$ for both τ_{01} and τ_{02}), and the slope for MALE was not statistically different from zero. Thus, the results in Table 6.6 were derived from the following reduced model:

$$\text{Level 1:} \quad \eta_{ij} = \beta_{0j} + \beta_{1j} \cdot NUMRISKS \tag{6.12}$$

$$\text{Level 2:} \quad \begin{cases} \beta_{0j} = \gamma_{00} + u_{0j} \\ \beta_{1j} = \gamma_{10} \end{cases}.$$

The combined model is thus: $\eta_{ij} = \gamma_{00} + \gamma_{10} \cdot NUMRISKS_{ij} + u_{0j}$.

In our analysis, the estimated logit for a child from a typical school ($u_{0j}=0$) and with no identified family risk factors (NUMRISKS = 0) is $\gamma_{00} = 1.45$ (s.e. = .05). This effect is statistically different from zero, $t(568) = 31.14$, $p < .001$. This suggests that for a child from a typical school with no family risks, the estimated probability of attaining proficiency is

$$\hat{p} = \frac{\exp(1.45)}{1+\exp(1.45)} = .81.$$

The negative effect for NUMRISKS, $\gamma_{10} = -.42$ (s.e. = .04), indicates that as the number of risk factors increases by one, the estimated logit *decreases* by .42 units; this effect is statistically different from zero, $t(6537) = -9.96$, $p < .001$. Exponentiating this slope, $\exp(\gamma_{10})$ yields $\exp(-.42)$, or 0.66. This value represents the effect of NUMRISKS on the odds of proficiency: as the number of risks increases by one, the odds of attaining proficiency is reduced by about one-third. For example, a child with NUMRISKS = 1 has a predicted logit $\hat{\eta}_{ij} = 1.45 + (-.42)*1 = 1.03$. Exponentiating this value gives exp(1.03) = 2.80, which reveals that for children with a single risk factor, the probability of attaining proficiency is larger than the probability of not attaining proficiency. However, the odds of attaining proficiency when NUMRISKS = 0 is much larger: exp(1.45) = 4.26. To compare these two odds, we can calculate the Odds Ratio (see formula (3)):

$$\frac{Odds(NUMRISKS = 1)}{Odds(NUMRISKS = 0)} = \frac{2.80}{4.26} = .66,$$

which is exactly exp(−.42). Thus, there is a 34% decrease in the odds as the number of risks increases by one (i.e., 100%*(OR − 1) = −34%). For a child with NUMRISKS = 4, the predicted logit is $\hat{\eta}_{ij} = 1.45 + (-.42)*4 = -.23$, yielding a corresponding odds of exp(−.23) = .79, and thus the estimated probability of attaining proficiency is .44. Children with the greatest number of family risks are at risk of not attaining proficiency in early numeracy (as defined here) by the end of first grade.

Logistic Contextual Models

While the previous models clarified the role of family risk on likelihood of proficiency in early numeracy and also indicated that gender was not a factor in numeracy proficiency at the end of first grade for this sample, the results of these first analyses also pointed to considerable residual variability in the intercepts across schools after adjusting for NUMRISKS, $\tau_{00} = .41$, $\chi^2(568) = 1022.19$, $p < .001$. The next set of analyses we conducted included several school-level variables to see if we could account for this residual variation. We included the measures of neighborhood climate (NBHOODCLIM) and school sector (PUBPRIV2) as predictors of the level-one intercepts and the level-one slopes for NUMRISKS. Since no between-school variability in the logit was found for the effect of NUMRISKS in the previous analysis, we anticipated no contribution from these level-two variables as predictors of the NUMRISKS slopes; however, we included these effects here to illustrate the interpretation of cross-level interactions in a multilevel logistic model. Table 6.7 contains the results of two analyses: one including NBHOODCLIM and PUBPRIV2 as predictors of both the intercepts and the slopes (using Level 1 and Level 2a models shown below) and the second providing the results of a reduced contextual model where only the intercepts are predicted from NBHOODCLIM and PUBPRIV2 (using Level 1 and Level 2b models, below). In both analyses, slope variability between-schools was constrained to zero, as supported through the previous analyses. Estimated logits and corresponding odds ratios are included in the table.

TABLE 6.7 Results for the Contextual Logistic Models: Model I Uses Level 2a for the School-Level Model; Model II Uses Level 2b

Fixed effects	Model I[a]		Model II[b]	
	Coefficient (SE)	Odds ratio	Coefficient (SE)	Odds ratio
Model for the intercepts (β_0)				
Intercept (γ_{00})	1.52 (.06)	4.57**	1.50 (.05)	4.48**
NBHOODCLIM (γ_{01})	-.11 (.02)	.89**	-.10 (.02)	.90**
PUBPRIV2[c] (γ_{02})	.42 (.12)	1.52**	.47 (.11)	1.60**
Model for NUMRISKS slope (β_1)				
Intercept (γ_{10})	-.37 (.06)	.69**	-.33 (.04)	.72**
NBHOODCLIM (γ_{11})	.01 (.01)	1.01	—	—
PUBPRIV2 (γ_{12})	.29 (.22)	1.33	—	—
Random effects (var. components)	Variance		Variance	
Intercept (τ_{00})	.34**		.34**	

** $p < .001$

a Deviance, under Laplace estimation: 18651.64, params. = 7

b Deviance, under Laplace estimation: 18654.075, params. = 5

c Public = 0; Private = 1.

Level 1: $\eta_{ij} = \beta_{0j} + \beta_{1j} \cdot NUMRISKS$ \hfill (6.13)

Level 2a: $\begin{cases} \beta_{0j} = \gamma_{00} + \gamma_{01} \cdot NBHOODCLIM + \gamma_{02} \cdot PUBPRIV2 + u_{0j} \\ \beta_{1j} = \gamma_{10} + \gamma_{11} \cdot NBHOODCLIM + \gamma_{12} \cdot PUBPRIV2 \end{cases}$

Level 2b: $\begin{cases} \beta_{0j} = \gamma_{00} + \gamma_{01} \cdot NBHOODCLIM + \gamma_{02} \cdot PUBPRIV2 + u_{0j} \\ \beta_{1j} = \gamma_{10} \end{cases}$

In combined form, Contextual Model I (Level 1 with Level 2a, above) can be written as:

$$\eta_{ij} = \gamma_{00} + \gamma_{01}(NBHOODCLIM)_j + \gamma_{02}(PUBPRIV2) + \gamma_{10}(NUMRISKS) + \quad (6.14)$$

$$\gamma_{11}(NBHOODCLIM * NUMRISKS) + \gamma_{12}(PUBPRIV2 * NUMRISKS) + u_{0j}.$$

Model I is a random intercepts and slopes-as-outcomes logistic regression model. Similarly, contextual Model II (Level 1 with Level 2b, above) can be written in combined form by eliminating the interaction terms from Equation 6.14 and is a random intercept logistic regression model. The effects in these contextual models are in log-odds. For both models, the results in Table 6.7 show that the main effects of NBHOODCLIM (γ_{01}) and PUBPRIV2 (γ_{02}) are statistically different from zero, and as expected for Model I, the cross-level interactions between both of these variables and NUMRISKS are not statistically significant (γ_{11} and γ_{12}, respectively). Therefore, their effects on the NUMRISKS slope are close to zero, and Model I and Model II are substantively similar. We begin with an interpretation of Model II, and then, to illustrate interpretation of cross-level interactions, we refer to Model I despite a lack of statistical significance for these cross-level interaction effects.

From Table 6.7, the intercept for Model II is $\gamma_{00} = 1.50$ ($p < .001$). This value represents the expected log-odds for a child who has no family risks (NUMRISKS = 0) and is in a public school (PUBPRIV2 = 0) and in a neighborhood with no serious crime or other problems (NBHOODCLIM = 0). Thus, the estimated odds for a child with these individual and school characteristics, exp(1.50), is 4.48, corresponding to a predicted probability of proficiency of .82 (from Equation 6.7). To assist in clarifying the results of the multilevel logistic model, this odds value of 4.48 can be called the "referent odds," that is, the prediction for the odds in the case when all predictors (school- and child-level) are zero. According to these referent odds, it is more likely for a child with no family risks in a public school with no neighborhood problems to be proficient in early numeracy than not.

According to the results for Model II, the estimated odds, and thus the predicted probability of proficiency, tend to decrease as severity of neighborhood climate and number of family risks increase, but the odds and predicted probability increase for children in private schools. Specifically, the effect of NBHOODCLIM on the log-odds is negative and statistically different from zero, controlling for both NUMRISKS and PUBPRIV2, $\gamma_{01} = -.10$ ($p < .001$). This effect suggests that when PUBPRIV2 and NUMRISKS are held constant, the odds of proficiency is expected to be lowered by .90 as the severity of neighborhood problems increases by 1-unit (OR = exp($-.10$) = .90). The effect of attending private school (PUBPRIV2) on proficiency, holding NUMRISKS and NBHOODCLIM constant, is positive and statistically significant, $\gamma_{02} = .47$ ($p < .001$). Thus, the odds of proficiency for children in private schools is 1.60 times greater than for children in public schools (OR = exp(.47) = 1.60), controlling for NBHOODCLIM and NUMRISKS. Overall, holding NBHOODCLIM and PUBPRIV constant, NUMRISKS has a negative and statistically significant effect on the log-odds for proficiency, $\gamma_{10} = -.33$ ($p < .001$), with an OR = exp($-.33$) = .72. With each 1-unit increase in the number of family risks, a child's odds of reaching proficiency in early numeracy decreases by nearly 28% (that is, 100%*(OR $-$ 1) = 100%*(.72 $-$ 1) = -28%), holding other effects constant.

As with all multilevel models, variability in the level-one slopes represents the between-schools variability in the relationships between level-one predictors and the proficiency outcome. In both Model I and Model II, the child-level effect of NUMRISKS was fixed since it was not detected to vary between schools in the earlier analyses. However, the results of Model II show that there is considerable residual variability in the school intercepts (log-odds of proficiency when NUMRISKS is zero) even after accounting for NBHOODCLIM and PUBPRIV2, with $\tau_{00} = .34$ ($p < .001$). Although we do not pursue this analysis further here, additional child- or school-level predictors might help to explain some of this variability.

Now we turn to the interpretation of Model I, which allows for cross-level interactions between each of the school-level predictors and NUMRISKS, the child-level predictor, on proficiency. Although neither of the predictors of the NUMRISKS slope was statistically significant, this example illustrates the challenges in interpreting multilevel models where effects of level-one explanatory variables may vary randomly or non-randomly. We will review these cross-level effects for demonstration purposes, although neither effect is statistically meaningful.

In Model I, NBHOODCLIM and PUBPRIV2 were included as predictors of the intercepts across schools as well as of the effect of a child's number of family risks characteristics (NUMRISKS) on child-level proficiency outcomes across schools. Thus, the intercepts and the slopes from the level-one equations are treated as outcomes in a regression model at level two.

The fixed effects in the equation predicting the slopes are referred to as cross-level interactions. They represent the effect of a school-level variable on a child-level predictor of proficiency. In essence, these effects tell us how the relationship between NUMRISKS and the log-odds tends to vary across schools, based on the school variables NBHOODCLIM and PUBPRIV2. We focus on these cross-level interactions since interpretation of main effects should only be undertaken cautiously when interaction is present (although, as noted earlier, that is not the case here).

For children in a public school (PUBPRIV2 = 0) with no crime or other problems identified in their neighborhood (NBHOODCLIM = 0), the effect of NUMRISKS on proficiency is negative and statistically different from zero ($\gamma_{10} = -.37$ ($p < .001$)). Across schools, the effect of NUMRISKS is not moderated by NBHOODCLIM; note that this effect is very close to zero, $\gamma_{11} = .01$ (n.s.) and that the associated odds ratio is nearly one. The effect of attending a private school on the effect of NUMRISKS is also not statistically significant, but it is in the expected direction; the harmful effect of NUMRISKS on proficiency is lessened for private school students relative to those in public schools, $\gamma_{12} = .29$ (n.s.). That is, for public school students with NBHOODCLIM = 0, the effect of NUMRISKS on the log-odds is $-.37$; this becomes $-.37 + .29 = -.08$ for children in private schools. The odds ratio for PUBPRIV2, $\exp(\gamma_{12}) = 1.33$, indicates that for a specific value of NUMRISKS and holding NBHOODCLIM constant, the odds of achieving proficiency are 1.33 times greater for private-school children than for children in public schools.

Note that the residual variance in the level-one intercepts is unchanged between Model I ($\tau_{00} = .34$) and Model II ($\tau_{00} = .34$), and both are significantly different from zero ($p < .01$). Additional level-two predictors of the intercept may be useful in decreasing this variability.

Model Comparisons

If the Laplace transformation is used for numerical integration of the likelihood function rather than an approximation based on PQL, deviances for nested models can be compared directly (Raudenbush et al., 2004). The deviances for the binary models based on Laplace rather than PQL are provided in the notes to each table presented in this chapter. In the summary below, we have listed the deviances in order of presentation:

Logistic Model	Deviance	Parameters Estimated
Empty	18,804.74	2
Random Coeffs	18,713.20	3
Contextual Model I	18,651.64	7
Contextual Model II	18,654.08	5

In general, a smaller deviance is preferred, and for nested models, the difference in deviance can be compared statistically. When models are nested, the difference of the deviances follows a chi-square distribution with degrees of freedom determined by the difference in number of estimated parameters. According to the deviance estimates for our four models, the random coefficients model with only NUMRISKS as a level-one predictor provides a better fit to the model than the empty model, $\chi^2_1 = (18,804.74 - 18,713.20) = 101.54$, $p < .01$. (Note that the coefficient for NUMRISKS was treated as fixed). Both of the contextual models result in a significantly smaller deviance than the empty model as well. However, comparing Models I and II, the difference in deviances is negligible, $\chi^2_2 = 2.44$, $p > .05$. With fewer parameters estimated, Model II is reasonably the better choice for estimating PROF45 among these alternatives.

Probability Predictions

A convenient way to clarify the interpretation of HGLM's is to use the model to calculate estimated probabilities based on varying levels of the explanatory variables. Table 6.8 contains predictions for a selection of values of the explanatory variables based on estimates in Model I that contained the cross-level interactions. Variable effects are often more challenging to interpret for HGLMs than for standard HLMs due to the logit metric and the additional required steps of transforming log-odds predictions to odds and then to probability. Looking at specific predictions can assist in interpretation. Although the few predictions provided in Table 6.8 are helpful for understanding the direction of effects in the relatively simple model presented here, complex designs may warrant a more detailed look at the results of cross-level interactions. Tate (2004) presents some useful strategies for interpreting cross-level effects in multilevel logistic models based

TABLE 6.8 Model Predictions Based on Logistic Model II

Prediction			Logits	Odds	Estimated probability
PUBPRIV2=0[a]	NUMRISKS=0	NBHOODCLIM=0	1.50	4.48	.82
	NUMRISKS=2	NBHOODCLIM=6	.23	1.25	.56
	NUMRISKS=4	NBHOODCLIM=12	−1.05	.35	.26
PUBPRIV2=1	NUMRISKS=0	NBHOODCLIM=0	1.97	7.19	.88
	NUMRISKS=2	NBHOODCLIM=6	.70	2.01	.69
	NUMRISKS=4	NBHOODCLIM=12	−.57	.56	.36

[a] For public schools, PUBPRIV2 = 0; PUBPRIV2 = 1 for private schools.

on approaches used in investigating simple effects for factorial analysis of variance designs.

Entries in Table 6.8 correspond with the results presented earlier. As children are exposed to greater numbers of family risks and increased severity of neighborhood problems, their likelihood of becoming proficient in early numeracy by the end of first grade diminishes. Further, this effect is stronger for children in public schools.

DATA EXAMPLES FOR ORDINAL OUTCOMES

Empty Model and Threshold Interpretation

In the multilevel logistic model, the outcome, PROF45, was dichotomized from an underlying six-level ordinal variable, PROFMATH (described in Table 6.1), and predictions based on the model could be used to estimate the probability of a child being "proficient" in early mathematics, as defined by having mastered at least through proficiency level 4. As with many variables in education and the behavioral sciences, dichotomizing an otherwise ordinal variable in this manner can result in a loss of information regarding individual- or context-level factors that overall might be related to a child's progression through these proficiency categories. The multilevel ordinal proportional odds model retains all the original values of the response variable for the analysis. The estimates from the resulting model summarize the effect of explanatory variables on the odds of being at or below any given proficiency category. Thus, the model provides for a simultaneous fitting of a series of logistic models corresponding to the different cumulative comparisons detailed in Table 6.2. As discussed earlier, the assumption of proportional odds implies that the effect of an explanatory variable across these separate simultaneous logistic models is constant and does not vary by level of response outcome.

The empty model, with no level-one or level-two predictors, provides a convenient starting point for understanding and interpreting multilevel ordinal models. Results of the empty model fit to the six-response category outcome for early mathematics proficiency PROFMATH are presented in Table 6.9. We used restricted PQL estimation for the ordinal models, and unit-specific estimates are presented (only the unit-specific estimates are available for ordinal models through the HLMv6.04 software). As with the logistic model, estimates are in log-odds and for ease of interpretation can be transformed to probabilities using Equation 6.7. The probability being estimated in ordinal models under the assumption of proportional odds is $P(R_{ij} \leq \text{category } k \mid \underline{x})$, that is, the probability, conditional on the explanatory variables, $\underline{x}$, that the proficiency level, or response R, for the ith student in

TABLE 6.9 Multilevel Ordinal Empty Model (Model I) and Ordinal Contextual Model (Model II)

Fixed effects	Model I		Model II	
	Coefficient (SE)	Odds ratio	Coefficient (SE)	Odds ratio
Model for the intercepts (β_0)				
Intercept (γ_{00})	-6.79 (.34)	.001**	-7.13 (.34)	.001**
NBHOODCLIM (γ_{01})			.12 (.01)	1.13**
PUBPRIV2[a] (γ_{02})			-.42 (.09)	.65**
Model for NUMRISKS slope (β_1)				
Intercept (γ_{10})			.39 (.04)	1.48**
For thresholds:				
δ_2	1.94 (.32)	6.99**	1.95 (.31)	7.03**
δ_3	3.41 (.34)	30.24**	3.43 (.33)	30.78**
δ_4	5.50 (.34)	244.86**	5.54 (.34)	255.10**
δ_5	7.85 (.34)	2574.22**	7.92 (.34)	2750.28**
Random effects (var. components)	Variance		Variance	
Var. in intercepts (τ_{00})	.57**		.31**	

*$p < .05$; **$p < .01$
[a] Public = 0; Private = 1.

the jth school is at or below category k, for $k = 0, 1, \ldots 5$. Since there are no predictors in the empty model, these cumulative probabilities correspond to overall estimates across all students in the sample at each cutpoint k.

Our example uses a $K = 6$ category response variable; thus, there are 5 $(K - 1)$ cumulative "splits" to the data, as described earlier in the section on the multilevel proportional odds model for ordinal outcomes and Table 6.2. The results of the empty model analysis presented in Table 6.9 include a series of threshold estimates corresponding to the natural cumulative splits represented by the proportional odds model. These threshold values can be used to estimate the intercepts for each of the five underlying cumulative analyses in the overall ordinal model. Following Equation 6.10, the empty model is as follows:

$$\text{Level 1:} \quad \eta_{kij} = \ln(Y'_{kij}) = \ln\left(\frac{P(R_{ij} \leq k)}{P(R_{ij} > k)}\right) = \beta_{0j} + \sum_{k=2}^{K-1} D_{kij}\delta_k \quad (6.15)$$

$$\text{Level 2:} \quad \beta_{0j} = \gamma_{00} + u_{0j}$$

Our results in Table 6.9 indicate that the estimated log-odds of being at or below proficiency level 0 (the lowest category) for a child in this sample is $\gamma_{00} = -6.79$, corresponding to an estimated odds of $\exp(-6.79) = .0011$ and estimated probability, $P(R_{ij} \leq \text{category } 0)$, of $.0011$ (see Equation 6.7). Recall from the descriptive statistics in Table 6.3 that only 9 of the 6539 students were in proficiency level 0 for this sample $(.0014)$; the estimate from the model matches the actual data fairly well. To estimate the log-odds, odds, and probability for the next cumulative comparison, $P(R_{ij} \leq \text{category } 1)$, we use the threshold estimate $d_2 = 1.95$ in addition to γ_{00}. The subscript for the threshold estimate, d_2, refers to the cumulative comparison being made, not to the specific value of the response outcome. In this case, the first comparison is for $P(R_{ij} \leq \text{category } 0)$; the second comparison is for $P(R_{ij} \leq \text{category } 1)$. Similarly, the remaining estimates for the log-odds, odds, and probabilities can be determined for all five cumulative comparisons; these are provided in Table 6.10, where they also are compared with the actual proportions derived for our sample.

The probability estimates from the empty model do appear to match the actual data. However, model estimates indicate that there is a substantial amount of variation between schools in the level-one intercepts, $\tau_{00} = .57$, $p < .01$. This suggests heterogeneity between schools in the probability of children being at or below a given proficiency level. Our next ordinal model is used to investigate how the individual- and school-level variables of NUMRISKS, NBHOODCLIM, and PUBPRIV2 may be associated with the probability of being at or below proficiency for any response category, k.

TABLE 6.10   Model Predictions Based on the Ordinal Empty Model

Model	Estimates for log odds	Estimates for odds	Estimates for $P(R_{ij} \leq$ cat. $k)$	Actual probability $P(R_{ij} \leq$ cat. $k)$
$\log(Y'_{1ij}) = \beta_0$	-6.787	.0011	.0011	.0011
$\log(Y'_{2ij}) = \beta_0 + \delta_2$ $-6.787 + 1.945 = -4.842$		.0079	.0078	.0095
$\log(Y'_{3ij}) = \beta_0 + \delta_3$ $-6.787 + 3.409 = -3.378$		.0341	.0330	.0388
$\log(Y'_{4ij}) = \beta_0 + \delta_4$ $-6.787 + 5.501 = -1.286$		.2764	.2165	.2271
$\log(Y'_{5ij}) = \beta_0 + \delta_5$ $-6.787 + 7.853 = 1.066$		2.904	.7438	.7147

Intraclass Correlation Coefficient

The ICC for ordinal data can be defined in the same way as for dichotomous outcomes (Snijders & Bosker, 1999). Two approaches using results from an empty model were described earlier in the section on intraclass correlation coefficients. We will apply the second definition presented there:

$$\text{ICC} = \frac{\tau_{00}}{\tau_{00} + 3.29} = .15,$$

where 3.29 corresponds to $(\pi^2/3)$, the variance of the logistic distribution. (Using the first method, the ICC also is .15). This value for the ICC is similar to what was obtained in the dichotomous proficiency analysis. This degree of clustering supports the utility of a multilevel analysis due to non-independence of the data.

Contextual Ordinal Model

The right-hand side of Table 6.9 provides the estimates for a contextual model of cumulative proficiency as follows:

$$\text{Level 1: } \eta_{kij} = \ln(Y'_{kij}) = \ln\left(\frac{P(R_{ij} \leq k)}{P(R_{ij} > k)}\right) = \beta_{0j} + \beta_{1j}NUMRISKS_{ij} + \sum_{k=2}^{K-1} D_{kij}\delta_k \quad (6.16)$$

$$\text{Level 2: } \begin{cases} \beta_{0j} = \gamma_{00} + \gamma_{01}NBHOODCLIM_j + \gamma_{02}PUBPRIV2_j + u_{0j} \\ \beta_{1j} = \gamma_{10} \end{cases}.$$

These equations represent a random intercepts model. Variability in the effect of NUMRISKS across schools was constrained to zero for purposes of this chapter and to correspond in structure to earlier models, but this constraint easily could be relaxed.

Tests of significance for the fixed effects and the variance components are similar methodologically to the logistic analysis presented earlier. That is, t-tests are used to test the fixed effects, and chi-square tests are applied to the variance components. Although the between-schools variance is reduced by approximately 46% based on the predictors in the contextual model,

$$\frac{\tau_{00}(\text{empty model}) - \tau_{00}(\text{contextual model})}{\tau_{00}(\text{empty model})} = \frac{.57 - .31}{.57} = .46,$$

there is still considerable residual variance remaining, $\tau_{00} = .31$, $\chi^2(566) = 1127.19$, $p < .01$.

Our results indicate that the effect of NUMRISKS on the cumulative log-odds of proficiency is positive and statistically different from zero, $\gamma_{10} = .39$, $p < .01$. Recall that in the cumulative model, the estimated probability is $P(R_{ij} \leq \text{cat. } k)$; thus, as the number of family risks increases, the probability of being at or below a given category, *rather than beyond that category*, tends to increase. Children with greater family risk are more likely to be at or below a given category. Although the parameter estimates have opposite signs between the logistic and cumulative logistic model, the interpretation is consistent and in the same direction.

School effects on the cumulative probability estimates were statistically significant and also in the same interpretive direction as the earlier logistic analysis. Children in schools with higher perceived severity of crime and related neighborhood issues are *more* likely to be at or below a given proficiency level, $\gamma_{01} = .12$, $p < .01$. Children in private schools are *less* likely to be at or below a given proficiency level, $\gamma_{02} = -.42$, $p < .01$; that is, by the rule of complements, children in private schools are more likely than their public school peers to be *beyond* a particular proficiency level.

To aid in interpretation of the model estimates, the predicted log-odds, odds, and probability can be determined for different values of the predictor variables. For each combination of values of the predictors, five probability estimates can be calculated for the data analyzed here, ranging from $P(R_{ij} \leq \text{cat. } 0)$ to $P(R_{ij} \leq \text{cat. } 4)$. Note that $P(R_{ij} \leq \text{cat. } 5) = 1.0$, and thus is not estimated. Each of the five cumulative probabilities is determined from its respective threshold estimate when calculating the estimated log-odds, as shown in the example in the section on empty model and threshold interpretation. Table 6.11 presents a series of cumulative probability predictions using values for the predictors chosen earlier for the logistic model. For space considerations, the log-odds and odds are not included in this table,

TABLE 6.11   Model Predictions Based on Ordinal Contextual Model for Selected Values of the Predictors

School type	Number of family risks	Severity of neighborhood problems	$P(R_{ij} \leq$ cat. 0)	$P(R_{ij} \leq$ cat. 1)	$P(R_{ij} \leq$ cat. 2)	$P(R_{ij} \leq$ cat. 3)	$P(R_{ij} \leq$ cat. 4)
Public	0	0	.0008	.0056	.0240	.1694	.6872
	0	6	.0017	.0116	.0487	.2978	.8204
	2	12	.0075	.0507	.1895	.6597	.9543
	2	0	.0018	.0122	.0513	.3096	.8285
	4	6	.0080	.0535	.1983	.6722	.9567
	4	12	.0164	.1052	.3396	.8100	.9787
Private	0	0	.0005	.0037	.0158	.1177	.5898
	0	6	.0011	.0076	.0324	.2172	.7493
	2	12	.0049	.0338	.1327	.5592	.9318
	2	0	.0011	.0080	.0342	.2269	.7597
	4	6	.0052	.0357	.1393	.5730	.9353
	4	12	.0108	.0714	.2518	.7361	.9678

but they must be calculated as a first step in finding the cumulative probabilities.

The resulting collection of probability estimates suggest that children in public schools who have the greatest number of family risks and are enrolled in schools in disadvantaged neighborhoods, as indicated by those with severe crime, trash, and other problems, consistently have the highest predicted probability of being *at or below* any given proficiency value (see sixth row in the table). Thus, these children are least expected, relative to their peers, to achieve proficiency in mathematics *beyond* any given category.

Assumption of Proportional Odds in Multilevel Ordinal Models

Estimates for the ordinal models presented above are based on the assumption of proportional odds, implying that the effects of the explanatory variables do not vary across the different cumulative comparisons being made. Thus, the parameter estimates summarize the effect of each variable across these splits. However, there is no currently available test for this assumption in the multilevel framework. An ad hoc approach to investigating the plausibility of proportional odds assumption involves fitting the series of binary logistic regressions represented by the cumulative model, following the comparisons in the last column of Table 6.2. This strategy frequently has been recommended when analyzing both multilevel and single-level ordinal data (see, for example, Bell & Dexter, 2000; Clogg & Shihadeh, 1994; O'Connell, 2006).

Table 6.12 shows the parameter estimates and odds ratios for the five underlying multilevel logistic models corresponding to the cumulative odds analysis. Of interest is the pattern of effects for each variable across these five logistic splits. The effects estimated in the proportional odds model summarize these effects, and thus, they should be quite similar, on average, across the five models if the assumption is feasible.

Recall that there are only 9 students who were at or below proficiency level 0 for our sample, so the estimates for that particular analysis are likely not reliable. Despite this small first group size, the parameter estimates in terms of log-odds and the odds ratios for two of our variables—NUMRISKS and NBHOODCLIM—do appear to be similar across the five analyses. Averaging the logistic ORs for each variable to approximate the expected odds ratio under the proportional odds assumption, we find an "average" OR of 1.75 for NUMRISKS and an "average" OR of 1.11 for NBHOODCLIM. These both are fairly consistent with the values estimated in the ordinal HGLM: 1.48 and 1.13, respectively. The effect of PUBPRIV2 does not exhibit such consistency ("average" OR = .36), so the distribution of this vari-

TABLE 6.12 Parameter Estimates and Odds Ratios (OR) for the Multilevel Logistic Models Corresponding to Cumulative Analyses for the Ordinal Contextual Model in Table 6.9

Response estimated Fixed effects	$R_{ij} \leq 0$ Coeff (SE) OR	$R_{ij} \leq 1$ Coeff (SE) OR	$R_{ij} \leq 2$ Coeff (SE) OR	$R_{ij} \leq 3$ Coeff (SE) OR	$R_{ij} \leq 4$ Coeff (SE) OR
Model for the intercepts (β_0)					
Intercept (γ_{00})	$-6.94 (.50)^{**}$ 0.00	$-5.25 (.21)^{**}$ 0.01	$-3.63 (.10)^{**}$ .03	$-1.50 (.06)^{**}$ 0.22	$.70 (.05)^{**}$ 1.97
NBHOODCLIM (γ_{01})	$.03 (.12)$ 1.03	$.09 (.05)^{*}$ 1.10	$.09 (.03)^{**}$ 1.10	$.10 (.02)^{**}$ 1.11	$.15 (.02)^{**}$ 1.16
PUBPRIV2 (γ_{02})	$-31.83 (4.1 \times 10^5)$ 0.00	$-1.45 (.73)^{*}$ 0.23	$-1.33 (.32)^{**}$ 0.26	$-.47 (.11)^{**}$ 0.62	$-.37 (.09)^{**}$ 0.69
Model for the NUMRISKS slopes (β_1)					
Intercept (γ_{10})	$.69 (.32)^{*}$ 1.99	$.67 (.13)^{**}$ 1.95	$.57 (.07)^{**}$ 1.76	$.33 (.04)^{**}$ 1.39	$.52 (.06)^{**}$ 1.68
Random effects (variance components)					
Var. in intercepts (τ_{00})	.134	.794	.340	$.339^{**}$	$.235^{**}$

$^{*} p < .05; ^{**} p < .01$

able across the proficiency categories, and the reasonableness of assuming a common odds ratio for the effect of attending a public or private school on proficiency, may be worth further investigation.

The assumption of proportional odds is an attractive one in terms of model parsimony, provided the intent of the research is to estimate an overall effect of a predictor variable on an ordinal outcome. While the proportional odds model is certainly the most widely used approach for analyzing ordinal data, there are popular alternatives, including continuation ratio HGLMs (Plewis, 2002) and mixed models that allow for non- or partial-proportional odds (Hedeker & Mermelstein, 1998). These approaches correspond well conceptually to similar alternatives in the single-level arena, many of which have been widely studied (e.g., Ananth & Kleinbaum, 1997; Greenland, 1994; O'Connell, 2006).

DISCUSSION

Multilevel logistic and ordinal models have wide appeal given the kinds of variables often studied in education and in social or behavioral psychology. The examples we discussed in this chapter were selected to illustrate the potential of these kinds of models and to provide a starting point for researchers who may be new to these methods. Our objective was to lay the methodological foundation for researchers to investigate significant research questions involving dichotomous and ordinal outcomes across multiple contexts. We structured our examples around the four model-building elements for generalized models suggested by Dobson (2002): expressing the response as a collection of predictor variables, parameter estimation and interpretation, quality of fit, and statistical inference and hypothesis testing—particularly with regard to the assumptions made by the multilevel logistic and ordinal models. Understanding the impact of contexts such as schools, classrooms, organizations, or communities on individual outcomes continues to emerge as a critical feature of many research studies. The examples and discussions provided in this chapter should prepare researchers to take advantage of multilevel methods when their outcomes of interest are measured using dichotomous or ordinal scales.

In our examples, the ordinal outcome variable was proficiency level computed from student responses to a series of clustered test items. A related critical application for HGLMs can be found within educational testing, where interest often first lies in the items that make up the reported scores. One issue of concern to educators and particularly to psychometricians is that of differential functioning of test items across different demographic groups, such as gender and ethnic, cultural, or racial groups. Logistic regression and ordinal logistic regression models have been used to model performance on dichotomously and ordinally scored test items as a function of student proficiency, group membership, and their interaction (Rogers & Swaminathan, 1993; Swaminathan & Rogers, 1994). In the case of items scored on an ordinal scale (such as where partial credit is assigned or responses to the item task are rated), a proportional odds or partial proportional odds model may be used. One of the strengths of logistic and ordinal regression procedures for investigating differential item functioning (DIF) is that they can be extended to take into account the hierarchical nature of student response data. Using multilevel models for assessing DIF not only allows for better estimation of DIF effects within schools or districts but also allows for a deeper analysis of factors that may explain or predict the presence of DIF.

Kamata (2001) provides in-depth discussion of how models for item-response theory can be viewed as HGLM's. Segawa (2005) extends several of these concepts to growth models for item-level data (i.e., three-level HGLM). Kamata, Bauer, and Miyazaki (2008) provide further demonstration of measurement models within a multilevel context. Rogers and Swaminathan (1998) developed Bayesian estimation procedures for fitting multilevel models for ordinal response data and applied them to investigate factors related to gender DIF in items from the National Assessment of Educational Progress (NAEP). Readers interested in methodology and applications for the analysis of item-level data within a multilevel framework would benefit from review of the few articles and chapters mentioned here.

SOME SOFTWARE OPTIONS

An excellent review of currently available software for multilevel modeling is included in chapter 12 in this volume (Roberts & McLeod, 2008). Not all currently available software is capable of fitting HGLM's (e.g., SPSS®), although software does tend to change rapidly enough that these procedures may be included in programming updates in the near future. We mention several potentially useful software packages here, but researchers do need to seek out documentation of the different estimation strategies and the particular models that these packages do or do not currently offer, as well as other packages that offer multilevel models for dichotomous, ordinal or other kinds of non-normal response variables.

In this chapter, we used HLMv6.04 (Raudenbush et al., 2004) to describe the features of HGLMs for dichotomous and ordinal data and to emphasize a conceptual understanding of the results of these models. The HLM software can be used to fit mixed models for continuous, dichotomous, and ordinal response data and is capable of fitting other non-linear functions as

238 A.A. O'CONNELL et al.

well (e.g., Poisson). The HLM website, http://www.ssicentral.com/hlm/, contains extensive downloadable examples with descriptions and explanations of results for HGLM.

The powerful and versatile SAS® software has three procedures for performing hierarchical or multilevel modeling: PROC MIXED, PROC GLIMMIX, and PROC NLMIXED. The MIXED procedure is used primarily for fitting linear mixed models of random effects and fixed effects to data. In this modeling approach, both intercepts and slopes are allowed to differ randomly, hence, leading to a multilevel model. PROC MIXED handles normally distributed response variables only. It assumes that the underlying distribution of random effects is normal, and random effects are entered linearly into the model. This procedure is identical to PROC GLM (for general linear models) if a model consists of fixed effects only.

PROC GLIMMIX fits generalized linear mixed models to data. This procedure handles response variables that are exponentially distributed. Like PROC MIXED, the GLIMMIX procedure assumes that the underlying distribution of random effects is normal, and it enters random effects linearly. This procedure is identical to PROC GENMOD (for generalized linear models) if a model consists of fixed effects only.

PROC NLMIXED is particularly suited for fitting nonlinear mixed models to data. Like PROC GLIMMIX, the NLMIXED procedure handles response variables that are exponentially distributed; it assumes that the underlying distribution of random effects is normal. Unlike the GLIMMIX procedure, PROC NLMIXED allows random effects to be entered linearly or non-linearly. When modeling generalized linear mixed models, PROC NLMIXED is more limited in the type of models allowed than PROC GLIMMIX is. Examples of the multilevel model approach performed by these three procedures and two macros (%GLIMMIX and %NLMIX), including examples for binomial and ordinal data, are available through SAS® version 9.1 Users Guide (SAS, 2004) and at http://support.sas.com/rnd/app/papers/glimmix.pdf and http://support.sas.com/documentation/onlinedoc/91pdf/index_913.html.

Plewis (2002) presents brief examples of the MLwiN® (Rasbash, et al., 2002) software approach to modeling multilevel ordinal data; this software is capable of fitting a variety of linear and non-linear mixed models. The Centre for Multilevel Modeling in Bristol, England, maintains a comprehensive website at http://www.cmm.bristol.ac.uk/ with data examples and some instructional support for modeling dichotomous or ordinal outcomes.

MIXOR®, a specialized software developed by Hedeker and Gibbons (1996) for mixed-effects ordinal regression analysis, is freely available online with a website that includes extensive application examples at http://tigger.uic.edu/hedeker/mix.html. Extensions to MIXOR include a suite of programs designed for mixed-effects models that can fit a variety of linear and non-linear situations.

Finally, R is a freeware package that has capacity for complex multilevel models including HGLM and has been used within that framework for item-response analyses and other educational or psychological applications. The developers maintain a comprehensive website with accessible documentation, example data sets and annotated analyses that continually are being updated and added to by its network of users; links to available resources can be accessed from http://www.r-project.org/.

NOTES

1. Other options include probit models, although these are not widely used in education. The logit model tends to be simpler to interpret, "because it can be written as a linear model for the logodds" (Fox, 1997, p. 448).
2. Information on access to the public-use ECLS-K data is available from NCES online at http://nces.ed.gov/ecls
3. The ECLS-K Users Guide explains that approximately 5% of children had response patterns that did not follow the Guttman model and attributes these patterns to guessing on multiple choice items.
4. Early releases of the ECLS-K data did not contain the highest proficiency score attained; these had to be derived from a series of dichotomous variables indicating pass/fail for each item cluster. Release of the third-grade data included highest proficiency scores for all earlier releases of the data, and those are the data used here.

REFERENCES

Agresti, A. (1989). Tutorial on modeling ordered categorical response data. *Psychological Bulletin, 105*, 290–301.

Agresti, A. (1990). *Categorical data analysis.* New York: John Wiley & Sons.

Agresti, A. (1996). *An introduction to categorical data analysis.* New York: John Wiley & Sons.

Ananth, C. V., & Kleinbaum, D. G. (1997). Regression models for ordinal responses: A review of methods and applications. *International Journal of Epidemiology, 26,* 1323–1333.

Armstrong, B.G., & Sloan, M. (1989). Ordinal regression models for epidemiologic data. *American Journal of Epidemiology, 129,* 191–204.

Bell, J.F., & Dexter, T. (2000). Using ordinal multilevel models to assess the comparability of examinations. *Multilevel Modeling Newsletter, 12*(2), 4–9.

Bender, R., &Benner, A. (2000). Calculating ordinal regression models in SAS and S-PLUS. *Biometrical Journal, 42,* 677–699.

Brant, R. (1990). Assessing proportionality in the proportional odds model for ordinal logistic regression. *Biometrics, 46,* 1171–1178.

Browne, W.J., Subramanian, S.V., Jones, K., & Goldstein, H. (2005). Variance partitioning in multilevel logistic models that exhibit overdispersion. *J.R. Statistical Society A, 168*(3), 599–613.

Cizek, G. J., & Fitzgerald, S. M. (1999). An introduction to logistic regression. *Measurement and Evaluation in Counseling and Development, 31,* 223–245.

Clogg, C.C., & Shihadeh, E.S. (1994). *Statistical models for ordinal variables.* Thousand Oaks, CA: Sage.

Dobson, A.J. (2002). *An introduction to generalized linear models* (2nd ed.). Boca Raton, FL: Chapman & Hall/CRC.

Evans, M., Hastings, N., & Peacock, B. (2000). *Statistical distributions* (3rd ed.). New York: Wiley

Fielding, A. (2003). Ordered category responses and random effects in multilevel and other complex structures. In Steven P. Reise and Naihua Duan (Eds.), *Multilevel modeling: Methodological advances, issues, and applications.* (p. 181–208). Mahwah, NJ: Lawrence Erlbaum Associates.

Fox, J. (1997). *Applied regression analysis, linear models, and related methods.* Thousand Oaks, CA: Sage.

Goldstein, H. (2002). *Multilevel statistical models* (3rd ed.). London: Oxford University Press.

Greenland, S. (1994). Alternative models for ordinal logistic regression. *Statistics in Medicine, 13,* 1665–1677.

Hedeker, D. & Gibbons, R.D. (1994). MIXOR: A computer program for mixed-effects ordinal regression analysis. *Computer Methods and Programs in Biomedicine, 49,* 157–76.

Hedeker, D. & Gibbons, R.D. (1996). A random-effects ordinal regression model for multilevel analysis. *Biometrics, 50,* 933–944.

Hedeker, D., & Mermelstein, R.J.(1998). A multilevel thresholds of change model for analysis of stages of change data. *Multivariate Behavioral Research, 33,* 427–455.

Hosmer, D. W., & Lemeshow, S. (2000). *Applied logistic regression* (2nd ed.). New York: John Wiley & Sons.

Kamata, A. (2001). Item analysis by the hierarchical generalized linear model. *Journal of Educational Measurement, 38,* 79–93.

Kamata, A., Bauer, D. J., & Miyazaki, Y. (2008). Multilevel measurement modeling. In A. A. O'Connell and D. B. McCoach (Eds.), *Multilevel modeling of educational data* (pp. 345–388). Charlotte, NC: Information Age Publishing.

Leyland, A.H. & Goldstein, H. (2001). *Multilevel modeling of health statistics.* New York: John Wiley and Sons.

Liao, T. F. (1994). *Interpreting probability models* (Quantitative Applications in the Social Sciences, No. 101). Thousand Oaks, CA: Sage.

Long, J.S. (1997). *Regression models for categorical and limited dependent variables.* Thousand Oaks, CA: Sage.

McCoach, D. B., & Black, A. C. (2008). Evaluation of model fit and adequacy. In A. A. O'Connell and D. B. McCoach (Eds.), *Multilevel modeling of educational data* (pp. 245–271). Charlotte, NC: Information Age Publishing.

McCullagh, P. (1980). Regression models with ordinal data (with discussion). *Journal of the Royal Statistical Society, B, 42*, 109–142.

McCullagh, P. & Nelder, J. (1989). *Generalized linear models* (2nd ed.). London: Chapman & Hall.

McCullach, C.E. & Searle, S. R. (2001). *Generalized, linear, and mixed models*. New York: John Wiley Sons, Inc.

Menard, S. (1995). *Applied logistic regression analysis*. Thousand Oaks, CA: Sage.

Menard, S. (2000). Coefficients of determination for multiple logistic regression analysis. *The American Statistician, 54*, 17–24.

National Center for Education Statistics (2002). *User's manual for the ECLS-K first grade public-use data files and electronic code book: NCES 2002-135*. Washington DC: US Department of Education.

Nelder, J.A., & Wedderburn, R.W. (1972). Generalized linear models. *Journal of the Royal Statistical Society, Series A, 135*, 370–384.

O'Connell, A.A., (2000). Methods for modeling ordinal outcome variables. *Measurement and Evaluation in Counseling and Development, 33*, 170–193.

O'Connell, A.A. (2006). *Logistic regression models for ordinal response variables*. Thousand Oaks, CA: Sage.

Pampel, F. C. (2000). *Logistic regression: A primer*. Thousand Oaks, CA: Sage.

Peng, C.Y.J., & Nichols, R. N. (2003). Using multinomial logistic models to predict adolescent behavioral risk. *Journal of Modern Applied Statistical Methods, 2*(1), 177–188.

Plewis, I. (2002). Modeling ordinal data using MlwiN. *Multilevel Modelling Newsletter, 14*(1). Retrieved from: http://multilevel.ioe.ac.uk/publref/newsletters.html.

Prochaska, J.O., & Velicer, W.F. (1997). The transtheoretical model of health behavior change. *American Journal of Health Promotion, 12*, 38–48.

Rasbash, J., Browne, W., Goldstein, H., Yang, M., Plewis, I., Woodhouse, G., et al. (2002). *A user's guide to MLwiN*. London: Centre for Multilevel Modelling.

Raudenbush, S.W. & Bryk, A. S. (2002). *Hierarchical linear models: Applications and data analysis methods* (2nd ed.). Newbury Park, CA: Sage.

Raudenbush, S., Bryk, A., Cheong, Y.F., & Congdon, R. (2004). *HLM 6: Hierarchical linear and nonlinear modeling*. Lincolnwood, IL: Scientific Software International.

Roberts, J. K., & McLeod, P. (2008). Software options for multilevel models. In A. A. O'Connell and D. B. McCoach (Eds.), *Multilevel modeling of educational data* (pp. 427–467). Charlotte, NC: Information Age Publishing.

Rogers, H. J., & Swaminathan, H. (1993). A comparison of the logistic regression and Mantel-Haenszel procedures for detecting differential item functioning. *Applied Psychological Measurement, 17*, 105–116.

Rogers, H. J., & Swaminathan, H. (1998, August). *A multilevel approach for investigating DIF*. Paper presented at the annual APA meeting, San Francisco.

Segawa, E. (2005). A growth model for multilevel ordinal data. *Journal of Educational and Behavioral Statistics, 30*, 369–396.

Snijders, T.A.B. & Bosker, R.J. (1999). *Multilevel analysis*. Thousand Oaks, CA: Sage.

Statistical Analysis System. (1997). SAS/STAT software: Changes and enhancements through release 6.12. Cary, NC: Author.

Statistical Analysis System (2004). SAS/STAT 9.1 user's guide. Cary, NC: SAS Institute Inc. available online http://support.sas.com/documentation/onlinedoc/91pdf/sasdoc_91/stat_ug_7313.pdf

Swaminathan, H., & Rogers, H. J. (1994, April). *Logistic regression procedures for detecting DIF in nondichotomous item responses.* Paper presented at the annual NCME meeting, New Orleans.

Tate, R. (2004). Interpreting Hierarchical Linear and Hierarchical Generalized Linear Models with Slopes as Outcomes. *Journal of Experimental Education, 73,* 71–95.

West, J., Denton, K., & Germino-Hausken, E. (2000). *America's kindergartners: Findings from the Early Childhood Longitudinal Study, Kindergarten Class of 1998–99: Fall 1998.* Washington, DC: United States Department of Education, National Center for Education Statistics. (NCES 2000-070)

Wong, G.Y., & Mason, W.M. (1985). The hierarchical logistic regression model for multilevel analysis. *Journal of the American Statistical Association, 80,* 513–524.

Zill, N., & West, J. (2001). *Entering kindergarten: A portrait of American children when they begin school.* Washington, DC: United States Department of Education, National Center for Education Statistics. (NCES 2001-035).

PART II

PLANNING AND EVALUATING MULTILEVEL MODELS

CHAPTER 7

EVALUATION OF MODEL FIT AND ADEQUACY

D. Betsy McCoach and Anne C. Black

"All models are false, but some are useful."
—Box, 1979, p. 202

How do researchers evaluate multilevel models? How should they choose among competing models? The utility of any model depends upon its ability to explain the phenomenon under investigation. Therefore, assessment of model adequacy should consider two aspects of the model: 1) model fit, or the use of model selection criteria to choose among competing models, and 2) the explanatory power of the model, or the ability of the predictors to explain scores on the outcome variable. While model fit is evaluated relative to other competing models, the explanatory power of the model may be evaluated both relative to competing models and in an absolute sense (i.e., does the model do a good or poor job of explaining scores on the outcome variable?). This chapter explains common measures of model adequacy within the multilevel modeling literature. Further, we briefly describe several areas of controversy or confusion surrounding measures of model adequacy. Finally, we provide recommendations for evaluating the adequacy of a multilevel model.

Multilevel Modeling of Educational Data, pages 245–272
Copyright © 2008 by Information Age Publishing

MODEL SELECTION CRITERIA

Model selection should be guided by theory and informed by data. Burnham and Anderson (2004) suggest that three general principles should guide model selection in the social sciences. First, parsimony is paramount. Adding additional parameters is likely to improve fit and cannot lead to worse model fit (Forster, 2000). The critical issue is whether the improvement in the fit of the model justifies the inclusion of the additional parameters. Second, Burnham and Anderson advocate the use of multiple working hypotheses. Using data to compare several plausible competing hypotheses often provides more useful information than comparing a given model to an often implausible null hypothesis. Third, one of the central tenets of scientific research is the use of quantitative information to judge the strength of evidence (Burnham & Anderson). Finally, researchers should examine the model to ensure that the estimated parameters make sense and seem plausible.

Model selection is a crucial part of the multilevel modeling process. How does the researcher select the appropriate model from among several competing models? Model selection requires striking a delicate balance between parsimony and complexity. The researcher's goal is to "arrive at a model that describes the observed data to a satisfactory extent but without unnecessary complications" (Snijders & Bosker, 1999, p. 91). The most common methods of model selection include hypothesis testing approaches and "information criteria," or index comparison, approaches. After briefly reviewing the concept of deviance, we explain how to use the chi-square difference test to compare the deviances of two nested models. We then review the use of index comparison approaches, such as the AIC and BIC, for model selection. Finally, we explain the use of R-squared type measures to determine the predictive power of the multilevel model. Researchers must consider both the fit and the predictive ability of a given multilevel model to determine the adequacy of the model.

Deviance

Maximum likelihood estimation techniques provide estimates for the values of the population parameters that maximize the probability of obtaining the observed data (Singer & Willett, 2003). A likelihood function "describes the probability of observing the sample data as a function of the model's unknown parameters" (Singer & Willett, p. 66). The parameter estimates are those estimates that maximize the likelihood function. When we use maximum likelihood (ML) to estimate the parameters of the model, the estimation also provides the likelihood, which easily can be transformed into a deviance statistic (Snijders & Bosker, 1999).

The deviance compares the log-likelihood of the specified model to the log-likelihood of a saturated model that fits the sample data perfectly (Singer & Willett, 2003, p. 117). Specifically, deviance = –2 (log-likelihood of the current model—log-likelihood of the saturated model) (–2LL) (Singer & Willett). Therefore, deviance is a measure of the badness of fit of a given model; it describes how much worse the specified model is than the best possible model (Singer & Willett). Deviance statistics cannot be interpreted directly since deviance is a function of sample size as well as the fit of the model. However, differences in deviance can be interpreted for competing models, if those models are hierarchically nested, use the same data set, and use full maximum likelihood estimation techniques to estimate the parameters.

In full maximum-likelihood estimation, the estimates of the variance and covariance components are conditional upon the point estimates of the fixed effects (Raudenbush & Bryk, 2002). When using full maximum likelihood (FIML), the number of parameters includes both the fixed effects and the variance and covariance components. Restricted maximum likelihood (REML) estimates of variance-covariance components adjust for the uncertainty about the fixed effects; FIML estimates do not (Raudenbush & Bryk). When the number of level-two units is large, REML and FIML results will produce similar estimates of the variance components. However, when there are few level-two units, the maximum likelihood estimates of the variance components (τ_{qq}) will be smaller than those produced by REML, and the REML results may be more realistic (Raudenbush & Bryk). The deviances of any two nested models that differ in terms of their fixed and/or random effects can be compared when using FIML. However, REML only allows for comparison of nested models that differ in their random effects (Snijders & Bosker, 1999, p. 89).

Hypothesis Testing

Hypothesis testing is one of the most commonly utilized model selection methods (Weaklim, 2004). In multilevel modeling, researchers often use chi-square difference tests to compare the fit of two different models. In addition, hypothesis tests are used to evaluate whether fixed effects, random level-one coefficients, and variance components are statistically significantly different from zero (Raudenbush & Bryk, 2002). Finally, general linear hypothesis testing using the Wald statistic allows researchers to test composite hypotheses about sets of fixed effects (Singer & Willett, 2003). Because this chapter is devoted to the determination of model fit issues, we focus our attention on the use of chi-square difference tests to determine the adequacy of the multilevel model.

Chi-square Difference Test

Two models are nested when one model is a subset of the other (Kline, 1998). In other words, in nested models, "the more complex model includes all of the parameters of the simpler model plus one or more additional parameters" (Raudenbush, Bryk, Cheong, & Congdon, 2000, p. 80–81). If two models are nested, the deviance statistics of two models can be compared directly. The deviance of the simpler model (D_1) minus the deviance of the more complex model (D_2) provides the change in deviance $(\Delta D = D_1 - D_2)$. The simpler model always will have at least as high a deviance as the more complex model, and generally the deviance of the more complex model will be lower than that of the simpler model. In large samples, the difference between the deviances of two hierarchically nested models is distributed as an approximate chi-square distribution with degrees of freedom equal to the difference in the number of parameters being estimated between the two models (de Leeuw, 2004). We refer to the number of parameters in the larger (less parsimonious) model as p_1 and the number of estimated parameters in the smaller (more parsimonious) model as p_2.

In evaluating model fit using the chi-square difference test, the more parsimonious model is preferred, as long as it does not result in significantly worse fit. In other words, if the model with the larger number of parameters fails to reduce the deviance by a substantial amount, the more parsimonious model is retained. Therefore, when the change in deviance (ΔD) exceeds the critical value of chi-square with $(p_1 - p_2)$ degrees of freedom, the difference in the deviances is statistically significant. In this situation, we favor the more complex model. However, if the more complex model does not result in a statistically significant reduction in the deviance statistic, we favor the more parsimonious model.

Full maximum likelihood estimation maximizes the likelihood of the sample data, whereas restricted maximum likelihood estimation maximizes the likelihood of the residuals (Singer & Willett, 2003, p. 118). In FIML, the number of reported parameters includes the fixed effects (the γ's) as well as the variance/covariance components. When using REML, the number of reported parameters includes only the variance and covariance components. To compare two nested models that differ in their fixed effects, it is necessary to use FIML estimation, not REML estimation. REML only allows for comparison of models that differ in terms of their random effects but have the same fixed effects. Because most programs use REML as the default method of estimation, it is important to remember to select FIML estimation to use ΔD to compare two hierarchically-nested models with different fixed effects.

An Example

Consider the following model:

$$Y_{ij} = \beta_{0j} + \beta_{1j}(IQ)_{ij} + r_{ij} \tag{7.1}$$

$$\beta_{0j} = \gamma_{00} + \gamma_{01}(SchoolSES)_j + u_{0j}$$

$$\beta_{1j} = \gamma_{10} + \gamma_{11}(SchoolSES)_j + u_{1j}$$

Remember, the number of estimated parameters in FIML is equal to the number of fixed effects (γ's) plus the number of variance covariance components. In this example, there are four fixed effects (γ_{00}, $\gamma_{01,}$ $\gamma_{10,}$ and γ_{11}). In addition, there are four variance covariance components (σ^2, the variance of r_{ij}; τ_{00}, the variance of u_{0j}; τ_{11}, the variance of u_{1j}; and τ_{01}, the covariance of u_{0j} and u_{1j}.). Therefore, there are eight estimated parameters in FIML. In contrast, the number of estimated parameters in REML is simply the number of variance/covariance components (σ^2, the variance of r_{ij}; τ_{00}, the variance of u_{0j}; τ_{11}, the variance of u_{1j}; and τ_{01}, the covariance of u_{0j} and u_{1j}.). In this example, there are four estimated parameters in REML.

Imagine we wanted to compare the model above to the following model, a model in which the SES/IQ slope remains constant across schools:

$$Y_{ij} = \beta_{0j} + \beta_{1j}(IQ)_{ij} + r_{ij} \tag{7.2}$$

$$\beta_{0j} = \gamma_{00} + \gamma_{01}(SchoolSES)_j + u_{0j}$$

$$\beta_{1j} = \gamma_{10} + \gamma_{11}(SchoolSES)_j$$

We are no longer estimating a variance for u_{1j} or the covariance of u_{1j} and u_{0j}. Therefore, model 2 contains six estimated parameters in FIML and two estimated parameters in REML. The difference between the deviance of model 1 and model 2 could be compared using either REML or FIML since the two models vary only in their variance-covariance components. Assume that the deviance of model 1 is 32, and the deviance of model 2 is 45; therefore, the difference between the deviances is 13. We compare this to the critical value of χ^2 with two degrees of freedom (which is 5.99). Because 13 is larger than 5.99, we reject the null hypothesis that the simpler model provides an equally good fit to the data, we determine that the simpler model fits significantly worse than the more complex model (the more complex model fits significantly better than the simpler model). Therefore, we conclude that we cannot make the proposed simplifications, and we opt in favor of the more complex model.

Finally, consider model 3, as compared to our initial model, model 1.

$$Y_{ij} = \beta_{0j} + \beta_{1j}(IQ)_{ij} + r_{ij} \tag{7.3}$$

$$\beta_{0j} = \gamma_{00} + \gamma_{01}(SchoolSES)_j + u_{0j}$$

$$\beta_{1j} = \gamma_{10} + u_{1j}$$

Model 3 eliminates the cross-level interaction between School SES and IQ. Model 3 contains seven estimated parameters in FIML (three fixed effects: γ_{00}, $\gamma_{01,}$ and $\gamma_{10,:}$ and four random effects: σ^2, τ_{00}, τ_{11}, and τ_{01}.) However, model 3 has four estimated parameters in REML, just as model 1 did. This demonstrates that models 1 and 3 are nested models in FIML but not in REML.

Other Model Selection Techniques

Using hypothesis testing procedures is one of the most commonly employed model selection methods in multilevel modeling. However, the hypothesis testing approach to model selection has been criticized on several grounds (Raftery, 1995). First, with large sample sizes, most null hypotheses are rejected. Therefore, the use of hypothesis tests for model selection can produce very complex models (Weaklim, 2004). Second, when a given model is selected from multiple models, p-values do not have the same interpretation as they do when only two models are considered, and p-values can be misleading in this situation (Raftery). "By choosing among a large number of variables, one increases the probability of finding 'significant' variables by chance alone" (Raftery, p. 118). In addition, classical hypothesis tests do not necessarily identify a single best model (Weaklim). While significance tests permit the researcher to reject or fail to reject the null hypothesis, significance tests do not actually provide evidence in support of the null hypothesis (Raftery). In other words, we have no evidence that the model we failed to reject is better than or preferable to the comparison model; we only can say that it is not significantly worse than the comparison model. Therefore, the more parsimonious model can be rejected, but it can never be 'confirmed' (Weaklim). By convention, researchers generally choose the most parsimonious model that is not rejected, selecting the simplest model unless there is statistical evidence suggesting the more complex model is preferable. However, this process cannot answer the question of which model is better. "Null hypothesis testing only provides arbitrary dichotomies (e.g., significant vs. non-significant), and in the all-too-often-seen case in which the null hypothesis is false on a priori grounds, the test result is superfluous" (Burnham & Anderson, 2004, p. 266). Since all models are simplifications of reality, all models are likely to be misspecified to a certain degree. Therefore, hypothesis tests do not provide guidance to help select an *imperfect* but parsimonious model (Gelman & Rubin, 1995). Further, hypothesis tests do not aid researchers in deciding whether the lack of fit of a parsimonious model is a problem in practice (Gelman & Rubin). Finally, hypothesis testing procedures do not quantify how *much* better a particular model is. Because hypothesis testing does not allow us to quantify the degree of fit or misfit; we cannot quantify the degree to which one model should be preferred over another.

However, the largest drawback of the hypothesis testing approach is that it only permits the comparison of nested models. It is often impossible to compare competing hypotheses using nested statistical models (Raftery, 1995). This is especially true when the models embody dissimilar or contradictory views of the process or phenomenon under examination (Raftery). Because hypothesis testing procedures only allow for comparison of nested models, if we wish to compare two models with different sets of predictors, we cannot use the chi-square difference test or any other hypothesis testing procedure. In this situation, model selection indices, such as the Akaike Information Criterion (*AIC*) and the Bayesian Information Criterion (*BIC*), are particularly helpful because they allow us to rank or compare models with different sets of parameters.

AIC and BIC

While model index comparison approaches, such as *AIC* and *BIC*, have received relatively little attention within the educational literature, their use is quite common within the sociological literature. (See, for example, *Sociological Methods and Research*, Volume 33(2), 2004, a special issue devoted to model selection issues in sociology). Information theoretic model selection represents, in some sense, the converse of classical hypothesis testing procedures (Bozdogan, 1987). Information theoretic techniques focus on "choosing a critical value which then determines, approximately, what the significance level is or might be" (Bozdogan, p. 363); whereas, in statistical significance testing, the researcher sets the probability of Type I error (alpha), which then determines the critical value.

There are several advantages to using the *AIC* or the *BIC* rather than relying upon deviance statistics and chi-square difference tests to evaluate the goodness of fit of a multilevel model. First, the *AIC* and *BIC* allow the comparison of non-nested models. As long as the sample remains constant, *AIC* and *BIC* allow the comparison of competing models, whether or not they are hierarchically nested. Further, selection indices such as the *AIC* and the *BIC* quantify the degree to which the given model represents an improvement over comparison models.

The Bayesian approach to model selection regards every competing model as the possible "true" model, and then estimates the likelihood that the model in question is, indeed, the correct model (Zucchini, 2000). For the *AIC*, the prediction of future data is the key criterion of the adequacy of a model (Kuha, 2004). Therefore, although the formulas for the *BIC* and the *AIC* appear similar, the philosophical underpinnings of the two approaches differ dramatically. The field of sociology tends to favor the *BIC*; whereas, econometricians tend to prefer the *AIC* (Kuha, 2004). Whether researchers should use the *AIC* or the *BIC* for model selection purposes has been the subject of much debate and scrutiny (Kuha, 2004; Weaklim, 1999, 2004). We choose to sidestep the controversy surrounding the choice of the *AIC* or the *BIC*. Rather, we believe that the combined use of the *AIC* and the *BIC* (in conjunction with chi-square difference tests for nested models) can be quite informative. While our explanations of the *AIC* and *BIC* are conceptually and mathematically shallow, we believe that they will serve the applied researcher. Those interested in the conceptual and methodological underpinnings of the *AIC* and the *BIC* should refer to Bozdogan (1987), Burnham and Anderson, (2004), Raftery (1995), Schwarz (1978), Wagenmeyers and Farrell (2004), and Zucchini (2000).

Not all software programs provide *AIC* and *BIC* measures in their output. HLM 6.04 does not provide estimates of *AIC* and *BIC*; however, SPSS, SAS, R, and MPLUS do provide these indices. Both the *AIC* and the *BIC* can be computed easily from the deviance statistic. Because *AIC* and *BIC* are computed from the deviance statistic, FIML generally is considered the most appropriate estimation method to use when computing information criteria (Verbeke & Molenberghs, 2000). However, a recent simulation study by Gurka (2006) suggests that information criteria such as the AIC and BIC also may perform at least as well under REML as they do under FIML. Further research is needed to determine whether information indices such as the AIC and BIC can be used with REML, but Gurka's results suggest that the use of information criteria under REML may not be as problematic as was once believed.

The Akaike Information Criterion (AIC). The formula for the *AIC* is shown below.

$$AIC = D + 2p \qquad (7.4)$$

where D is deviance and p = the number of parameters estimated in the model.

To compute the *AIC*, simply multiply the number of parameters by two and add this product to the deviance statistic. As you will recall, the deviance (or –2log-likelihood [–2LL]) represents the degree "of inaccuracy, badness of fit, or bias when the maximum likelihood estimators of the parameters of a model are used" (Bozdogan, 1987, p. 356). The second term, $2p$, imposes a penalty based on the complexity of the model. When there are several competing models, the model with the lowest AIC value is considered to be the best model. Because the AIC's penalty term is equal to $2p$, the deviance must decrease by more than 2 per additional parameter in order to favor the model with greater numbers of parameters.

Compare this to the chi-square difference test for model selection. The critical value of χ^2 with one degree of freedom at $\alpha = .05$ is 3.84. Therefore, when comparing two models that differ by one degree of freedom, the chi-square difference test actually imposes a more stringent criterion for rejecting the simpler model. In fact, this is true for comparisons of models that differ by seven or fewer parameters. Therefore, using the chi-square difference test will result in an equivalent or more parsimonious model than using the AIC when comparing models that differ by seven or fewer parameters. However, when comparing models that differ by more than seven parameters, the AIC will favor more parsimonious models.

The Bayesian Information Criterion (BIC). The BIC is equal to the sum of the deviance and the product of the natural log of the sample size and the number of parameters. The formula for the BIC is shown below.

$$BIC = D + \ln(n) * p \qquad (7.5)$$

where D is deviance (–2LL),
p = the number of parameters estimated in the model, and
n = the sample size.

Therefore, the BIC imposes a penalty on the number of parameters that is impacted directly by the sample size. In multilevel models, it is not entirely clear which sample size should be used with the BIC: the number of units at the lowest level, the number of units at the highest level, or some weighted average of the two. SAS PROC MIXED uses the number of independent sampling units as the sample size when computing the BIC. In contrast, SPSS and R use the level-one sample size in their computation of the BIC. Therefore, even though SPSS and SAS will produce identical –2LL and AIC values, the BIC value will differ across these programs. Since the BIC imposes a steeper per parameter penalty as the sample size increases, the BIC value produced by SPSS and R will be larger than the BIC value produced by SAS, and it will tend to favor more parsimonious models. MPLUS also uses the level-one sample size in the computation of BIC. However, because growth models in MPLUS would typically be formulated in the wide or multivariate format, the effective sample size used for the computation of the

BIC in MPLUS is the number of people in the sample. Thus, the choice of sample size for the computation of the *BIC* is not without controversy. Future research should address the impact of this choice on model selection. In the meantime, researchers should carefully consider which sample size they are implicitly or explicitly using in their computation of the *BIC*.

However, even at small sample sizes, the *BIC* will favor more parsimonious models than the *AIC* or traditional chi-square difference tests. Given a sample size as low as 50, the penalty for the *BIC* is 3.912 times the number of parameters. In contrast, the penalty for the *AIC* is two times the number of parameters, and the rejection region for traditional chi-square difference tests is 3.84 for one parameter, 5.99 for two parameters, etc.

The model with the lowest *BIC* is considered to be the best fitting model. Raftery (1995) provided guidelines for interpreting changes in *BIC*. Subtract the *BIC* for model 2 from the *BIC* for model 1 to compute a *BIC* difference ($BIC_1 - BIC_2$). Raftery suggests that *BIC* differences of 0–2 provide weak evidence favoring model 2 over model 1, *BIC* differences of 2–6 provide positive evidence for favoring model 2, *BIC* differences of 6–10 provide strong evidence favoring model 2, and *BIC* differences above 10 provide very strong evidence favoring model 2 over model 1.

The central question in model selection is how much additional information a given parameter must add to justify its inclusion (Weaklim, 2004). Figure 7.1 provides a graph of the decision values for the chi-square differ-

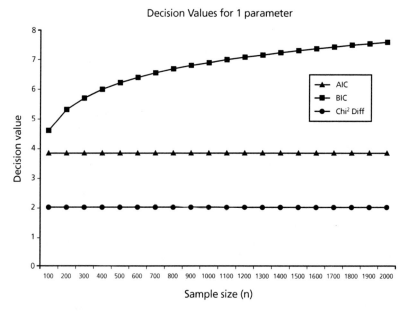

Figure 7.1 Critical decision values for *AIC*, *BIC*, and chi-square difference measures with successive increases in sample size of 100.

ence test, the *AIC*, and the *BIC* for two nested models that differ by one parameter at a variety of sample sizes. The y-axis shows the change in deviance
necessary to favor the more complex model over the simpler model. In the
figure, this quantity is called the "decision value." The figure clearly shows
that for one-parameter tests, the *AIC* placed the least stringent criterion for
favoring the more complex model. The *BIC* places the most stringent criterion for favoring the more parsimonious model, and the penalty that the
BIC imposes becomes increasingly stringent as the sample size increases.
However, the relationship between the *BIC* and the sample size is curvilinear, and increasing the sample size has very little impact on the decision
value of the *BIC* once the sample reaches 10,000 or greater. For example,
the penalty for a sample size of 10,000 is 9.21; the penalty for a sample size
of 20,000 is 9.90; the penalty for a sample size of 30,000 is 10.31.

Figure 7.2 provides a graph of the decision values for the chi-square difference test, the *AIC*, and the *BIC* with sample sizes of 200, 1000, and 5000
for nested models as a function of the change in the number of parameters.
When comparing models that differ by a small number of parameters (sev-
en or fewer), the *AIC* will result in the most complex models. The *BIC* will
always favor more parsimonious models than the *AIC* or the chi-square difference test, and this effect is especially pronounced at larger sample sizes.

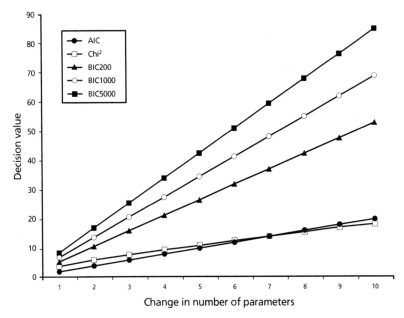

Figure 7.2 Critical decision values for *AIC*, *BIC*, and chi-square difference measures
where *n* = 200, 1000, and 5000, as number of parameters increases from 1 to 10.

In conclusion, of the three model selection techniques, *BIC* favors the most parsimonious models, regardless of sample size. The *AIC* and the chi-square difference test often will provide similar results. However, the chi-square difference test favors more parsimonious models for smaller changes in the number of parameters, and the *AIC* favors more parsimonious models in the case of larger changes in the number of parameters. The *BIC* explicitly takes sample size into consideration, while chi-square and *AIC* do not. It is important to remember that the chi-square difference test only can be used to compare nested models. However, the *AIC* and the *BIC* can be used to compare both nested and non-nested models. Our recommendation is to examine *AIC*, *BIC*, and chi-square difference tests (for nested models). Most of the time, the three methods will converge upon the same decision. When there is a discrepancy among the three indices, we recommend using professional judgment and knowledge of the research area to guide decision making.

Example

To illustrate the use of the hypothesis testing and model selection approaches, we turn our attention to Table 7.1, which contains fixed and random effects estimates for six different models, and to Table 7.2, which contains their associated fit statistics. We illustrate a model-building approach to model the between- and within-school variability of students' reading achievement at the beginning of kindergarten using the Early Childhood Longitudinal Study, Kindergarten Cohort (ECLS-K). (See chapters 2 and 6 of this volume (Stapleton & Thomas, 2008, and O'Connell, Goldstein, Rogers, & Pens, 2008, respectively) for details about the ECLS-K dataset.) The sample size for this analysis includes 7215 first-time kindergarteners in 578 kindergartens. To enable comparison of models that differed in their fixed effects using the chi-square difference test and to compute the *BIC* and *AIC* values, we estimated all models using FIML. The models in Table 7.1 utilize a small set of student- and school-level predictors to explain students' reading achievement in the fall of the kindergarten year. Student-level variables include age and SES. School-level variables include school type (public/private), the percentage of students who receive free lunch in the school (a measure of school *SES*), and the percentage of minority students in the school. Model 1 is the baseline model. As a control variable, it includes the number of months of kindergarten the student attended prior to taking the reading achievement test. Model 2 adds the student's age at kindergarten entry as a level-one predictor. As seen in Table 7.1, the fixed effect of SES is statistically significant (the parameter estimate is .36; the standard error is

TABLE 7.1 Fixed Effects and Variance Components for ECLS-K Example Analyses

Fixed effects	Parameter	Model 1 (baseline)	Model 2 (adds age of kindergarten entry)	Model 3 (adds SES)	Model 4 (SES—with no random slope)	Model 5 (adds sector and % free lunch)	Model 6 (adds % minority)
For Intercept (β_0)							
Intercept	γ_{00}	20.86 (.73)	20.88 (.72)	19.97 (.55)	20.09 (.56)	19.22 (.52)	19.23 (.52)
Private	γ_{01}					1.08 (.35)	1.06 (.35)
% free lunch	γ_{02}					−.05 (.01)	−.05 (.01)
% minority	γ_{03}						.003 (.01)
For SES slope (β_1)							
Intercept	γ_{10}			3.91 (.15)	3.88 (.13)	3.71 (.18)	3.71 (.18)
Private	γ_{11}					−1.38 (.40)	−1.4 (.41)
% free lunch	γ_{12}					−.02 (.01)	−.025 (.01)
% minority	γ_{13}						.003 (.01)
For K exp. (β_2)							
Intercept	γ_{20}	1.28 (.33)	1.28 (.33)	1.73 (.25)	1.74 (.25)	1.92 (.23)	1.92 (.23)
For entry age (β_3)							
Intercept	γ_{30}		.36 (.02)	.36 (.02)	.36 (.02)	.35 (.02)	.36 (.02)
Public	γ_{31}						
Var. comp.							
	τ_{00}	13.79 (1.13)	13.52 (1.11)	5.19 (.61)	5.38 (.59)	3.80 (.52)	3.78 (.52)
	τ_{01}			2.19 (.45)		2.01 (.41)	1.99 (.41)
	τ_{11}			2.19 (.68)		2.17 (.65)	2.15 (.65)
	σ^2	60.48 (1.05)	58.70 (1.01)	54.61 (.97)	55.47 (.96)	54.32 (.96)	54.33 (.96)
Number of parameters		4	5	8	6	12	14

TABLE 7.2   Pseudo-R^2 and Model Fit Measures for the ECLS-K Examples

Pseudo-R^2 and model fit	Model 1 (baseline)	Model 2 (adds age of kindergarten entry)	Model 3 (adds SES)	Model 4 (SES—with no random slope)	Model 5 (adds sector and % free lunch)	Model 6 (adds % minority)
Proportional reduction in variance—Level one		.03	.10	.08	.10	.10
Prop. reduction in prediction error—Level one		0.03	.19	0.18	0.22	0.22
Proportional reduction in variance—Level two		0.02	.62	0.61	0.72	0.73
Prop. reduction in prediction error—Level two		0.02	.48	0.47	0.56	0.56
Level-two R^2 slope (Raudenbush & Bryk, 2002)					.009	.02
Deviance	50,819.43	50,608.21	49,847.04	49,890.46	49,725.25	49,724.82
AIC	50,827.43	50,618.21	49,863.04	49,902.46	49,749.25	49,752.82
BIC (n= the number of level-2 units)	50,844.87	50,640.01	49,897.92	49,928.62	49,801.57	49,813.86
BIC (n= the number of level-1 units)	50,854.966	50,662.63	49,918.11	49,943.76	49,831.86	49,848.58
Number of parameters	4	5	8	6	12	14

.02). However, we are most interested in using the change in deviance and the *AIC* and *BIC* to assess the fit of the two models.

To use the chi-square difference test to compare the two models, we compute the change in deviance (ΔD) and the change in the number of estimated parameters (Δp) and compare these values to the critical value of chi-square with Δp degrees of freedom. First, we compare model 1, the baseline model, to model 2, a model which adds (grand-mean centered) age of kindergarten entry as a level-one predictor. The change in deviance is $50{,}819.43 - 50{,}608.21 = 211.22$. The change in the number of parameters is $5 - 4 = 1$. We compare 211.22 to the critical value of chi-square with one degree of freedom, which is 3.84. Because $211.22 > 3.84$, we reject the null hypothesis that the two models fit the data equally well, and we favor the more complex model. The additional parameter results in improved model fit.

Using *AIC*, we favor the model with the smaller *AIC* value. Table 7.2 shows that the deviance for model 1 is 50,819.43 with 4 parameters. Therefore the *AIC* is $50{,}819.43 + 2*4$, or 50,827.43. The *AIC* for model 2 is $50{,}608.21 + 5*2$, or 50,618.21. Using *AIC*, we conclude that the model that includes age is superior to the model that does not include age.

Finally, we compare the *BIC* values for the two models. For these examples, we used the number of level-two units as the sample size for the computation of the *BIC*. For completeness and for comparison purposes, Table 7.2 provides 2 different *BIC* estimates: the *BIC* computed using the number of level-2 units as the effective sample size and the *BIC* computed using the number of level-1 units as the effective sample size.

Using $n = $ the number of level 2 units, the *BIC* for model 1 in Table 7.2 is $50{,}819.43 + 4*\ln(578)$, or 50,844.87. The BIC for model 2 is $50{,}608.21 + 5*\ln(578)$, or 50,640.01. The *BIC* for model 2 is smaller than the *BIC* for model 1, so we again conclude that model 2 provides better fit to the data than model 1. In addition, the change in *BIC* (204.86) is greater than 10. Therefore, according to Raftery's (1995) rules of thumb, the difference in *BIC* provides very strong evidence for favoring model 2 over model 1. In this case, we would draw the same conclusions regarding model selection if we were to use the *BIC* computed using the level-one sample size.

Model 3 includes SES as a student-level predictor of beginning kindergarten reading. The slope of SES is random; therefore, the inclusion of SES adds three additional parameters to the model: one fixed effect (γ_{10}) and two random effects (τ_{01} and τ_{11}). The fixed effect of SES is statistically significant, and both additional random effects (τ_{01} and τ_{11}) are also statistically significant. However, to assess the model fit, we examine the effects of adding these three parameters on the change in deviance, the *AIC*, and the *BIC*. Adding these three additional parameters decreases the deviance from 50,608.21 to 49,847.04. This change in deviance of 761.17 exceeds the critical value of 7.82, the critical value of chi-square with three degrees of freedom at $\alpha = .05$. In addition, the *AIC* is substantially smaller in the model that includes SES (49,863.04) than in the model without SES (50,618.21). Finally, the change in *BIC* from model 2 (50,640.01) to model 3 (49,897.92) is 742.09. This difference in *BIC* provides very strong evidence for favoring model 3 over model 2 (Raftery, 1995).

Finally, let us examine what happens when we add the percentage of minority students as a level-two (school-level) predictor, and compare the resulting model (model 6) to the previous model (model 5). First, the percentage of minority students does not exert a statistically significant influence on either the intercept (γ_{03}) or on the SES slope (γ_{13}). When we compare the two models using the chi-square difference test, the change in deviance is .42 (49,725.25 – 49.724.82) for a two-parameter change in the model. This is below the critical value of chi-square with two degrees of freedom (5.99); therefore, we fail to reject the null hypothesis and conclude that the more parsimonious model (without percentage minority students) does not provide a statistically significantly poorer fit to the data than the model that includes those two parameters. Further, the *AIC* is smaller for the model that does not include percentage of minority students (49,749.25 for model 5 vs. 49,752.82 for model 6). Finally, the *BIC* is smaller for model 5 (49,801.57) than for model 6 (49,813.86), and this difference (12.29) is larger than 10. Therefore, this difference in *BIC* provides very strong evidence for favoring model 5 over model 6 (Raftery, 1995).

Summary—Model Selection Criteria

These examples, in combination with Figures 7.1 and 7.2, demonstrate that much of the time, the chi-square difference test, the *AIC*, and the *BIC* will converge, and point toward the selection of the same model. In other situations, the *AIC*, *BIC*, and chi-square difference tests may lead to conflicting conclusions. When these results diverge, the researcher must make a difficult decision about whether he or she favors model parsimony or model complexity. In borderline cases in which the change in deviance between two models is relatively small, the *BIC* favors the more parsimonious model while the *AIC* (and the chi-square difference test) favors the more complex model. In these situations, it is very important for the researchers to use their substantive knowledge and judgment to reach a conclusion about the "best model." Kuha (2004) suggests that when the *AIC* and the *BIC* err, "the *AIC* tends to favor models that are too large, and *BIC* models that are too small. Thus, an optimistic interpretation of these results is that even a disagreement at least suggests bounds for the range of acceptable models" (Kuha, p. 222). Very little research has specifically examined the AIC and BIC within a multilevel framework. However, Whittaker & Furlow (2006) conducted a simulation study to examine the performance of the AIC and the BIC under a number of different conditions when estimating two-level hierarchical linear models. They found that when the information indices did not select the correct model, the AIC tended to select the more parameterized (less parsimonious) model, whereas the BIC tended to select the less parameterized (more parsimonious) model. In this situation, we suggest considering substantive and theoretical issues as well as empirical and statistical ones. Cudeck and Henley (1991) also provide advice that is useful in this regard. They suggest that when evaluating the relative performance of competing models, often the best that can be done is to state clearly the criteria that are used in the comparison, in conjunction with descriptions of the models, characteristics of the data, and the purpose for which the models were constructed; moreover, this is actually a useful accomplishment whose value should not be minimized. Finally, when two competing models appear to fit the data (almost) equally well, replication studies using a new sample may be the most effective way to determine which model is truly "the best."

In conclusion, it is important to remember that the researcher plays an important role in the evaluation of model fit. No mechanical data analytic procedure for evaluating model fit should override human judgment (Browne, 2000). Examining changes in deviance in combination with model selection indices, such as the *AIC* and the *BIC*, seems to be the most prudent course of action for evaluating model fit. The rules of thumb presented earlier provide guidance for the researcher; however, they should not be used blindly or mechanically.

REDUCTION IN VARIANCE ESTIMATES

Complementary to the use of model fit criteria for model evaluation and selection, analogs of the squared multiple correlation, R^2, may be used to assess the ability of a given model to explain the data. In ordinary multiple regression, the squared multiple correlation between the outcome variable and the linear combination of weighted predictor variables represents the proportion of variance explained by the regression model and can be converted (by multiplication by 100) to a percent of total variability explained by the specified linear combination of predictor variables. In this case, the value of R^2 is, by calculation as a ratio of sums of squared deviation scores, always non-negative. Its value always increases or remains stable with the addition of predictor variables into the model (the value of R^2 is never reduced under these conditions) and can serve as a stand-alone measure of the predictive capability of a model.[1]

As multilevel modeling of data has become increasingly accessible to researchers, attention has been given to the need for a comparable measure of variance explained for these models. Because variance components can exist at each level of the multilevel model, the concept of "explained variance" becomes more complex. Several estimates may be needed for a single model, and R^2 may take on reduced,[2] or even negative, values with the addition of predictors. This portion of the chapter provides guidelines for calculating and interpreting these (sometimes anomalous) estimates and presents the two predominant methods.

The first method for computing and interpreting the multilevel model version of R^2, also sometimes referred to as *pseudo-R^2* (Singer & Willett, 2003), produces an R^2 statistic for each parameter estimate in the model (Raudenbush & Bryk, 2002). The statistic is interpreted as the *proportional reduction in variance* for that parameter estimate that results from the use of one model as compared to a base, or comparison, model. The statistic only can be computed and interpreted as the value of one model relative to another model and should not be interpreted as an explanation of the absolute amount of variance in the criterion variable.

The second method of deriving the multilevel R^2 statistic (Snijders & Bosker, 1994, 1999) results in separate measures of *proportional reduction in prediction error* for levels one (the prediction of Y_{ij}) and two (the prediction of $\overline{Y}_{j}$) of the random intercepts only model. These estimates, too, represent changes in the amount of residual variance that result from the application of one model relative to a comparison model but make use of total estimated variance in their computation, as $\hat{\sigma}^2 + \hat{\tau}_{00}$ provides a reasonable estimate of the sample variance of Y (Snijders & Bosker, 1994).

In using R^2 with multilevel models, it is important to remain mindful of the unique interpretation of each estimate in drawing conclusions about model value.

R^2 as Proportional Reduction in Variance

At level one, the individual level, r_{ij} represents the random error associated with the measurement of individual i in group j (Singer & Willett, 2003) in relation to the estimated level-two group mean. Each level-one error is assumed to be normally distributed with a constant variance, represented as σ^2 (Raudenbush & Bryk, 2002). At the individual level, the proportional reduction in within-groups variance is calculated by first subtracting the level-one variance of the new model from that of the base model. The ratio of that difference to the base model level-one variance is interpreted "as a proportion reduction in that variance" (Kreft & deLeeuw 1998, p. 118). That statistic is computed

$$\frac{\hat{\sigma}_b^2 - \hat{\sigma}_f^2}{\hat{\sigma}_b^2} \tag{7.6}$$

where $\hat{\sigma}_b^2$ = the estimated level-one variance for the base model and $\hat{\sigma}_f^2$ = the estimated level-one variance for the fitted model (Raudenbush & Bryk, 2002).

At level two, population variance components estimates are represented by $\hat{\tau}_{qq}$ and are given for the intercepts[3] (β_{0j}) and each slope estimate (β_{1j}, $\beta_{2j}...,\beta_{qj}$) that is not fixed to equal zero and, therefore, is permitted to be random. At level two, the proportional reduction in the variance of the intercepts, β_{0j}, is computed

$$\frac{\hat{\tau}_{00_b} - \hat{\tau}_{00_f}}{\hat{\tau}_{00_b}} \quad (7.7)$$

where $\hat{\tau}_{00_b}$ = the estimated variance of the intercepts in the base model and $\hat{\tau}_{00_f}$ = the estimated variance of the intercepts in the fitted model.

The result is a proportional reduction in variance that can be attributed to the predictor(s) unique to the fitted model (Raudenbush & Bryk, 2002).

Likewise, the proportional reduction in the variance of a given slope, β_{qj}, is calculated

$$\frac{\hat{\tau}_{qq_b} - \hat{\tau}_{qq_f}}{\hat{\tau}_{qq_b}} \quad (7.8)$$

where $\hat{\tau}_{qq_b}$ = the estimated variance of slope q in the base model and $\hat{\tau}_{qq_f}$ = the estimated variance of slope q in the fitted model.

Once a base model has been established, subsequent multilevel models can be compared to it to determine the resulting proportional reduction in variance. Note that level-two proportion reduction in variance statistics only can be compared for models with the same level-one model (Raudenbush & Bryk, 2002, p. 150). The estimated reduction is computed separately for each parameter estimate (Raudenbush & Bryk, 2002; Singer & Willett, 2003). For comparison of variance estimates at level one, the null model, which contains only a random intercept and no level-one predictor variables, typically is used as the base model, and other level-one models that include level-one predictors are compared to this null model. For comparison of variance estimates at level two, the level-one fitted model (containing level-one but no level-two predictor variables) is used as the base model for comparison of subsequent models containing level-two predictor variables.

Example

Table 7.2 contains variance components for several models fit to the ECLS-K data set, where the outcome is reading achievement of students in the fall of their kindergarten year. Model 1, which includes a level-one covariate, a measure of exposure to kindergarten (in months of instruction), serves as the base model. Model 2 includes an additional student-level predictor, (grand-mean centered) age at kindergarten entry. To determine the proportional reduction in level-one residual variance that resulted from the addition of the "age" predictor, the estimated student-level variances are compared according to Equation 7.6 above: $(60.48 - 58.70)/60.48 = .029$. This result indicates that only about 3% of the within-group variance, after accounting for months of kindergarten exposure, is attributable to student age at kindergarten entry. The bulk of the variance at this level is not explained by model 2.

The level-two variance estimates (τ_{00}) for the two models are compared as in Equation 7.7: $(13.79 - 13.52)/13.79 = .019$. As might be expected, the between-groups variance is reduced by a negligible amount (less than 2%) with the addition of the level-one predictor in model 2.

Model 5 (which includes *SES*, kindergarten exposure, and age of kindergarten entry as level-one predictors, and school sector and percent free lunch as level-two predictors) was compared to model 3 (a nested model that did not include the level-two predictors) to estimate proportional reduction in variance of the SES-achievement slopes (β_{1j}) using Equation 7.8: $(2.19 - 2.17)/(2.19) = .01$. We conclude that the level-two predictors, *school sector* and *percent free lunch*, in the fitted model do not explain any appreciable variance in the slope when compared to model 3.

The Confounding of Variance Estimates

As stated earlier, the concept of explained variance in multilevel models is different from that in OLS regression models as the former may involve multiple variance component estimates. An additional complexity of the concept in multilevel modeling relates to the confounding of variance component estimates across levels. We examine how the level-two variance component estimate in the random intercepts only model may be dependent on the specified level-one model.

When a significant level-one predictor is added to a random intercepts only model, the level-one variance component is reduced. This is to be expected. However, under these conditions, the level-two variance component, τ_{00} also may be affected (Raudenbush & Bryk, 2002). Its value may increase or decrease with the addition of the level-one predictor. One explanation for the change is that, as level-one predictors are added to the random intercept models, the meaning of β_{0j} may change. Without any predictors in the model, this estimate represents the mean for group j on the outcome variable. As predictors are added, the interpretation of β_{0j} becomes the outcome for a person in group j whose value is zero for all level-one predictors (Raudenbush & Bryk, 2002). Unless all level-one variables are group mean centered, it is clear that this estimate, and its variance, τ_{00} should change with the addition of variables in the level-one model. In the example above, the intercept for model 1 represents the average reading achievement for group j after adjusting for months of kindergarten exposure. In model 2, the intercept becomes the reading achievement for a student in school j whose entry age is equal to the grand-mean age of kindergarten entry because we have grand-mean centered the age variable.

In the random intercepts model, it is possible for level-two proportion reduction of variance statistics to be reduced or become negative with the addition of predictor variables at level one. This possibility conflicts with our interpretation of the traditional R^2 in OLS multiple regression as a sum of squares ratio and highlights another complexity in using an analog of R^2 in multilevel modeling. Essentially, because of the method by which variance components are estimated, while adding a level-two variable will decrease the estimate of τ_{00} and leave σ^2 relatively unchanged, adding a group-mean centered variable at level one will decrease the estimate of σ^2 *while increasing* the estimate of τ_{00} (Snijders & Bosker, 1994). When a fixed effect has been added to the model, Snijders and Bosker (1999) suggest that decreases in the proportion of variance explained of .05 or more in large sample studies also may be diagnostic of model misspecification.

To illustrate this phenomenon with the ECLS-K data set, we compared a model using group-mean centered SES at level one to the base model (model 1). The resulting estimate of σ^2 for the fitted model was 57.01 and for τ_{00} was 14.07. The proportion reduction in variance for level one was

$$\frac{\hat{\sigma}_b^2 - \hat{\sigma}_f^2}{\hat{\sigma}_b^2} = \frac{60.52 - 57.01}{60.52} = .06$$

where $\hat{\sigma}_b^2$ = the level-one variance for the base model and $\hat{\sigma}_f^2$ = the level-one variance for the fitted model. Group-mean centered SES explained approximately 6% of the within-groups variance.

At level two, the proportion of reduction in variance was

$$\frac{\hat{\tau}_{00_b} - \hat{\tau}_{00_f}}{\hat{\tau}_{00_b}} = \frac{13.79 - 14.07}{13.79} = -.02$$

where $\hat{\tau}_{00_b}$ = the level-two variance for the base model and $\hat{\tau}_{00_f}$ = the level-two variance for the fitted model. This illustrates that the inclusion of group-mean centered variables actually can increase variance at level two.

For comparison, we estimated the proportion of variance reduction for a model using *grand-mean centered* SES. For this model, $\hat{\sigma}^2$ was 57.28, and $\hat{\tau}_{00}$ was 5.58, resulting in a variance reduction estimate at level one of .05 and at level two of .60. Thus, where essentially no level-two variance was explained (in comparison to the base model) when the level-one predictor SES was group-mean centered, 60% of the variance was explained using grand-mean centering. A great deal of variability between schools on mean reading achievement can be accounted for by differences in student-level SES; however, within schools, this predictor explains a small proportion of the variance in achievement, indicating selection effects at the school level.

Generally speaking, group-mean centering will decrease σ^2 but increase τ_{00} (Snijders & Bosker, 1994). Therefore, the inclusion of a group-mean centered variable results in a reduction of unexplained variance at level one and an increase in unexplained variance at level two. For detailed discussion about the topic of centering variables and its effect on estimated variance reduction, we refer the reader to the existing literature (Enders & Tofighi, 2007; Hox, 2002; Kreft & deLeeuw, 1998; Raudenbush & Bryk, 2002; Snijders & Bosker, 1994, 1999).

R^2 as Proportional Reduction in Prediction Error

An alternative to estimating parameter-specific proportional reduction in variance that compensates for the confounding of variance estimates, R^2 can be computed as a *proportional reduction of prediction error*. This method of variance reduction estimation uses the total, rather than parameter-specific, variance estimates for each model in the comparison. R^2 is computed separately for levels one (the prediction of Y_{ij}) and two (the prediction of $\bar{Y}_{.j}$) (Snijders & Bosker, 1994, 1999). Given a random intercepts only model, the prediction error for individual outcomes (Y_{ij}) is equal to the sum of the level-one and level-two variance components,

$$\hat{\sigma}^2 + \hat{\tau}_{00}. \tag{7.9}$$

The proportional reduction of prediction error at level one for this model relative to the base or null model, R_1^2,

$$= 1 - \frac{\left(\hat{\sigma}^2 + \hat{\tau}_{00}\right)_f}{\left(\hat{\sigma}^2 + \hat{\tau}_{00}\right)_b} \tag{7.10}$$

where $(\sigma^2 + \tau_{00})_f$ = the prediction error for the fitted model and $(\sigma^2 + \tau_{00})_b$ = the prediction error for the base model.

Applying this formula to evaluate model 2 above relative to the base model (model 1), where $\hat{\sigma}^2 + \hat{\tau}_{00} = 74.27$ for model 1 and $\hat{\sigma}^2 + \hat{\tau}_{00} = 72.22$ for model 2, the *level-one* proportional reduction in prediction error, R_1^2, is $1 - (72.22/74.27) = .03$

At level two, the prediction error for the group mean, $\bar{Y}_{.j}$,

$$= \frac{\hat{\sigma}^2}{n_j} + \hat{\tau}_{00}. \tag{7.11}$$

where n_j represents the number of units in the level-2 cluster, j. When the numbers of units within a level-two cluster is unbalanced, there are a few options for the value of n_j (Hox, 2002; Snijders & Bosker, 1994). The researcher can determine a priori a value that is representative of all groups, use the average group size, or use the harmonic mean of the groups, calculated as $N/[\Sigma_j(1/n_j)]$ (Snijders & Bosker, 1999).

The level-two proportional reduction in the prediction error, R_2^2,

$$= 1 - \frac{\left(\dfrac{\hat{\sigma}^2}{n_j} + \tau_{00} \right)_f}{\left(\dfrac{\hat{\sigma}^2}{n_j} + \tau_{00} \right)_b} \tag{7.12}$$

where

$$\left(\frac{\hat{\sigma}^2}{n_j} + \tau_{00} \right)_f$$

is the prediction error variance for the fitted model and

$$\left(\frac{\hat{\sigma}^2}{n_j} + \tau_{00} \right)_b$$

is the prediction error variance for the base model.

Applying Formula 12 to evaluate the change in variance at level two (comparing model 2 with model 1), given a representative value of $n = 12$,

$$R_2^2 = 1 - \frac{\dfrac{58.7}{12} + 13.52}{\dfrac{60.48}{12} + 13.79} = .02.$$

The relative size of values of R^2 at either level resulting from the two variance reduction estimation methods (whether they are similar or one estimate is larger than the other), depends on the effect of the predictor(s) in the model at that level. When a predictor significantly reduces the variance component at level one, and not at level two, the level-one proportion of reduction in variance estimate will be larger than the proportional reduction in prediction error variance at that level because the latter takes into account the small effect on the level-two variance. The opposite will be true for the level-two reduction in variance estimates, where the proportional reduction in prediction error variance will be the larger estimate at that level (because of the inclusion of the change to $\hat{\sigma}^2$ in that formula). The reverse relationships will occur when a predictor variable in a model results in a significant reduction in level-two variance and has little effect on the variance estimate for level one.

A benefit of the R^2-as-proportional reduction in prediction error is the (relatively) predictable "behavior" of R^2 under given conditions. When models are specified correctly and group size is constant at n, population values of R_1^2 and R_2^2 will be reduced when explanatory variables are removed, given the assumption that the variance components at levels one and two (r_{ij} and u_{0j}) are uncorrelated with all predictor variables, X_{ij} (Snijders & Bosker, 1994, 1999). However, sample estimates of R_1^2 and R_2^2 still may decrease when predictors are added or increase when predictors are deleted from the model (Snijders & Bosker, 1994, p. 355). Roberts and Monaco (2006) provide an example of the possibility of negative modeled variance using the proportional reduction in error variance model. A large reduction in value of R^2 with the addition of an explanatory variable into a model may be diagnostic of possible misspecification of the larger model (Snijders & Bosker, 1994). One "important type" of model misspecification is the restricting of predictor variables to have the same within- and between-group regression coefficients when they actually are different in the population (p. 356).

Estimating Variance Reduction in Three-Level Models

Snijders and Bosker (1999) provide a formula for estimating variance at level one of the three-level random intercept model. This simply involves adding the variance component from the third level to the formula for level-one variance in the two-level model (Formula 9), such that the total estimated variance equals the sum of the variance components at each level:

$$\hat{\sigma}^2 + \hat{\tau}_{00} + \hat{\varphi}_{00} \tag{7.13}$$

The level-one proportional reduction in residual variance then is calculated:

$$1 - \frac{(\hat{\sigma}^2 + \hat{\tau}_{00} + \hat{\varphi}_{00})_f}{(\hat{\sigma}^2 + \hat{\tau}_{00} + \hat{\varphi}_{00})_b} \tag{7.14}$$

where φ_{00} represents the variance component at level three (Snijders & Bosker, 1999).

Variance Reduction Estimates in Models with Random Slopes

In a model with random slopes, the relationship between the predictor variable and the dependent variable varies by cluster, and the variance component (τ_{qq}) estimates the variability in this relationship across clusters. According to Hox (2002), if the multilevel model contains random slopes, it is "inherently more complex, and the concept of explained variance has no unique definition" (p. 63). Estimating R_1^2 and R_2^2 for models with random slopes involves "tedious" calculation (see Snijders & Bosker, 1994). However, they can be estimated easily by omitting the random slopes and re-estimating "the models as random intercept models with the same fixed parts" (Snijders & Bosker, 1999, p. 105). The variance components from the fixed-slope model then should be used to calculate R_1^2 and R_2^2 as for random intercepts models, described earlier (Formulas 10 and 12). This typically results in estimates that are close approximations of those for the random slopes model (Snijders & Bosker, 1999).

Summary—Reduction in Variance Estimates

In conclusion, the various multilevel R^2-type statistics described above provide measures to compare one model to another in terms of its ability to account for the variability in a given data set. They are not, however, without their limitations, regardless of method of estimation. We briefly have presented two methods to estimate the proportional reduction in variance. Conclusions about the relative "value" of a model should be made carefully, with the unique definition of the variance reduction estimate in mind. When models have random slopes, R^2 does not have a unique definition (Hox, 1998; Kreft et al., 1995). The relationship between the level-one predictor and the dependent variable varies across level-two units, and the level-two variance estimate is not constant in these models (Snijders & Bosker, 1999). With these caveats in mind, multilevel R^2 measures can provide a useful tool to compare the predictive ability of various multilevel models.

CONCLUSION

Measures of model fit and model adequacy discussed in this chapter provide the researcher with fairly objective methods to compare multilevel models. However, researchers disagree about the appropriateness of these measures, and their use has been somewhat controversial. Therefore, it is important to use these measures thoughtfully and selectively, with attention to their limitations. Future methodological research should examine the properties and performance of these indices to define more clearly their utility to inform model selection in multilevel applications.

NOTES

1. Reporting adjusted R^2 in addition to R^2 is recommended when comparing regression equations with varying numbers of predictors. Adjusted R^2 is a corrected estimate of proportion of explained variance, accounting for sample size and number of predictors in the model (Green & Salkind, 2003).
2. Throughout this chapter, the symbol, R^2 is used to represent the proportional reduction in variance in the multilevel model. However, it should not be assumed that this statistic is the mathematical equivalent of, or analogous to, the squared multiple correlation R^2 used with OLS multiple regression.
3. The value and interpretation of the intercept, and variance of the intercept, at level two is influenced by the "location" of the X variable (i.e., the decision about whether and how X is centered) in level one (Raudenbush & Bryk, 2002).

REFERENCES

Box, G. E. (1979). Robustness in the strategy of scientific model building. In R. L. Lauer & G. N. Wilkinson (Eds.), *Robustness in Statistics* (pp. 201–236). New York: Academic Press.

Bozdogan, H. (1987). Model selection and Akaike's Information Criterion (AIC): The general theory and its analytical extensions. *Psychometrika, 52,* 345–270.

Browne, M. W. (2000). Cross validation methods. *Journal of Mathematical Psychology, 44,* 108–132.

Burnham, K. P., & Anderson, D. R. (2004). Multimodel inference: Understanding AIC and BIC in model selection. *Sociological Methods and Research, 33,* 261–304.

Cudeck, R., & Henly, S. J. (1991). Model selection in covariance structures analysis and the problem of sample size: A clarification. *Psychological Bulletin, 109,* 512–519.

de Leeuw, J. (2004). Multilevel analysis: Techniques and applications (Book review). *Journal of Educational Measurement, 41,* 73–77.

Enders, C. K. & Tofighi, D. (2007). Centering predictor variables in cross-sectional multilevel models: A new look at an old issue. *Psychological Methods, 12,* 121–138.

Forster, M. R. (2000). Key concepts in model selection: Performance and generalizability. *Journal of Mathematical Psychology, 44,* 205–231.

Gelman, A., & Rubin, D. B. (1995). Avoiding model selection in Bayesian social research. *Sociological Methodology, 25,* 165–173.

Green, S. B., & Salkind, N. J. (2003). *Using SPSS for Windows and Macintosh: Analyzing and understanding data* (3rd ed.). Upper Saddle River, N.J.: Prentice Hall.

Gurka, M. J. (2006). Selecting the best linear mixed model under REML. *The American Statistician, 60, 1,* 19–26.

Hox, J. (2002). *Multilevel analysis techniques and applications.* Mahwah, N.J.: Lawrence Erlbaum Associates.

Kline, R. B. (1998). *Principles and practice of structural equation modeling.* New York: The Guilford Press.

Kreft, I. G. G., de Leeuw, J., & Aiken, L. S. (1995). The effect of different forms of centering in hierarchical linear models. *Multivariate Behavioral Research, 30,* 1–21.

Kreft, I. & de Leeuw, J. (1998). *Introducing multilevel modeling.* Thousand Oaks, CA: Sage Publications.

Kuha, J. (2004). AIC and BIC: Comparisons of assumptions and performance. *Sociological Methods and Research, 33,* 188–229.

O'Connell, A. A., Goldstein, J., Rogers, H. J., & Peng, C. Y. J. (2008). Logistic and ordinal multilevel models. In A. A. O'Connell and D. B. McCoach (Eds.), *Multilevel modeling of educational data* (pp. 199–242). Charlotte, NC: Information Age Publishing.

Raftery, A. E. (1995). Bayesian model selection in social research. *Sociological Methodology, 25,* 111–163.

Raudenbush, S. W., & Bryk, A. S. (2002). *Hierarchical linear models.* Thousand Oaks, CA: Sage Publications.

Raudenbush, S. W., Bryk, A. S., Cheong, Y. F., & Congdon, R. (2000). *HLM 5: Hierarchical linear and non-linear modeling.* Chicago: Scientific Software International.

Roberts, J. K., & Monaco, J. P. (2006, April). *Effect size measures for the two-level linear multilevel model.* Paper presented at the annual meeting of the American Educational Research Association, San Francisco, CA.

Schwarz, G. (1978). Estimating the dimension of a model. *The Annals of Statistics, 6,* 461–464.

Singer, J. D., & Willett, J. B. (2003). *Applied longitudinal data analysis: Modeling change and event occurrence.* Oxford: Oxford University Press.

Snijders, T., & Bosker, R. (1994). Modeled variance in two-level models. *Sociological Methods & Research, 22*(3), 342–363.

Snijders, T., & Bosker, R. (1999). *Multilevel analysis.* Thousand Oaks, CA: Sage Publications.

Stapleton, L. M., & Thomas, S. L. (2008). The use of national datasets for teaching and research: Sources and issues. In A. A. O'Connell and D. B. McCoach (Eds.), *Multilevel modeling of educational data* (pp. 11–57). Charlotte, NC: Information Age Publishing.

Verbeke, G., & Molenberghs, G. (2000). *Linear mixed models for longitudinal data.* New York: Springer-Verlag.

Wagenmakers, E., & Farrell, S. (2004). AIC model selection using Akaike weights. *Psychonomic Bulletin and Review, 11,* 192–196.

Weaklim, D. L. (1999). A critique of the Bayesian Information Criterion for model selection. *Sociological Methods and Research, 27,* 359–397.

Weaklim, D. L. (2004). Introduction to the special issue on model selection. *Sociological Methods and Research, 33,* 167–187.

Whittaker, T. A., & Furlow, C. F. (2006, April). A comparison of model selection criteria for hierarchical linear modeling. Paper presented at the annual conference of the American Educational Research Association, San Francisco, CA.

Zucchini, W. (2000). An introduction to model selection. *Journal of Mathematical Psychology, 44,* 41–61.

CHAPTER 8

POWER, SAMPLE SIZE, AND DESIGN

Jessaca Spybrook

INTRODUCTION

Thus far, the majority of the chapters in this book have focused on the analysis of multilevel data. However, before a researcher can analyze the data, he/she must plan the study and determine the necessary sample size to detect effects of a given magnitude. This chapter concentrates on how to plan studies with adequate power to detect treatment effects when the treatment conditions are assigned at random to whole groups. The focus here is on randomized experiments because they are the most effective way to establish causal relationships (Boruch, 1997; Cook & Payne, 2002; Slavin, 2002). This approach, however, can be adapted to quasi-experiments and observational studies.

In educational contexts, interventions often are targeted towards entire groups, e.g., classrooms, grade levels, or entire schools; thus, clusters of people are randomized instead of individuals (Bloom, 2005). Some prominent examples include the Comer School Development Program (CSDP) evaluations (Cook et al., 1999; Cook, Murphy, & Hunt, 2000), the Even Start evaluation (St. Pierre, Swartz, Murray, & Deck, 1996), and more recently, the Success For All (SFA) evaluation (Borman et al., 2005). In both the CSDP and SFA evaluations, entire schools were assigned randomly to either the program or a control condition. In the first evaluation of Even Start, a literacy program for parents and children, whole families were assigned randomly into treatment conditions.

The Education Sciences Reform Act of 2002 (U.S. Department of Education, 2002) strongly encourages the use of experiments to determine what works in education. Randomizing schools and classrooms for studies of educational interventions is often more feasible than randomizing individual students. Further, educational interventions often are delivered by teachers within classrooms. Therefore, even if students are assigned randomly to conditions, there likely would be some sort of "classroom effect." For all of these reasons, the frequency of cluster randomized trials in education is likely to increase in the future.

One of the difficulties associated with designing cluster randomized trials is that the unit of analysis is often the individual but the unit of randomization is the cluster. Thus, there are two sources of variability: between-cluster variability and within-cluster variability. Both sources of variability must be accounted for in the design of cluster randomized trials, making planning cluster randomized trials more complicated than planning single level trials.

There is a growing body of literature on power, sample size, and design considerations for cluster randomized trials. The importance of the number of clusters for achieving adequate power is now widely recognized (Donner & Klar, 2000; Hox, 2002; Moerbeek, VanBreukelen, & Berger, 2000; Murray, 1998; Raudenbush, 1997; Schochet, 2005; Snijders & Bosker, 1993). In addition, the use of covariates and blocking to enhance the power in cluster randomized trials is also well established (Bloom, 2005; Bloom, Richburg-Hayes, & Black, 2005; Martin, Diehr, Perrin, & Koepsell, 1993; Raudenbush, Martinez, & Spybrook, 2005; Schochet, 2005). More sophisticated designs, such as repeated measures within individuals within clusters and randomizing clusters within multiple treatment sites, also have been explored (Murray 1998; Raudenbush & Liu, 2000, 2001; Schochet, 2005). Books by Murray (1998) and Donner and Klar (2000) focus on the design of cluster randomized trials in health related fields.

There are many different designs that rely on the random assignment of clusters to treatment conditions; a discussion of all these possibilities is beyond the scope of this chapter (see Murray, 1998, and Raudenbush, Spybrook, Liu, & Congdon, 2006, for more comprehensive reviews). This chapter focuses on two fundamental designs: simple two-level cluster randomized trials, with and without a cluster-level covariate, and multi-site cluster randomized trials. A simple two-level cluster randomized trial is one in which an intervention is administered to an intact groups of individuals, or clusters. Since the intervention is delivered at the cluster level, entire clusters are assigned randomly

TABLE 8.1   Graphical Display of a Two-Level Cluster Randomized Trial and a Multi-Site Cluster Randomized Trial

	Two-level cluster randomized trial	Multi-site cluster randomized trial
Levels in the hierarchy	Two	Three
Analysis unit	Level one	Level one
Treatment unit	Level two	Level two
Blocking	No	Yes

to the treatment or control condition. However, the individual is still the primary unit of interest, or the unit of analysis. Similar to a simple two-level cluster randomized trial, the unit of analysis in a multi-site cluster randomized trial is the individual, and the unit of randomization is the cluster. However, in a multi-site cluster randomized trial, there is an additional level, known as the site, or block. Clusters are assigned randomly to the treatment or control condition within each site. A multi-site cluster randomized trial can be conceived as a two-level cluster randomized trial repeated across sites. Table 8.1 is a graphical depiction of the two designs.

The first section of this chapter defines some of the key statistical concepts related to power. The following sections describe each design, examine the models, and provide the statistical background for calculating the power of the study. These sections also include an example of each design and describe how to use the *Optimal Design* software (Liu, Spybrook, Congdon, Martinez, & Raudenbush, 2006) to calculate the power to detect the treatment effect. The chapter concludes with a discussion of the practical considerations for planning an experiment when clusters are assigned at random to treatment conditions.

STATISTICAL POWER

The statistical power of a study is the probability of rejecting the null hypothesis when a specific alternative hypothesis is true. For example, in a study comparing the outcomes of two groups, power is the probability of rejecting the null hypothesis that the outcomes of two groups are equal when, in fact, there is a difference of a given magnitude. In other words, power is the probability of reaching the conclusion that the two groups are different, given that they are, in fact, different. Since the discussion of power is linked to discussions of hypothesis testing and significance levels, it is important to have a clear definition of each of these terms before proceeding.

In a two-treatment design, the most common null hypothesis states that there is no difference between the outcome for the treatment group and the control group in the population. The alternative hypothesis states that there is a difference between the population parameters for the two groups. The probability of rejecting the null hypothesis when it is true, denoted α, is called the Type I error rate. This also is known as the significance level. A Type I error occurs when the researcher finds a statistically significant difference between two groups when their scores do not, in fact, differ in the population. Typically, alpha is set at .05 so that when the null hypothesis is true, there is only a 5% chance of making a Type I error. Suppose, however, that the null hypothesis is false. A Type II error arises when a false null hypothesis is retained mistakenly. The probability of retaining a false null hypothesis, the Type II error rate, is denoted as β. In this case, the researcher incorrectly concludes that the population parameters of the two groups do not differ. In other words, when committing a Type II error, the researcher overlooks a "true" difference. The two types of errors are illustrated in Table 8.2.

If the null hypothesis is true (first row of Table 8.2), the correct decision is to retain it, and the probability of this correct decision is as follows: Probability (Retain $H_0 \mid H_0$ is true) = $1 - \alpha$. The incorrect decision is the Type I error—rejecting the true H_0. When H_0 is true, this error will occur with probability α. On the other hand, if the null hypothesis is false (second row of Table 8.2), the correct decision is to reject it. The probability of making this correct decision is defined as power: Probability (Reject $H_0 \mid H_0$ is false) = $1 - \beta$. The incorrect decision, known as the Type II error, occurs with probability β, that is Probability (Type II error $\mid H_0$ false) = β.

To illustrate the relationship between a Type I error, Type II error, and statistical power, imagine a simple t-test comparing the means for two independent groups. The null hypothesis states there is no difference in the population means, and the alternative hypothesis states that the population mean for one group is greater than the mean for the other group (a one-sided hypothesis test). Figure 8.1 displays the t-distribution under the null hypothesis and the t-distribution under the alternative hypothesis. Note that the mean of the t-distribution of the null hypothesis is set to zero.

TABLE 8.2 Possible Errors in Hypothesis Testing

	Do not reject the null hypothesis	Reject the null hypothesis
Null hypothesis is true	No error (Probability = $1 - \alpha$)	Type I error (Probability = α)
Null hypothesis is false	Type II error (Probability = β)	No error (Power) (Probability = $1 - \beta$)

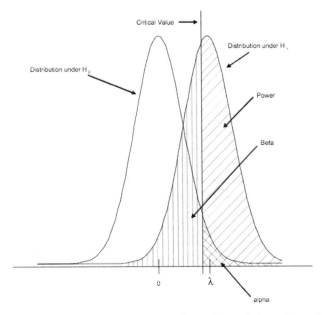

Figure 8.1   The relationship between alpha (Type I error), beta (Type II error), and statistical power.

The mean of the statistical distribution under the alternative hypothesis is λ, known as the non-centrality parameter. The non-centrality parameter is defined as

$$\lambda = \frac{\beta}{se(\bar{Y}_E - \bar{Y}_C)} = \frac{\beta}{se(\hat{\beta})} \, , \tag{8.1}$$

where

> β is the true mean difference between the two groups, $\mu_E - \mu_C$, and
> $\hat{\beta}$ is the estimated mean difference between the two groups.

Thus, the non-centrality parameter is a ratio of the true difference between the groups to the standard error of the estimated difference between the two groups. From Figure 8.1, it is clear that as λ increases, or as the true difference in standard error units increases, the statistical power also increases. Intuitively, this makes sense. The larger the true difference between the two groups, the more likely it is that the researcher will detect this difference.

Note that the non-centrality parameter is closely related to the test-statistic for a t-test. The test statistic is

$$t = \frac{\hat{\beta}}{\text{se}(\bar{Y}_E - \bar{Y}_C)} = \frac{\hat{\beta}}{\text{se}(\hat{\beta})}. \qquad (8.2)$$

Both the non-centrality parameter and the test statistic are ratios that feature the standard error of the estimate in the denominator. In statistical terms, the precision of the estimate is defined as the reciprocal of the error variance (Raudenbush & Bryk, 2002). The smaller the standard error, the more precise the estimate is. Thus, decreasing the variance (or standard error) of the estimate is equivalent to increasing the precision of the estimate. A more precise estimate results in a larger test statistic and non-centrality parameter, leading to greater statistical power. Power greater than or equal to 0.80 often is recognized by the research community to be sufficient, though some researchers seek 0.90 as a minimum (Cohen, 1988).

CLUSTER RANDOMIZED TRIALS

The natural clustering in our education system involves multiple hierarchies. Students are nested within classrooms within schools within districts. Given that educational interventions often are administered at the classroom, school, or district level, experiments that randomize groups are particularly relevant for the study of educational phenomena. In fact, educational interventions usually are designed to affect whole groups (Bloom, Bos, & Lee, 1999; Boruch & Foley, 2000). Group-randomized trials allow researchers to test the effectiveness of these group-level interventions. For example, comprehensive school reforms target entire schools. Thus, it makes sense to implement the treatment at the school level even though the primary interest is at the student level. The evaluations of the Comer School Development Program (Cook et al., 1999; Cook et al., 2000) and the Success For All Program (Borman et al., 2005) exemplify group-randomized trials designed to test the effectiveness of school reform models. These trials rely on the random assignment of schools to treatment conditions, where the outcome of interest is student achievement. Therefore, designing trials with adequate power to detect the effect of the intervention is critical.

In a cluster randomized trial, holding α constant, the power of a test is a function of the cluster size, n, the total number of clusters, J, the within-cluster variation, σ^2, the between-cluster variation, τ, and the true mean difference between groups, γ_{01}. Given the variance components and the true mean difference between groups, the power in cluster randomized trials is dominated by the number of clusters, not the number of subjects within a cluster (Snijders & Bosker, 1993). Therefore, to increase the power, in general, it is best to increase the number of clusters. However, increasing the number of clusters may be far more expensive than adding additional subjects within a cluster. Obviously, this can be problematic because all research projects operate under budgetary constraints. For example, imagine that a research team wants to test the effectiveness of a new math program which will be implemented school-wide. Since the program is implemented at the school level, entire schools need to be randomized to the new program or the control condition. Individual math achievement, the outcome of interest, will be assessed using a standardized math test. If the test is one that the schools already use, testing a large number of students does not incur much additional cost for the evaluation. However, adding more clusters, or schools, is costly. Adding a new school requires securing an agreement with school leaders to participate, training additional teachers in the new program, buying the necessary supplies for a school, and paying for data collectors to travel to the school. Because adding more schools may not always be possible, it becomes critical to try to increase the power by manipulating other features of the design.

The true mean difference between groups also contributes to the power of the test. Larger group differences result in studies with higher power. Though the phenomenon under investigation greatly determines this difference, researchers can try to create conditions to maximize the effect of the treatment. Some strategies include implementing the treatment with high fidelity, increasing the duration of the treatment, and minimizing spillover effects (Bloom, 2005). The variance of the mean difference also influences power; reducing this variance increases the power of the test. By including cluster-level covariates in the design and analysis of a cluster randomized trial, researchers can try to reduce this variation to increase power. The next section describes the model for a cluster randomized trial.

The Model

A cluster randomized trial is a two-level design in which students are nested within clusters (Raudenbush & Bryk, 2002). Thinking back to the math program example introduced in the earlier section on cluster randomized trials, students represent the level-one units, and schools represent the level-two units. Using the notation of Raudenbush and Bryk, the unstandardized model for this cluster randomized trial in hierarchical form is given in Equations 8.3 and 8.4. Maximum likelihood (ML) estimation commonly is used to estimate the parameters in these types of multilevel models. For a discussion of estimation techniques, see Hox (2002) or Raudenbush (1997). The level-one, or student-level, model is

$$Y_{ij} = \beta_{0j} + e_{ij} \quad \text{with } e_{ij} \sim N(0, \sigma^2), \tag{8.3}$$

where

> $i = 1, \ldots, n$ students per school,
> $j = 1, \ldots, J$ schools,
> β_{0j} is the mean for school j,
> e_{ij} is the error associated with each student, and
> σ^2 is the within-school variance.

The level-two, or school-level, model is

$$\beta_{0j} = \gamma_{00} + \gamma_{01} W_j + u_{oj} \quad \text{with } u_{0j} \sim N(0, \tau), \tag{8.4}$$

where

> γ_{00} is the grand mean given that data are coded $-\frac{1}{2}$ for the control group and $\frac{1}{2}$ for the experimental group and there are equal sample sizes in the 2 groups,
> γ_{01} is the mean difference between the treatment and control group, or the main effect of treatment,
> W_j is an indicator variable in which $-\frac{1}{2}$ represents the control group and $\frac{1}{2}$ represents the experimental group,
> u_{0j} is the random effect associated with each cluster, and
> τ is the variance between clusters.

The mixed model is

$$Y_{ij} = \gamma_{00} + \gamma_{01} W_j + u_{0j} + e_{ij} \quad \text{with } u_{0j} \sim N(0, \tau) \, e_{ij} \sim N(0, \sigma^2). \tag{8.5}$$

The main effect of treatment, or the difference between treatment average and control average, is of central interest. It is estimated by

$$\hat{\gamma}_{01} = \bar{Y}_E - \bar{Y}_C, \tag{8.6}$$

where

> $\bar{Y}_E$ is the mean for the experimental group and
> $\bar{Y}_C$ is the mean for the control group.

When each treatment has an equal number, $J/2$, of clusters, the variance of the main effect of treatment is estimated by

$$\text{var}(\hat{\gamma}_{01}) = \frac{4(\tau + \sigma^2 / n)}{J}, \tag{8.7}$$

where

 n is the total number of participants per cluster,
 J is the total number of clusters,
 σ^2 is the variance within cluster, and
 τ is the variance between clusters (Raudenbush, 1997).

Note that the variance term has two components of error, e_{ij} and u_{0j}, due to the multilevel structure of the data. The variance components are multiplied by 4 because the proportion of schools randomized into the treatment group (P) is .50. The more general form of the formula contains an expression that multiplies P by $1 - P$ in the denominator (Bloom et al., 2005). The product of P and $1 - P$ is .25, and dividing a number by .25 is equivalent to multiplying the number by 4.0; therefore, whenever there are $J/2$ clusters for both the treatment condition and the control condition, the numerator is multiplied by a factor of 4 (see Raudenbush, 1997).

For illustration purposes, all examples in this chapter make the assumption of equal allocation of clusters. However, this may not always be the case. Treatment clusters may be much more expensive than control clusters; as such, researchers may want fewer treatment clusters and more control clusters. For information on the effects of unequal allocation of clusters on the variance of the treatment effect, readers should refer to Bloom (2005).

Testing the Treatment Effect

Hypothesis testing can be used to determine if the difference between the means of the two populations is "statistically significant." This means that it is unlikely that we would observe a difference of this magnitude if the true difference in the population were equal exactly to zero. In this case, the null hypothesis is that there is no difference between the means or that there is no treatment effect. For a two-tailed hypothesis test, the alternative hypothesis states that there is a difference in the means or that there is a treatment effect. These hypotheses can be stated in symbols as follows:

$$H_0: \gamma_{01} = 0$$
$$H_1: \gamma_{01} \neq 0.$$

If each cluster contains an equal number of participants, one can use the results of a two-factor nested ANOVA to test the main effect of treatment (Kirk, 1982).[1] If there are an unequal number of participants in each cluster, it is permissible to substitute the harmonic mean for the number of participants per cluster because it provides a good approximation for the calculation (Raudenbush, 1997). The harmonic mean is $n_{harmonic} = J / \sum n_j^{-1}$. The harmonic mean is a weighted mean and tends to be smaller than the arithmetic mean; therefore, it provides a more conservative estimate of the sample size for power calculations.

Recall that the example used in the section on statistical power uses a t-test, which is appropriate for cases with only two groups. However, the t-test is a specific case of the F-test, which can be used to compare two or more groups. The F-test is presented in the remaining sections in order to provide the more general case for testing differences in population means (see Kirk, 1982, for more details). In the cluster randomized trial, the F-statistic is the ratio of treatment variance to cluster variance. The F-statistic is defined as

$$F\text{-}statistic = \frac{(MS_{treatment})}{(MS_{cluster})}.$$ (8.8)

Note the F-statistic converges to the ratio of expected mean squares, which is defined as

$$\frac{E(MS_{treatment})}{E(MS_{cluster})} = \frac{n\tau + \sigma^2 + nJ\gamma_{01}^2/4}{n\tau + \sigma^2} = 1 + \frac{nJ\gamma_{01}^2/4}{n\tau + \sigma^2}$$ (8.9)

and can be rewritten as

$$\frac{E(MS_{treatment})}{E(MS_{cluster})} = 1 + \lambda \text{ where } \lambda = \frac{nJ\gamma_{01}^2/4}{n\tau + \sigma^2} \text{ (Raudenbush, 1997).}$$ (8.10)

If the null hypothesis is true (e.g., if $\lambda = 0$), the F-statistic follows a central F-distribution with one degree of freedom for the numerator and $J - 2$ degrees of freedom for the denominator. Under the central F-distribution, the F-statistic is approximately one. In other words, there is no variation between treatments, so $\gamma_{01} = 0$, and the $nJ\gamma_{01}^2/4$ term in the numerator of the expected mean square ratio is zero. In this case, $\lambda = 0$; thus, the ratio of expected mean squares reduces to

$$\frac{E(MS_{treatment})}{E(MS_{cluster})} = \frac{n\tau + \sigma^2}{n\tau + \sigma^2} = 1 + \lambda = 1.$$

If the null hypothesis is false, meaning that there is a treatment difference ($\gamma_{01} \neq 0$), the F-statistic follows a non-central F-distribution with one degree of freedom for the numerator and $J-2$ degrees of freedom for the denominator. Then, the ratio of expected mean squares becomes the non-central F-distribution, characterized by a non-centrality parameter, λ (see Equation 8.10) which can be rewritten as

$$\lambda = \frac{\gamma_{01}^2}{4(\tau + \sigma^2 / n) / J} = \frac{\gamma_{01}^2}{\text{var}(\hat{\gamma}_{01})}. \qquad (8.11)$$

Note that λ, the non-centrality parameter, is the ratio of the squared main effect to the variance of the estimate of the treatment effect. Equation 8.11 clearly shows that the non-centrality parameter, λ, is a function of γ_{01}, n, J, τ, and σ^2.

The non-centrality parameter is related strongly to the power of the test. As λ increases, the F-statistic increases, thereby increasing the probability of rejecting the null hypothesis. Recall that the denominator of the non-centrality parameter is identical to the variance of the treatment effect, or

$$\text{var}(\hat{\gamma}_{01}) = \frac{4(\tau + \sigma^2 / n)}{J};$$

thus, decreasing the variance of the treatment effect increases λ. Recall that the standard error of the treatment effect is the square root of the variance of the treatment effect:

$$\text{se}(\hat{\gamma}_{01}) = \sqrt{\frac{4(\tau + \sigma^2 / n)}{J}}. \qquad (8.12)$$

Notice that increasing n and J will decrease the standard error, or increase the precision of the estimate, thereby increasing the power. However, increasing J has more of an effect than increasing n. The next two sections take a closer look at how the cluster size and the number of clusters affect the power of the test.

Cluster Size, n

Cluster size, n, refers to the number of participants in each cluster. In general, increasing n decreases the standard error of the treatment effect (Equation 8.12), increasing the power. However, at some point, increasing n without increasing the number of clusters, J, provides no further benefit. In Equation 8.12, as $n \rightarrow \infty$, $\text{se}(\hat{\gamma}_{01}) = 2\sqrt{\tau / J}$. This expression will not tend to zero unless $\tau = 0$ or $J \rightarrow \infty$.

Number of Clusters, J

As the total number of clusters, J, increases, the power to detect significant differences also increases. As mentioned earlier, the number of clusters has a stronger influence on power than the cluster size. As J increases, the power approaches one, regardless of n. This is because as J increases towards infinity, the standard error (Equation 8.12) gets infinitely small. This causes the non-centrality parameter to increase towards infinity, which results in the power approaching one. Therefore, to achieve the desired power, one can increase J. However, increasing J, or adding additional clusters, may not be feasible due to budgetary or other constraints.

Intraclass Correlation, ρ

The intraclass correlation, ρ, is a ratio of the variability between clusters to the total variability:

$$\rho = \frac{\tau}{\tau + \sigma^2}, \tag{8.13}$$

where

τ is the variation between clusters,
σ^2 is the variation within clusters, and
$\tau + \sigma^2$ is the total variation.

Note that this is the same intraclass correlation that can be calculated from a one-way random effects ANOVA (Raudenbush & Bryk, 2002). For United States data sets on school achievement with schools as clusters, ρ typically ranges between 0.10 and 0.20 (Schochet, 2005). Because $\tau + \sigma^2$ is the total variation, it can be standardized to equal one. Then it follows from Equation 8.13 that $\rho = \tau$ and $1 - \rho = \sigma^2$. As ρ increases, more of the variation is due to between-cluster variability. Replacing τ and σ^2 with ρ and $1 - \rho$ in the standard error formula (Equation 8.12), the standard error of the estimated effect of treatment can be rewritten as

$$se(\hat{\gamma}_{01}) = \sqrt{\frac{4(\rho + (1 - \rho) / n)}{J}}. \tag{8.14}$$

From Equation 8.14, it is apparent that increased values of ρ increase the standard error or decrease the precision of the estimate, thus decreasing the power of the test. Also, as ρ increases, the effect of n decreases. Therefore, if there is a lot of variability between clusters, more power is gained by increasing the number of clusters sampled. The key idea for ρ is that power increases as ρ decreases for a fixed n and J.

Standardized Effect Size

To make results from any study comparable to other studies, it is common to report effects in a standardized metric. This sometimes is referred to as a standardized model. Standardizing a model means that effect sizes do not depend on the nature of the original measurement scale used for the outcome variable. In a standardized model, the intraclass correlation coefficient, ρ, and the standardized effect size, δ, are used instead of σ^2, τ, and γ_{01}. The treatment effect is the difference between the means of the two groups. The standardized effect size, δ, is defined as the difference in the population means of the two groups divided by the estimated standard deviation of the outcome variable

$$\delta = \frac{\gamma_{01}}{\sqrt{\sigma^2 + \tau}},$$ (8.15)

where

$\gamma_{01} = \mu_E - \mu_C$,
μ_E is the population mean for the experimental group, and
μ_C is the population mean for the control group.

Given σ^2 and τ, the standardized effect size, δ, is estimated by

$$\hat{\delta} = \frac{\bar{y}_E - \bar{y}_C}{\sqrt{\sigma^2 + \tau}}$$ (8.16)

and

$$\text{se}(\hat{\delta}) = \sqrt{\frac{4(\rho + (1-\rho)/n)}{J}}.$$ (8.17)

These standardized effect sizes then are used to represent the magnitude of a treatment effect in a common metric. A general rule of thumb is that standardized effect sizes above 0.80 are considered large, between 0.50 and 0.80 are considered medium, and between 0.20 and 0.50 are considered small (Cohen, 1988). However, these are simply guidelines and should be interpreted with caution. Existing literature may serve as a better guide of reasonable effect size estimates. Small effect sizes, though more difficult to detect, are frequently very realistic in education settings. For example, Kane (2004) found that normal growth among elementary students in reading and math achievement was approximately 0.25 standard deviations per year. Thus, a program that might raise scores by 0.10 standard deviation units during one school year would have a considerable effect on achievement. Although a larger sample size is required to detect a smaller effect size, designing a study to detect a small treatment effect may be necessary. In planning a study, the researcher must specify a desired minimum effect size to calculate the power of the test. Researchers typically estimate this effect size using existing literature from similar studies, pilot data, or from analyses of observational data collected on a similar topic area.

The non-centrality parameter, λ (Equation 8.11), which is strongly related to the power of the test, can be redefined in terms of the effect size, δ, and the intraclass correlation, ρ, as shown below:

$$\lambda = \frac{nJ\delta^2 / 4}{n\rho + (1-\rho)} = \frac{J\delta^2}{4(\rho + (1-\rho)/n)}. \tag{8.18}$$

Using Equation 8.18, it is possible for a researcher to calculate the power of the test using n, J, δ, and ρ. The *Optimal Design* software (Liu et al., 2006) employs the standardized notation.

Example for Cluster Randomized Trial

The example in this section provides the details for the math example introduced earlier. Recall that a team of researchers want to test whether a new math series is superior to the standard series. The researchers propose a cluster randomized trial with students nested within schools. There are 40 schools willing to participate in the experiment. They assign 20 schools to the treatment, the new math series, and 20 schools to the control, the standard math series. To determine whether students using the new math series perform better than the students using the regular math series, they use a special math test that normally is not administered to students, so they decide to limit the number of students taking the test. They secure 25 students from one classroom within each school. The null hypothesis states that, on average, math achievement will be the same for students using the regular math series (control group) and students using the new math series (experimental group). The alternate hypothesis states that average math achievement for the experimental group is greater than that of the control group. The researchers want to be able to detect a minimum effect size of 0.25. Based on past studies, they expect 8% of the total variation in the outcome will lie between schools, so $\rho = 0.08$. Under these constraints, what power do the researchers have to detect an effect size of 0.25?

There are a variety of programs available for power analyses, including *GPOWER* (Erdfelder, Faul, & Buchner, 1996), *PINT* (Snijders, Bosker, & Guldemond, 2003), and *Optimal Design* (Liu et al., 2006). The examples in this chapter use the *Optimal Design* (OD) software. Some details for using the OD Software are provided in this chapter. In addition, the software and a complete user manual are freely available on http://sitemaker.umich.edu/group-based.

Upon opening the OD program, the main screen lists the different design options. Because the example is a cluster randomized trial, the user selects the cluster randomized trials module. All of the subheadings under power for the main effect of treatment (continuous outcome) offer the researcher an opportunity to explore the power of the study as a function of one specific design element. Each option produces a graph with power on the y-axis and the specified design element on the x-axis. For example, power vs. cluster size allows the researcher to see how the power changes (y-axis on the graph) as the cluster size increases (x-axis on the graph) for fixed J, ρ, and δ. The five subheadings under power for the main effect of treatment function similarly, so once the user is familiar with one option, the others follow easily.

To explore the power as a function of the effect size, the user selects power vs. effect size (delta). The buttons along the top of the screen allow the user to enter the significance level, α; the intraclass correlation, ρ; the total number of clusters, J; the number of individuals per cluster, n; and the proportion of variance explained by the level-two covariate, R_{L2}^2. (Our example does not yet include a level-two covariate. This feature is explained in the example in the next section.) The remaining buttons on the top of the screen offer the researcher additional screen options and are described in detail in the manual. In this example, because the effect size is allowed to vary along the x-axis, the user must enter the intraclass correlation, ρ, the total number of clusters, J, and the number of individuals per cluster, n, to construct a power curve.

Setting $\rho = .08$, $J = 40$, and $n = 25$ produces the power curve in Figure 8.2. The curve reveals power = .62 for an effect size of 0.25. Since a Type II error equals 1—power, we also can interpret this result as meaning that approximately 38% of the time, researchers would not be able to detect an effect size of 0.25. To achieve power = .80, researchers would have to increase the minimum detectable effect size to 0.31. Thus, by increasing the desired effect size, the power also increases.

A common misconception is that large clusters result in studies with high power. To explore how the number of students per cluster affects the power, the user may allow the within-cluster sample size to vary along the x-axis by selecting the power vs. cluster size option. Using the prior

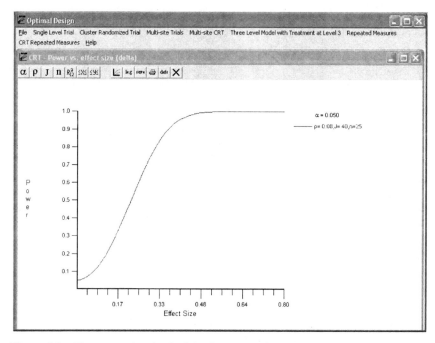

Figure 8.2 Cluster randomized trial—Power vs. effect size.

example as a guide, setting $\rho = .08$, $J = 40$, and $\delta = 0.25$ allows the user to see the power, assuming that there are up to 400 students in the school and that the researchers want to test all the students. The power curve is in Figure 8.3.

It appears that the threshold for a power of .80 is about 60 students. This means that adding more persons per cluster does not increase the power after approximately 60 students. If it is expensive to test individual students, it would not be cost-effective to test more students above the threshold because no additional power is gained.

To illustrate how the number of clusters affects the power, suppose that the researcher wants to know how many total clusters of size 25 are necessary to detect an effect size of 0.25 with power = .80. For this, the user allows J, the number of clusters, to vary along the x-axis by selecting power vs. number of clusters, J, and entering the information similarly to the examples above. The power curve is displayed in Figure 8.4.

Notice that unlike the within-cluster sample size, as the number of clusters increases, the power increases towards 1.0. With the information above, a total of approximately 60 clusters is required to achieve power = .80.

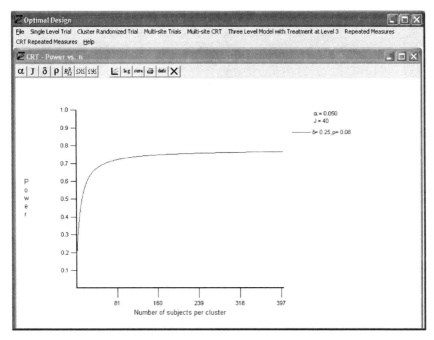

Figure 8.3   Cluster randomized trial—Power vs. cluster size.

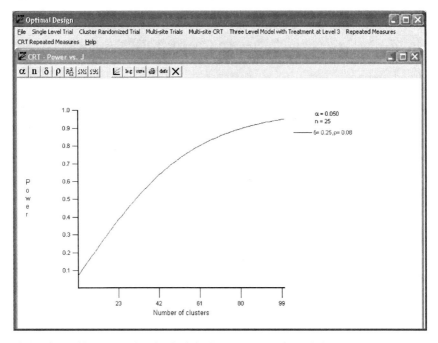

Figure 8.4   Cluster randomized trial—Power vs. number of clusters.

CLUSTER RANDOMIZED TRIALS
WITH A CLUSTER-LEVEL COVARIATE

From the previous example and discussion, it is clear that the number of clusters has a greater effect on the power than the number of people within each cluster. However, the cost of a study frequently limits the number of clusters. One method to combat this problem is to include a level-two covariate in the design and analysis of a cluster randomized trial. Including a cluster-level covariate may reduce the number of clusters necessary to achieve a specified level of power. This section focuses specifically on including a covariate at the cluster level. This may be an aggregated covariate, such as pre-test scores aggregated across schools or school socioeconomic status (SES). Cluster-level covariates are often less expensive and easier to collect than individual-level covariates. Because the gain in precision is very similar for either type of covariate, it may be advantageous to collect a cluster-level covariate (Bloom, 2005). For a more complete discussion of the effect of cluster-level covariates on statistical power, see Bloom (2005) or Bloom et al. (2005).

Including a covariate in the design of a cluster randomized trial adds an additional component that influences the power of the test: the strength of the correlation between the covariate and the true cluster mean outcome. The strength of the correlation between the covariate and the true cluster mean is denoted as $\rho_{x\beta_0}$. Using this notation, β_{0j} represents the true mean outcome for cluster j, and X_j represents the covariate. The conditional level-two variance, or unexplained variance after accounting for the covariate, is denoted as τ_{1x}. The stronger the correlation, $\rho_{x\beta_0}$, the smaller the conditional level-two variance, τ_{1x}. The relationship between the conditional and unconditional level-two variance can be expressed as $\tau_{1x} = (1 - \rho_{x\beta_0}^2)\tau$. Recall that by decreasing the level-two variance, the estimate of the treatment effect is more precise; therefore, the power increases.

The Model

In hierarchical form, the level-one model for a cluster randomized trial with a cluster-level covariate is the same as Equation 8.3. The level-two model, or cluster-level model, differs from a simple cluster randomized trial because it includes a term for the cluster-level covariate. The model is

$$\beta_{0j} = \gamma_{00} + \gamma_{01}W_j + \gamma_{02}X_j + u_{oj} \quad \text{with } u_{0j} \sim N(0, \tau_{1x}), \quad (8.19)$$

where

γ_{00} is the grand mean,

γ_{01} is the mean difference between the treatment and control group or the main effect of treatment,

γ_{02} is the regression coefficient for the cluster-level covariate,

W_j is an indicator variable where $-\frac{1}{2}$ represents the control group and $\frac{1}{2}$ represents the experimental group,

X_j is the cluster-level covariate, centered around its group mean,

u_{0j} is the random effect associated with each cluster, and

τ_{1x} is the residual variance between clusters.

Note that the between-cluster variance, τ_{1x}, is now the residual variance conditional on the cluster-level covariate X. For simplicity, assume there is no interaction between the cluster-level covariate, X, and the treatment group, W. This is known as the homogeneity of regression slopes assumption. The power analyses assume there is no interaction (Raudenbush et al., 2006). It is not possible to check the homogeneity of regression slopes assumption until the data have been collected. Note that if later interaction tests reveal there is an interaction, the initial power estimates will not be accurate.

Similar to the cluster randomized trial without a covariate, of central interest is the treatment effect, or the difference between the treatment average and control average, adjusting for the covariate. However, now the main effect of treatment is estimated by

$$\hat{\gamma}_{01} = \bar{Y}_E - \bar{Y}_C - \hat{\gamma}_{02}(\bar{X}_E - \bar{X}_C), \tag{8.20}$$

where

$\bar{Y}_E$ is the mean for the experimental group,

$\bar{Y}_C$ is the mean for the control group,

$\bar{X}_E$ is the covariate mean for the experimental group, and

$\bar{X}_C$ is the covariate mean for the control group.

The estimated main effect of treatment resembles the estimated effect without the covariate; however, now it is adjusted for treatment group differences in the covariate. The variance of the main effect of treatment is estimated by the following:

$$\text{var}(\hat{\gamma}_{01}) = \frac{4(\tau_{1x} + \sigma^2 / n)}{J}\left[1 + \frac{1}{J-4}\right], \tag{8.21}$$

where

n is the total number of participants per cluster,

J is the total number of clusters, and

τ_{1x} is the conditional level-two variance, $(1-\rho_{x\beta_0}^2)\tau_{1x}$ (Raudenbush, 1997).

Testing the Treatment Effect

Similar to the case without a covariate, hypothesis testing can be used to determine if the main effect of treatment is "statistically significant." If the data are balanced, one can use the results of a nested analysis of covariance with random effects for clusters and fixed effects for the treatment and covariate (Kirk, 1982). The test statistic is an F-statistic, which compares the adjusted treatment variance to the adjusted cluster variance. The F-statistic is defined as

$$F\text{-statistic} = \frac{MS^*_{treatment}}{MS^*_{clusters}}, \tag{8.22}$$

where $MS^*_{treatment}$ and $MS^*_{cluster}$ are now adjusted for the covariate. Note that the F-statistic converges to the ratio of expected mean squares, defined as

$$\frac{E(MS^*_{treatment})}{E(MS^*_{clusters})} = 1 + \lambda_x. \tag{8.23}$$

The F-test follows a non-central F-distribution, $F(1, J-3, \lambda_x)$ in the case of a cluster-level covariate where the non-centrality parameter, λ_x, is

$$\lambda_x = \frac{J\gamma_{01}^2}{4(\tau_{1x} + \sigma^2/n)} \tag{8.24}$$

and

$$\tau_{1x} = (1 - \rho_{x\beta_o}^2)\tau. \tag{8.25}$$

From Equations 8.24 and 8.25, it is obvious that the stronger the correlation, $\rho_{x\beta_0}$, the smaller τ_{1x} and the greater the increase in the power of the test. For example, a covariate that has a correlation of .60 with the cluster level mean will reduce the between-cluster variation by 36% whereas a correlation of .80 will reduce the between-cluster variation by 64%. In educational studies, pre-tests tend to be the most powerful covariates.

Note that the non-centrality parameter with and without the covariate are closely related. The main difference in the formula is the presence of the conditional between-cluster variance. However, if the correlation between the covariate and the cluster-level mean is zero, the between-cluster variance is not reduced. In other words, the conditional and unconditional between-cluster variance is the same. In this case, the non-centrality parameter reduces to the non-centrality parameter in the case of no covariate.

In most cases, the correlation is positive, and there is a reduction of between-cluster variance. However, one consequence of including a covariate is that we lose one degree of freedom. In the case of no covariate, the F-test follows a non-central F-distribution, $F(1, J-2, \lambda)$, whereas in the covariate case, there is one less degree of freedom, $F(1, J-3, \lambda_x)$. This may be a potential problem in a study with a limited number of clusters.

Standardized Effect Size

The non-centrality parameter can be defined using standardized effect size notation. Recall that in Equation 8.24, the non-centrality parameter was defined as

$$\lambda_x = \frac{J\gamma_{01}^2}{4(\tau_{1x} + \sigma^2 / n)}.$$

Replacing $\tau_{1x} = (1 - \rho_{x\beta_0}^2)\tau$, constraining $\tau + \sigma^2 = 1$, and defining

$$\delta = \frac{\gamma_{10}}{\sqrt{\tau + \sigma^2}},$$

λ_x can be rewritten as a function of δ, ρ, and $\rho_{x\beta_0}$:

$$\lambda_x = \frac{J\delta^2}{4[(1 - \rho_{x\beta_0}^2)\rho + (1 - \rho)/n]}. \tag{8.26}$$

The only difference in the non-centrality parameter in the case of the cluster-level covariate is the correction factor, $(1 - \rho_{x\beta_0}^2)$. The correction factor only affects ρ, the between-cluster variation, since the covariate is a cluster-level covariate.

Example of CRT with a Cluster-level Covariate

Imagine the researchers in the math example include a cluster-level covariate. Recall that they estimated $\rho = .08$, desired a minimum effect size of 0.25, and had 40 clusters and 25 subjects per cluster. The power to detect an effect was only .62. Suppose the researchers have access to last year's average math test scores for the schools. Bloom (2005) has shown that a correlation of approximately .75 between pretest and posttest is well within the reasonable range. Therefore, it is reasonable to anticipate that average school pre-test scores explain 56% of the variation in true school-level mean posttest scores. What is the power when the researchers include the covariate in the design and analysis?

Returning to the original power curve for power vs. effect size (δ) displayed in Figure 8.2, it can be modified to reflect the information in the cluster-level covariate by selecting the R^2_{L2} icon. Recall that R^2_{L2} represents the proportion of variance in cluster means that is explained by the cluster-level covariate. The power curves in Figure 8.5 compare the power with and without the cluster-level covariate information.

The trajectory reveals that the power to detect an effect size of 0.25 increases from approximately .62 to .80 when the cluster-level covariate is included in the design and analysis.

Although the use of a covariate can substantially increase power in a cluster randomized trial, there are caveats. First, if there is very little initial between-cluster variation, including a cluster-level covariate will result in only smalls gain in power. For example, if the unconditional between-cluster variation is only 0.02, it is already so small that reducing it will not increase the power substantially. Second, choice of the covariate must be specified during the design phase, prior to any data analysis. Post-hoc searching expeditions cannot be used to identify appropriate covariates, and they will produce biased tests of the significance of the treatment effect. If point estimates of the treatment effect look very different with and without adjustment of the covariate, critics may suspect opportunistic choice of the co-

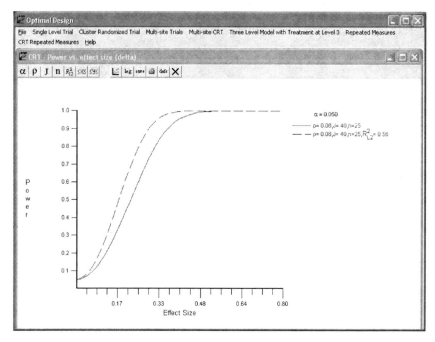

Figure 8.5 Cluster randomized trial with and without a cluster-level covariate—Power vs. effect size.

variate and question the reliability of the results (Raudenbush et al., 2005). Third, covariates are continuous variables; discrete variables, such as race or gender, cannot be used as possible covariates. Finally, as mentioned, the researcher should check the assumption that the covariate association with the outcome is the same across treatment groups (Kirk, 1982).

MULTI-SITE CLUSTER RANDOMIZED TRIALS

Although a simple two-level cluster randomized trials is appropriate in many cases, there are studies that involve another level of nesting. Imagine a case in which students are nested within schools that are nested within districts. The districts are quite different from each other, including rural, urban, and suburban districts. The researchers are concerned that randomizing across districts may not be effective. For example, if the randomization process resulted in all the suburban districts receiving the treatment, half of the rural districts receiving the treatment, and no urban districts receiving the treatment, attributing any achievement gains to the treatment would be problematic because the students in the different districts likely would be different with respect to academic achievement prior to the treatment. The multi-site cluster randomized trial avoids this dilemma by randomizing within sites/blocks, or in this case, within districts. This ensures that an equal proportion of schools within each district receive the treatment. In essence, the multi-site cluster randomized trial is the simple two-level cluster randomized trial repeated across sites. An example of this design is the evaluation of the *Early Elementary Mathematics Curricula* conducted by Mathematica Policy Research, Inc. (http://www.mathcurriculastudy.com/profile.asp). This evaluation involved 20 districts. Within districts, schools were assigned to treatment conditions. Student math achievement was the main outcome of interest.

The technique described above, randomizing units within sites/blocks, is commonly known as blocking and is used frequently in experimental designs that randomize individuals (Kirk, 1982). The concept of blocking can be extended to a cluster randomized trial. The use of pre-randomization blocking can improve the precision of the estimates and increase the power of the tests. To use pre-randomization blocking, the researcher identifies sites or blocks in which clusters are very similar with respect to the outcome variable. This reduces the heterogeneity within sites, increasing the precision of the treatment effect estimate, hence increasing the power of the test for the main effect of treatment. One advantage attributed to blocking rather than covariance analysis (such as that used in the previous example) is that a blocking variable may be a continuous or a discrete variable. For example, a researcher may block on average school SES or the percentage of minority students in a school.

A design using blocking before randomizing groups can be thought of as a multi-site cluster randomized trial, an extension of the cluster randomized trial (Raudenbush et al., 2006). In a multi-site cluster randomized trial, the site is the block, and clusters are assigned randomly to treatment and control within each site. Sometimes, the sites are natural administrative units, for example, schools in which classrooms are assigned randomly to treatment or control. Other times, the sites are made up of groups of units that have similar characteristics, such as schools that have a similar racial and ethnic composition. Then, the schools within each site are assigned randomly to treatment or control.

To illustrate, recall the earlier example: researchers want to test the effectiveness of a new math program. Suppose that the ethnic composition of the school is related to school mean math achievement, which makes it possible to assign the schools to "blocks" that are similar on ethnic composition. Within each block, schools are randomized to receive the new math program or the regular program.

Designing a multi-site cluster randomized trial requires that the researcher calculate the power for the average treatment effect since a separate treatment effect is estimated for each site. Blocking reduces the variance in the estimate of the treatment effect because by dividing schools into blocks, the between-block variance is removed from the error variance (Kirk, 1982). If the between-block component is large, removing it greatly reduces the variance of the estimate.

The power to detect the main effect of treatment in a multi-site cluster randomized trial is slightly more complicated than in a cluster randomized trial. In a typical multi-site cluster randomized trial, power is a function of the following while holding α constant: minimum detectable effect size, δ; the intraclass correlation, ρ; the effect size variability, σ_{δ}^2; the number of sites, K; the number of clusters per site, J; and the cluster size, n (Raudenbush et al., 2006).

The effect size variability, σ_{δ}^2, is not estimable in a cluster randomized trial because only one effect size, the standardized difference between the control and experimental groups, is calculated. However, in a multi-site cluster randomized trial, the experiment is replicated within sites. Therefore, there are effect size estimates for each site. Hence, it is also possible to estimate the variance of the effect size. In cases where the researcher suspects the variance of the effect size is large, it may be useful to calculate the power for the variance of the treatment effect (Raudenbush & Liu, 2001).

It is important to think about whether the sites in a multi-site cluster randomized trial should be considered fixed or random. In some cases, the sites will be regarded as randomly sampled from a larger universe or "population" of possible sites. The larger universe is the target of generalization. For example, if schools are sampled and then classrooms are assigned at random to treatments within schools, the target of any generalizations often will be the larger universe of schools from which schools in the study are regarded as a representative sample.

In other cases, the sites will be regarded as fixed. Consider a program designed to teach students about the dangers of drugs. The outcome for the study is students' attitude towards drugs, which is measured by a questionnaire. The researchers hypothesize that the school setting—suburban, urban, or rural—affects students' attitude towards drugs. Thus, they want to block on the setting. In this case, suburban, urban, and rural are not regarded as sampled from a population of settings but rather as fixed blocks or sites. The researchers are only able to draw inferences to these specific blocks. In cases with small numbers of blocks, it is difficult to try to draw inferences to a larger universe; therefore, the fixed effects approach is more logical. Whether the sites are viewed as random or fixed affects both the data analysis and the power analysis (Raudenbush et al., 2006). Both cases are discussed in the remaining sections.

The Random Effects Model

The random effects model is appropriate when sites are viewed as randomly sampled from a larger population. Data from a multi-site cluster randomized trial can be represented as a three-level model: persons nested within clusters nested within sites. The level-one model, or person-level model, is (Raudenbush et al., 2006)

$$Y_{ijk} = \pi_{0jk} + e_{ijk} \quad \text{with } e_{ijk} \sim N(0, \sigma^2), \tag{8.27}$$

where

$i = 1, \ldots, n$ persons per cluster,
$j = 1, \ldots, J$ clusters per site,
$k = 1, \ldots, K$ sites,
π_{0jk} is the mean for cluster j in site k,
e_{ijk} is the error associated with each person, and
σ^2 is the within-cluster variance.

The level-two model, or cluster-level model, is

$$\pi_{0jk} = \beta_{00k} + \beta_{01k}W_{jk} + r_{0jk} \quad \text{with } r_{0jk} \sim N(0, \tau_\pi), \quad (8.28)$$

where

> β_{00k} is the mean for site k,
> β_{01k} is the treatment effect at site k,
> W_{jk} is an indicator variable where $-\frac{1}{2}$ represents the control group
> and $\frac{1}{2}$ represents the experimental group,
> r_{0jk} is the random effect associated with each cluster, and
> τ_π is the variance between clusters within sites.

The level-three model, or site-level model, is

$$\beta_{00k} = \gamma_{000} + u_{00k} \quad \text{with } \mathrm{var}(u_{00k}) \sim \tau_{\beta_{00}}$$

$$\beta_{01k} = \gamma_{010} + u_{01k} \quad \text{with } \mathrm{var}(u_{01k}) \sim \tau_{\beta_{11}} \quad \mathrm{cov}(u_{00k}, u_{01k}) = \tau_{\beta_{01}}, \quad (8.29)$$

where

> γ_{000} is the grand mean,
> γ_{010} is the average treatment effect ("main effect of treatment"),
> u_{00k} is the random effect associated with each site mean,
> u_{01k} is the random effect associated with each site treatment effect,
> $\tau_{\beta_{00}}$ is the variance between site means,
> $\tau_{\beta_{11}}$ is the variance between sites on the treatment effect, and
> $\tau_{\beta_{01}}$ is the covariance between site-specific means and site-specific
> treatment effects.

The random effects, u_{00k} and u_{01k}, typically are assumed bivariate normal in distribution. The two quantities, the main effect of treatment, γ_{010}, and the variance of the treatment effect, $\tau_{\beta_{11}}$ are the most interesting. Note that this model is a random effects model. In a fixed effects model, the variance of the treatment effect, $\tau_{\beta_{11}}$, would be zero.

Testing the Average Treatment Effect

The average treatment effect is denoted as γ_{010} in level three of the model. Given a balanced design, it is estimated by

$$\hat{\gamma}_{010} = \bar{Y}_E - \bar{Y}_C, \quad (8.30)$$

where

$\bar{Y}_E$ is the mean for the experimental group and
$\bar{Y}_C$ is the mean for the control group.

The estimated main effect of treatment resembles the main effect of treatment in the cluster randomized trial; however, now the summation is over clusters and sites. Thus, the variance of the treatment effect is slightly more complicated than in a cluster randomized trial. It is estimated by

$$\text{var}(\hat{\gamma}_{010}) = \frac{\tau_{\beta_{11}} + 4(\tau_\pi + \sigma^2 / n) / J}{K} \tag{8.31}$$

(Raudenbush & Liu, 2000). The main difference in the variance of the treatment effect in a multi-site cluster randomized trial compared to a cluster randomized trial is that now there are four sources of variability: the within-cluster variance, σ^2; the between-cluster variance or within-site variance, τ_π; the between-site variance, $\tau_{\beta_{00}}$; and the between-site variance in the treatment effect, $\tau_{\beta_{11}}$.

If the data are balanced, one can use the results of a nested analysis of variance with random effects for the clusters and sites and fixed effects for the treatment (Kirk, 1982). Similar to prior tests, the test statistic is an *F* statistic, which now compares the treatment variance to the treatment by site variance. The *F*-statistic is defined as

$$F\text{statistic} = \frac{MS_{treatment}}{MS_{treatmentXsite}}. \tag{8.32}$$

If the null hypothesis is false, the *F*-test follows a non-central *F*-distribution, $F(1, K-1; \lambda)$. Recall that the non-centrality parameter, λ, is a ratio of the squared-treatment effect to the variance of the treatment effect estimate, or

$$\lambda = \frac{\gamma_{010}^2}{\text{var}(\hat{\gamma}_{010})} = \frac{K\gamma_{010}^2}{\tau_{\beta_{11}} + 4(\tau_\pi + \sigma^2 / n) / J}. \tag{8.33}$$

Looking at the formula, it is clear that *K*, the number of sites, has the greatest impact on the power. It is especially important to have a large *K* if there is a lot of between-site variance in the treatment effect. Increasing *J* also increases the power, but it is not as important as *K*. *J* becomes more important if there is a lot of variability between clusters within sites. Finally, increasing *n* does increase the power, but *n* has the smallest effect of the three sample sizes. Increasing *n* is most beneficial if there is a lot of variability within clusters. In addition to K, J, and n, a larger effect size increases power.

Note that $\tau_{\beta_{11}}$, the between-site variance of the treatment effect, appears in the denominator of the non-centrality parameter. If the variance of the treatment effect across sites is large, it is particularly important to have a large number of sites to counteract the increase in variance. However, if the variability of the impact across sites is very large, it may be masking the true treatment effect. The importance of the variance of the treatment effect is discussed in a later section.

Standardized Notation

In the standardized model, the within-cluster variance, σ^2, and the between-cluster variance, τ_π, sum to one. The intraclass correlation, ρ, is defined as

$$\rho = \frac{\tau_\pi}{\tau_\pi + \sigma^2}.$$

Note that this is the intraclass correlation within blocks. In other words, the between-block variability is removed, so ρ is the between-cluster variance relative to the total variance within blocks. Constraining $\tau_\pi + \sigma^2 = 1$, it can be rearranged so $\tau_\pi = \rho$ and $\sigma^2 = 1 - \rho$. This notation is the same as the notation for the standardized model for the cluster randomized trial.

In standardized notation, the non-centrality parameter, λ, can be rewritten as

$$\lambda = \frac{K\delta^2}{\sigma_\delta^2 + 4[\rho + (1-\rho)/n]/J}, \tag{8.34}$$

where

ρ is the intraclass correlation

$$\rho = \frac{\tau_\pi}{\tau_\pi + \sigma^2},$$

or the variance between clusters relative to the between and within cluster variation within blocks;

δ is the standardized main effect of treatment,

$$\delta = \frac{\gamma_{010}}{\sqrt{\tau_\pi + \sigma^2}}; \text{ and}$$

σ_δ^2 is the variance of the standardized treatment effect,

$$\sigma_\delta^2 = \frac{\tau_{\beta_{11}}}{\tau_\pi + \sigma^2}$$

(Raudenbush et al., 2006).

Note that in a multi-site cluster randomized trial, the variance of the effect size is standardized in addition to the treatment effect. The magnitude of the effect size variability depends on the desired minimum detectable effect. For example, a standardized effect size variance of 0.10 is the same as a standard error of approximately $\sqrt{0.10} = 0.31$. If a researcher desires a minimum detectable effect of 0.50, a standard error of 0.31 is quite large and would result in a 95% prediction interval ranging from −0.11 to 1.11, indicating a lot of uncertainty in the estimate. For a standardized effect size of 0.50, a standardized effect size variance of 0.01 (or standard error of 0.10) is more reasonable and would yield a 95% prediction interval ranging from 0.30 to 0.70.

Example—Multi-site Cluster Randomized Trial

Suppose in our previous math example the researchers block prior to randomization. They decide to block on school SES. By consulting prior school research studies, the researchers hypothesize that blocking on school SES will explain approximately 40% of the variation in the outcome. They still secure 40 schools, but prior to random assignment of the schools, they match the schools according to SES. Note that they now have 20 sites, or matched pairs. The researchers assume that the intraclass correlation prior to blocking is approximately .08. The researchers still are interested in detecting a minimum effect size equal to approximately 0.25. The researchers assume that the effect size variability = 0.01. What is the power under this design?

In the *Optimal Design* software (Liu et al., 2006), the multi-site cluster randomized trial module operates similarly to the cluster randomized trial module. However, the user must specify three additional components: the total number of sites, K; the percent of variance explained by the blocking variable, B; and the effect size variability, σ_δ^2. Because the within-block intraclass correlation (described earlier) is frequently unknown to the researcher and may be difficult to estimate, the program asks for the intraclass correlation prior to blocking as well as the percent of variance explained by the blocking variable and then calculates the within-block intraclass correlation.

Selecting power vs. effect size (delta) and specifying $n = 25$, $J = 2$, $K = 20$, $\rho = .08$, $B = 0.40$, and $\sigma_\delta^2 = 0.01$, reveals the power curve in Figure 8.6.

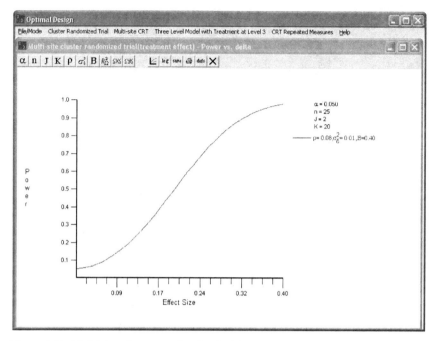

Figure 8.6   Multi-site cluster randomized trial—Power vs. effect size for a random effects model.

For an effect size of about 0.25, the power is approximately .71. Recall that in the first example, the power for a simple cluster randomized trial with 40 clusters and no covariate was only .62. To achieve power of .71 in a simple cluster randomized trial with no covariate, 50 clusters would be necessary. Therefore, blocking in this design achieves the same level of power with 10 fewer schools.

Testing the Variance of the Treatment Effect

The tests described in this section are only applicable under the random effects model where it is assumed that the treatment effect varies randomly across the sites. The design, with treatments randomized to clusters within sites, allows an estimate of this variability since each site has its own treatment effect. If the variability across sites is very large, it may be masking the true treatment effect. For example, imagine a multi-site cluster randomized trial that reports a standardized treatment effect estimate of 0.23. The researchers claim that the new math program improves scores by 0.23 standard units. However, they fail to report that the standardized treatment effect variability across sites is 0.30. The high variance may be masking the fact that some types of schools benefit from the program while other types of schools actually suffer from the program. For example, there may be a differential effect by location, where rural schools that adopt the program see positive effects but urban schools that adopt the program see negative or no effects. Thus, the researchers would need to investigate moderating site characteristics. Reporting the average treatment effect alone may be very misleading and is not recommended (Raudenbush & Liu, 2000).

The variance of the treatment effect is critical in determining the interpretation of a treatment effect estimate; therefore, it is important to be able to detect large treatment effect variability with adequate power. In standardized notation, the null and alternative tests for the treatment effect variability are

$$H_0 : \sigma_\delta^2 = 0$$

$$H_1 : \sigma_\delta^2 > 0$$

The null hypothesis states that the variance of the treatment impact across sites is null, whereas the alternative hypothesis states that it is greater than zero. (The variance can never be negative, so this is always a directional hypothesis.) The test for the variance of the treatment effect is an F-test. The F-statistic is defined as

$$F\text{-}statistic = \frac{(MS_{treatmentXsite})}{(MS_{within-cell})}. \tag{8.35}$$

The F-statistic follows a central F-distribution with df $= K - 1$, $K(J - 2)$. The ratio of the expectation of the numerator to the expectation of the denominator is (Kirk, 1982)

$$\frac{E(MS_{treatmentXsite})}{E(MS_{within-cell})} = 1 + \frac{J\sigma_\delta^2}{4[\rho + (1-\rho)/n]}. \tag{8.36}$$

Note that the power is based on the following: the number of sites, K; the number of clusters per site, J; the number of people per cluster, n; the standardized effect size variability, σ_δ^2, and the intra-cluster correlation, ρ.

Under the null hypothesis, one expects σ_δ^2 to be zero; thus, the ratio of the expected mean squares should be one. As σ_δ^2 increases, the ratio of expected mean squares gets larger, which increases the power of the test. Thus, the number of clusters within each site is critical for increasing the power to detect the variance of the treatment effect across sites. Increasing K also increases the power, through the degrees of freedom, but is not as important as increasing J. Note that this is the opposite of what was found in the case of power for the treatment effect, where K was the most significant factor in increasing power and J was less important.

Looking at Equation 8.36, it is clear that it will be difficult to achieve adequate power to detect small values of σ_δ^2, like 0.01, unless J is extremely large, which is unlikely. However, this is not very problematic because a researcher's primary concern is to be able to detect larger treatment effect variability; small values will not influence the interpretation of the treatment effect.

THE FIXED EFFECTS MODEL

The fixed effects model is appropriate when sites are viewed as fixed effects, meaning that generalizations are restricted to the actual sites in the study. The model for the fixed effects approach is identical to the random effects model with a crucial exception: the site-specific contributions, u_{00k} and u_{01k}, are designated as fixed constants rather than random variables. In this model, there is one main reference effect and $K-1$ site-specific effects. There is no random effect size variability, σ_δ^2, since the treatment effect does not vary randomly across sites.

The models help illustrate the difference between treating the sites as fixed or random effects. The level-one and level-two models for a fixed effects case are identical to models (8.27) and (8.28) in the random effects case. The level-three model, or site-level model, differs and can be written as

$$\beta_{00k} = \gamma_{000} + \sum_{k=1}^{K-1} D_k u_{00k}$$

$$\beta_{01k} = \gamma_{010} + \sum_{k=1}^{K-1} D_k u_{01k}, \tag{8.37}$$

where

γ_{000} is the reference group overall mean,
γ_{010} is the reference group treatment effect,
D_k is a site-specific dummy variable,
u_{00k} are the treatment-by-site interaction effects, which are fixed effects associated with each site mean and are constrained to have a mean of zero, and
u_{01k} are the treatment-by-site interaction effects, which are fixed effects associated with each site treatment effect and are constrained to have a mean of zero (Raudenbush et al., 2006).

Similar to the random effects case, the treatment effect, γ_{010}, is one of the primary quantities of interest. However, in the fixed effects case, the treatment-by-site interaction effects, u_{01k}, are also of interest, whereas in the random effects case, the random treatment effect variability, σ_δ^2, is of interest.

Testing the Average Treatment Effect

If the data are balanced, one can use the results of a nested analysis of variance with random effects for the clusters and fixed effects for sites, treatments, and site-by-treatment interaction (Kirk, 1982). The test statistic is an F-statistic, which compares treatment variance to within-cell variance. The F-statistic is defined as

$$F\text{-}statistic = \frac{MS_{treatment}}{MS_{within-cell}}. \tag{8.38}$$

If the null hypothesis is false, the F-test follows a non-central F-distribution, $F(1, K(J-2); \lambda)$, where

$$\lambda = \frac{KJ\gamma_{010}^2}{4(\tau_\pi + \sigma^2 / n)}. \tag{8.39}$$

Recall that the larger the non-centrality parameter, the greater the power of the test. By looking at the formula, it is clear that KJ, the total number of clusters, has the greatest impact on the power. Increasing n does increase the power but has the smallest effect of the three sample sizes. Increasing n is most beneficial if there is a lot of variability within clusters. In addition to larger values of K, J, and n, a larger effect size increases power.

Standardized Notation

The non-centrality parameter, λ, can be rewritten in terms of the standardized model

$$\lambda = \frac{KJ\delta^2}{4[\rho + (1-\rho) / n]}, \tag{8.40}$$

where

ρ is the intraclass correlation,

$$\rho = \frac{\tau_\pi}{\tau_\pi + \sigma^2},$$

or the variance between clusters relative to the between and within cluster variation within blocks, and
δ is the standardized main effect of treatment,

$$\delta = \frac{\gamma_{010}}{\sqrt{\tau_\pi + \sigma^2}}.$$

Example of Fixed Effects Multi-site Cluster Randomized Trial

Fixed effects models are most appropriate when the researchers are not trying to generalize beyond the sample. Suppose for example that a team of researchers plans to test an intervention designed to improve reading achievement. The researchers select three sites, an urban, suburban, and rural district. Within each site, they randomize eight schools each to the treatment and control groups. They plan to test 15 students from one classroom within each school. Prior to blocking, they expect that the intraclass correlation will be .10. The researchers hypothesize blocking will explain 40% of the between site variation. What is the minimum detectable effect size if they want power equal to .80?

The only difference in doing a fixed effects and random effects power analyses using the OD software is the setting for the effect size variability, σ_δ^2. In a fixed effects model, the user sets $\sigma_\delta^2 = 0$. Selecting power vs. effect size (delta) in the multi-site cluster randomized trials (MSCRT) module and specifying $n = 15$, $J = 16$, $K = 3$, $\rho = .10$, $B = 0.40$, and $\sigma_\delta^2 = 0$ reveals the power curve in Figure 8.7.

For power = .80, the minimum detectable effect size is approximately 0.29.

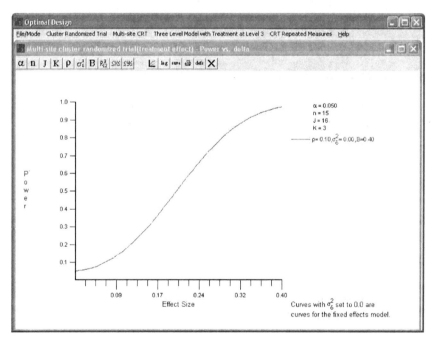

Figure 8.7   Multi-site cluster randomized trial—Power vs. effect size for a fixed effects model.

Testing Site-by-Treatment Variation

Operationally, the test of the site-by-treatment variation in the case of the fixed effects model is identical to that in the case of the random effects model. The null hypothesis, however, differs. Recall that in the case of the random effects model, the null hypothesis states

$$H_0 : \tau_{\beta_{11}} = 0,$$

or for the standardized random effects model,

$$H_0 : \sigma_\delta^2 = 0.$$

However, in the fixed effects model, the site-specific treatment effects are fixed constants rather than random variables. Thus, in the non-standardized model

$$H_0 : \sum_{k-1}^{K} u_{01k}^2 = 0.$$

As in the random effects case, this hypothesis can be tested using

$$F[K-1, K(J-2)] = \frac{MS_{treatmentXsite}}{MS_{within-cell}}. \tag{8.41}$$

When the F-test indicates rejection of H_0, one emphasizes the estimation of site-specific treatment effects, also known as "simple main effects," or post hoc procedures designed to identify subsets of sites for which the treatment effect is homogeneous (see Kirk, 1982, p. 317).

DISCUSSION

This chapter describes two major designs that randomize entire clusters instead of individuals: cluster randomized trials with and without a cluster-level covariate and multi-site cluster randomized trials. In general, simple cluster randomized trials yield the least amount of power because these trials do not use additional information that may be available. The number of clusters drives the power and may seem overwhelming to researchers, particularly because additional clusters are typically expensive. One strategy for making the best use of resources for studies on a fixed budget is to find the optimal allocation of individuals and clusters. In a simple cluster randomized trial, the optimal allocation of individuals and clusters minimizes the variance of the treatment effect and maximizes the power for a fixed budget. For details regarding the optimal allocation of individuals and clusters, see Headrick & Zumbo, 2005; Moerbeek, VanBreukelen, & Berger, 2000; and Raudenbush, 1997.

Researchers often seek to increase the power of the test by including a covariate or employing blocking. Deciding whether to use a covariance analysis or to block can be complicated. If a variable is available that could be used as a covariate or a blocking variable, using it as a covariate tends to increase the power over using it as a blocking variable (Raudenbush et al., 2005). However, the assumptions for an analysis of covariance are more restrictive than the assumptions for a design that includes blocking. In addition to less stringent restrictions, blocking often appeals to researchers because it increases the face validity of the design. In many cases, researchers block on a salient characteristic to improve face validity and then use a covariance adjustment to try to increase the power. For a more complete discussion of the tradeoffs of blocking and covariance adjustment on power in cluster randomized trials, see Raudenbush et al., 2006.

Researchers involved in planning cluster randomized trials need to be familiar with the statistical models and to understand how the design parameters affect the power of the test. There are also practical considerations that researchers face when planning cluster randomized trials. First, the researcher must decide on the appropriate design. Aside from the designs mentioned in the chapter, other possibilities might include a three-level design with treatment at level three (students within classrooms within schools where treatment is at the school level) or a cluster randomized trial with repeated measures (repeated measures on students within a classroom where treatment is implemented at the classroom level) (Raudenbush et al., 2006). In order to select the correct design, researchers should identify the unit of analysis, the unit of treatment, and the clustering levels involved. For example, consider the math curriculum evaluation discussed earlier. Recall that entire schools are assigned randomly to either the new curriculum or the regular curriculum. To determine the effectiveness of the new curriculum, the researchers plan to analyze students' scores on a standardized math test. In this case, students are the unit of analysis, and schools are the unit of treatment. However, the curriculum is implemented in numerous classrooms within each school, and if the researchers expect variation across classrooms, they may need to include the classroom level and alter the design to be a three level design with treatment at level three. Information regarding the classrooms and type of math program, (i.e., scripted or flexible) would be helpful in deciding whether or not the treatment is likely to vary across classrooms. This, in turn, would help the researcher to determine the appropriate design to use for the power analysis.

In either case, researchers must have reasonable estimates of the design parameters in order to conduct a power analysis. Because cluster randomized trials in education are relatively new, finding estimates of effect sizes and intraclass correlations can be difficult. One option is to conduct a pilot study to estimate the parameters. A second option is to estimate the parameters using data from large observational studies, such as NELS (http://nces.ed.gov/surveys/nels88/) or ECLS (http://nces.ed.gov/ecls/). A third option is to search the existing literature for studies that have been conducted on similar outcomes for estimates of effect sizes and intraclass correlations. Recent work by Bloom et al. (2005) provides empirical estimates of intraclass correlations and effect sizes for studies that focus on academic achievement. As more trials are conducted, it is important to continue to publish intraclass correlations and effect sizes to enhance the planning of future studies. Ensuring that studies have adequate power to detect the treatment effect is an important first step in conducting high quality cluster randomized trials in education.

NOTE

1. This is the same result we would obtain using a two-level hierarchical linear model (Equations 8.1 and 8.2), estimated by means of restricted maximum likelihood.

REFERENCES

Bloom, H. S. (2005). Randomizing groups to evaluate place-based programs. In H. S. Bloom (Ed.), *Learning more from social experiments: Evolving analytic approaches* (pp. 115–172). New York: Russell Sage Foundation.

Bloom, H. S., Bos, J. M., & Lee, S. W. (1999). Using cluster random assignment to measure program impacts: Statistical implications for the evaluation of education programs. *Evaluation Review, 23*, 445–469.

Bloom, H. S., Richburg-Hayes, L., & Black, A. R. (2005). *Using covariates to improve precision: Empirical guidance for studies that randomize schools to measure the impacts of educational interventions.* New York: MDRC.

Borman, G. D., Slavin, R. E., Cheung, A., Chamberlain, A., Madden, N., & Chambers, B. (2005). Success for All: First-year results from the national randomized field trial. *Educational Evaluation and Policy Analysis, 27*, 1–22.

Boruch, R. F. (1997). *Randomized experiments for planning and evaluation: A practical guide.* Thousand Oaks, CA: Sage Publications.

Boruch, R. F., & Foley, E. (2000). The honestly experimental society. In L. Bickman (Ed.), *Validity and social experiments: Donald Campbell's legacy* (pp. 199–239). Thousand Oaks, CA: Sage Publications, Inc.

Cohen, J. (1988). *Statistical power analyses for the behavioral sciences*. Hillsdale, NJ: Lawrence Erlbaum Associates, Inc.

Cook, T. D., Habib, F. N., Phillips, M. P., Settersten, R. A., Shagle, S. C., & Degirmencioglu, S. M. (1999). Comer's School Development Program in Prince George's County, Maryland: A theory-based evaluation. *American Educational Research Journal, 36*, 543–597.

Cook, T. D., Murphy, R. F., & Hunt, H. D. (2000). Comer's School Development Program in Chicago: A theory-based evaluation. *American Educational Research Journal, 37*, 535–597.

Cook, T .D., & Payne, M. (2002). Randomized experiments in educational policy research: A critical examination of the reasons the educational evaluation community has offered for not doing them. *Educational Evaluation and Policy Analysis, 24*, 175–199.

Donner, A., & Klar, N. (2000). *Design and analysis of cluster randomization trials in health research*. London: Arnold Publishers.

Erdfelder, E., Faul, F., & Buchner, A. (1996). GPOWER: A general power analysis program. *Behavior Research Methods, Instruments, & Computers, 28*, 1–11.

Headrick, T. C., & Zumbo, B. D. (2005). On optimizing multi-level models: Power under budget constraints. *Australian and New Zealand Journal of Statistics, 47*(2), 219–229.

Hox, J. J. (2002). *Multilevel analysis: Techniques and applications*. Mahwah, NJ: Lawrence Erlbaum Associates, Inc.

Kane, T. J. (2004). *The impact of after-school programs: Interpreting the results of four recent evaluations*. New York: W.T. Grant Foundation.

Kirk, R. E. (1982). *Experimental design: Procedures for the behavioral sciences*. Belmont, CA: Brooks/Cole Publishing Company.

Liu, X., Spybrook, J., Congdon, R., Martinez, A., & Raudenbush, S. W. (2006). *Optimal design for longitudinal and multilevel research. V1.77* [Computer software]. Retrieved from http://sitemaker.umich.edu/group-based.

Mathematica Policy Research, Inc. (2005). *A national study of early elementary math curricula*. Retrieved January 17, 2007 from http://www.mathcurriculastudy.com/profile.asp

Martin, D. C., Diehr, P., Perrin, E. B., & Koepsell, T. D. (1993). The effect of matching on the power of randomized community intervention studies. *Statistics in Medicine, 12*, 329–338.

Moerbeek, M., Van Breukelen, J. P., & Berger, M. P. F. (2000). Design issues for experiments in multi-level populations. *Journal of Educational and Behavioral Statistics, 25*(3), 271–284.

Murray, D. M. (1998). *Design and analysis of group-randomized trials*. New York: Oxford University Press, Inc.

Raudenbush, S. W. (1997). Statistical analysis and optimal design for cluster randomized trials. *Psychological Methods, 2*, 173–185.

Raudenbush, S. W. (2003). The quantitative assessment of neighborhood social environments. In I. Kawachi and L. Berkman (Eds.), *Neighborhoods and health*, (pp. 121–131). Oxford: University Press.

Raudenbush, S. W. & Bryk, A. S. (2002). *Hierarchical linear models: Applications and data analysis methods*. Thousand Oaks, CA: Sage Publications.

Raudenbush, S. W. & Liu, X. (2000). Statistical power and optimal design for multi-site randomized trials. *Psychological Methods, 5,* 199–213.

Raudenbush, S. W. & Liu, X. (2001). Effects of study duration, frequency of observation, and sample size on power in studies of group differences in polynomial change. *Psychological Methods, 6,* 387–401.

Raudenbush, S. W., Martinez, A., & Spybrook, J. (2005). *Strategies for improving precision in group-randomized experiments.* New York: W.T. Grant Foundation.

Raudenbush, S. W., Spybrook, J., Liu, X., & Congdon, R. (2006). *Optimal design for longitudinal and multilevel research: Documentation for the "Optimal Design"* [Computer software manual]. Retrieved from *http://sitemaker.umich.edu/group-based*

Schochet, P. (2005). *Statistical power for random assignment evaluations of education programs.* Princeton, NJ: Mathematica Policy Research, Inc.

Slavin, R. (2002). Evidence-based educational policies: Transforming educational practice and research. *Educational Researcher, 31*(7), 15–21.

Snijders, T. A. B., & Bosker, R. J. (1993). Standard errors and sample sizes for two-level research. *Journal of Educational Statistics, 18,* 237–259.

Snijders, T. A. B., Bosker, R. J., & Guldemond, H. (2003). *Power analysis in two-level designs v2.11*[Computer software]. Retrieved from http://stat.gamma.rug.nl/snijders/multilevel.htm

St. Pierre, R. G., Swartz, J. P., Murray, S., & Deck, D. (1996). *Improving family literacy: Findings from the national Even Start evaluation.* Cambridge, Mass: Abt Associates.

U.S. Department of Education. (2002). *Education Sciences Reform Act of 2002.* Retrieved January 17, 2007 from http://www.govtrack.us/congress/billtext.xpd?bill=h107-5598

U.S. Department of Education. (n.d.). *National Education Longitudinal Study of 1988.* Retrieved January 17, 2007 from http://nces.ed.gov/surveys/nels88/.

U.S. Department of Education. (n.d.). *Early Childhood Longitudinal Study.* Retrieved January 17, 2007 from http://nces.ed.gov/ecls/.

PART III

EXTENDING THE MULTILEVEL FRAMEWORK

CHAPTER 9

MULTILEVEL METHODS FOR META-ANALYSIS

Sema A. Kalaian and Rafa M. Kasim

Unlike the applications of multilevel modeling presented in the previous and upcoming chapters in this book, where the researchers have multilevel structured raw data, the present chapter deals with meta-analytic data that represents published descriptive summary results of the primary research studies. Multilevel meta-analysis methods view the study subjects as being nested within the sample of studies from the population of primary studies that address the same research question. Therefore, the meta-analytic data is conceptualized as having a hierarchical structure, where groups of subjects are nested within the primary studies that are included in the meta-analytic review.

Meta-analysis, or research synthesis, is defined as a systematic, scientific quantitative method for aggregating and synthesizing descriptive summary results from a collection of published studies that investigate the same research question (Glass, 1976). Generally, the main purpose of meta-analysis is to synthesize quantitatively the results from the primary studies and to reconcile any apparent contradictions in a specific focus of research (Glass, 1976; Hedges, 1982, 1994; Hedges & Olkin, 1985; Kalaian & Raudenbush, 1996).

Multilevel Modeling of Educational Data, pages 315–343
Copyright © 2008 by Information Age Publishing

315

The meta-analysis process includes several steps: formulating a research problem, locating the primary studies, evaluating the primary studies, coding and analyzing the meta-analytic data, and disseminating the findings. Therefore, conducting a meta-analytic review is much like conducting a scientific research study, except that the meta-analytic data are the descriptive and summary statistics obtained from each of the primary research studies and not the raw data. Group means, standard deviations, sample sizes, correlation coefficients, proportions, and odds ratios are examples of such published summary statistics. These descriptive statistics are used to calculate an effect size index and its variance for each of the primary studies. Thus, in a typical meta-analysis, each of the primary study's outcomes is converted to a common standardized effect size metric with common means and standard deviations for quantitative research synthesis purposes. Consequently, these calculated effect sizes and their variances are modeled, and coded study and sample characteristics serve as predictor variables to try to explain variation across the effect sizes.

Since Glass's introduction of the term "meta-analysis" to the social and behavioral research in 1976, countless meta-analytic reviews have been conducted across many different disciplines. Medicine, health, education, social and behavioral sciences, business, and marketing are some of the disciplines that often employ meta-analytic reviews (e.g., Becker, Shram, Chang, Kino, & Quitieri, 1992; Kalaian, Mullan, & Kasim, 1999). With the significant increase of meta-analytic reviews, the demands for new developments of meta-analytic approaches also have increased. To date, three meta-analytic approaches have been developed and used by meta-analysts. These approaches are the fixed-effects approach (Hedges, 1981, 1994; Hedges & Olkin, 1985), the random-effects approach (Hedges & Olkin; Raudenbush, 1994), and the mixed-effects approach (Raudenbush & Bryk, 1985, 2002). However, the fixed-effects approach is the most commonly used approach because of its analytical simplicity.

One of the most significant decisions a meta-analyst must make is choosing between the fixed-effects approach (Hedges, 1982, 1994; Hedges & Olkin, 1985) and the mixed-effects approach (Goldstein, 1995; Kalaian & Raudenbush, 1996; Raudenbush & Bryk, 1985, 2002) to analyze the meta-analytic data. In the fixed-effects approach for analyzing meta-analytic data, the meta-analyst assumes that (a) the primary studies represent the entire population of primary studies with a common single population effect size that underlies all the primary studies and (b) the observed variations in the primary studies' effect sizes constitute a systematic variance attributable to sample and study characteristics plus some sampling error. This sampling error is considered the sole source of error in the fixed-effects approach.

On the other hand, in the multilevel approach (mixed-effects or random-effects regression), the meta-analyst assumes that the primary studies under review are samples from the population of studies. Accordingly, an estimate of a study's effect size is considered a function of a true population effect size, a within-studies sampling error, and a random between-studies error. This random between-studies error variation is the key component for distinguishing the mixed-effects approach from the fixed-effects approach. It is estimated via the multilevel approach and can be modeled and explained using study and sample characteristics (Hox, 2002; Kalaian & Kasim, 2004; Raudenbush & Bryk, 2002). Therefore, the multilevel approach combines the features of the fixed-effects and random-effects approaches in one model, where the known study and sample characteristics are considered as *fixed effects* and the remaining unexplained variations in the true effects magnitudes are considered as *random effects*. Thus, contrary to the fixed-effects approach, the meta-analyst using the mixed-effects approach assumes that there are differences in the effect sizes beyond those due to sampling error.

Since the conception of meta-analysis methods, numerous fixed and mixed effects univariate (a single outcome from each primary study) and multivariate (multiple outcomes from each primary study) meta-analytic techniques have been developed for estimating, synthesizing, and integrating different types of effect size indices. In addition to the decision to choose between either the fixed- or mixed-effects approach, choosing between univariate and multivariate meta-analysis methods is another significant decision that should be made by the meta-analyst before analyzing the data. If the meta-analyst has a single outcome and, consequently, a single effect size from each primary study, then the univariate meta-analysis methods should be used for analyzing the meta-analytic data. On the other hand, if the meta-analyst has two or more somewhat correlated outcomes in each study and, consequently, two or more correlated effect sizes, then the multivariate meta-analysis methods should be used to analyze the data.

This chapter presents the conceptualizations of univariate and multivariate meta-analysis using multilevel methods for meta-analysis. To illustrate and compare their applications, we apply these two methods to a subset of studies of the Scholastic Aptitude Test (SAT) coaching effectiveness, reviewed previously by Kalaian (1994) and Kalaian and Raudenbush (1996).

UNIVARIATE MULTILEVEL META-ANALYSIS

This section presents the application of the univariate multilevel metaanalytic methods to experimental research studies. We define the notations used in multilevel meta-analysis; then we provide a detailed application of the univariate multilevel meta-analysis approach. To illustrate the univariate multilevel meta-analysis methods, we utilize the SAT-Verbal and

SAT-Math sub-samples of the SAT coaching data reported and analyzed by Kalaian (1994), Kalaian and Raudenbush (1994), and Kalaian and Raudenbush (1996).

Notation for the Univariate Meta-Analysis

To conduct a univariate multilevel meta-analysis, the researcher first locates K primary studies that answer the same research question. For example, the primary studies can be randomized experimental studies comparing an experimental group to a control group on a specific outcome measure. However, the studies need not be experimental in nature. Rather, the primary studies in a meta-analysis may consist of two-group comparative studies. The differences between the coached and uncoached groups on SAT scores in the collection of the SAT coaching effectiveness studies, or between male and female comparisons on an outcome measure in gender differences studies, are examples of two-group comparative studies. Alternatively, the meta-analytic data may consist of K primary correlational studies, where each of these primary studies tests the relationships between two variables (e.g., the relationship between homework assignments and achievement). Likewise, data from primary studies with other types of research designs can be combined and meta-analyzed. Thus, the methods for estimating effect sizes from the primary studies vary according to the primary studies' research designs, the outcome's metric, and the statistical procedures used. As such, the first step in a typical meta-analytic application is the calculation of meaningful and comparable effect sizes for each of the individual primary studies. These effect sizes are standardized indices of the primary studies' outcomes that help the meta-analyst to combine these outcomes across various studies. Without this standardization process, the primary studies cannot be combined quantitatively and summarized, especially when there are variations among primary studies in terms of design, measurements, metrics, and type of scales. Different types of effect size indices are used in different meta-analytic reviews depending on the meta-analysis research question and the type of the outcome variable.

In this chapter, the effect size index for measuring the effectiveness of an experimental treatment is based on the standardized mean difference (outlined below). For example, a study with a single outcome measure (e.g., math achievement scores) for an experimental and a control group would yield a single effect size. However, it is important to note that other types of effect sizes can be estimated in meta-analysis depending on the measurement scale of the primary studies' outcomes. Correlation coefficients, variances, odds-ratios, and proportions are examples of such outcomes. This chapter presents notations and formulas for calculating effect sizes for experimental designs. Each of K randomized experimental studies compares an outcome measure of an experimental treatment condition (E) to the same outcome of a control condition (C) in study i ($i = 1, 2, \ldots, K$), where K is the number of primary studies.

The estimated standardized mean difference between experimental and control groups for a single outcome measure (Glass, 1976; Hedges, 1994) in the ith study is defined as

$$g_i = \frac{\bar{Y}_i^E - \bar{Y}_i^C}{S_i}, \qquad (9.1)$$

where $\bar{Y}_i^E$ and $\bar{Y}_i^C$ are the experimental and control group means in the ith study, respectively. S_i is the square root of the pooled within-groups variances, S_i^2, and is estimated as follows:

$$S_i^2 = \frac{(n_i^E - 1)(S_i^E)^2 + (n_i^C - 1)(S_i^C)^2}{(n_i^E - 1) + (n_i^C - 1)}, \qquad (9.2)$$

where $(S_i^E)^2$ and $(S_i^C)^2$ are the experimental and control groups' estimated variances for the outcome measure in study i, respectively. n_i^E and n_i^C are the sample sizes for the experimental and control groups in study i, respectively.

If the sample sizes within each study are small (10 or less subjects), the effect size, g_i, is an upwardly biased estimator of the population effect size, δ_i. Thus, the bias is considered as a function of the sample sizes of the experimental and control groups for each of the primary studies. This biased effect size, g_i, for each primary study can be corrected with the following simple multiplicative formula (Hedges, 1981):

$$d_i = \left(1 - \frac{3}{4m_i - 1}\right) g_i, \quad m_i = n_i^E + n_i^C - 2. \qquad (9.3)$$

The sampling variance, $\hat{\sigma}_{(d_i)}^2$, of the effect size, d_i, for study i can be estimated as follows (Hedges, 1981):

$$\hat{\sigma}_{(d_i)}^2 = \frac{n_i^E + n_i^C}{n_i^E n_i^C} + \frac{d_i^2}{2(n_i^E + n_i^C)}, \qquad (9.4)$$

where n_i^E and n_i^C are the sample sizes for the experimental and control groups in study i, respectively, and d_i^2 is the square of the effect size for study i.

Computational Illustration

For illustrative purposes, we provide the computational details for the above biased and unbiased estimates of the standardized mean difference (effect size) and their variances for the SAT-Math subset of the SAT coaching studies. In this chapter, for computational illustration purposes, we will use Zuman's (1988) SAT coaching primary study, which is one of the SAT coaching effectiveness studies reported in Kalaian (1994) and Kalaian and Raudenbush (1996). For Zuman's SAT coaching study, the mean of the SAT-Math scores for the experimental group (coached group) was 446, and the standard deviation was 82.9. The mean of the SAT-Math scores for the control group (uncoached group) for this specific study was 383, and the standard deviation was 104.7. The sample sizes for the coached and not coached groups for this specific study were 16 and 17, respectively. Thus, using Equation 9.2, the pooled SAT-Math variances of the experimental and control groups, S_M^2, is

$$S_M^2 = \frac{(16-1)(82.9)^2 + (17-1)(104.7)^2}{(16-1)+(17-1)} = 8983.213.$$

For the computational illustrations in this section, we use the subscript M to represent SAT-Math. Using Equation 9.1, the estimated biased SAT-Math effect size, g_M, for this primary study is

$$g_M = \frac{446-383}{S_M} = \frac{446-383}{94.78} = 0.67.$$

The unbiased effect size of the SAT-Math, d_M, using Equation 9.3 is

$$d_M = \left(1 - \frac{3}{4(16+17-2)-1}\right)0.67 = 0.65.$$

Equation 9.4 provides the estimated variance of the SAT-Math effect size, $\hat{\sigma}_{(d_M)}^2$ as

$$\hat{\sigma}_{(d_M)}^2 = \frac{16+17}{(16)(17)} + \frac{(0.65)^2}{2(16+17)} = 0.128.$$

Univariate Multilevel Meta-Analysis Model

Generally, the effect sizes, d_i's, from the K primary studies and their variance estimates, $\hat{\sigma}_{(d_i)}^2$, provide the data for the two-level multilevel meta-analysis model (Raudenbush & Bryk, 2002). The first level is the *within-study (level-one) model* and the second level is the *between-studies (level-two) model*. The two levels of a univariate multilevel model for meta-analysis are described below.

Univariate Within-Study (Level-One) Model

In the within-study (level-one) model for the multilevel meta-analysis, the estimated study effect size, d_i, for each of the K primary studies in the review is expressed as a function of a true population effect size, δ_i, plus a sampling error, e_i, that is unique to study i.

$$d_i = \delta_i + e_i, \quad \text{where } e_i \sim N(0, \sigma_e^2) \quad i = 1, 2, \ldots, K. \tag{9.5}$$

The estimated effect sizes from the K primary studies are assumed to be independent and approximately normally distributed with a mean of zero and known sampling error variance σ_e^2. The sampling error is assumed to be known because in meta-analysis the original raw data is not available and the sampling variances of the effect sizes are calculated from the summary statistics of the primary studies.

Univariate Between-Studies (Level-Two) Model

In the between-studies (level-two) model of the multilevel meta-analysis, the true effect size from each primary study typically is expressed in two distinct multilevel models that have different forms and interpretations. The first form represents an *unconditional multilevel model*, in which no explanatory variables are included at either level one or level two. Results from the unconditional model serve two important purposes. First, the unconditional model helps the meta-analyst in assessing and estimating the overall weighted average effect size. Second, the unconditional model helps the meta-analyst to estimate and examine heterogeneity in the primary studies' effect sizes in order to assess and make a decision about the need for modeling this heterogeneity in the subsequent conditional between-studies models.

The second form is the *conditional multilevel model*, in which explanatory predictor variables are included at either or both levels of the hierarchy. If the results of the unconditional model indicate there is substantial heterogeneity in the effect sizes of the primary studies, then the meta-analyst proceeds to estimate one or more conditional models. In the conditional model, it is assumed that the effect size parameter, δ_i, for each primary study is a function of the true effect size, known study and sample characteristics, and random error. The conditional model allows the meta-analyst to try to explain the variations among the studies' effect sizes.

Unconditional Univariate Between-Studies (Level-Two) Model. The unconditional model, in which no explanatory variables are included in the model at either level one or level two, is the first of several multilevel models in any multilevel modeling. It serves as a baseline model that can be compared with subsequent more complex multilevel models. The unconditional model allows the meta-analyst to estimate the overall average weighted effect size across all primary studies and to test whether it is statistically significantly different from zero. Additionally, the unconditional model can be used to estimate the variability of the true effect sizes across the K primary studies and to test the homogeneity of these true effect sizes across all the primary studies. Specifically, the unconditional model provides a test for the following null hypothesis: $H_0: \delta_1 = \delta_2 = \ldots = \delta_K$.

In level two of the unconditional model, the true effect size parameter for each of the K studies is viewed as a function of an overall average effect size, γ_0, plus a unique random error U_i, for study i:

$$\delta_i = \gamma_0 + U_i, \quad \text{where } U_i \sim N(0, \tau). \tag{9.6}$$

Here, τ is the variance of U_i and has a χ^2 distribution with $K-1$ degrees of freedom. It represents the amount of variation in the true effect sizes. A significant χ^2 value indicates the existence of a significant variation (heterogeneity) in the effect sizes across the K primary studies. Thus, given a significant χ^2 finding from the initial unconditional multilevel analysis, interest turns into explaining the variability among the effect sizes. This usually is accomplished by modeling this variability using study and sample characteristics as predictors in the conditional between-studies (level-two) models.

Conditional Univariate Between-Studies (Level-Two) Models. The conditional model extends the unconditional multilevel model by including information about the primary studies and their sample characteristics as potential predictors to account for and explain some of the variation (heterogeneity) among the true effect sizes. A between-study (level-two) conditional model for a primary study i takes the following regression form:

$$\delta_i = \gamma_0 + \gamma_1 W_{1i} + \gamma_2 W_{2i} + \ldots \gamma_q W_{qi} + U_i, \quad \text{where } U_i \sim N(0, \tau), \tag{9.7}$$

where, δ_i is the true effect size and U_i is the unique random error for study i ($i = 1, 2, \ldots, K$) after accounting for study and sample characteristics. The q set of W's represent study characteristics with $(q+1)$ regression coefficients, γ's (q regression slopes – $\gamma_1, \gamma_2, \ldots, \gamma_q$ – and an intercept, γ_0). U_i represents the amount of residual variance across the effect sizes, δ_i, that is left unexplained after modeling the effect sizes by the known study and sample characteristics. τ is the residual variance of these random errors.

HIERARCHICAL LINEAR MODELING (HLM) SOFTWARE

The HLM 6 Software (Raudenbush, Bryk, Cheong, & Congdon, 2004) can be used to analyze meta-analytic data. However, using HLM for meta-analysis requires the use of different settings and techniques. Typically, in most meta-analytic studies, the sampling variance of the level-one effect size is, itself, estimated from each of the primary studies' descriptive data. Thus, in meta-analysis, the sampling variance of each effect size estimate is considered known, and it usually is estimated from the summary statistics of each primary study. Hence, multilevel meta-analysis often is referred to as a multilevel V-known analysis. To use the HLM 6 software to conduct a meta-analysis, we need to use the "V-known" routine within the HLM 6 software. This routine is included in the HLM 6 software package and is designed specifically to analyze univariate as well as multivariate meta-analytic data.

This V-known routine is used for analyzing data in which the level-one variances and covariances are assumed to be known and are obtained from the available summary statistics from each primary study (e.g., meta-analytic data). Unlike the other multilevel applications presented in the other chapters of this book, the univariate and multivariate multilevel meta-analysis via the V-known option of HLM2 within the HLM 6 software requires a single ASCII data file, as described below. Typically, the analysis can be accomplished in a "batch" or "interactive" mode. However, it can be accomplished in a "windows" mode for the univariate meta-analysis only (i.e., single effect size) (Raudenbush et al., 2004, p. 189).

Analyzing Univariate Meta-Analytic Data Using HLM 6 Software

For the univariate multilevel meta-analysis, the HLM 6 software requires a single ASCII data input file consisting of one row of data for each of the primary studies in the meta-analytic review. Thus, each row contains the meta-analytic data information (e.g., study ID, study's estimated effect size, sampling variance for the estimated effect size, and coded study and sample characteristics) in the following specified order:

1. Study ID in character format
2. Effect size index (d_i) in numeric format
3. Sampling variance ($\hat{\sigma}^2_{(d_i)}$) of the effect size in numeric format
4. Explanatory variables (study and sample characteristics) in numeric format.

The SPSS format for the SAT coaching data file for the illustrative example (see Figure 9.1) in the next section requires the variables to be in the following order: study ID, effect size (diSATM), variance of the effect size (Var_Mat), Logarithmic transformed Coaching Hours (logHR). The data then can be saved in an ASCII format file (see Figures 9.2 and 9.3). The

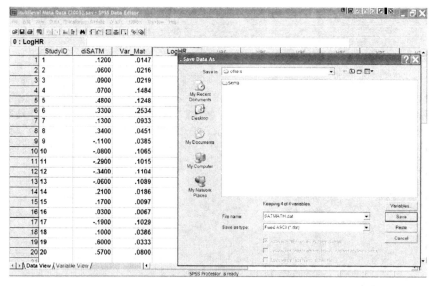

Figure 9.1   A screenshot of saving the SAT-Math coaching data from the SPSS data editor.

StudyID	diSATM	Var_Mat	LogHR
1	1	.1200	.0147
2	2	.0600	.0216
3	3	.0900	.0219
4	4	.0700	.1484
5	5	.4800	.1248
6	6	.3300	.2534
7	7	.1300	.0933
8	8	.3400	.0451
9	9	-.1100	.0385
10	10	-.0800	.1065
11	11	-.2900	.1015
12	12	-.3400	.1104
13	13	-.0600	.1089
14	14	.2100	.0186
15	15	.1700	.0097
16	16	.0300	.0067
17	17	-.1900	.1029
18	18	.1000	.0386
19	19	.6000	.0333
20	20	.5700	.0800

Figure 9.2   A screenshot of saving the SAT-Math coaching data as ASCII file from the SPSS data editor.

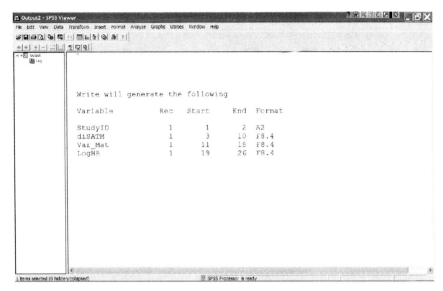

Figure 9.3   A screenshot of the specifications of the created ASCII file for the SAT-Math coaching data.

ASCII format file becomes the data input file to create the MDM (Multivariate Data Matrix) file needed by the HLM software. This MDM file is used for subsequent multilevel analyses of the meta-analytic data. For detailed explanation on how to create the MDM file and how to run the multilevel analysis, the reader should refer to the "V-known" option of the HLM2 within the HLM 6 software (Raudenbush et al., 2004, p. 184).

For this chapter, we are using the HLM 6 software to analyze the univariate meta-analytic data. However, it is important to note that the multilevel analysis of meta-analytic data can be accomplished by using other commercial software, such as MLwiN (Rasbash et al., 2000) or SAS Proc Mixed (Littell, Miliken, Stroup, & Wolfinger, 1996). These other software packages have different data requirements than HLM. For example, they need special data set-up and constraints in order to handle multilevel meta-analytic data. The reader should refer to these software manuals for guidance on how to conduct multilevel meta-analyses.

Illustrative Example: SAT Coaching Data

To illustrate the univariate multilevel meta-analysis methods, we use a subset of the meta-analytic data used by Kalaian (1994), Kalaian and Raudenbush (1994), and Kalaian and Raudenbush (1996). The chosen subset includes studies that reported the effectiveness of coaching programs for both SAT-Math and SAT-Verbal scores. For a complete listing of the SAT coaching studies, the reader should refer to either Kalaian (1994) or Kalaian and Raudenbush (1996). Two key research questions guided their conduct of the meta-analysis review. The first research question was, "What is the effect of SAT coaching on SAT-Math and SAT verbal scores?" The second research question was "Do different coaching durations influence the effectiveness of the SAT coaching programs?"

Table 9.1 includes a subset of the primary studies reported by Kalaian (1994) and Kalaian and Raudenbush (1996). We use this subset for methodological illustration purposes only; for complete data results, readers should refer to these original publications. The example data file includes unbiased SAT-Math and SAT-Verbal effect sizes (Hedges, 1981), variances and covariances of the multivariate effect sizes (illustrated later in this chapter), and coaching duration. The purpose of this chosen subset of primary

TABLE 9.1 Scholastic Attitude Test (SAT) Coaching Studies Data

Study	Year	d_1	d_2	Hours	$\hat{\sigma}^2_{(d_1)}$	$\hat{\sigma}_{(d_1,d_2)}$	$\hat{\sigma}^2_{(d_2)}$
Evans & Pike (A)	1973	.1300	.1200	21	.0147	.0097	.0147
Evans & Pike (B)	1973	.2500	.0600	21	.0218	.0143	.0216
Evans & Pike (C)	1973	.3100	.0900	21	.0221	.0144	.0219
Laschewer	1986	.0000	.0700	9	.1484	.0979	.1484
Zuman (B)	1988	.1300	.4800	24	.1216	.0805	.1248
Coffin	1987	-.2300	.3300	18	.2517	.1640	.2534
Davis	1985	.1300	.1300	15	.0933	.0615	.0933
Frankel	1960	.1300	.3400	30	.0445	.0294	.0451
Whitla	1962	.0900	-.1100	10	.0385	.0254	.0385
Curran (A)	1988	-.1000	-.0800	6	.1066	.0703	.1065
Curran (B)	1988	-.1400	-.2900	6	.1007	.0665	.1015
Curran (C)	1988	-.1600	-.3400	6	.1092	.0721	.1104
Curran (D)	1988	-.0700	-.0600	6	.1089	.0718	.1089
Dear	1958	-.0200	.2100	15	.0186	.0123	.0186
Dyer	1953	.0600	.1700	15	.0096	.0064	.0097
FTC	1978	.1500	.0300	40	.0067	.0044	.0067
Keefauver	1976	.1700	-.1900	14	.1029	.0675	.1029
Lass	1961	.0200	.1000		.0385	.0254	.0386
Reynolds & Oberman	1987	.0400	.6000	63	.0320	.0211	.0333
Zuman (A)	1988	.5400	.5700	27	.0797	.0521	.0800

Note: d_1 is the SAT-Verbal effect size.
d_2 is the SAT-Math effect size.
Hours is Duration of SAT coaching in hours.

SAT coaching studies is to illustrate both the univariate and multivariate meta-analysis methods presented in this chapter; therefore, the reader is cautioned against inferring any substantive conclusions about the effectiveness of the SAT coaching programs on SAT-Math and SAT-Verbal scores based on these demonstrations. We chose this subset because the V-known routine of the HLM2 within the HLM 6 software requires the complete set of the multiple effect sizes and cannot handle multivariate data with missing effect sizes. We explain and demonstrate the multivariate multilevel meta-analysis method later in this chapter. For complete listing of the SAT coaching studies, coding procedures, inclusion and exclusion criteria used, and coaching effectiveness results and findings, refer to the work by Kalaian (1994) and by Kalaian and Raudenbush (1996).

Univariate Multilevel Meta-Analysis Results

The results of the coaching effects on the SAT-Verbal and SAT-Math subsets are used to illustrate the univariate multilevel meta-analysis method. The values of the 20 SAT-Verbal effect sizes that were estimated (using Equations 9.1–9.4) ranged from –0.23 to 0.54; the values of the 20 SAT-Math effect sizes that were estimated (using Equations 9.1–9.4) ranged from –0.34 to 0.60 (see Table 9.1).

The box plots in Figure 9.4 indicate greater variability in the SAT-Math effect sizes than in the SAT-Verbal effect sizes. Figure 9.4 also shows the

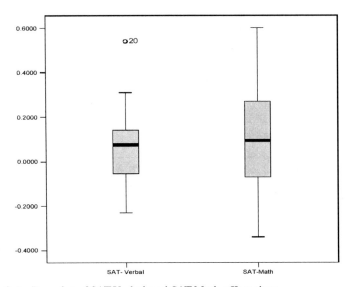

Figure 9.4   Box plot of SAT-Verbal and SAT-Math effect sizes.

existence of an outlier in the SAT-Verbal effect sizes. This outlier effect size is from Zuman's (1988) study. We decided to keep this primary study in our illustrative data set.

Table 9.2 presents the results of the univariate unconditional multilevel meta-analysis (Equation 9.6) via the HLM 6 software for the SAT-Verbal effect sizes. The overall weighted average of the 20 SAT-Verbal effect sizes is $\gamma_0 = 0.109$ with a standard error of 0.039 and is significantly different from zero. A chi-square value of 9.979 with 19 degrees of freedom for testing the variability of the effect sizes ($\tau = 0.00001$), indicates that these effect sizes are homogenous and came from a population of common SAT coaching effect sizes.

Table 9.3 presents the results for the univariate unconditional multilevel meta-analysis for the SAT-Math effect sizes using the HLM 6 software. The overall weighted average of the 20 SAT-Math effect sizes is $\gamma_0 = 0.120$ with a standard error of 0.0395. Similar to the SAT-Verbal results, SAT-Math results show that the mean of the effect sizes is significantly different from zero, and the effect sizes are homogeneous ($\tau = 0.0004$, $\chi^2(19) = 0.428$, $p = 0.369$).

Typically, an insignificant chi-square test for the variability of the effect sizes suggests that no further action from the meta-analyst is required. Thus, given non-significant chi-square values for both SAT subtests' (SAT-Math and SAT-Verbal) effect sizes, there is no need to fit a univariate conditional multilevel meta-analysis model. However, we chose to fit the conditional

TABLE 9.2   Unconditional Univariate Multilevel Meta-Analysis Results for the Effects of Coaching on the SAT-Verbal Scores

Parameter	Fixed effects				Random effects		
	Coefficient	S.E.	t	p-value	τ	χ^2	p-value
Average SAT-Verbal effects, γ_0	0.109	0.039	2.797	0.012	0.000	9.979	>.500

Note: The degrees of freedom = 19.

TABLE 9.3   Unconditional Univariate Multilevel Meta-Analysis Results for the Coaching Effects on the SAT-Math Scores

Parameter	Fixed effects				Random effects		
	Coefficient	S.E.	t	p-value	τ	χ^2	p-value
Average SAT-Math effects, γ_0	0.120	0.0395	3.034	0.007	0.000	20.428	0.369

Note: The degrees of freedom = 19.

TABLE 9.4   Conditional Univariate Multilevel Meta-Analysis Results for the Effects of SAT-Math Coaching

Parameter	Fixed effects				Random effects		
	Coefficient	S.E.	t	p-value	τ	χ²	p-value
Intercept, γ_0	−0.134	0.163	−0.827	0.419			
Log (hrs), γ_1	0.091	0.055	1.66	0.114	0.08	18.718	0.409

Note: The degrees of freedom = 18.

multilevel meta-analysis model to the SAT-Math coaching effect sizes for the completeness of the multilevel meta-analysis presentation and illustration. In our conditional multilevel meta-analysis model, we used coaching duration in hours as an explanatory (predictor) variable to try to explain some of the non-significant variation in the SAT-Math effect sizes.

The SAT coaching duration for these 20 samples ranged from 6 to 63 hours, with an average duration of 19.31 hours and a standard deviation of 14 hours. Most of the coaching hours were concentrated at the lower end of the distribution, creating a positively skewed distribution; therefore, we performed a natural logarithmic transformation of the coaching variable prior to using it as a predictor variable in the conditional multilevel meta-analysis model (Kalaian, 1994; Kalaian & Raudenbush, 1996).

The results of the univariate conditional between-studies modeling of the SAT-Math effect sizes (Table 9.4) show that logarithmically transformed hours of SAT coaching has a non-statistically significant positive effect on SAT-Math effect sizes ($\gamma_1 = 0.091$, standard error = 0.055, t-ratio = 1.66, $p = 0.114$). Furthermore, a non-significant chi-square value of 18.718 with 18 degrees of freedom ($p = 0.409$) for testing the variability, τ, in the effect of SAT coaching duration on the SAT-Math effect sizes indicates a homogeneity among the SAT coaching effect sizes across all studies after controlling for the SAT coaching duration.

MULTIVARIATE MULTILEVEL META-ANALYSIS

In the illustrative SAT coaching example presented above, there were two outcomes from each primary SAT coaching study (SAT-Math and SAT-Verbal) that we analyzed separately using univariate meta-analysis methods. In this section, we will demonstrate the simultaneous analysis of the same SAT coaching meta-analytic data set with two outcomes using multivariate multilevel methods. These SAT coaching outcomes are measurements from the same sample of individuals and, therefore, are correlated to some extent. Generally, when a meta-analyst faces the challenge of summarizing independent empirical primary studies on several correlated outcome measures, multivariate meta-analysis techniques become the most appropriate analytical tool (Gleser & Olkin, 1994; Hedges & Olkin, 1985; Kalaian, 1994; Kalaian & Kasim, 2004; Kalaian & Raudenbush, 1996).

Multivariate meta-analysis methods have several methodological and substantive advantages over the univariate approaches. First, the multivariate analysis takes into account the correlation between the multiple outcome measures, leading to better and more precise parameter estimates. Second, the meta-analyst can pose and answer comprehensive multivariate research questions that cannot be answered by using the univariate meta-analysis methods. For example, the research question of whether the exploratory study characteristics relate differently to the effect sizes of the different multivariate outcomes (Kalaian & Kasim, 2004; Kalaian & Raudenbush, 1996) cannot be answered using univariate meta-analysis methods.

Multivariate multilevel meta-analysis methods do the following: (a) estimate the magnitude of the effect sizes for the multiple correlated outcomes from the primary studies; (b) assess the variances and covariances among these multivariate effect sizes across the primary studies, taking into account the correlations between these correlated outcomes; and (c) explain the between-study variances and covariances of the multiple effect sizes using known study and group characteristics as explanatory predictor variables in the specified multilevel model. Thus, unlike the univariate case, the estimation process used in the multivariate case accounts for the correlation between the multiple effect sizes from each study.

Notation for the Multivariate Meta-Analysis

The meta-analytic data for the multivariate multilevel meta-analysis consists of K primary studies investigating common research questions that involve multiple correlated outcome measures. In this section, we present meta-analytic methods for calculating the multivariate effect sizes and their variances and covariances for randomized experimental studies. Then, we apply the multivariate multilevel meta-analysis model to the K randomized experimental research studies, each comparing p outcomes of an experimental treatment group (E) to p outcomes of a control group (C), where p denotes the number of outcome measures in each of the primary experimental studies. For example, if each of the primary studies under review has two outcome measures ($p = 2$), then the total number of outcome measures across all K studies is equal to $2K$ or pK (number of studies, K, multiplied by the number of outcomes, p).

In the multivariate meta-analytic context, the measure of the effectiveness of an experimental treatment (effect size) is based on the multivariate standardized mean difference (Gleser & Olkin, 1994; Kalaian, 1994; Kalaian & Kasim, 2004; Kalaian & Raudenbush, 1996) and can be estimated for each of the multiple outcome measures from each primary study. For instance, a study with two related outcome measurements (e.g., SAT-Math and SAT-Verbal scores) for an experimental and a control group in an experimental primary study would yield two multivariate effect sizes, one for the SAT-Math scores and the other for the SAT-Verbal scores (Becker, 2000; Gleser & Olkin, 1994; Kalaian; Kalaian & Raudenbush).

Let Y_{ip}^E and Y_{ip}^C represent the experimental and control groups' outcome measures for each of the p multiple outcomes for study i. The estimated standardized mean difference (Hedges, 1994) between the experimental and control groups for the pth outcome measure, in the ith study is

$$g_{ip} = \frac{\bar{Y}_{ip}^E - \bar{Y}_{ip}^C}{S_{ip}}, \tag{9.8}$$

where $\bar{Y}_{ip}^E$ and $\bar{Y}_{ip}^C$ are the ith study's experimental and control group means, respectively, for the pth outcome measure. S_{ip} is the square root of the pooled within-groups variance estimate for the pth outcome in the ith study, S_{ip}^2. This pooled within-groups variance can be estimated as follows:

$$S_{ip}^2 = \frac{(n_{ip}^E - 1)(S_{ip}^E)^2 + (n_{ip}^C - 1)(S_{ip}^C)^2}{(n_{ip}^E - 1) + (n_{ip}^C - 1)}, \tag{9.9}$$

where $(S_{ip}^E)^2$ and $(S_{ip}^C)^2$ are the experimental and control groups' variances for the pth outcome measure for study i, respectively. n_{ip}^E and n_{ip}^C are the sample sizes for the experimental and control groups, respectively.

As in the univariate case, the estimated multivariate effect size, g_{ip}, is a biased estimate of the population effect size, δ_{ip}, especially when the sample sizes are small. An unbiased estimator can be calculated (Hedges, 1981; Hedges & Olkin, 1985) as follows:

$$d_{ip} = \left(1 - \frac{3}{4m_{ip} - 1}\right)g_{ip}, \quad \text{where } m_{ip} = n_{ip}^E + n_{ip}^C - 2. \tag{9.10}$$

For a fixed value of δ_{ip}, this multivariate effect size estimator, d_{ip}, is asymptotically normally distributed with mean, δ_{ip}, and estimated variance,

$$\hat{\sigma}_{(d_{ip})}^2 = \frac{n_{ip}^E + n_{ip}^C}{n_{ip}^E n_{ip}^C} + \frac{d_{ip}^2}{2(n_{ip}^E + n_{ip}^C)}. \tag{9.11}$$

It is important to note that Equations 9.8 through 9.11 are similar to Equations 9.1 to 9.4, respectively, for estimating the biased and unbiased univariate effect sizes and their variances with one exception: a subscript, p, is added to represent the effect size for the pth outcome variable from the primary studies.

In the multivariate meta-analytic data, the multiple effect sizes usually are correlated. Consequently, we need to estimate the covariances between any pair of the multiple effect sizes in addition to the variances for each of the multiple effect sizes. For instance, for our SAT coaching example presented above, we have two effect sizes (SAT-Math and SAT-Verbal) for each of the K primary studies. Therefore, we need to estimate the variances of these effect sizes as well as the covariance between the SAT-Math and SAT-Verbal effect sizes for each study, i. In general, the covariance between any pair of the multiple effect sizes from each primary study can be estimated as follows:

$$\hat{\sigma}_{(d_{ip},d_{ip'})} = \frac{n_{ip}^E + n_{ip}^C}{n_{ip}^E n_{ip}^C} \, r_{ip,ip'} + \frac{d_{ip} d_{ip'} r_{ip,ip'}^2}{2(n_{ip}^E + n_{ip}^C)}, \tag{9.12}$$

where $r_{ip,ip'}$ is the correlation coefficient between any pair of the outcome measures in each of the primary studies.

Computational Illustration

The same subsample of the primary studies that we used to illustrate univariate multilevel meta-analysis is used to demonstrate the multivariate meta-analysis and to compare the results of both methods. For example, Zuman's study, used above to illustrate the univariate meta-analysis methods and in which the interest was only the SAT-Math coaching effectiveness, also reports the effects of SAT coaching on SAT-Verbal scores. In Zuman's study, the mean of the SAT-Verbal scores for the experimental group (in this case, the coached group) was 373, and the standard deviation was 73.3. The mean of the SAT-Verbal scores for the control group (in this case, the uncoached group) was 385, and the standard deviation was 56.7. The sample sizes for the coached and uncoached groups were 16 and 17, respectively. Earlier, we computed the SAT-Math pooled variances. Now we use the same process to compute the SAT-Verbal pooled variance for Zuman's study, S_V^2 using Equation 9.9 as follows:

$$S_V^2 = \frac{(16-1)(73.3)^2 + (17-1)(56.7)^2}{(16-1)+(17-1)} = 4259.084.$$

The subscript, V, represents SAT-Verbal. The estimated biased effect size, g_v, for the SAT-Verbal using Equation 9.8 is

$$g_V = \frac{375-385}{S_V} = \frac{375-385}{65.26} = -0.153.$$

The unbiased effect size for the SAT-Verbal, d_v, using Equation 9.10 is

$$d_V = \left(1 - \frac{3}{4(16+17-2)-1} \right)(-0.153) = -0.149.$$

The estimated variance of the SAT-Verbal effect size, $\hat{\sigma}^2_{(d_V)}$, using Equation 9.11 is

$$\hat{\sigma}^2_{(d_V)} = \frac{16+17}{(16)(17)} + \frac{(-0.149)^2}{2(16+17)} = 0.122.$$

It is important to note that we already have estimated the SAT- Math effect size and its variance for Zuman's (1988) primary study during the computational illustration of the univariate multilevel meta- analysis methods. These estimates were 0.65 and 0.128, respectively (see the earlier univariate computational illustration section).

The SAT manual reports that the correlation coefficient between SAT-Math and SAT-Verbal ($r_{V,M}$) is 0.66. This correlation is used to estimate the covariances between the SAT-Verbal and SAT-Math effect sizes. For multivariate meta-analytic data, we usually do not have access to the original raw data; consequently, we cannot calculate the correlation coefficient between any pair of variables. Therefore, the published correlation coefficient between any pair of outcomes should be used from the reported existing literature (e.g., manuals, reports). Thus, the estimated covariance between the SAT-Math and SAT-Verbal effect sizes using Equation 9.12 is

$$\hat{\sigma}_{(d_V, d_M)} = \frac{16+17}{(16)(17)}(0.66) + \frac{(0.65)(-0.149)(0.66)^2}{2(16+17)}$$

$$= 0.079.$$

Multivariate Multilevel Meta-Analysis Model

As in the univariate multilevel meta-analysis model, the presentation of the multivariate multilevel meta-analysis model in two stages (levels) clarifies the logic of the hierarchical structure of the multivariate meta-analytic data. At the first stage (level one), a "within-study" model specifies the multiple correlated effect sizes as a function of their true multiple effect sizes and their associated multivariate sampling errors. At the second stage (level two), a "between-studies" model specifies the distribution of the multiple true effect sizes from the first stage as a function of multiple true average effect sizes (one true average effect size for each of the multiple correlated outcomes) and unexplained multivariate random errors.

Multivariate Within-Study (Level-One) Model

In the multivariate within-study (level-one) model, the observed vector of unbiased multiple correlated effect sizes, $\underline{d}_i$, of study i, depends upon a vector of population effect sizes, $\underline{\delta}_i$, plus a vector of multiple sampling error estimates, $\underline{e}_i$, for each primary study. Thus, the basic multivariate within-study model for study i, can be represented as

$$\underline{d}_i = \underline{\delta}_i + \underline{e}_i, \quad i = 1, 2, \ldots, K, \tag{9.13}$$

where $\underline{d}_i$ is a $(p \times 1)$ vector of observed multivariate effect sizes for study i. $\underline{\delta}_i$ is a $(p \times 1)$ vector of true multivariate effect sizes for study i, and $\underline{e}_i$ is a $(p \times 1)$ vector of multivariate sampling errors. Here, p is the number of multiple outcomes from each of the primary studies, assuming that there are no missing effect sizes across studies. Unfortunately, the standard V-known routine of the HLM 6 software for analyzing multilevel meta-analysis data cannot handle multivariate meta-analytic data with missing effect sizes. However, the meta-analytic methodological developments by Kalaian (1994) and Kalaian and Raudenbush (1996) provide analytical solutions to this incomplete multivariate effect sizes problem. We refer the reader to these two resources for details about how multivariate incomplete data can be analyzed using the HLM 6 software.

The multivariate multilevel within-study model for each primary study can be expressed in more general compact matrix form as

$$\mathbf{d} = \delta + \mathbf{e}, \tag{9.14}$$

where

$$\mathbf{e} \sim N(0, \Sigma). \tag{9.15}$$

Here $\mathbf{d}$, δ, and $\mathbf{e}$ are $(P \times 1)$ vectors with $P = K\,p$. P is the total number of multiple outcomes across all of the K primary studies. Σ is the diagonal sampling variance-covariance matrix of the multivariate effect sizes from all the K primary studies with K variance-covariance sub-matrices, $\hat{\Sigma}_i$, along the diagonal. Entries for the variance-covariance matrix of the K submatrices, $\hat{\Sigma}_i$, one variance-covariance matrix for each of the primary studies, are estimated using Equations 9.11 and 9.12. Assuming independence of the individual primary studies, the estimated sampling variance covariance matrix $\hat{\Sigma}$ has a $(P \times P)$ dimension with variance-covariance, $\hat{\Sigma}_i$ sub-matrices in the diagonal, and blocks of zero matrices in the off-diagonals. This general overall sampling variance-covariance matrix can be represented as

$$
\hat{\Sigma} = \begin{bmatrix}
\hat{\Sigma}_1 & 0 & . & \cdots & 0 \\
0 & \hat{\Sigma}_2 & . & \cdots & 0 \\
. & . & . & \cdots & . \\
. & . & . & \cdots & . \\
0 & 0 & . & \cdots & \hat{\Sigma}_K
\end{bmatrix}.
\tag{9.16}
$$

Multivariate Between-Studies (Level-Two) Model

At the second stage of the multilevel meta-analysis (level two), the multivariate between-studies model can be expressed in two forms and usually is used sequentially for different meta-analytic purposes. The first step involves estimating the *multivariate unconditional between-studies model,* in which no predictor variables are included in the model. In the unconditional multivariate meta-analytic model, we assume that the multiple effect size parameters vector, $\underline{\delta}_i$, vary around a grand mean vector plus a random error vector. As in the univariate unconditional between studies (level-two) models, the results of the unconditional model allow us to test the homogeneity of the multivariate effect sizes across the K primary studies and to assess the need for subsequent multivariate conditional modeling if heterogeneity is detected. The second step involves estimating *the multivariate conditional between-studies model.* In the conditional multivariate meta-analytic model, we assume that the multiple effect size parameters, $\underline{\delta}_i$, depend on known study and sample characteristics plus a random error. These two level-two models are presented below.

Multivariate Unconditional Between-Studies Model

In this model, the true multivariate effect size parameters vector for each primary study, $\underline{\delta}_i$, are viewed as varying randomly around an overall multivariate grand mean vector, $\underline{\gamma}$, plus a unique random error vector, $\underline{U}_i$:

$$
\underline{\delta}_i = \underline{\gamma} + \underline{U}_i, \quad \underline{U}_i - N(\underline{0}, \underline{\tau}).
\tag{9.17}
$$

The complete multivariate unconditional between-studies model for all the primary studies includes all the $\underline{\delta}_i$ and $\underline{U}_i$ vectors and is represented in the following general matrix form:

$$
\boldsymbol{\delta} = \boldsymbol{\gamma} + \mathbf{U}, \quad \mathbf{U} \sim \mathbf{N}(\mathbf{0}, \boldsymbol{\tau}).
\tag{9.18}
$$

In the multivariate case, τ is the multivariate unconditional conditional variance-covariance matrix of the multiple effect sizes. δ and U are (P $\times$ 1) vectors with $P = K \times p$. P is the total number of multiple outcomes across all K primary studies.

The χ^2 test statistic is used to test the variance-covariance matrix of the multivariate between-studies errors, τ. A significant χ^2 value for testing the homogeneity of the multivariate effect size vectors across K primary studies ($H_0: \underline{\delta}_1 = \underline{\delta}_2 = \ldots = \underline{\delta}_K$) indicates that the multivariate effect size vectors are heterogeneous, or inconsistent, across all of the primary studies. To understand the heterogeneity among the multivariate effect sizes, study and sample characteristics can be used to explain some of this heterogeneity using multivariate conditional between-studies models.

Multivariate Conditional Between-Studies Model. In this multivariate conditional between-studies model, which is an extension of the multivariate unconditional between-studies model, we use information about study and sample characteristics to account for some of the variation among the multiple correlated effect sizes. In other words, we try to explain some of the variations in the multivariate effect size parameters through methodological, contextual, or treatment variations in the set of collected primary studies under consideration. This between-study model can be represented as follows:

$$\underline{\delta}_i = \underline{W}_i \underline{\gamma} + \underline{U}_i, \quad \underline{U}_i - N(\underline{0}, \tau), \tag{9.19}$$

where $\underline{\delta}_i$ and $\underline{U}_i$ are ($p \times 1$) vectors, p is the number of outcomes in each primary study, and K is the number of primary studies. $\underline{W}_i$ is a ($p \times q$) matrix of q known study characteristics, and $\underline{\gamma}$ is a ($q \times 1$) vector of between-study parameters. q is the number of predictor variables in the model. Here, we assume that $\underline{U}_i$ has a multivariate normal distribution with mean vector $\underline{0}$ and conditional variance-covariance matrix $\underline{\tau}$.

By sequentially stacking all the $\underline{\delta}_i$ vectors from all the studies, we will have the complete multivariate conditional between-studies model that can be represented in general matrix form as

$$\delta = W\gamma + U, \quad U \sim N(0, \tau). \tag{9.20}$$

τ is the multivariate conditional variance-covariance matrix of the multiple effect sizes. In other words, τ is the amount of unexplained parameter variation and co-variation left after accounting for the various effects of known study and sample characteristics. δ and U are ($P \times 1$) vectors with $P = K \times p$. P is the total number of multiple outcomes across all of the K primary studies. W is a ($P \times q$) matrix of known study characteristics and γ is a ($q \times 1$)

vector of between-study parameters. q is the number of predictor variables in the model.

In the unconditional multivariate multilevel between-studies model, the χ^2 test statistic is used to test the homogeneity of the residual variance-covariance matrix of the multivariate between-studies errors, τ. When testing the homogeneity of the multivariate effect size vectors across the K studies $(H_0\colon \underline{\delta}_1 = \underline{\delta}_2 = \ldots = \underline{\delta}_K)$, a significant χ^2 value indicates that a statistically significant amount of between-study variability remains to be explained among the multivariate effect sizes, even after accounting for certain study characteristics (predictors).

ANALYZING MULTIVARIATE META-ANALYTIC DATA USING HLM 6 SOFTWARE

As in the univariate multilevel analysis, the multivariate multilevel meta-analysis via the V-known option of the HLM2 in the HLM 6 software package requires a single ASCII data file and can be accomplished only in batch or interactive mode (Raudenbush et al., 2004).

To analyze the multivariate meta-analytic data, HLM 6 software requires an ASCII data file with a row of the multivariate meta-analytic data for each of the primary studies in the meta-analytic review. Each row of data contains the following information in the following specified variable order:

1. Study ID in character format.
2. Multiple effect size indices. For example, for primary studies with two outcomes, the order of the multiple effect sizes will be (d_1, d_2) in numeric format.
3. Variances and covariances of the effect sizes. For example, for studies with two outcomes (d_1, d_2), the order of the variances and the covariance of the two effect sizes should be $(\hat{\sigma}^2_{(d_1)}, \hat{\sigma}_{(d_1, d_2)}, \hat{\sigma}^2_{(d_2)})$ in numeric format.
4. Explanatory variables (study and sample characteristics) in numeric format in any order chosen by the meta-analyst.

Using the V-known routine of the HLM 2 within the HLM 6 software requires each primary study to have a complete set of multivariate outcomes. For example, for the SAT coaching studies that have two outcomes (SAT-Verbal and SAT-Math), we must have two outcomes from each primary study. Thus, the primary studies with missing outcomes need to be excluded from the meta-analytic data set in order to use the HLM 6 software and/or any other software for meta-analysis. As mentioned earlier, the reader should refer to Kalaian (1994) and Kalaian and Raudenbush (1996) for a detailed explanation of how to analyze multivariate meta-analytic data with missing effect sizes (incomplete meta-analytic data).

The ASCII meta-analytic data file is used to create the MDM file. This file is needed for subsequent multivariate multilevel meta-analysis modeling purposes. The reader should refer to the "V-known" option of the HLM2 within the HLM 6 manual (Raudenbush et al., 2004, p. 184) for a detailed explanation on how to create the MDM file and how to run the multivariate multilevel analysis.

For our multivariate meta-analytic data, the multivariate SAT coaching data (SAT-Verbal and SAT-Math) first is entered into the SPSS data editor (see Figure 9.5). The SPSS data file then is exported into an ASCII file with a specified format (see Figure 9.6). This data format is needed when creating the MDM file for analyzing the multivariate meta-analytic data via the HLM 6 software.

As it is shown in Figure 9.5, the data for our example are entered and represented in the SPSS data file in the following order:

1. Study Identification (Study ID)
2. The two effect sizes (diSATV and diSATM)
3. The SAT-Verbal variance (Var_Ver)
4. The covariance between the two effect sizes (Cov_MV)
5. The SAT-Math variance (Var_Mat)
6. The logarithmic transformed coaching hours (Hours).

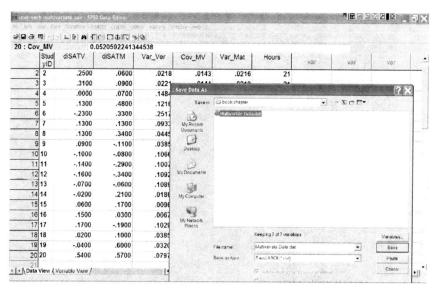

Figure 9.5 A screenshot of setting up and saving the multivariate SAT coaching data (SAT-Math and SAT-Verbal) as an ASCII File from the SPSS data editor.

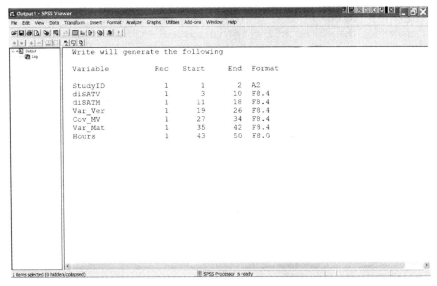

Figure 9.6 A screenshot of the specifications of the created ASCII File for the multivariate SAT coaching data.

Figures 9.5 and 9.6 illustrate this process for the SAT dataset with two SAT outcomes (SAT-Verbal and SAT-Math). Note that the saved ASCII file in Figure 9.6 has a format that corresponds to the following variable order (StudyID, diSATV, diSATM, Var_Ver, Cov_MV, Var_Mat, and Hours).

Once the MDM file for the HLM 6 software is created from the ASCII file, it is used to execute the multilevel analysis for any specified multilevel model (e.g., unconditional and conditional models). Again, we recommend that the reader refer to the HLM 6 software manual (Raudenbush et al., 2004, p. 184) for a detailed explanation on how to create the MDM file and how to execute and run the multivariate multilevel analysis.

Multivariate Multilevel Meta-Analysis Results

The unconditional results (Table 9.5) of the multivariate multilevel meta-analysis via HLM 6 indicate that the overall multivariate weighted average estimate of the 20 SAT-Verbal effect sizes is $\gamma_{10} = 0.103$ standard deviation units with a standard error of 0.042. As in the univariate case, these results indicate that the SAT-Verbal effect sizes are homogenous ($\tau = 0.004$, $\chi^2 = 10.001$, $p > 0.500$). In addition, Table 9.5 indicates that the overall multivariate weighted average of the 20 SAT-Math effect sizes is $\gamma_{20} = 0.131$ standard deviation units with a standard error of 0.055. The multivariate SAT-Math

TABLE 9.5   Unconditional Multivariate Multilevel Meta-Analysis Results for the Effects of the SAT-Verbal and SAT-Math Coaching

Parameter	Fixed effects				Random effects		
	Coefficient	S.E.	t	p-value	τ	χ^2	p-value
Average SAT-Verbal effects, γ_{10}	0.103	0.042	2.449	0.024	0.004	10.001	>.500
Average SAT-Math effects, γ_{20}	0.131	0.055	2.620	0.017	0.014	20.517	0.364

Notes: (1) The degrees of freedom = 19.

(2) Since this was multivariate multilevel meta-analysis, HLM estimates the random between-studies covariance between SAT-Verbal and SAT-Math effect sizes ($\tau_{21} = -0.069$).

results also show that these effect sizes are homogeneous ($\tau = 0.014$, $\chi^2 = 20.517$, $p = 0.364$).

Again, these multivariate results are different from the univariate unconditional multilevel results because they are adjusted for the covariance between the SAT-Verbal and SAT-Math subtests. For example, the overall SAT-Verbal average effect size using the univariate unconditional meta-analysis methods is 0.109 with a standard error of 0.039, while the overall SAT-Verbal average effect size using the multivariate unconditional meta-analysis methods is 0.103 with a standard error of 0.042. Similarly, the overall SAT-Math average effect size using the univariate unconditional meta-analysis methods is 0.120 with a standard error of 0.0395, while the overall SAT-Math average effect size using the multivariate unconditional meta-analysis methods is 0.131 with a standard error of 0.050.

As in the univariate case, non-significant χ^2 values indicate homogeneity of the multivariate SAT-Verbal and SAT-Math effect sizes. Given a result of non-significant χ^2 value, there is no need to proceed with the fitting of the multivariate conditional multilevel models. However, we chose to model these effect sizes using hours of coaching as a predictor variable for completeness and continuity of the multivariate multilevel application presented above.

The results of the conditional multilevel model (Table 9.6) show that logarithmically transformed hours of SAT coaching has a non-significant effect on SAT-Verbal effect sizes ($\gamma_{11} = 0.046$, standard error = 0.06, t-ratio = 0.764, $p = 0.455$). Furthermore, these results indicate that the residual variance-covariance, τ, adjusted for coaching duration as a predictor variable in modeling SAT-Verbal effect sizes, is not significant ($\tau = 0.003$, $\chi^2 = 8.824$, $p > 0.500$). Coaching duration has a non-statistically significant effect on the prediction of SAT-Math effect size ($\gamma_{21} = 0.145$, standard error = 0.071, t-ratio = 2.043, $p = 0.056$). As expected, these results show that the residual variance-covariance

TABLE 9.6 Conditional Multivariate Multilevel Meta-Analysis Results for the Effects of the SAT-Verbal and SAT-Math Coaching

Parameter	Fixed effects				Random effects		
	Coefficient	S.E.	t	p-value	τ	χ^2	p-value
SAT-Verbal							
Intercept, γ_{10}	0.039	0.181	−0.214	0.833			
Log (hrs), γ_{11}	0.046	0.060	0.764	0.455	0.003	8.824	>.500
SAT-Math							
Intercept, γ_{20}	−0.284	0.210	−1.356	0.192			
Log (hrs), γ_{21}	0.145	0.071	2.043	0.056	0.015	18.963	0.394

Notes: (1) The degrees of freedom = 18.
(2) Since this was multivariate multilevel meta-analysis, HLM estimates the random between-studies covariance between SAT-Verbal and SAT-Math effect sizes ($\tau_{21} = -0.0066$).

of the effect sizes, adjusted for coaching duration as a predictor variable in modeling SAT-Math effect sizes, also is not statistically significant ($\tau = 0.015$, $\chi^2 = 18.963$, $p = 0.394$).

These multivariate results are different from the univariate conditional multilevel results presented in the univariate multilevel meta-analysis section of this chapter because the multivariate results account for the covariance between the SAT-Verbal and SAT-Math effect sizes. For example, using the univariate conditional meta-analysis methods, the fixed effects regression coefficient for the Log (hrs) for SAT-Math, is 0.091 with a standard error of 0.055. In contrast, using the multivariate conditional meta-analysis methods, the fixed effects regression coefficient for the Log (hrs) for SAT-Math, is 0.145 with a standard error of 0.071.

CONCLUSION

In summary, the major goal of meta-analytic methods is to estimate quantitative summary measures for the effect sizes from all the primary studies under review, such as an overall weighted effect size for the effect sizes from the collection of primary studies. Once these weighted effect sizes are estimated, meta-analytic methods are used to assess the heterogeneity of these effect sizes across the primary studies. If the heterogeneity among the effect sizes is significantly large, this heterogeneity is modeled using study and sample characteristics to explain some of the variability among the effect sizes. In this chapter, we illustrated and presented these procedures using the univariate and multivariate multilevel modeling approaches to meta-analysis.

According to the results of the multilevel analysis of the illustrative example (SAT coaching studies), it is clear that the univariate and the multivariate multilevel approaches yielded different results. In general, these differences depend on the strength of the correlation between the pairs of the multiple outcome variables. For example, our results indicated that using the multivariate multilevel meta-analysis methods yielded slightly different estimates of effect sizes. Also, in this example, the multivariate analyses produced larger standard errors than the results of the univariate multilevel meta-analysis methods. Thus, because of the methodological and substantive advantages of the multivariate meta-analytic methods compared to the univariate meta-analysis methods, we recommend using the multivariate meta-analysis methods whenever the meta-analyst encounters multiple, correlated outcomes from the primary studies. Using multivariate meta-analysis methods leads to more accurate and precise estimates because multivariate meta-analysis takes into account the relationships between the outcome variables in the primary studies.

As with any research design, meta-analytic methods have advantages and shortcomings. Objectivity of the findings, increased statistical power, and improved generalizability of the results are examples of such advantages. Publication bias and the file drawer problem are some of the limitations of meta-analytic methods.

In conclusion, meta-analysis is a quantitative method for integrating and synthesizing a cumulative body of research studies that test the same research hypothesis. In the research area in which a meta-analysis is to be employed, researchers carefully must choose and specify one or more meta-analytic approaches in a fashion that is consistent with the objectives and assumptions of the meta-analysis.

REFERENCES

Becker, B. J. (2000). Multivariate meta-analysis. In H. E. A. Tinsley and S. D. Brown (Eds.). *Handbook of applied multivariate statistics and mathematical modeling* (pp. 499–525). San Diego: Academic Press.

Becker, B. J., Shram, C. M., Chang, L., Kino, M. M., & Quitieri, M. (1992). Models of science achievement: Forces affecting male and female performance in school science. In T. D. Cook, H. Cooper, D. S. Cordray, H. Hartmann, L. V. Hedges, R. J. Light, et al. (Eds.), *Meta-analysis for exploration: A casebook* (pp. 209–281). New York: Russell Sage Foundation.

Glass, G. V. (1976). Primary, secondary, and meta-analysis. *Educational Researcher, 5,* 3–8.

Gleser, L. J., & Olkin, I. (1994). Stochastically dependent effect sizes. In H. Cooper, & L.V. Hedges (Eds.), *The handbook of research synthesis* (pp. 339–355). New York: Russell Sage Foundation.

Goldstein, H. (1995). *Multilevel statistical models.* London: Edward Arnold/New York: Halsted.

Hedges, L. V. (1981). Distribution theory for Glass's estimator of effect size and related estimators. *Journal of the American Statistical Association, 74,* 311–319.

Hedges, L. V. (1982). Fitting continuous models to effect size data. *Journal of Educational Statistics, 7,* 245–270.

Hedges, L. V. (1994). Fixed effects models. In H. Cooper, and L. V. Hedges (Eds.), *The handbook of research synthesis* (pp. 285–299). New York: Russell Sage Foundation.

Hedges, L. V., & Olkin, I. (1985). *Statistical methods for meta-analysis.* Orlando, FL: Academic Press.

Hox, J. (2002). *Multilevel analysis: Techniques and applications.* Mahwah, NJ: Lawrence Erlbaum Associates.

Kalaian, H. A. (1994). A multivariate mixed linear model for meta-analysis. Unpublished doctoral dissertation, Michigan State University.

Kalaian, S. A., & Kasim, R. M. (2004). Comparison between multivariate fixed-effects and mixed-effects meta-analytic approaches. *Academy of Management Research Methods 2004 Forum, No. 9.* Retrieved January 25 from http://aom.pace.edu/rmd/2004forum.html

Kalaian, H. A., & Raudenbush, S.W. (1994, April). *Scholastic aptitude test coaching effectiveness: A multivariate hierarchical linear meta-analysis approach.* Paper presented at the annual meeting of the American Educational Research Association, New Orleans, Louisiana.

Kalaian, H. A., & Raudenbush, S.W. (1996). A multivariate linear model for meta-analysis, *Psychological Methods, 1,* 227–235.

Kalaian, H. A., Mullan, P. B., & Kasim, R. M. (1999). What can studies of problem-based learning tell us? Synthesizing and modeling PBL effects on national board of medical examination performance: Hierarchical linear modeling meta-analytic approach. *Advances in Health Sciences Education, 4,* 209–221.

Littell, R. C., Miliken, G. A., Stroup, W. W., & Wolfinger, R. D. (1996). *SAS system for mixed models.* Cary, NC: SAS Institute, Inc.

Rasbash, J., Browne, W., Goldstein, H., Yang, M., Plewis, I., Healy, M., et al. (2000). *A user's guide to MlwiN.* London: Multilevel Models Project, University of London.

Raudenbush, S. W. (1994). Random effects models. In H. Cooper, and L. V. Hedges (Eds.), *The handbook of research synthesis* (pp. 301–321). New York: Russell Sage Foundation.

Raudenbush, S. W., & Bryk, A. S. (1985). Empirical Bayes meta-analysis. *Journal of Educational Statistics, 10,* 75–98.

Raudenbush, S. W., & Bryk, A. S. (2002). *Hierarchical linear models: Applications and data analysis methods.* Newbury Park, CA: Sage Publications.

Raudenbush, S. W., Bryk, A. S., Cheong, Y., & Congdon, R. T. (2004). *HLM 6: Hierarchical linear and nonlinear modeling.* Chicago: Scientific Software International.

Zuman, J. P. (1988, April). *The effectiveness of special preparation for the SAT: An evaluation of a commercial coaching school.* Paper presented at the annual meeting of the American Educational Research Association, New Orleans, Louisiana. (ERIC Document Reproduction Service No. ED 294 900).

CHAPTER 10

MULTILEVEL MEASUREMENT MODELING

Akihito Kamata, Daniel J. Bauer, and Yasuo Miyazaki

Multilevel modeling can be utilized for psychometric analyses, and such a use of multilevel modeling techniques is referred to as multilevel measurement modeling (MMM) (e.g., Beretvas & Kamata, 2005). Typically, traditional psychometric models, including classical test theory (CTT) and item response theory (IRT) models, do not consider a nested structure of the data, such as students nested within schools. However, data in educational research frequently have such a nested data structure, especially when data are collected by multi-stage sampling. The strength of MMM becomes important when we analyze psychometric data that have such a nested structure. MMM appropriately analyzes data by taking into account both within- and between-cluster variations of the data. Also, since multilevel modeling is essentially an extension of a regression model to multiple levels, the flexibility of MMM offers the opportunity to incorporate covariates and interaction effects. As discussed in previous chapters of this book, another advantage of a multilevel approach is that it can accommodate unbalanced data, using all of the available information in the data.

This chapter is organized into six main parts. First, a brief introduction to traditional measurement models is provided. Second, MMM for continu-

Multilevel Modeling of Educational Data, pages 345–388
Copyright © 2008 by Information Age Publishing
All rights of reproduction in any form reserved.

ous test components using Hierarchical Linear Models (HLM) is demonstrated. Third, MMM for dichotomously-scored test components using Hierarchical Generalized Linear Models (HGLM) is introduced. Fourth, MMM with covariates is demonstrated for the HGLM approach. Fifth, limitations of HLM/HGLM approaches are discussed. Lastly, an alternative multilevel structural equation modeling (SEM) approach is introduced. Throughout the chapter, a data set from a state-wide testing program is analyzed for illustration purposes.

MEASUREMENT MODELS—TRADITIONAL PERSPECTIVES

Since it is essential to understand measurement models from traditional perspectives, this section briefly reviews classical test theory and item response theory.

Classical Test Theory

In classical test theory (CTT; e.g., Crocker & Algina, 1986; Lord & Novick, 1968; Traub, 1994), an observed score on a test component (e.g., item) is the sum of the underlying true score plus error of measurement. For an observed score on test component (e.g., item) i (X_i),

$$X_i = T_i + E_i, \tag{10.1}$$

where T_i is the true score and E_i is the error score of the test component. Statistically, T_i is the expected value of X_i. On the other hand, E_i is a random variable with mean = 0 and unknown variance, $\mathrm{var}(E_i)$.

Depending on the assumptions made about the true and error scores, there are several types of CTT models. These are (strictly) parallel, essentially parallel, (strictly) tau-equivalent, essentially tau-equivalent, and congeneric measures, in (approximately) descending order of strictness of the assumptions. The minimum requirements for the least strict condition (congeneric condition) are that (a) all the test components (e.g., items) measure the same construct; (b) the true scores (T_i) and error scores (E_i) are uncorrelated; and (c) error scores (E_i) are uncorrelated across test components. Other measures need to satisfy these three requirements, in addition to other requirements for T_i and E_i, as described below.

If $T_i = T_{i'}$ and $\mathrm{var}(E_i) = \mathrm{var}(E_{i'})$ for any test components (e.g., items) i and i' $(i \neq i')$, the test components are said to be strictly parallel. If the error variances are the same across test components (e.g., items) but the true scores between test components are different only by a constant $a_{ii'}$

($T_i = T_{i'} + a_{ii'}$ for components i and i' [$i \neq i'$]), the components are said to be essentially parallel. When the true scores differ by only a constant, the implication is that the variances of the true scores across examinees remain the same across test components. More practically, the essentially parallel condition implies that the difference in true scores is the difference in their test component difficulties (e.g., item difficulties), while the reliabilities of test components are equal. If $T_i = T_{i'}$ for all i and i' ($i \neq i'$) but $\text{var}(E_i)$ are not the same, the test components are strictly tau-equivalent. This is a situation where the difficulties of test components (e.g., items) are the same while the reliabilities of test components are different. If $T_i = T_{i'} + a_{ii'}$ for all i and i' ($i \neq i'$), where $a_{ii'}$ is a constant, and $\text{var}(E_i)$ are not the same, the test components are essentially tau-equivalent. This is a situation where the difficulties of test components (e.g., items difficulties) are not the same and the reliabilities of test components are not equal. Under the parallel and tau-equivalent conditions (including their essential conditions), true scores of test components are perfectly correlated. From a factor analytic perspective, parallel and tau-equivalent conditions are represented by homogeneous factor loadings for test components, indicating equal test component (e.g., item) discriminations. Finally, when $T_i \neq T_{i'}$, which implies that $\text{var}(T_i) \neq \text{var}(T_{i'})$ for any test components (e.g., items) i and i' ($i \neq i'$), and $\text{var}(E_i) \neq \text{var}(E_{i'})$, test components are said to be congeneric. Under the congeneric condition, true scores of test components do not have unit correlations. From a factor analytic perspective, the congeneric condition is represented by heterogeneous factor loadings for test components, indicating non-equal test component (e.g., item) discriminations. Assumptions for the five test conditions are summarized in Table 10.1. For more detailed discussions on the differences in the assumptions, see Traub (1994), and Miyazaki (2005).

One important characteristic of the classical test theory (CTT) model is that the observed variables X_i are treated as continuous, even when test components (e.g., items) are scored dichotomously or polytomously. Also,

TABLE 10.1   Assumptions of the Five CTT Conditions

	$T_i = T_{i'}$?	$\text{Var}(E_i) = \text{Var}(E_{i'})$?	Correlation between true scores
(Strictly) Parallel	Yes	Yes	1
Essentially parallel	No, but $T_i = T_{i'} + a_{ii'}$	Yes	1
(Strictly) Tau-equivalent	Yes	No	1
Essentially tau-equivalent	No, but $T_i = T_{i'} + a_{ii'}$	No	1
Congeneric	No	No	Not 1

well-known Cronbach's alpha (an index of internal consistency and measurement reliability under a single administration of a test) is derived based on the CTT framework.

Item Response Theory

Item response theory (IRT) models represent another class of measurement models. For dichotomously scored test items, there are several well-recognized IRT models, such as the Rasch model, the 2-parameter logistic model (2PL), and the 3-parameter logistic model (3PL). The 2PL model can be written as

$$\log\left(\frac{p_{ij}}{1-p_{ij}}\right) = \alpha_i(\theta_j - \beta_i), \tag{10.2}$$

where θ_j is the ability of an examinee j, α_i is the discrimination of item i, and β_i is the difficulty of item i. The metric of θ_j and β_i are typically in a standardized scale, where 0 is the center of the distribution with a standard deviation of 1. When the discrimination is equal for all items in the test and it is constrained to be 1, the model becomes

$$\log\left(\frac{p_{ij}}{1-p_{ij}}\right) = \theta_j - \beta_i \tag{10.3}$$

and is known as the Rasch model. Since the difference between θ_j and β_i is directly a logit quantity, the metric of θ_j and β_i are typically in the logit scale, where 0 indicates a typical ability or difficulty.

The most prominent difference between the CTT and the IRT models is that IRT models treat item response data as a categorical variable rather than as a continuous variable. On the other hand, there is a link between IRT models and CTT models. For example, assumptions about error scores and true scores are similar between 2PL and the congeneric condition and between the Rasch model and essentially tau-equivalent condition (see Miyazaki, 2005). Also, 2PL and the Rasch models are special cases of a factor analytic model (see Kamata & Bauer, 2008; Takane & de Leeuw, 1987).

MULTILEVEL MEASUREMENT MODEL BY HLM AND HGLM APPROACHES

This section presents multilevel measurement models with continuous and dichotomous measurement indicators (test components). When a measurement model is formulated by a linear multilevel model such as HLM (Raudenbush & Bryk, 2002) with test components or items (measurement indicators) that are continuous variables, it corresponds to a classical test theory model. Alternatively, when a measurement model is formulated by a generalized linear multilevel model such as HGLM (Raudenbush & Bryk) with test components or items (measurement indicators) that are categorical variables, the model corresponds to an item response theory model, such as the Rasch model. Whereas CTT and IRT models implicitly assume simple random sampling, multilevel measurement modeling can accommodate data collected by a complex sampling method, such as multistage sampling. Multilevel modeling can accommodate CTT or IRT models into its framework, and thus, it can be used to conduct psychometric analyses for clustered data, such as measures collected from children clustered within classrooms or schools.

Illustrative Data[1]

The example data set includes the fourth-grade mathematics assessment from a statewide testing program in the United States. A total of 3,312 students (N) from 30 schools (K) were sampled, where schools first were selected randomly from the population of schools. For the examples presented here, we use three of the five subscales from the mathematics assessment (eight measurement items, seven algebraic thinking items, and seven data analysis/probability items). Because it is assumed that the subscales measure a single construct, mathematics proficiency, the scale score for the whole test was created simply as the sum of the three subscale scores. All items in these three subscales were scored dichotomously (correct or incorrect). For our first example, illustrating a MMM with continuous measurement indicators, the scale score for each subscale was obtained by computing the proportion of items correct for each subscale. Proportion scores, rather than total scores, were used because each subscale had a different numbers of items. Further, the proportion score for each subscale was multiplied by 10 (this was done solely for the purpose of working with larger numbers that would be easier to present and interpret). Descriptive statistics are provided in Table 10.2. These subscale scores were treated as three measurement indicators (test components) in our first illustration using HLM. After introducing the HGLM formulation, the individual items are used instead as measurement indicators. Therefore, 22 measurement indicators were used for the HGLM analyses.

HLM Approach for the Multilevel Measurement Modeling

In the HLM approach, scores of the test components (subscales, in this illustrative analysis) are treated as continuous variables. Without consider-

TABLE 10.2 Descriptive Statistics for the Sample Data

a. Student level (N = 3312)

Subscale	Minimum	Maximum	Mean	SD
1. Measurement	0	10	5.605	2.510
2. Algebraic thinking	0	10	4.874	2.555
3. Data analysis/probability	0	10	5.556	2.464
Total	0	30	16.035	6.355

b. School level (K = 30)

	Minimum	Maximum	Mean	SD
Number of students	20	228	110.40	47.544
School mean subscale 1 (measurement)	3.45	7.40	5.554	0.935
School mean subscale 2 (algebraic thinking)	3.37	6.85	4.793	0.901
School mean subscale 3 (data analysis/probability)	3.82	7.89	5.513	0.920
School mean total	10.72	21.69	15.860	2.649

ing the nesting of students within schools, the conventional coefficient alpha for the total score of the three subscales was .798 (obtained by the SPSS Reliability procedure). The corresponding standard error of measurement for the total score was estimated as $6.355 \times \sqrt{1-.798} = 2.856$.[2]

Many problems may arise as a consequence of ignoring nested data structures when making statistical inferences. These negative effects are well documented in multilevel modeling textbooks, such as Hox (2005) and Raudenbush and Bryk (2002). However, few studies have focused specifically on the effect of ignoring nested data structures in psychometric analyses. Among them, Raudenbush, Rowan, and Kang (1991) demonstrated that coefficient alpha is inherently ambiguous if nesting is ignored in school-based studies because it measures neither the reliability of school-level measures nor the reliability of student-level measures. Instead, there are actually two types of internal consistency that have clear interpretability in a multilevel design: one at the student level and another at the school level. In the following examples, we will demonstrate how to obtain these two measures of internal consistency, provide their interpretations, and describe how they compare to the conventional coefficient alpha.

To take into account group membership, a multilevel measurement model can be formulated as a three-level hierarchical linear model. We first consider a standard univariate three-level HLM, where the level-one measurement errors are assumed to be homogeneous across groups. This assumption is equivalent to the essentially parallel condition described earlier, where it is assumed that the subtest true scores differ only in their means and not in their dispersion; that is, scores differ only according to the difficulty of the subtest, and error variances are equal for all subtests. As mentioned earlier, discriminations are assumed equal for the three subtests under this condition.

The level-one model can be written as

$$Y_{ijk} = \pi_{0jk} + \pi_{1jk}D2_{ijk} + \pi_{2jk}D3_{ijk} + \varepsilon_{ijk}, \qquad (10.4a)$$

where Y_{ijk} is the score on subscale i for student j in school k ($i = 1,\ldots, 3$; $j = 1,\ldots, J_k$ where J_k is the number of students in school k; $k = 1,\ldots, 30$), $D2_{ijk}$ is an indicator taking on a value of 1 if the response i for student j in school k belongs to subscale 2 (algebraic thinking) and 0 if not, and $D3_{ijk}$ is an indicator taking on a value of 1 if the response i belongs to subscale 3 (data analysis/probability) and 0 if not.[3] In this setup, subscale 1 serves as the reference subscale. The intercept, π_{0jk} is the true score of subscale 1 (measurement) for student j in school k. The remaining coefficients are interpreted relative to the reference subscale: π_{1jk} is the true score difference between subscale 2 and subscale 1, and π_{2jk} is the true score difference between subscale 3 and subscale 1. Therefore, the true score of subscale 2 for student j in school k is $\pi_{0jk} + \pi_{1jk}$, and the true score of subscale 3 for student j in school k is $\pi_{0jk} + \pi_{2jk}$. Furthermore, the measurement errors, ε_{ijk}, are assumed to be normally distributed with a mean of zero and constant variance, σ^2. These measurement errors also are assumed to be independent of one another. The latter assumption is equivalent to the assumption of uncorrelated errors in classical test theory.[4] The single value for the error variance, σ^2, represents the homogeneous error variance across subscales assumed for parallel measures.

The level-two model is the student-level model, where π_{0jk}, π_{1jk}, and π_{2jk} are treated as outcome variables. In order to reflect the proposition that all three of the subscales measure a common construct, only the intercept π_{0jk} is treated as random. Accordingly, the level-two equations are

$$\pi_{0jk} = \beta_{00k} + r_{0jk}$$
$$\pi_{1jk} = \beta_{10k} \qquad , \qquad (10.4b)$$
$$\pi_{2jk} = \beta_{20k}$$

where β_{00k} is the mean subscale-1 mathematics score for school k, β_{10k} is the mean difference between subscale-1 and subscale-2 mathematics scores for school k, and β_{20k} is the mean difference between subscale-1 and subscale-3 mathematics scores for school k. The random effect, r_{0jk}, is interpreted as mathematics proficiency level for student j in school k and as independent and normally distributed with mean of 0 and variance τ_π.

The level-three model is the school-level model. Only the intercept, β_{00k}, was assumed to vary randomly across schools. Therefore, the level-three equations are

$$\beta_{00k} = \gamma_{000} + u_{00k}$$

$$\beta_{10j} = \gamma_{100} \qquad , \qquad (10.4c)$$

$$\beta_{20j} = \gamma_{200}$$

where γ_{000} is the grand mean of subscale-1 score; γ_{100} is the grand mean difference between subscales 1 and 2, γ_{200} is the grand mean difference between subscales 1 and 3. The random effect, u_{00k}, is independent and normally distributed with mean of 0 and variance τ_β. This variance allows for variation in the school-level mean mathematics scores.

To better understand the model formulated above, we write the combined model, which joins the three levels:

$$Y_{ijk} = \gamma_{000} + \gamma_{100}D_{2ijk} + \gamma_{200}D_{3ijk} + r_{0jk} + u_{00k} + \varepsilon_{ijk}. \qquad (10.4d)$$

From the CTT perspective, $\gamma_{000} + \gamma_{100}D_{2ijk} + \gamma_{200}D_{3ijk} + r_{0jk} + u_{00k}$ is the true score for subscale i for student j in school k, and ε_{ijk} is the random measurement error. The true score consists of three sources of variation: subscale, student, and school. Since two dummy variables, D_{2ijk} and D_{3ijk}, are indicators of subscale 2 and 3 and do not depend on student (j) and school (k), the fixed effects part of the true score, $\gamma_{000} + \gamma_{100}D_{2ijk} + \gamma_{200}D_{3ijk}$, can be interpreted as subscale difficulties, and the random effects, $r_{0jk} + u_{00k}$, can be interpreted as student overall mathematics proficiency, which is represented as the sum of student proficiency relative to the school mean and the school mean relative to the grand mean. Since the subscale difficulties differ and the errors are assumed to have homogeneous variances, the HLM model formulated above assumes an essentially parallel structure.

Results of fitting this three-level model to the example data are presented in Table 10.3. Note that by default the model is estimated using full maximum likelihood (FML) as opposed to restricted maximum likelihood (REML) (the default for the two-level HLM).[5]

The estimate of the student-level reliability, denoted as α_π, is obtained as .768, which is slightly lower than the estimate obtained from the conventional approach ($\alpha = .798$), which ignored the nested data structure. The value .768 was computed by substituting the estimates of variances ($\hat{\tau}_\pi = 2.998$ and

TABLE 10.3   Results from Three-Level Psychometric Model

a. Fixed Effects

	Estimate	Standard error	t-ratio	df	p-value
γ_{000}	5.547	.158	35.180	29	<.001
γ_{100}	-.731	.041	-18.057	9933	<.001
γ_{200}	-.050	.041	-1.230	9933	.219

b. Variance Components

	Estimate	Standard error	df	Chi-Square	p-value	Reliability
Level 1						
σ^2	2.717	.047				
Level 2						
τ_π	2.998	.098	3282	9358.894	<.001	.768
Level 3						
τ_β	.683	.188	29	527.171	<.001	.936

c. Model Summary

Deviance	# of parameter estimated
43053.238	6

$\hat{\sigma}^2 = 2.717$) and the number of subscales within student ($n = 3$) into the following formula:[6]

$$\hat{\alpha}_\pi = \frac{\hat{\tau}_\pi}{\hat{\tau}_\pi + \hat{\sigma}^2 / n} = \frac{2.998}{2.998 + 2.717 / 3} = .768. \qquad (10.5)$$

This formula, where n is the number of test components, corresponds to the general "reliability" formula in multilevel modeling (e.g., Raudenbush & Bryk, 2002, p. 270). The reduction in the reliability coefficient occurred because the reliability obtained from a traditional model that ignores nesting is inflated due to the correlation of scores observed within the same school. In fact, the estimate of intraclass correlation (ICC), a correlation between the latent adjusted means within the same school is

$$\mathrm{cor}(\pi_{0jk}, \pi_{0j'k}) = \frac{\tau_\beta}{\tau_\beta + \tau_\pi} = .186$$

for $j \neq j'$, which is not an ignorable magnitude of correlation (for more detailed discussion on the impact of the magnitude of the ICC, see, for example, Snijders & Bosker, 1999, p. 46).

The reliability of the school mean ($\bar{Y}_{\bullet\bullet k}$) was very high at .936. This value is computed by taking the average of the reliability coefficients for each school,

$$\alpha_\beta = \frac{1}{K}\sum \alpha_{\beta k}, \tag{10.6}$$

where

$$\alpha_{\beta k} = \frac{\hat{\tau}_\beta}{\hat{\tau}_\beta + \hat{\tau}_\pi / J_k + \hat{\sigma}^2 / J_k n}, \tag{10.7}$$

which were presented in Equations 10.14 and 10.16 in Raudenbush et al. (1991).[7] Here, J_k is the number of students for school k, and other terms have been defined above. In the formula, the school-level reliability, α_β, approaches one as J_k goes to infinity. In our data, the average number of students per school is 110; hence, the reliability of the school mean mathematics scores is very high at .936.

The implication of this difference in reliability at the school- versus student-level is that we can be much more confident in assigning a mathematics proficiency score to the school as a whole than any given student within the school. In other words, we more confidently can differentiate and rank order schools in terms of school performance on mathematic achievement than we can distinguish students within schools.

Measurement Models by Multivariate Three-Level Models

In this section, use of multivariate HLM for MMM is demonstrated. As mentioned earlier, the measurement model we considered in the previous section corresponds to the essentially parallel measures CTT structure, which requires that relatively strong assumptions be met (true scores are different only by test component difficulties, and equal component reliabilities). Not all of these assumptions are necessary for the scores to be interpretable; therefore, we may wish to relax some of the assumptions and test the fit empirically. We will use the multivariate module of HLM[8] software for this purpose. For other ways of applying multivariate HLM, such as to multiple outcomes and to repeated measures designs, the reader is referred to Raudenbush and Bryk (2002) and Thum (1997).

The first model we consider is the unrestricted model, where no structure is given to the variances/covariances of the level-one subtest true scores. This most unrestricted model imposes no structure on the covariance matrix and serves as the baseline model for comparison to more restrictive models.[9] The second model allows the level-one error variance to differ over the three subscales, while the covariances among the three subscales are constrained to be the same. The weaker assumptions of this model correspond to the essentially tau-equivalent CTT model. Third, the homogeneous level-one error variance model is presented. The homogeneous level-one error variance model has only two covariance parameters: the level-one error variance and the level-two between-cluster variance. Thus, it is the simplest model and has the most restrictive covariance structure. The homogeneous level-one error variance model corresponds to an essentially parallel measure CTT model where error variances of measurement are homogeneous but true score means are heterogeneous. It also corresponds to the previous three-level psychometric model that was fit through a univariate approach.

Unrestricted Model

The level-one model consists of two equations. The first equation links the incomplete data vector (i.e., observed data) and the complete data vector (observed data and missing data) via a set of indicator variables so that

$$Y_{ijk} = IND1_{ijk}Y^*_{1jk} + IND2_{ijk}Y^*_{2jk} + IND3_{ijk}Y^*_{3jk} \qquad (10.8a)$$

for $i = 1, \ldots, 3$, $j = 1, \ldots, 3312$, and $k = 1, \ldots, 30$, where Y_{ijk} is the ith observation of mathematics achievement subscale score for student j in school k, and through the three indicator variables ($IND1$, $IND2$, $IND3$) is linked to the complete data vector $(Y^*_{1jk}, Y^*_{2jk}, Y^*_{3jk})$ of the three subscale scores for student j in school k. $IND1$ is the indicator variable for subscale 1 (measurement) of mathematics: it takes the value of one if the observation is from subscale 1 of mathematics and zero if not. Similarly, $IND2$ and $IND3$ are indicator variables for subscale 2 (algebraic thinking) and subscale 3 (data analysis/probability). Thus, the indicator variables differentiate which of the three subscales the observed value of Y_{ijk} measures.

The second part of the level-one model describes the measurement model for the outcome variables:

$$Y^*_{pjk} = \pi_{0jk} + \pi_{1jk}D2_{pjk} + \pi_{2jk}D3_{pjk} + e_{pjk} \quad (p = 1, 2, \text{ and } 3), \qquad (10.8b)$$

where Y^*_{pjk} is the pth subscale score student j in school k would have displayed if the score had been observed, π_{0jk} is the true score of subscale 1 for student j in school k, π_{1jk} is the difference score between subscales 1 and 2 for student j in school k, and π_{2jk} is the difference score between subscales 1 and 3 for student j in school k. $D2_{ij}$ is an indicator taking on a value of one if the response i belongs to subscale 2 (algebraic thinking) and zero otherwise, and $D3_{ij}$ is an indicator taking on a value of one if the response i belongs to subscale 3 (data analysis/probability) and 0 otherwise. The residual, e_{pjk}, is a random error associated with the pth subscale score, Y^*_{pjk}, an element of complete latent data. The second equation can be represented succinctly in matrix form as a multivariate linear model with 3 outcome variables:

$$\mathbf{Y}^*_{jk} = \begin{pmatrix} Y^*_{1\,jk} \\ Y^*_{2\,jk} \\ Y^*_{3\,jk} \end{pmatrix} = \begin{pmatrix} 1 & D2_{1\,jk} & D3_{1\,jk} \\ 1 & D2_{2\,jk} & D3_{2\,jk} \\ 1 & D2_{3\,jk} & D3_{3\,jk} \end{pmatrix} \begin{pmatrix} \pi_{0\,jk} \\ \pi_{1\,jk} \\ \pi_{2\,jk} \end{pmatrix} + \begin{pmatrix} e_{1\,jk} \\ e_{2\,jk} \\ e_{3\,jk} \end{pmatrix} = \begin{pmatrix} 1 & 0 & 0 \\ 1 & 1 & 0 \\ 1 & 0 & 1 \end{pmatrix} \begin{pmatrix} \pi_{0\,jk} \\ \pi_{1\,jk} \\ \pi_{2\,jk} \end{pmatrix} + \mathbf{e}_{jk}. \quad (10.8c)$$

We assume that $\mathbf{e}_{jk}$ has a multivariate normal distribution with a mean of vector $\mathbf{0}$ and an arbitrary 3×3 covariance matrix,

$$\Delta = \begin{pmatrix} \delta_{11} & \delta_{12} & \delta_{13} \\ \delta_{12} & \delta_{22} & \delta_{23} \\ \delta_{13} & \delta_{23} & \delta_{33} \end{pmatrix}, \quad (10.8d)$$

which involves six unique parameters. Then at level two, to let this covariance matrix, Δ, represent the overall between-student (within-school) variances and covariances among the three subtests, we constrain all the coefficients in Equation 10.8b (π's). That is,

$$\pi_{0\,jk} = \beta_{00k}$$
$$\pi_{1\,jk} = \beta_{10k} \quad . \quad (10.8e)$$
$$\pi_{2\,jk} = \beta_{20k}$$

The above model specification simply formulates the standard multivariate linear model for the complete data vector. We can see this by obtaining the combined model for the complete data vector, $\mathbf{Y}^*_{jk}$, by combining Equations 10.8c and 10.8e:

$$\mathbf{Y}^*_{jk} = A\beta_k + \mathbf{e}_{jk}, \quad (10.8f)$$

where

$$A = \begin{pmatrix} 1 & 0 & 0 \\ 1 & 1 & 0 \\ 1 & 0 & 1 \end{pmatrix}$$

and $\beta_k = (\beta_{00k}, \beta_{10k}, \beta_{20k})^T$. From this Equation, we can confirm that the variance-covariance matrix, Δ, in fact, represents the dispersion of the complete data, $\mathbf{Y}^*_{jk}$, within schools, i.e., $\Delta = \text{var}(\mathbf{e}_{jk}) = \text{var}(\mathbf{Y}^*_{jk} \mid \beta_k)$. Note that consistent with the absence of a specific measurement model, no structure has been imposed on this covariance matrix. Later models will differ in this regard.

The level-three units are schools. The level-three model that we formulate assumes only that the intercept varies across schools. This implies that some schools have higher average mathematics proficiency than others. Therefore,

$$\beta_{00k} = \gamma_{000} + u_{00k}$$

$$\beta_{10k} = \gamma_{100} \qquad , \qquad (10.8g)$$

$$\beta_{20k} = \gamma_{200}$$

where u_{00k} are independent, normally distributed with mean of 0 and variance of τ_β. Thus, the overall covariance structure for the complete data, $\mathbf{Y}^*_{jk}$, is

$$\text{var}(\mathbf{Y}^*_{jk}) = E[\text{var}(\mathbf{Y}^*_{jk} \mid \beta_k)] + \text{var}[E(\mathbf{Y}^*_{jk} \mid \beta_k)] = \Delta + A \, \text{var}(\beta_k) A^T = \Delta + \tau_\beta J_3,$$

where J_3 is a 3×3 matrix of all 1's.[10]

Results of fitting this model to the illustrative data are summarized in Table 10.4. The number of parameters estimated is 10 for this unrestricted model; three for fixed effects, six for the unique variances and covariances in Δ matrix, and τ_β, the variance of the first subscale (which is the reference group) at the school level.[11]

Heterogeneous Level-One Variance Model

The second model is the heterogeneous level-one variance model. For this model, the first equation at level one is the same as the unrestricted model (Equation 10.8a). The second equation of the level-one model includes the error term, e_{pjk},

$$Y^*_{pjk} = \pi_{0jk} + \pi_{1jk} D2_{pjk} + \pi_{2jk} D3_{pjk} + e_{pjk} \quad (p = 1,2,3), \qquad (10.9a)$$

but here the e_{pjk} are independent and normally distributed with mean of 0 and constant variance of σ_1^2, σ_2^2, and σ_3^2 for the three subscales, respectively. The level-two equations are

$$\pi_{0jk} = \beta_{00k} + r_{0jk}$$

$$\pi_{1jk} = \beta_{10k} \qquad , \qquad (10.9b)$$

$$\pi_{2jk} = \beta_{20k}$$

TABLE 10.4   Results for the Unrestricted Model for Three Subscales

a. Fixed Effects

	Estimate	Standard error	t-ratio	df	p-value
γ_{000}	5.548	.158	35.176	29	<.001
γ_{100}	-.731	.040	-18.191	3311	<.001
γ_{200}	-.050	.040	-1.240	3311	.215

b. Variance and Covariance Components

	Estimate	Standard error
Level 1 & 2		
$\text{var}(e_{0jk})$	5.684	.140
$\text{var}(e_{1jk})$	5.926	.110
$\text{var}(e_{2jk})$	5.535	.137
$\text{cov}(e_{0jk}, e_{1jk})$	3.128	.115
$\text{cov}(e_{0jk}, e_{2jk})$	2.935	.146
$\text{cov}(e_{1jk}, e_{2jk})$	2.932	.112
Level 3		
τ_β	.684	.188

c. Summary

Deviance	# of parameter estimated
43044.647	10

Note: The heading "Level 1 & 2" indicates that r_{jk} represents the student-level variability of a multivariate outcome, although it was used as the level-1 term in the model equation.

where r_{0jk} is normally distributed with mean of 0 and variance of τ_π. The level-three equations are exactly the same as for the unrestricted model (Equation 10.8g). Thus, the covariance matrix Δ is now structured as

$$\Delta = \begin{pmatrix} \tau_\pi + \sigma_1^2 & \tau_\pi & \tau_\pi \\ \tau_\pi & \tau_\pi + \sigma_2^2 & \tau_\pi \\ \tau_\pi & \tau_\pi & \tau_\pi + \sigma_3^2 \end{pmatrix}. \tag{10.9c}$$

The results for the heterogeneous level-one variance model for the sample data are presented in Table 10.5. Note that the number of estimated parameters in the heterogeneous model is now eight, two more than the homogeneous model.

Homogeneous Level-One Variance Model
The last multivariate multilevel model to be fitted is the homogeneous level-one variance model, which is equivalent to the standard three-level HLM

TABLE 10.5 Results for the Heterogeneous Level-One Variance Model

a. Fixed Effects

	Estimate	Standard error	t-ratio	df	p-value
γ_{000}	5.547	.158	35.176	29	<.001
γ_{100}	−.731	.041	−17.986	9933	<.001
γ_{200}	−.050	.040	−1.246	9933	.213

b. Variance and Covariance Components

	Estimate	Standard error
Level 1		
σ_1^2	2.619	.089
σ_2^2	2.857	.094
σ_3^2	2.675	.090
Level 2		
τ_π	2.997	.098
Level 3		
τ_β	.684	.188

c. Summary

Deviance	# of parameter estimated
43049.851	8

demonstrated previously. In this model the equal error variance assumption is further imposed for the previous model. Model equations are unchanged from the previous model. Thus, in the second equation of the level-one model, Equation 10.9a, the errors e_{pjk} are still independent and normally distributed with mean of 0. However, the variances are now assumed to be equal for the three subscales. Thus, the covariance matrix Δ is now structured as

$$\Delta = \begin{pmatrix} \tau_\pi + \sigma^2 & \tau_\pi & \tau_\pi \\ \tau_\pi & \tau_\pi + \sigma^2 & \tau_\pi \\ \tau_\pi & \tau_\pi & \tau_\pi + \sigma^2 \end{pmatrix}. \tag{10.10}$$

The results of the data analysis assuming a homogeneous level-one variance model are presented in Table 10.6.

Notice that the parameter estimates both for fixed and for random effects, as well as the value of the deviance at convergence, are the same as the ones obtained from the standard three-level HLM (see Table 10.3), which were demonstrated earlier in this chapter. These results confirm that the MMM based on the multivariate HLM with homogenous level-one variance is equivalent to the MMM based on the standard univariate three-level HLM.

TABLE 10.6   Results for the Homogeneous Level-One Variance Model

a. Fixed Effects

	Estimate	Standard error	t-ratio	df	p-value
γ_{000}	5.547	.158	35.180	29	<.001
γ_{100}	−.731	.041	−18.057	9933	<.001
γ_{200}	−.050	.040	−1.230	9933	.219

b. Variance and Covariance Components

	Estimate	Standard error
Level 1		
σ^2	2.717	.047
Level 2		
τ_{π}	2.998	.098
Level 3		
τ_{β}	.683	.188

c. Summary

Deviance	# of parameter estimated
43053.238	6

Finally, we compare the three nested models by deviance tests to evaluate which model is most appropriate for the data. The results in Table 10.7 indicate that the homogeneous level-one variance model is the best fitting model among the three for these data, since the change of the deviance was not significant for either the heterogeneous level-one variance model or the unrestricted model at .05 level of significance (see Chapter 7 of this volume (McCoach & Black, 2008) for details on model comparison).

HGLM Approach for Multilevel Measurement Model

The previous section described multilevel measurement models for continuous measurement indicators. Although this assumption is suitable in certain circumstances, such as the illustrative analysis in previous sections, it is often the case that measurement indicators are categorical variables. In fact, the item-level response data in the illustrative data example consists entirely of dichotomous items. Therefore, if one wishes to use the items as measurement indicators, it will be more appropriate to treat measurement indicators as categorical variables. Other examples include ordered categorical items, such as Likert-type scale items in an attitude survey. In these cases, generalized multilevel linear or nonlinear models that are equivalent to well-known

TABLE 10.7 Summary of the Three Models by Considering Nested Data Structure

a. Deviance

Model	Parameters estimated	Deviance
1. Unrestricted model	10	43044.647
2. Heterogeneous level-1 variance model	8	43049.851
3. Homogeneous level-1 variance model	6	43053.238

b. Deviance Test

	Chi-square	df	p-value
Model 3 vs. Model 2	3.387	2	.182
Model 2 vs. Model 1	5.204	2	.072
Model 3 vs. Model 1	8.590	4	.071

item response models, such as the Rasch model or the two-parameter item response theory (IRT) model, can be specified for the data.

It is still an option to use a linear multilevel model for categorically-measured indicator variables. Specifically, for dichotomous indicator variables, a linear probability model can be fit using the untransformed 0, 1 dichotomous responses as the outcomes (item responses); thus, the predicted dependent variable corresponds to the probability of observing the event, such as supplying a correct answer rather than an incorrect answer. However, this is not a desirable approach for several reasons, such as possibility of out-of range predicted probability values. Chapter 6 of this volume (O'Connell, Goldstein, Rogers, & Peng, 2008) and Long (1997), for example, provide detailed discussions of the problems associated with the linear probability model.

A more desirable approach to modeling categorical indicator variables is to use a generalized linear model (GLM) extension of the multilevel linear model, such as the hierarchical generalized linear model (HGLM) (O'Connell et al., 2008; Raudenbush & Bryk, 2002), specifically, one using the logit link. In this section, we assume that the responses are scored dichotomously in a manner similar to our example data.[12] Let $Y_{ijk} = 1$ if the ith response is correct for student j of school k and $Y_{ijk} = 0$ otherwise, and let μ_{ijk} be the probability of $Y_{ijk} = 1$. This probability varies randomly across students. However, conditioning on this probability, we have $Y_{ijk}|\mu_{ijk} \sim$ Bernoulli with $E(Y_{ijk}|\mu_{ijk}) = \mu_{ijk}$ and $\text{var}(Y_{ijk}|\mu_{ijk}) = \mu_{ijk}(1 - \mu_{ijk})$. Then, a multilevel measurement model[13] can be written for the example data set as

$$\text{logit}(\mu_{ijk}) = \gamma_i + r_{jk} + u_k, \tag{10.11}$$

where γ_i is the effect of item i. Student ability variation within school, $r_{jk} \sim N(0, \sigma_{r_k}^2)$ and the school mean ability variation $u_k \sim N(0, \sigma_u^2)$ are assumed. This model is equivalent to the Rasch model, where $-\gamma_i$ is the item difficulty for item i and $r_{jk} + u_k$ is the trait level for person j in school k. The multilevel measurement model takes into account within-school (or between-students for each school) variability, as well as between-school variability, while the Rasch model is a single-level model that only considers between-students variability for all schools combined. This distinction is analogous to the difference between the three-level MMM discussed in the previous section relative to conventional CTT models. In fact, Equation 10.11 can be simplified to a two-level model by not considering the level-three variation,

$$\text{logit}(\mu_{ij}) = \pi_i + r_j. \tag{10.12}$$

In this case, the model is equivalent to the Rasch model, where $-\pi_i$ is the item difficulty for item i and r_j is the trait level for person j.[14]

Models in Equations 10.11 and 10.12 are HGLMs based on a logit link function, with a three-level HGLM for Equation 10.11 and a two-level HGLM for Equation 10.12. The quantity being predicted is the log of the odds of getting item i correct for the jth child in the kth school; the model in Equation 10.12 assumes there are no school differences. However, some constraints need to be imposed to identify the parameters of the model. Several different ways to parameterize the model have been suggested, as well as different estimation methods and optimization methods. For example, Kamata (2001) demonstrated that this can be modeled in the framework of HGLM using one item as a reference item and including an intercept term. Also, it is possible to estimate parameters in the model by constraining the mean item difficulties to be zero without specifying a reference item (e.g., Cheong & Raudenbush, 2000).

Parameter estimation can be accomplished by delete several different methods, including the penalized quasi likelihood (PQL), Laplace approximation, Gaussian numerical integration of log-likelihood, and fully Bayesian Markov Chain Monte Carlo (MCMC) methods. Rijmen, Tuerlinckx, Meulders, Smits, and Balazs (2005) compared these estimation methods and demonstrated that all estimators performed equally well in reasonable conditions. In the examples below, we use the HLMv6 software, which utilizes PQL estimation. Roberts and Herrington (2005) demonstrated how to set up and analyze data for these models in several different software packages.

Equation 10.11 is fit by a three-level HGLM for the example data, which is analogous to the homogeneous level-one variance model in the linear case, except that the outcomes (items) are treated as dichotomous rather than continuous. In the illustrative data, there are 22 items. Therefore, the level-one equation is the item-level model and can be written as

$$\text{logit}(\mu_{ijk}) = \pi_{0jk} + \sum_{q=1}^{21} \pi_{qjk} D_{qijk}, \tag{10.13}$$

where D_{qijk} is the qth indicator variable that takes a value of one if $q = i$ for item i. There is no error term in Equation 10.13 because it is absorbed by the link function (O'Connell et al., 2008). One item is used as a reference item, and the other item difficulties are assessed relative to the reference item. Thus, $q = 1, \ldots, 21$, rather than up to 22 ($8 + 7 + 7 = 22$ items). Then, the level-two equations are

$$\pi_{0jk} = \beta_{00k} + r_{0jk}, \tag{10.14}$$
$$\pi_{qjk} = \beta_{q0k}$$

where $q = 1, \ldots, 21$. The slopes are not random because the item difficulties are assumed to be equal across individual students. The level-three equations are

$$\beta_{00k} = \gamma_{000} + \mu_{00k}, \tag{10.15}$$
$$\beta_{q0k} = \gamma_{q00}$$

The slopes are not random because the item difficulties are assumed to be equal across schools. As a result, γ_{000} is the difficulty of the reference item, and γ_{q00} is the difference between item i (for $q = i$) and the reference item in their difficulties. The ability of student j in school k is $r_{0jk} + u_{00k}$. Both r_{0jk} and u_{00k} are assumed to be normally distributed with means of zero and unknown variances.[15] The results of this model are presented in Table 10.8.

The difficulty of item 40 (the reference item) was estimated to be .344 (γ_{000}) logits, indicating it is .344 logits higher than the mean ability. Other values indicated in Table 10.8a are differences in their difficulties compared to item 40. For example, item 6 is more difficult than item 40 by .178; thus, its difficulty is $.344 + .178 = .522$. On the other hand, item 7 is easier than item 40 by .408, so its difficulty is $.344 - .403 = -.059$. Notice that $\text{se}(\gamma_{i00})$ for item 40 is the standard error for the item's difficulty while the standard errors for the remaining estimated parameters are standard errors for the difference in difficulty from that of item 40. For this model, the variances of the student abilities are provided in the bottom panel of Table 10.8b. The within-school variance was estimated as $\sigma^2 = \text{var}(r_{0jk}) = .694$, while the between-school variance was estimated as $\tau = \text{var}(u_{00k}) = .162$. This implies that the intraclass correlation in latent mathematics ability is

$$\frac{\tau}{\sigma^2 + \tau} = .162 / (.694 + .162) = .189.$$

In other words, 18.9% of the variability in mathematics ability can be ascribed to differences between schools as opposed to variability among students within schools.

TABLE 10.8   Results of Example Data Analysis by HGLM – Unconditional Model

a. Fixed Effects

Item	γ_{i00}	$se(\gamma_{i00})$
Measurement		
6	.178	.054
7	−.403	.053
8	.023	.053
10	−.028	.053
28	.061	.053
31	−1.342	.055
39	.883	.057
40*	.344	.084
Algebraic thinking		
14	−.555	.053
16	−.265	.053
17	−.785	.053
19	−1.266	.055
21	−.006	.053
35	−.508	.053
36	.399	.054
Data analysis		
4	.377	.054
25	−.485	.053
26	.507	.055
29	−.977	.054
30	−.201	.053
33	−.874	.054
38	1.061	.058

b. Random Effects

	Estimate	Standard Error
Level 2		
$var(r_{0jk})$	.694	.016
Level 3		
$var(u_{00k})$	.162	.047

* This item was used as the reference item in the model. Therefore, the parameter listed for this item is the estimate of the intercept γ_{000}.

Model Extensions with a Covariate

Both HLM and HGLM models can be extended easily to include covariates and additional variance and covariance components. For example, assume we have an additional person-level predictor (X_{jk}) in the three-level HGLM measurement model and that our interest is in the main effects of the additional person-level predictor and the interaction effect between the additional predictor and the item indicator $(D_{ijk}X_{jk})$. We can still use Equation 10.13 as the level-one model. The level-two equations become

$$\pi_{0jk} = \beta_{00k} + \beta_{01k}X_{jk} + r_{0jk},$$
$$\pi_{qjk} = \beta_{q0k} + \beta_{q1k}X_{jk} \tag{10.16}$$

where $q = 1, \ldots, 21$. Here, β_{01k} is the main effect of the person-level predictor, and β_{q1k} is the person by item interaction effect. Furthermore, if we also are interested in the random variation of the person by item interaction effect across the level-three units, the level-three equations become

$$\beta_{00k} = \gamma_{000} + u_{00k}$$
$$\beta_{01k} = \gamma_{010}$$
$$\beta_{q0k} = \gamma_{q00} \tag{10.17}$$
$$\beta_{q1k} = \gamma_{q10} + u_{q1k}$$

where $q = 1, \ldots, 21$ and u_{q1k} is the random effect of the interaction effect. In addition to the fixed effects (γ_{000}, γ_{010}, γ_{q00}, and γ_{q10}), the variance and covariance components, var(r_{0jk}), var(u_{00k}), var(u_{q1k}), and cov(u_{00k}, u_{q1k}), are estimated.

If X_{jk} is a dichotomous variable that represents two subpopulations of test examinees, the interaction effect γ_{q10} is a differential item functioning (DIF) parameter that enables one to detect potential item bias. When subgroups of examinees have different probability of answering an item correctly, given the same level of abilities, we say the item displays DIF.[16] Furthermore, this three-level formulation of the model is equivalent to the "random effect DIF model" presented by Cheong (2006) and Kamata, Chaimongkol, Genc, and Bilir (2005). In this context, one's interest is in estimating the magnitude of γ_{q10} (the mean magnitude of DIF across schools) and var(u_{q1k}) (the randomly varying DIF magnitude across schools). Also, cov(u_{00k}, u_{q1k}) indicates how the mean performance of students and DIF magnitude are related at the school level.

For demonstration, one student-level variable, enrollment in a free or subsidized lunch program, is used. Fifty-seven percent of the students in the sample were enrolled in free or subsidized lunch programs. Using the HGLM option in the HLM software, we fit the model by arbitrarily treating the last item (item 40) in the measurement subscale as a reference item. We needed further constraints to fix the magnitude of the fixed interaction effect (DIF magnitude; γ_{i10} in Equation 10.17) for identification reasons. Our preliminary data exploration indicated the magnitude of the DIF for the third item in the measurement subscale was near zero (γ_{i10} = .0001 for this item). Therefore, its effect was constrained to be zero, and the parameter was dropped from the model. Accordingly, var(u_{i1k}) was also constrained to be zero for this item.

Seven items displayed statistically significant DIF (DIF estimates were larger than twice their standard errors). These items are indicated by asterisks in Table 10.9. Each had negative values, indicating that students who participated in free or subsidized lunch programs had significantly lower odds of correct answers for the indicated items, given the same level of ability. For item 33 in the data analysis subscale, for example, the odds of a correct answer for students who received free or subsidized lunch was only 70% (exp[–.351] = .704) as high as the odds of success for students who were not receiving free or subsidized lunch. For the seven items that displayed significant DIF, random effects were further estimated in a separate model.[17] Six of these items displayed statistically significant variability, indicating variation in the degree of DIF across schools. For example, the estimate of var(u_{i1k}) was .230 for item 33. In conjunction with the estimate of the fixed effect, it can be interpreted that the 95% of logits for DIF on item 33 are in the range of $-.351 \pm 1.96\sqrt{.230} = [-1.291, .589]$, assuming the normality of the distribution of DIF across schools.

By examining the estimated cor(u_{00k}, u_{i1k}) in Table 10.9, we see that the correlations are all positive among the seven items with significant DIF. Positive correlations indicate that DIF was higher for schools with higher mean performance. These seven items had negative DIF magnitudes, indicating students with free or subsidized lunch had lower odds of correct answer, given the same level of ability. At a glance this may seem counter-intuitive. However, given that the mean interaction effect (DIF) was a negative value, stronger interaction effects are actually values of DIF closer to zero. In other words, the interaction effect resulted in DIF values that were more positive (or closer to zero) in schools with higher mean performance.

Summary and Limitations of the HLM/HGLM Approach

To this point, we have demonstrated how to fit measurement models using hierarchical linear and generalized linear models. These approaches are different in how they treat measurement indicator variables; conse-

TABLE 10.9 Estimates of Fixed and Random Effects for the Interaction Effect

Item	Fixed effects γ_{i10}	se	Random effects $\text{var}(u_{i1k})$	$\text{cor}(u_{00k}, u_{i1k})$
Measurement				
6	−.247*	.113	.072**	.134
7	.000**	—		
8	.024	.133		
10	−.297*	.110	.059**	.436
28	−.149	.111		
31	−.066	.107		
39	−.307*	.117	.078**	.573
40	.000**	—		
Algebraic thinking				
14	.139	.128		
16	−.155	.103		
17	−.284*	.117	.144**	.453
19	−.069	.108		
21	.007	.110		
35	−.072	.105		
36	−.417*	.105	.010	.476
Data analysis				
4	−.199	.113		
25	−.182	.107		
26	−.264*	.114	.091**	.643
29	−.040	.122		
30	−.037	.142		
33	−.351*	.128	.230**	.499
38	.111	.124		

* Magnitudes are greater than twice the standard errors.
** Magnitudes are significant at $\alpha = .05$ based on chi-square test.

quently, their link functions are different. However, they are very similar in other ways. Therefore, HLM and HGLM approaches are discussed together in this section.

The basic approach of these multilevel measurement models is to conceive of the measured variables or item responses as the lowest level of a three-level model with levels corresponding to the observed measures (level one), persons (level two), and groups (level three). In the case where there are no groups (i.e., ignoring school membership, or when school differences were not part of the research design), the model reduces to a simple random intercept model, where the random intercept now accounts for the dependence among the repeated measures (items) within person and, hence, constitutes the latent factor or trait. In the linear case (with continuous measurement indicators), this corresponds to a confirmatory factor model assuming equal factor loadings, or an essentially tau-equivalent structure that assumes equal discrimination. For dichotomous items, a random intercept model produces the well-known Rasch model, which also assumes equal discrimination across items. In both cases, differences in the difficulties of test components are modeled by including the fixed effects of dummy variables for each measure.

One advantage of formulating these models in the HLM/HGLM framework as compared to the traditional (single-level) CTT or IRT frameworks is that these measurement models can be extended to allow for variance components in the latent factors or traits at both the individual and group level. When the full three-level model is specified, this allows for variability in the factor means (item subscales) across groups, as well as within-group variability in individual levels on the latent factor. As such, the total variance of the latent factor can be decomposed into between- and within-school components. The intraclass correlation obtained from this decomposition of the latent variable typically exceeds the magnitude of the intraclass correlations for the measured variables, reflecting disattenuation for measurement error (Raudenbush et al., 1991). Another advantage is that observed predictors can be included in the model at either the individual and/or group level to explain the two components of variance.

There are, however, some limitations to incorporating measurement models into HLM or HGLM. One limitation is the assumption that the discrimination power (factor loadings) are equal (or at least known a priori) for all test components. Ideally, these model parameters could be estimated directly from the data, just as typically is done in confirmatory factor analysis and two-parameter item response models. Many empirical applications of linear factor models and item response models where the factor loadings differ across the observed measures suggest the need for this modeling flexibility.

By assuming equal factor loadings, we are assuming that the relationships between the observed measures and the latent factor are equivalent across all test components. In test-scoring, it is considered desirable for a measurement instrument to possess such a property (see e.g., Embretson & Reise, 2000). Thus, when this equivalence assumption is consistent with the data, it provides for a parsimonious and useful measurement model for the instrument. On the other hand, a less restrictive model would allow the factor loadings or item discriminations to vary, rather than constraining them to be equal a priori. This constraint is more difficult to impose for binary items because a model that contains item-specific discrimination parameters is not a hierarchical generalized linear model anymore (Rijmen et al., 2003). More generally, a fundamental limitation of the HLM/HGLM approach is that the random coefficients are related to the observed repeated measures via a design matrix, which, by definition, must consist of known values (see Bauer, 2003). The random intercept that constitutes the latent factor or trait is defined by inserting a column of ones into the design matrix for the random effects. To overcome this limitation, one must leave the HLM/HGLM framework so that the design matrix can be replaced by a matrix that allows the inclusion of both known values (e.g., covariates) and unknown values (e.g., factor loadings or discrimination parameters).

For binary items, Rijmen, Tuerlinckx, De Boeck, and Kuppens (2003) and Rijmen and Briggs (2004) provide an example of such an approach using a non-linear mixed model. According to their approach, a 2PL IRT model can be modeled by treating a logit of the probability of the response as a linear function. We assume that the distribution of the latent trait is an arbitrary distribution, such as a standard normal distribution. Also, we assume that the probability of observing 1 rather than 0 for the dependent variable is defined by the cumulative standard logistic distribution. One limitation is that the available software (e.g., **PROC NLMIXED** in SAS) is limited to the formulation of two-level models. (This does not preclude the inclusion of level-three covariates. In fact, we do not have to distinguish the level of hierarchy for fixed effects, such as covariates in the model.) Thus, we cannot estimate the variance and covariance components of the level-three model, such as $\mathrm{var}(u_{00k})$, $\mathrm{var}(u_{q1k})$, and $\mathrm{cov}(u_{00k}, u_{q1k})$ from Equation 10.17.

An additional limitation of the HLM/HGLM approach concerns the simultaneous modeling of several latent variables. Multiple latent variables can, in fact, be estimated by removing the intercept from the model and estimating random effects for predictors coded one or zero to differentiate groupings among the observed measures or items (see e.g., Cheong & Raudenbush, 2000; Kamata & Cheong, 2008; Raudenbush et al., 1991). However, the structure applied to the covariance matrix among these latent variables often is quite limited. Typically, the covariances would be left unstructured, indicating that each latent factor is correlated with every other latent factor and that there are no structural relations between them. The need to allow for such effects is demonstrated by the popularity of structural equation models that include regressions among latent variables. Both predictors and outcomes can be defined as latent variables and estimates of the effects can be obtained that are unbiased by measurement error.

Another limitation of the HLM/HGLM approach to incorporating latent variables in hierarchical models is that it imposes a highly structured model on the within-group and between-group variability of the observed measures. Specifically, the HLM/HGLM approach assumes that the group means of these measures vary randomly across groups but that the variation in the factor means entirely accounts for this variability. As will be discussed later in more detail, this assumption implies that (1) the same factor structure (e.g., dimensionality) holds both within-groups and between-groups; (2) the factor loadings (or discrimination parameters) are identical at both levels of the model; and (3) there are no group-mean differences in the observed measures that are not due to variation in the factor means (or other covariates included in the model). Although HLM/HGLM approach is a parsimonious and easily understood model, these restrictions may not always be consistent with theory or hold in practice. Ideally, these restrictions should be tested and relaxed when inconsistent with the data.

Given these limitations of the HLM/HGLM approach to the design and analysis of measurement models, we will conclude this section by discussing some additional alternative methods. One alternative is the Generalized, Linear, Latent and Mixed Model (GLLAMM) of Skrondal and Rabe-Hesketh (2004), an add-on program for STATA. This model allows for the estimation of factor loadings or discrimination parameters, the specification of structural relations between latent variables, and differences in the between-group and within-group model structure. This model is very general. However, because the estimation requires numerical integration, specifications including several latent variables and/or other random effects can be computationally intensive. In fact, GLLAMM allows us to formulate the same model used in the example data analyses based on Equations 10.16 and 10.17, along with discrimination parameters. In this example, however, we had eight random effects at level three of the model (seven random DIF and one school-level variance of latent abilities), and this number of random effects, unfortunately, makes numerical integration computationally impractical. One strategy to avoid such a large number of random effects is to simplify the model, for instance, by estimating a random DIF effect for one item at a time, which results in two random effects at level three but seven separate data analyses. This approach is much more feasible computationally; however, all random DIF effects except the one being investigated are constrained to be zero in each analysis. This may or may not be a reasonable assumption. It is hoped that improved computational algorithms for these types of model will be available in the future.

Another approach that has the same flexibility, with the exception that it is applicable only for linear models, is the two-level structural equation model (SEM). It is this approach that we discuss in greater detail in the next section, relaxing the assumptions of the HLM/HGLM approach discussed previously.

TWO-LEVEL STRUCTURAL EQUATION MODEL

SEM is a multivariate method that generalizes regression, path analysis, and factor analysis. At its core, SEM represents the integration of measurement models (e.g., factor analysis) with simultaneous equations (e.g., path analysis). It allows for the definition of multiple latent variables and structural relations among the latent variables. Many HLMs can be fit as single-level SEMs using a multivariate approach wherein the level-one observations are construed to be separate variables. This relation is well-known for growth models (Willett & Sayer, 1994) but also holds more generally (Bauer, 2003; Curran, 2003). As an alternative to the single-level approach, the covariance matrix of the measured variables can be modeled simultaneously at both the within- and between-group level in a two-level SEM (Goldstein & McDonald, 1988; McDonald & Goldstein, 1989; Muthén, 1994; Muthén & Satorra, 1995). To demonstrate this extension, we first describe the single-level (standard) SEM and then proceed to allow for an additional level of nesting, such as data obtained from children within classrooms or children within schools.

The measurement model of the linear SEM can be defined by the following equation:

$$\mathbf{y}_j = \mathbf{v} + \mathbf{\Lambda}\mathbf{\eta}_j + \mathbf{\varepsilon}_j. \tag{10.18}$$

This is effectively just a linear regression of the vector of n observed variables, $\mathbf{y}_j$, on the latent variables, $\mathbf{\eta}_j$ for person j. $\mathbf{y}_j$ is an $n \times 1$ vector that contains scores or responses to i measurement indicators, while $\mathbf{\eta}_j$ is a $P \times 1$ vector that contains latent scores for P latent factors. As such, the notation reads as follows: $\mathbf{v}$ are intercepts ($n \times 1$ vector), $\mathbf{\Lambda}$ are slopes (factor loadings) ($n \times P$ matrix), and $\mathbf{\varepsilon}_j$ are residuals ($n \times 1$ vector). For the previous illustrative data analysis with continuous measurement indicators (HLM formulation), $n = 3$ with 3 subscales and $P = 1$ with one latent factor (mathematics ability) to be measured. Of importance, the residuals, $\mathbf{\varepsilon}_j$, are assumed to be normally distributed with means of zero and $n \times n$ covariance matrix $\mathbf{\Theta}$ (often, but not necessarily, assumed to be diagonal, reflecting independent residuals or local independence).

The latent variable model of the SEM can then be written as

$$\mathbf{\eta}_j = \mathbf{\alpha} + \mathbf{B}\mathbf{\eta}_j + \mathbf{\zeta}_j. \tag{10.19}$$

This, too, is simply a linear regression; only this time, latent variables are regressed on other latent variables. The intercepts and slopes of this latent variable regression are given by $\mathbf{\alpha}$ ($P \times 1$ vector) and $\mathbf{B}$ ($P \times P$ matrix), respectively, and $\mathbf{\zeta}_j$ are the residuals ($P \times 1$ vector). The residuals are assumed to be normally distributed with means of zero and $P \times P$ covariance matrix, $\mathbf{\psi}$. These latent variable residuals also are assumed to be uncorrelated with the residuals from the measurement model. Note that it is not always necessary to include latent variable regressions in an SEM. If there is no latent variable regression in an SEM (for instance, in a confirmatory factor analysis), the **B** matrix is a null matrix. Then, the intercepts, α, are interpreted simply as factor means, and ψ is the covariance matrix of the latent factors. However, including latent variable regressions (via a non-null **B** matrix) allows the researcher to examine structural relations that are unbiased by measurement error, including causal chains involving several latent variables (e.g., indirect or mediated effects).

These equations and assumptions imply that the mean vector and covariance matrix of the measured variables are

$$\mu = \nu + \Lambda(I - B)^{-1}\alpha,$$

$$\Sigma = \Lambda(I - B)^{-1}\psi\left[(I - B)^{-1}\right]'\Lambda' + \Theta. \tag{10.20}$$

Here, **I** is a $P \times P$ identity matrix. If no latent variable regressions are present in the model (**B** is a null matrix), then these equations simplify considerably to

$$\mu = \nu + \Lambda\alpha,$$

$$\Sigma = \Lambda\psi\Lambda' + \Theta. \tag{10.21}$$

Readers may be familiar with these equations as giving the structure of a confirmatory factor model (see e.g., Bollen, 1989). To ease the exposition of the two-level SEM, it is the simpler model in Equation 10.21 that we will focus on here, though extensions to the full model in Equation 10.20 are straightforward.

In practice, maximum likelihood typically is used to find the estimates for the model parameters that most likely would have given rise to the observed data. In estimating the (single-level) SEM model, the log-likelihood is summed over individuals in the sample, requiring the assumption that the data vectors (responses to measurement indicators) for any two individuals are independent. Further detail on the single-level SEM may be sought from a number of excellent texts, including Bollen (1989), Kaplan (2000), or Kline (2005).

The two-level SEM differs from the foregoing single-level model in assuming that data are obtained from multiple individuals randomly sampled from each of many groups in the population. To account for the correlations among individuals within groups, it is assumed that the intercepts of the measured variables vary randomly over groups. The factor model can then be written as

$$y_{jk} = \nu_k + \Lambda_W \eta_{jk} + \varepsilon_{jk}, \tag{10.22}$$

where k indexes group, and the subscripting of the intercept vector indicates that intercepts vary randomly over groups. Within groups, the latent factors are assumed to be normally distributed with mean vector α and covariance matrix ψ_W, and the residuals are assumed to be normally distributed with means of zero and covariance matrix Θ_W. A key assumption is that these covariance matrices are homogeneous across all groups. As such, for any given group k (i.e., fixing v_k to a specific value), the (pooled) within-group covariance matrix is given by essentially the same equation as the standard SEM Equation 10.21, namely

$$\Sigma_W = \Lambda_W \psi_W \Lambda_W' + \Theta_W, \tag{10.23}$$

where the W subscript indicates "within-groups."

The key difference between the two-level SEM and the standard single-level SEM involves the additional component of variability due to the random intercepts. These intercepts are assumed to be independent of the other terms in Equation 10.22 and normally distributed across groups:

$$v_k \sim N(v, \Sigma_B). \tag{10.24}$$

Here, v captures the average intercepts of the indicators over groups, and the covariance matrix Σ_B refers to the between-groups covariance, or the covariance due to group mean (intercept) differences. The insight behind multilevel SEM is to impose an additional factor structure on this covariance matrix (Ansari, Jedidi, & Dube, 2002; Goldstein & McDonald, 1988; McDonald & Goldstein, 1989; Muthén, 1994; Muthén & Satorra, 1995). The resulting equation is

$$\Sigma_B = \Lambda_B \psi_B \Lambda_B' + \Theta_B. \tag{10.25}$$

Similar expressions could be given for the full multilevel SEM with latent variable regressions. Note that while the structure applied to the within- and between-groups covariance matrices appears very similar, the differential subscripting of the matrices by W or B, respectively, indicates that the parameter estimates or even the factor structure of the model can differ between the two parts of the model.

To summarize, under the assumption that the groups differ only in their intercepts, the total covariance matrix can be partitioned into a (pooled) within-groups component, reflecting associations observed within groups, and a between-groups component, reflecting associations observed between groups (due to the group mean differences). A model is fit simultaneously to these two covariance matrices. Sample estimates of Σ_W and Σ_B can be computed and provide sufficient statistics for estimating the model by an approximate maximum likelihood estimator (Muthén's maximum likelihood, or MUML; Muthén, 1995; Muthén & Satorra, 1995). More recently, a true full information maximum likelihood estimator also has become available in several SEM software programs.[18]

Relationship to the HLM Approach

Although superficially quite different, the two-level SEM and the HLM approach to fitting measurement models presented earlier in this chapter are, in fact, similar in many ways. Namely, both the two-level SEM and the HLM approach assume that the means of the observed variables vary randomly over groups. In the two-level SEM, it is the vector of intercepts that varies, whereas in the HLM approach, it is the vector of factor means. For example, the intercepts for every item can vary randomly in the SEM, but in HLM, only the factor mean scores can vary. The latter model is, in fact, more restrictive. This can be seen in equation form where the two-level SEM assumes that the group means for the measured variables, μ_k, can be expressed as

$$\mu_k = \nu_k + \Lambda_W \alpha. \tag{10.26}$$

This follows from the fact that in Equation 10.22 only the intercepts vary over groups (and the latent factors are distributed identically over groups, with mean vector α). By adding and subtracting the mean vector for ν_k, Equation 10.26 can then be rewritten as

$$\mu_k = \nu + \Lambda_W \alpha + (\nu_k - \nu), \tag{10.27}$$

where the covariance matrix for the last term, the random component, is Σ_B and has the structure given in Equation 10.25. The HLM approach assumes that this random component actually arises due to group differences in the factor means. Thus, in the HLM approach, the model for the group means can be written as

$$\mu_k = \nu + \Lambda_W \alpha + \Lambda_W (\alpha_k - \alpha), \tag{10.28}$$

where α_k is the vector of randomly varying factor means. Notice that this model differs from Equation 10.27 only in that the term $(\nu_k - \nu)$, reflecting random intercepts, has been replaced by the term $\Lambda_W (\alpha_k - \alpha)$, reflecting random factor means.

Since there are fewer latent factors than observed measures, the HLM approach reduces the number of random effects and results in a very parsimonious model. From Equation 10.28, we can derive the implied covariance matrix of μ_k in the HLM approach to be

$$\Sigma_B = \Lambda_W \psi_B \Lambda_W', \tag{10.29}$$

where ψ_B now is interpreted as the covariance matrix for the random factor means. By comparing Equations 10.25 and 10.29, we can see that the HLM approach assumes that the factor loading matrix (and hence factor structure) is equal at the within and between levels and that there is no residual variability at the between level (i.e., $\Lambda_B = \Lambda_W$ and $\Theta_B = 0$; Rabe-Hesketh, Skrondal, & Pickles, 2004). Thus, the HLM approach assumes a more restricted model than the SEM approach. Within the two-level SEM, one can fit a model with these same restrictions and test (via likelihood ratio) whether the restrictions are tenable for the data.

Two other advantages of the two-level SEM also are worth noting. One important advantage is that the factor loadings at both levels of the model can be estimated and need not be pre-specified by the analyst. This permits the estimation of two-level congeneric measurement models and measurement models including cross loadings, etc. Another advantage of the two-level SEM is that we can extend the preceding equations to allow for causal relations among latent factors at both the individual and group levels (similar to the single-level SEM). In contrast, the HLM approach typically assumes the covariance matrix among the latent factors to be unrestricted. We now demonstrate the features of the two-level SEM with our empirical example.

Example Analyses

To demonstrate some of the advantages of the two-level SEM, we now re-analyze the math scale data introduced earlier, comprised of the three sub-scale scores for mathematics proficiency. We used M*plus* to fit these models (Muthén & Muthén, 2004), although other SEM software, such as LISREL and EQS, is equally capable of fitting multilevel SEMs. The three-level HLM analysis of the data reported earlier, with equal residual variances across items represented by Equations 10.4a–10.4c, can be written as a two-level SEM with the following specifications

$$\mathbf{v} = \begin{bmatrix} 0 \\ \gamma_{100} \\ \gamma_{200} \end{bmatrix}; \; \Lambda_W = \Lambda_B = \begin{bmatrix} 1 \\ 1 \\ 1 \end{bmatrix}; \tag{10.30}$$

$$\alpha = \begin{bmatrix} \gamma_{000} \end{bmatrix}; \; \Theta_W = \sigma^2 \mathbf{I}; \; \Theta_B = 0; \; \psi_W = \begin{bmatrix} \tau_\pi \end{bmatrix}; \; \psi_B = \begin{bmatrix} \tau_\beta \end{bmatrix}.$$

Note that the symbols within these matrices correspond to the HLM notation used to report the earlier results and not the typical SEM notation. The fit of this model, as judged by the unrestricted model in HLM represented by Equations 10.8a–10.8f, was seen to be good. However, it should be noted that the unrestricted model in a two-level SEM differs from the unrestricted model in HLM. The unrestricted HLM estimated earlier included the three means and six unique variances/covariances in Σ_W plus one school-level variance, totaling 10 parameters. From the standpoint of the two-level SEM, this is not really an unrestricted model, as it assumes that all six unique elements in Σ_B can be explained by the single parameter τ_β. That is, the mean and covariance structure for the three subscales implied by the unrestricted HLM (see notation defined for Equations 10.8d through 10.8f) are

$$\mu = \begin{bmatrix} \gamma_{000} \\ \gamma_{000} + \gamma_{100} \\ \gamma_{000} + \gamma_{200} \end{bmatrix}, \quad \Sigma_W = \Delta = \begin{bmatrix} \delta_{11} & & \\ \delta_{21} & \delta_{22} & \\ \delta_{31} & \delta_{32} & \delta_{33} \end{bmatrix},$$

$$\Sigma_B = \tau_\beta J_3 = \begin{bmatrix} \tau_\beta & & \\ \tau_\beta & \tau_\beta & \\ \tau_\beta & \tau_\beta & \tau_\beta \end{bmatrix}.$$

(10.31)

Thus, this "unrestricted" model actually imposes a highly restrictive structure on the between-groups covariance matrix. In contrast, in the unrestricted two-level SEM, Σ_W and Σ_B both are estimated freely (each including six unique and unconstrained elements), along with the means for the three measures, totaling 15 parameters for this data. The unrestricted model for the three subscales in the two-level SEM is then

$$\mu = \begin{bmatrix} \mu_1 \\ \mu_2 \\ \mu_3 \end{bmatrix}, \quad \Sigma_W = \begin{bmatrix} \sigma_{W11} & & \\ \sigma_{W21} & \sigma_{W22} & \\ \sigma_{W31} & \sigma_{W32} & \sigma_{W33} \end{bmatrix}, \quad \Sigma_B = \begin{bmatrix} \sigma_{B11} & & \\ \sigma_{B21} & \sigma_{B22} & \\ \sigma_{B31} & \sigma_{B32} & \sigma_{B33} \end{bmatrix}. \quad (10.32)$$

Using the truly unrestricted two-level SEM for comparison, the model in Equation 10.30 is, in fact, rejected with $\chi^2(9) = 85.62$, $p < .001$. The M*plus* syntax for this analysis is provided in Appendix C-1.

The next model we consider is nearly identical to Equation 10.30 but relaxes the assumption of equality for the factor loadings:

$$v = \begin{bmatrix} 0 \\ \gamma_{100} \\ \gamma_{200} \end{bmatrix}; \quad \Lambda_W = \Lambda_B = \begin{bmatrix} 1 \\ \lambda_2 \\ \lambda_3 \end{bmatrix};$$

(10.33)

$$\alpha = \begin{bmatrix} \gamma_{000} \end{bmatrix}; \quad \Theta_W = \sigma^2 I; \quad \Theta_B = 0; \quad \psi_W = \begin{bmatrix} \tau_\pi \end{bmatrix}; \quad \psi_B = \begin{bmatrix} \tau_\beta \end{bmatrix}.$$

In this model, we clearly see that the two-level SEM allows for both differences in intercepts (difficulty) and factor loadings (discrimination) across the measured variables. Freeing these two factor loadings results in a significant improvement in model fit relative to the model in Equation 10.31, $\chi^2(2) = 7.61$, $p = .022$. This improvement in fit is not sufficient to result in a good fitting model overall. Relative to the unrestricted model, the model in Equation 10.33 still is rejected: $\chi^2(7) = 78.01$, $p < .001$. The M*plus* syntax for this analysis is provided in Appendix C-2.

We next estimated a model that allowed for the estimation of different factor loadings and residual variances within- and between-groups:

$$\mathbf{v} = \begin{bmatrix} 0 \\ \gamma_{100} \\ \gamma_{200} \end{bmatrix}; \ \boldsymbol{\Lambda}_W = \begin{bmatrix} 1 \\ \lambda_{W2} \\ \lambda_{W3} \end{bmatrix}; \ \boldsymbol{\Lambda}_B = \begin{bmatrix} 1 \\ \lambda_{B2} \\ \lambda_{B3} \end{bmatrix};$$

$$\boldsymbol{\alpha} = \begin{bmatrix} \gamma_{000} \end{bmatrix}; \ \boldsymbol{\Theta}_W = \sigma_W^2 \mathbf{I}; \ \boldsymbol{\Theta}_B = \sigma_B^2 \mathbf{I}; \ \boldsymbol{\psi}_W = \begin{bmatrix} \tau_\pi \end{bmatrix}; \ \boldsymbol{\psi}_B = \begin{bmatrix} \tau_\beta \end{bmatrix}.$$

$$(10.34)$$

By removing the equality constraints on $\boldsymbol{\Lambda}_W$ and $\boldsymbol{\Lambda}_B$, we are allowing the within-groups relation between the factor and observed variables to differ from the between-groups relation between the factor and the observed variable group means. The addition of residual variance at the group level admits the possibility that not all of the variability in the group means is due to differences in the common factor mean. Some group-level variance is specific to each measured variable. The addition of the three new parameters in this model resulted in a dramatic improvement in model fit relative to the model in Equation 10.34: $\chi^2(3) = 72.07$, $p < .001$. Furthermore, the model in Equation 10.34 could not be rejected by comparison to the unrestricted model: $\chi^2(4) = 5.94$, $p = .204$, indicating that this model adequately recovers the relations between the three observed measures at both the student and school levels. The estimates of the factor loadings and variance components from this model are reported in Table 10.10. The M*plus* syntax is provided in Appendix C-3.

In fact, Table 10.10 shows that although this model fits better than the original HLM, the differences in the estimates are rather minor. The estimated factor loadings are all close to one, and the residual variance for the random intercepts, though significantly different from zero, is small (.061). The within-schools factor variance estimate is trivially larger (3.041, relative to 2.998 in the HLM model), and the between-schools factor variance estimate shows a somewhat larger difference (.718, relative to .683 in the HLM model). Given the high power of the current analyses, these differences were statistically significant but might not be substantively meaningful. In other applications, larger differences between the two approaches could occur.

TABLE 10.10 Parameter Estimates and Standard Errors for Two-Level SEM in Equation (10.34)

Parameter	Estimate	Standard error
λ_{W2}	1.026	.027
λ_{W3}	0.964	.026
λ_{B2}	0.950	.093
λ_{B3}	0.932	.092
σ_W^2	2.653	.046
σ_B^2	0.061	.016
τ_π	3.041	.135
τ_β	0.718	.217

Limitations of the Two-Level SEM

Thus, we see that the two-level SEM offers some additional flexibility for fitting hierarchical models with latent variables. Our example illustrated some of these added features but not others, for instance, the ability to model causal relations among latent factors (see Liang & Bentler, 2004, for an example and useful discussion of the full multilevel SEM). The two-level SEM approach does, however, have its own limitations. The commonly used MUML (Muthén maximum likelihood) estimator requires complete data on the observed indicators of the latent factors and makes the assumption that the observed variables are continuous-normal (to construct the pooled within covariance matrix). More recently, some SEM software has introduced a full-information maximum likelihood estimator that can accommodate missing data and/or other scale types. For other scale types, however, numerical integration methods that become infeasible for large models with many random effects are implemented.

A final limitation applies to both the two-level SEM and the HLM approach equally. Generally, both approaches assume that the measured variables differ only in their intercepts (item difficulties) across groups. That is, there are no random slopes (item discriminations) in the models. More ideally, the full range of HLMs presently fit to observed outcome variables also would be available for latent outcome variables. For instance, the prediction of one latent variable, achievement, by another latent variable, peer acceptance, might have a random slope that, in turn, depends on a group-level variable, classroom climate. While some SEM software (e.g., M*plus*; Muthén & Muthén, 2004) now permits the estimation of random slopes in latent variable models, this requires numerical integration, so the number of latent variables or random effects is limited in practice. Bayesian approaches (e.g., Markov Chain Monte Carlo methods; Ansari et al., 2002) may prove more flexible, but these approaches bring their own difficulties (e.g., long computing times, difficulty determining convergence). Thus, although many advances have been made in the fitting of hierarchical models with latent variables, much work still remains to be done.

CONCLUSION

In this chapter, we presented multilevel measurement models from the HLM, HGLM, and multilevel SEM perspectives. While traditional measurement models, such as CTT and IRT models, do not take into account the dependency of measures within groups, such as schools, we demonstrated the possibilities of modeling such a nested data structure in measurement models, both for continuous and dichotomous measurement indicators. Also, we presented example data analyses to model different classical test theory assumptions to test their fit to the data with continuous measurement indicators, as well as a model with dichotomous measurement indicators that includes a covariate and additional variance-covariance components in the group-level of the model. Although our discussion was limited to a unidimensional case, similar modeling can be employed for multidimensional cases (e.g., Cheong & Raudenbush, 2000; Kamata & Cheong, 2007). Also, our discussion indicated there are many issues that need further improvement, including computational issues for three-level models with item discrimination parameters for categorical measurement indicators and models with random item discrimination parameters. It is our hope that further advancement will be made in these areas.

NOTES

1. A computer generated data set and supplemental document with syntax for HLM and M*plus* can be obtained through the book web site. The data set on the web is similar in design but not the same as the one used in this chapter for data security reasons.
2. These values could be reproduced by formulating a two-level HLM where the level-one units are subscales and the level-two units are students by taking the ratio of the level-one error variance to the total error variance. (For details, see Miyazaki & Skaggs, in press).
3. There are other ways to parameterize the effect of subscales. For example, see Cheong & Raudenbush (2000) and Kamata & Cheong (2007).
4. Some of the assumptions can be relaxed as we will show in the section of Measurement Models by Multivariate 3-level Model.
5. The HLM syntax for this analysis is provided in Appendix A-1.
6. When this formula is applied to the results for a two-level measurement model ignoring the nested data structure, $\alpha = .798$, will be reproduced (see Miyazaki & Skaggs, in press) in HLM output.

7. Note that the average had to be taken because of the different number of student (J_k). If J_ks were constant, the average was unnecessary, as we did in Equation 10.5.
8. In HLM software (Raudenbush, Bryk, Cheong, Congdon, & Du Toit, 2004), the only option available for multivariate hierarchical linear models is full maximum likelihood.
9. As we will see later, this is not truly an unrestricted model from the multilevel confirmatory factor analysis perspective.
10. Thus, this unrestricted model is not completely unrestricted and will be considered again from a Structural Equation Modeling perspective later in this chapter.
11. HLM syntax for this analysis is provided in Appendix A-2. This syntax produces results for the following two models as well.
12. Extensions to models for polytomously scored items also are shown in Rijmen et al. (2003), Shin (2003), and Williams and Beretvas (2006).
13. This equation is expressed as a combined form with simplified subscripts to highlight its equivalency to the Rasch model. HGLM formulation will be presented later in this section
14. See Beretvas and Kamata (2005) and Kamata (2001) for more details about the relationship between HGLM and the Rasch model.
15. The HLM syntax for this analysis is provided in Appendix B-1.
16. See, for example, Holland and Wainer (1993) and Zumbo (1999) for detailed introduction to DIF.
17. The HLM syntax for this analysis is provided in Appendix B-2.
18. For many years, the MUML estimator was the only estimator available in conventional software for estimating two-level SEMs. This estimator is exact if the number of individuals in each cluster is the same (i.e., balanced) but approximate otherwise. Given the more recent addition of true ML estimation to conventional software (even for unbalanced designs), it is hard to imagine an application where MUML would now be preferable to ML.

ACKNOWLEDGEMENTS

Authors started this work when they were involved in the 2004–2005 program on Latent Variable Models in the Social Sciences (LVSS) at the Statistical and Applied Mathematical Sciences Institute (SAMSI), Research Triangle Park, NC. Authors are thankful for the opportunities and support from the SAMSI.

REFERENCES

Ansari, A., Jedidi, K., & Dube, L. (2002). Heterogeneous factor analysis models: A Bayesian approach. *Psychometrika, 67,* 49–78.
Bauer, D. J. (2003). Estimating multilevel linear models as structural equation models. *Journal of Educational and Behavioral Statistics, 28,* 135–167.

Beretvas, S. N., & Kamata, A. (2005). The multilevel measurement model: Introduction to the special issue. *Journal of Applied Measurement, 6,* 247–254.

Bollen, K. A. (1989). *Structural equations with latent variables.* New York: John Wiley & Sons.

Cheong, Y. F. (2006). Analysis of school context effects on differential item functioning using hierarchical generalized linear models. *International Journal of Testing, 6,* 57–79.

Cheong, Y. F., & Raudenbush, S. W. (2000). Measurement and structural models for children's problem behaviors. *Psychological Methods, 5,* 477–495.

Crocker, L., & Algina, J. (1986). *Introduction to classical and modern test theory.* Fort Worth, TX: Harcourt.

Curran, P. J. (2003). Have multilevel models been structural equation models all along? *Multivariate Behavioral Research, 38,* 529–569.

Embretson, S. E., & Reise, S. P. (2000). *Item response theory for psychologists.* Mahwah, NJ: Lawrence Erlbaum.

Goldstein, H. I., & McDonald, R. P. (1988). A general model for the analysis of multilevel data. *Psychometrika, 53,* 455–467.

Holland, P. W., & Wainer, H. (1993). *Differential item functioning.* Hillsdale, NJ: Lawrence Erlbaum.

Hox. J. (2005). *Multilevel analysis: Techniques and applications.* Mahwah, NJ: Lawrence Erlbaum.

Kamata, A. (2001). Item analysis by the hierarchical generalized linear model. *Journal of Educational Measurement, 38,* 79–93.

Kamata, A., & Bauer, D. J. (2008). A note on the relationship between factor analytic and item response theory models. *Structural Equation Modeling: A Multidisciplinary Journal, 15,* 136–193.

Kamata, A. Chaimongkol, S., Genc, E., & Bilir, M. K. (2005, April). *Random-effect differential item functioning across group unites by the hierarchical generalized linear model.* Paper presented at the annual meeting of American Educational Research Association, Montreal, Canada.

Kamata, A., & Cheong, Y. F. (2007). Multilevel Rasch models. In M. von Davier & C. H. Carstensen (Eds.), *Multivariate and mixture distribution Rasch models: Extensions and applications* (pp. 271–232). New York: Springer.

Kaplan, D. (2000). *Structural equation modeling: Foundations and extensions.* Thousand Oaks, CA: Sage Publications.

Kline, R. B. (2005). *Principles and practice of structural equation modeling* (2nd ed.). New York: Guilford Press.

Liang, J., Bentler, P. M. (2004). An EM algorithm for fitting two-level structural equation models. *Psychometrika, 69,* 101–122.

Long, J. S. (1997). *Regression models for categorical and limited dependent variables.* Thousand Oaks, CA: Sage Publications.

Lord, F. M., & Novic, M. R. (1968). *Statistical theories of mental test scores.* Reading, MA: Addison-Wesley.

McCoach, D. B., & Black, A. C. (2008). Evaluation of model fit and adequacy. In A. A. O'Connell and D. B. McCoach (Eds.), *Multilevel modeling of educational data* (pp. 245–271). Charlotte, NC: Information Age Publishing.

382 A. KAMATA, D.J. BAUER, and Y. MIYAZAKI

McDonald, R. P., & Goldstein, H. (1989). Balanced versus unbalanced designs for linear structural relations in two-level data. *British Journal of Mathematical and Statistical Psychology, 42,* 215–232.

Miyazaki, Y. (2005). Some links between classical and modern test theory via the two-level hierarchical generarized linear model. *Journal of Applied Measurement, 6*(3), 289–310.

Miyazaki, Y., & Skaggs, G. (in press). Linking classical test theory and two-level hierarchical linear models. *Journal of Applied Measurement.*

Muthén, B. O. & Satorra, A. (1995). Complex sample data in structural equation modeling. *Sociological Methodology, 25,* 267–316.

Muthén, B. O. (1994). Multilevel covariance structure analysis. *Sociological Methods & Research, 22,* 376–398.

Muthén, L. K., & Muthén, B. O. (2004). *Mplus User's Guide* (3rd ed.). Los Angeles, CA: Muthén & Muthén.

O'Connell, A. A., Goldstein, J., Rogers, H. J., & Peng, C. Y. J. (2008). Multilevel logistic models for dichotomous and ordinal data. In A. A. O'Connell and D. B. McCoach (Eds.), *Multilevel modeling of educational data* (pp. 199–242). Charlotte, NC: Information Age Publishing.

Rabe-Hesketh, S., Skrondal, A., & Pickles, A. (2004). Generalized multilevel structural equation modelling. *Psychometrika 69,* 167–190.

Raudenbush, S., Bryk, A., Cheong, Y. F., Congdon, R., & Du Toit, M. (2004). *HLM 6: hierarchical linear and nonlinear modeling.* Chicago: Scientific Software International.

Raudenbush, S. W., & Bryk, A. S. (2002). *Hierarchical linear models: applications and data analysis methods* (2nd ed.). Thousand Oaks, CA: Sage.

Raudenbush, S. W., Rowan, B., & Kang, S. J. (1991). A multilevel, multivariate model for studying school climate with estimation via the EM algorithm and application to U.S. high-school data. *Journal of Educational Statistics, 16*(4). 295–330.

Rijmen, F., & Briggs, D. (2004). Multiple person dimensions and latent item predictors. In P. De Boeck, & M. Wilson (Eds.), *Explanatory item response models: A generalized linear and nonlinear approach.* (pp. 247–265). New York: Springer.

Rijmen, F., Tuerlinckx, F., De Boeck, P., & Kuppens, P. (2003). A nonlinear mixed model framework for item response theory. *Psychological Methods, 8,* 185–205.

Rijmen, F., Tuerlinckx, F., Meulders, M., Smits, D. J. M., & Balazs, K. (2005). Mixed model estimation methods for the Rasch model. *Journal of Applied Measurement, 6,* 273–288.

Roberts, J. K., & Herrington, R. (2005). Demonstration of software programs for estimating multilevel measurement model parameters. *Journal of Applied Measurement, 6,* 255–272.

Shin, S. (2003). *A polytomous nonlinear mixed model for item analysis.* Unpublished doctoral dissertation, University of Texas at Austin, Austin, TX.

Skrondal, A., & Rabe-Hesketh, S. (2004). *Generalized latent variable modeling: Multilevel, longitudinal, and structural equation models.* Boca Raton: Chapman & Hall/CRC.

Takane, Y., & de Leeuw, J. (1987). On the relationship between item response theory and factor analysis of discretized variables. *Psychometrika, 52,* 393–408.

Thum, Y. M. (1997). Hierarchical linear models for multivariate behavioral data. *Journal of Educational and Behavioral Statistics, 22,* 77–108.

Traub, R. (1994). *Reliability for the Social Sciences.* Thousand Oaks, CA: Sage.

Willett, J. B., & Sayer, A. G. (1994). Using covariance structure analysis to detect correlates and predictors of individual change over time. *Psychological Bulletin, 116*, 363–381.

Williams, N. J., & Beretvas, S. N. (2006). DIF identification using HGLM for polytomous items. *Applied Psychological Measurement, 30*, 22–42.

Zumbo, B. D. (1999). *A handbook on the theory and methods for differential item functioning: Logistic regression modeling as a unitary framework for binary and Likert-type (ordinal) item scores.* Ottawa, ON: Directorate of Human Resources Research and Evaluation, Department of National Defense.

APPENDIX A

HLM syntax with 3 continuous measurement indicators

1. Univariate Analysis

```
#WHLM CMD FILE FOR hlm3.mdm
nonlin:n
numit:100
stopval:0.0000010000
level1:MATH10_3=INTRCPT1+D2+D3+RANDOM
level2:INTRCPT1=INTRCPT2+random/
level3:INTRCPT2=INTRCPT3+random/
level2:D2=INTRCPT2/
level3:INTRCPT2=INTRCPT3/
level2:D3=INTRCPT2/
level3:INTRCPT2=INTRCPT3/
fixtau2:3
fixtau3:3
accel:5
level1weight:none
level2weight:none
level3weight:none
varianceknown:none
hypoth:n
resfil1:n
resfil2:n
resfil3:n
constrain:N
laplace:N,0
graphgammas:C:\HLM Book Chapter\three level model\grapheq.geq
lvr-beta:n
title:3 level CTT model
output:C:\HLM Book Chapter\three level model\ctt hlm3.txt
fulloutput:n
fishertype:2
```

2. Multivariate Analyses

```
#WHLM CMD FILE FOR mctt_31.mdm
numit:100
stopval:0.0000010000
level1:MATH10_3-INTRCPT1+D2+D3+RANDOM
level2:INTRCPT1=INTRCPT2+random
level3:INTRCPT2=INTRCPT3+random
level2:D2=INTRCPT2
level3:INTRCPT2=INTRCPT3
level2:D3=INTRCPT2
level3:INTRCPT2=INTRCPT3
fixtau2:3
fixtau3:3
accel:5
hypoth:n
graphgammas:C:\HLM Book Chapter\M10c_3var\MHLM3\grapheq.geq
r_e_model:het11var
title:Multivariate 3 level CTT model
output:C:\HLM Book Chapter\M10c_3var\MHLM3\mctt_31.txt
fulloutput:n
```

APPENDIX B

HLM syntax for 22 dichotomous measurement indicators

1. Unconditional Model

```
#WHLM CMD FILE FOR Ch12_2.mdm
nonlin:binomial
microit:50
macroit:200
stopmicro:0.0000010000
stopmacro:0.0001000000
level1:RESPON=INTRCPT1+I4+I6+I7+I8+I10+I14+I16+I17+I19+I21+I
       25+I26+I28+I29+I30+I31+I33+I35+I36+I38+I39+RANDOM
level2:INTRCPT1=INTRCPT2+random/
level3:INTRCPT2=INTRCPT3+random/
level2:I4=INTRCPT2/
level3:INTRCPT2=INTRCPT3/
level2:I6=INTRCPT2/
level3:INTRCPT2=INTRCPT3/
level2:I7=INTRCPT2/
level3:INTRCPT2=INTRCPT3/
```

.
.
.

```
level2:I39=INTRCPT2/
level3:INTRCPT2=INTRCPT3/
fixsigma2:1.000000
fixtau2:3
fixtau3:3
accel:5
level1weight:none
level2weight:none
level3weight:none
varianceknown:none
hypoth:n
resfil1:n
resfil2:n
resfil3:n
constrain:N
laplace:N,50
graphgammas:F:\Chapter12\Ch12_2a.geq
lvr-beta:n
title:no title
output:F:\Chapter12\Ch12_2a.out
fulloutput:n
fishertype:2
```

2. Model with Level-2 Covariate and Its Random Effect at Level-3

```
#WHLM CMD FILE FOR Ch12_2.mdm
nonlin:binomial
microit:50
macroit:200
stopmicro:0.0000010000
stopmacro:0.0001000000
level1:RESPON=INTRCPT1+I4+I6+I7+I8+I10+I14+I16+I17+I19+I21+I
      25+I26+I28+I29+I30+I31+I33+I35+I36+I38+I39+RANDOM
level2:INTRCPT1=INTRCPT2+LUNCH+random/
level3:INTRCPT2=INTRCPT3+random/
level3:LUNCH=INTRCPT3/
level2:I4=INTRCPT2/
level3:INTRCPT2=INTRCPT3/
level2:I6=INTRCPT2+LUNCH/
level3:INTRCPT2=INTRCPT3/
level3:GROUP=INTRCPT3+random/
```

```
level2:I7=INTRCPT2/
level3:INTRCPT2=INTRCPT3/



.
.
.



level2:I39=INTRCPT2/
level3:INTRCPT2=INTRCPT3/
fixsigma2:1.000000
fixtau2:3
fixtau3:3
accel:5
level1weight:none
level2weight:none
level3weight:none
varianceknown:none
hypoth:n
resfill1:n
resfil2:n
resfil3:n
constrain:N
laplace:N,50
graphgammas:F:\Chapter12\Ch12_2b.geq
lvr-beta:n
title:no title
output:F:\Chapter12\Ch12_2b.out
fulloutput:n
fishertype:2
```

APPENDIX C

M*plus* syntax for 2-level SEM with 3 continuous measurement indicators

1. Model with Unit Factor Loadings

```
TITLE: CTT one factor, two levels, unit loadings,
       homoscedastic;
DATA: FILE IS Ch12_3.dat;
VARIABLE:
NAMES ARE student school lunch i1-i21 area1 area2 area3;
USEVARIABLES school area1 area2 area3;
CLUSTER IS school;
```

```
MISSING IS .;
ANALYSIS:
TYPE = MEANSTRUCTURE TWOLEVEL;
ESTIMATOR = ML;
MODEL:
%BETWEEN%
math_b by area1@1;
math_b by area2@1 (1);
math_b by area3@1 (2);
area1@0 area2@0 area3@0;
[area1*5 area2*5 area3*5];
math_b*.7;
%WITHIN%
math_w by area1@1;
math_w by area2@1 (1);
math_w by area3@1 (2);
math_w*3;
area1*2.7 (3);
area2 (3);
area3 (3);
```

2. Model with Heterogeneous Loadings ($\Lambda_W = \Lambda_B$)

```
TITLE: CTT one factor, two levels, free loadings,
       homoscedastic;
DATA: FILE IS Ch12_3.dat;
VARIABLE:
NAMES ARE student school lunch i1-i21 area1 area2 area3;
USEVARIABLES school area1 area2 area3;
CLUSTER IS school;
MISSING IS .;
ANALYSIS:
TYPE = MEANSTRUCTURE TWOLEVEL;
ESTIMATOR = ML;
MODEL:
%BETWEEN%
math_b by area1@1;
math_b by area2*1 (1);
math_b by area3*1 (2);
area1@0 area2@0 area3@0;
[area1*5 area2*5 area3*5];
math_b*.7;
%WITHIN%
math_w by area1@1;
```

```
math_w by area2*1 (1);
math_w by area3*1 (2);
math_w*3;
area1*2.7 (3);
area2 (3);
area3 (3);
```

3. Model with Heterogeneous Loadings ($\Lambda_W \neq \Lambda_B$)

```
TITLE: CTT one factor, two levels, within and between
       loadings and intercepts;
DATA: FILE IS Ch12_3.dat;
VARIABLE:
NAMES ARE student school lunch i1-i21 area1 area2 area3;
USEVARIABLES school area1 area2 area3;
CLUSTER IS school;
MISSING IS .;
ANALYSIS:
TYPE = MEANSTRUCTURE TWOLEVEL;
ESTIMATOR = ML;
MODEL:
%BETWEEN%
math_b by area1@1;
math_b by area2*1;
math_b by area3*1;
!M10MCB@0 M10MCD@0 M10MCE@0;
area1 (1);
area2 (1);
area3 (1);
[area1*5 area2*5 area3*5];
math_b*.7;
%WITHIN%
math_w by area1@1;
math_w by area2*1;
math_w by area3*1;
math_w*3;
area1*2.7 (2);
area2 (2);
area3 (2);
```

PART IV

MASTERING THE TECHNIQUE

CHAPTER 11

REPORTING RESULTS FROM MULTILEVEL ANALYSES

**John M. Ferron, Kristin Y. Hogarty, Robert F. Dedrick,
Melinda R. Hess, John D. Niles, and Jeffrey D. Kromrey**

OVERVIEW

In recent years there have been dramatic advances in the field of multilevel modeling. These advances, coupled with the addition of new features and options for statistical output in current multilevel software programs such as HLM, SAS PROC MIXED and MLwiN (Roberts & McLeod, 2008), have posed challenges to researchers attempting to communicate the results of these models to audiences with varying levels of statistical and research expertise. Unlike the area of structural equation modeling for which recommendations and guidelines have been presented to enhance the communication value of the results (Boomsma, 2000; Hoyle & Panter, 1995; McDonald & Ho, 2002; Raykov, Tomer, & Nesselroade, 1991), the field of multilevel modeling has provided few guidelines for conveying research findings.

A recent review of the reporting practices of articles from education and related journals (Ferron et al., 2006) supports the need for guidelines. In this review, Ferron et al. analyzed 98 multilevel modeling articles from 19

Multilevel Modeling of Educational Data, pages 391–426
Copyright © 2008 by Information Age Publishing

journals with an educational or related focus (e.g., *American Educational Research Journal, Child Development*) to determine how authors addressed the following issues: (a) model development and specification; (b) data considerations including distributional assumptions, outliers, measurement error, power, and missing data; (c) estimation procedures; and (d) hypothesis testing and statistical inference including inferences about variance parameters and fixed effects. Overall, the results indicated that in many cases not enough information was presented to allow readers to fully interpret the results or replicate the analyses. Additionally, the use of different terminology such as variance estimates versus random effects and the use of terms (e.g., standardized) left undefined by authors present challenges to understanding the results of multilevel analyses.

This chapter offers suggestions for *what* to present when reporting results of multilevel analyses and options for *how* to present these results using text, tables, and figures. The assumption underlying these guidelines is that the organization and presentation of multilevel models and their results have the potential to critically impact the utility and understanding of multilevel research. These guidelines reflect the realities that are present in most current publishing opportunities (e.g., space restrictions in paper journals); although, with the advent of online publication, issues such as length of articles and the number of illustrations and tables may be less critical. Because a single chapter cannot include guidelines for every type of multilevel model, it is important to clarify that the focus of this chapter is primarily on what might be termed "traditional" multilevel models. This chapter considers linear models of continuous outcomes where the random effects are assumed normally distributed. This allows consideration of two-level applications where individuals are nested in contexts, such as students nested in schools, and applications where observations are nested within individuals, such as growth curve models. Models in which the outcome is represented by binary, count, or ordinal data are not considered (see O'Connell, Goldstein, Rogers, & Peng, 2008, and Raudenbush & Bryk, 2002, for discussions of these types of applications), nor are multilevel structural equation models (SEM; Muthén & Muthén, 1998–2004) or multilevel item response models (Kamata, 2001; Kamata, Bauer, & Miyazaki, 2008).

As with any set of guidelines, flexibility is needed to take into account the requirements of the publication outlet and the intended audience. For example, a novice reader of multilevel studies may be able to interpret graphs of a growth curve model more easily than a complex equation with coefficients. Reactions to these guidelines by journal editors and researchers experienced in multilevel modeling can be used to further refine criteria for reporting multilevel results.

The organization of this chapter parallels the sections and subsections of many journal articles: (a) research questions, (b) literature review, (c) method, (d) results, and (e) discussion. Each section of the journal article can play a role in enhancing the interpretability and value of results from multilevel studies. The first section of this chapter presents some common research questions addressed through the use of two-level models. Following this section, we discuss how the literature review might be used to provide a rationale for multilevel analyses, including advantages and disadvantages of this approach. The method section consists of five subsections and offers suggestions for communicating information about: (a) participants, including the number at each level of analysis, sampling procedures, and missing data; (b) type and limitations of the research design; (c) variables, including how the variables were coded and procedures used to address measurement quality; (d) models, including the use of equations for model specification, the centering of predictors, the process for defining the model, and the approach used to evaluate model integrity; and (e) estimation and inference, including technical details of the algorithms for parameter estimation and approaches used for making inferences about variance parameters, fixed effects, and level-one coefficients. The results section consists of two subsections and offers guidelines for presenting: (a) preliminary results on data quality and (b) results directly tied to the research questions. The discussion section presents the core elements that should be part of the discussion in any research study and identifies some elements that are unique to multilevel modeling. Finally, a list of questions that generally should be answerable by the reader of a well-written report of a multilevel modeling application is provided in the form of a checklist. This checklist summarizes the guidelines and suggestions presented in this chapter.

RESEARCH QUESTIONS

As a starting point for communicating the purpose of the study and the appropriateness of using a multilevel approach, the researcher needs to clearly state the questions under investigation. Once these questions have been stated, the statistical models that are aligned with these questions, along with their corresponding assumptions, can be specified. Results linked to these models and ultimately to the research questions then can be presented.

There are a variety of multilevel designs focusing on different types of research questions. With these different research questions come correspondingly different types of results, including preliminary results checking assumptions and those focused directly on the research questions, as well as multiple formats for presenting results.

For example, multilevel designs in which individuals are measured within some larger unit, such as a classroom, often address questions related to how much of the variability in an outcome is associated with within- and between-group differences, as well as the extent to which various within- and between-group factors account for this variability. In contrast, multilevel designs in which individuals are measured repeatedly over time often address questions related to the form of change (e.g., linear, nonlinear), variation in growth parameters (e.g., intercept and slope), and factors associated with the variation in the growth parameters (e.g., gender). Table 11.1 presents examples of some research questions addressed in two-level multilevel studies and the types of data structures associated with these questions.

LITERATURE REVIEW

In research reports of multilevel analyses, the literature review should describe how the multilevel nature of the research problem under investigation has been addressed in the past. For example, has past research dealt with the unit of analysis issue by ignoring the independence assumption or by aggregating nested data within units? To provide a connection with the current application of multilevel modeling, relevant methodological issues addressed in prior research should be discussed. Through this discussion, the rationale of using a multilevel approach to address the specific questions under investigation can be provided along with the advantages and disadvantages of the multilevel approach. Controversies that are being discussed in the multilevel literature that are relevant to the current investigation can be presented (e.g., use of pseudo R^2 values, use of Akaike's Information Criterion [AIC] and the Bayes Information Criterion [BIC] for model selection). The author of the literature review also can clarify whether the current multilevel application is a replication of a previous study, an extension of prior research, or a new line of inquiry.

The literature review also should foreshadow some of the methodological decisions that are made in the multilevel modeling phase of the study. For example, if some or all of the predictors in the models were selected based on *a priori* considerations (i.e., theory or previous research versus exploratory analyses and tests of significance), the connection with the previous research should be explicit. Similarly, if past research and/or theory were used to justify decisions about other modeling issues such as the variance-covariance structures or centering of predictors, these links need to be made clear. Boote and Beile (2005) have provided additional criteria in developing the literature review for research studies in general; these include providing a rationale for what previous literature to include or exclude and a discussion of the practical and theoretical significance of the research problem.

TABLE 11.1   Examples of Research Questions Addressed by Two-Level Multilevel Designs

General question	Applied question
	Individuals nested within units
1. How much of the variation in an outcome is there within- and between-groups?	How much of the variation in eighth-grade mathematics achievement is within schools? How much is between schools?
2. What is the proportional reduction in the within-group variance when a within-group predictor is added to the model?	What proportion of the within-group variation in eighth-grade mathematics achievement is associated with students' seventh-grade mathematics achievement?
3. What is the relationship between a selected within-group factor and an outcome?	What is the relationship between students' seventh-grade mathematics achievement and students' eighth-grade mathematics achievement?
4. Does the relationship between a selected within-group factor and an outcome vary across the level two units?	Does the relationship between students' seventh-grade mathematics achievement and students' eighth-grade mathematics achievement vary across schools?
5. What is the proportional reduction in the between-group variance in a level two parameter (i.e., intercept) when a between-group predictor is added to the model?	What proportion of the variability in average eighth-grade mathematics achievement is associated with school SES?
6. What is the relationship between a selected between-group factor and an outcome?	What is the effect of a school mathematics instructional program on average school mathematics achievement for eighth graders?
7. To what extent is the relationship between a selected within-group factor and an outcome moderated by a selected between-group factor?	To what extent is the relationship between students' seventh-grade mathematics achievement and students' eighth-grade mathematics achievement moderated by the school's mathematics program?
	Observations nested within individuals
8. Is the functional form of individual change linear, quadratic, or cubic?	What is the functional form of individual change in reading achievement from grades 1 to 5?
9. To what extent do individuals vary in initial status on an outcome?	To what extent do first graders differ in their initial status in reading achievement?
10. To what extent do individuals vary in their rate of change on an outcome?	To what extent does the rate of change in reading achievement of elementary students vary across individuals?
11. What is the relationship between selected individual characteristics and initial status?	To what extent do boys and girls differ in their initial reading achievement?
12. What is the relationship between selected individual characteristics and rate of change?	To what extent do boys and girls differ in their rate of reading achievement change?
13. What is the relationship between individuals' initial status and their rate of change?	What is the relationship between initial reading achievement and the rate of change in reading achievement?

METHOD

Participants

Issues of sample size, sample characteristics, sampling procedures, and power are more complex in multilevel models because of the multiple units of analysis. For a multilevel design in which individuals, such as students, are nested within some larger units, such as schools, simply reporting the total number of students or the total number of schools is not sufficient because the distribution of students across schools can impact model specification and the precision of the parameter estimates. In addition, communicating information about sample sizes requires presenting a rationale for the number of units selected at each level. This rationale may rely on statistical power analyses that include considerations of expected effect sizes, alpha levels, and anticipated attrition and missing data rates (Mok, 1995; Raudenbush, 1997; Raudenbush & Liu, 2000; Spybrook, 2008).

Table 11.2 provides one approach to communicating sample sizes at each level of analysis for a multilevel unbalanced design (unequal sample sizes across units) involving 600 students from 86 schools. If the dataset is large, it may not be practical to provide a table like Table 11.2. In this case, researchers could present descriptive information, including the average number of level-one units per level-two unit, as well as the minimum and maximum number of level-one units. For example, the information in Table 11.2 could be summarized by indicating that there were 86 schools, with the number of students ranging from 1 to 10 per school, with an average of about 7 students per school.

TABLE 11.2   Example of Table for Summarizing Sample Sizes for Students Nested Within Schools in a Two-Level Design

Number of students per school	Number of schools with specified number of students	Cumulative frequency of schools	Cumulative frequency of students
1	11	11	11
2	3	14	17
3	6	20	35
4	2	22	43
5	3	25	58
6	2	27	70
7	10	37	140
8	10	47	220
9	10	57	310
10	29	86	600

TABLE 11.3 Example of Table for Summarizing Sample Sizes for Two-Level Growth Curve Design

Number of time points observed	Number of individuals	% of individuals	Cumulative frequency of individuals
1	10	7.1	10
2	20	14.2	30
3	16	11.4	46
4	21	15.0	67
5	73	52.1	140

For a multilevel design in which individuals are measured repeatedly over time, the distribution of the number of observed time points should be specified. For example, reporting the number of individuals with two data points, three data points, etc. allows readers to evaluate the possibility of identifying nonlinear models and the precision of the parameter estimates from these more complex models (see Table 11.3).

Investigators also should describe the type of sampling procedures that were implemented and discuss if the same sampling procedures were employed at different levels. For example, schools may be selected randomly, and students within those schools may be selected randomly, providing a probability sample at each level. A mixed sampling approach, employing probability sampling at one level and nonprobability methods at another level, also may occur. For example, schools may be selected randomly, but the sample of students at each school may come from teachers who were willing to participate. In studies using existing data, the original database may have been collected using complex sampling methods (Stapleton & Thomas, 2008). In these circumstances, researchers should communicate the type of sampling such as cluster, stratified, or disproportionate, and the implications for the use of sampling weights. For datasets that make available multiple sets of sampling weights, it should be clear what sampling weights were used in the analysis.

Whatever the sampling approach, it is important to describe the final dataset in sufficient detail to allow other researchers to be able to critique or replicate the study. Part of this description should be a discussion of missing data at each level, the degree to which missingness is related to the variables being studied, the method used to handle missing data, and the corresponding consequences, such as introduction of bias and reduction in power (for additional discussion on missing data see Collins, Schafer, & Kam, 2001; Little & Rubin, 1987; Roy & Lin, 2002). Finally, as part of the description of the participants, authors may acknowledge that they complied with all applicable federal, state, and local regulations and standards related to the ethical treatment of human subjects.

Research Design

The research design and procedures of the study should be reported in sufficient detail to allow readers to replicate the study, to judge whether human subjects were treated ethically, and to critically interpret the results. A challenge in communicating information about the research design is that there is a lack of universally accepted terminology (Maciejewski, Diehr, Smith, & Hebert, 2002). For this reason, researchers need to describe the essential characteristics of the design (e.g., use of experimental manipulation of variables, use of longitudinal data collection) as well as the limitations of the design. Attention should be drawn to how extraneous variables were controlled through methods such as randomization, matching, or statistical adjustments at one or more levels of the analysis. Because these methods can be implemented in a variety of ways, actual implementation procedures need to be detailed.

Description of the design also may involve defining terms that might be used differently across disciplines (for example, omitted variable versus unmeasured confounder). For details on design issues in multilevel studies, see Murray (1998) and Murray, Varnell, and Blitstein (2004). By clearly communicating the design and its limitations, researchers will help readers to judiciously interpret the results of the multilevel anaylsis.

Variables

Clear descriptions and definitions of the variables under investigation are essential in communicating information about the research design. Issues that should be addressed include how the variables were coded (e.g., dummy/effect coding), procedures used to form composite variables (e.g., items used to form a subscale), procedures used to form aggregate level-two variables (e.g., average SES of all students at the school, versus average SES of the students at the school who participated in the study), and at which level(s) the variables were measured in the multilevel models. One way to convey these details efficiently is through the inclusion of a codebook in an appendix that provides information about the variables and their measurement (Lee & Loeb, 2000; Marks, 2000).

Measurement quality of the variables in terms of reliability and validity is also of critical importance. Most measures in educational studies contain error, and these errors, if not accounted for, can bias estimates of variance parameters, variance ratios, fixed effects, and the standard errors of fixed effects (Woodhouse, Yang, Goldstein, & Rasbash, 1996). Consequently, researchers need to provide psychometric information on the variables used in the multilevel analysis. Reliance on estimates of reliability or validity provided in technical manuals or previously reported research is typically not sufficient because such estimates are sample specific (Thompson & Vacha-Haase, 2000). In situations in which the measurement error is substantial, researchers may consider analytical methods for specifying and adjusting for the measurement error (Longford, 1993; Woodhouse et al., 1996).

It is helpful to divide the study variables by the level at which they are measured (e.g., level one, level two, etc.). Researchers investigating a variable that is measured at different levels (e.g., student SES vs. SES of the school) need to present psychometric information about the variable at each level and discuss how the variable may have different meanings at different levels. In addition to presenting the variables at each level of analysis, the role(s) played by the variables in the study should be specified (e.g., outcome, predictor, covariate). The role delineation becomes important as the researcher attempts to communicate the multilevel models under investigation. For example, in a study examining the question of whether the relationship between student SES and student mathematics achievement (i.e., slope) varies across different types of schools, the researcher might identify student SES as a predictor and specify the β coefficient representing this relationship as random. In another study examining the effects of an instructional program on mathematics achievement, student SES may be used as a control variable, and therefore, the researcher might fix the variance of the β coefficient to zero.

Models

In view of the complexity of multilevel models, researchers need to address multiple issues in their descriptions of their models. First, the statistical models need to be specified clearly and fully. Second, the method used to center/scale each variable in the model should be provided. Third, the process used to derive the models should be communicated to help the reader understand the degree to which the analyses were exploratory or confirmatory in nature. Finally, the methods used to examine the integrity of the model should be detailed to help the reader evaluate the resulting inferences.

Specification

In multilevel modeling, the statistical models need to be presented in an understandable manner so that readers can gauge the appropriateness of the models for addressing the research questions as well as for replicating the analyses. Although it is possible to communicate a multilevel model in words, verbal descriptions are often ambiguous or incomplete, and thus may not be an efficient way to communicate the model. A more effective strategy to specify the multilevel model is through the use of one or more equations for each level of the model. Some software programs, such as HLM (Raudenbush, Bryk, Cheong, & Congdon, 2004), generate the equations that specify the model, facilitating insertion into a manuscript.

Consider a researcher who is studying students nested in schools. The researcher may be interested in the effects of student seventh-grade mathematics achievement (Math7) and student SES (SES) on student eighth-grade mathematics achievement (Math8). A level-one model could be developed to describe Math8 as a function of Math7 and SES within a specific school:

$$\text{Math8}_{ij} = \beta_{0j} + \beta_{1j}\,\text{Math7}_{ij} + \beta_{2j}\,\text{SES}_{ij} + r_{ij}, \tag{11.1}$$

where Math8_{ij} is the eighth-grade mathematics achievement score for the ith student in the jth school, β_{0j} is the intercept of the regression equation predicting Math8 in the jth school, β_{1j} is the regression coefficient indexing the strength of the association of Math7 with Math8 in the jth school, β_{2j} is the regression coefficient indexing the strength of the association of student SES with Math8 in the jth school, and r_{ij} is the error, which is assumed to be normally distributed with a covariance of Σ.

When students are nested in schools, as in this example, Σ commonly is assumed to be $\sigma^2 \mathbf{I}$, where σ^2 is the variance and $\mathbf{I}$ is a $n \times n$ Identity Matrix, where n is the number of level-one units. This implies that the errors are modeled as if they were sampled independently from a normal distribution with variance, σ^2. If multilevel models are used for longitudinal data in which repeated measures are nested within individuals, one may want to relax this assumption to allow for the correlation among errors that are close together in time. A variety of alternative structures including first-order autoregressive have been discussed and presented in the methodological literature (Wolfinger, 1993). Note that one step in communicating the model is to be clear about the assumed structure of Σ.

After specifying the level-one model, the level-two model is specified. Returning to the example, the level-two model could be used to consider the effects of school context on Math8. Assume the researcher believes, either through theory or previous research, that the level of Math8 in the school depends on whether the school is using an experimental mathematics instructional program (Program) and the school SES (SchoolSES), and that Program also moderates the effects of Math7 on Math8. The level-two model would use Program and School SES as predictors of some of the co-efficients of the level-one model. One possible specification could be:

$$\beta_{0j} = \gamma_{00} + \gamma_{01} \text{ Program}_j + \gamma_{02} \text{ SchoolSES}_j + u_{0j} \qquad (11.2)$$

$$\beta_{1j} = \gamma_{10} + \gamma_{11} \text{ Program}_j + u_{1j} \qquad (11.3)$$

$$\beta_{2j} = \gamma_{20}, \qquad (11.4)$$

where Program_j is coded 0 if school j is a control school that does not use the experimental mathematics program and coded 1 if school j is using the experimental program; SchoolSES_j is the measure of school-level SES at school j; and u_{0j} and u_{1j} are level-two errors, which are assumed to be normally distributed with a covariance of $\mathbf{T}$. In this example, $\mathbf{T}$, could be specified in several ways. One way is as a 2×2 unstructured covariance matrix,

$$\mathbf{T} = \begin{bmatrix} \tau_{00} & \\ \tau_{10} & \tau_{11} \end{bmatrix}, \qquad (11.5)$$

which would imply that there was random variability in the intercepts (τ_{00}) and in the regression coefficients associated with Math7 (τ_{11}) and that the errors associated with the intercepts and Math7 coefficients may covary with each other (τ_{10}). One may find that the data support constraining a variance to zero, thus reducing the number of elements estimated in $\mathbf{T}$. Alternatively, one might define the covariance structure so that a greater number of variance components are estimated. For example, the researcher also may allow the coefficients associated with student-level SES to vary randomly; in this case, an error term, u_{2j}, would be added to Equation 11.4, and $\mathbf{T}$ would become a 3-by-3 matrix. Part of communicating the model involves letting the reader know what structure was assumed for $\mathbf{T}$.

Although it is common in the educational literature to see multilevel models communicated using regression equations for each level of the model, it is also possible to combine the regression equations into a single equation. By substituting the level-two model for β_{0j}, β_{1j}, and β_{2j} in the level-one model, the following combined model would be obtained:

$$\text{Math8}_{ij} = \gamma_{00} + \gamma_{01} \text{ Program}_j + \gamma_{02} \text{ SchoolSES}_j + \gamma_{10} \text{ Math7}_{ij} + \qquad (11.6)$$
$$\gamma_{11} \text{ Program}_j * \text{Math7}_{ij} + \gamma_{20} \text{ SES}_{ij} + u_{0j} + u_{1j} \text{ Math7}_{ij} + r_{ij} ,$$

which has the same form as the mixed linear model,

$$\mathbf{y} = \mathbf{X}\boldsymbol{\beta} + \mathbf{Z}\nu + \boldsymbol{\varepsilon}, \qquad (11.7)$$

where **y** is a vector of outcome data, β is a vector of fixed effects, **X** and **Z** are known model matrices, ν is a vector of random effects, and ε is a vector of errors (Henderson, 1975). Again, the structure of the covariance matrices needs to be made explicit. Using mixed model notation, one typically refers to the covariance matrix of the level-one errors as **R** and to the covariance matrix of the level-two errors as **G**. For the above example, one could indicate that the blocks of **R** were specified as $\sigma^2\mathbf{I}$ and that the blocks of **G** were specified as 2 by 2 and unstructured,

$$\mathbf{G} = \begin{bmatrix} g_{11} & \\ g_{21} & g_{22} \end{bmatrix}, \tag{11.8}$$

where g_{11} is the random variance in the intercepts, g_{22} is the random variance in the regression coefficients associated with Math7, and g_{21} is the covariance between the errors associated with the intercepts and the Math7 coefficients.

The choice of using equations for each level or a single equation should be based on the judgment of which method will communicate most easily to the intended audience. Information for making this decision can be gleaned from consulting previous issues of the target journal to determine how multilevel models typically are communicated. If it is judged that the equations provide too much technical detail for the typical reader, an appendix could be included (for an example, see Marsh, Köller, & Baumert, 2001).

Centering of Predictors

Centering of the level-one and level-two predictors has implications for interpreting the results of multilevel models (Kreft & de Leeuw, 1998; Kreft, de Leeuw, & Aiken, 1995; Morrell, Pearson, & Brant, 1997; Raudenbush & Bryk, 2002) and, therefore, is an important consideration in reporting the results. In the example specified in Equations 11.1–11.5, suppose the seventh-grade mathematics achievement (Math7) was measured on a scale ranging from 200 to 800, student SES was dummy coded (0 = eligible for free or reduced lunch, 1 = not eligible), school SES was defined as the proportion of students in the school not eligible for free or reduced lunch, and the mathematics program variable was dummy coded (0 = control school, 1 = mathematics program school). If Math7 was kept in its natural metric, γ_{00} would be the predicted eighth-grade mathematics achievement (Math8) for a student in a control school with 0% of the students not eligible for free or reduced lunch, who is individually eligible for free or reduced lunch, and who has a Math7 score of zero. Since a Math7 score of zero is not possible, this coefficient is difficult to interpret in a substantively meaningful way. The effect of the instructional program in this model, γ_{01}, would be interpreted as the difference in the effectiveness of the two programs when Math7 was zero (again, a value that is not particularly informative). Difficulties also would arise in interpreting the variance components. For example, the random variance in the intercepts, τ_{00}, would be the between-school variation in predicted Math8 scores for students who are eligible for free or reduced lunch and who have Math7 scores of zero. Centering or rescaling prior mathematics achievement makes the interpretation of the coefficients and variance components more meaningful.

One approach to scaling predictor variables is to subtract the grand mean of the predictor variable from each score $(x_{ij} - \bar{x}_{..})$; this can be done for variables at level one or at level two. Using grand-mean centering of Math7 and school SES in our example, γ_{00} is the predicted Math8 score for students in a control school with sample average school SES, who are individually eligible for free or reduced lunch, and who have a sample average Math7 score. Similarly, the effect of instructional program, γ_{01}, is interpreted as the difference in the effectiveness of the two programs for students having the sample average of seventh-grade mathematics achievement and the same individual and school SES.

A second approach to scaling the predictor variable is to subtract the level-two unit mean of the predictor variable from each score $(x_{ij} - \bar{x}_{.j})$; this centering process can only be done for level-one predictors. Using group-mean centering of Math7 and grand-mean centering of school SES in our example, γ_{00} is interpreted as the predicted Math8 score for a student in a control school with sample average school SES, who is individually eligible for free or reduced lunch, and whose Math7 score was at the sample average for his or her school. The effect of the experimental program, γ_{01}, is interpreted as the difference in the effectiveness of the two programs for students who are at their school's sample average level of mathematics achievement and have the same individual SES.

A third approach to scaling a predictor variable is to subtract a theoretically meaningful value (k) from each score $(x_{ij} - k)$. This approach is similar to grand-mean centering in that a constant is subtracted from each score. The β_{0j} is interpreted as the expected outcome for individuals at the specific value that has been set by the researcher. For example, in a growth curve model examining change in mathematics achievement from grades 1 through 8, a researcher may center the grade predictor at grade 8. In this case, β_{0j} is interpreted as the expected value of the outcome for a student in eighth grade.

The differences in the substantive interpretation of these regression coefficients (fixed effects) illustrate the importance of clearly delineating the type of centering that has been employed. In addition, centering has consequences for interpreting the variance components. For example, the variance in the intercepts will depend on how the intercepts are defined, which in turn depends on the centering. Vague statements that "all predictors were centered" or that "mean centering was employed to facilitate interpretation of the models" are not sufficient to insure proper interpretation of the results. If model estimates are presented in tables, the researcher should use a table note to describe the type of centering used so that interpretation of parameter estimates readily follows.

Process for Defining the Model

In some situations researchers are able to use theory and past research to define the multilevel model(s) prior to examining their data. In these situations the data are used as a check to verify the reasonableness of the model but not as a means for building the model. Consequently, hypothesis testing for key parameters and the construction of confidence intervals around an effect of interest are relatively straightforward. When researchers rely on the data to help define the model, the research is more exploratory and strong inference becomes considerably more difficult. To critically examine the inferences made, the reader needs to fully understand the degree to which the data were used to develop the model.

Consider, for example, the model specified in Equations 11.1–11.5. Suppose the researcher had made a strong argument supporting the details of the model specification and that the only decision based on the data was to allow the errors in the level-two equations to covary. A reader concerned that this decision may have been incorrect could think through the potential consequences of estimating a covariance parameter that has a value of zero in the population. This type of misspecification can negatively affect the precision in estimating other parameters in the model (Verbeke, 1997) and sometimes leads to estimation difficulties (Van den Noortgate & Onghena, 2003; Verbeke, 1997). The reader may conclude that the potential misspecification has negligible consequences for interpretation if estimation difficulties were not encountered and a reasonable level of precision was obtained for the parameter estimates.

Alternatively (again considering the model specified in Equations 11.1–11.5), suppose the researcher arrived at this model after considering 12 potential predictors of variability in the intercepts and regression coefficients. The presented model contains only the predictors that were statistically significant. Again the reader may wish to consider the consequences of possible misspecifications. Relevant variables may have been omitted from the model (a possible consequence of insufficient power), which might lead to substantial biasing of the effect estimates of the included predictors. In this case, readers may judge the potential misspecifications to have substantial enough ramifications to alter the way they evaluate the results.

Evaluation of Model Integrity

A variety of statistical tools may be employed to obtain information about the integrity and trustworthiness of a model. Researchers may examine fit indices, the degree to which data are consistent with modeling assumptions, and the sensitivity of parameter estimates to outliers and changes in model specification. Such examinations may provide support for, or indicate appropriate caveats related to, the fidelity of model estimates. The clear explication of the results of investigations of model integrity, including what approaches were taken, what results were obtained, and what these results suggest about the model reported, is important in interpreting the study results.

Fit indices may be used to guide selection among alternative models. The fit indices most commonly used are the deviance statistic (Raudenbush et al., 2004), AIC (Akaike, 1974), and BIC (Schwartz, 1978). More details about model fit indices are provided in Chapter 7 of this volume (McCoach & Black, 2008). It is also important to note, however, that not all multilevel software packages provide all these estimates of model fit and that not all researchers use the same indices. Consequently, it is important to be specific about how model fit was assessed.

Distributional assumptions (normality and equal variance) are made about the errors at each level in the model. Violations can be suggestive of specification errors and can lead to biases in the standard errors at both levels of the model (Raudenbush & Bryk, 2002). The multilevel modeling results also can be influenced by outliers. There are multiple methods available to screen data for violations of assumptions (Jiang, 2001; Raudenbush & Bryk, 2002; Teuscher, Herrendorfer, & Guiard, 1994) and the presence of outliers (Longford, 2001). Given the variety of methods available, researchers need to not only communicate that data were screened for violations of assumptions and outliers but to note the specific methods used.

Also available are approaches for assessing the *impact* of outliers, assumption violations, and alternative specification decisions. Bayesian techniques, such as the Gibbs sampling methods as well as other strategies and algorithms, can be used to examine the impact of extreme observations at either level one or level two of the model (Seltzer, Novak, Choi, & Lim, 2002). Models can be estimated with and without a transformation of a nonnormal outcome variable to examine the impact of nonnormality on the results (for an example, see Kochenderfer-Ladd & Wardrop, 2001). Models also can be estimated under multiple plausible covariance structure specifications to examine the impact of specification decisions on inferences (Ferron, Dailey, & Yi, 2002). Because multiple methods are available to assess the degree to which inferences are sensitive to modeling decisions, researchers should communicate the specifics of any methods utilized.

Collectively, techniques employed to provide evidence of model robustness and sensitivity of parameter estimates to changes in model specification will serve to enhance the trustworthiness of an estimated model. For readers to critically evaluate the results presented and the inferences made, they need to know the particulars of the methods used to evaluate model integrity.

Estimation and Inference

Technical details about estimation of the multilevel model and approaches to statistical inference allow readers to evaluate strengths and weaknesses of the methods selected and to permit replication. As such, these technical details should be viewed as an integral part of reporting the results. A variety of issues are subsumed under this topic, including estimation algorithms and the inferential methods used to conduct hypothesis tests and construct confidence intervals.

Estimation

A variety of methods are available for the estimation of parameters, each with its own strengths and weaknesses. As such, estimation methods and algorithms should be identified explicitly in the discussion of parameter estimation. In addition, identification of the specific software program and version used for estimation is helpful for readers interested in technical details about the analysis. In discussing the technical details, it also should be communicated whether estimation problems were encountered (e.g., improper variance estimates) and, if they were, how they were addressed.

Common methods of estimation for multilevel models include maximum likelihood (ML), restricted maximum likelihood (REML), and Bayesian (Kreft & de Leeuw, 1998; Raudenbush & Bryk, 2002). These methods of estimation can be carried out using many different algorithms, thus underscoring the need for definitive information regarding estimation methods and algorithms employed. For example, ML estimation may be accomplished using the expectation-maximization (EM) algorithm, the Newton-Raphson algorithm, the Fisher scoring algorithm, or iterative generalized least squares (IGLS), while Bayesian estimation may be accomplished using the Gibbs sampler. These algorithms have been programmed into many different software programs. Thus, one researcher may accomplish REML estimation using the EM algorithm programmed into HLM (Raudenbush et al., 2004), another may accomplish REML estimation using restricted iterative generalized least squares (RIGLS) using MLwiN (Rasbash, Steele, Browne, & Prosser, 2004), while a third may accomplish REML using the Newton-Raphson algorithm programmed in SAS PROC MIXED (SAS Institute Inc., 2000).

Reporting of the estimation method, estimation algorithm, software program, and whether estimation problems were encountered can be communicated effectively in a single sentence in the description of the data analysis, a footnote, or a technical appendix. The use of less common estimation approaches, such as bootstrapping, robust ML, and robust REML methods (Carpenter, Goldstein, & Rasbash, 1999; Meijer, Van der Leeden, & Busing, 1995; Richardson & Welsh, 1995), may require more explication, possibly in an appendix.

Estimation methods typically will produce point estimates of each parameter in the multilevel model and these estimates are often valuable in addressing particular research questions. Additional information about the parameter estimates often is provided to aid the researcher in making inferences, possibly taking the form of hypothesis tests and/or confidence intervals for parameters of interest. Clear communication of the types of estimates calculated and details about the approach employed are important for valid interpretation of such inferential statistics. When considering the options available, it becomes important to distinguish between inferences made about variance parameters (elements in Σ and $\mathbf{T}$), fixed effects (γ's), and random level-one coefficients (e.g., β_{0j}).

Inferences about Variance Parameters

The simplest approach to creating a confidence interval (CI) for a variance parameter is to use the standard error of the variance parameter estimate, computed from the inverse of the information matrix. By adding and subtracting 1.96 times the standard error of the parameter estimate, one can create a 95% CI, assuming a normal sampling distribution. This approach, however, has limitations, especially when the sample size is small or the variance parameter is near zero (Littell, Milliken, Stroup, & Wolfinger, 1996; Raudenbush & Bryk, 2002). For such data, researchers may consider other options, including the Satterthwaite approach (Littell et al., 1996), bootstrapping (Carpenter et al., 1999; Meijer et al., 1995), a method based on local asymptotic approximations (Stern & Welsh, 2000), and, if the data are balanced, an approach based on a set of quadratic forms (Yu & Burdick, 1995). These alternative methods can lead to different results. If other researchers are to critically evaluate or replicate the analysis, they need to know the specific methods used. Consequently, this is another technical detail that should be reported.

For researchers wishing to test hypotheses regarding variance parameters, a similar variety of choices is available. The simplest approach would be to conduct a z-test by dividing the estimate by its standard-error. Although this approach is asymptotically valid, like the standard error based CIs noted previously, it becomes questionable when the sampling distribution cannot be assumed normal. Alternative approaches include a likelihood ratio χ^2 (Littell et al., 1996), an approximate χ^2 test described by Raudenbush and Bryk (2002), bootstrapping (Carpenter et al., 1999; Meijer et al., 1995), and a likelihood ratio test based on the local asymptotic approximation (Stern

& Welsh, 2000). Again, different choices can lead to different results and thus the method should be reported.

Inferences about Fixed Effects

Inferences about fixed effects may be obtained from confidence intervals for the effects of interest. For example, a 95% CI could be constructed around the point estimate by adding and subtracting 1.96 times the standard error. This approach assumes a normal sampling distribution, which can be demonstrated asymptotically, but which becomes questionable for smaller samples. Consequently, one may utilize a critical t-value with v degrees of freedom. Several methods for defining the degrees of freedom have been given (Giesbrecht & Burns, 1985; Kenward & Roger, 1997), and some software packages allow for different definitions to be specified. An alternative to assuming an approximate t-distribution is to turn to bootstrapping to construct the confidence intervals.

Hypothesis tests also can be conducted using t- or F-tests with approximate degrees of freedom. Again, different approximations have been suggested, and thus, researchers need to be clear about the method used for obtaining the degrees of freedom for these tests. Several alternatives to these approximate tests have been discussed. These include a test based on a Bartlett-corrected likelihood ratio statistic (Zucker, Lieberman, & Manor, 2000), a permutation test (Reboussin & DeMets, 1996), and bootstrapping. Researchers using one of these methods should specify the approach that was used and the rationale.

Inferences about Level-One Coefficients

Researchers also may be interested in estimating the random level-one coefficients and making inferences about these coefficients. For example, a researcher who is interested in estimating the effects of seventh-grade mathematics achievement on eighth-grade mathematics achievement may wish to obtain a separate effect estimate for each school. Again, there are multiple choices for estimation and inference, and it is important for the researcher to convey the choices made.

One approach would be to estimate the level-one model separately for each school using ordinary least squares (OLS) estimation methods, in which case standard methods are available for constructing confidence intervals and testing hypotheses about coefficients. With this approach the estimate for a specific school is based only on information from that school, which may be just a few observations. By failing to use the information from the other schools, the obtained estimate is not as precise as it could be.

An alternative is to obtain Empirical Bayes estimates, which consider all available information. Empirical Bayes estimates tend to pull each school's effect estimate toward a value predicted by the model, with the amount of adjustment depending upon the uncertainty in the effect estimate being considered and the variability in the effect estimates. This process biases the estimates but provides values that tend to be closer to the parameter values than those based on OLS estimation, resulting in a smaller expected mean square error (Raudenbush & Bryk, 2002). For Empirical Bayes estimates, the standard errors can be computed and used for the creation of confidence intervals or z-tests of statistical significance.

RESULTS

Researchers may consider reporting at least two types of results: (a) preliminary results that address the properties and quality of the data (e.g., measures of central tendency, reliability of outcomes, predictors, and level-one coefficients such as intercepts and slopes), missing data patterns and relationships of missing data to relevant variables, model assumptions including normality and homogeneity of variance, and model building steps; and (b) primary results directly addressing the research questions. Two examples are used to illustrate various approaches to reporting results. The first considers a two-level model examining mathematics achievement of students nested in schools; the second involves a two-level growth curve model of reading achievement.

Preliminary Results

Tables presenting descriptive univariate information about the variables under investigation (e.g., mean, standard deviation, range, skewness, kurtosis) and correlations among variables are common in published research. With a few format changes in these tables, important information about the variables in the multilevel models can be communicated efficiently. Examples of this type of information are illustrated based on data for the two-level mathematics achievement example in Table 11.4 (univariate statistics) and Table 11.5 (correlations). Dividing the study variables by the level at which they are measured provides information about the potential variables available for model building at each level and their distributional properties. Inclusion of sample sizes for each variable provides information about missing data, with implications for issues related both to statistical power and to potential convergence and estimation problems in model development.

TABLE 11.4   Example of Table for Presenting Descriptive Data for Variables in Two-Level Model with Students Nested Within Schools

Variable	N	M	SD	Skewness	Kurtosis	Outliers
			Level one			
Math8	2000	303.25	31.06	0.20	0.45	None
Math7	1967	303.15	51.12	−0.01	−0.12	None
Student SES	2000	0.25				
			Level two			
School SES	40	0.25	0.16	−0.21	0.28	None
Program	40	0.50				

Note: Math8 is eighth-grade mathematics achievement; Math7 is seventh-grade mathematics achievement; Student SES is coded 0 if eligible for free or reduced lunch and 1 if not eligible; School SES equals the proportion of students in the study at a school that are not eligible for free or reduced lunch; Program is coded 0 for a control school and 1 for a program school; and an outlier was defined as an observation exceeding 1.5 interquartile ranges beyond the 1st or 3rd quartile.

TABLE 11.5   Example of Table for Presenting Pearson Product Moment Correlations for Variables in Two-Level Model with Students Nested Within Schools

	Level one (N = 1967)		
	Math8	**Math7**	**Student SES**
Math8	1.00		
Math7	0.59	1.00	
Student SES	0.18	0.14	1.00
	Level two (J = 40)		
	School SES	**Program**	
School SES	1.00		
Program	−0.02	1.00	

Note: Math8 is eighth-grade mathematics achievement; Math7 is seventh-grade mathematics achievement; Student SES is coded 0 if eligible for free or reduced lunch and 1 if not eligible; School SES equals the proportion of students in the study at a school that are not eligible for free or reduced lunch; Program is coded 0 for a control school and 1 for a program school; the N of 1967 is based on listwise deletion.

As part of the presentation of descriptive information, it is important to distinguish what outcome variables are being examined in the research questions and then to present descriptive information about these outcomes. The potential for confusion on this issue can be illustrated with the growth curve modeling example for reading achievement in which a researcher was interested in examining changes in reading achievement from grades 1 to 5 and the factors associated with these changes. The researcher may identify reading achievement as the outcome variable and then only present descriptive statistics and psychometric information, such as reliability estimates, for reading achievement at each grade level. Given that the researcher's focus is on *changes* in reading achievement, the outcome variable is technically the slope parameter estimate and, therefore, descriptive information (minimum, maximum, mean, standard deviation, skewness, kurtosis) both for EB and OLS slope estimates along with reliability estimates should be presented. Similar information should be presented if intercepts (e.g., initial status in a growth curve) are the focus of the research questions (see Table 11.6). The reliability estimates for the slope and intercept parameters, which are calculated in some software programs, can be used to make decisions about whether these coefficients should be specified as fixed or random and also provide information about the extent to which relationships between predictors and the coefficients may be attenuated.

An alternative way to communicate information about the distribution of intercepts and slopes efficiently is to provide a graphical display of the reading trajectories. If the number of level-two units is too large for a clear visual display of *all* units, the researcher could provide a visual display based on a random sample of the level-two units (see Figure 11.1). In addition to

TABLE 11.6 Example of Table for Summarizing Reading Achievement for Two-Level Growth Curve Model

Outcome	*N*	Min	Max	*M*	*SD*	Skewness	Kurtosis	Outliers
OLS								
Intercept (initial status)	100	168.5	273.5	220.0	24.5	0.01	–0.48	None
Slope (yearly change)	100	–30.4	150.6	53.9	37.1	0.23	–0.05	None
EB								
Intercept (initial status)	100	186.6	247.7	220.0	13.7	–0.23	–0.07	None
Slope (yearly change)	100	–33.2	148.5	53.9	35.9	0.19	–0.08	None

Note: OLS is Ordinary Least Squares; EB is Empirical Bayes; the time variable was scaled in yearly increments from grades 1 to 5 with zero corresponding to the beginning of the study (grade 1); an outlier was defined as an observation exceeding 1.5 interquartile ranges beyond the 1st or 3rd quartile; and reliability of OLS regression coefficient estimates for intercepts and slopes were .80 and .45, respectively.

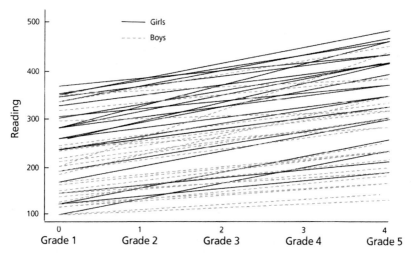

Figure 11.1 Example of fitted OLS linear regressions of reading achievement on grade level for a random sample of 50 students.

Stem	Leaves
1.0	
.9	23
.8	125679
.7	1245677899
.6	01446678899
.5	012233446788999
.4	00012233344445678899
.3	00112233444455566
.2	0111223458
.1	144789
.0	3689

Figure 11.2 Example of a stem-and-leaf plot presenting R^2 values for fitted OLS regressions of reading achievement on grade level for 100 students.

summarizing the slope and intercept distributions, it is also useful to summarize R^2 values (see Figure 11.2) for the individual OLS regression models. Displays summarizing the R^2 values for different growth models (linear or quadratic) then could be used to support decisions about the choice of model while at the same time providing a scaffold for the multilevel results addressing the research questions. Another way of summarizing the level-one regression would be to include a table listing the R^2 values along with the OLS level-one equations.

As part of these preliminary analyses, the researcher should communicate details about the data that may impact modeling in the primary analyses. It is important to discuss issues of nonnormality, heteroscedasticity, multicollinearity, and outliers. Potential violations of the underlying assumptions need to be examined thoroughly and communicated clearly to the reader. In addition to reporting any anomalies that are found during data screening, researchers should document analysis decisions that are made in light of the data. For example, a researcher may transform a variable to improve normality or use an alternative covariance structure to address heteroscedasticity. In situations where how to proceed is somewhat ambiguous, researchers also should provide information on the degree to which the results are sensitive to the data anomalies or alternative modeling decisions. Given the space requirements of many journals, the results of data screening activities will need to be summarized concisely, and some of the technical details may need to be handled through footnotes, or an appendix.

Preliminary analyses should include computing the intraclass correlation coefficient (ICC). The ICC, derived from an unconditional model with no within- and between-group predictors (also called the one-way random effects ANOVA model, or the empty model), provides baseline information for evaluating the relative contributions of within- and between-group predictors.

Primary Results

In presenting the primary results from multilevel analyses, researchers should provide a listing of all estimated parameters for each model that is interpreted, while also striving to focus the reader's attention on the specific estimates and results that address the research questions. This can be challenging because the links between the questions, models, and statistical results are not always as apparent as they would be in applications using simpler statistical models. Focus can be achieved by adding visual cues such as bold-faced type in tables (see Wainer, 1997), by including statements interpreting the key parameter estimates in the narrative, and by illustrating effects using graphical displays.

Example 1: Students Nested within Schools

Consider again the example where eighth-grade mathematics achievement is being predicted based on seventh-grade mathematics achievement, student SES, school SES, and whether or not the school had used the mathematics program. Suppose the primary purpose of the research is to estimate the effects of the mathematics program on eighth-grade mathematics achievement and the degree to which the program's effect depends on prior achievement (seventh-grade mathematics achievement) of the students. The researcher may wish to start by pointing the reader to a table with the complete listing of the parameter estimates and an indication of the precision of these estimates (e.g., standard errors or confidence intervals). There are several ways to structure such a table. One possibility is to use the format shown in Table 11.7, where predictors are listed in rows, and columns are used for different models. This format parallels a relatively standard way of reporting and comparing multiple regression models, which may facilitate a reader's understanding of the results. This table includes symbols commonly used to refer to fixed effects (e.g., γ_{00}, γ_{10}) and variance estimates (e.g., σ^2, τ_{00}) along with brief descriptors. The included symbols match those used when the model was specified (Equations 11.1–11.5) to facilitate the connection of the estimates in the table to the parameters in the model. An alternative method for tabular representation of multilevel analysis results can be found in Ethington (1997).

Since the primary focus of this analysis is on estimating the effect of the mathematics instructional program, the narrative should provide an interpretation of the estimated program effect ($\hat{\gamma}_{01}$), which as noted previously would depend on how the variables were scaled or centered. For example, assuming grand-mean centering of Math7, the effect estimate, $\hat{\gamma}_{01}$, would be interpreted in a statement such as: "students with a sample average level of seventh-grade mathematics achievement who are in a school with the mathematics instructional program are predicted to have an eighth-grade mathematics achievement score that is $\hat{\gamma}_{01}$ points higher than similar students in a control school."

Attention should also be drawn to the cross-level interaction effect (γ_{11}), which suggests that the difference in expected eighth-grade mathematics achievement between programs is not constant across seventh-grade achievement levels. A graphical display of predicted eighth-grade mathematics achievement as a function of seventh-grade mathematics achievement and program (see Figure 11.3) could be constructed using the equations with estimated parameter values. This graph helps to communicate the degree to which the program effect differs for students of varying levels of seventh-grade mathematics achievement.

An alternative display could be constructed by graphing the program effect as a function of seventh-grade mathematics achievement, where the program effect is defined as the difference in expected eighth-grade mathematics achievement between comparable program and control students at a specified level of seventh-grade mathematics achievement. Confidence interval bands then could be added (Tate, 2004), and the range of seventh-grade mathematics achievement scores for which the difference between programs is statistically significant would become apparent. An example using 95% confidence interval bands is provided in Figure 11.4.

TABLE 11.7   Example of Table Summarizing REML Parameter Estimates for Two-Level Model of Eighth-Grade Mathematics Achievement

Parameter	Unconditional model			Full model		
	Parameter estimate	SE	95% CI	Parameter estimate	SE	95% CI
Fixed effects						
Intercept (γ_{00})	303.10	0.85	301.43 to 304.77	299.76	1.12	297.57 to 301.95
Math7 (γ_{10})	—	—	—	0.44	0.05	0.34 to 0.53
Student SES (γ_{20})	—	—	—	5.87	1.06	3.79 to 7.95
School SES (γ_{02})	—	—	—	6.62	3.61	−0.45 to 13.69
Program (γ_{01})	—	—	—	1.90	0.85	0.23 to 3.57
Program*Math7 (γ_{11})	—	—	—	−0.24	0.01	−0.26 to −0.22
Variance estimates						
Level-one variance (σ^2)	784.53	24.93	735.67 to 833.39	358.43	11.46	335.97 to 380.89
Intercept variance (τ_{00})	2.77	3.45	0 to 9.53	5.31	2.89	0 to 10.97
Slope variance (τ_{11})	—	—	—	0.05	0.02	0.01 to 0.09
Error covariance (τ_{10})	—	—	—	0.36	0.18	0.01 to 0.71

Note: Math7 is seventh-grade mathematics achievement grand-mean centered; Student SES is coded 0 if eligible for free or reduced lunch and 1 if not eligible; School SES is the grand-mean centered proportion of students in the study at a school that are not eligible for free or reduced lunch; Program is coded 0 for a control school and 1 for a program school; CIs constructed using 1.96*SE; level-one sample size equals 1967; level-two sample size equals 40; and the intra-class correlation (ICC) derived from the unconditional model equals .0035.

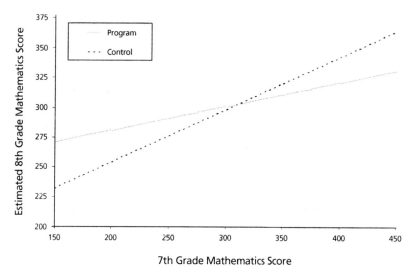

Figure 11.3 Graphical illustration of the effect of the mathematics program on eighth-grade mathematics achievement as a function of seventh-grade mathematics achievement for low SES students from a school with average SES.

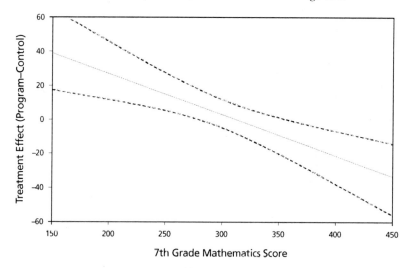

Figure 11.4 Graphical illustration of the mathematics program effect (solid line) and 95% confidence interval (dotted lines) as a function of seventh-grade mathematics achievement.

In addition to graphical displays designed to illustrate effects of interest, researchers sometimes compute pseudo R^2 values, giving the proportion of the variance at a particular level associated with the effect of interest (Kreft & de Leeuw, 1998; McCoach & Black, 2008; Snijders & Bosker, 1994).

Given that alternative calculations have been debated in the literature, it is important to specify the particular method used to estimate the pseudo R^2 value. In addition, it is important to be aware that the use of such indices is controversial and thus researchers providing these indices should do so carefully and in a manner that recognizes the limitations of the methods. For applications illustrating the use of pseudo R^2 values, see McCoach and Black, 2008, and Singer and Willett (2003).

Some researchers have provided standardized effect estimates by standardizing the regression coefficients from the multilevel model (Purcell-Gates, Degener, Jacobson, & Soler, 2002). Different methods can be used to standardize (e.g., across total sample versus within level-two units), and thus, it is important to communicate the details of the standardization process. As with pseudo R^2 values, the standardization of regression coefficients is controversial. For example, Willett, Singer, and Martin (1998) concluded that standardized regression coefficients may be misleading and caution against their use. Others have argued that for experimental studies, such as cluster-randomized trials, standardized effect sizes should be calculated and presented (Spybrook, 2008). Before presenting this type of information, researchers should critically evaluate whether it adds to their results and, if so, to present the information along with a discussion of the limitations of standardization.

Example 2: Growth Curve Model

As a second example, consider a longitudinal study of changes in reading achievement over the elementary years, where the research questions focus on the form of change (e.g., linear, nonlinear), the variation in growth parameters (e.g., intercept and slope), and gender differences in initial status and changes in reading achievement. After preliminary results have been presented, a table listing variance and covariance estimates, fixed effects, and fit indices for models where different growth trajectory forms were assumed can be useful to summarize information pertinent to questions of trajectory form and variability. Assume the researcher considered three models (an intercept only model, a linear growth trajectory model, and a quadratic growth trajectory model) and that for each, Σ was assumed to be $\sigma^2 I$ and T was assumed to be unstructured. One way of presenting the results for comparison of the models is provided in Table 11.8.

After identifying an appropriate form for the growth trajectories and determining the variability in the growth parameters, the researcher could address the question of the degree to which the growth trajectories differ for boys and girls. Assume the quadratic growth curve model best fit the data based on the AIC and BIC and that there was sufficient variation in the intercepts, linear, and quadratic terms, to use each of the growth parameters as an outcome in the examination of gender differences. The

TABLE 11.8   Example of Table Summarizing REML Parameter Estimates for Two-Level Growth Curve Models of Reading Achievement

Parameter	Intercept only model		Linear model		Quadratic model	
	Parameter estimate	95% CI	Parameter estimate	95% CI	Parameter estimate	95% CI
Fixed Effects						
Intercept (γ_{00})	327.8 (6.12)	315 to 339	219.9 (2.30)	215 to 224	210.2 (1.53)	207 to 213
Time: Linear (γ_{10})			53.9 (3.80)	46.5 to 61.4	73.4 (1.30)	70.8 to 75.9
Time^2: Quadratic (γ_{20})					-4.86 (0.90)	-6.63 to -3.09
Variance Estimate						
Level one (σ^2)	11076 (799.0)	9510 to 12642	524.0 (43.62)	438 to 609	75.3 (7.65)	60 to 90
Intercept (τ_{00})	1497 (561.5)	396 to 2597	275.9 (89.54)	100 to 451	198.7 (39.03)	122 to 275
Linear (τ_{11})			1326.0 (200.0)	934 to 1718	69.6 (25.51)	19 to 119
Intercept, Linear (τ_{10})			-493.3 (111.2)	-711 to -275	88.8 (22.45)	45 to 133
Quadratic (τ_{22})					73.3 (11.73)	50 to 96
Intercept, Quadratic (τ_{20})					-13.3 (15.05)	-43 to 16
Linear, Quadratic (τ_{21})					16.1 (11.73)	-7 to 39
	AIC	BIC	AIC	BIC	AIC	BIC
Fit Indices	6124.4	6129.6	4990.1	5000.5	4444.3	4462.5

Note: Time is scaled in years and is centered so that zero corresponds to the beginning of first grade; standard errors (SE) follow parameter estimates in parentheses; for variance estimates τ_{00}, τ_{11}, and τ_{22} are residual variances, while τ_{10}, τ_{20}, and τ_{21} are residual covariances; CIs were constructed using 1.96*SE; AIC = Akaike's Information Criterion; BIC = Bayes Information Criterion; estimates based on 100 students, all with five observations.

TABLE 11.9 Example of Table Summarizing REML Parameter Estimates for the Model Relating Gender to Reading Growth Curves

		Intercepts (π_{0i})	Linear terms (π_{1i})	Quadratic terms (π_{2i})
Fixed effects				
Intercept (β_{p0})	Estimate	201.44	66.99	−5.06
	SE	1.95	1.57	1.26
	95% CI	197.6 to 205.3	63.9 to 70.1	−7.6 to −2.6
Gender (β_{p1})	Estimate	17.48	12.79	0.39
	SE	2.76	2.21	1.78
	95% CI	12.0 to 22.9	8.4 to 17.1	−3.1 to 3.9
Variances	Estimate	123.5	29.5	74.0
	SE	27.9	19.9	11.4

Note: Time is scaled in years and is centered so that zero corresponds to the beginning of first grade; Gender is dummy coded (0 = Male, 1 = Female); residual level-one variance, σ^2, is 75.3, and the error covariances between intercept and linear, intercept and quadratic, and linear and quadratic terms are $\tau_{10} = 32.1$, $\tau_{20} = -15.1$, and $\tau_{21} = 14.8$; CIs were constructed using degrees of freedom estimated through the containment method; estimates based on 100 students, each with five observations.

multilevel model using gender as a predictor of each growth parameter could be arranged using a format that parallels Table 11.7 or Table 11.8, or alternatively, it could be arranged so that the columns corresponded to the growth parameters (intercept, linear term, quadratic term) and the rows correspond to the variables used to predict each growth parameter. This type of arrangement is provided in Table 11.9.

The interpretation of the coefficient describing the effect of a predictor such as gender on an intercept parameter is relatively straightforward once the type of centering has been specified, and it parallels the interpretation of an effect for a predictor variable in a multiple regression model. However, the interpretation of a coefficient describing the effect of a predictor such as gender on either the linear or quadratic parameter estimate is more complex and, in fact, addresses the question of a cross-level interaction (i.e., does gender moderate the relationship between time and reading achievement?). Given this complexity, it is suggested that a graphical display of this cross-level interaction be constructed using the equations with estimated parameter values and then presented to aid interpretation (see Figure 11.5 for an example).

In summary, several suggestions have been made for communicating preliminary and primary results. Preliminary results should be presented that include univariate summaries of the variables under investigation, the correlations among these variables, summaries of the distributions of the random level-one coefficients, and the ICC. Primary results should include

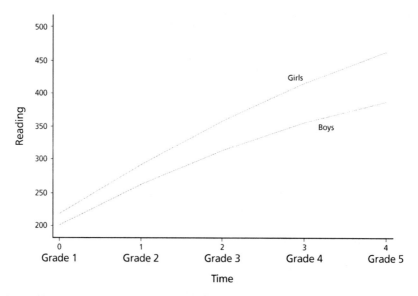

Figure 11.5 Graphical illustration of the predicted reading achievement trajectories of girls and boys based on a quadratic model with time measured in years and centered so zero corresponds to the beginning of first grade.

all parameter estimates of interpreted models (typically in a table) along with indications of the precision of these estimates (i.e., standard errors or confidence intervals). These tabular results should be supplemented with narrative interpretation, effect size calculations, and/or graphical displays to bring attention to the specific estimates or results that address the research questions.

DISCUSSION

The discussion section provides researchers an opportunity to evaluate, interpret, and qualify the results of the study. Researchers should provide a concise statement about the relationship between the results and the original research questions, emphasizing any practical as well as theoretical implications. Description of the limitations of the study resulting from the type of design, sampling, measurement procedures, and analysis should be provided. Researchers can link their findings to past research and articulate the degree to which the results are generalizable based on the study design and analyses.

General guidelines for discussing the results of empirical studies, such as those provided in the *Publication Manual of the American Psychological Asso-*

ciation (American Psychological Association, 2001) or the *American Medical Association Manual of Style* (Iverson et al., 1998), should be augmented by consideration of specific issues relative to multilevel modeling. Such issues might include: (a) what information is provided by the multilevel approach that was not provided in previous investigations that relied on the use of more traditional analyses (e.g., multiple regression) and (b) how the results may have been impacted by the decisions made during the multilevel model development and estimation.

SUMMARY

This chapter has provided a series of suggestions organized around the sections traditionally reported in published research. Some suggestions echo general recommendations made for reporting research, discussing issues such as sampling, variable selection, research design, and the connection between research questions and analyses (e.g., AERA Task Force on Reporting Research Methods, 2006). Other suggestions are more specific to multilevel modeling, focusing on issues such as estimation and inference, the nature of multilevel data, and reporting multilevel results.

To summarize these suggestions, a list of questions was developed that generally should be answerable by the *reader* of a well-written report of a multilevel modeling application. Mirroring the structure of a research report, these questions are organized into five categories: (1) research study (e.g., What sampling strategy was used?), (2) model specification (e.g., How many models were estimated?), (3) estimation and inference (e.g., What method of estimation was used?), (4) data (To what degree were data consistent with distributional assumptions?), and (5) results (Which specific results addressed each research question?). These questions are presented in the form of a checklist in Table 11.10.

Those preparing reports of multilevel modeling applications could use this checklist as a tool, asking themselves whether the consumer of the research report could answer these questions. Alternatively, one might ask colleagues to review a manuscript and attempt to answer the questions. The ability of colleagues to answer the questions may suggest areas that warrant additional attention and clarification.

The manner in which multilevel results are organized and presented has the potential to critically impact the utility, understanding, and credibility of the research. This belief motivated the writing of this chapter and informed the development of suggestions as to *what* to present and *how* to present multilevel results. These suggestions will need to be evaluated critically in the context of novel applications and may need further refinement as the techniques used in multilevel modeling evolve. Nonetheless,

TABLE 11.10 Checklist for Report of Multilevel Study

Could the reader answer the following general questions about the study?	Yes	N/A
What were the purposes/research questions for the study?		
Was the literature reviewed consistent with the study purposes and methods?		
What sampling strategy was used at each level (e.g., probability)?		
What sampling weights, if any, were used?		
How many units were at each level of the analysis?		
How were lower-level units distributed across upper-level units?		
Was a power analysis used to determine the number of units at each level?		
What study design was used (e.g., experimental, quasi-experimental)?		
What variables were used in the analyses?		
What is the validity evidence for each variable?		
What is the reliability evidence for each variable?		

Could the reader answer the following questions about model specification?	Yes	N/A
How many models were estimated?		
What were the fixed effects in each estimated model?		
What was the covariance structure of each estimated model?		
What process was used to define the fixed effects for each model?		
What process was used to define the covariance structure for each model?		
What method was used to evaluate model fit?		
How was each variable centered, coded, or scaled?		

Could the reader answer the following questions about estimation and inference?	Yes	N/A
What software and version were used?		
What method of estimation was used (e.g., REML, ML)?		
Were estimation problems (e.g., improper variance estimates) encountered?		
If estimation problems were encountered, how were they addressed?		
What methods were used to make inferential statements?		

Could the reader answer the following questions about the data?	Yes	N/A
What was the structure of the data (e.g., students nested in schools)?		
How were the variables and level one coefficients distributed?		
To what degree were variables correlated?		
Were data missing? And if so, how were they treated?		
To what degree did missing data impact the results?		
Were there outliers? And if so, how were they identified and handled?		
To what degree did outliers influence the results?		
To what degree were the data consistent with the distributional assumptions?		
To what degree were the results sensitive to questionable assumptions?		

Could the reader answer the following questions about the results?	Yes	N/A
Which specific results addressed each research question?		
What was the ICC?		
What was the estimated value of each parameter in each interpreted model?		
How precise was each estimate (e.g., SE, CI)?		
How do the limitations impact interpretation?		

Note: N/A = Not applicable

it is hoped that these suggestions will be useful to researchers reporting multilevel modeling applications and will serve to improve the consistency and clarity of the reported results from multilevel analyses.

REFERENCES

AERA Task Force on Reporting Research Methods. (2006). *Standards for reporting on empirical social science research in AERA publications.* Retrieved February 1, 2007, from http//www.aera.net/?id=1480

Akaike, H. (1974). A new look at the statistical model of identification. *IEEE Transaction on Automatic Control, 19,* 716–723.

American Psychological Association. (2001). *Publication manual of the American Psychological Association.* Washington, DC: author.

Boomsma, A. (2000). Reporting analyses of covariance structures: Teacher's corner. *Structural Equation Modeling, 7,* 461–483.

Boote, D. N., & Beile, P. (2005). Scholars before researchers: On the centrality of the dissertation literature review in research preparation. *Educational Researcher, 34,* 3–15.

Carpenter, J., Goldstein, H., & Rasbash, J. (1999). A non-parametric bootstrap for multilevel models. *Multilevel Modeling Newsletter, 11,* 2–5.

Collins, L. M., Schafer, J. L., & Kam, C. M (2001). A comparison of inclusive and restrictive strategies in modern missing data procedures. *Psychological Methods, 6,* 330–351.

Ethington, C. A. (1997). A hierarchical linear modeling approach to studying college effects. *Higher Education: Handbook of Theory and Research, 12,* 165–194.

Ferron, J., Dailey, R., & Yi, Q. (2002). Effects of misspecifying the first-level error structure in two-level models of change. *Multivariate Behavioral Research, 37,* 379–403.

Ferron, J., Hess, M. R., Hogarty, K. Y., Dedrick, R. F., Kromrey, J. D., Lang, T. R., et al. (2006, April). *Multilevel modeling: A review of methodological issues and applications.* Paper presented at the annual meeting of the American Educational Research Association, San Francisco, CA.

Giesbrecht, F., & Burns, J. (1985). Two-stage analysis based on a mixed model: Large-sample asymptotic theory and small-sample simulation results. *Biometrics, 41,* 477–486.

Henderson, C. R. (1975). Best linear unbiased estimation and prediction under a selection model. *Biometrics, 31,* 423–447.

Hoyle, R. H., & Panter, A. T. (1995). Writing about structural equation models. In R. H. Hoyle (Ed.), *Structural equation modeling concepts, issues, and applications* (pp. 158–176). Thousand Oaks, CA: Sage Publications.

Iverson, C., Flanagin, A., Fontanarosa, P. B., Glass, R. M., Glitman, P., Lantz, J. C., et al. (1998). *American Medical Association Manual of Style* (9th ed.). Philadelphia: Lippincott Williams & Wilkins.

Jiang, J. M. (2001). Goodness-of-fit tests for mixed model diagnostics. *The Annals of Statistics, 29,* 1137–1164.

Kamata, A. (2001). Item analysis by the hierarchical generalized linear model. *Journal of Educational Measurement, 38,* 79–93.

Kamata, A., Bauer, D. J., & Miyazaki, Y. (2008). Multilevel measurement modeling. In A. A. O'Connell & D. Betsy McCoach (Eds.), *Multilevel modeling of educational data* (pp. 345–390). Charlotte, NC: Information Age Publishing.

Kenward, M., & Roger, J. (1997). Small sample inference for fixed effects from restricted maximum likelihood. *Biometrics, 53,* 983–997.

Kochenderfer-Ladd, B., & Wardrop, J. L. (2001). Chronicity and instability of children's peer victimization experiences as predictors of loneliness and social satisfaction trajectories. *Child Development, 72,* 134–151.

Kreft, I. G. G., & de Leeuw, J. (1998). *Introducing multilevel models.* London: Sage.

Kreft, I. G. G., de Leeuw, J., & Aiken, L. S. (1995). The effect of different forms of centering in hierarchical linear models. *Multivariate Behavioral Research, 30,* 1–21.

Lee, V. E., & Loeb, S. (2000). School size in Chicago elementary schools: Effects on teachers' attitudes and students' achievement. *American Educational Research Journal, 37,* 3–31.

Littell, R., Milliken, G., Stroup, W., & Wolfinger, R. (1996). *SAS system for mixed models.* Cary, NC: SAS Institute Inc.

Little, R. J., & Rubin, D. B. (1987). *Statistical analysis with missing data.* New York: John Wiley & Sons.

Longford, N. (1993). Regression analysis of multilevel data with measurement error. *British Journal of Mathematical and Statistical Psychology, 46,* 301–311.

Longford, N. (2001). Simulation-based diagnostics in random-coefficient models. *Journal of the Royal Statistical Society Series A-Statistics in Society, 164,* 259–273.

Ma, X., Ma, L., & Bradley, K. D. (2008). Using multilevel modeling to investigate school effects. In A. A. O'Connell and D. Betsy McCoach (Eds.), *Multilevel modeling of educational data* (pp. 59–110). Charlotte, NC: Information Age Publishing.

Maciejewski, M. L., Diehr, P., Smith, M. A., & Hebert, P. (2002). Common methodological terms in health services research and their symptoms. *Medical Care, 40,* 477–484.

Marks, H. M. (2000). Student engagement in instructional activity: Patterns in the elementary, middle, and high school years. *American Educational Research Journal, 37,* 153–184.

Marsh, H. W., Köller, O., & Baumert, J. (2001). Reunification of East and West German school systems: Longitudinal multilevel modeling study of the big-fish-little-pond effect on academic self concept. *American Educational Research Journal, 38,* 321–350.

McCoach, D. B., & Black, A. C. (2008). Evaluation of model fit and adequacy. In A. A. O'Connell and D. Betsy McCoach (Eds.), *Multilevel modeling of educational data* (pp. 245–272). Charlotte, NC: Information Age Publishing.

McDonald, R. P., & Ho, M. R. (2002). Principles and practice in reporting structural equation analysis. *Psychological Methods, 7,* 68–82.

Meijer, E., Van der Leeden, R., & Busing, F. (1995). Implementing the bootstrap multilevel model. *Multilevel Modeling Newsletter, 7,* 7–11.

Mok, M. (1995). Sample size requirements for 2-level designs in educational research. *Multilevel Modeling Newsletter, 7*, 11–15.

Morrell, C. H., Pearson, J. D., & Brant, L. J. (1997). Linear transformations of linear mixed-effect models. *The American Statistician, 51*, 338–343.

Murray, D. M. (1998). *Design and analysis of group randomized trials.* New York: Oxford University Press.

Murray, D. M., Varnell, S. P., & Blitstein, J. L. (2004). Design and analysis of group-randomized trials: A review of methodological developments. *American Journal of Public Health, 94*, 423–432.

Muthén, L. K., & Muthén, B. O. (1998–2004). *Mplus user's guide* (3rd ed.). Los Angeles: Muthén & Muthén.

O'Connell, A. A., Goldstein, J., Rogers, H. J., & Peng, C. Y. J. (2008). Multilevel logistic models for dichotomous and ordinal data. In A. A. O'Connell & D. Betsy McCoach (Eds.), *Multilevel modeling of educational data* (pp. 199–244). Charlotte, NC: Information Age Publishing.

Purcell-Gates, V., Degener, S. C., Jacobson, E., & Soler, M. (2002). Impact of authentic adult literacy instruction on adult literacy practices. *Reading Research Quarterly, 37*, 70–92.

Rasbash, J., Steele, F., Browne, W., & Prosser, B. (2004). *A user's guide to MLwiN version 2.0.* London: Institute of Education.

Raudenbush, S. W. (1997). Statistical analysis and optimal design for cluster randomized trials. *Psychological Methods, 2*, 173–185.

Raudenbush, S. W., & Bryk, A. S. (2002). *Hierarchical linear models: Applications and data analysis methods* (2nd ed.). Newbury Park, CA: Sage Publications.

Raudenbush, S. W., Bryk, A. S., Cheong, Y., & Congdon, R. (2004). *HLM 6: Hierarchical linear and nonlinear modeling.* Chicago: Scientific Software International.

Raudenbush, S. W., & Liu, X. (2000). Statistical power and optimal design for multisite randomized trials. *Psychological Methods, 5*, 199–213.

Raykov, T., Tomer, A., & Nesselroade, J. R. (1991). Reporting structural equation modeling results in *Psychology and Aging*: Some proposed guidelines. *Psychology and Aging, 6*, 499–503.

Reboussin, D. M., & DeMets, D. L. (1996). Exact permutation inference for two sample repeated measures data. *Communications in Statistical Theory and Methods, 25*, 2223–2238.

Richardson, A., & Welsh, A. (1995). Robust restricted maximum likelihood in mixed linear models. *Biometrics, 51*, 1429–1439.

Roberts, J. K., & McLeod, P. (2008). Software options for multilevel models. In A. A. O'Connell & D. Betsy McCoach (Eds.), *Multilevel modeling of educational data* (pp. 427–468). Charlotte, NC: Information Age Publishing.

Roy, J., & Lin, X. (2002). Analysis of multivariate longitudinal outcomes with nonignorable dropouts and missing covariates: Changes in methadone treatment practices. *Journal of the American Statistical Association, 97*, 40–52.

SAS Institute Inc. (2000). *SAS/Proc MIXED* (Version 8) [Computer program]. Cary, NC: SAS Institute Inc.

Schwartz, G. (1978). Estimating the dimensions of a model. *Annals of Statistics, 6*, 461–464.

Seltzer, M., Novak, J., Choi, K., & Lim, N. (2002). Sensitivity analysis for hierarchical models employing t level one assumptions. *Journal of Educational and Behavioral Statistics, 27,* 181–222.

Singer, J. D., & Willett, J. B. (2003). *Applied longitudinal data analysis: Modeling change and event occurrence.* New York: Oxford University Press.

Snijders, T. A. B., & Bosker, R. J. (1994). Modeled variance in two-level models. *Sociological Methods and Research, 22,* 342–363.

Spybrook, J. (2008). Power, sample size, and design. In A. A. O'Connell and D. Betsy McCoach (Eds.), *Multilevel modeling of educational data* (pp. 273–314). Charlotte, NC: Information Age Publishing.

Stapleton, L. M., & Thomas, S. L. (2008). The use of national datasets for teaching and research. In A. A. O'Connell & D. Betsy McCoach (Eds.), *Multilevel modeling of educational data* (pp. 11–58). Charlotte, NC: Information Age Publishing.

Stern, S., & Welsh, A. (2000). Likelihood inference for small variance components. *Canadian Journal of Statistics, 28,* 517–532.

Tate, R. (2004). Interpreting hierarchical linear and generalized linear models with slopes as outcomes. *Journal of Experimental Education, 73,* 71–95.

Teuscher, F., Herrendorfer, G., & Guiard, G. (1994). The estimation of skewness and kurtosis of random effects in the linear model. *Biometrical Journal, 36,* 661–672.

Thompson, B., & Vacha-Haase, T. (2000). Psychometrics is datametrics: The test is not reliable. *Educational and Psychological Measurement, 60,* 174–195.

Van den Noortgate, W., & Onghena, P. (2003). Combining single-case experimental data using hierarchical linear models. *School Psychology Quarterly, 18,* 325–346.

Verbeke, G. (1997). Linear mixed models for longitudinal data. In G. Verbeke & G. Molenberghs (Eds.), *Linear mixed models in practice: A SAS-oriented approach* (pp. 63–153). New York: Springer.

Wainer, H. (1997). Some multivariate displays of NAEP results. *Psychological Methods, 2,* 34–63.

Willett, J. B., Singer, J. D., & Martin, N. C. (1998). The design and analysis of longitudinal studies of development and psychopathology in context: Statistical models and methodological recommendations. *Development and Psychopathology, 10,* 395–426.

Wolfinger, R. (1993). Covariance structure selection in general mixed models. *Communications in Statistics—Simulation, 22,* 1079–1106.

Woodhouse, G., Yang, M., Goldstein, H., & Rasbash, J. (1996). Adjusting for measurement error in multilevel analysis. *Journal of the Royal Statistical Society-A, 159,* 201–212.

Yu, Q., & Burdick, R. (1995). Confidence-intervals on variance components in regression-models with balanced (Q–1)-Fold nested error structure. *Communications in Statistics -Theory and Methods, 24,* 1151–1167.

Zucker, D., Lieberman, O., & Manor, O. (2000). Improved small sample inference in the mixed linear model: Bartlett correction and adjusted likelihood. *Journal of the Royal Statistical Society-B, 62,* 827–838.

CHAPTER 12

SOFTWARE OPTIONS FOR MULTILEVEL MODELS

J. Kyle Roberts and Patrick McLeod

INTRODUCTION

This is somewhat of a difficult chapter to write as it almost certainly will be dated even before it is published. As software companies and developers continually update their products, changes to routines are made almost daily. Thus, it makes sense for a researcher in hierarchical linear modeling (HLM) to specialize and become expert in one package and continually update his or her own knowledge of changes in that package, rather than trying to remain fluent in the updates of multiple packages. However, this piece of advice comes with the caveat that while some users may prefer one package for certain types of models, this package simply may not be able to model other data structures (e.g., dichotomous outcomes, multivariate response models). Therefore, selecting a software package is a two-stage process of identifying the most appropriate package for use and then recognizing the limitations of that package, as well as which packages potentially could overcome these limitations.

Multilevel Modeling of Educational Data, pages 427–463
Copyright © 2008 by Information Age Publishing
All rights of reproduction in any form reserved.

History of the Development of Software

The development of multilevel models consistently is traced back to the work of Robinson (1950), with the recognition of contextual effects in research. Put simply, Robinson discovered that nesting structures in data can be a major contributing factor to the development of individual differences within and across those nesting structures. Therefore, data analyses that neglect these structures potentially could lead to erroneous interpretations of correlational data structures.

Although Robinson was arguably one of the first individuals to recognize the need for multilevel modeling in analyzing correlational data structures, powerful computing technologies did not exist in the 1950's, and thus, no great progress was made in this area. Likewise, Lindley and Smith (1972) coined the term "hierarchical linear models" for the method to analyze such data through Bayesian estimation, but until the development of the EM algorithm (Dempster, Laird, & Rubin, 1977), such models were, at best, strenuous exercises in complex covariance components.

The growth of the microcomputer almost paralleled these developments. As computer technology developed, so did the software packages that could estimate these types of models. Before the formalization of some of these packages, researchers were forced to write their own Fortran or C++ code or follow a lengthy step-by-step process through a program like MATHE-MATICA. Currently, a researcher has numerous packages from which to choose in estimating multilevel models. With each new update, the software becomes easier and easier to use and manipulate. In fact, while many programs require the researcher to generate "code" to estimate a model, some packages currently have "point and click" options. This development comes with a caution, however, and Singer (1998) states it well: "Statistical software does not a statistician make" (p. 350). As can be seen in the other chapters in this volume, these are complicated models to estimate and should be approached with great caution. The fact that some of these procedures come included in a larger package (e.g., SAS) may actually contribute to the misuse of these models.

Organization of the Chapter

This chapter is organized into nine different sections. The first eight sections are designated for explanation of some selected software packages. The last section provides a side-by-side comparison of the models and methodologies available for each of the packages. Although there are multiple software options for fitting multilevel models, we have chosen to restrict our discussion to what we perceive are some of the more frequently used packages. These packages are MLwiN, HLM, SAS, S-PLUS, R, SPSS, M*plus*, and STATA. Other packages that will not be discussed include LISREL, MIXREG, SYSTAT, and WINBUGS. For further discussion, the Centre for Multilevel Modelling at the Institute of Education in London hosts an excellent website that has software reviews for all of the above mentioned packages (http://www.cmm.bristol.ac.uk/).

This chapter includes a discussion of the resources available for reference, the types of models available, data setup procedures, analysis specifications, the interpretation of output files, the graphing capabilities for each of the packages, and a brief summary of their strengths and weaknesses. The last section of the chapter provides a side-by-side comparison of each of the packages, along with some recommendations about which programs are most appropriate for fitting different models.

In each section, we will be using the publicly available dataset illustrated in Roberts (2004). This dataset may be obtained in multiple formats at http://www.hlm-online.com/datasets/ This dataset contains scores from 160 students in 16 schools on two variables: a science achievement variable and a composite variable measuring urbanicity, a synthetic variable that measures the degree to which an individual is in a more- or less-urban setting. Higher scores on the urbanicity variable tend to indicate more impoverished settings. Throughout the demonstrations of each statistical package, the common model used is a two-level model with random effects for the intercept and the slope coefficient for the urbanicity variable. Thus, the level-one structural model is

$$science_{ij} = \beta_{0j} + \beta_{1j}urbanicity_{ij} + r_{ij}, \tag{12.1}$$

with level-two equations,

$$\beta_{0j} = \gamma_{00} + u_{0j} \tag{12.2a}$$

$$\beta_{1j} = \gamma_{10} + u_{1j}. \tag{12.2b}$$

Table 12.1 contains the resulting estimates from this fitted model, based on restricted maximum likelihood (REML) estimation in the HLMv6.04 software package.

Although the intent of this chapter is to give the reader a brief overview of each of the selected packages, this short manuscript does not replace the instruction that comes in the manuals accompanying each package. Furthermore, as packages change frequently, readers are encouraged to investigate software before purchasing.

TABLE 12.1   Two-level Model Estimates Based on Roberts (2004) Data Example

Fixed effects:	Estimate	S.E.
Intercept, γ_{00}	22.391	2.717
Urbanicity, γ_{10}	−0.867	0.130
Random effects:		
Level-1 effect, σ^2	0.271	
School mean, τ_{00}	113.602	
Urbanicity slope, τ_{11}	0.252	
$COV(u_{0j}, u_{1j})$, τ_{01}	−3.344	
Fit:		
Deviance	412.171	
AIC	424.171	
BIC	442.547	

Note 1: Estimation is via REML, within HLMv6.04.
Note 2: In Roberts (2004), the random effects are labeled differently but have the same meaning.

MLwiN 2.0

Development of the Package

The MLwiN package first was developed as a DOS-based system by the team at the Centre for Multilevel Modelling at London's Institute of Education. The precursors to MLwiN 2.0, MLn and ML3, were mostly command interface driven rather than the graphical user interface (GUI) available in the current version. While the GUI interface does make the package more user-friendly, the underlying command interface is still available for use, making MLwiN less of a static program by giving the researcher access to routines which are not "point and clickable." This can be especially helpful when a variable needs to be transformed or dummy-coded variables need to be created. The one difficulty, however, is that utilizing the command interface is a skill that is covered only rudimentarily in the user's manual.

The GUI interface is a great plus for this package. For beginning users, this is a great strength for both this package and the HLM package. Being able to see the actual notation for the model that is being estimated places these two packages somewhat above other software. However, this comes at a cost: the screens are so specialized in these two packages because they are built to run only multilevel models. If other data manipulation is necessary, MLwiN is somewhat cumbersome because data must be exported to another package and then imported back into MLwiN. MLwiN can estimate models with either iterative generalized least squares (IGLS) or restrictive iterative generalized least squares (RIGLS), as well as through penalized quasi-likelihood (PQL), second-order PQL, marginal quasi-likelihood, and second-order MQL.

Types of Models Available

MLwiN will allow the researcher to specify a model with up to five levels, which is a great strength over the other packages but begs the question of whether or not an analysis with five levels is appropriate or interpretable. However, should a researcher ever need such a model, this is the package to use. MLwiN is able to fit multiple types of models for data types including normal response, binomial, Poisson, negative binomial, repeated measures, nominal and ordered multinomial, cross-classified, multiple membership and cross-classified models, survival and time series, as well as multivariate normal data.

Data Setup Procedures

Earlier versions of MLwiN only had the capability of ASCII text input; however, the newer versions allow the user to "paste" datasets from the clipboard (SPSS datasets work with this paste function). MLwiN uses a single dataset to perform analyses; it does not require splitting the data into multiple datasets for each level. MLwiN does, however, require a "constant" to be included in the dataset in order to estimate the intercept. A simple variable with a value of one for each case in the dataset will meet this requirement. In the case of more complicated models (binomial for example), this constant must be specified as more than one variable. This is done because MLwiN requires that the parameter n_i (the denominator for the binomial distribution parameter) be specified as equal to one for all units. Therefore, one of the constants will be used to estimate the intercept or grand mean, and the second constant will be used in the estimation of the variance component for the binomial dataset. Although this would seem overly cumbersome, the manual does a great job of walking users through this setup process.

In addition to the usual higher-level grouping variable(s), MLwiN requires an individual id variable for each case in the dataset. These variables, along with the variables for the constant(s), can be created within the command interface.

Analysis Specifications

The default in MLwiN is to use IGLS for normal response model estimation. Restrictive IGLS, Markov Chain Monte Carlo (MCMC), and Bootstrap are also available for these models as well as for the repeated measures and multiple membership models. The binary, Poisson, and negative binomial models may be estimated with penalized quasi-likelihood, marginal quasi-likelihood, MCMC, and bootstrap methods. Specifying a model is simply a "point and click" endeavor after the data file has been input into MLwiN. Once a dependent variable has been selected with the appropriate number of levels, covariates/predictors can be added to the model simply by selecting "Add Term" and then defining whether or not that variable should include a random term.

Interpreting Output Files

MLwiN is a great learning tool for the novice multilevel modeling researcher. Output and command specification files are in a "what you see is what you get" (WYSIWYG) format. In MLwiN, it is not always possible to build and run a "final" model without first producing estimates for simpler models. While it is sometimes more expedient to be able to go straight to a final model, MLwiN relies on previous estimates as a starting point for estimating more complicated models, thereby requiring the final model to be built in stages. These additional steps force the researcher to use a model building approach and to explore aspects of the data that might have been overlooked previously. Figure 12.1 contains a screen shot of the final MLwiN results for the model shown in Equations 12.1, 12.2a and 12.2b. The

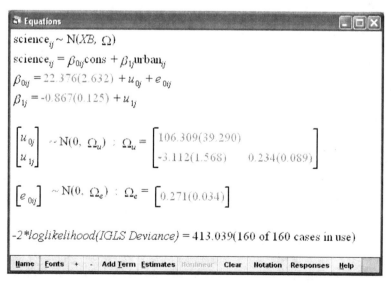

Figure 12.1 MLwiN equations window output from estimating Roberts (2004) data.

slight differences in estimates between the MLwiN results and those shown in Table 12.1 are due to the estimation strategy used (IGLS versus REML, respectively).

Graphing Capabilities

MLwiN has a fairly powerful graphing package that allows for customized graphs, including Trellis graphs. Trellis graphics are an array of the same graph type by the levels of some factor variables. In MLwiN, the graphing functions are interactive; the user can click anywhere on a graph and the closest point estimate and group membership will be displayed. The MLwiN manual devotes an entire chapter to the graphics capabilities of this package. The package also contains excellent graphing functions for running model diagnostics. For example, a researcher can identify an outlier simply by clicking on it, thus providing the opportunity to "mask" that outlier so that it does not unduly influence other observations. Figure 12.2 provides an example of one of the graphing functions applied to the Roberts (2004) data, displaying the level-one regression models for each of the 16 schools.

Strengths and Weaknesses

MLwiN is an exceptionally powerful package for modeling hierarchical and multilevel data. The ability to build models dynamically in a format

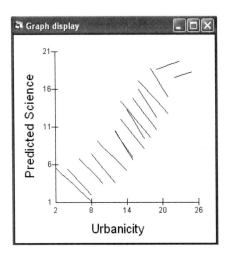

Figure 12.2   Graphing example from MLwiN: Regression of science on urbanicity for each of 16 schools.

that the user actually can view (instead of having to write "code" as in some other programs) is a great strength. The fact that MLwiN was built specifically to handle multilevel data is another strength, because it incorporates functions that may be crucial to model building. For example, some Bayesian models are difficult to estimate and use a lot of processing time. MLwiN allows the user to run a "burn-in" period on complicated Markov Chain Monte Carlo (MCMC) models, the estimates from which will be used to initialize the start of the MCMC.

While being a strictly multilevel application is a great strength, it is also somewhat of a weakness. Sometimes, simple functions, such as grand-mean centering, are difficult to perform. Although MLwiN does have a powerful commands window tool that can be used to perform a multitude of statistical functions, learning this new command language can prove a daunting task. (The documentation in the manual is not as extensive as the Help Menu topics distributed with the software). As is the case for most of the software packages reviewed, the researcher can become somewhat frustrated trying to find where all of the model output is stored. MLwiN stores information in free columns within the dataset, and it often surprises new users to find that the variance/covariance matrix for the fixed effects can be found in column c1099 (c99 in older versions). Despite these weaknesses, MLwiN is still a superb package for fitting multilevel data.

HLM 6.0

Development of the Package

Like MLwiN, the HLM package is designed solely for use with hierarchical and multilevel data. The package has been in development since the mid-1980's, and version 6 was released in 2004. HLM has become a popular package because of the link to the hierarchical linear modeling text by Raudenbush and Bryk (2002), and because of the WYSIWYG format that allows users to "point and click" their models. The development of the package has been overseen mainly by Raudenbush and Bryk and also by Richard Congdon.

Types of Models Available

In addition to the two-level linear models, HLM can fit three-level models as well as certain types of cross-classified models. Through the hierarchical generalized linear models routine, HLM can fit a series of nonlinear models, including binomial, Poisson, multinomial, and ordinal models. HLM also can fit multivariate models with the HMLM routine. Fitting each of these models in HLM requires the use of separate subroutines (cf., HLM2, HLM3, HMLM, HMLM2, and HCM2), but the basic look and feel of the HLM interface is consistent across all of these subroutines, making the transition to more complicated models easier.

Data Setup Procedures

Data setup in HLM is different than in other packages. HLM uses a series of data inputs from data files equal to the number of levels being investigated. For a two-level model, the researcher is encouraged to create two separate datasets, one for each level. Although a single level-one dataset may be analyzed in HLM, the manual advises researchers against building an analysis in this manner when the level-one dataset is large (Raudenbush, Bryk, Cheong, Congdon, & duToit, 2004). If the datasets are split into levels, the level-one dataset has to contain a level-two "id" variable and be sorted by that variable (all cases in each group must appear together). This sorting is a simple function that can be run in any external data processing program. The level-two dataset contains the grouping variable and any other variables that are measured at the second level. This process of "splitting" the dataset adds an additional step to the data setup because most datasets have the lowest level variables nested inside higher level variables; however, it is easy to create separate data files using custom programmed routines in packages like SPSS, S-PLUS, R, and SAS. These files then are "married" into a MDM (multivariate data matrix) file that can be used by HLM for further data analysis (in HLMv5 and earlier versions, this file was known as a SSM file). One potentially frustrating aspect of this type of data structuring is the need to "recreate" the MDM file every time a change is made to the data. For a very basic example, suppose a researcher is investigating a growth model and after testing the linear growth model, wanted to include polynomials as measures of the growth trend. In order to do this, these polynomials would need to be created in another software package, and then the files would be reintroduced into HLM to create a new MDM file.

Analysis Specifications

After creating the MDM file, the model may be specified easily. As the MDM data file was created in two steps via datasets at each level, the model to be estimated also must be created at each level. Unlike other programs, such as S-PLUS or SAS, the user actually has the benefit of seeing model equations at each level of the hierarchy. The program also will generate a

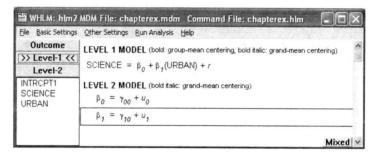

Figure 12.3   Screen Shot of Model Specification within HLM.

combined model by clicking on the "Mixed" button on the GUI interface. Regardless, the ability to separate the model into the corresponding and appropriate level-specific equations is a wonderful benefit of this package. Specifying the model is then a simple process of "point and click." After first selecting the level-one outcome variable, other variables then can be added to and deleted from the model simply by clicking in the appropriate place. HLM allows the user to specify a variable as either group-mean centered or grand-mean centered; these transformations are performed directly within the HLM package. A screen-shot example of a model corresponding to Equations 12.1, 12.2a and 12.2b can be seen in Figure 12.3.

Although there is not enough room in this manuscript to describe every step in the process of running the model through the HLM software, a complete description of the steps necessary to fit the model shown in Figure 12.3 may be downloaded at http://www.hlm-online.com/datasets/education/data1_hlm.pdf.

Interpreting Output Files

Once the model has been specified and run, HLM generates a report that is opened in Microsoft Notepad (or any other text editor). There is a considerable amount of information in this file, so we will only show a portion of the output here (entries in bold correspond to some of the entries in Table 12.1):

```
Summary of the model specified (in equation format)
----------------------------------------------------
Level-1 Model
   Y = B0 + B1*(URBAN) + R

Level-2 Model
   B0 = G00 + U0
   B1 = G10 + U1
```

```
Final estimation of fixed effects:
------------------------------------------------------------------
                                  Standard  Approx.
Fixed Effect          Coefficient   Error  T-ratio  df   P-value
------------------------------------------------------------------
For INTRCPT1, B0
    INTRCPT2, G00     22.391241  2.716968    8.241  15   0.000
For URBAN slope, B1
    INTRCPT2, G10     -0.867005  0.129808   -6.679  15   0.000
------------------------------------------------------------------


The outcome variable is SCIENCE
Final estimation of variance components:
------------------------------------------------------------------
Random Effect    Standard   Variance   df  Chi-square  P-value
                 Deviation  Component
------------------------------------------------------------------
INTRCPT1, U0     10.65844   113.60241  15  1626.56233   0.000
URBAN slope, U1   0.50199     0.25200  15    19.72077   0.000
level-1, R        0.52025     0.27066
------------------------------------------------------------------


Statistics for current covariance components model
--------------------------------------------------
Deviance = 412.171305
Number of estimated parameters = 4
```

From the output above, we can see that the fixed effect for the intercept is estimated to be 22.391 and the fixed effect for the slope of "urban" is −0.867. These are the same results shown in Table 12.1. Other sources of information that might be of interest to the researcher, such as residuals, fitted values, and OLS estimates, are saved as a residual file in either SPSS, SAS, Stata, SYSTAT, or free format. To create these residual files, the user must specify that these values be saved by clicking on the level-one residuals and the level-two residuals buttons within the basic settings menu.

Graphing Capabilities

HLM has some very nice "canned" graphing functions that help the user build relatively complex graphs, such as the level-one school equations from the Roberts (2004) data in Figure 12.4. HLM allows for box and whisker plots, scatter plots, and line plots that include a level-two classification variable, as well as a series of model-based graphs, including equation graphing, graphing of residuals, and empirical Bayes and OLS estimate plots of confidence intervals. Although HLM's graphical capacities are more limited than some of the other programs, each new version of HLM seems to

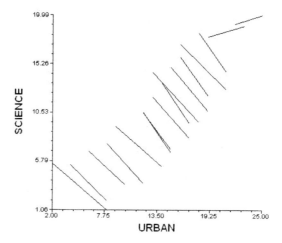

Figure 12.4   Graphing example from HLM: Regression of science on urbanicity ("urban") for each of 16 schools.

provide improved graphical capacities. In S-PLUS, a user simultaneously can compare two models by overlaying the graphs from each of the models using the Trellis graphing function (note, however, that this requires a fairly skilled user). In HLM, such graphics are not possible.

Strengths and Weaknesses

Like MLwiN, HLM is a powerful package for users focused solely on fitting multilevel models. However, it also is plagued with the same problems as MLwiN in that many data-handling routines must be run in an external software package and then imported back into HLM. Across the development of the different versions, HLM has made great gains in the area of graphic handling. In addition, this software package allows the user to actually see the model being built. The package is a great complement to the HLM text by Raudenbush and Bryk (2002), and has a very extensive user's manual (Raudenbush et al., 2004) that has strong links between the aforementioned text and the software package.

SAS

Development of the Package

The SAS statistical package has been the core product of the SAS Institute since it began operation with seven employees in Raleigh, North Carolina in 1976. Today, SAS is best known for its extensible macro language and diverse yet powerful services such as SAS Business Intelligence and SAS Enterprise Intelligence. SAS statistical core, now part of SAS Analytics, is still one of the premier options for many forms of statistical analysis, including multilevel models. The SAS Foundation installation (installation including the core of SAS and most of SAS's additional development services such as Enterprise Miner) is currently available for nearly all major operating systems including Microsoft Windows, Solaris, and Linux. SAS is only available at version 6.12 for Macintosh OS X.

Types of Models Available

The SAS workhorse for multilevel modeling is PROC MIXED. This procedure allows the user to fit multilevel models, growth models, and hierarchical models (cf., Singer, 1998, for a concise history of PROC MIXED). SAS also implements procedures for nonlinear mixed models, PROC NLMIXED and GLIMMIX. Both PROC NLMIXED and GLIMMIX allow the estimation of non-linear models, whereas PROC MIXED handles linear mixed models.

Data Setup Procedures

SAS uses a single data set to perform analyses. Working with data in SAS is different than using SPSS or STATA. Whereas most statistical packages interact directly with the operating system and file path structure of the machine on which they are installed, SAS uses an internal library structure to write to and call from data. The data step in SAS is the core of the data importation and manipulation. Since SAS's implementation of a GUI system, the easiest way to bring data into SAS and assign it to the WORK library is to import it using the Import Data Wizard. This wizard allows the user to import data seamlessly into the WORK library from such common file formats as Microsoft Excel spreadsheets, Microsoft Access databases, comma separated values files, and ASCII delimited text files.

Analysis Specifications

The SAS syntax for specifying a two-level model with random effects and generating empirical Bayes estimates is straightforward; unfortunately for the first-time user, the number of options for model generation can be daunting. The syntax below fits the model shown in Equations 12.1, 12.2a and 12.2b.

```
proc mixed data = mlm noclprint noitprint covtest;
 class group;
 model science = urban
 / solution ddfm = bw notest outp=dataout;
 random intercept urban / subject = group type = un solution;
run;
```

In SAS, a "PROC" is a procedure; the PROC step specifies the analysis. The first line of code tells SAS to use the procedure MIXED (proc mixed) on the data object named mlm (data = mlm). The option noclprint instructs the SAS system to suppress the printing of the class-level information table (a listing of the identifiers for each of the "groups" in the present example) and the option noitprint instructs the SAS system to suppress the printing of the iteration history table; removal of these commands provides more extensive output. The option covtest produces asymptotic standard errors and Wald Z-tests for the variance and covariance parameters.

The statement specifications class, model, and random all specify the model and analysis; class identifies the classification variable for this analysis as group. The class group statement is unnecessary if the data are sorted by group, and omitting this statement will speed optimization. The model statement instructs SAS to analyze a model with science as a dependent variable and urban as the independent variable/covariate. The solution specification instructs SAS to use the between/within method for calculating the denominator degrees of freedom for tests of fixed effects (Singer, 1998), and the notest option suppresses the Type III hypothesis tests of the fixed effects (these tests can be reported through the solution option, however). The outp=dataout command writes the output from the mixed procedure to a file named dataout. This file is used later to graph the predicted model. The random statement is the most important piece of the puzzle; it contains the specifications for calculation of random effects, for the covariance structure, and for the generation of the empirical Bayes estimates. In this example, the "random intercept urban" command specifies a random intercept model in which the variable urban is allowed to have random slopes. After the "/," the nesting structure is specified by the command "subject = group" which identifies the variable group as the level-two identifier. The "type = un" command allows for an unstructured variance-covariance matrix. The default option is "type = vc" which invokes the variance components structure, allowing for a different variance component for each random effect (but no covariance). The "solution" command instructs SAS to print the estimates for the fixed effects, and the "run" statement indicates to SAS to now run the identified code.

Interpreting Output Files

Even with the example code written to suppress the output of the class-level information table and iteration history table, SAS still generates quite a bit of output. Native SAS output uses a file type called List files (*.lst). The easiest way to bridge this SAS system file type into more commonly available file types, assuming the researcher is working with a desktop installation of SAS, is to right click on the Output window, select File, then Save As, and in the resulting dialog box select the option RTF files under Save As Type. RTF (Rich Text Format) files are easily readable in Microsoft Word, Open Office, and Corel WordPerfect. The example code produces the following (abridged) output file:

```
Covariance Parameter Estimates
                            Standard    Z
Cov Parm Subject  Estimate   Error    Value    Pr Z
UN(1,1) GROUP      113.60    43.5264    2.61   0.0045
UN(2,1) GROUP      -3.3463    1.7746   -1.89   0.0593
UN(2,2) GROUP       0.2520    0.09939   2.54   0.0056
Residual            0.2707    0.03386   7.99   <.0001


Fit Statistics

-2 Res Log Likelihood       412.2
AIC (smaller is better)     420.2
AICC (smaller is better)    420.4
BIC (smaller is better)     423.3


Null Model Likelihood Ratio Test

DF   Chi-Square   Pr > ChiSq
 3      350.63      <.0001


The SAS System


The Mixed Procedure


Solution for Fixed Effects

                       Standard
Effect     Estimate     Error     DF   t Value   Pr > |t|
Intercept   22.3912    2.7170     15     8.24     <.0001
URBAN       -0.8670    0.1298    143    -6.68     <.0001
```

Solution for Random Effects

Effect	GROUP	Estimate	Standard Error	DF	t Value	Pr > |t|
Intercept	1	-15.3528	2.7602	158	-5.56	<.0001
URBAN	1	0.1201	0.1558	158	0.77	0.4418
Intercept	2	-13.4900	2.7772	158	-4.86	<.0001
URBAN	2	-0.00728	0.1637	158	-0.04	0.9646
Intercept	3	-10.7226	2.8359	158	-3.78	0.0002
URBAN	3	0.04421	0.1632	158	0.27	0.7868
Intercept	4	-7.2610	2.9126	158	-2.49	0.0137
URBAN	4	-0.09373	0.1699	158	-0.55	0.5819
Intercept	5	-6.2056	2.9165	158	-2.13	0.0349
URBAN	5	0.08207	0.1578	158	0.52	0.6038
Intercept	6	3.6377	3.4612	158	1.05	0.2949
URBAN	6	-0.4300	0.2014	158	-2.14	0.0343
Intercept	7	2.1597	3.2627	158	0.66	0.5090
URBAN	7	-0.3110	0.1883	158	-1.65	0.1006
Intercept	8	2.5028	3.1490	158	0.79	0.4279
URBAN	8	-0.1260	0.1674	158	-0.75	0.4529
Intercept	9	9.1791	3.5944	158	2.55	0.0116
URBAN	9	-0.4350	0.1973	158	-2.20	0.0289
Intercept	10	4.5760	3.2082	158	1.43	0.1557
URBAN	10	-0.09870	0.1699	158	-0.58	0.5621
Intercept	11	8.5914	3.3742	158	2.55	0.0118
URBAN	11	-0.2035	0.1759	158	-1.16	0.2490
Intercept	12	13.9689	3.6910	158	3.78	0.0002
URBAN	12	-0.4109	0.1927	158	-2.13	0.0345
Intercept	13	8.8764	3.2846	158	2.70	0.0076
URBAN	13	-0.01729	0.1638	158	-0.11	0.9161
Intercept	14	18.8103	3.9965	158	4.71	<.0001
URBAN	14	-0.4061	0.1966	158	-2.07	0.0405
Intercept	15	-9.6672	3.5218	158	-2.74	0.0068
URBAN	15	1.1381	0.1669	158	6.82	<.0001
Intercept	16	-9.6030	4.1094	158	-2.34	0.0207
URBAN	16	1.1550	0.1851	158	6.24	<.0001

The above "Solution for Fixed Effects" are computed as 22.391 for the global intercept and −0.867 for the global slope. The "Solution for Random Effects" are then the empirical Bayes estimates for the intercept and slope coefficient for each of the 16 schools. SAS produces these values as part of the output, while the provision of these results is generally post hoc in other software packages. Since we specified "type = un", SAS also produces the variance and covariance parameter estimates. In this table, UN(1,1) represents the variance estimate for the intercept, UN(2,2) is the variance of the slope coefficients, and UN(2,1) is the covariance between these two effects.

Graphing Capabilities

Producing publication-quality graphics in SAS is done through the procedure GPLOT. Rougher graphics can be produced during analysis using PROC PLOT, but they will not be publication quality. PROC GPLOT was used to produce the two way graph in Figure 12.5 using the following code

```
axis1 order =(1 to 25 by 1) minor = none label = (a = 90 "Predicted
      Science");
axis2 order = (1 to 25 by 1) minor = none label =("Urban");

proc gplot data = dataout;
 plot pred*urban=group / nolegend haxis=axis2 vaxis=axis1;
run;
```

The first two lines of this SAS code create the labels for the two axes of the graph. Notice in `proc gplot` command that the dataset being used is `dataout` and not `mlm`. This is because we previously asked SAS to store the predicted values in the `dataout` file (see the "outp = dataout" option in the `solution` statement of the `model` command). The second line in the `gplot` command simply specifies which variables to be graphed.

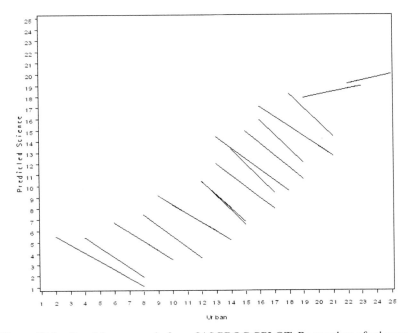

Figure 12.5 Graphing example from SAS PROC GPLOT: Regression of science on urbanicity ("urban") for each of 16 schools.

Strengths and Weaknesses

SAS has several strengths. First, utilizing PROC MIXED allows the user to employ a wide array of options to specify and estimate multilevel models. For advanced users of SAS, it is relatively easy to write new programs to create a new type of analysis. In addition, researchers can conduct all data manipulation and analysis in the same package. Finally, SAS, like S-PLUS, uses object-oriented language. Therefore, users can specify and analyze multiple datasets and perform multiple operations simultaneously. This framework structure in SAS makes it an obvious choice when users want to perform complicated simulations and Monte Carlo investigations. As with most command-language based software programs, the learning curve in the SAS programming language is a difficult, but rewarding, hill to climb.

S-PLUS 7.0

Development of the Package

The S-PLUS package evolved from the S programming language developed by John Chambers at Bell Labs in 1976. Since then, S was acquired by MathSoft and later incorporated into the Insightful Corporation which now distributes S-PLUS, the user-end application of the S programming language. S-PLUS uses a series of routines stored in "libraries" to run different statistical analyses. The current application for running linear multilevel models is the lme (which stands for linear mixed effects), which is part of the larger nlme (which stands for non-linear mixed effects) library developed by Pinheiro and Bates (2002).

S-PLUS is an object-oriented language. For the user, this means that data, commands, output, and graphics easily can be used in multiple formats and multiple objects can be accessed simultaneously. For example, in S-PLUS a researcher could randomly generate 10,000 datasets, run an analysis on each dataset, save a specific part of the output in a constantly appended data file, and then run an analysis on that saved part of the output. Other packages, such as SPSS and STATA, do not allow multiple datasets to be opened simultaneously; however, this is not a problem for S-PLUS's object-oriented language.

Types of Models Available

S-PLUS uses a set of different routines to fit different multilevel models. Available in the GUI are the linear and nonlinear mixed-effects models.

S-PLUS is actually a programming language platform; therefore, the GUI writes code in the background for the user using the lme and nlme functions, respectively. Other routines are not available as part of the GUI package but still are loaded with S-PLUS and can be run from the commands window. The correlatedData library contains both the glme and gee functions for fitting binomial and autoregressive longitudinal data. The MASS library can fit binomial data with penalized quasi-likelihood estimation with the glmmPQL function and negative binomial models with the glm.nb function.

Data Setup Procedures

S-PLUS requires that data be nested inside a single stacked dataset in order to fit a multilevel model. There must be a unique case for each level-one unit. For example, if there were 10 students inside a given school, the dataset would contain 10 rows of data, each with the same level-two identifier. S-PLUS also has the ability to import data from a host of other software packages as well as from ASCII text.

Analysis Specifications

In order to carry out different data analyses, S-PLUS uses a series of functions, which contain arguments for specifying the type of model to be fit. For example, the lm function is used to run a linear regression (linear model) and the aov function is used to specify an ANOVA. Discussing all of the different functions in S-PLUS used to fit multilevel models would take a considerable amount of space; therefore, this chapter focuses only on the lme (linear mixed effects) function.

In this function, there are a list of required arguments and other optional arguments. The basic structure of the function is

```
lme(data, fixed, random, correlation, weights, method),
```

where data is the original data file, fixed is the formula describing the fixed-effects part of the model, and random is the formula describing the random-effects of the model. The first three arguments must be included in the analysis; the last three are optional. The optional argument correlation is used to define the within-group correlation structure. The optional weights argument is used to describe the within-group heteroscedasticity function. The method argument defines the estimation method (i.e., maximum likelihood [ML] or restricted maximum likelihood [REML]). Other functions such as the glme function in the correlatedData library utilize other estimation methods, such as PQL, restricted PQL, MQL, and restricted MQL.

In analyzing the Roberts (2004) dataset, here referred to as example.data, the lme function would be specified as

```
lme.out<-lme(data=example.data, fixed=SCIENCE~URBAN,
random=~URBAN|GROUP)
```

By first typing lme.out<- in the Commands Window, S-PLUS actually will take the output obtained through running the function lme and place it into a new object called lme.out. Any name can be used as an object as long as that name is not already a function. Hence, lme.out will work as the name of an object, but lme would not. In the command line above, the fixed effects are specified as follows: scores on the outcome variable "SCIENCE" are estimated by (~) scores on the variable "URBAN." In the random command, the variables for which random effects are desired appear to the left of the "|" and the grouping variable appears to the right. To specify a random intercepts only model, the "URBAN" variable in the random part of the command line simply would be replaced by a "1" so that the line would read

```
random=~1|GROUP
```

S-PLUS can also handle three-level models through the same command line. If the researcher wanted to include level-two and level-three grouping structures of classrooms and schools, respectively, the random statement for a random intercepts model would read:

```
random=~1|SCHOOL/CLASSROOM
```

Interpreting Output Files

Once the object lme.out has been created, the summary of the output from the analysis can be displayed by typing summary(lme.out) in the Commands Window. Doing so will yield the following:

```
Linear mixed-effects model fit by REML
 Data: example.data
 AIC         BIC          logLik
 424.1713    442.5469     -206.0857
```

```
Random effects:
 Formula: ~ URBAN | GROUP
 Structure: General positive-definite
             StdDev         Corr
(Intercept) 10.6584840   (Inter
 URBAN       0.5019958   -0.625
 Residual    0.5202538

Fixed effects: SCIENCE ~ URBAN
               Value    Std.Error    DF    t-value    p-value
(Intercept)   22.39124   2.717018    143   8.241111   <.0001
 URBAN        -0.86701   0.129811    143  -6.678989   <.0001

Standardized Within-Group Residuals:
      Min           Q1          Med           Q3          Max
 -2.376494   -0.7914869   0.007393824   0.6221058   2.169879

Number of Observations: 160
Number of Groups: 16
```

The fixed effects are 22.391 for the intercept and –0.867 for the slope of the URBAN variable. The variance components are displayed as standard deviations and can be computed either by squaring these values or by typing the command VarCorr(lme.out). The empirical Bayes estimates of the random effects μ_{0j} can be obtained by typing ranef(lme.out) in the commands window.

Graphing Capabilities

One of the great strengths of S-PLUS is its powerful graphics capabilities. S-PLUS can plot a wide variety of typical graphs and Trellis graphs. However, this powerful tool comes with a caveat: figuring out exactly what to display in a graph is not always a simple endeavor. To view a graph of each of the group-predicted regression lines from the model represented above, modifying the code to include the command plot(augPred(lme.out)) will yield the result in Figure 12.6. However, having all of these prediction lines appear on top of each other in one graph, as in Figures 12.2 and 12.4, is a much more difficult task that requires a fair amount of programming. The good news is that if a graph can be conceived, S-PLUS probably can create it. The bad news is that you may have to have a great deal of knowledge in the S-PLUS language to produce the desired results.

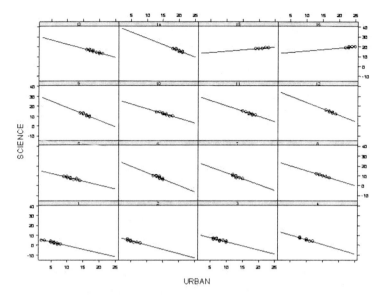

Figure 12.6   Graphing example in S-PLUS: Regression of science on urbanicity ("urban") for each of 16 schools.

Strengths and Weaknesses

S-PLUS is a very powerful package that encompasses a variety of tools for data analysis. The routines created to run a multilevel analysis are relatively powerful. The wonderful thing about this package is the "open source" nature of each of the functions. For an advanced user of S-PLUS, it is relatively easy to "tweak" the functions in order to create a new type of analysis or procedure. The problem is, however, that the learning curve for this package is fairly steep. Fitting simple models in this package is fairly straightforward, but more complicated models require a fair amount of expertise in the S-PLUS language and programming. This knowledge does have its rewards, however, as S-PLUS is a superior package for simulating data and for resampling, both of which are tools that can help further the growing field of multilevel modeling.

R

Those who are familiar with the R programming language probably know it as the free open-sourced version of S-PLUS. In fact, both packages are based on the S programming language and use commands that are remarkably similar in both form and execution. R originally was written by Gentleman and Ihaka at the University of Auckland. The first version of R was released in 2000. The original goal of R was to make a "leaner" S language-based system that did not have the same memory hampering problems that S-PLUS had in its early stages of development. As R has evolved, its strength has become that it is a powerful free software package with a network of users who write code that is shared openly among other users. Although S-PLUS supports more of a GUI design, recent programs in R, such as R-Commander developed by John Fox (2005), give it the same feel as the S-PLUS interface.

As the code for running a linear multilevel model in R is exactly the same as running the model in S-PLUS, it does not bear repeating here. The `nlme` package (for linear and non-linear mixed effects models) run in R uses the same set of commands used by the `nlme` library in S-PLUS (available at http://cran.r-project.org/). There are some subtle differences, however. First, R does not allow the user to run the `plot(augPred(lme.object))` command to produce the graph seen in Figure 12.6. This graph can still be produced, but it must be done with a `groupedData` object. Second, the commands for running more complicated models like binary response models, are different in R. In S-PLUS, the correlatedData library is used to fit binary response models, whereas the `lme4` package in R is used to fit these models.

Recently, new routines have been introduced to R that also allow for the fitting of multilevel models. In addition to the `nlme` library, the `lme4` package contains the routine "`lmer`" which is also capable of running these models. This library is very similar to `nlme` in terms of its functionality, but the main benefit that it has is that the computations are based on analysis of sparse matrices. This allows `lmer` to analyze data at much faster rates than previous versions of `nlme` (Bates, 2006a).

The `lmer` command syntax is slightly different than the `nlme` syntax. In `lmer` the command line takes the form

```
lmer(formula, data, family, method, control , start, subset,
weights, na.action, offset, model, x, y, ...)
```

A thorough description of all of the arguments in this command line can be obtained by typing `?lmer` at any command prompt in R. The format of the command line is mostly similar to `lme`, with the exception of the fact that `lme` splits the commands for the fixed and random parts of the command, whereas `lmer` simply has a single "formula" command line. Part of the reasoning behind this change is that multilevel models are sometimes better thought of as a single linear (in this case) equation instead of a series of two equations (or levels) estimated separately (D. Bates, personal communication, April 6, 2006). Therefore, the syntax necessary to run the model in Equations 12.1, 12.2a, and 12.2b would be

```
ex1<-lmer(SCIENCE ~ URBAN + (URBAN|GROUP), example.data)
```

The above command line may be read as the variable "SCIENCE" being estimated by "urban" plus the random effects for both "URBAN" and for the intercept defined by the level-two grouping variable "GROUP." Just as with S-PLUS, if a three-level model were to be specified with level-two and level-three grouping structures of classrooms and schools respectively (these are not real variables in the dataset but are meant as heuristic), the command line for this model would read as follows:

```
ex1<-lmer(SCIENCE ~ URBAN + (URBAN|SCHOOL/CLASSROOM), example.data)
```

Typing the command summary(ex1) will produce the following results:
```
Linear mixed-effects model fit by REML

Formula: SCIENCE ~ URBAN + (URBAN | GROUP)
 Data: example.data
 AIC         BIC          logLik        MLdeviance    REMLdeviance
 424.1713    442.6223     -206.0857     413.2216      412.1713
Random effects:
 Groups Name           Variance    Std.Dev.   Corr
 GROUP(Intercept)      113.60403   10.65852
 URBAN                 0.25200     0.50200    -0.625
 Residual              0.27066     0.52025
# of obs: 160, groups: GROUP, 16

Fixed effects:
               Estimate    Std. Error   DF      t value    Pr(>|t|)
(Intercept)    22.39124    2.71703      158     8.2411     6.152e-14***
URBAN          -0.86700    0.12981      158     -6.6790    3.884e-10***
---
Signif. codes: 0 '***' 0.001 '**' 0.01 '*' 0.05 '.' 0.1 ' ' 1

Correlation of Fixed Effects:
 (Intr)
URBAN -0.641
```

This output is remarkably similar to the S-Plus lme output. One notable difference is that the *df* has changed from previous versions of the package (see the S-PLUS output from above). The reasoning behind this *df* change is a discussion that could easily take up another volume and a problem that probably won't be resolved in the near future. For an interesting discussion of the problems related to *df* and *p*-values in multilevel models, see Bates (2006b).

The only disadvantage to using R, as opposed to S-PLUS, is that it doesn't support a graphical user interface (GUI) design. However, even this drawback has been overcome partially with the development of the R-Commander program by Fox (2005). Regardless, R is an extremely powerful package using object-oriented language. Coupled with the fact that the software is free, R is a very inviting package. The one caveat is that this package, like S-PLUS, has a steep learning curve. Learning new code is like learning a new language; however, the payoff may well be worth the effort.

SPSS 14.0

Development of the Package

The multilevel modeling routine in SPSS was first added in version 11.5. Built on two routines, SPSS utilizes both MIXED and VARCOMP to fit multilevel models. However, the VARCOMP command only provides the user with estimates of the variance components and not the fixed effects for any covariates included in the model. Therefore, this section only will include discussion of the MIXED routine. SPSS does have a "point and click" method of fitting multilevel models using the Linear option under the Mixed Models pull-down menu, but for reasons of space, it is easier to present the syntax here.

Types of Models Available and Data Setup Procedures

In addition to the two-level random-effects model, SPSS can fit three-level models. Cross-classified and multivariate normal response models also can be fit through the same MIXED routine. SPSS can fit models with either maximum likelihood (ML) or restricted maximum likelihood (REML) estimation methods. However, SPSS is not able to fit non-normal response models, models with binomial outcomes, or models with ordinal outcomes. Although SPSS does provide relatively clean output with a number of options, the higher-level residuals cannot be saved in SPSS. These can be estimated using the MATRIX command, but the process is rather cumbersome.

The data file to be analyzed must be imported into the Data Editor (.sav) and stacked in a format where each row of data represents a single person in a group (or occasion within a person in the case of repeated measures models). The outcome and covariates are specified in the first line of the MIXED command (shown below).

Analysis Specifications

The MIXED command has a relatively straightforward structure. First, an empty Syntax Editor must be opened in SPSS so that the command parameters may be specified. After also opening the dataset in the Data Editor, fitting the model from Equations 12.1, 12.2a, and 12.2b using the Roberts (2004) data would be accomplished with the following commands

```
MIXED science WITH urban
      /FIXED = urban
      /RANDOM = INTERCEPT urban | SUBJECT(group) COVTYPE(UN)
      /METHOD = ML
      /PRINT = COVB G HISTORY SOLUTION TESTCOV
      /SAVE = FIXPRED (fix_pred) PRED (tot_pred) RESID (resid).
```

The first line specifies that the MIXED command is to be run where the dependent variable "science" is predicted WITH the covariate "urban." If a factor were to be included in the model, it also would be included here but specified with the BY command rather than the WITH command. The /FIXED subcommand specifies the fixed effects to be estimated from the variable list given in the first line. In this line, polynomials could be added to a repeated measures model where a variable for "time" was included in the model and then "time*time" and "time*time*time" were added on the /FIXED command line.

The /RANDOM line specifies the random effects for the model and also provides the grouping structure for the two-level model. In this case, we have allowed random effect estimates for the intercept and the slope of urban, shown in the commands to the left of the "|". The command "SUBJECT(group)" indicates that "group" is the cluster-level variable. In this line, we also specify that the covariance structure is unstructured using COVTYPE(UN). As mentioned previously, we can fit the model through either ML or REML estimation procedures by specifying either approach on the /METHOD subcommand (REML is the default procedure) in the fourth line.

In the /PRINT subcommand, we have asked SPSS to output the asymptotic covariance matrix of the fixed-effects parameter estimates (COVB), random effect covariance structure (G), the iteration history (HISTORY), the final estimates of the fixed and random effects (SOLUTION), and the tests for the covariance parameters (TESTCOV).

The final line of the command syntax (/SAVE) saves three casewise statistics to the data file. The FIXPRED command creates a variable called "fix_pred" containing the regression means without the random effects (like performing a regression analysis for each group without using maximum likelihood and empirical Bayes). The PRED command saves the predicted values from the model into a variable called "tot_pred"; these are the empirical Bayes estimates. The RESID command saves the residual values $(Y_{ij} - \hat{Y}_{ij})$ into a variable called "resid". The $\hat{Y}_{ij}$ is the empirical Bayes predicted value. All of these values can be seen in the data file after the analysis is run.

Interpreting Output Files

Running the above command syntax will produce a considerable amount of information, only a portion of which will be discussed here. First, it should be noted that SPSS outputs five different information criteria of model fit, including the chi-square (–2 * log likelihood), the Akaike Information Criterion (AIC), Hurvich and Tsai's Criterion (AICC), Bozdogan's Criterion (CAIC), and the Schwarz Bayesian Criterion (BIC). Figure 12.7 shows the estimates of the fixed effects and covariance parameters for the common model being demonstrated in this chapter.

SPSS estimates the fixed effect for the intercept to be 22.381 and the fixed effect estimate for the slope of urban at –0.866. As was mentioned previously, viewing the level two residuals is not an option SPSS provides in the output but may be estimated using the MATRIX command in conjunction with multiple COMPUTE statements (Leyland, 2004, details the steps necessary to compute these estimates). The residual, or level-one, variance is estimated to be 0.271, and the variances for the model intercept and slope of "urban" are estimated to be 106.013 and 0.235, respectively.

Strengths and Weaknesses

Although SPSS is a relatively straightforward package, it handles a limited number of models. SPSS uses separate command lines to estimate the

Estimates of Fixed Effects[a]

Parameter	Estimate	Std. Error	df	t	Sig.	95% Confidence Interval	
						Lower Bound	Upper Bound
Intercept	22.380802	2.628171	15.667	8.516	.000	16.799698	27.961906
urban	-.866076	.125623	15.665	-6.894	.000	-1.132849	-.599303

a. Dependent Variable: science.

Estimates of Covariance Parameters[a]

Parameter		Estimate	Std. Error	Wald Z	Sig.
Residual		.270698	.033869	7.993	.000
Intercept + urban	UN (1,1)	106.0128	39.456980	2.687	.007
[subject = group]	UN (2,1)	-3.111117	1.610682	-1.932	.053
	UN (2,2)	.234903	.090189	2.605	.009

a. Dependent Variable: science.

Figure 12.7   Output example from SPSS.

fixed and random parts of the model. This may be helpful to some who like to conceive of models as coming from two sets of equations rather than one combined model. The REPEATED subcommand makes fitting multivariate normal models easy, as well as provides a method of fitting a range of correlation functions. The REPEATED command allows for unbalanced repeated measures data and can be used in this case to extend to missing multivariate responses. These positives, however, are outweighed by SPSS's inability to fit any model other than a normal response model. The question could then be asked, "Is it worthwhile to learn to fit multilevel models using SPSS?" The answer to this question is more a matter of convenience rather than statistics. As many researchers already use SPSS for other statistical analyses, some most likely will decide to work with MIXED rather than have to purchase another package. This convenience has the limitations of a small number of models, however, as well as the inability to provide any graphical capabilities within the MIXED routine.

Mplus 4.1

Development of the Package

Mplus was first released in 1998 with the intent of providing users with a powerful tool to conduct analysis with latent variables. Many statisticians think of Mplus primarily as a tool for conducting structural equation modeling (SEM) analysis; however, the software has been expanded to include exploratory factor analysis, latent class analysis, mixture modeling, Monte Carlo studies, and now multilevel analysis. Since the design of this package is primarily around an SEM framework, it is helpful to conceptualize the multilevel model as being a special case of a structural equation model in order to use this package.

Types of Models Available

Mplus only allows for models with two levels; however, three-level models are available by using the wide format option in a repeated measures model. Mplus estimates multilevel models through either the limited information estimator for use with models with continuous outcomes, random intercepts, and no missing data, or through full-information maximum likelihood allowing for continuous and categorical outcomes and missing data. This capability allows the Mplus user to specify a series of multilevel models, including regression, confirmatory factor analysis, growth modeling, discrete time-

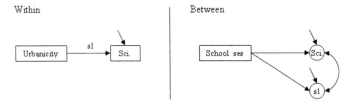

Figure 12.8 Example of a multilevel SEM model.

survival analysis, mixture analysis, growth mixture analysis, and latent class analysis. As previously mentioned, M*plus* conceptualizes the MLM model as an SEM equation. For example, the two-level model in Equations 12.3 and 12.4 can be expressed in SEM format as shown in Figure 12.8.

Level-1

$$science_{ij} = \beta_{0j} + \beta_{1j} urbanicity_{ij} + r_{ij} \tag{12.3}$$

Level-2

$$\beta_{0j} = \gamma_{00} + school\_ses_j + u_{0j} \\ \beta_{1j} = \gamma_{10} + school\_ses_j + u_{1j} \tag{12.4}$$

Data Setup Procedures

M*plus* reads data as an ASCII text file with the file-type extension .dat. Most software packages are able to export data in this format, so data input is not really an issue. The difficulty, however, is in remembering which columns of data correspond with which variable names. For small datasets, this is not a big problem, but it could prove problematic with larger datasets. In the command code, discussed later, the data file must be stored in the same root directory as the command file.

Analysis Specifications

M*plus* is command-driven software and has its own language and specifications. As such, the learning curve for initial command file setup in M*plus* can be quite steep. Regardless, the M*plus* language is fairly straightforward, and the manual does a relatively good job of describing the steps necessary to run a model. In fitting the Roberts (2004) data, the input file generated is

```
TITLE: This is a file to run the Roberts (2004) multilevel data
DATA: FILE IS example2.dat;
VARIABLE: NAMES ARE group science urban;
 WITHIN = urban;
 CLUSTER = group;
ANALYSIS: TYPE = TWOLEVEL RANDOM;
MODEL:
 %WITHIN%
 s | science ON urban;
SAVEDATA: FILE IS ebayes.dat;
 SAVE=FSCORES;
```

In the VARIABLE command, the names of the variables in the dataset are identified in the order in which they appear in the ASCII text (.dat) file. This is also the area where the WITHIN (level-one) variables and the BE-TWEEN (level-two) variables are specified. In the Roberts dataset, no level-two variables were specified; therefore, the BETWEEN command is not included here. Although the dependent variable "science" is a level-one variable, it does not have to be specified in the WITHIN command because it is assumed to be measured at the lowest level. The CLUSTER command identifies the grouping variable. The ANALYSIS command specifies the type of model; in this case, it is a two-level model with random effects.

In the MODEL command, the formula for the multilevel model is speci-fied. In this case, the model is defined as a random intercepts and random slopes model. The intercepts are random by the default because this is a multilevel model. The command "science ON urban" means that science (the DV) is regressed on urban (the IV). The command "s |" indicates that the slope for the "urban" variable is allowed to vary randomly across schools. A level-two predictor of either the intercept or slope would also be defined in the MODEL command. For example, suppose that the level-two predictor called "school_ses" were added as a predictor of both the intercept and the slope of "urban," as shown in Figure 12.8. The additional commands to specify this level-two predictor model would be

```
%BETWEEN%
science s ON school_ses;
```

In the final command, SAVEDATA, the FSCORES command will allow the creation of a .dat file containing the empirical Bayes estimates of the ran-dom effects.

Interpreting Output Files

The command file above results in the following (appended) output:

```
TESTS OF MODEL FIT
Loglikelihood
 H0 Value -210.113

Information Criteria
 Number of Free Parameters 5
 Akaike (AIC) 430.225
 Bayesian (BIC) 445.601
 Sample-Size Adjusted BIC 429.773
 (n* = (n + 2) / 24)

MODEL RESULTS
             Estimates    S.E.      Est./S.E.
Within Level
 Residual Variances
 SCIENCE     0.275        0.036     7.663
Between Level
 Means
 SCIENCE    22.335        2.600     8.589
 S          -0.865        0.120    -7.204
 Variances
 SCIENCE    96.271       23.786     4.047
 S           0.209        0.114     1.839
```

Most of the output is self-explanatory. The maximum likelihood estimate of the intercept for the model is 22.335, which is labeled "Means...Science". The fixed effect for the slope, or the value associated with the path previously defined between "urban" and "science" as "S", is –0.865.

Strengths and Weaknesses

M*plus* has somewhat limited graphing functions. Although these graphing functions continue to be developed with newer releases, the availability of some of the more complicated graphs are difficult to create and sometimes not possible.

Most SEM researchers are already familiar with the power of M*plus* as a tool for fitting structural equation models. These same researchers now have a tool in a powerful package to fit multilevel models in a framework that is already familiar to them, which is a huge strength of this package. Although probably easy for the SEM researcher, the task of having to learn notation for multilevel models as well as SEM notation could prove daunting for the novice multilevel modeler. Therefore, this is probably not the best package to recommend for someone just getting started in this field unless they are already comfortable with the SEM framework. Even for the advanced user, having to think in terms of paths rather than in terms of equations can be frustrating. Regardless, the breadth of the types of models that can be fit with this package make it great for fitting multilevel models. In addition, M*plus* shines as an SEM package and handles multilevel SEM quite well. However, one large disadvantage of M*plus* is that three-level organizational models cannot be estimated.

STATA 9

Development of the Package

STATA is currently in its ninth version and is available for Windows, Macintosh, and Unix users. Although the package now has a GUI, the real strength of this package, like SAS and S-PLUS, is the language that STATA uses. Although much more powerful than using the GUI alone, the command language does come at a bit of a cost in that the learning curve is quite steep. However, unlike R, SAS, and S-PLUS, STATA is not based on an object-oriented language, and as such, multiple datasets may not be opened or created simultaneously. This poses no problems for estimating the multilevel model of a single dataset but somewhat limits STATA's ability to run simulations and Monte Carlo investigations.

Types of Models Available

STATA uses three main commands to fit linear variance-components models. The first two, xtreg and xtmixed, belong to a larger xt family of commands that are used for fitting panel data using random-effect estimation. The gllamm (generalized linear latent and mixed models) command also can be used to fit linear models. Of these three commands, only xtmixed and gllamm can be used to fit both random-intercept and random-slope models. The xtmixed command will be used to demonstrate fitting the Roberts (2004) data.

Dichotomous and binary response models can be fit with the gllamm and gee commands. The gllamm command also can be used to fit ordinal and count data and three-level models. The xtmixed command will fit three-level models as well as cross-classified random effects.

Data Setup Procedures

STATA requires that data be nested in a single stacked dataset in order to fit a multilevel model. Therefore, there must be a unique case for each level-one unit. For example, if there were 10 students inside a given school, the dataset would contain 10 rows of data, each with the same level-two identifier. STATA has the ability to import data from an ASCII text using any of the three commands: infile, infix, and insheet. STATA also can accept data pasted into the data editor window from other data handling programs.

Analysis Specifications and Output Files

Once the data have been read into STATA, the variables available for use in the analysis will appear in the "Variables" window. The command that we use to fit the multilevel model in this example is the xtmixed command. Recall from above, however, that we also could use gllamm to fit the model or use xtreg if this were a random-intercept only model. The command line to run the model is

```
xtmixed science urban || group: urban, cov(unstr) mle
```

Immediately after the xtmixed command, the fixed part of the equation is specified. In this case, science is the dependent variable, and urban is the covariate/predictor. STATA automatically assumes that there is only one dependent variable and also inserts a "constant" to estimate the value for the intercepts. The next command "| |" specifies the random portion of the model. In this case, the group variable describes the nesting structure of the model and the covariate urban is included to estimate random effects for the slope. The command cov(unstr) is used to tell STATA that the covariance matrix should be unstructured. The default in STATA is to set the covariance and correlation at zero. Finally, the model is estimated with maximum likelihood estimation via the mle command. Running this model will produce the following results:

```
Performing EM optimization:

Performing gradient-based optimization:

Iteration 0: log likelihood = -206.58458
Iteration 1: log likelihood = -206.58419
Iteration 2: log likelihood = -206.58419

Computing standard errors:

Mixed-effects ML regression Number of obs = 160
Group variable: group Number of groups = 16

  Obs per group: min = 10
  avg = 10.0
  max = 10
```

```
Wald chi2(1) = 47.53
Log likelihood = -206.58419 Prob > chi2 = 0.0000
```

science	Coef.	Std. Err.	z	P>|z|	[95% Conf. Interval]
urban	-.8660764	.1256234	-6.89	0.000	-1.112294 -.6198591
_cons	22.3808	2.628171	8.52	0.000	17.22968 27.53192

Random-effects Parameters	Estimate	Std. Err.	[95% Conf. Interval]
group: Unstructured			
sd(urban)	.4846681	.0930423	.3326888 .7060747
sd(_cons)	10.29625	1.916086	7.14948 14.82805
corr(urban,_cons)	-.6234374	.1627997	-.8489995 -.205682
sd(Residual)	.5202865	.0325484	.4602487 .588156

```
LR test vs. linear regression: chi2(3) = 343.62 Prob > chi2 = 0.0000
```

From the above output, the fixed effect for the slope of urban is estimated at –.866, and the intercept (labeled _cons) is estimated to be 22.381. In the "Random-effects Parameters," the standard deviation for each of the random effects and the residual are presented. Squaring these values provides the variance measures.

Obtaining the empirical Bayes estimates in STATA is not as straightforward as in other programs. They are saved into the memory of STATA but must be extracted with the predict command by

```
predict reff*, reffects
```

Running this command will produce two new columns in the dataset called reff1 and reff2. The reff1 variable contains the predictions for the random slopes of urban, and reff2 contains the predictions for the random intercepts. These are not the actual values for the slope and intercept for each group but instead the predicted deviations around the grand values $\hat{\gamma}_{00}$ and $\hat{\gamma}_{10}$. We can obtain the actual predicted values by typing the commands

```
gen inter_eb=reff2 + _b[_cons]
gen slope_eb = reff1 + _b[urban]
```

The variables inter_eb and slope_eb are now added to the data file and can be viewed in the data editor. As an aside, these variables may be appended so that only one estimate for each group is displayed with the commands

```
by group, sort: gen f = _n==1
list group inter_eb slope_eb if f==1
```

which will produce

```
+-------------------------------------+
|    group   inter_eb     slope_eb    |
|-------------------------------------|
  1. | 1       7.035718    -.7462909   |
 11. | 2       8.895245    -.873138    |
 21. | 3      11.66553     -.822382    |
 31. | 4      15.12298     -.9599397   |
 41. | 5      16.1874      -.7850651   |
|-------------------------------------|
 51. | 6      25.98181    -1.293594    |
 61. | 7      24.52494    -1.176069    |
 71. | 8      24.88588     -.9924154   |
 81. | 9      31.51446    -1.298473    |
 91. | 10     26.95829     -.9651392   |
|-------------------------------------|
101. | 11     30.95904    -1.069137    |
111. | 12     36.29395    -1.274143    |
121. | 13     31.25546     -.8836451   |
131. | 14     41.09571    -1.267743    |
141. | 15     12.80025      .2674876   |
|-------------------------------------|
151. | 16     12.91617      .2824648   |
+-------------------------------------+
```

Graphing Capabilities

STATA comes with a very powerful graphing package that is able to incorporate all types of graphs. To create the graph for the predicted lines for each group, run the following commands

```
estimates store randmodel
predict prrandmodel, fitted
sort group urban
twoway(line prrandmodel urban, connect(ascending))
```

The last line is the command to actually produce the graph, but the first three commands are needed to produce the fitted values from the specified model. Figure 12.9 contains the graph produced by the syntax shown

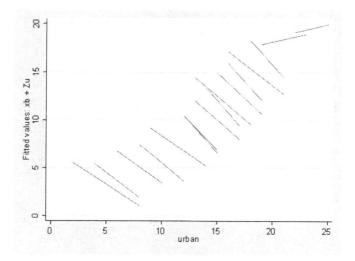

Figure 12.9 Graphing example in STATA: Regression of science on urbanity ("urban") for each of 16 schools.

above. STATA also can produce a graph in which each group's predicted regression line is in a separate graph, but they are appended together in Trellis format (like the S-PLUS example in Figure 12.6) using the command

```
twoway (line prrandmodel urban), by(group)
```

Strengths and Weaknesses

STATA is a very powerful package that encompasses a variety of tools for data analysis. The routines created to run a multilevel analysis are relatively powerful. Although there is more than just one routine available to run multilevel models, the syntax required for each command is slightly different and users could find themselves frustrated in that sequences of commands would be different between xtmixed and gllamm. For example, fitting a random intercept model in xtmixed would require the command

```
xtmixed science || group, cov(unstr) mle
```

whereas the same procedure run in gllamm would need to be formatted as

```
gllamm science, i(group) adapt
```

The wonderful thing about this package is the ability to write and reuse routines that are common to multilevel models through creating "do-files" in STATA. For example, it would be possible to create a command routine that would produce the intraclass correlation from a null multilevel ANOVA model by writing an .ado file to run this command. The STATAlist user's group (a link is available on the STATA website) is also a great resource for finding and developing new .ado files to run new routines. In fact, the `gllamm` routine originally began as a user-developed .ado file.

FINAL COMMENTS ON THE SOFTWARE PACKAGES

Given this brief review of the eight selected software packages, some general comments can be made concerning their use. First, nothing is inherently wrong with any of the packages, and none of them produce errant results. Slight differences in results emerge, however, based on estimation method and algorithms embedded within each package. Just like selecting a new car to drive, sometimes decisions are made based on comfort, and sometimes decisions are made on economics. Knowing this, here are some general comments.

The programs with the most "programmability" are SAS, S-PLUS, Stata, and R. If there is any thought that you might want to run simulations or actually generate some statistics not part of a canned routine, then it would be best to go with these programs. As an added bonus, these packages have wonderful graphing functions. However, as was noted previously, learning any of these languages takes time and dedication.

The HLM and MLwiN packages seem to be the two packages that best facilitate understanding and interpretation of the models. Once data have been input into these packages, fitting a model is simply a "point and click" exercise. Actually seeing the input model (instead of having to write code) is a great bonus contained only in these two packages. MLwiN has the added strength in that the estimates are then superimposed on the inputted model (in HLM an output file must be opened). Both of these packages are very powerful for fitting multilevel models, but their utility outside the realm of multilevel modeling is extremely limited. The other packages (M*plus*, SPSS, and STATA) are also good packages for fitting these models, but each of these has some problems in the breadth of models that can be fit. M*plus* is certainly the best package if you want to combine SEM and HLM analyses.

Given space limitations, this chapter has provided only the briefest introduction to each of the aforementioned software packages. As a means of cross comparison, Table 12.2 presents a side-by-side comparison of each of the packages in terms of the types of models they can accommodate, along with distributional shapes, estimation methods, and link functions. Please keep in mind, however, that this table could be obsolete within 1 month of printing this book as software packages continually are updated and expand

TABLE 12.2   A Comparison of Multilevel Software Packages

	MLwiN	HLM	SAS	S-PLUS	R	SPSS	Mplus	STATA
Types of models								
Normal response	X	X	X	X	X	X	X	X
Binary/Binomial	X	X	X	X	X		X	X
Repeated measures	X	X	X	X	X	X	X	X
Multinomial	X	X	X	X	X		X	X
Cross-classified	X	X	X	X	X			X
Multivariate	X	X	X	X	X	X	X	X
Nonlinear	X	X	X	X	X		X	X
Survival Data	X		X	X	X		X	X
Meta-analysis	X	X	X	X	X			X
Distributional shape								
Gaussian	X	X	X	X	X	X		X
Inverse Gaussian			X	X	X			X
Poisson	X	X	X	X	X			X
Binomial	X	X	X	X	X			X
Extra binomial	X	X	X	X	X			X
Gamma			X	X	X			X
Estimation methods								
Full maximum likelihood		X	X	X	X	X	※	X
Restricted maximum likelihood		X	X	X	X	X		X

Penalized quasi-likelihood	X	X		X	X
Second-order PQL	X			X	
Restricted PQL	X	X		X	X
Marginal quasi-likelihood	X			X	
Second-order MQL	X				
Restricted MQL		X	X	X	
Laplace			X	X	X
Adaptive Gaussian quadrature			X	X	X
Link functions					
Logit	X	X	X	X	X
Probit	X	X	X	X	X
Cumulative logit		X	X	X	X
Inverse			X	X	X
Log	X	X	X	X	X
Complementary log-log	X		X	X	X
Square root		X	X	X	
Power			X	X	X
Reciprocal		X		X	X

Note: * The *Mplus* manual (Muthén & Muthén , 1998–2006, p. 426) describes the three estimation procedures available as "(1) maximum likelihood parameter estimates with conventional standard errors and chi-square test statistic, (2) maximum likelihood parameter estimates with standard errors and chi-square test statistic that are robust to non-normality and non-independence of observations . . . computed using a sandwich estimator, and (3) maximum likelihood parameter estimates with standard errors approximated by first-order derivatives and a conventional chi-square test statistic."

ed. In some of the packages, a functionality may be available but not within the library discussed in this chapter. For example, in R, `lmer` will not perform optimization by adaptive Gaussian quadrature, but the `glmmML` library will. Exceptions like this are also the case in S-PLUS, SAS, and STATA.

Finally, users who would like to know more about the software packages may want to access the following resources.

- MLwiN—The manual that ships with the software package (also downloadable as a .pdf file from http://www.cmm.bristol.ac.uk/) is a great resource. The Hox (2002) text also uses MLwiN to illustrate many of the datasets analyzed.
- HLM—Both the manual that ships with HLM and the Raudenbush and Bryk (2002) text are excellent resources. Software is available from http://www.ssicentral.com/hlm/
- SAS—The Singer (1998) article is still used as a top resource for multilevel models in SAS. UCLA has a great companion website to this article at http://www.ats.ucla.edu/stat/paperexamples/singer/ that shows how to fit this dataset in other packages. The software is available from http://www.sas.com/
- S-PLUS and R—The Pinheiro and Bates (2000) text is the definitive resource on the `nlme` package. Descriptions for the correlatedData, lme4, nlme, and lmer packages are available for download from the Insightful (http://www.insightful.com) and CRAN (http://cran.r-project.org/) websites.
- SPSS—The SPSS website (http://www.spss.com/) has a technical report entitled "Linear mixed-effects models in SPSS" that is helpful; to obtain the document, one must complete a free registration with SPSS. The recent Peugh and Enders (2005) article will also be helpful to SPSS users.
- M*plus*—The manual that ships with M*plus* is extremely helpful. UCLA also has a series of excellent lectures on video given by Bengt Muthén, which is available at http://www.ats.ucla.edu/stat/mplus/seminars/mlmMplus_JH/. The software is available from http://www.statmodel.com/
- STATA—Stata Press has released an excellent book by Rabe-Hesketh and Skrondal (2005), which provides detail on fitting multilevel models. The software is available from http://www.stata.com/

REFERENCES

Bates, D. (2006a). *Comparing least squares calculations.* Retrieved December 18, 2006, from http://cran.r-project.org/doc/vignettes/Matrix/Comparisons.pdf

Bates, D. (2006b). *lmer, p-values and all that.* Retrieved May 29, 2006, from https://stat.ethz.ch/pipermail/r-help/2006-May/094765.html

Dempster, A. P., Laire, N. M., & Rubin, D. B. (1977). Maximum likelihood from incomplete data via the EM algorithm. *Journal of the Royal Statistical Society, Series B, 39,* 1–38.

Fox, J. (2005). The R Commander: A basic-statistics graphical user interface to R. *Journal of Statistical Software, 14,* 1–41.

Hox, J. J. (2002). *Multilevel analysis: Techniques and applications.* Mahway, NJ: Erlbaum

Leyland, A. H. (2004). *A review of multilevel modeling in SPSS.* Retrieved May 1, 2006, from http://www.cmm.bristol.ac.uk/learning-training/multilevel-m-software/reviewspss.pdf

Lindley, D. V. & Smith, A. F. M. (1972). Bayes estimates for the linear model. *Journal of the Royal Statistical Society, Series B, 34,* 1–41.

Muthén, L. K., & Muthén, B. O. (1998–2006). *Mplus user's guide* (4th ed.). Los Angeles: Muthén & Muthén.

Peugh, J. & Enders, C. (2005). Using the SPSS mixed procedure to fit cross-sectional and longitudinal multilevel models. *Educational and Psychological Measurement, 65,* 717–741.

Pinheiro, J. C., & Bates, D. M. (2000). *Mixed-effects models in S and S-PLUS.* New York: Springer.

Rabe-Hesketh, S. & Skrondal, A. (2005). *Multilevel and longitudinal modeling using Stata.* College Station, TX: Stata Press.

Raudenbush, S., & Bryk, A. (2002). *Hierarchical linear models* (2nd ed.). Newbury Park, CA: Sage.

Raudenbush, S. Bryk, A. Cheong, Y. F., & Congdon, R., & du Toit, M. (2004). *HLM6: Hierarchical linear and non-linear modeling.* Lincolnwood, IL: Scientific Software International.

Roberts, J. K. (2004). An introductory primer on multilevel and hierarchical linear modeling. *Learning Disabilities: A Contemporary Journal, 2*(1), 30–38.

Robinson, W. S. (1950). Ecological correlations and the behavior of individuals. *Sociological Review, 15,* 351–357.

Singer, J. D. (1998). Using SAS PROC MIXED to fit multilevel models, hierarchical models, and individual growth models. *Journal of Educational and Behavioral Statistics, 24,* 323–355.

CHAPTER 13

ESTIMATION PROCEDURES FOR HIERARCHICAL LINEAR MODELS

Hariharan Swaminathan and H. Jane Rogers

As described in the previous chapters, hierarchical linear models are appropriate for situations in which observations are grouped into clusters and in which the clusters, in turn, may belong to larger units. In order to make valid inferences about the parameters of interest, the nested structure of the data must be taken into account during estimation of parameters. Faulty inferences can be drawn about important effects if the structure of the data is ignored. The purpose of this chapter is to describe estimation procedures for hierarchical linear models. The focus here is on linear models for which the outcome variable is continuous. The procedures to be described apply conceptually to models where the outcome variable is dichotomous or ordinal, though modifications are needed to accommodate the non-linear nature of the model; this chapter does not address estimation procedures for such models.

We begin with estimation procedures for fixed effects in the simplest case of known variance components. Well-known ordinary least squares (OLS) or generalized least squares (GLS) regression procedures are adequate and

Multilevel Modeling of Educational Data, pages 469–519
Copyright © 2008 by Information Age Publishing
All rights of reproduction in any form reserved.

appropriate for this case. The statistical foundations of these procedures are presented as an aid in understanding the more complex procedures subsequently discussed. Estimation procedures for the more common case of unknown variance components are then described. Maximum likelihood and Bayesian procedures are appropriate in this case. These procedures, as well as the Newton-Raphson and E-M algorithms commonly used in their implementation, are discussed. A simple example is used throughout the chapter to illustrate the various estimation procedures. Our goal in this chapter is to provide an introduction to the estimation procedures that are available and the algorithms used in their implementation but not to provide complete computational details of any single method. Rather, the chapter is intended to provide a framework and serve as a starting point for the motivated reader seeking to gain a thorough understanding of estimation procedures for hierarchical models.

To illustrate the issues involved in estimation, consider a simple example of a hierarchical model, where individuals are grouped in clusters and are measured on a variable of interest. The model for the score y_{ij} of individual i ($i = 1, 2, ..., n_j$) in cluster j ($j = 1, 2, ..., J$), where n_j is the number of individuals in cluster j and J is the number of clusters, may be expressed as[1]

$$y_{ij} = \mu_j + e_{ij}. \tag{13.1}$$

In the above expression, μ_j is the mean of cluster j, and e_{ij} is the within-cluster error, or deviation of the score of person i in cluster j from the cluster mean. These errors are assumed to have mean zero and variance σ^2. If the clusters are drawn at random from a population of clusters, then μ_j is a random variable such that

$$\mu_j = \gamma_0 + u_j, \tag{13.2}$$

where u_j represents the deviation of the cluster j mean from the overall mean and is assumed to have mean zero and variance τ^2. Thus, τ^2 indicates the variation of cluster means around the population mean γ_0. The models given in Equations 13.1 and 13.2 can be regarded as a two-level model, where at level one (Equation 13.1), μ_j is a random variable, called a *random effect*, and at level two (Equation 13.2), the parameter γ_0 is called a *fixed effect*. The parameters of interest are the fixed effect, γ_0, and the *variance components*, σ^2 and τ^2. In some situations, it is also of interest to estimate the random coefficients, μ_j.

As an example of a situation in which these models are appropriate, suppose we are interested in determining the mean achievement level in a certain subject area of students at a particular grade level in a school district. A random sample of schools is obtained and the achievement levels of the

TABLE 13.1   Example: Data and Descriptive Statistics for a Simple Hierarchical Model

	Cluster 1	Cluster 2	Cluster 3	Cluster 4	Cluster5
	2	6	7	10	1
	6	7	8	8	2
	4	8	9	9	3
Mean	4.0	7.0	8.0	9.0	2.0
S.D.	2.0	1.0	1.0	1.0	1.0

students in the schools are measured. The models given in Equations 13.1 and 13.2 reflect this data structure. Suppose that the primary interest in this case is to estimate γ_0, the mean achievement level of students in the district, and the standard error of the estimate.

To make this example concrete, data collected on five (randomly selected) clusters (schools) with three observations per cluster ($n_j = 3, j = 1, \ldots, 5$) are shown in Table 13.1. We shall use these data throughout the chapter to illustrate the estimation procedures we discuss.

The "naïve" approach would be to ignore the cluster structure and estimate the mean of the total group. The estimate of the mean, $\hat{\gamma}_0$, would be 6.0, and the estimate of the variance, $\hat{\sigma}^2$, would be 8.43. Hence the standard error of the estimate of γ_0, $SE(\hat{\gamma}_0)$, is $\sqrt{8.43 / 15} = 0.750$ (Kirk, 1995). However, as we know from the sampling literature (Kish, 1965), this approach underestimates the standard error because of its failure to take into account the random variation of the cluster means.

As an attempt at a more appropriate approach, we could take into account the cluster structure and write a model that indicates that the cluster means vary around the population mean, i.e.,

$$\bar{y}_j = \gamma_0 + \varepsilon_j, \tag{13.3}$$

where ε_j is the error with mean zero and variance σ_ε^2. If the sample sizes in the clusters are equal ($n_j = n$), then the estimate of γ_0 under this model is simply the average of the cluster means, i.e.,

$$\hat{\gamma}_0 = \frac{1}{J} \sum_{j=1}^{J} \bar{y}_j. \tag{13.4}$$

When the cluster sizes are unequal, $\hat{\gamma}_0$ is not a simple average of the cluster means; rather, it is a weighted average. In the interest of simplicity, we will derive the variance of $\hat{\gamma}_0$ only for the case of equal cluster sizes, as is the case in our example. Since the sample means are assumed to be independent, the variance of $\hat{\gamma}_0$ is

$$Var(\hat{\gamma}_0) = Var\left(\frac{1}{J}\sum_{j=1}^{J}\bar{y}_j\right) = \frac{1}{J^2}\sum_{j=1}^{J}Var(\bar{y}_j).$$

According to the sampling distribution of the mean, $Var(\bar{y}_j) = \sigma_\varepsilon^2/n_j = \sigma_\varepsilon^2/n$ if the clusters are of equal size n. Thus, in this case,

$$Var(\hat{\gamma}_0) = \frac{J}{J^2}Var(\bar{y}_j) = \frac{1}{J}\frac{\sigma_\varepsilon^2}{n}.$$

The estimate of the standard error of $\hat{\gamma}_0$ is $\sqrt{Var(\hat{\gamma}_0)} = \hat{\sigma}_\varepsilon / \sqrt{nJ}$. To complete the computation, we need an estimate of σ_ε^2. Under the assumption that the observations are independently and identically distributed, the best estimate of σ_ε^2 is the pooled within-cluster variance,

$$\sum_{j=1}^{J}\sum_{i=1}^{n_j}(y_{ij} - \bar{y}_j)^2 / (N - J) \quad \text{(Kirk, 1995)}.$$

For the example, the cluster means are 4, 7, 8, 9, 2, and the estimate of γ_0 is 6.0, as before. The ANOVA table from the SPSS General Linear Model procedure is given in Table 13.2.

The estimate of the error variance, σ_ε^2, from Table 13.2 , is 1.600, and hence the standard error of the estimate of γ_0 is $\sqrt{1.6/(3\times 5)} = 0.326$. The SPSS analysis also gives the 95% confidence interval for γ_0 as [5.272, 6.728].

The two approaches described above produce identical estimates of the population mean. However, the "naïve" approach ignores the variation in the cluster means. The analysis based on the model in Equation 13.3 is better than the naïve approach because it takes into account the cluster structure and uses the pooled within-cluster variance rather than the total variance to obtain an estimate of the standard error of $\hat{\gamma}_0$. Nevertheless, it underestimates the standard error because it does not take into account the random component u_j in the estimation of the cluster means (Equa-

---

TABLE 13.2   ANOVA Results for the Data in Table 13.1

Source	Sum of squares	df	Mean square
Cluster (*between*)	102.000	4	25.500
Error (*within*)	16.000	10	1.600
Total	118.000	14	

Note: Dependent Variable: *y*

tion 13.2). An alternative way to look at this is to note that, as we shall see below, the random component u_j introduces dependencies in the observations within clusters. This dependence among the observations violates the assumption of independence that was necessary to compute the pooled within cluster-variance and results in the incorrect estimation of the standard error of $\hat{\gamma}_0$. This incorrect determination of the standard error results in a larger value of the test statistic, leading to inflated Type I error rates in inferences about γ_0.

To see how failing to take into account the error u_j in the model underestimates the standard error of $\hat{\gamma}_0$, we combine the models given in Equations 13.1 and 13.2 into a single model:

$$y_{ij} = \gamma_0 + u_j + e_{ij}. \tag{13.5}$$

The model given in Equation 13.5 resembles a one-way analysis of variance model. However, in the one-way ANOVA model, the clusters are not sampled from a population, so u_j is a fixed effect, often estimated as the difference between the cluster mean and the grand mean. In the present case, u_j is a random variable; hence, the model given in Equation 13.5 is the classic one-way *random effects* model with the assumption that the mean of u_j, or its expected value, written as $E(u_j)$, is zero and $Var(u_j) = \tau^2$.

The variance of e_{ij} is σ^2, hence, the variance of y_{ij} under the assumption that u_j and e_{ij} are independent, is

$$Var(y_{ij}) = Var(\gamma_0 + u_j + e_{ij}) = Var(u_j + e_{ij}) = \tau^2 + \sigma^2.$$

Furthermore, within cluster j, the covariance between the observations i and k is

$$Cov(y_{ij}, y_{kj}) = Cov(\gamma_0 + u_j + e_{ij}, \gamma_0 + u_j + e_{kj})$$
$$= Cov(u_j, u_j) = Var(u_j) = \tau^2,$$

as e_{ij}, e_{kj} and u_j are mutually independent. Thus, in a random effects model, the observations within a cluster are not independent. The correlation, ρ, between observations y_{ij}, y_{kj}, known as the *intraclass correlation*, is thus

$$\rho = Cov(y_{ij}, y_{kj}) / \sqrt{Var(y_{ij})Var(y_{kj})} = \tau^2 / (\tau^2 + \sigma^2).$$

The intraclass correlation, ρ, approaches one as the variation among the clusters (τ^2) increases relative to the error variance (σ^2) and is zero when there is no variation among the clusters. As pointed out earlier, the dependence among the observations within a cluster violates the assumption of independence in the computation of pooled within-cluster variance, resulting in an incorrect estimation of the standard error.

In order to estimate γ_0 and the standard error of the estimate of γ_0 correctly, we rewrite the model in Equation 13.5 by averaging over individuals in group j, i.e.,

$$\bar{y}_j = \gamma_0 + u_j + \bar{e}_j. \tag{13.6}$$

If we let $u_j + \bar{e}_j = \varepsilon_j$, then we obtain a model that looks exactly like that in Equation 13.3. The estimate of γ_0 is the same as that given in Equation 13.4, i.e., the grand mean, $\bar{y}$. In deriving the variance of γ_0, we once again will limit our attention to the case of equal cluster sizes, as needed for our example. In this case, $Var(\bar{e}_j) = \sigma^2/n$, so the variance of $\hat{\gamma}_0$ is obtained as

$$Var(\hat{\gamma}_0) = Var\left(\frac{1}{J}\sum_{j=1}^{J}\bar{y}_j\right) = \frac{1}{J^2}\sum_{j=1}^{J}Var(\bar{y}_j) = \frac{1}{J^2}\sum_{j=1}^{J}Var\left(u_j + \bar{e}_j\right)$$

$$= \frac{1}{J^2}\sum_{j=1}^{J}\left(\tau^2 + \frac{\sigma^2}{n}\right) = \frac{1}{J}(\tau^2 + \frac{\sigma^2}{n}).$$

The correct standard error of $\hat{\gamma}_0$, $\sqrt{Var(\hat{\gamma}_0)}$, can be computed now. However, in order to compute it, estimates of the variance components τ^2 and σ^2 are needed.

Recall that in a one-way random effects model, the expected Mean Sum of Squares Between, $E(MSB)$, and the expected Mean Sum of Squares Within, $E(MSW)$, are given by the expressions (Kirk, 1995)

$$E(MSB) = \sigma^2 + n\tau^2, \ E(MSW) = \sigma^2,$$

assuming equal cluster sizes with n observations in each cluster. From these expressions, it follows that

$$\frac{E(MSB) - E(MSW)}{n} = E\left[\frac{(MSB - MSW)}{n}\right] = \frac{\sigma^2 + n\tau^2 - \sigma^2}{n} = \tau^2.$$

Hence, the estimate of σ^2, $\hat{\sigma}^2$, is MSW, and the estimate of τ^2, $\hat{\tau}^2$, is $(MSB - MSW)/n$.

For the example above (see Table 13.2), $\hat{\sigma}^2 = MSW = 1.600$, and $\hat{\tau}^2 = (25.500 - 1.600)/3 = 7.967$. These are the correct estimates of the parameters for this example. With $n = 3$, the estimate of the variance of $\hat{\gamma}_0$ is

$$Var(\hat{\gamma}_0) = \frac{7.967 + \dfrac{1.600}{3}}{5} = 1.700.$$

The standard error of the estimate is $\sqrt{1.700} = 1.304$. As can be seen, the standard error is almost 4 times larger than the standard error obtained by ignoring the variance of u_j. The 95% confidence interval for γ_0 based on a model that does not take into account all the sources of variance is [5.272, 6.728], while the confidence interval based on the appropriate model is [2.380, 9.620]. If in truth, $\gamma_0 = 8.0$, for example, and this hypothesis was tested, we would reject the hypothesis according to the former (incorrect) procedure but not the latter. Thus, in this case, an erroneous decision to reject the null hypothesis would be made as a result of using an incorrect estimation procedure.

The model given in Equations 13.1 and 13.2 is the simplest example of a multilevel or hierarchical model. Nevertheless, this simple example illustrates the problems inherent in the estimation of parameters, and in particular, that of estimating the standard errors in such models. Faulty inferences can be drawn about important effects when sources of variance at multiple levels are not taken into account. Therefore, it is critical that appropriate estimation procedures be used.

A variety of estimation procedures may be employed in the estimation of parameters in multilevel models. The estimation procedures described in the following sections are the Ordinary Least Squares (OLS) procedure, the Generalized Least Squares (GLS) procedure, the Maximum Likelihood (ML) Procedure, the Restricted or Residual Maximum Likelihood (REML) procedure, and Bayesian procedures. In simple cases, as in the example above where the sample sizes were equal, these procedures yield similar or identical results; however, in complex models, these estimation procedures may not always yield identical results. The choice of estimation procedure depends on factors such as heterogeneity of variances, properties of the estimators (e.g., bias), and philosophical considerations (Bayesian versus frequentist perspectives). Subsequent sections discuss these issues in more detail.

MODELS AND NOTATION

Before beginning the discussion of estimation procedures, it is useful to review the models to be considered and the notation that will be used. In the linear regression model where the dependent variable y is related to a set of predictors, $x_1, \ldots, x_p$, the model is

$$y = \beta_0 + \beta_1 x_1 + \beta_2 x_2 + \ldots + \beta_p x_p + e. \tag{13.7}$$

When N individuals are observed on y and on the set $(x_1, \ldots, x_p)$, the model for individual i is

$$y_i = \beta_0 + \beta_1 x_{i1} + \beta_2 x_{i2} + \ldots + \beta_i x_{ij} + \ldots + \beta_p x_{ip} + e_i. \tag{13.8}$$

Using matrix notation, the model in Equation 13.8 can be expressed as (Searle, 1971)

$$\mathbf{y} = \mathbf{X}\boldsymbol{\beta} + \mathbf{e}, \tag{13.9}$$

where

$$\mathbf{y} = \begin{bmatrix} y_1 \\ y_2 \\ \cdot \\ \cdot \\ \cdot \\ y_N \end{bmatrix}, \quad \mathbf{X} = \begin{bmatrix} 1 & x_{11} & \cdots & x_{1p} \\ 1 & x_{21} & \cdots & x_{2p} \\ \cdot & \cdot & \cdots & \cdot \\ \cdot & \cdot & \cdots & \cdot \\ \cdot & \cdot & \cdots & \cdot \\ 1 & x_{N1} & \cdots & x_{Np} \end{bmatrix}, \quad \boldsymbol{\beta} = \begin{bmatrix} \beta_0 \\ \beta_1 \\ \cdot \\ \cdot \\ \cdot \\ \beta_p \end{bmatrix}, \quad \mathbf{e} = \begin{bmatrix} e_1 \\ e_2 \\ \cdot \\ \cdot \\ \cdot \\ e_N \end{bmatrix}.$$

$$\quad (N \times 1) \qquad\qquad (N \times p+1) \qquad\qquad (p+1 \times 1) \quad (N \times 1)$$

In the model represented by Equations 13.8 and 13.9, the errors, e_i, and hence y_i, usually are assumed to be independently and identically distributed (Searle, 1971), i.e.,

$$Var(\mathbf{e}) = Var(\mathbf{y}) = \sigma^2 I,$$

where I is an $(N \times N)$ identity matrix.

In multilevel applications, the level-one model is as given in Equation 13.7, and the model for person i in cluster j ($j = 1, \ldots, J$) is expressed as

$$y_{ij} = \beta_0 + \beta_{1j} x_{ij1} + \beta_{2j} x_{ij2} + \ldots + \ldots + \beta_{pj} x_{ijp} + e_{ij}. \tag{13.10}$$

At level two, the variation in the level-one regression coefficients is modeled as

$$\begin{aligned} \beta_0 &= \gamma_{00} + \gamma_{01} w_1 + \gamma_{02} w_2 + \ldots + \gamma_{0k} w_k + u_0 \\ \beta_1 &= \gamma_{10} + \gamma_{11} w_1 + \gamma_{12} w_2 + \ldots + \gamma_{1k} w_k + u_1 \\ &\quad\ldots\ldots \\ \beta_p &= \gamma_{p0} + \gamma_{p1} w_1 + \gamma_{p2} w_2 + \ldots + \gamma_{pk} w_k + u_p \end{aligned}, \tag{13.11}$$

where $w_1, \ldots, w_k$ are level-2 predictors. In matrix notation, the level-two model can be expressed as

$$\boldsymbol{\beta} = \mathbf{W}\boldsymbol{\gamma} + \mathbf{u}. \tag{13.12}$$

To see how the matrix and the vector of parameters are formed, consider a simple example where the dependent variable at level one (student) is mathematics achievement. Suppose that the independent variable at level one is Mathematics Aptitude (MA), that is,

$$y = \beta_0 + \beta_1 MA + e.$$

If two school-level variables, w_1, w_2 are used to explain the variation across schools in β_0, β_1, and β_2, then we have the level-two model:

$$\beta_0 = \gamma_{00} + \gamma_{01}w_1 + \gamma_{02}w_2 + u_0$$
$$\beta_1 = \gamma_{10} + \gamma_{11}w_1 + \gamma_{12}w_2 + u_1$$

In matrix notation, the level-two model is

$$\begin{bmatrix} \beta_0 \\ \beta_1 \end{bmatrix} = \begin{bmatrix} 1 & w_1 & w_2 & 0 & 0 & 0 \\ 0 & 0 & 0 & 1 & w_1 & w_2 \end{bmatrix} \begin{bmatrix} \gamma_{00} \\ \gamma_{01} \\ \gamma_{02} \\ \gamma_{10} \\ \gamma_{11} \\ \gamma_{12} \end{bmatrix} + \begin{bmatrix} u_0 \\ u_1 \end{bmatrix} = \begin{bmatrix} \mathbf{w}_1 \\ \mathbf{w}_2 \end{bmatrix} \begin{bmatrix} \gamma_{00} \\ \gamma_{01} \\ \gamma_{02} \\ \gamma_{10} \\ \gamma_{11} \\ \gamma_{12} \end{bmatrix} + \begin{bmatrix} u_0 \\ u_1 \end{bmatrix}, \quad (13.13)$$

where $\mathbf{w}_1 = [1 \ w_1 \ w_2 \ 0 \ 0 \ 0]$ and $\mathbf{w}_2 = [0 \ 0 \ 0 \ 1 \ w_1 \ w_2]$. In terms of the observations, the model given by Equation 13.10 can be written as

$$\mathbf{y}_j = \mathbf{X}_j \boldsymbol{\beta}_j + \mathbf{e}_j, \quad (13.14)$$

where $\boldsymbol{\beta}_j$ is the $(p + 1 \times 1)$ vector of regression coefficients in group j and X_j is the matrix of observations on the predictors in group j. The level-two model given in Equation 13.11 can be expressed as

$$\boldsymbol{\beta}_j = \mathbf{W}_j \boldsymbol{\gamma} + \mathbf{u}_j, \quad (13.15)$$

where $\mathbf{W}_j$ is the matrix of observations on a set of predictors in group j at level two and $\boldsymbol{\gamma}$ is the vector of level-two regression coefficients, which are treated as fixed effects (Raudenbush & Bryk, 2002). For the example in Equation 13.13, the matrix $\mathbf{W}_j$ is

$$W_j = \begin{bmatrix} \mathbf{w}_{1j} \\ \mathbf{w}_{2j} \end{bmatrix}.$$

Because the coefficients $\beta_0, \beta_1, \ldots, \beta_p$ come from the same unit of analysis (in this example, school), we cannot assume that they are independent. The dependence amongst these elements is reflected in the joint distribution of the random effects $u_{0j},\ u_{1j}, u_{2j}, \ldots, u_{pj}$. We shall assume that $\mathbf{u}_j$ is a vector of random variables distributed normally with mean vector zero and variance-covariance matrix T, i.e.,

$$\mathbf{u}_j \sim N(0,T).$$

The diagonal elements of T are the variances of the elements of β, and the off-diagonal elements are their covariances. For the example given above with two level-two predictors, the matrix T is

$$T = \begin{bmatrix} \tau_{00} & & \\ \tau_{10} & \tau_{11} & \\ \tau_{20} & \tau_{21} & \tau_{22} \end{bmatrix},$$

where $\tau_{00} = Var(\beta_0)$, $\tau_{11} = Var(\beta_1)$, $\tau_{22} = Var(\beta_2)$, $\tau_{10} = Cov(\beta_0,\beta_1)$, $\tau_{20} = Cov(\beta_0,\beta_2)$, and $\tau_{21} = Cov(\beta_1,\beta_2)$. We shall also assume that T is the same across all groups.

For the example introduced at the start of the chapter, the model for the observations in cluster j is $y_{ij} = \mu_j + e_{ij}$ and can be expressed as

$$\mathbf{y}_j = \begin{bmatrix} 1 \\ 1 \\ 1 \end{bmatrix} \mu_j + \mathbf{e}_j. \tag{13.16}$$

The model above is a special case of the model given in Equation 13.14. Here, the matrix X_j is a (3×1) vector of ones, and β_j is the scalar μ_j, corresponding to one dependent variable at the second level. Clearly, X_j is the same across the five clusters. At level two, $\mu_j = \gamma_0 + u_j$. In this case,

$$\mu_1 = 1\gamma_0 + u_1 = W_1\gamma_0 + u_1$$
$$\mu_2 = 1\gamma_0 + u_2 = W_2\gamma_0 + u_2$$
$$\mu_3 = 1\gamma_0 + u_3 = W_3\gamma_0 + u_3$$
$$\mu_4 = 1\gamma_0 + u_4 = W_4\gamma_0 + u_4$$
$$\mu_5 = 1\gamma_0 + u_5 = W_5\gamma_0 + u_5 .$$

Thus, in terms of Equation 13.15, W_j $(j = 1, \ldots, 5)$ are all (1×1) matrices, each having 1 as its element, and the fixed parameter vector γ is a scalar, γ_0.

With this background, we now turn to procedures for estimating the parameters of the model.

ESTIMATION PROCEDURES WITH KNOWN VARIANCE COMPONENTS

The basic estimation issue for multilevel models is that of estimating the parameters such as γ_0 along with the variance components τ^2 and σ^2. It also may be of interest to estimate the random coefficients, such as in the example used in the previous section, where the parameters μ_j characterize "school effects." While in some cases, as in the previous example, the variance components do not affect the estimation of the fixed effects, they always are needed for computing the standard errors of the estimates. More often than not, the estimation of fixed effects must take into account the variance components. The variance components may be estimated first (using, for example, generalizations of the procedures described in the example) and treated as known during the estimation of fixed effects, or they may be estimated simultaneously with the fixed effects. Most of the estimation procedures commonly employed use the latter approach; however, it is instructive to demonstrate how estimation simplifies in the case of known (previously estimated) variance components. Two estimation procedures that are appropriate and adequate in this situation are Ordinary Least Squares (OLS) estimation and Generalized Least Squares (GLS) estimation. The focus in this section is on estimating the fixed effects γ; a later section discusses estimation of the level-one random coefficients.

Ordinary Least Squares Estimation

Estimation of the parameters in the linear regression model given in Equation 13.9 is performed by the method of least squares. The Ordinary Least Squares estimation procedure is appropriate when the errors are assumed to be independent and homoscedastic, that is, the variance of the errors is of the form $\sigma^2 I$. In this case, the vector of regression coefficients β that minimizes the function

$$\sum_{i=1}^{N} e_i^2 = \mathbf{e'e} = (\mathbf{y} - \mathbf{X}\beta)'(\mathbf{y} - \mathbf{X}\beta) \tag{13.17}$$

is taken as the Ordinary Least Squares (OLS) Estimator of β. This requires finding the value of β that satisfies

$$\frac{\partial}{\partial \beta}(\mathbf{e}'\mathbf{e}) = \frac{\partial}{\partial \beta}(\mathbf{y} - \mathbf{X}\beta)'(\mathbf{y} - \mathbf{X}\beta) = \frac{\partial}{\partial \beta}(\mathbf{y}'\mathbf{y} - 2\beta'\mathbf{X}'\mathbf{y} + \beta'\mathbf{X}'\mathbf{X}\beta) \qquad (13.18)$$

$$= -2\mathbf{X}'\mathbf{y} + 2\mathbf{X}'\mathbf{X}\beta = 0.$$

Solving for β, we obtain

$$\hat{\beta} = (\mathbf{X}'\mathbf{X})^{-1}\mathbf{X}'\mathbf{y}, \qquad (13.19)$$

provided that $(\mathbf{X}'\mathbf{X})^{-1}$ is not singular. The estimator given in Equation 13.19 is the OLS estimator of β (Searle, 1971). If we treat the matrix $\mathbf{X}$ as fixed, then $\hat{\beta}$ is a linear function of the observations $\mathbf{y}$ and hence is a *linear estimator* of β. The OLS estimator is an unbiased estimator of β, i.e., $E(\hat{\beta}) = \beta$. From Searle (1971), the variance-covariance matrix of $\hat{\beta}$ is

$$Var(\hat{\beta}) = \sigma^2[(X'X)^{-1}].$$

It can be shown that among all unbiased linear estimators of β, the OLS estimator has the minimum variance. Thus, the OLS estimator $\hat{\beta}$ is known as the Best Linear Unbiased Estimator (BLUE) of β. If, in addition, we assume that $\mathbf{e} \sim N(0, \sigma^2 I)$, then:

$$\hat{\beta} \sim N(\beta, \sigma^2[X'X]^{-1}). \qquad (13.20)$$

The result given above regarding the sampling distribution of $\hat{\beta}$ is important for drawing inferences about the elements of β.

To estimate the level-two fixed effects, we first note that an equivalent expression to that given in Equation 13.20 is

$$\hat{\beta}_j = \beta_j + \varepsilon_j, \qquad (13.21)$$

where $\varepsilon_j \sim N(0, \sigma^2[X'_j X_j]^{-1})$. (Strictly speaking, the assumption of normality is not necessary at this point; it is needed only for determining the distribution of the estimates and for testing hypotheses about the parameters of interest.) Combining Equation 13.21 with the level-two model in Equation 13.15, we obtain

$$\hat{\beta}_j = W_j \gamma + u_j + \varepsilon_j = W_j \gamma + \delta_j, \qquad (13.22)$$

where $\delta_j = u_j + \varepsilon_j$. Because W_j and γ are constants and given that $Var(\varepsilon_j) = \sigma^2[X'_j X_j]^{-1}$ and the variance-covariance matrix of u_j is T, the variance-covariance matrix of $\hat{\beta}_j$, $Var(\hat{\beta}_j)$, assuming that ε_j and u_j are independent, is

$$Var(\hat{\beta}_j) = Var(\mathbf{u}_j + \varepsilon_j) = \mathbf{T} + \sigma^2(\mathbf{X}'_j \mathbf{X}_j)^{-1} \equiv \Delta_j. \qquad (13.23)$$

The level-two model given in Equation 13.22 is analogous to a multivariate linear model with multiple dependent variables, with the dependent variables being the level-one regression coefficients. If the same explanatory variables are used for β_0, β_1, and β_2 (that is, the W_j matrices are equal) and if the same number of observations are used across the level-one units (that is $\sigma^2[\mathbf{X}'_j\mathbf{X}_j]^{-1}$ is the same across the level-one units), then the variance-covariance matrices of the $\hat{\boldsymbol{\beta}}_j$ are the same across the level-one units, and we have, at level two, the classic multivariate regression model (Swaminathan, 1989a). In this case, the OLS procedure is appropriate for estimating parameters.

The ordinary least squares criterion to be minimized at level two is

$$\sum_{j=1}^{J} (\hat{\boldsymbol{\beta}}_j - \mathbf{W}_j\boldsymbol{\gamma})' (\hat{\boldsymbol{\beta}}_j - \mathbf{W}_j\boldsymbol{\gamma}).$$

Following the steps given in Equations 13.17–13.19 for obtaining the least squares estimators for the parameters in the model given in Equation 13.9, the least squares estimator of the fixed effects γ is obtained as

$$\hat{\boldsymbol{\gamma}} = (\sum_{j=1}^{J} \mathbf{W}'_j\mathbf{W}_j)^{-1}(\sum_{j=1}^{J} \mathbf{W}'_j\hat{\boldsymbol{\beta}}_j).$$

In the example in Section 1, where there are five clusters and no predictors at either level, the model for the observations in cluster j is as given in Equation 13.16. Here, the X matrix in each group is a (3×1) column vector of ones. These data satisfy the requirement mentioned above for the OLS procedure to be appropriate, that is, that the X_j matrices are equal for all dependent variables. The vector β_j is the scalar μ_j and the matrix W_j is the scalar 1. Hence, for the example,

$$(\sum_{j=1}^{J} \mathbf{W}'_j\mathbf{W}_j)^{-1} = (\sum_{j=1}^{5} 1 \times 1)^{-1} = 1/5;$$

$$(\sum_{j=1}^{J} \mathbf{W}'_j\hat{\boldsymbol{\beta}}_j) = (\sum_{j=1}^{5} 1 \times \hat{\beta}_{0j}) = (\sum_{j=1}^{5} 1 \times \bar{y}_j) = (\sum_{j=1}^{5} \bar{y}_j).$$

Simplifying these equations, we obtain the OLS estimate of γ_0 as

$$(\sum_{j=1}^{5} \bar{y}_j)/5 = 6.0,$$

the same value that was obtained previously.

The sampling variance of the OLS estimator, $Var(\hat{\boldsymbol{\gamma}})$, is given as

$$Var(\hat{\gamma}) = (\sum_{j=1}^{J} \mathbf{W}_j' \mathbf{W}_j)^{-1} \left[\sum_{j=1}^{J} \mathbf{W}_j' \Delta_j \mathbf{W}_j \right] (\sum_{j=1}^{J} \mathbf{W}_j' \mathbf{W}_j)^{-1}, \qquad (13.24)$$

where Δ_j is as given in Equation 13.23. When $\gamma = \gamma_0$, as in our earlier example, $W_j = 1$, $T_{1\times1} = \tau^2$, $(\mathbf{X}_j'\mathbf{X}_j)^{-1} = 1/3$; hence,

$$\Delta_j = \left(\tau^2 + \frac{\sigma^2}{3} \right).$$

Substituting these values in Equation 13.24, we obtain the sampling variance of $\hat{\gamma}_0$ as

$$\frac{1}{5} \left(\tau^2 + \frac{\sigma^2}{3} \right) = 1.7,$$

as obtained earlier.

Generalized Least Squares Estimation

As noted in the previous section, the OLS estimator is appropriate in situations where the errors are homoscedastic, that is, the error variances are homogeneous. In the example given above, Δ_j is the same across the clusters because of equal cluster sizes. If the clusters have unequal numbers of observations, then the variance Δ_j will vary across the clusters. In this case, it is advantageous to use an estimation procedure that takes into account the heterogeneity of Δ_j across clusters and gives more weight to observations that have smaller variance. The Generalized Least Squares (GLS) estimator described in this section has this property. This procedure will produce estimates that, overall, have smaller sampling variance, that is, estimates that are more *efficient* than OLS estimators, whenever there is heterogeneity in the variances.

The Generalized Least Squares estimator is also appropriate in other situations. At the second level in a multilevel model, a researcher may decide to use different explanatory variables for the different first-level regression coefficients; this is akin to using different predictor variables for the dependent variables in a multivariate general linear model. For example, in a multivariate analysis of covariance situation, rather than using the same set of covariates for each dependent variable, the researcher may decide to use different covariates for different dependent variables. Such a model with different predictor variables for different dependent variables first was introduced by Zellner (1962), who called this model the Seemingly Unrelated Regressions (SUR) model. In this situation, the error variance-covariance matrices are heterogeneous, and hence, GLS estimators are more appropriate than OLS estimators.

In the single-level regression model where $\mathbf{y} = X\boldsymbol{\beta} + \mathbf{e}$, if

$$Var(\mathbf{y}) = Var(\mathbf{e}) = \Sigma,$$

where Σ is not of the form $\sigma^2 I$, then the objective function to be minimized in estimation is

$$\varphi = (\mathbf{y} - X\boldsymbol{\beta})'\Sigma^{-1}(\mathbf{y} - X\boldsymbol{\beta}).$$

The estimator $\hat{\boldsymbol{\beta}}$ that minimizes the function is known as the Generalized Least Squares Estimator of $\boldsymbol{\beta}$. Finding the first derivative of φ, setting it to zero, and solving for $\boldsymbol{\beta}$, we obtain the GLS estimator of $\boldsymbol{\beta}$ as

$$\hat{\boldsymbol{\beta}} = (X'\Sigma^{-1}X)^{-1}X'\Sigma^{-1}\mathbf{y}. \tag{13.25}$$

Note that when $\Sigma = \sigma^2 I$, the GLS estimator reduces to the OLS estimator. The expression given in Equation 13.25 shows that in obtaining the GLS estimates, the observations $\mathbf{y}$ are weighted inversely by the elements of the variance-covariance matrix Σ. Observations that have a large variance will receive smaller weight than the observations that have smaller variance. In this sense, GLS estimates are "weighted" estimates, where the weights are the precision (inverse of the variance) of the observations.

We now apply these results to the multilevel case. Since the Δ_j are not the same across clusters, the OLS procedure is not appropriate for the estimation of γ. The objective function to be minimized in this case becomes

$$\sum_{j=1}^{J}(\hat{\boldsymbol{\beta}}_j - W_j\boldsymbol{\gamma})'\Delta_j^{-1}(\hat{\boldsymbol{\beta}}_j - W_j\boldsymbol{\gamma}),$$

and the GLS estimator of γ is obtained analogously to that in Equation 13.25 as

$$\hat{\boldsymbol{\gamma}} = (\sum_{j=1}^{J}W_j'\Delta_j^{-1}W_j)^{-1}(W_j'\Delta_j^{-1}\hat{\boldsymbol{\beta}}_j). \tag{13.26}$$

The sampling variance of $\hat{\boldsymbol{\gamma}}$, $Var(\hat{\boldsymbol{\gamma}})$, is

$$Var(\hat{\boldsymbol{\gamma}}) = Var\left[(\sum_{j=1}^{J}W_j'\Delta_j^{-1}W_j)^{-1}(\sum_{j=1}^{J}W_j'\Delta_j^{-1}\hat{\boldsymbol{\beta}}_j)\right].$$

Noting that $Var(A\mathbf{x}) = A\ Var(\mathbf{x})A'$ for any matrix A, the expression above simplifies to

$$Var(\hat{\boldsymbol{\gamma}}) = (\sum_{j=1}^{J} W_j' \Delta_j^{-1} W_j)^{-1}.$$

For the example provided earlier, $W_j = 1$, $X' = [1\ \ 1\ \ 1]$, $(X'X)^{-1} = 1/3$, and Δ_j, as given in Equation 13.23, reduces to

$$\tau^2 + \frac{\sigma^2}{3}$$

for all clusters. Since Δ_j does not vary across clusters, the OLS and GLS estimates and their sampling variances coincide. However, if the clusters are of different sizes, then the two estimates will differ since Δ_j is a function of $(X_j'X_j)^{-1}$, which depends on the sample size. In the example, had the cluster sizes differed, the weights for the cluster means would be

$$[\tau^2 + \frac{\sigma^2}{n_j}]^{-1}.$$

Thus, clusters with large sample sizes will receive a greater weight than those with small sample sizes. Naturally, when $n_j = n$, all cluster means receive the same weight.

SIMULTANEOUS ESTIMATION OF FIXED EFFECTS AND VARIANCE COMPONENTS

The methods described in the previous sections provide a useful and necessary background for our development of parameter estimation procedures in multilevel models. These procedures are based on the assumption that the variance components are known or can be estimated separately prior to the estimation of effects. In reality, variance components rarely are known. However, in the case of balanced data, as in the example provided at the beginning of this chapter, the variance components and the fixed effects can be estimated separately; the correct estimates of the fixed effects and the variance components and correct standard errors of the fixed effects will be obtained. In the unbalanced case and in more complex multilevel models, the fixed effects and the variance components must be estimated together. In this section, we discuss procedures that are appropriate for the more common situation of simultaneous estimation of the fixed effects and the variance components.

Maximum Likelihood Estimation

The Maximum Likelihood (ML) procedure is widely used in a variety of estimation problems. In some cases, as we shall see, the ML estimator coincides with OLS and GLS estimators, and in such instances, these estimators, rather than ML estimators, are used because of their simplicity. The Maximum Likelihood procedure is particularly useful when the models are complex and the sampling distribution of the estimators cannot be determined. The major advantage of the ML procedure is that large sample (asymptotic) properties of maximum likelihood estimators, such as their distributions and standard errors, are known; with this knowledge, confidence intervals can be constructed for the parameters of interest, and hypotheses concerning the parameters can be tested.

The Maximum Likelihood Estimator (MLE) of a vector of parameters θ is the value of θ for which the *likelihood function* attains its maximum value, where the likelihood is a function of the data given the parameters. To define the likelihood function, let $f(y:\theta)$ be the density function of a continuous random variable y with parameter vector θ and let $y_1,\ldots,y_n$ be independent realizations of y with *joint* distribution denoted as $g(y:\theta)$. The joint distribution is a function of the unknown parameters θ. The possible values of θ form the *parameter space*. Once the data are observed, the joint distribution loses its probabilistic meaning and becomes a mathematical function of the parameters, known as the *likelihood function*. Loosely speaking, the likelihood function gives the likelihood (probability) of observing a given sample of data as a function of the unknown parameters. To obtain the maximum likelihood estimators, that is, to find the value of θ that maximizes the likelihood function, we set to zero the first derivative of the likelihood function with respect to θ and solve the resulting set of *likelihood equations*.

To make these concepts concrete, we shall obtain maximum likelihood estimators of the mean μ and variance σ^2 of a random variable y. Assume that observations are drawn from a normal distribution. The normal density function $f(y_i:\mu,\sigma^2)$ is

$$f(y_i:\mu,\sigma^2) = \frac{1}{\sqrt{2\pi\sigma^2}}\exp\{-\frac{1}{2\sigma^2}(y_i-\mu)^2\}. \qquad (13.27)$$

Since the observations are independent, the joint distribution of $y_1,\ldots,y_n$, $g(y:\theta)$, is the product of the densities given in Equation 13.27, i.e.,

$$g(y_1,\ldots,y_n:\mu,\sigma^2) = \prod_{i=1}^{n} f(y_i:\mu,\sigma^2) = \prod_{i=1}^{n}\frac{1}{\sqrt{2\pi\sigma^2}}\exp\{-\frac{1}{2\sigma^2}(y_i-\mu)^2\},$$

where $\prod$ is the product symbol indicating that the terms are to be multiplied. Thus,

$$g(y_1,\ldots,y_n : \mu,\sigma^2) = \frac{1}{(2\pi\sigma^2)^{n/2}} \exp\{-\frac{1}{2\sigma^2} \sum_{i=1}^{n}(y_i-\mu)^2\}.$$

Once the data are observed, $g(y_1,\ldots,y_n:\mu,\sigma^2)$ is denoted as $L(y_1,\ldots,y_n:\mu,\sigma^2)$, the likelihood function. Since the logarithm of a product is the sum of the logarithms, it is easier to work with the logarithm of the likelihood function (*Log Likelihood*) than the likelihood itself. Another reason for working with the Log Likelihood is that the second derivative of the Log Likelihood plays an important role in maximum likelihood estimation. The Log Likelihood, in this case, is

$$\log L(y_1,\ldots,y_n : \mu,\sigma^2) = \frac{n}{2}\log(\frac{1}{2\pi\sigma^2}) + \log[\exp\{-\frac{1}{2\sigma^2}\sum_{i=1}^{n}(y_i-\mu)^2\}] \qquad (13.28)$$

$$= -\frac{n}{2}\log(2\pi) - \frac{n}{2}\log(\sigma^2) - \frac{1}{2\sigma^2}\sum_{i=1}^{n}(y_i-\mu)^2.$$

The log of the likelihood function reaches its maximum at the same values of the parameters as does the likelihood function itself, so nothing is lost by working with the Log Likelihood.

Suppose that σ^2 is known and that we want to determine the value of μ that maximizes the likelihood function. Differentiating the log of the likelihood function with respect to μ, we obtain

$$\frac{\partial}{\partial\mu}\log L(y_1,\ldots,y_n : \mu,\sigma^2) = \frac{1}{\sigma^2}\sum_{i=1}^{n}(y_i-\mu).$$

Setting this derivative to zero and solving the resulting likelihood equation results in

$$\sum_{i=1}^{n}(y_i-\mu) = 0 \Leftrightarrow \mu = \frac{1}{n}\sum_{i=1}^{n}y_i = \bar{y}.$$

Thus, $\bar{y}$ is the MLE of μ. To determine the MLE of σ^2, we substitute the estimate of $\mu = \bar{y}$ in the likelihood function and evaluate the derivative with respect to σ^2:

$$\frac{\partial}{\partial\sigma^2}\log L(y_1,\ldots,y_n : \mu,\sigma^2) = -\frac{n}{2}\frac{1}{\sigma^2} + \frac{1}{2(\sigma^2)^2}\sum_{i=1}^{n}(y_i-\bar{y})^2.$$

Setting this derivative to zero and solving the likelihood equation, we find that the MLE of σ^2 is

$$\hat{\sigma}^2 = \frac{1}{n}\sum_{i=1}^{n}(y_i - \bar{y})^2. \tag{13.29}$$

As is well known, the divisor in the expression above must be $(n-1)$ in order to obtain an unbiased estimate of σ^2 (Kirk, 1995). The MLE of σ^2 given in Equation 13.29 is a biased estimate. In this simple case, the bias can be corrected by multiplying the estimate by the factor $n/(n-1)$.

To obtain maximum likelihood estimates of the parameters for the regression model $\mathbf{y} = X\boldsymbol{\beta} + \mathbf{e}$, we first need to determine the joint distribution of $y_1, y_2, \ldots, y_n$. If we assume that $\mathbf{e} \sim N(\mathbf{0}, \boldsymbol{\Sigma})$, then $\mathbf{y} \sim N(X\boldsymbol{\beta}, \boldsymbol{\Sigma})$. Hence, the joint distribution of $\mathbf{y} = [y_1\ y_2\ \cdots\ y_n]$ is

$$f(\mathbf{y}) = \frac{1}{(2\pi)^{n/2}|\boldsymbol{\Sigma}|^{1/2}}\exp\{-\frac{1}{2}(\mathbf{y}-X\boldsymbol{\beta})'\boldsymbol{\Sigma}^{-1}(\mathbf{y}-X\boldsymbol{\beta})\}.$$

The log of the likelihood, therefore, is

$$\log L(y:\boldsymbol{\beta},\boldsymbol{\Sigma}) = -\frac{n}{2}\log(2\pi) - \frac{1}{2}\log|\boldsymbol{\Sigma}| - \frac{1}{2}(y-X\boldsymbol{\beta})'\boldsymbol{\Sigma}^{-1}(y-X\boldsymbol{\beta}). \tag{13.30}$$

From Equation 13.30, it is clear that the MLE of $\boldsymbol{\beta}$ is the value that minimizes

$$(\mathbf{y} - X\boldsymbol{\beta})'\boldsymbol{\Sigma}^{-1}(\mathbf{y} - X\boldsymbol{\beta}).$$

Since the function to be minimized is the same as the function for the GLS procedure, the ML and GLS estimates coincide. If we assume that $\boldsymbol{\Sigma} = \sigma^2 I$, as assumed in ordinary least squares regression,

$$\log L(\mathbf{y}:\boldsymbol{\beta},\sigma^2) = -\frac{n}{2}\log(2\pi) - \frac{1}{2}\log|\sigma^2 I| - \frac{1}{2\sigma^2}(\mathbf{y}-X\boldsymbol{\beta})'(\mathbf{y}-X\boldsymbol{\beta}) \tag{13.31}$$

$$= -\frac{n}{2}\log(2\pi) - \frac{n}{2}\log(\sigma^2) - \frac{1}{2\sigma^2}(\mathbf{y}-X\boldsymbol{\beta})'(\mathbf{y}-X\boldsymbol{\beta}).$$

In deriving the likelihood function above, we have used the result that $|\sigma^2 I| = (\sigma^2)^n$. From Equation 13.31, it can be seen that the MLE of $\boldsymbol{\beta}$ is the value that minimizes $(\mathbf{y} - X\boldsymbol{\beta})'(\mathbf{y} - X\boldsymbol{\beta})$. This function is the same function used for obtaining OLS estimates. In fact, Gauss, in developing his celebrated Least Squares Criterion, arrived at it through the normal density function, using a method similar to that provided above.

To obtain the ML estimate of σ^2, we find the derivative of $\log L$ with respect to σ^2:

$$\frac{\partial}{\partial \sigma^2} \log L(\mathbf{y} : \boldsymbol{\beta}, \sigma^2) = -\frac{n}{2\sigma^2} + \frac{1}{2(\sigma^2)^2} (\mathbf{y} - X\boldsymbol{\beta})' (\mathbf{y} - X\boldsymbol{\beta}).$$

Solving the likelihood equation, we obtain the MLE of $\hat{\sigma}^2$ as

$$\hat{\sigma}^2 = \frac{1}{n}(\mathbf{y} - X\hat{\boldsymbol{\beta}})' (\mathbf{y} - X\hat{\boldsymbol{\beta}}), \tag{13.32}$$

where $\hat{\boldsymbol{\beta}} = (X'X)^{-1}X'\mathbf{y}$.

The estimate given in Equation 13.32 is biased; an unbiased estimate of the error variance is obtained by using a divisor of $(n-p-1)$ (Searle, 1971) rather than n.

For the two-level model, combining levels one and two yields the model

$$\mathbf{y}_j = X_j W_j \boldsymbol{\gamma} + X_j \mathbf{u}_j + \mathbf{e}_j = A_j \boldsymbol{\gamma} + X_j \mathbf{u}_j + \mathbf{e}_j, \tag{13.33}$$

where $A_j = X_j W_j$. Now

$$Var(\mathbf{y}_j) = Var(X_j \mathbf{u}_j + \mathbf{e}_j) = X_j T X_j' + \sigma^2 I \equiv \boldsymbol{\Psi}_j. \tag{13.34}$$

Thus, under the assumption that $\mathbf{u}_j$ and $\mathbf{e}_j$ are multivariate normally distributed,

$$\mathbf{y}_j \sim N(A_j \boldsymbol{\gamma}, \boldsymbol{\Psi}_j). \tag{13.35}$$

The likelihood function is, therefore,

$$L(\mathbf{y} : \boldsymbol{\gamma}, \sigma^2, T) = k \prod_{j=1}^{J} \frac{1}{|\boldsymbol{\Psi}_j|^{1/2}} \exp\{-\frac{1}{2}(\mathbf{y}_j - A_j\boldsymbol{\gamma})' \boldsymbol{\Psi}_j^{-1}(\mathbf{y}_j - A_j\boldsymbol{\gamma})\}, \tag{13.36}$$

where k is a constant. The log of the likelihood, dropping the constant, is

$$\log L(\mathbf{y} : \boldsymbol{\gamma}, \sigma^2, T) = -\frac{1}{2}\sum_{j=1}^{J} \log |\boldsymbol{\Psi}_j| - \frac{1}{2}\sum_{j=1}^{J}(\mathbf{y}_j - A_j\boldsymbol{\gamma})' \boldsymbol{\Psi}_j^{-1}(\mathbf{y}_j - A_j\boldsymbol{\gamma}). \tag{13.37}$$

The maximum likelihood estimates are obtained by setting the vector of first derivatives of the log likelihood function to zero and solving the likelihood equations. Letting $\boldsymbol{\theta}$ denote the vector of parameters, the likelihood equations are

$$\frac{\partial}{\partial \boldsymbol{\theta}} \log L(\mathbf{y} : \boldsymbol{\gamma}, T, \sigma^2) = \begin{bmatrix} \dfrac{\partial}{\partial \boldsymbol{\gamma}} \log L(\mathbf{y} : \boldsymbol{\gamma}, T, \sigma^2) \\[2ex] \dfrac{\partial}{\partial \sigma^2} \log L(\mathbf{y} : \boldsymbol{\gamma}, T, \sigma^2) \\[2ex] \dfrac{\partial}{\partial T} \log L(\mathbf{y} : \boldsymbol{\gamma}, T, \sigma^2) \end{bmatrix} = \mathbf{0}.$$

As an illustration, consider the ML estimation of the parameters γ_0 and the variance components τ^2 and σ^2 for the simple one-way random-effects anova example described earlier. Within cluster j, the model given in Equation 13.33 simplifies to

$$\mathbf{y}_j = \gamma_0 \begin{bmatrix} 1 \\ 1 \\ 1 \end{bmatrix} + u_j \begin{bmatrix} 1 \\ 1 \\ 1 \end{bmatrix} + \mathbf{e}_j = \gamma_0 \mathbf{1}_j + u_j \mathbf{1}_j + \mathbf{e}_j,$$

where $\mathbf{1}_j$ is the $(n_j \times 1)$ vector whose elements are ones. With the usual assumptions $E(u_j) = 0$, $E(\mathbf{e}_j) = 0$, and $Cov(u_j, \mathbf{e}_j) = 0$ we obtain the mean vector of $\mathbf{y}_j$ as $E(\mathbf{y}_j) = \gamma_0 \mathbf{1}$. Using the fact noted earlier that $Var(A\mathbf{x}) = AVar(\mathbf{x})A'$ for any matrix A, the variance-covariance matrix of $\mathbf{y}_j$ is

$$Var(\mathbf{y}_j) \equiv \boldsymbol{\Sigma}_j = \mathbf{1}_j \tau^2 \mathbf{1}_j' + \sigma^2 I_j = \tau^2 \mathbf{1}_j \mathbf{1}_j' + \sigma^2 I_j. \qquad (13.38)$$

The product $\mathbf{11}'$ is a $(n_j \times n_j)$ matrix of ones and I_j is the $(n_j \times n_j)$ identity matrix; hence, $Var(\mathbf{y}_j)$ is a $(n_j \times n_j)$ matrix with diagonal elements $(\sigma^2 + \tau^2)$ and off-diagonal elements τ^2. The above result shows immediately that the variance of an observation in cluster j is $(\sigma^2 + \tau^2)$ and that the covariance between any pair of observations in cluster j is τ^2. Assuming that $\mathbf{y}_j$ is multivariate normal, using Equation 13.30, the likelihood function in cluster j is obtained as

$$\log L(\mathbf{y}_j : \gamma_0, \sigma^2, \tau^2) = -\frac{n}{2} \log(2\pi) - \frac{1}{2} \log|\boldsymbol{\Sigma}_j| - \frac{1}{2} (\mathbf{y}_j - \gamma_0 \mathbf{1}_j)' \boldsymbol{\Sigma}_j^{-1} (\mathbf{y}_j - \gamma_0 \mathbf{1}_j).$$

For the variance-covariance matrix $\boldsymbol{\Sigma}$ given in Equation 13.38,

$$\boldsymbol{\Sigma}_j^{-1} = \frac{1}{\sigma^2} \left(I_j - \frac{\omega}{(1 + n_j \omega)} \mathbf{1}_j \mathbf{1}_j' \right),$$

where $\omega = \tau^2 / \sigma^2$ and the determinant $|\Sigma_j| = (\sigma^2)^{n_j}(1+n_j\omega)$. It is less cumbersome to obtain the derivatives of the log of the likelihood with respect to σ^2 and ω rather than with respect to σ^2 and τ^2. Once σ^2 and ω are estimated, the estimate of τ^2 can be obtained as the product of the estimates of σ^2 and ω.

With the expressions for Σ^{-1} and $|\Sigma|$, the likelihood function can be simplified as

$$\log L(\mathbf{y}_j : \gamma_0, \sigma^2, \omega) = -\frac{n_j}{2}\log(2\pi) - \frac{n_j}{2}\log\sigma^2 - \frac{1}{2}\log(1+n_j\,\omega)$$

$$-\frac{1}{2\sigma^2}(\mathbf{y}_j - \gamma_0\mathbf{1}_j)'\left[I_j - \left(\frac{\omega}{1+n_j\omega}\right)\mathbf{1}_j\mathbf{1}_j'\right](\mathbf{y}_j - \gamma_0\mathbf{1}_j).$$

The log of the complete likelihood (over the J clusters) is

$$\log L(\mathbf{y} : \gamma_0, \sigma^2, \omega) = \sum_{j=1}^{J}\log L(\mathbf{y}_j : \gamma_0, \sigma^2, \omega).$$

The derivatives of $\log L(\mathbf{y}:\gamma_0, \sigma^2, \tau^2)$ with respect to γ_0, σ^2, τ^2 are needed to obtain the ML estimators of the fixed effect γ_0 and the variance components σ^2 and τ^2. These derivatives are given below:

$$\frac{\partial}{\partial\gamma_0}\log L = \frac{1}{\sigma^2}\left\{\sum_{j=1}^{J}\sum_{i=1}^{n_j}\frac{1}{(1+n_j\omega)}(y_{ij} - \gamma_0)\right\}$$

$$\frac{\partial}{\partial\sigma^2}\log L = \frac{1}{2(\sigma^2)^2}\left\{\sum_{j=1}^{J}\sum_{i=1}^{n_j}(y_{ij}-\gamma_0)^2 - \sum_{j=1}^{J}\frac{\omega}{(1+n_j\omega)}\left[\sum_{i=1}^{n_j}(y_{ij}-\gamma_0)\right]^2 - N\sigma^2\right\}$$

$$\frac{\partial}{\partial\omega}\log = \frac{1}{2\sigma^2}\sum_{j=1}^{J}\frac{1}{(1+n_j\omega)^2}\left[\sum_{i=1}^{n_j}(y_{ij}-\gamma_0)\right]^2 - \frac{1}{2}\sum_{j=1}^{J}\frac{n_j}{(1+n_j\omega)}.$$

Setting the first derivative with respect to γ_0 equal to zero, we obtain the ML estimator of γ_0 as a weighted combination of the cluster means, $\bar{y}_j$:

$$\hat{\gamma} = \left\{\sum_{j=1}^{J}\frac{n_j\bar{y}_j}{(1+n_j\omega)}\right\} / \left\{\sum_{j=1}^{J}\frac{n_j}{(1+n_j\omega)}\right\}.$$

The weights are functions of the cluster size n_j, σ^2, and τ^2. This expression can be obtained as a special case of Equation 13.26. Thus, the ML estimator is also the GLS estimator. When sample sizes are equal across clusters, the first derivative reduces to

$$\frac{\partial}{\partial \gamma_0} \log L = \frac{1}{\sigma^2(1+n\omega)} \left\{ \sum_{j=1}^{J} \sum_{i=1}^{n} (y_{ij} - \gamma_0) \right\}.$$

Setting the first derivative equal to zero and solving the resulting likelihood equation results in $\hat{\gamma}_0$ being equal to the overall mean (as given in Equation 13.4).

Maximum Likelihood Estimation with the Newton-Raphson Procedure

While in some situations, the likelihood equations can be solved analytically, that is, in closed form, it is not the case in general. A closed-form solution is possible for the estimation of γ_0 in the example provided above for the balanced case. However, in the unbalanced case, the three likelihood equations must be solved simultaneously. Since these are not linear equations, explicit solutions are not possible. These equations must be solved by trial and error, that is, iteratively. Procedures for the iterative solution of equations are referred to as numerical methods. A simple numerical method would be as follows: (i) start with a value of ω and determine the value of γ_0; (ii) with these values of ω and γ_0, determine σ^2; (iii) update the value of ω using the values of γ_0 and σ^2; (iv) repeat steps (i) to (iii) until the values of these parameters do not change from cycle to cycle, i.e., convergence occurs. In the balanced design, γ_0 does not depend on the other parameters, and its value is obtained immediately as the grand mean.

To apply the procedure described above to the simple example we have used throughout, we need starting values for the parameters. Denote these as τ_0^2 and σ_0^2. The correct estimates of the parameters obtained in the first section of the chapter were 7.967 and 1.6, respectively. For illustrative purposes, we will choose starting values that are not too close to these values: $\hat{\sigma}_0^2 = 1.0$ and $\hat{\tau}_0^2 = 5.0$. In the first iteration, $\hat{\gamma}_0$ is immediately calculated as 6.0. With a convergence criterion of .00001, convergence is reached in eight iterations, giving a value of 1.6 for σ^2 and 6.2668 for τ^2. While the value for σ^2 agrees with the result obtained earlier, τ^2 is underestimated, indicating that the ML estimator of the variance component τ^2 is biased.

An alternative to the iterative procedure described above is the Newton-Raphson procedure for solving the likelihood equations. Suppose that the equation to be solved involving a single unknown is $f(x) = 0$. According to the Newton-Raphson procedure, if x_i is an approximate solution to this equation's iteration i, then a more accurate solution x_{i+1} is

$$x_{i+1} = x_i - \frac{f(x_i)}{f'(x_i)}. \tag{13.39}$$

This procedure is repeated until the change value between iterations is less than a prescribed criterion. Figure 13.1 provides a geometric inter-

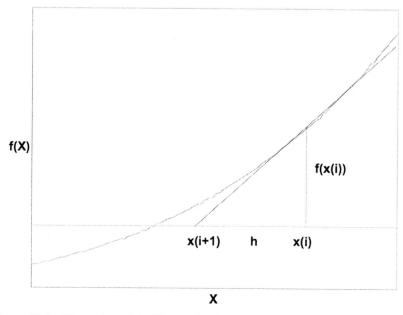

Figure 13.1 Illustration of the Newton-Raphson procedure.

pretation for the above iterative scheme. Since $f'(x_i)$ is the slope at x_i, it follows that $f(x_i)/h = f'(x_i)$ so that $h = f(x_i)/f'(x_i)$. Thus, the new value $x_{i+1} = x_i - h$. The Equation 13.39 follows directly.

In the situation where several parameters must be estimated (in our example the parameters are γ_0, σ^2, ω), there are several likelihood equations that must be solved simultaneously. Let θ denote the vector of parameters $[\theta_1\ \theta_2\ \dots\ \theta_m]$,

$$\frac{\partial}{\partial \theta} \log L$$

denote the vector of m first derivatives of the log likelihood function, and

$$\frac{\partial^2}{\partial \theta \partial \theta'} \log L$$

denote the $(m \times m)$ matrix of second derivatives. Then the matrix extension of the Newton-Raphson procedure given in Equation 13.39 is

$$\theta_{i+1} = \theta_i - \left[\frac{\partial^2}{\partial \theta \partial \theta'} \log L\right]_{\theta_i}^{-1} \left[\frac{\partial}{\partial \theta} \log L\right]_{\theta_i}, \qquad (13.40)$$

where θ_I is the vector of parameter estimates at iteration I and the first and second derivatives are evaluated at these values. The symmetric matrix of second derivatives for our example is

$$
\frac{\partial^2}{\partial\theta\,\partial\theta'}\log L =
\begin{bmatrix}
\dfrac{\partial^2 \log L}{\partial\gamma_0^2} & \dfrac{\partial^2 \log L}{\partial\gamma_0\partial\sigma^2} & \dfrac{\partial^2 \log L}{\partial\gamma_0\partial\omega} \\[2ex]
\dfrac{\partial^2 \log L}{\partial\sigma^2\partial\gamma_0} & \dfrac{\partial^2 \log L}{\partial(\sigma^2)^2} & \dfrac{\partial^2 \log L}{\partial\sigma^2\partial\omega} \\[2ex]
\dfrac{\partial^2 \log L}{\partial\omega\,\partial\gamma_0} & \dfrac{\partial^2 \log L}{\partial\omega\,\partial\sigma^2} & \dfrac{\partial^2 \log L}{\partial\omega^2}
\end{bmatrix}.
$$

To begin the Newton-Raphson procedure, starting values are specified for the parameters. Procedures for obtaining starting values are discussed in the next section. Once suitable starting values are specified for the parameters, the first and second derivatives can be computed. The matrix of the second derivatives is inverted and the iterative procedure given in Equation 13.40 is set in motion. For the balanced case, the starting value for γ_0 will have no effect on the iterative procedure; the procedure will converge immediately to the grand mean.

In the case of our example, the second derivatives for the example are relatively straightforward to obtain; these are not provided here. Using the Newton-Raphson procedure described above and with starting values set at $\hat\gamma_{00} = 5.0$, $\hat\sigma_0^2 = 1.0$, and $\hat\tau_0^2 = 5.0$, $\hat\gamma_0$ immediately was obtained as 6.0, the grand mean. With a convergence criterion of .00001, convergence was reached in six iterations, yielding $\hat\sigma^2 = 1.6$ and $\hat\tau^2 = 6.2668$. The iteration history is provided in Table 13.3. As noted previously, τ^2 is underestimated.

TABLE 13.3 Results of Maximum Likelihood Estimation with the Newton-Raphson Algorithm

Parameter	Values at start of iteration					
	1	2	3	4	5	Final
γ	5.0000	6.0000	6.0000	6.0000	6.0000	6.0000
τ^2	5.0000	6.0587	6.1971	6.2503	6.2662	6.2667
σ^2	1.0000	1.2548	1.4716	1.5796	1.5994	1.6000
Change values						
h_1	−1.0000	0.0000	0.0000	0.0000	0.0000	0.0000
h_2	−1.0587	−0.1384	−0.0532	−0.0159	−0.0005	0.0000
h_3	−0.2548	−0.2168	−0.1080	−0.0198	−0.0006	0.0000

While, in general, the first derivative of the likelihood function is relatively easy to obtain, determining the matrix of second derivatives is more difficult. The matrix calculus developed by McDonald and Swaminathan (1973) and Magnus and Neudecker (1988), among others, provides a simplified step-by-step procedure for evaluating the derivatives of complex matrix functions.

Starting Values and Issues in Optimization

The numerical procedures employed in the section above require starting values for the parameters. Starting values should be chosen carefully, particularly in the case of the Newton-Raphson algorithm, as the algorithm will converge either very slowly or not at all if the starting value is too far from the local/global maximum. In the present context, a reasonable starting value for the fixed effect γ is the OLS estimator $\hat{\gamma}_0$, obtained using Equation 13.19. The pooled within-cluster variance provides a good starting value for σ^2, while a reasonable starting value for the variance-covariance matrix T, denoted as T_0, is obtained by computing the variance-covariance matrix of $\hat{\beta}_j$ across the groups, i.e.,

$$T_0 = \frac{1}{(J-r-1)} \sum_{j=1}^{J} (\hat{\beta}_j - W_j\hat{\gamma}_0)(\hat{\beta}_j - W_j\hat{\gamma}_0)',$$

where r is the number of level-two predictors.

While the Newton-Raphson procedure is one of the most widely used procedures for optimization, it has some drawbacks. The first is that the procedure described above is valid only for unconstrained optimization in which no restrictions are placed on the values that a parameter can take. This is obviously a problem in estimating variance components that are constrained to be positive. It may happen that the algorithm converges to a negative value. A common practice in the case of negative estimates of variance is to set the values to zero; obviously, these estimates are not interpretable. Alternative estimation algorithms, such as the E-M algorithm described in the next section, may avert this problem.

The second drawback is that, as with any optimization algorithm, the Newton-Raphson procedure may locate only a local maximum and not the global maximum. The properties of the ML estimators are obtained only when the ML estimate corresponds to the global maximum. While there is no guarantee that an algorithm will locate the global maximum, the starting values used may affect the outcome because if the starting value is near a local maximum, the algorithm will converge to that local maximum. If this problem is suspected, then useful diagnostic information can be obtained by changing the starting value and determining whether the algorithm converges to the same final value. Dennis and Schnabel (1996) provide a detailed discussion of optimization procedures and issues.

Properties of ML Estimators

In general, the ML estimators of the variance components (such as σ^2) in the presence of fixed parameters (such as β) are biased. Despite this, ML estimators have the following advantages: Maximum Likelihood estimators are asymptotically (a) consistent, (b) functions of sufficient statistics if sufficient statistics exist, (c) efficient, and (d) normally distributed (Kendall & Stuart, 1969).

The asymptotic normality of ML estimators is used frequently in drawing inferences in complex models in which exact sampling distributions of the estimators cannot be determined. Obviously, when using the asymptotic normality property, the variance of the estimator is needed. In general, if $\hat{\theta}$ is the ML estimator of θ, then asymptotically (Kendall & Stuart, 1969),

$$Var(\hat{\theta}) = -\left\{E\left[\frac{\partial^2}{\partial\theta^2}\log L\right]_{\theta=\hat{\theta}}\right\}^{-1}.$$

As an example, let us obtain the variance of the ML estimator of the mean ($\bar{y}$). The second derivative of the log of the likelihood function given in Equation 13.28 with respect to μ is

$$\frac{\partial^2}{\partial\mu^2}\log L(y_1,\ldots,y_n : \mu,\sigma^2) = \frac{\partial}{\partial\mu}\left\{\frac{2}{2\sigma^2}\sum_{i=1}^{n}(y_i - \mu)\right\} = -\frac{n}{\sigma^2}.$$

Inverting and taking the expected value, we obtain

$$-E\left\{\frac{\partial^2}{\partial\mu^2}\log L\right\}^{-1} = \frac{\sigma^2}{n},$$

the usual formula for the sampling variance of $\bar{y}$.

The quantity

$$\mathcal{I} = -E\left[\frac{\partial^2}{\partial\theta^2}\log L\right]$$

is known as the Fisher's Information Function, or simply the Information Function, and was introduced by R.A. Fisher in connection with maximum likelihood estimation (Kendall & Stuart, 1969). It is the reciprocal of the variance and a natural by-product of the final stage of the Newton-Raphson algorithm. While its primary use is in inference, it has been used in other contexts. In the field of measurement, the information function plays a critical role within the Item Response Theory framework for test development and for such uses as Computer Adaptive Testing (Hambleton, Swaminathan, & Rogers, 1991).

The information function for the multiparameter case is

$$\mathcal{I} = -E\left[\frac{\partial^2 \log L}{\partial\theta\,\partial\theta'}\right]. \tag{13.41}$$

This information function is calculated at the convergence of the Newton-Raphson algorithm using the ML estimates. The inverse of the information matrix is the asymptotic variance-covariance matrix of the ML estimators. The square roots of the diagonal elements of the variance-covariance matrix are the standard errors of the parameter estimates. It should be noted that the information function and the standard errors are based on asymptotic theory and may not be correct in small samples. In the multilevel case, Longford (1993) has noted that the asymptotic results hold as the number of clusters increases, rather than as the cluster size increases.

When the likelihood function is complex, it may not be possible to obtain an analytical expression for the information function. In such cases, the matrix of second derivatives at the final stage of the Newton-Raphson algorithm is taken as an approximation to the information function.

In some cases it is efficient to use the information function defined above instead of the matrix of second derivatives in the Newton-Raphson procedure. The advantage is that the information function is positive-definite (positive in the single parameter case), whereas the matrix of second derivatives need not be positive-definite. When it is not, the procedure will not converge. When the information function or matrix is used in the Newton-Raphson procedure, the procedure is termed Fisher's Method of Scoring (Kendall & Stuart, 1969). Longford (1987, 1989) described the Fisher scoring algorithm in the multilevel case.

Maximum Likelihood Estimation with the E-M Algorithm

The E-M algorithm is introduced most easily in the context of the simple example used throughout this chapter. Recall that the model in the example is a one-way random effects model, $y_{il} = \gamma_0 + u_j + e_{ij}$, with $Var(u_j) = \tau^2$, and $Var(e_j) = \sigma^2$. If u_j is *observed*, all the parameters of interest can be estimated without any difficulty. For example, if u_j is observed, $y_{ij}^* = (y_{ij} - u_j)$ is observed, and the parameters can be estimated as follows:

$$\hat{\gamma}_0 = \frac{\sum_{j=1}^{J}\sum_{i=1}^{n_j} y_{ij}^*}{N}; \quad \hat{\tau}^2 = \frac{\sum_{j=1}^{J} u_j^2}{J}; \quad \hat{\sigma}^2 = \frac{\sum_{j=1}^{J}\sum_{i=1}^{n_j}(y_{ij}^* - \hat{\gamma}_0)^2}{N}.$$

In this case the set (y_{ij}, u_j) is the *complete data*. With complete data, the quantities

$$\sum_{j=1}^{J}\sum_{i=1}^{n_j} y_{ij}^*, \quad \sum_{i=1}^{n_j} u_j^2, \quad \sum_{j=1}^{J}\sum_{i=1}^{n_j}(y_{ij}^* - \hat{\gamma}_0)^2$$

are sufficient statistics for estimating the parameters γ_0, τ^2, and σ^2.

Since the u_j are not observed, the set (y_{ij}) is considered *incomplete data*, and the set (u_j) is considered *missing*. As in all missing value situations, the task is to devise a procedure to replace the missing values by observable quantities in order to carry out the estimation of parameters.

Dempster, Laird, and Rubin (1977) developed an algorithm for estimating parameters in complex models; they showed that substituting the conditional expectations of the sufficient statistics of the missing values in the likelihood function, maximizing the resulting likelihood function to obtain parameter estimates, and iterating the process results in a sequence of estimates that converges to a local or global maximum of the likelihood function. The first step in the process is the Expectation step, in which expected values are computed, followed by the Maximization step, in which the likelihood is maximized, hence the procedure is known as the E-M Algorithm.

For our example, we need the conditional expectation of u_j. In this simple case, conditioning on $\bar{y}_j$ is equivalent to conditioning on y_{ij} since the model can be expressed in terms of either y_{ij} or $\bar{y}_j$ as shown in Equations 13.5 and 13.6. The conditional expectation of u_j given $\bar{y}_j$ is given by the usual regression formula:

$$E(u_j \mid \bar{y}_j) = E(u_j) + \frac{Cov(u_j, \bar{y}_j)}{Var(\bar{y}_j)}[\bar{y}_j - E(\bar{y}_j)]. \tag{13.42}$$

From Equation 13.6, it can be seen that $E(\bar{y}_j) = \gamma_0$. By the assumptions of the model, $E(u_j) = 0$. The variance of $\bar{y}_j$, as shown previously, is

$$Var(\bar{y}_j) = \tau^2 + \frac{\sigma^2}{n_j}.$$

The covariance between u_j and $\bar{y}_j$ is

$$Cov(u_j, \bar{y}_j) = Cov(u_j, \mu_j + \bar{e}_j) = Cov(u_j, \mu_j) + Cov(u_j, \bar{e}_j) = Cov(u_j, u_j) + 0 = \tau^2.$$

Substituting these expressions in Equation 13.42, we obtain

$$E(u_j \mid \bar{y}_j) = E(u_j) + \tau^2 \left[\tau^2 + \frac{\sigma^2}{n_j} \right]^{-1} (\bar{y}_j - \gamma_0) = \lambda_j (\bar{y}_j - \gamma_0) \equiv u_j^*,$$

where

$$\lambda_j = \frac{\tau^2}{(\tau^2 + \sigma^2 / n_j)}.$$

We will replace u_j with its expectation, u_j^*, in the computation of the sufficient statistics.

To start the E-M algorithm, we need initial values of the parameters, γ_0, τ^2, and σ^2. Denote these as γ_{00}, τ_0^2, and σ_0^2. The initial values for τ^2 and σ^2 for the example may be obtained by carrying out an ANOVA on the data, as was reported in Table 13.2. Once the initial values are obtained, λ_{j0}, and hence $u_{j0}^* = \lambda_{j0}(\bar{y}_j - \gamma_{00})$, are determined. The value of u_{j0}^* is used subsequently in the computation of the sufficient statistic for γ_0 and the estimation of γ_0.

The sufficient statistics for τ^2 and σ^2 require the conditional expectation of u_j^2. To obtain $E(u_j \mid \bar{y}_j)^2$, we note that by definition,

$$Var(u_j \mid \bar{y}_j) \equiv v_j = E\{ [u_j - E(u_j)] \mid \bar{y}_j \}^2 = E \{ [u_j - u_j^*] \mid \bar{y}_j \}^2.$$

Since

$$E \{(u_j - u_j^*) \mid \bar{y}_j \}^2 = E \{(u_j^2 - 2u_j u_j^* + u_j^{*2}) \mid \bar{y}_j \} = E \{(u_j^2 - u_j^{*2}) \mid \bar{y}_j \},$$

it follows that

$$E(u_j^2 \mid \bar{y}_j) = u_j^{*2} + v_j,$$

where the variance of $u_j \mid \bar{y}_j$ is, from standard regression theory, (Morrison, 1990),

$$v_j = Var(u_j) [1 - \frac{Cov(u_j, \bar{y}_j)^2}{Var(u_j)Var(\bar{y}_j)}] = \tau^2 [1 - \frac{(\tau^2)^2}{\tau^2(\tau^2 + \sigma^2/n_j)}] = \tau^2(1 - \lambda_j).$$

In the maximization step, the likelihood is maximized to obtain the ML estimates:

$$\hat{\gamma}_0 = \frac{\sum_{j=1}^{J} \sum_{i=1}^{n_j} (y_{ij} - u_j^*)}{N}, \tag{13.43}$$

$$\hat{\tau}^2 = \frac{\sum\limits_{j=1}^{J}[(u_j^{*2} + v_j]}{J},$$

(13.44)

$$\hat{\sigma}^2 = \frac{\sum\limits_{j=}^{J}\sum\limits_{i=1}^{n_j}[(y_{ij} - \hat{\gamma}_0 - u_j^*)^2 + v_j]}{N}.$$

(13.45)

To summarize, the E-M algorithm proceeds as follows:

Step 0: Obtain initial values for the parameters, γ_0, τ^2, σ^2 , and λ_j.
Step 1: E-Step: With the values for the parameter estimates, compute the expectations:

$$E(u_j \mid \bar{y}_j) = u_j^* = \lambda_j(\bar{y}_j - \gamma_0),$$

$$E(u_j^2 \mid \bar{y}_j) = u_j^{*2} + v_j,$$

$$E\{(y - \gamma_0 - u_j)^2 \mid \bar{y}_j\} = (y - \gamma_0 - u_j^*)^2 + v_j.$$

Step 2: M-Step: Compute the ML estimates of the parameters by substituting the expectations obtained in the E-step in Equations
13.43–13.45.
Step 3: Repeat Step 1 and Step 2; check for convergence. Convergence
is reached when the estimates in Step 2 change by less than some
preset criterion from one cycle to the next. If convergence has not
been reached, repeat Steps 1 and 2.

For the five-group example with which we have been working, the initial
values were set as previously: $\gamma_{00} = 5$; $\tau_0^2 = 5$; $\sigma_0^2 = 1$. With these initial values,
$\lambda_j = \tau^2/[\tau^2 + \sigma^2/n_j] = 5/[5+1/3] = .9375$. Since the number of observations is
the same in the groups, λ_j does not vary across groups. The computational
steps and the iterative sequence are summarized in Table 13.4.

With a convergence criterion of .00001, convergence was reached in 56
iterations. The number of iterations is large; however, since only elementary computations are carried out, the procedure runs quickly. Note once
again that the estimator of τ^2 is biased.

The basic steps in the E-M algorithm described above can be extended
immediately to the general multilevel model $\mathbf{y}_j = X_j W_j \boldsymbol{\gamma} + X_j \mathbf{u}_j + \mathbf{e}_j$, where
$\mathbf{e}_j \sim N(\mathbf{0}, \sigma^2 I)$ and $\mathbf{u}_j \sim N(\mathbf{0}, \mathbf{T})$. If $\mathbf{u}_j$ were observed, then the maximum likelihood estimators of the parameters (which in this case, because of the nor-
mality assumption, coincide with the OLS estimators) would be

TABLE 13.4 Results of Maximum Likelihood Estimation with the E-M Algorithm

Parameter	Iteration					
E-step	1	2	3	4	...	Final (56)
λ_j	0.9375	0.9385	0.9336	0.9308	...	0.9216
V_j	5.3333	0.4410	0.4782	0.4897	...	0.4915
u_1^*	-0.9375	-0.9971	-1.0458	-1.0971	...	-1.8315
u_2^*	1.8750	1.8183	1.7550	1.6954	...	0.9332
u_3^*	2.8125	2.7568	2.6887	2.6263	...	1.8457
u_4^*	3.7500	3.6953	3.6223	3.5571	...	2.7763
u_5^*	-2.8125	-2.8741	-2.9130	-2.9130	...	3.6747
M-step						
γ	5.0624	5.1202	5.1786	5.2354	...	5.9884
τ^2	7.1680	7.2041	7.0801	6.9662	...	6.2668
σ^2	1.4096	1.5367	1.5783	1.5921	...	1.6000
Change values						
h_1	0.0625	0.0567	0.0584	0.0568	...	0.0000
h_2	2.1679	0.3616	0.1240	0.1139	...	0.0000
h_3	0.4096	0.1271	0.0416	0.0139	...	0.0000

$$\hat{\gamma} = \sum_{j=1}^{J}(W_j'X_j'X_jW_j)^{-1}\sum_{j=1}^{J}W_j'X_j'(\mathbf{y}_j - X_j\mathbf{u}_j), \qquad (13.46)$$

$$\hat{T} = \frac{\sum_{j=1}^{J}\mathbf{u}_j\mathbf{u}_j'}{J},$$

$$\hat{\sigma}^2 = \frac{\sum_{j=1}^{J}\mathbf{e}_j'\mathbf{e}_j}{N} = \frac{\sum_{j=1}^{J}(\mathbf{y}_j - X_jW_j\gamma - X_j\mathbf{u}_j)'(\mathbf{y}_j - X_jW_j\gamma - X_j\mathbf{u}_j)}{N}.$$

Since $\mathbf{u}_j$ is not observed, we find the conditional mean of $\mathbf{u}_j$ given the observation $\mathbf{y}_j$ and use it to calculate expected values of the "missing" $\mathbf{u}_j$.

The joint density of $(\mathbf{u}_j, \mathbf{y}_j)$ is multivariate normal:

$$\begin{bmatrix} \mathbf{u}_j \\ \mathbf{y}_j \end{bmatrix} \sim N\left(\begin{bmatrix} 0 \\ X_jW_j\gamma \end{bmatrix}, \begin{bmatrix} T & TX_j' \\ X_jT & \Delta_j \end{bmatrix}\right),$$

where $\Delta_j = (X_j'TX_j + \sigma^2 I)$. The conditional density of $\mathbf{u}_j|\mathbf{y}_j$ is normal with mean $\mathbf{u}_j^*$, where

$$\mathbf{u}_j^* = TX_j'\Delta_j^{-1}(\mathbf{y}_j - X_jW_j\boldsymbol{\gamma}),$$

and dispersion matrix V_j, where

$$V_j = T - TX_j'\Delta_j^{-1}X_jT$$

(Morrison, 1990). These expressions simplify for the example with five groups with three observations in each group to yield the results described earlier.

To estimate $\boldsymbol{\gamma}$, the conditional expectation of $\mathbf{u}_j$, $\mathbf{u}_j^*$, must be substituted in Equation 13.46. This substitution yields, in the M-step, the estimator

$$\hat{\boldsymbol{\gamma}} = \sum_{j=1}^{J}(W_j'X_j'X_jW_j)^{-1}\sum_{j=1}^{J}W_j'X_j'(\mathbf{y}_j - X_j\mathbf{u}_j^*). \tag{13.47}$$

To estimate T, the conditional expectation of $\mathbf{u}_j\mathbf{u}_j'$ must be obtained. Since, by definition, the variance-covariance matrix of $\mathbf{u}_j$ conditional on $\mathbf{y}_j$ is

$$E\{(\mathbf{u}_j - \mathbf{u}_j^*)(\mathbf{u}_j - \mathbf{u}_j^*)' \,|\, \mathbf{y}_j\} = V_j,$$

it follows that

$$E(\mathbf{u}_j\mathbf{u}_j' \,|\, \mathbf{y}_j) = \mathbf{u}_j^*\mathbf{u}_j'^* + V_j.$$

Thus, in the M-step, the estimator of T is

$$\hat{T} = \frac{\sum_{j=1}^{J}[\mathbf{u}_j^*\mathbf{u}_j'^* + V_j]}{J}. \tag{13.48}$$

Now,

$$\mathbf{e}_j'\mathbf{e}_j = (\mathbf{y}_j - X_jW_j\hat{\boldsymbol{\gamma}} - X_j\mathbf{u}_j)'\,(\mathbf{y}_j - X_jW_j\hat{\boldsymbol{\gamma}} - X_j\mathbf{u}_j) \tag{13.49}$$

$$= (\mathbf{y}_j - X_jW_j\hat{\boldsymbol{\gamma}})'(\mathbf{y}_j - X_jW_j\hat{\boldsymbol{\gamma}}) - 2(\mathbf{y}_j - X_jW_j\hat{\boldsymbol{\gamma}})'X_j\mathbf{u}_j + \mathbf{u}_j'X_j'X_j\mathbf{u}_j,$$

and hence, the expectation of $\mathbf{u}_j'X_j'X_j\mathbf{u}_j$ needs to be evaluated. Since $\mathbf{u}_j'X_j'X_j\mathbf{u}_j$ is a scalar, it can be expressed as

$$\mathbf{u}_j'X_j'X_j\mathbf{u}_j = \mathrm{Tr}(\mathbf{u}_j'X_j'X_j\mathbf{u}_j) = \mathrm{Tr}(X_j'X_j\mathbf{u}_j\mathbf{u}_j'),$$

using the well known result, $\mathrm{Tr}(AB) = \mathrm{Tr}(BA)$. Thus,

$$E(\mathbf{u}'_j X'_j X_j \mathbf{u}_j \mid \mathbf{y}_j) = E(\mathrm{Tr}\,[X'_j X_j \mathbf{u}_j \mathbf{u}'_j] \mid \mathbf{y}_j) \tag{13.50}$$

$$= \mathrm{Tr}\, E(X'_j X_j \mathbf{u}_j \mathbf{u}'_j \mid \mathbf{y}_j) = \mathrm{Tr}\,[X'_j X_j (\mathbf{u}^*_j \mathbf{u}'^*_j + V_j)]$$

$$= \mathbf{u}^{*\prime}_j X'_j X_j \mathbf{u}^*_j + \mathrm{Tr}\,[(X'_j X_j) V_j].$$

Substituting Equation 13.50 into Equation 13.49 and simplifying, we obtain

$$\mathbf{e}'_j \mathbf{e}^*_j = (\mathbf{y}_j - X_j W_j \hat{\gamma} - X_j \mathbf{u}^*_j)' (\mathbf{y}_j - X_j W_j \hat{\gamma} - X_j \mathbf{u}^*_j) + \mathrm{Tr}\,[(X_j X'_j) V_j].$$

In the M-step, the maximum likelihood estimates of the parameter σ^2 is

$$\hat{\sigma}^2 = \frac{\sum_{j=1}^{J} \mathbf{e}'^*_j \mathbf{e}^*_j}{N}. \tag{13.51}$$

The E-M algorithm proceeds as follows:

Step 0: Obtain initial values for the parameters, γ, T, σ^2. (Procedures for obtaining starting values were discussed in the previous section.)

Step 1: **E-Step:** With the values for parameter estimates, compute the expectations:

$$E(\mathbf{u}_j) = TX'_j \Delta_j^{-1}(\mathbf{y}_j - X_j W_j \gamma)$$

$$E(\mathbf{u}_j \mathbf{u}'_j) = \mathbf{u}^*_j \mathbf{u}'^*_j + V_j,$$

$$E(\mathbf{e}'_j \mathbf{e}_j) = (\mathbf{y}_j - X_j W_j \hat{\gamma} - X_j \mathbf{u}^*_j)' (\mathbf{y}_j - X_j W_j \hat{\gamma} - X_j \mathbf{u}^*_j) + \mathrm{Tr}[(X_j X'_j) V_j]$$

Step 2: **M-Step:** Use these expectations in Equations 13.47, 13.48, and 13.51 to obtain the MLE estimates of the parameters.

Step 1 and Step 2 are repeated until convergence occurs.

The variance-covariance matrix of the ML estimates of γ, is obtained as the inverse of the information matrix given in Equation 13.41. In this case, the information matrix for γ is given by (Bryk & Raudenbush, 1992):

$$\mathcal{I}(\gamma) = \sigma^2 X'\{I - X[X'X + \sigma^2 T^{-1}]X'\}X.$$

The standard errors of the γ parameters are the square roots of the diagonal elements of the variance-covariance matrix. As previously noted, these standard errors are based on asymptotic theory, and when the number of clusters is small, the estimates of the standard errors may not be accurate.

The E-M algorithm is a general procedure that, in most cases, is easy to implement. In the case of linear models, the expectation step is easy to carry out, and in the case of normally distributed variables, the maximization step is accomplished easily. However, as demonstrated with the simple illustration of estimating parameters in five groups, the E-M algorithm converges very slowly. Raudenbush (1995) notes that the HLM program uses an Aitkin accelerator to speed convergence of the E-M algorithm. An alternative would be to combine the E-M and a more quickly converging algorithm, such as the Newton-Raphson. While the E-M algorithm is slow, it is more robust to poor starting values than is the Newton-Raphson procedure; it will always converge to a global maximum and will never produce negative variance estimates (de Leeuw & Kreft, 1995); therefore, it could be used during the early stages of estimation before switching over to the quicker Newton-Raphson algorithm.

Restricted ML Estimation

As pointed out earlier, one of the problems with maximum likelihood estimation is that the estimates of the variance components are biased. The reason for this is that the complete likelihood function in Equation 13.36 involves the vector of fixed parameters γ, which must be estimated along with the variance components, and the loss in degrees of freedom that arises in the estimation of fixed effects is not taken into account in the maximum likelihood estimation of the variance components. A solution to this problem is contained in the following fact: if in the combined two-level model $\mathbf{y} = XW\gamma + X\mathbf{u} + \mathbf{e}$ we can transform $\mathbf{y}$ so that its expected value is zero, the vector γ will not appear in the likelihood function. If we can find such a transformation in the present case, the fixed effects will not appear in the likelihood function, and the estimation of the variance components can take place without any reference to the fixed effects, resulting in unbiased estimates of the variance components.

To accomplish this, Patterson and Thompson (1971) suggested a procedure that uses "error contrasts" to remove the fixed effects. Error contrasts arc a set of linear combinations of the outcome variables such that the expected values of the transformed variables are zero. Since $E(\mathbf{y}) = XW\gamma = A\gamma$, where $A = XW$, it follows that $E(C'\mathbf{y}) = C'A\gamma = \mathbf{0}$, and hence choosing C' such that $C'A = O$ makes $C'\mathbf{y}$ a set of error contrasts. The goal is to find a matrix C such that $C'A = O$, that is, a matrix C that is orthogonal to A. The error matrix $[I - A(A'A)^{-1}A']$ is orthogonal to A, i.e.,

$$[I - A(A'A)^{-1}A']A = A - A(A'A)^{-1}A'A = O.$$

However, the error matrix is not of full rank, so we take a basis of the matrix to use as C. Since the rank of the error matrix is $(N - r - 1)$, where r is the number of fixed effects, the matrix C can be taken as any $(N - r - 1)$ columns of the error matrix.

To illustrate the use of error contrasts and to make it manageable, consider a one-level regression model. For simplicity, consider an example smaller in size but similar to the one presented earlier: four clusters consisting of four levels of a fixed factor, with two observations per cell. The matrix X corresponding to the simplest dummy coding and the C matrix are presented below. Since the matrix X is (8×4) of rank 4, the error matrix is (8×8) of rank 4. The (8×4) C matrix is the basis for the error matrix.

$$
X = \begin{bmatrix} 1 & 1 & 0 & 0 \\ 1 & 1 & 0 & 0 \\ 1 & 0 & 1 & 0 \\ 1 & 0 & 1 & 0 \\ 1 & 0 & 0 & 1 \\ 1 & 0 & 0 & 1 \\ 1 & 0 & 0 & 0 \\ 1 & 0 & 0 & 0 \end{bmatrix}; \quad C' = \begin{bmatrix} 1 & -1 & 0 & 0 \\ -1 & 1 & 0 & 0 \\ 1 & 0 & -1 & 0 \\ -1 & 0 & 1 & 0 \\ 1 & 0 & 0 & -1 \\ -1 & 0 & 0 & 1 \\ 1 & 0 & 0 & 0 \\ -1 & 0 & 0 & 0 \end{bmatrix}
$$

Since, in general, C is of dimension $((N - p - 1) \times N)$, the vector $C'\mathbf{y}$ is a set of $(N - p - 1)$ variables. Moreover, $C'\mathbf{y} \sim N(C'X\boldsymbol{\beta}, \sigma^2 C'C)$, and hence the likelihood function is

$$
L(C'\mathbf{y} : \sigma^2) = \frac{1}{(2\pi)^{N-p-1} |\sigma^2 C'C|} \exp - \frac{1}{2}(C'\mathbf{y})' [\sigma^2 C'C]^{-1}(C'\mathbf{y}).
$$

Since $|\sigma^2 C'C| = (\sigma^2)^{N-p-1} |C'C|$, differentiating the log likelihood with respect to σ^2, we obtain

$$
\frac{\partial}{\partial \sigma^2} \log(C'\mathbf{y} : \sigma^2) = -\frac{(N - p - 1)}{2\sigma^2} + \frac{1}{2(\sigma^2)^2} \mathbf{y}'C(C'C)^{-1}C'\mathbf{y}.
$$

Setting this derivative equal to zero, we obtain the Restricted ML (REML) estimator of σ^2 as

$$
\hat{\sigma}_R^2 = \frac{\mathbf{y}'C(C'C)^{-1}C'\mathbf{y}}{(N - p - 1)} = \frac{\mathbf{y}'[I - X(X'X)^{-1}X]\mathbf{y}}{(N - p - 1)}.
$$

Estimation based on the likelihood function of the error contrasts generally is known as Restricted Maximum Likelihood (REML) or Residual Maximum Likelihood estimation (Longford, 1993; Kreft & de Leeuw, 1998) and results in unbiased estimates. Using the result obtained by Harville (1974), the restricted likelihood function of the two-level model can be expressed as

$$\log L(\mathbf{y} : \sigma^2, T) = -\frac{1}{2}\sum_{j=1}^{J}\log\left|\Psi_j\right| - \frac{1}{2}\sum_{j=1}^{J}\log\left|A_j'\Psi_j A_j\right| - \qquad (13.52)$$

$$\frac{1}{2}\sum_{j=1}^{J}(\mathbf{y}_j - A_j\boldsymbol{\gamma})'\Psi_j^{-1}(\mathbf{y}_j - A_j\boldsymbol{\gamma}).$$

The restricted Log Likelihood differs from the complete Log likelihood given in Equation 13.37 by the addition of the term

$$-\frac{1}{2}\sum_{j=1}^{J}\log\left|A_j'\Psi_j A_j\right|.$$

The maximization proceeds in the same way as with the maximum likelihood estimation.

Applying this procedure to the data in our example using the E-M algorithm with starting values as set previously, the procedure converged in eight iterations. The iteration history is given in Table 13.5. Note that the

TABLE 13.5   Results of Restricted Maximum Likelihood Estimation with the E-M Algorithm

Parameter	Value at start of iteration					
E-step	1	2	3	4	...	Final (8)
λ_j	0.9375	0.9385	0.9336	0.9308	...	0.9216
V_j	5.3333	0.4410	0.4782	0.4897	...	0.4915
u_1^*	−0.9375	−0.9971	−1.0458	−1.0971	...	−1.8315
u_2^*	1.8750	1.8183	1.7550	1.6954	...	0.9332
u_3^*	2.8125	2.7568	2.6887	2.6263	...	1.8457
u_4^*	3.7500	3.6953	3.6223	3.5571	...	2.7763
u_5^*	−2.8125	−2.8741	−2.9130	−2.9130	...	3.6747
M-step						
γ	5.0000	6.0000	6.0000	6.0000	...	6.0000
τ^2	5.0000	7.2266	7.7932	7.9297	...	7.9670
σ^2	1.0000	1.4099	1.5390	1.5803	...	1.5998
Change values						
h_1	−1.0000	0.0000	0.0000	0.0000	...	0.0000
h_2	−2.2266	−0.5667	−0.1364	−0.0306	...	0.0001
h_3	−0.4099	−0.1291	−0.0412	−0.0133	...	0.0005

estimate of τ^2 is 7.967, the correct value. The Newton-Raphson algorithm provided similar results, so these are not reported here.

The clear advantage of REML estimation over full ML estimation is that REML estimators of the variance components are unbiased. However, care should be exercised in choosing REML over full ML procedures when comparing the fit of nested models. In examining deviance statistics for evaluating the relative fit of nested models (see McCoach & Black, 2008), the REML procedure should only be used if the models being compared have the same fixed components and differ only in their random components (Kreft & de Leeuw, 1998). This problem does not arise when using full ML procedures.

Dempster et al. (1977) and Dempster, Rubin, and Tsutakawa (1981) showed that the restricted ML procedure can be conceptualized as a Bayesian approach in which the parameter γ is treated as a random variable. (We shall return to this procedure in the section on Bayesian approaches.) In this context, Dempster et al. (1981) considered the traditional ML procedure as a maximum likelihood procedure with "fixed" γ parameters and labeled it Maximum Likelihood Fixed (MLF). In contrast, they argued that in the restricted maximum likelihood procedure, the parameter γ is considered random, and so labeled the procedure Maximum Likelihood Procedure Random (MLR). Since in the Dempster-Rubin-Tsutakawa formulation, the parameter is integrated out, the procedure also can be described as a *marginal maximum likelihood* procedure. The MLR approach is implemented in the HLM6 software (Raudenbush, Bryk, Cheong, & Congdon, 2004). The restricted maximum likelihood procedure defined in terms of error contrasts (REML) and MLR yield identical results.

ESTIMATION OF RANDOM COEFFICIENTS

The focus in the previous sections was on the estimation of the fixed effects, γ. Quite often, it is of interest to estimate the level-one random coefficients, β_j. In the simple example used throughout, the five clusters constituted a random sample from a population. When the cluster means differ considerably from each other, i.e., the between-cluster variation is large, the sample mean $\bar{y}_j$ is a good estimator of μ_j. If on the other hand, the between-cluster variation is zero, the overall mean is the best estimator of μ_j. The advantage of using the overall mean is that it is more efficient than $\bar{y}_j$ when the between cluster variation is zero since the error variance is much smaller due to the larger sample size.

When neither of these two extreme situations occurs, an estimator that weights the individual cluster mean and the overall mean is desirable. When data are collected on multiple clusters, it is advantageous to use the information available in the other clusters to stabilize the estimator of a particular cluster mean and to increase its efficiency.

To demonstrate how the random coefficients are estimated, let us return to the example used in earlier sections, where the model for the observations is

$$y_{ij} = \mu_j + e_{ij}$$
$$\mu_j = \gamma_0 + u_j ,$$

with $Var(e_{ij}) = \sigma^2$ and $Var(u_j) = \tau^2$. In this context, we are interested in estimating the random coefficient μ_j. This problem can be formulated as "predicting" μ_j from the observed cluster means $\bar{y}_j$. To carry out this prediction, we need the regression equation that relates μ_j to the observed values $\bar{y}_j$.

From standard regression theory (Morrison, 1990), given either the assumption of bivariate normality or a linear relationship, the regression of μ_j on $\bar{y}_j$, denoted as $E(\mu_j | \bar{y}_j)$, is

$$E(\mu_j | \bar{y}_j) = E(\mu_j) + \frac{Cov(\mu_j, \bar{y}_j)}{Var(\bar{y}_j)} [\bar{y}_j - E(\bar{y}_j)]. \qquad (13.53)$$

From Equation 13.6, $E(\bar{y}_j) = \gamma_0$. Also, because $\mu_j = \gamma_0 + u_j$, $E(\mu_j) = \gamma_0$. The variance of $\bar{y}_j$, as shown previously, is

$$Var(\bar{y}_j) = \tau^2 + \frac{\sigma^2}{n_j}.$$

The covariance between μ_j and $\bar{y}_j$ is

$$Cov(\mu_j, \bar{y}_j) = Cov(\mu_j, \mu_j + \bar{e}_j) = Var(\mu_j) + 0 = \tau^2.$$

Substituting these values in Equation 13.53, we obtain the regression equation

$$E(\mu_j | \bar{y}_j) = \gamma_0 + \frac{\tau^2}{\left(\tau^2 + \frac{\sigma^2}{n_j}\right)} (\bar{y}_j - \gamma_0) = \gamma_0 + \lambda_j (\bar{y}_j - \gamma_0). \qquad (13.54)$$

Replacing γ_0 by its estimate, $\bar{y}_.$, we have

$$E(\mu_j | \bar{y}_j) = \lambda_j \bar{y}_j + (1 - \lambda_j) \bar{y}_.. \qquad (13.55)$$

Thus, the mean of the conditional distribution of $\mu_j | \bar{y}_j$ is a function of the observed mean of cluster j and the grand mean, weighted by the *reliabil-*

ity λ_j, defined as the ratio of the parameter variance (or true score variance) τ^2 to the total variance $(\tau^2 + \sigma^2/n_j)$. If the reliability is high, more weight is given to the cluster mean, while if the reliability is low, more weight is given to the overall mean (Raudenbush & Bryk, 2002). Clearly, the reliability is affected by the precision with which the group mean is estimated. Holding the sample size constant, the reliability will be large when τ^2, the variation among the cluster means, is large.

For the data in the example in Section 1, $\hat{\tau}^2 = 7.967$; $\hat{\sigma}^2 = 1.600$; $n_j = 3$. Hence,

$$\lambda = \frac{\hat{\tau}^2}{\hat{\tau}^2 + \dfrac{\hat{\sigma}^2}{n}} = \frac{7.967}{7.967 + \dfrac{1.600}{3}} = 0.937,$$

and $1-\lambda = 1 - 0.937 = 0.063$. The grand mean $\bar{y}_. = 6.0$. Thus, the predicted value of μ_j from $\bar{y}_j$, is the *regressed* or *shrunken* estimate of the cluster mean μ_j. These regressed estimates for the five clusters are given in Table 13.6.

As can be seen, the estimates are regressed towards the grand mean. Cluster 5, with mean 2.0, is farthest from the grand mean of 6.0, and hence its estimate is regressed upwards to 2.251. Cluster 4, with the highest mean of 9.0, is regressed down towards the grand mean. The movement towards the grand mean is modest because the reliability, .937, is very high. If the reliability was 1.0, there would not have been any regression towards the mean. On the other hand, if the reliability was zero, all the estimates would have regressed completely to the grand mean of 6.0.

As we shall see later, this regressed or weighted estimator coincides with the Bayes estimator of the parameter μ_j (Lindley & Smith, 1972; Lord & Novick, 1968). It was first used by Kelley in 1927 to estimate the true score of an individual. If the reliability of the test is low, the true score estimate will regress towards the group mean. In our case, the estimator is weighted by the "reliability" and "shrunk" toward the grand mean. Lindley and Smith (1972), in the context of Bayesian estimation, have shown that this esti-

TABLE 13.6   Estimates of μ_j for the Data in Table 13.1

Cluster	Mean $\bar{y}_j$	Estimate of μ_j .9372*$\bar{y}_j$ + .0628* $\bar{y}_.$
1	4	4.126
2	7	6.937
3	8	7.874
4	9	8.812
5	2	2.251

Note: $\bar{y}_. = 6.0$

mator has the smallest expected mean squared error among all estimators (Raudenbush & Bryk, 2002).

In the general multilevel case given in Equations 13.14 and 13.15, we are interested in predicting the random coefficient vector $\boldsymbol{\beta}_j$ from the best within-group estimator of $\boldsymbol{\beta}_j$, that is, the OLS estimator of $\boldsymbol{\beta}_j$ (Raudenbush & Bryk, 2002). The generalization of Equation 13.52 to the multivariate regression of $\boldsymbol{\beta}_j$ on $\hat{\boldsymbol{\beta}}_j$, is

$$E(\boldsymbol{\beta}_j \mid \hat{\boldsymbol{\beta}}_j) = E(\boldsymbol{\beta}_j) + Cov(\boldsymbol{\beta}_j, \hat{\boldsymbol{\beta}}_j)[Var(\hat{\boldsymbol{\beta}}_j)]^{-1}[\hat{\boldsymbol{\beta}}_j - E(\hat{\boldsymbol{\beta}}_j)].$$

From Equation 13.15, $E(\boldsymbol{\beta}_j) = W_j\boldsymbol{\gamma}$. As $\hat{\boldsymbol{\beta}}_j$ is an unbiased estimator of $\boldsymbol{\beta}_j$, $E(\hat{\boldsymbol{\beta}}_j) = E(\boldsymbol{\beta}_j) = W_j\boldsymbol{\gamma}$. From Equation 13.22,

$$Cov(\boldsymbol{\beta}_j, \hat{\boldsymbol{\beta}}_j) = Cov(\boldsymbol{\beta}_j, W_j\boldsymbol{\gamma} + \mathbf{u}_j + \mathbf{e}_j) = Cov(\boldsymbol{\beta}_j, \mathbf{u}_j) = T.$$

Using Equation 13.23, we obtain

$$\begin{aligned}
E(\boldsymbol{\beta}_j \mid \hat{\boldsymbol{\beta}}_j) &= W_j\boldsymbol{\gamma} + T\Delta_j^{-1}[\hat{\boldsymbol{\beta}}_j - W_j\boldsymbol{\gamma}] \\
&= \Lambda_j\hat{\boldsymbol{\beta}}_j + (I - \Lambda_j)W_j\hat{\boldsymbol{\gamma}}
\end{aligned} \tag{13.56}$$

where $\Lambda_j = T\Delta_j^{-1}$ and $\hat{\boldsymbol{\beta}}_j$ is the OLS estimator given in Equation 13.19. The matrix $\Lambda_j = T\Delta_j^{-1}$ is the multivariate analog of the univariate reliability coefficient. In this case, the estimator is shrunk towards the predicted value, $W_j\hat{\boldsymbol{\gamma}}$. Raudenbush and Bryk (2002) have provided several examples of the regressed or shrunken estimate.

BAYESIAN PROCEDURES

Bayesian statistical theory provides a natural framework for multilevel models. Much of the estimation theory discussed in the previous sections can be recast in the Bayesian framework. Under Bayesian theory, parameters are treated not as constants but as random variables. This treatment is a reflection of our uncertainty about the parameters both before and after collecting data. We indicate our prior uncertainty by specifying a probability distribution for the parameter that represents our belief about the parameter and the extent of our uncertainty prior to collecting data. Once data are gathered, our uncertainty about the parameter is reduced but not eliminated; we obtain a revised belief distribution, or posterior probability distribution, that reflects the new state of our knowledge about the parameter. The key feature that distinguishes Bayesian estimation theory from classical theory is that we can make probabilistic statements about the parameters of interest given the data. Under the classical approach, we are limited to making probabilistic statements about the data, given values of the (fixed) parameters; this limitation leads to the convoluted chain of reasoning that causes many beginning students of statistics difficulty in understanding inference, especially in interpreting confidence intervals.

The well-known Bayes Theorem provides the means for combining the prior distribution with the data to produce the posterior distribution. According to Bayes Theorem, the probability of event A given event B, $P[A|B]$, is

$$P[A|B] = \frac{P[B|A]P[A]}{P[B]}.$$

For continuous variables, the probabilities above are replaced by probability density functions:

$$f(y|x) = \frac{f(x|y)f(y)}{f(x)}. \tag{13.57}$$

To apply this theorem to the context of parameter estimation, let y denote the set of parameters to be estimated, and let $f(y)$ denote the density function that characterizes the researcher's prior belief or information about the parameters y. Let x denote the observed data. Then, $f(x|y)$ is the likelihood of the data x given the parameters y, and $f(y|x)$ represents the revised belief distribution about the parameters after the data are observed. This revised belief distribution is referred to as the posterior distribution of the parameters. The function $f(x)$ is a function of the data only; it does not involve the parameters, and is a constant once the data are observed. Therefore, Equation 13.57 can be expressed as

$$\text{Posterior Distribution} \propto \text{Likelihood} \times \text{Prior Distribution}. \tag{13.58}$$

From this expression, we see that the posterior distribution is the prior distribution modified after the data are observed.

Let us now apply these concepts to the multilevel model. In the classical approach, the parameter γ in the combined two-level model, $y_j = X_j W_j \gamma + X_j u_j + e_j$, is considered a fixed parameter. In contrast, within the Bayesian framework γ is considered a random variable. The parameters σ^2 and the matrix T also are considered random variables. Thus, inferences about γ, σ^2, and T are made by obtaining the joint posterior distribution of these parameters. In the full Bayesian approach, prior distributions must be specified for all the parameters of interest to obtain the posterior distribution of the parameters.

To obtain the posterior distribution of the parameters, γ, σ^2, and T, we need (a) the model for the data and (b) the prior distribution of the parameters. The model for the data is captured in our statement about the distribution $f(\mathbf{y})$ of the random variable $\mathbf{y}$ in group j (Equations 13.34 and 13.35): $\mathbf{y}_j \sim N(X_j W_j \gamma, \Psi_j)$, where $\Psi_j = X_j T X_j' + \sigma^2 I$. In the Bayesian framework, the distribution of $\mathbf{y}_j$ is expressed as

$$\mathbf{y}_j \mid \gamma, \sigma^2, T \sim N(X_j W_j \gamma, \Psi_j)$$

to state explicitly the fact that the data structure depends on the unknown parameters γ, σ^2, and T. With the assumption that the $\mathbf{y}_j$ ($j = 1, \ldots, J$) are independent, the joint distribution $f(\mathbf{y}_1, \ldots, \mathbf{y}_J \mid \gamma, \sigma^2, T)$ can be determined. Once the data are observed, this distribution is the likelihood function:

$$L(\mathbf{y}_1, \ldots, \mathbf{y}_J \mid \gamma, \sigma^2, T) = \prod_{j=1}^{J} f(\mathbf{y}_j \mid \gamma, \sigma^2, T) \equiv L(\mathbf{y} \mid \gamma, \sigma^2, T). \quad (13.59)$$

The exact form of the likelihood function is given in Equation 13.36. The only difference between the likelihood function defined in Equation 13.36 and the function in Equation 13.59 is the notation that shows that in the Bayesian framework we view the likelihood function as being conditional on the unknown parameters rather than a function of the parameters as is the case in the classical framework. To specify the prior distribution of the parameters γ, σ^2, and T, we assume *a priori* that they are independent, or equivalently,

$$f(\gamma, \sigma^2, T) = f(\gamma) f(\sigma^2) f(T).$$

With these specifications and applying Equation 13.58, we obtain the posterior distribution of γ, σ^2, and T as

$$f(\gamma, \sigma^2, T \mid y_1, \ldots, y_J) \propto L(\mathbf{y} \mid \gamma, \sigma^2, T) f(\gamma) f(\sigma^2) f(T) \quad (13.60)$$

$$\propto \prod_{j=1}^{J} \frac{1}{|\Psi_j|^{1/2}} \exp\{-\frac{1}{2}(\mathbf{y}_j - A_j \gamma)' \Psi_j^{-1} (\mathbf{y}_j - A_j \gamma)\}$$

$$\times f(\gamma) f(\sigma^2) f(T).$$

If we take $f(\gamma)$, $f(\sigma^2)$, and $f(T)$, to be constants, that is, if we assume that the parameters have uniform distributions, we find that the posterior distribution in Equation 13.60 is proportional to the likelihood function, the difference being that posterior distribution is still a distribution of the parameters and permits probabilistic statements about the parameters. If point estimates of the parameters are required, then the mode, mean, or the median of the posterior distribution can be taken as a point estimate. Since the mode is obtained by maximizing the posterior distribution, the posterior modal estimates coincide with the ML estimates. In this sense, it can be argued that ML estimation is a special case of Bayesian estimation procedure when uniform distributions are assumed for the priors.

The posterior distribution $f(\gamma,\sigma^2,T|y_1,\ldots,y_j)$ is a joint distribution of the parameters, and if point estimates of the parameters are obtained using the above distribution, the uncertainty in the parameters is not taken into account. For example, the point estimate of γ does not reflect the uncertainty in σ^2 and T. Similar considerations apply to the point estimates of σ^2 and T. To take into account the uncertainty in the parameters, the value of γ must be obtained by "averaging" over all the values of σ^2 and T. That is, we need the posterior distribution of each of the parameters γ, σ^2, T by "averaging" over the other two. These distributions are referred to as *marginal* distributions and are obtained by integrating the joint posterior over the region of the other parameters. Point estimates based on these marginal distributions do reflect the uncertainty in the other parameters.

The marginal distributions described above require multidimensional integrals and hence are difficult to obtain in general. However, in some situations, the integration can be carried out analytically. One such case is the marginal (but joint) distribution of σ^2 and T obtained by integrating over γ. Since uniform distributions were assumed for these parameters, the resulting posterior distribution is identical in form to the Restricted Likelihood Function (Equation 13.52), derived by Dempster et al. (1981). Thus, inference based on the REML or the MLR procedure can be viewed as being contained within the Bayesian framework. It should be noted, however, that Dempster et al. (1981) did not provide a complete Bayesian framework for the MLR procedure. They treated only the parameter γ as a random variable and not σ^2 or T, in contrast to the presentation here. In this sense, the restricted likelihood function is not a posterior distribution of σ^2 and T.

The uniform prior distributions specified above are considered *improper* prior probability distributions in that the area under the uniform density curve is not finite. To avoid this problem, the uniform prior distribution often is justified by expressing it as a limiting form of the normal distribution with mean zero and a *very large* variance (Dempster et al., 1981; Zellner, 1971). While the uniform distribution can be justified as a prior distribution for a parameter such as γ because the parameter space includes positive as well as negative values, this is not the case for the parameters σ^2 or T. Since σ^2 cannot take on negative values, the uniform distribution is not an appropriate prior distribution. Jeffreys (1939), in laying down the foundation for statistical inference, showed that a non-informative prior distribution for σ^2 is proportional to $(\sigma^2)^{-1}$. Correspondingly, for the matrix T, the non-informative prior distribution is proportional to $|T|^{-1}$, where $|T|$ is the determinant of T.

Rather than using non-informative prior distributions, informative priors may be specified for parameters. For example, instead of assuming a non-informative prior distribution for γ, the prior distribution can be specified as $\gamma \sim N(\mu_\gamma, \Gamma)$. In this case, specific values for μ_γ and Γ need to be provided. While this may be possible in situations where the investigator may have accumulated considerable information, in general, it is not reasonable to assume that the investigator has such precise information. Lindley and Smith (1972) have provided a framework in which *hyper prior distributions* can be specified for the parameters of the prior distribution; that is, the parameters of the prior distribution have distributions themselves. It is this framework that has been used in multilevel estimation procedures (Bryk & Raudenbush, 1992; Raudenbush & Bryk, 2002). In this case, specifying non-informative priors for the parameters μ_γ and Γ, as described above, is appropriate. An alternative is to estimate these parameters along with γ, σ^2, and T. This procedure is called Empirical Bayes (EB) estimation (Bryk & Raudenbush, 1992; Gelman et al., 1995; Raudenbush & Bryk, 2002).

Informative prior distributions for variance components are slightly more complex. The reader is referred to Box and Tiao (1973), Gelman, Carlin, Stern, and Rubin (1995), or Zellner (1971) for details.

The estimation of random coefficients β_j provides a classic scenario for Bayesian estimation. In fact, the estimation of the random coefficients, rather than the fixed effect γ, was the primary focus of Lindley and Smith (1971) and Rubin (1989). Under the Bayesian approach, the level-one model is expressed in distributional form as

$$\mathbf{y}_j \mid \boldsymbol{\beta}_j, \sigma^2 \sim N(X\boldsymbol{\beta}_j, \sigma^2 I),$$

and the level-two model is expressed as

$$\boldsymbol{\beta}_j \mid \boldsymbol{\gamma}, T \sim N(W_j\boldsymbol{\gamma}, T).$$

If there are no level-two predictors, the expression above becomes $\boldsymbol{\beta}_j \mid \boldsymbol{\mu}_\beta, T \sim N(\boldsymbol{\mu}_\beta, T)$, where $\boldsymbol{\mu}_\beta$, T are the parameters of the prior distribution of $\boldsymbol{\beta}_j$. Swaminathan (1989b) provided a Bayesian framework for estimating the parameters $\boldsymbol{\beta}_j$ by specifying an inverse chi-square distribution for σ^2, a uniform distribution for $\boldsymbol{\mu}_\beta$, and the inverted Wishart distribution for T, and integrating out $\boldsymbol{\mu}_\beta$, σ^2, and T to obtain the marginal posterior distribution of $\boldsymbol{\beta}_j$. Alternatively, an empirical Bayes approach could be used and the parameters $\boldsymbol{\mu}_\beta$ and T estimated along with $\boldsymbol{\beta}_j$ and σ^2. If $\boldsymbol{\mu}_\beta$ is replaced by $W_j\boldsymbol{\gamma}$ and estimated along with T, $\boldsymbol{\beta}_j$, and σ^2, the estimator defined in Equation 13.53 obtains.

The above derivation simplifies considerably for the example we have used throughout. For this example, the model for the data is $y_{ij} \sim N(\mu_j, \sigma^2)$. Our prior belief about μ_j is $\mu_j \sim N(\gamma_0, \tau^2)$. Since the mean $\bar{y}_j$ is a sufficient statistic for μ_j, the posterior distribution can be expressed conditionally on $\bar{y}_j$ rather than on the observations in cluster j. Using Equation 13.58, the posterior distribution of μ_j is

$$f(\mu_j \mid \bar{y}_j, \sigma^2, \gamma_0, \tau^2) \propto f(\bar{y}_j \mid \mu_j, \sigma^2) f(\mu_j \mid \gamma_0, \tau^2). \qquad (13.61)$$

Since the likelihood $f(\bar{y}_j \mid \mu_j, \sigma^2)$ has the form of a normal distribution and the prior distribution is normal, the posterior distribution will be normal. The Bayes estimator is the mean of the posterior distribution and is identical to that given in Equation 13.54:

$$E(\mu_j \mid \bar{y}_j, \sigma^2, \gamma_0, \tau^2) = \lambda_j \bar{y}_j + (1 - \lambda_j)\gamma_0.$$

When the estimated values for σ^2, γ_0, τ^2 are substituted, we obtain the Empirical Bayes (EB) estimator, given in Equation 13.55.

The Bayes estimator assumes that the parameters of the prior distributions are known, while the EB procedure replaces these parameters with their estimated values. To take full advantage of the Bayesian framework, we need to specify prior distributions for these parameters (as indicated by Swaminathan, 1989b). Using these informative priors will result in a joint posterior distribution of the cluster means, $f(\mu_1, \dots, \mu_j, \sigma^2, \gamma_0, \tau^2 \mid \bar{y}_j)$, in contrast to the posterior distribution in Equation 13.61, which is a posterior distribution only of the cluster mean μ_j. By integrating out σ^2, γ_0, and τ^2, we obtain the joint posterior distribution of the cluster means, $f(\mu_1, \dots, \mu_j \mid \bar{y}_j)$. Swaminathan, Hambleton, and Algina (1975) used this approach in the context of estimating proportions in J clusters and obtained joint modal estimators of the parameters. While the joint modal estimators of μ_j have the same structure as in Equations 13.54 and 13.55 (a weighted estimate of the cluster means and overall mean), the weights λ_j will differ considerably.

While joint estimators are adequate, they are not ideal in all situations. O'Hagan (1976) showed that marginal estimators behave better that joint estimators, and marginal means are better point estimates than marginal modes. Obtaining marginal distributions and computing the means (and variances) require the evaluation of multidimensional integrals. Until recently, procedures for evaluating such integrals were not widely known to statisticians, although they have been used in physics since the 1940s. With the introduction of Monte Carlo techniques using Gibbs sampling by Geman and Geman (1984), evaluation of higher order integrals has become routine in statistics. With these techniques, the functions to be integrated are decomposed into a fixed function and a probability density function.

Random values are generated from the probability density function and using these values, the integrals are evaluated. The Markov-Chain Monte-Carlo (MCMC) procedure is based on this principle. The Gibbs Sampler provides a sampling scheme for generating random numbers from a specified probability density function. Raudenbush and Bryk (2002) provide a clear introduction to MCMC methods. For a detailed description of MCMC procedures, the reader is referred to Gelman et al. (1995).

The MCMC procedure is implemented in the freeware WinBUGS (Spiegelhalter, Thomas, Best, & Lunn, 2003.) While Gibbs sampling is computationally intensive and it may not be clear when the procedure has converged (Draper, 1995), the new version of WinBUGS does include some convergence diagnostics to aid the user in determining if convergence has occurred. This software is being used widely for Bayesian analysis and, within the last several years, has revolutionized the practical application of Bayesian procedures.

CONCLUSION

Whenever observations are grouped into clusters and clusters are sampled randomly from a population, statistical models for the data must reflect this structure in order for parameters to be estimated correctly and valid inferences to be made. Failure to take into account the structure of the data can lead to faulty inferences. Our purpose in this chapter was to introduce the commonly used procedures and algorithms that are appropriate for estimating parameters in multilevel models.

Multilevel models can be formulated as mixed models or models with random coefficients. While the mixed-model formulation is general, the random coefficient model is more intuitive and provides a greater insight into the models for the beginner. The random coefficient model formulation was presented here partly for this reason and also because this formulation fits naturally into a Bayesian inferential framework.

The Maximum Likelihood, Restricted Maximum Likelihood, and Bayesian procedures are the most widely used estimation procedures in such computer software as SPSS, SAS, HLM6 (Raudenbush et al., 2004), and VARCL (Longford, 1990); hence, these were described in some detail. The two most commonly used algorithms in ML and REML estimation, the Newton-Raphson and E-M algorithm, were described and their use demonstrated through a simple example. While the Ordinary Least Squares and the Generalized Least Squares procedures are not used for simultaneously estimating the fixed effects and the variance components, they were described here because they provide the foundation for the more complex estimation procedures and are used as starting values in various stages of the E-M algorithm and in the EB estimation of random coefficients. An estimation procedure that was not discussed in this chapter is the Iterative Generalized Least Squares (IGLS) procedure (Goldstein, 1986) used in the MLwiN (Rasbash, Steele, Browne, & Prosser, 2005) software. This procedure uses the Generalized Least Squares procedure as the building block in estimation of the fixed effects and random components. Goldstein (1986) showed that when normality assumptions are made, the IGLS procedure is identical to the ML procedure. Longford (1993) and Raudenbush and Bryk (2002) showed that the iterative procedure is identical to the Newton-Raphson procedure. Readers interested in this procedure are referred to Goldstein (1986, 2002).

Maximum likelihood procedures based on the complete likelihood function yield unbiased estimates of the fixed effects but biased estimates of the variance components. Restricted maximum likelihood procedures produce unbiased estimates of the variance components by removing the fixed parameters from the likelihood function and hence are recommended when the variance components are of interest. However, care should be taken in using this procedure when comparing the fit of nested models.

In implementing either the full or restricted maximum likelihood procedure, the E-M algorithm or the Newton-Raphson algorithm may be used. The Newton- Raphson and the Fisher's Scoring algorithm are the most widely used algorithms (SAS, SPSS, VARCL) while the E-M algorithm, along with Fisher scoring, is used in the HLM6 software. The E-M algorithm is the proverbial tortoise, reliable but slow, and hence, it is enhanced using convergence acceleration techniques (Raudenbush, 1995). The Newton-Raphson algorithm converges quickly, in general, but is susceptible to poor starting values and local maxima and can produce inadmissible estimates of the variance components.

Multilevel models fit naturally into a Bayesian framework. In fact, Bryk and Raudenbush (1992) have shown that estimation procedures used in the HLM software can be formulated completely within a Bayesian framework. The full and restricted maximum likelihood estimation procedures can be viewed as special cases of Bayesian estimation techniques. The advantage of Bayesian procedures is that through the specification of prior distributions the uncertainty in the parameters can be modeled, and by obtaining marginal posterior distributions, the effect of uncertainty in one set of parameters on estimation of another parameter can be taken into account. As Rubin (1989) notes, as problems become more difficult, it becomes more important to be fully Bayesian. However, the full Bayesian approach requires the evaluation of higher-order integrals, is computer intensive, and was not attempted until recently except by a handful of dedicated Bayesians. However, with the development of MCMC procedures employing the Gibbs sampling technique and now the ready availability of software for implementing these procedures, Bayesian techniques have become more accessible and widely used. The theoretical elegance of the Bayesian framework and its natural application to multilevel models make it a powerful unifying approach for estimation and inference. As Draper (1995) predicted, fully Bayesian methods using some form of MCMC procedure will become the industry standard for multilevel analysis in the very near future.

While an exhaustive coverage of estimation procedures was beyond the scope of this chapter, we hope that we have achieved our goal of motivating the reader to seek a deeper understanding of estimation procedures and issues in multilevel models.

NOTE

1. Terminology used in this chapter differs slightly from earlier chapters but is necessary to develop and support the concepts and procedures presented.

REFERENCES

Bryk, A. S. & Raudenbush, S. W. (1992). Hierarchical linear models: Applications and data analysis methods. Thousand Oaks, CA: Sage Publications.

Box, G. E. P., & Tiao, G. C. (1973). *Bayesian inference in statistical analysis.* Reading, MA: John Wiley & Sons.

De Leeuw, J., & Kreft, I.G. (1995). Questioning multilevel models. *Journal of Educational and Behavioral Statistics, 20,* 171–189.

Dempster, A. P., Laird, N. M., & Rubin, D. B. (1977). Maximum likelihood from incomplete data via the E-M algorithm. *Journal of the Royal Statistical Society, Series B, 39,* 1–8.

Dempster, A.P., Rubin, D.B., Tsutakawa, R.K. (1981). Estimation in covariance components models. *Journal of the American Statistical Association, 76,* 341–353.

Dennis, J. E., & Schnabel, R. B. (1996). *Numerical methods for unconstrained optimization and nonlinear equations.* Philadelphia, PA: Society for Industrial and Applied Mathematics.

Draper, D. (1995). Inference in hierarchical modeling in the social sciences. *Journal of Educational and Behavioral Statistics, 20,* 115–148.

Gelman, A., Carlin, J. B., Stern, H. S., & Rubin, D. B. (1995). *Bayesian data analysis.* New York: Chapman & Hall.

Geman, S., & Geman, D. (1984). Stochastic relaxation, Gibbs distributions and the Bayesian restoration of images. *IEEE Transactions on Pattern Analysis and Machine Intelligence, 6,* 721–741.

Goldstein, H. (1986). Multilevel mixed linear model analysis using iterative generalized least squares. *Biometrika, 73,* 43–56.

Goldstein, H. (2002). Multilevel statistical models (3rd ed.). London: Arnold Publishing.

Harville, D. A. (1974). Bayesian inference for variance components using only error contrasts. *Biometrika, 61*, 383–385.

Hambleton, R. K., Swaminathan, H., & Rogers, H. J. (1991). *Fundamentals of item response theory.* Newbury Park, CA: Sage Publications.

Jeffreys, H. (1939). *Theory of probability.* Oxford : Oxford University Press.

Kendall, M. G., & Stuart, A. (1969). *The advanced theory of statistics* (Vol. 2). London: Charles Griffin.

Kirk, R. E. (1995). *Experimental design: Procedures for the behavioral sciences.* (3rd ed.) Belmont, CA: Wadsworth.

Kish, L. (1965). *Survey sampling.* New York: John Wiley.

Kreft, I. G., & de Leeuw, J. (1998). *Introducing multilevel modeling.* Thousand Oaks, CA: Sage.

Lindley, D. V., & Smith, A. F. M. (1972). Bayes estimates for the linear model. *Journal of the Royal Statistical Society, Series B, 34*, 1–41.

Longford, N. T. (1987). A fast scoring algorithm for maximum likelihood estimation in unbalanced models with nested random effects. *Biometrika, 74*, 817–827.

Longford, N. T. (1989). Fisher scoring algorithm for variance component analysis of data with multilevel structure. In. R. D. Bock (Ed.), *Multilevel analysis of educational data* (pp. 297–310). Orlando, FL: Academic Press.

Longford, N.T. (1990). VARCL—Software for variance components analysis of data with nested random effects (maximum likelihood). Technical Report. Educational Testing Service: Princeton, NJ.

Longford, N. T. (1993). *Random coefficient models.* Oxford: Clarendon Press.

Lord, F. M. & Novick, M. R. (1968). *Statistical theories of mental test scores.* Reading, MA: Addison-Wesley Publishing Company.

Magnus, J. R., & Neudecker, H. (1988). *Matrix differential calculus with applications in statistics and econometrics.* New York: John Wiley.

McCoach, D. B., & Black, A. C. (2008). Evaluation of model fit and adequacy. In A. A. O'Connell and D. B. McCoach (Eds.), *Multilevel modeling of educational data* (pp. 245–271). Charlotte, NC: Information Age Publishing.

McDonald, R. P. & Swaminathan, H. (1973). A simple matrix calculus with applications to multivariate analysis. *General Systems*, XVIII, 37–54.

Morrison, D. F. (1990). *Multivariate statistical methods* (3rd ed). New York: McGraw-Hill Publishing Company.

O'Hagan, A. (1976). On posterior joint and marginal models. *Biometrika, 63*, 329–333.

Patterson, H. D., & Thompson, R. (1971). Recovery of inter-block information when block sizes are unequal. *Biometrika, 58*, 545–554.

Rasbash, J., Steele, F., Browne, M., & Prosser, B. (2005). A user's guide to MLwiN Version 2.0. Bristol, UK: Center for Multilevel Modelling. Retrieved 12/20/06 from http://www.cmm.bristol.ac.uk/MLwiN/download/manuals.shtml.

Raudenbush, S. W. (1995). Reexamining, reaffirming, and improving application of hierarchical models. *Journal of Educational and Behavioral Statistics, 20*, 210–220.

Raudenbush, S.W. & Bryk, A. S. (2002). *Hierarchical linear models: Applications and data analysis methods* (2nd ed.). Thousand Oaks, CA: Sage Publications.

Raudenbush, S., Bryk, A., Cheong, Y. F., & Congdon, R. (2004). *HLM 6: Hierarchical linear and nonlinear modeling.* Lincolnwood, IL: Scientific Software International.

Rubin, D. B. (1989). Some applications of multilevel models to educational data. In R. D. Bock (Ed.) *Multilevel analysis of educational data.* New York: Academic Press.

Searle, R. (1971). *Linear models.* New York: John Wiley.

Spiegelhalter, D., Thomas, A., Best, N., & Lunn, D. (2003). WINBUGS 4 User Manual. Retrieved 12/20/2006, from http://www.mrc-bsu.cam.ac.uk/bugs/.

Swaminathan, H. (1989a). Interpreting the results of multivariate analysis of variance. In B. Thompson (Ed.) *Advances in social science methodology* Greenwich: Jai Press.

Swaminathan, H. (1989b). Multilevel data analysis: A discussion. In R. D. Bock (Ed.) *Multilevel analysis of educational data.* New York: Academic Press.

Swaminathan, H., Hambleton, R. K., & Algina, J. (1975). A Bayesian decision theoretic procedure for use with criterion-referenced tests. *Journal of Educational Measurement, 12,* 87–98.

Zellner, A. (1962). An efficient method of estimating seemingly unrelated regressions and tests for aggregation bias. *Journal of the American Statistical Association, 57,* 348–368.

Zellner, A. (1971). *An introduction to Bayesian inference in econometrics.* New York: Wiley.

ABOUT THE CONTRIBUTORS

Daniel Bauer is an Assistant Professor in the L.L. Thurstone Psychometric Laboratory at the University of North Carolina at Chapel Hill. His research focuses on extending, evaluating, and applying multilevel models (and mixed-effects models), structural equation models, and mixture models, particularly as they may elucidate the study of social development. His papers have been published in *Psychological Methods, Journal of Educational and Behavioral Statistics, Multivariate Behavioral Research, Sociological Methods and Research,* and *Structural Equation Modeling,* and he currently serves on the editorial boards of *Psychological Methods, Psychological Assessment,* and *Multivariate Behavioral Research.*

Natasha S. Beretvas is an Associate Professor in the Quantitative Methods area of Educational Psychology at the University of Texas at Austin, where she teaches courses on statistics, including advanced seminars on meta-analysis and factor analysis. Her research interests lie in the application and evaluation of statistical and psychometric modeling, with a focus on methodological dilemmas in meta-analysis and multilevel modeling. She is the author of several book chapters and peer-reviewed articles.

Anne C. Black is a doctoral candidate in the Measurement, Evaluation, and Assessment program in the Educational Psychology department at the University of Connecticut. Her research interests include statistical modeling of educational phenomena, effects of missing data on parameter estimation and statistical inference, single-subject research design, and applied behavior analysis. Upon completion of her degree, she plans to pursue a career in academia.

Multilevel Modeling of Educational Data, pages 521–527
521

Kelly D. Bradley is an Assistant Professor in the Department of Educational Policy Studies and Evaluation at the University of Kentucky. She teaches quantitative research and methods courses. Her areas of expertise are survey research and Rasch measurement. Teacher quality issues, especially in math and science, are at the forefront of her research agenda. Dr. Bradley holds a M.S. in statistics from the University of South Carolina, a B.S. in mathematics and sociology and a B.A. in mathematics education from Fairmont State College, and a Ph.D. in Quantitative Research, Evaluation, and Measurement in Education from The Ohio State University.

Robert F. Dedrick is an Associate Professor of Educational Measurement and Research at the University of South Florida. He received his undergraduate degree in Psychology from Bucknell University and his Ph.D. in Educational Psychology from the University of Michigan. He teaches courses in research methods and measurement. His research interests include issues related to the mentoring of doctoral students and the assessment of children. He currently is involved in a national study examining the development of children adopted from China. His work has been published in *Educational and Psychological Measurement, Psychological Assessment,* and *Sociology of Education.*

John M. Ferron is a Professor of Educational Measurement and Research at the University of South Florida and teaches methods for analyzing quantitative research data, including multilevel modeling, interrupted time series analysis, structural equation modeling, and factor analysis. His research interests include the development and understanding of methods used to analyze educational data. This work has been published in the *Journal of Educational and Behavioral Statistics, Multivariate Behavioral Research,* the *Journal of Experimental Education, Educational and Psychological Measurement, Psychometrika,* and the *Encyclopedia of Statistics in Behavioral Science.*

Jessica Goldstein is an Assistant Professor in Residence in the Measurement, Evaluation, and Assessment program at the University of Connecticut. Dr. Goldstein currently is working with the Connecticut State Department of Education on the development of an online formative assessment system. Her prior work includes data analysis on research projects funded by the National Science Foundation, the American Educational Research Association, and the Connecticut Department of Education, specifically focused on the analysis of large-scale databases, hierarchical linear modeling, and survey research.

Melinda R. Hess is the Director of the Center for Research, Evaluation, Assessment, and Measurement at the University of South Florida. Her interests include exploring strengths and weaknesses of methods of analysis, factors of research design that impact precision and accuracy of results, and consequences of practices used to report results. Her work has been published in *Educational and Psychological Measurement, Journal of Educational and Behavioral Statistics, Journal of College Teaching & Learning,* and *Multiple Linear Regression Viewpoints* and has won two Distinguished Paper awards at research conferences. She currently serves as co-editor of the *Florida Journal of Educational Research.*

Kristine Y. Hogarty is the Director of Assessment for the College of Education at the University of South Florida. Her experiences include instrument development, research design and data analysis in Education, Criminology, Business and Industry. Her primary research interests are applied statistics and data analysis. Her work has been published in *Behavior Research Methods, Instruments, & Computers, Educational and Psychological Measurement, Journal of College Teaching & Learning, Journal of Police and Criminal Psychology, Journal of Research on Computing in Education, Journal of Research in Education, Multiple Linear Regression Viewpoints,* and *Psychometrika.*

Janet K. Holt is an Associate Professor of Educational Research and Evaluation at Northern Illinois University, where she teaches statistics, research, and measurement in the Department of Educational Technology, Research, and Assessment. Currently, her primary research focus is on statistical methods for modeling developmental change, and she has applied growth modeling methods to the study of math and science persistence of women and minorities, early development of speech, and modeling change across critical transitions. She is Past President of the Mid-Western Educational Research Association and serves on the editorial boards and reviews for several educational and psychological journals.

Sema Kalaian is an Associate Professor of Statistics and Measurement at Eastern Michigan University. She was a recipient of the "Best Paper" award from the American Educational Research Association (AERA) and the "Distinguished Paper Award" from the Society for the Advancement of Information Systems (SAIS). Her research interests focus on the development of statistical methods and its applications. Much of her methodological work has concentrated on multivariate meta-analytic techniques for combining evidence from multiple primary studies. Other research interests include the applications of hierarchical linear modeling and structural equation modeling to large-scale multilevel and longitudinal data sets.

Akihito Kamata is an Associate Professor of Educational Measurement and Statistics in the Department of Educational Psychology and Learning Systems at Florida State University. His research interests focus on methods and applications of item response theory, multilevel modeling, and structural equation modeling for analysis and modeling of test data.

Rafa M. Kasim is an Assistant Professor of Statistics and Research Design Methods at Kent State University. He received his Ph.D. in statistics and research design from the college of Education at Michigan State University. His major area of professional interest is multilevel modeling, measurement, and quantitative methods. His current work focuses on exploring efficient ways of estimating effect sizes for single subject design studies through multilevel models. Some of his publish work appears in the *American Journal of Drug and Alcohol Abuse, Advances in Health Sciences Education, Journal of Educational and Behavioral Statistics*, and *Journal of Substance Abuse Treatment*.

Jeffrey D. Kromrey is a Professor in the Department of Educational Measurement and Research at the University of South Florida. His research interests focus primarily on methodological issues in quantitative data analysis. His work has won five distinguished paper awards at research conferences, and he was awarded the Researcher of the Year in 1997 by the Florida Educational Research Association and the President's Award for Faculty Excellence in 2003. He is a former editor of *Review of Educational Research* and currently serves as editor of *Florida Journal of Educational Research* and executive editor of *Journal of Experimental Education*.

Lingling Ma currently is working on her doctorate in the Department of Curriculum and Instruction at the University of Kentucky. Her research is anchored in quantitative research methodology and large-scale assessment, with a focus on hierarchical linear modeling and longitudinal analysis. She has conducted research studies on educational assessment, school effectiveness, program evaluation, teacher supply and demand, and college teaching and learning, with research papers published in *Evaluation Review and Studies in Educational Evaluation*.

Xin Ma is a Full Professor in the Department of Curriculum and Instruction at the University of Kentucky. He is a Fellow of the (United States) National Academy of Education and a recipient of the Early Career Contribution Award from the Committee for Scholars of Color in Education of the American Educational Research Association. He was a Canada Research Chair and the former Director of the Canadian Center for Advanced Studies of National Databases at the University of Alberta. Dr. Ma's research interests include mathematics education, school effectiveness, policy research, and advanced quantitative methods.

D. Betsy McCoach is an Assistant Professor in the Educational Psychology Department in the Neag School of Education at the University of Connecticut, where she teaches graduate courses in measurement, educational statistics, and research design. Her methodological research interests include hierarchical linear modeling, instrument design, factor analysis, structural equation modeling, longitudinal analysis, and quantitative research methodology. Dr. McCoach's substantive research interest is the underachievement of academically able students. Dr. McCoach is the co-editor of the *Journal of Advanced Academics.*

Patrick M. McLeod is currently a Research Consultant with the University of North Texas's Academic Computing Services group providing research support and statistical support to UNT's research community while focusing on development of SAS and Stata support products. He was born and raised in Denton, Texas. He graduated from Denton High School in 1991 and attended Texas A&M University and the University of North Texas, where he earned a B.A. in Social Science in 1998. He has worked in mainframe operations, as a graduate research assistant, in landscaping, in telecommunications, and in computer security. He would like to thank Dr. Kyle Roberts for giving him the opportunity to work on this book chapter.

Yasuo Miyazaki is an Assistant Professor in the Department of Educational Leadership and Policy Studies in the School of Education at Virginia Polytechnic Institute and State University. His primary research interests include hierarchical linear/nonlinear modeling, growth modeling, hierarchical measurement models, and school effects.

John D. Niles is a Visiting Associate Professor in the Department of Educational Measurement and Research at the University of South Florida. He teaches courses in educational measurement and evaluation. He has done extensive measurement work in social studies education within the Caribbean. His research interests include achievement trends within the Caribbean and multilevel modeling.

Ann Aileen O'Connell is an Associate Professor in the School of Educational Policy and Leadership at The Ohio State University, where she teaches courses in graduate-level statistical methods, including multilevel modeling, logistic regression, sampling and survey research methods, and multivariate analysis. Her collection of published work emphasizes research applications using these and other advanced methodologies in the field of HIV-prevention and for program evaluation in health and education. Dr. O'Connell's work has appeared in journals including *Women and Health, Evaluation and the Health Professions, Measurement and Research in Counseling and Development, MMWR,* and *Journal of Modern Applied Statistical Methods,* and she recently has published a book with Sage Publications on the treatment of ordinal response data.

Joanne C. Y. Peng is presently a Professor of Inquiry Methodology and Adjunct Professor of Statistics at Indiana University—Bloomington. She received her Ph.D. from University of Wisconsin at Madison. Her research interests include logistic regression modeling, missing data methods, and research design.

J. Kyle Roberts is an Associate Professor of Literacy, Language, and Learning in the School of Education and Human Development at Southern Methodist University. Dr. Roberts is the founder and past president of the Hierarchical Linear Modeling (HLM) Special Interest Group of the American Educational Research Association (2004). His research interests include applications of multilevel analysis to complex educational data and value-added assessment.

Jane H. Rogers is an Associate Professor in the Measurement, Evaluation, and Assessment Program of the Neag School of Education at the University of Connecticut, where she teaches courses in educational statistics, measurement, and item response theory. She received her Bachelor's and Master's degrees at the University of New England in Australia and her Ph. D. in Psychology at the University of Massachusetts, Amherst. Her research interests are in applications of item response theory, assessment of differential item functioning, and educational statistics. She is co-author of a book on item response theory and has published papers on a wide range of psychometric issues.

Jessaca Spybrook is a senior researcher at The Evaluation Center at Western Michigan University. Her research focuses on improving the design and analysis of large-scale evaluations of education interventions. She has consulted on the design of numerous evaluations and coauthored software that assists the researcher in the planning of experiments. Dr. Spybrook holds a master's in applied statistics and a doctorate in education from the University of Michigan.

Laura Stapleton holds a quantitative psychology position at University of Maryland, Baltimore County. After 10 years working in institutional research undertaking applied studies of universities, she earned her Ph.D. in Measurement, Statistics, and Evaluation at the University of Maryland in 2001. For 4 years, she was an Assistant Professor of Quantitative Methods in Educational Psychology at the University of Texas. Her research centers on collection and statistical modeling of survey data, especially in covariance structure modeling frameworks. Her research examines item development and problems in using traditional statistical analysis when survey respondents are not obtained through simple random sampling procedures.

Hariharan Swaminathan is Professor of Education at the University of Connecticut. He has coauthored two books on item response theory and has published widely in the areas of Bayesian analysis, psychometrics, and multivariate statistics. He has served on the GRE Board and the NAEP Design and Analysis Committee and currently serves on the Board of Directors of NCME, Scientific Review panel of IES, and the editorial boards of *Educational and Psychological Measurement, Applied Psychological Measurement,* and *Journal of Educational Measurement.* He has received the College Outstanding Teacher Award at the University of Massachusetts and is the recipient of the APA Jacob Cohen Award for Distinguished Teaching and Mentoring.

Scott L. Thomas is Associate Professor of Higher Education at the Institute of Higher Education at the University of Georgia. Dr. Thomas's current work focuses on latent variable multilevel models and social network analysis. His work in this area includes *An Introduction to Multilevel Modeling* (with Ron Heck, published by Taylor and Francis/Psychology Press) and related articles in a variety of refereed journals. His work can be found in journal articles and book chapters in a wide variety of areas.

CPSIA information can be obtained at www.ICGtesting.com
Printed in the USA
269086BV00002BA/40/P